Theory of Asset Pricing

The Addison-Wesley Series in Finance

Berk/DeMarzo
Corporate Finance

Copeland/Weston/Shastri
Financial Theory and Corporate Policy

Dufey/Giddy
Cases in International Finance

Eakins
Finance: Investments, Institutions, and Management

Eiteman/Stonehill/Moffett
Multinational Business Finance

Gitman
Principles of Managerial Finance

Gitman
Principles of Managerial Finance—Brief Edition

Gitman/Joehnk
Fundamentals of Investing

Gitman/Madura
Introduction to Finance

Hughes/MacDonald
International Banking: Text and Cases

Madura
Personal Finance

Marthinsen
Risk Takers: Uses and Abuses of Financial Derivatives

McDonald
Derivatives Markets

Megginson
Corporate Finance Theory

Melvin
International Money and Finance

Mishkin/Eakins
Financial Markets and Institutions

Moffett
Cases in International Finance

Moffett/Stonehill/Eiteman
Fundamentals of Multinational Finance

Pennacchi
Theory of Asset Pricing

Rejda
Principles of Risk Management and Insurance

Solnik/McLeavey
International Investments

Titman/Martin
Valuation: The Art and Science of Making Strategic Investments

Theory of Asset Pricing

GEORGE PENNACCHI

University of Illinois,
Urbana–Champaign

PEARSON

Addison
Wesley

Boston San Francisco New York
London Toronto Sydney Tokyo Singapore Madrid
Mexico City Munich Paris Cape Town Hong Kong Montreal

Publisher: Greg Tobin
Editor in Chief: Denise Clinton
Senior Acquisitions Editor: Donna Battista
Assistant Editor: Allison Stendardi
Managing Editor: Nancy Fenton
Senior Production Supervisor: Meredith Gertz
Cover Designer: Charles Spaulding
Supplements Editor: Heather McNally
Media Producer: Bridget Page
Senior Marketing Manager: Roxanne Hoch
Senior Prepress Supervisor: Caroline Fell
Senior Manufacturing Buyer: Carol Melville
Production Coordination, Composition, Text Design: Windfall Software, using ZzTEX
Illustrations: LM Graphics

Library of Congress Cataloging-in-Publication Data

Pennacchi, George Gaetano.
   Theory of asset pricing / George Pennacchi.
     p.   cm.
   Includes bibliographical references and index.
   ISBN 0-321-12720-X (alk. paper)
  1. Capital assets pricing model.   2. Securities.   I. Title.
   HG4636.P4 2007
   332.63′2042—dc22

                         2006039325

ISBN-13: 978-0-321-12720-4
ISBN-10: 0-321-12720-X

1 2 3 4 5 6 7 8 9 10—CRW—11 10 09 08 07

To Peggy, George J., Laura, and Sally

Contents

Preface

The genesis of this book came from my experience teaching asset pricing theory to beginning doctoral students in finance and economics. What I found was that no existing text included all of the major theories and techniques of asset valuation that students studying for a Ph.D. in financial economics should know. While there are many excellent books in this area, none seemed ideal as a stand-alone text for a one-semester first course in theoretical asset pricing. I chose topics for this book that I believe are most valuable to someone at the start of a career in financial research. Probably the two features that most distinguish this book from others are its broad coverage and its user-friendliness.

Contents of this book have been used for over a decade in introductory finance theory courses presented to doctoral students and advanced masters students at the University of Illinois at Urbana-Champaign. The book presumes that students have a background in mathematical probability and statistics and that they are familiar with constrained maximization (Lagrange multiplier) problems. A prior course in microeconomics at the graduate or advanced undergraduate level would be helpful preparation for a course based on this book. However, I have found that doctoral students from mathematics, engineering, and the physical sciences who had little prior knowledge of economics often are able to understand the course material.

This book covers theories of asset pricing that are the foundation of current theoretical and empirical research in financial economics. It analyzes models of individual consumption and portfolio choice and their implications for equilibrium asset prices. In addition, contingent claims valuation techniques based on the absence of arbitrage are presented. Most of the consumption-portfolio choice models assume individuals have standard, time-separable expected utility functions, but the book also considers more recent models of utility that are not time separable or that incorporate behavioral biases. Further, while much of the analysis makes standard "perfect markets" assumptions, the book also examines the impact of asymmetric information on trading and asset prices. Many of the later chapters build on earlier ones, and important topics reoccur as models of increasing complexity are introduced to address them. Both discrete-time and continuous-time models are presented in a manner that attempts to be intuitive, easy to follow, and that avoids excessive formalism.

As its title makes obvious, this book focuses on theory. While it sometimes contains brief remarks on whether a particular theory has been successful in explaining empirical findings, I expect that doctoral students will have additional exposure to an empirical investments seminar. Some of the material in the book may be skipped if time is limited to a one-semester course. For example, parts of the binomial option pricing material covered in Chapter 7 may be cut if students have seen this material in a masters-level derivatives course. Any or all of the chapters in Part V, Additional Topics in Asset Pricing, also may be omitted. In my teaching, I cover Chapter 15 on behavioral finance and asset pricing, in part because current research on this topic is expanding rapidly. However, if reviewer response is any indication, there are strongly held opinions about behavioral finance, and so I suspect that some readers will choose to skip this material altogether while others may wish to see it expanded.

Typically, I also cover Chapter 16, which outlines some of the important models of asymmetric information that I believe all doctoral students should know. However, many Ph.D. programs may offer a course entirely devoted to this topic, so that this material could be deleted in that circumstance. Chapters 17 and 18 on modeling default-free and defaultable bond prices contain advanced material that I typically do not have time to cover during a single semester. Still, there is a vast amount of research on default-free term structure models and a growing interest in modeling default risk. Thus, in response to reviewers' suggestions, I have included this material because some may find coverage of these topics helpful for their future research.

A final note on the end-of-chapter problems: Most of these problems derive from assignments and exams given to my students at the University of Illinois. The solutions are available for instructor download at www.aw.com/finance.

Acknowledgments

I owe a debt to the individuals who first sparked my interest in financial economics. I was lucky to have been a graduate student at MIT during the early 1980s where I could absorb the insights of great financial economists, including Fischer Black, Stanley Fischer, Robert Merton, Franco Modigliani, Stewart Myers, and Paul Samuelson. Also, I am grateful to my former colleague at Wharton, Alessandro Penati, who first encouraged the writing of this book when we team taught a finance theory course at Università Bocconi during the mid-1990s. He contributed notes on some of the book's beginning chapters.

Many thanks are due to my colleagues and students at the University of Illinois who provided comments and corrections to the manuscript. In addition, I have profited from the valuable suggestions of many individuals from other universities who reviewed drafts of some chapters. I am particularly indebted to the following individuals who provided extensive comments on parts of the book: Mark Anderson, Gurdip Bakshi, Evangelos Benos, Michael W. Brandt, Murillo Campello, David Chapman, Gregory Chaudoin, Mikhail Chernov, Michael Cliff, Pierre Collin-Dufresne, Bradford Cornell, Michael Gallmeyer, Christos Giannikos, Antonio Gledson de Carvalho, Olesya Grishchenko, Hui Guo, Jason Karceski, Mark Laplante, Dietmar Leisen, Sergio Lence, Tongshu Ma, Galina Ovtcharova, Kwangwoo Park, Christian Pedersen, Glenn Pedersen, Monika Piazzesi, Allen Poteshman, James Reineck, Peter Ritchken, Saurav Roychoudhury, Nejat Seyhun, Timothy Simin, Chester Spatt, P. V. Viswanath, Qinghai Wang, and Hong Yan.

The level of support that I received from the staff at Addison-Wesley greatly exceeded my initial expectations. Writing a book of this scope was a time-consuming process that was made manageable with their valuable assistance. Senior Acquisitions Editor Donna Battista deserves very special thanks for her encouragement and suggestions.

Last but not least my wife Peggy and our triplets George, Laura, and Sally deserve recognition for the love and patience they have shown me. Their enthusiasm buoyed my spirits and helped bring this project to fruition.

Theory of Asset Pricing

PART I

SINGLE-PERIOD PORTFOLIO CHOICE AND ASSET PRICING

CHAPTER 1

Expected Utility and Risk Aversion

Asset prices are determined by investors' risk preferences and by the distributions of assets' risky future payments. Economists refer to these two bases of prices as investor "tastes" and the economy's "technologies" for generating asset returns. A satisfactory theory of asset valuation must consider how individuals allocate their wealth among assets having different future payments. This chapter explores the development of expected utility theory, the standard approach for modeling investor choices over risky assets. We first analyze the conditions that an individual's preferences must satisfy to be consistent with an expected utility function. We then consider the link between utility and risk aversion and how risk aversion leads to risk premia for particular assets. Our final topic examines how risk aversion affects an individual's choice between a risky and a risk-free asset.

Modeling investor choices with expected utility functions is widely used. However, significant empirical and experimental evidence has indicated that individuals sometimes behave in ways inconsistent with standard forms of expected utility. These findings have motivated a search for improved models of investor preferences. Theoretical innovations both within and outside the expected utility paradigm are being developed, and examples of such advances are presented in later chapters of this book.

1.1   Preferences When Returns Are Uncertain

Economists typically analyze the price of a good or service by modeling the nature of its supply and demand. A similar approach can be taken to price an asset. As a starting point, let us consider the modeling of an investor's demand for an asset. In contrast to a good or service, an asset does not provide a current consumption benefit to an individual. Rather, an asset is a vehicle for saving. It is a component of an investor's financial wealth representing a claim on *future* consumption or purchasing power. The main distinction between assets is the difference in their future payoffs. With the exception of assets that pay a risk-free return, assets' payoffs are random. Thus, a theory of the demand for assets needs to specify investors' preferences over different, uncertain payoffs. In other words, we need to model how investors choose between assets that have different probability distributions of returns. In this chapter we assume an environment where an individual chooses among assets that have random payoffs at a single future date. Later chapters will generalize the situation to consider an individual's choices over multiple periods among assets paying returns at multiple future dates.

Let us begin by considering potentially relevant criteria that individuals might use to rank their preferences for different risky assets. One possible measure of the attractiveness of an asset is the average, or *expected value*, of its payoff. Suppose an asset offers a single random payoff at a particular future date, and this payoff has a discrete distribution with n possible outcomes $(x_1, \ldots, x_n)$ and corresponding probabilities $(p_1, \ldots, p_n)$, where $\sum_{i=1}^{n} p_i = 1$ and $p_i \geq 0$.[1] Then the expected value of the payoff (or, more simply, the expected payoff) is $\bar{x} \equiv E[\tilde{x}] = \sum_{i=1}^{n} p_i x_i$.

Is it logical to think that individuals value risky assets based solely on the assets' expected payoffs? This valuation concept was the prevailing wisdom until 1713, when Nicholas Bernoulli pointed out a major weakness. He showed that an asset's expected payoff was unlikely to be the only criterion that individuals use for valuation. He did it by posing the following problem, which became known as the St. Petersberg paradox:

> Peter tosses a coin and continues to do so until it should land "heads" when it comes to the ground. He agrees to give Paul one ducat if he gets heads on the very first throw, two ducats if he gets it on the second, four if on the third, eight if on the fourth, and so on, so that on each additional throw the

---

1. As is the case in the following example, n, the number of possible outcomes, may be infinite.

number of ducats he must pay is doubled.[2] Suppose we seek to determine Paul's expectation (of the payoff that he will receive).

Interpreting Paul's prize from this coin flipping game as the payoff of a risky asset, how much would he be willing to pay for this asset if he valued it based on its expected value? If the number of coin flips taken to first arrive at a heads is i, then $p_i = \left(\frac{1}{2}\right)^i$ and $x_i = 2^{i-1}$ so that the expected payoff equals

$$\bar{x} = \sum_{i=1}^{\infty} p_i x_i = \frac{1}{2}1 + \frac{1}{4}2 + \frac{1}{8}4 + \frac{1}{16}8 + \cdots \qquad (1.1)$$

$$= \frac{1}{2}(1 + \frac{1}{2}2 + \frac{1}{4}4 + \frac{1}{8}8 + \cdots$$

$$= \frac{1}{2}(1 + 1 + 1 + 1 + \cdots = \infty$$

The "paradox" is that the expected value of this asset is infinite, but intuitively, most individuals would pay only a moderate, not infinite, amount to play this game. In a paper published in 1738, Daniel Bernoulli, a cousin of Nicholas's, provided an explanation for the St. Petersberg paradox by introducing the concept of *expected utility*.[3] His insight was that an individual's utility or "felicity" from receiving a payoff could differ from the size of the payoff and that people cared about the expected utility of an asset's payoffs, not the expected value of its payoffs. Instead of valuing an asset as $\bar{x} = \sum_{i=1}^{n} p_i x_i$, its value, V, would be

$$V \equiv E\left[U\left(\tilde{x}\right)\right] = \sum_{i=1}^{n} p_i U_i \qquad (1.2)$$

where U_i is the utility associated with payoff x_i. Moreover, he hypothesized that the "utility resulting from any small increase in wealth will be inversely proportionate to the quantity of goods previously possessed." In other words, the greater an individual's wealth, the smaller is the added (or marginal) utility received from an additional increase in wealth. In the St. Petersberg paradox, prizes, x_i, go up at the same rate that the probabilities decline. To obtain a finite valuation, the trick is to allow the utility of prizes, U_i, to increase more slowly than the rate that probabilities decline. Hence, Daniel Bernoulli introduced the principle of a *diminishing marginal utility of wealth* (as expressed in his quote above) to resolve this paradox.

---

2. A ducat was a 3.5-gram gold coin used throughout Europe.

3. An English translation of Daniel Bernoulli's original Latin paper is printed in *Econometrica* (Bernoulli 1954). Another Swiss mathematician, Gabriel Cramer, offered a similar solution in 1728.

The first complete axiomatic development of expected utility is due to John von Neumann and Oskar Morgenstern (von Neumann and Morgenstern 1944). Von Neumann, a renowned physicist and mathematician, initiated the field of *game theory*, which analyzes strategic decision making. Morgenstern, an economist, recognized the field's economic applications and, together, they provided a rigorous basis for individual decision making under uncertainty. We now outline one aspect of their work, namely, to provide conditions that an individual's preferences must satisfy for these preferences to be consistent with an expected utility function.

Define a *lottery* as an asset that has a risky payoff and consider an individual's optimal choice of a lottery (risky asset) from a given set of different lotteries. All lotteries have possible payoffs that are contained in the set $\{x_1, \ldots, x_n\}$. In general, the elements of this set can be viewed as different, uncertain outcomes. For example, they could be interpreted as particular consumption levels (bundles of consumption goods) that the individual obtains in different states of nature or, more simply, different monetary payments received in different states of the world. A given lottery can be characterized as an ordered set of probabilities $P = \{p_1, \ldots, p_n\}$, where of course, $\sum_{i=1}^{n} p_i = 1$ and $p_i \geq 0$. A different lottery is characterized by another set of probabilities, for example, $P^* = \{p_1^*, \ldots, p_n^*\}$. Let $\succ$, $\prec$, and $\sim$ denote preference and indifference between lotteries.[4]

We will show that if an individual's preferences satisfy the following five conditions (axioms), then these preferences can be represented by a real-valued utility function defined over a given lottery's probabilities, that is, an expected utility function $V(p_1, \ldots, p_n)$.

AXIOMS:

1. *Completeness*
   For any two lotteries P^* and P, either $P^* \succ P$, or $P^* \prec P$, or $P^* \sim P$.

2. *Transitivity*
   If $P^{**} \succeq P^*$ and $P^* \succeq P$, then $P^{**} \succeq P$.

3. *Continuity*
   If $P^{**} \succeq P^* \succeq P$, there exists some $\lambda \in [0, 1]$ such that $P^* \sim \lambda P^{**} + (1 - \lambda)P$, where $\lambda P^{**} + (1 - \lambda)P$ denotes a "compound lottery"; namely, with probability λ one receives the lottery P^{**} and with probability $(1 - \lambda)$ one receives the lottery P.

---

4. Specifically, if an individual prefers lottery P to lottery P^*, this can be denoted as $P \succ P^*$ or $P^* \prec P$. When the individual is indifferent between the two lotteries, this is written as $P \sim P^*$. If an individual prefers lottery P to lottery P^* or she is indifferent between lotteries P and P^*, this is written as $P \succeq P^*$ or $P^* \preceq P$.

These three axioms are analogous to those used to establish the existence of a real-valued utility function in standard consumer choice theory.[5] The fourth axiom is unique to expected utility theory and, as we later discuss, has important implications for the theory's predictions.

4. *Independence*

For any two lotteries P and P^*, $P^* \succ P$ if for all $\lambda \in (0,1]$ and all P^{**}:

$$\lambda P^* + (1 - \lambda)P^{**} \succ \lambda P + (1 - \lambda)P^{**}$$

Moreover, for any two lotteries P and $P^\dagger$, $P \sim P^\dagger$ if for all $\lambda \in (0,1]$ and all P^{**}:

$$\lambda P + (1 - \lambda)P^{**} \sim \lambda P^\dagger + (1 - \lambda)P^{**}$$

To better understand the meaning of the independence axiom, note that P^* is preferred to P by assumption. Now the choice between $\lambda P^* + (1 - \lambda)P^{**}$ and $\lambda P + (1 - \lambda)P^{**}$ is equivalent to a toss of a coin that has a probability $(1 - \lambda)$ of landing "tails," in which case both compound lotteries are equivalent to P^{**}, and a probability λ of landing "heads," in which case the first compound lottery is equivalent to the single lottery P^* and the second compound lottery is equivalent to the single lottery P. Thus, the choice between $\lambda P^* + (1 - \lambda)P^{**}$ and $\lambda P + (1 - \lambda)P^{**}$ is equivalent to being asked, prior to the coin toss, if one would prefer P^* to P in the event the coin lands heads.

It would seem reasonable that should the coin land heads, we would go ahead with our original preference in choosing P^* over P. The independence axiom assumes that preferences over the two lotteries are independent of the way in which we obtain them.[6] For this reason, the independence axiom is

---

5. A primary area of microeconomics analyzes a consumer's optimal choice of multiple goods (and services) based on their prices and the consumer's budget contraint. In that context, utility is a function of the quantities of multiple goods consumed. References on this topic include (Kreps 1990), (Mas-Colell, Whinston, and Green 1995), and (Varian 1992). In contrast, the analysis of this chapter expresses utility as a function of the individual's wealth. In future chapters, we introduce multiperiod utility functions where utility becomes a function of the individual's overall consumption at multiple future dates. Financial economics typically bypasses the individual's problem of choosing among different consumption goods and focuses on how the individual chooses a total quantity of consumption at different points in time and different states of nature.

6. In the context of standard consumer choice theory, λ would be interpreted as the amount (rather than probability) of a particular good or bundle of goods consumed (say, C) and $(1 - \lambda)$ as the amount of another good or bundle of goods consumed (say, C^{**}). In this case, it would not be reasonable to assume that the choice of these different bundles is independent. This is due to some goods being substitutes or complements with other goods. Hence, the validity of the independence axiom is linked to outcomes being uncertain (risky), that is, the interpretation of λ as a probability rather than a deterministic amount.

also known as the "no regret" axiom. However, experimental evidence finds some systematic violations of this independence axiom, making it a questionable assumption for a theory of investor preferences. For example, the Allais paradox is a well-known choice of lotteries that, when offered to individuals, leads most to violate the independence axiom.[7] Machina (Machina 1987) summarizes violations of the independence axiom and reviews alternative approaches to modeling risk preferences. In spite of these deficiencies, the von Neumann–Morgenstern expected utility theory continues to be a useful and common approach to modeling investor preferences, though research exploring alternative paradigms is growing.[8]

The final axiom is similar to the independence and completeness axioms.

5. *Dominance*
Let P^1 be the compound lottery $\lambda_1 P^\ddagger + (1 - \lambda_1)P^\dagger$ and P^2 be the compound lottery $\lambda_2 P^\ddagger + (1 - \lambda_2)P^\dagger$. If $P^\ddagger \succ P^\dagger$, then $P^1 \succ P^2$ if and only if $\lambda_1 > \lambda_2$.

Given preferences characterized by the preceding axioms, we now show that the choice between any two (*or more*) arbitrary lotteries is that which has the higher (*highest*) expected utility.

The completeness axiom's ordering on lotteries naturally induces an ordering on the set of outcomes. To see this, define an "elementary" or "primitive" lottery, e_i, which returns outcome x_i with probability 1 and all other outcomes with probability zero; that is, $e_i = \{p_1, \ldots, p_{i-1}, p_i, p_{i+1}, \ldots, p_n\} = \{0, \ldots, 0, 1, 0, \ldots 0\}$ where $p_i = 1$ and $p_j = 0 \ \forall j \neq i$. Without loss of generality, suppose that the outcomes are ordered such that $e_n \succeq e_{n-1} \succeq \ldots \succeq e_1$. This follows from the completeness axiom for this case of n elementary lotteries. Note that this ordering of the elementary lotteries may not necessarily coincide with a ranking of the elements of x strictly by the size of their monetary payoffs, since the state of nature for which x_i is the outcome may differ from the state of nature for which x_j is the outcome, and these states of nature may have different effects on how an individual values the same monetary outcome. For example, x_i may be received in a state of nature when the economy is depressed, and monetary payoffs may be highly valued in this state of nature. In contrast, x_j may be received in a state of nature characterized by high economic expansion, and monetary payments may not be as highly valued. Therefore, it may be that $e_i \succ e_j$ even if the monetary payment corresponding to x_i was less than that corresponding to x_j.

---

7. A similar example is given in Exercise 2 at the end of this chapter.
8. This research includes "behavioral finance," a field that encompasses alternatives to both expected utility theory and market efficiency. An example of how a behavioral finance utility specification can impact asset prices will be presented in Chapter 15.

From the continuity axiom, we know that for each e_i, there exists a $U_i \in [0, 1]$ such that

$$e_i \sim U_i e_n + (1 - U_i)e_1 \tag{1.3}$$

and for $i = 1$, this implies $U_1 = 0$ and for $i = n$, this implies $U_n = 1$. The values of the U_i weight the most and least preferred outcomes such that the individual is just indifferent between a combination of these polar payoffs and the payoff of x_i. The U_i can adjust for both differences in monetary payoffs and differences in the states of nature during which the outcomes are received.

Now consider a given arbitrary lottery, $P = \{p_1, \ldots, p_n\}$. This can be considered a compound lottery over the n elementary lotteries, where elementary lottery e_i is obtained with probability p_i. By the independence axiom, and using equation (1.3), the individual is indifferent between the compound lottery, P, and the following lottery, given on the right-hand side of the following equation:

$$p_1 e_1 + \cdots + p_n e_n \sim p_1 e_1 + \cdots + p_{i-1}e_{i-1} + p_i \left[U_i e_n + (1 - U_i)e_1 \right]$$
$$+ p_{i+1}e_{i+1} + \cdots + p_n e_n \tag{1.4}$$

where we have used the indifference relation in equation (1.3) to substitute for e_i on the right-hand side of (1.4). By repeating this substitution for all i, $i = 1, \ldots, n$, we see that the individual will be indifferent between P, given by the left-hand side of (1.4), and

$$p_1 e_1 + \cdots + p_n e_n \sim \left(\sum_{i=1}^{n} p_i U_i \right) e_n + \left(1 - \sum_{i=1}^{n} p_i U_i \right) e_1 \tag{1.5}$$

Now define $\Lambda \equiv \sum_{i=1}^{n} p_i U_i$. Thus, we see that lottery P is equivalent to a compound lottery consisting of a Λ probability of obtaining elementary lottery e_n and a $(1 - \Lambda)$ probability of obtaining elementary lottery e_1. In a similar manner, we can show that any other arbitrary lottery $P^* = \{p_1^*, \ldots, p_n^*\}$ is equivalent to a compound lottery consisting of a Λ^* probability of obtaining e_n and a $(1 - \Lambda^*)$ probability of obtaining e_1, where $\Lambda^* \equiv \sum_{i=1}^{n} p_i^* U_i$.

Thus, we know from the dominance axiom that $P^* \succ P$ if and only if $\Lambda^* > \Lambda$, which implies $\sum_{i=1}^{n} p_i^* U_i > \sum_{i=1}^{n} p_i U_i$. So defining an expected utility function as

$$V(p_1, \ldots, p_n) = \sum_{i=1}^{n} p_i U_i \tag{1.6}$$

will imply that $P^* \succ P$ if and only if $V(p_1^*, \ldots, p_n^*) > V(p_1, \ldots, p_n)$.

The function given in equation (1.6) is known as von Neumann–Morgenstern expected utility. Note that it is linear in the probabilities and is unique up to a linear monotonic transformation.[9] This implies that the utility function has "cardinal" properties, meaning that it does not preserve preference orderings for all strictly increasing transformations.[10] For example, if $U_i = U(x_i)$, an individual's choice over lotteries will be the same under the transformation $aU(x_i) + b$, but not a nonlinear transformation that changes the "shape" of $U(x_i)$.

The von Neumann–Morgenstern expected utility framework may only partially explain the phenomenon illustrated by the St. Petersberg paradox. Suppose an individual's utility is given by the square root of a monetary payoff; that is, $U_i = U(x_i) = \sqrt{x_i}$. This is a monotonically increasing, concave function of x, which here is assumed to be simply a monetary amount (in units of ducats). Then the individual's expected utility of the St. Petersberg payoff is

$$V = \sum_{i=1}^{n} p_i U_i = \sum_{i=1}^{\infty} \frac{1}{2^i} \sqrt{2^{i-1}} = \sum_{i=2}^{\infty} 2^{-\frac{i}{2}} \tag{1.7}$$

$$= 2^{-\frac{2}{2}} + 2^{-\frac{3}{2}} + \cdots$$

$$= \sum_{i=0}^{\infty} \left(\frac{1}{\sqrt{2}}\right)^i - 1 - \frac{1}{\sqrt{2}} = \frac{1}{2 - \sqrt{2}} \cong 1.707$$

which is finite. This individual would get the same expected utility from receiving a certain payment of $1.707^2 \cong 2.914$ ducats since $V = \sqrt{2.914}$ also gives expected (and actual) utility of 1.707. Hence, we can conclude that the St. Petersberg gamble would be worth 2.914 ducats to this square-root utility maximizer.

However, the reason that this is not a complete resolution of the paradox is that one can always construct a "super St. Petersberg paradox" where even expected utility is infinite. Note that in the regular St. Petersberg paradox, the probability of winning declines at rate 2^i, while the winning payoff increases at rate 2^i. In a super St. Petersberg paradox, we can make the winning payoff increase at a rate $x_i = U^{-1}(2^{i-1})$ and expected utility would no longer be finite. If we take the example of square-root utility, let the winning payoff be $x_i = 2^{2i-2}$; that is, $x_1 = 1$, $x_2 = 4$, $x_3 = 16$, and so on. In this case, the expected utility of the super St. Petersberg payoff by a square-root expected utility maximizer is

$$V = \sum_{i=1}^{n} p_i U_i = \sum_{i=1}^{\infty} \frac{1}{2^i} \sqrt{2^{2i-2}} = \infty \tag{1.8}$$

---

9. The intuition for why expected utility is unique up to a linear transformation can be traced to equation (1.3). Here the derivation compares elementary lottery i in terms of the least and most preferred elementary lotteries. However, other bases for ranking a given lottery are possible.

10. An "ordinal" utility function preserves preference orderings for *any* strictly increasing transformation, not just linear ones. The utility functions defined over multiple goods and used in standard consumer theory are ordinal measures.

Should we be concerned that if we let the prizes grow quickly enough, we can get infinite expected utility (and valuations) for any chosen form of expected utility function? Maybe not. One could argue that St. Petersberg games are unrealistic, particularly ones where the payoffs are assumed to grow rapidly. The reason is that any person offering this asset has finite wealth (even Bill Gates). This would set an upper bound on the amount of prizes that could feasibly be paid, making expected utility, and even the expected value of the payoff, finite.

The von Neumann–Morgenstern expected utility approach can be generalized to the case of a continuum of outcomes and lotteries having continuous probability distributions. For example, if outcomes are a possibly infinite number of purely monetary payoffs or consumption levels denoted by the variable x, a subset of the real numbers, then a generalized version of equation (1.6) is

$$V(F) = E[U(\widetilde{x})] = \int U(x)\, dF(x) \tag{1.9}$$

where $F(x)$ is a given lottery's cumulative distribution function over the payoffs, x.[11] Hence, the generalized lottery represented by the distribution function F is analogous to our previous lottery represented by the discrete probabilities $P = \{p_1, \ldots, p_n\}$.

Thus far, our discussion of expected utility theory has said little regarding an appropriate specification for the utility function, $U(x)$. We now turn to a discussion of how the form of this function affects individuals' risk preferences.

1.2 Risk Aversion and Risk Premia

As mentioned in the previous section, Daniel Bernoulli proposed that utility functions should display diminishing marginal utility; that is, $U(x)$ should be an increasing but concave function of wealth. He recognized that this concavity implies that an individual will be risk averse. By risk averse we mean that the individual would not accept a "fair" lottery (asset), where a fair or "pure risk" lottery is defined as one that has an expected value of zero. To see the relationship between fair lotteries and concave utility, consider the following example. Let there be a lottery that has a random payoff, $\widetilde{\varepsilon}$, where

$$\widetilde{\varepsilon} = \begin{cases} \varepsilon_1 & \text{with probability } p \\ \varepsilon_2 & \text{with probability } 1-p \end{cases} \tag{1.10}$$

---

11. When the random payoff, $\widetilde{x}$, is absolutely continuous, then expected utility can be written in terms of the probability density function, $f(x)$, as $V(f) = \int U(x) f(x)\, dx$.

The requirement that it be a fair lottery restricts its expected value to equal zero:

$$E\left[\tilde{\varepsilon}\right] = p\varepsilon_1 + (1-p)\varepsilon_2 = 0 \tag{1.11}$$

which implies $\varepsilon_1/\varepsilon_2 = -(1-p)/p$, or solving for p, $p = -\varepsilon_2/(\varepsilon_1 - \varepsilon_2)$. Of course, since $0 < p < 1$, ε_1 and ε_2 are of opposite signs.

Now suppose a von Neumann–Morgenstern expected utility maximizer whose current wealth equals W is offered the above lottery. Would this individual accept it; that is, would she place a positive value on this lottery?

If the lottery is accepted, expected utility is given by $E\left[U\left(W + \tilde{\varepsilon}\right)\right]$. Instead, if it is not accepted, expected utility is given by $E\left[U\left(W\right)\right] = U\left(W\right)$. Thus, an individual's refusal to accept a fair lottery implies

$$U\left(W\right) > E\left[U\left(W + \tilde{\varepsilon}\right)\right] = pU\left(W + \varepsilon_1\right) + (1-p)U\left(W + \varepsilon_2\right) \tag{1.12}$$

To show that this is equivalent to having a concave utility function, note that $U\left(W\right)$ can be rewritten as

$$U(W) = U\left(W + p\varepsilon_1 + (1-p)\varepsilon_2\right) \tag{1.13}$$

since $p\varepsilon_1 + (1-p)\varepsilon_2 = 0$ by the assumption that the lottery is fair. Rewriting inequality (1.12), we have

$$U\left(W + p\varepsilon_1 + (1-p)\varepsilon_2\right) > pU\left(W + \varepsilon_1\right) + (1-p)U\left(W + \varepsilon_2\right) \tag{1.14}$$

which is the definition of U being a concave function. A function is concave if a line joining any two points of the function lies entirely below the function. When $U(W)$ is concave, a line connecting the points $U(W + \varepsilon_2)$ to $U(W + \varepsilon_1)$ lies below $U(W)$ for all W such that $W + \varepsilon_2 < W < W + \varepsilon_1$. As shown in Figure 1.1, $pU(W + \varepsilon_1) + (1-p)U(W + \varepsilon_2)$ is exactly the point on this line directly below $U(W)$. This is clear by substituting $p = -\varepsilon_2/(\varepsilon_1 - \varepsilon_2)$. Note that when $U(W)$ is a continuous, second differentiable function, concavity implies that its second derivative, $U''(W)$, is less than zero.

To show the reverse, that concavity of utility implies the unwillingness to accept a fair lottery, we can use a result from statistics known as Jensen's inequality. If $U(\cdot)$ is some concave function and $\tilde{x}$ is a random variable, then Jensen's inequality says that

$$E[U(\tilde{x})] < U(E[\tilde{x}]) \tag{1.15}$$

Therefore, substituting $\tilde{x} = W + \tilde{\varepsilon}$ with $E[\tilde{\varepsilon}] = 0$, we have

$$E\left[U(W + \tilde{\varepsilon})\right] < U\left(E\left[W + \tilde{\varepsilon}\right]\right) = U(W) \tag{1.16}$$

which is the desired result.

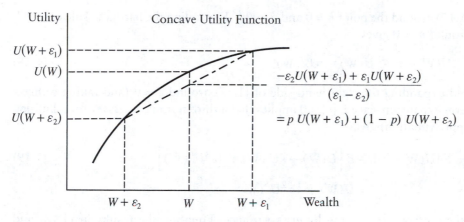

Figure 1.1 ——Fair Lotteries Lower Utility

We have defined risk aversion in terms of the individual's utility function.[12] Let us now consider how this aversion to risk can be quantified. This is done by defining a *risk premium*, the amount that an individual is willing to pay to avoid a risk.

Let π denote the individual's risk premium for a particular lottery, $\tilde{\varepsilon}$. It can be likened to the maximum insurance payment an individual would pay to avoid a particular risk. John W. Pratt (Pratt 1964) defined the risk premium for lottery (asset) $\tilde{\varepsilon}$ as

$$U(W - \pi) = E\left[U(W + \tilde{\varepsilon})\right] \tag{1.17}$$

$W - \pi$ is defined as the *certainty equivalent* level of wealth associated with the lottery, $\tilde{\varepsilon}$. Since utility is an increasing, concave function of wealth, Jensen's inequality ensures that π must be positive when $\tilde{\varepsilon}$ is fair; that is, the individual would accept a level of wealth lower than her expected level of wealth following the lottery, $E\left[W + \tilde{\varepsilon}\right]$, if the lottery could be avoided.

To analyze this Pratt risk premium (Pratt 1964), we continue to assume the individual is an expected utility maximizer and that $\tilde{\varepsilon}$ is a fair lottery; that is, its expected value equals zero. Further, let us consider the case of $\tilde{\varepsilon}$ being "small" so that we can study its effects by taking a Taylor series approximation of equation

---

12. Based on the same analysis, it is straightforward to show that if an individual strictly prefers a fair lottery, his utility function must be convex in wealth. Such an individual is said to be risk-loving. Similarly, an individual who is indifferent between accepting or refusing a fair lottery is said to be risk-neutral and must have utility that is a linear function of wealth.

(1.17) around the point $\widetilde{\varepsilon} = 0$ and $\pi = 0$.[13] Expanding the left-hand side of (1.17) around $\pi = 0$ gives

$$U(W - \pi) \cong U(W) - \pi U'(W) \tag{1.18}$$

and expanding the right-hand side of (1.17) around $\widetilde{\varepsilon} = 0$ (and taking a three-term expansion since $E[\widetilde{\varepsilon}] = 0$ implies that a third term is necessary for a limiting approximation) gives

$$E[U(W + \widetilde{\varepsilon})] \cong E\left[U(W) + \widetilde{\varepsilon}U'(W) + \tfrac{1}{2}\widetilde{\varepsilon}^2 U''(W)\right] \tag{1.19}$$

$$= U(W) + \tfrac{1}{2}\sigma^2 U''(W)$$

where $\sigma^2 \equiv E[\widetilde{\varepsilon}^2]$ is the lottery's variance. Equating the results in (1.18) and (1.19), we have

$$\pi = -\tfrac{1}{2}\sigma^2 \frac{U''(W)}{U'(W)} \equiv \tfrac{1}{2}\sigma^2 R(W) \tag{1.20}$$

where $R(W) \equiv -U''(W)/U'(W)$ is the Pratt-Arrow measure of absolute risk aversion (Pratt 1964; Arrow 1971). Note that the risk premium, π, depends on the uncertainty of the risky asset, σ^2, and on the individual's coefficient of absolute risk aversion. Since σ^2 and $U'(W)$ are both greater than zero, concavity of the utility function ensures that π must be positive.

From equation (1.20) we see that the concavity of the utility function, $U''(W)$, is insufficient to quantify the risk premium an individual is willing to pay, even though it is necessary and sufficient to indicate whether the individual is risk averse. In order to determine the risk premium, we also need the first derivative, $U'(W)$, which tells us the marginal utility of wealth. An individual may be very risk averse ($-U''(W)$ is large), but he may be unwilling to pay a large risk premium if he is poor since his marginal utility is high ($U'(W)$ is large).

To illustrate this point, consider the following *negative exponential* utility function:

$$U(W) = -e^{-bW}, b > 0 \tag{1.21}$$

Note that $U'(W) = be^{-bW} > 0$ and $U''(W) = -b^2 e^{-bW} < 0$. Consider the behavior of a very wealthy individual, that is, one whose wealth approaches infinity:

$$\lim_{W \to \infty} U'(W) = \lim_{W \to \infty} U''(W) = 0 \tag{1.22}$$

---

13. By describing the random variable $\widetilde{\varepsilon}$ as "small," we mean that its probability density is concentrated around its mean of 0.

As $W \to \infty$, the utility function is a flat line. Concavity disappears, which might imply that this very rich individual would be willing to pay very little for insurance against a random event, $\tilde{\varepsilon}$, certainly less than a poor person with the same utility function. However, this is not true, because the marginal utility of wealth is also very small. This neutralizes the effect of smaller concavity. Indeed,

$$R(W) = \frac{b^2 e^{-bW}}{b e^{-bW}} = b \tag{1.23}$$

which is a constant. Thus, we can see why this utility function is sometimes referred to as a *constant absolute-risk-aversion* utility function.

If we want to assume that absolute risk aversion is declining in wealth, a necessary, though not sufficient, condition for this is that the utility function have a positive third derivative, since

$$\frac{\partial R(W)}{\partial W} = -\frac{U'''(W)U'(W) - [U''(W)]^2}{[U'(W)]^2} \tag{1.24}$$

Also, it can be shown that the coefficient of risk aversion contains all relevant information about the individual's risk preferences. To see this, note that

$$R(W) = -\frac{U''(W)}{U'(W)} = -\frac{\partial \left(\ln \left[U'(W) \right] \right)}{\partial W} \tag{1.25}$$

Integrating both sides of (1.25), we have

$$-\int R(W) dW = \ln[U'(W)] + c_1 \tag{1.26}$$

where c_1 is an arbitrary constant. Taking the exponential function of (1.26), one obtains

$$e^{-\int R(W) dW} = U'(W) e^{c_1} \tag{1.27}$$

Integrating once again gives

$$\int e^{-\int R(W) dW} dW = e^{c_1} U(W) + c_2 \tag{1.28}$$

where c_2 is another arbitrary constant. Because expected utility functions are unique up to a linear transformation, $e^{c_1} U(W) + c_1$ reflects the same risk preferences as $U(W)$. Hence, this shows one can recover the risk preferences of $U(W)$ from the function $R(W)$.

Relative risk aversion is another frequently used measure of risk aversion and is defined simply as

$$R_r(W) = WR(W) \tag{1.29}$$

In many applications in financial economics, an individual is assumed to have relative risk aversion that is constant for different levels of wealth. Note that this assumption implies that the individual's absolute risk aversion, $R(W)$, declines in direct proportion to increases in his wealth. While later chapters will discuss the widely varied empirical evidence on the size of individuals' relative risk aversions, one recent study based on individuals' answers to survey questions finds a median relative risk aversion of approximately 7.[14]

Let us now examine the coefficients of risk aversion for some utility functions that are frequently used in models of portfolio choice and asset pricing. *Power* utility can be written as

$$U(W) = \frac{1}{\gamma} W^\gamma, \gamma < 1 \tag{1.30}$$

implying that $R(W) = -\frac{(\gamma-1)W^{\gamma-2}}{W^{\gamma-1}} = \frac{(1-\gamma)}{W}$ and, therefore, $R_r(W) = 1 - \gamma$. Hence, this form of utility is also known as *constant relative risk aversion*. *Logarithmic* utility is a limiting case of power utility. To see this, write the power utility function as $\frac{1}{\gamma} W^\gamma - \frac{1}{\gamma} = \frac{W^\gamma - 1}{\gamma}$.[15] Next take the limit of this utility function as $\gamma \to 0$. Note that the numerator and denominator both go to zero, such that the limit is not obvious. However, we can rewrite the numerator in terms of an exponential and natural log function and apply L'Hôpital's rule to obtain

$$\lim_{\gamma \to 0} \frac{W^\gamma - 1}{\gamma} = \lim_{\gamma \to 0} \frac{e^{\gamma \ln(W)} - 1}{\gamma} = \lim_{\gamma \to 0} \frac{\ln(W) W^\gamma}{1} = \ln(W) \tag{1.31}$$

Thus, logarithmic utility is equivalent to power utility with $\gamma = 0$, or a coefficient of relative risk aversion of unity: $R(W) = -\frac{W^{-2}}{W^{-1}} = \frac{1}{W}$ and $R_r(W) = 1$.

Quadratic utility takes the form

$$U(W) = W - \frac{b}{2} W^2, b > 0 \tag{1.32}$$

---

14. The mean estimate was lower, indicating a skewed distribution. Robert Barsky, Thomas Juster, Miles Kimball, and Matthew Shapiro (Barsky et al. 1997) computed these estimates of relative risk aversion from a survey that asked a series of questions regarding whether the respondent would switch to a new job that had a 50-50 chance of doubling their lifetime income or decreasing their lifetime income by a proportion λ. By varying λ in the questions, they estimated the point where an individual would be indifferent between keeping their current job or switching. Essentially, they attempted to find λ^* such that $\frac{1}{2} U(2W) + \frac{1}{2} U(\lambda^* W) = U(W)$. Assuming utility displays constant relative risk aversion of the form $U(W) = W^\gamma/\gamma$, then the coefficient of relative risk aversion, $1 - \gamma$, satisfies $2^\gamma + \lambda^{*\gamma} = 2$. The authors warn that their estimates of risk aversion may be biased upward if individuals attach nonpecuniary benefits to maintaining their current occupation. Interestingly, they confirmed that estimates of relative risk aversion tended to be lower for individuals who smoked, drank, were uninsured, held riskier jobs, and invested in riskier assets.

15. Recall that we can do this because utility functions are unique up to a linear transformation.

Note that the marginal utility of wealth is $U'(W) = 1 - bW$ and is positive only when $b < \frac{1}{W}$. Thus, this utility function makes sense (in that more wealth is preferred to less) only when $W < \frac{1}{b}$. The point of maximum utility, $\frac{1}{b}$, is known as the "bliss point." We have $R(W) = \frac{b}{1-bW}$ and $R_r(W) = \frac{bW}{1-bW}$.

Hyperbolic absolute-risk-aversion (HARA) utility is a generalization of all of the aforementioned utility functions. It can be written as

$$U(W) = \frac{1-\gamma}{\gamma}\left(\frac{\alpha W}{1-\gamma} + \beta\right)^{\gamma} \tag{1.33}$$

subject to the restrictions $\gamma \neq 1$, $\alpha > 0$, $\frac{\alpha W}{1-\gamma} + \beta > 0$, and $\beta = 1$ if $\gamma = -\infty$. Thus, $R(W) = \left(\frac{W}{1-\gamma} + \frac{\beta}{\alpha}\right)^{-1}$. Since $R(W)$ must be > 0, it implies $\beta > 0$ when $\gamma > 1$. $R_r(W) = W\left(\frac{W}{1-\gamma} + \frac{\beta}{\alpha}\right)^{-1}$. HARA utility nests constant absolute-risk-aversion ($\gamma = -\infty$, $\beta = 1$), constant relative-risk-aversion ($\gamma < 1$, $\beta = 0$), and quadratic ($\gamma = 2$) utility functions. Thus, depending on the parameters, it is able to display constant absolute risk aversion or relative risk aversion that is increasing, decreasing, or constant. We will revisit HARA utility in future chapters as it can be an analytically convenient assumption for utility when deriving an individual's intertemporal consumption and portfolio choices.

Pratt's definition of a risk premium in equation (1.17) is commonly used in the insurance literature because it can be interpreted as the payment that an individual is willing to make to insure against a particular risk. However, in the field of financial economics, a somewhat different definition is often employed. Financial economists seek to understand how the risk of an asset's payoff determines the asset's rate of return. In this context, an asset's risk premium is defined as its expected rate of return in excess of the risk-free rate of return. This alternative concept of a risk premium was used by Kenneth Arrow (Arrow 1971), who independently derived a coefficient of risk aversion that is identical to Pratt's measure. Let us now outline Arrow's approach. Suppose that an asset (lottery), $\tilde{\varepsilon}$, has the following payoffs and probabilities (which could be generalized to other types of fair payoffs):

$$\tilde{\varepsilon} = \begin{cases} +\epsilon & \text{with probability } \frac{1}{2} \\ -\epsilon & \text{with probability } \frac{1}{2} \end{cases} \tag{1.34}$$

where $\epsilon \geq 0$. Note that, as before, $E[\tilde{\varepsilon}] = 0$. Now consider the following question. By how much should we change the expected value (return) of the asset, by changing the probability of winning, in order to make the individual indifferent between taking and not taking the risk? If p is the probability of winning, we can define the risk premium as

$$\theta = prob \; (\tilde{\varepsilon} = +\epsilon) - prob \; (\tilde{\varepsilon} = -\epsilon) = p - (1-p) = 2p - 1 \qquad (1.35)$$

Therefore, from (1.35) we have

$$prob \; (\tilde{\varepsilon} = +\epsilon) \equiv p = \frac{1}{2}(1+\theta)$$

$$\qquad (1.36)$$

$$prob \; (\tilde{\varepsilon} = -\epsilon) \equiv 1 - p = \frac{1}{2}(1-\theta)$$

These new probabilities of winning and losing are equal to the old probabilities, $\frac{1}{2}$, plus half of the increment, θ. Thus, the premium, θ, that makes the individual indifferent between accepting and refusing the asset is

$$U(W) = \frac{1}{2}(1+\theta)U(W+\epsilon) + \frac{1}{2}(1-\theta)U(W-\epsilon) \qquad (1.37)$$

Taking a Taylor series approximation around $\epsilon = 0$ gives

$$U(W) = \frac{1}{2}(1+\theta)\left[U(W) + \epsilon U'(W) + \tfrac{1}{2}\epsilon^2 U''(W)\right] \qquad (1.38)$$

$$+ \frac{1}{2}(1-\theta)\left[U(W) - \epsilon U'(W) + \tfrac{1}{2}\epsilon^2 U''(W)\right]$$

$$= U(W) + \epsilon\theta U'(W) + \tfrac{1}{2}\epsilon^2 U''(W)$$

Rearranging (1.38) implies

$$\theta = \tfrac{1}{2}\epsilon R(W) \qquad (1.39)$$

which, as before, is a function of the coefficient of absolute risk aversion. Note that the Arrow premium, θ, is in terms of a probability, while the Pratt measure, π, is in units of a monetary payment. If we multiply θ by the monetary payment received, ϵ, then equation (1.39) becomes

$$\epsilon\theta = \tfrac{1}{2}\epsilon^2 R(W) \qquad (1.40)$$

Since ϵ^2 is the variance of the random payoff, $\tilde{\varepsilon}$, equation (1.40) shows that the Pratt and Arrow measures of risk premia are equivalent. Both were obtained as a linearization of the true function around $\tilde{\varepsilon} = 0$.

The results of this section showed how risk aversion depends on the shape of an individual's utility function. Moreover, it demonstrated that a risk premium, equal to either the payment an individual would make to avoid a risk or the individual's required excess rate of return on a risky asset, is proportional to the individual's Pratt-Arrow coefficient of absolute risk aversion.

1.3 Risk Aversion and Portfolio Choice

Having developed the concepts of risk aversion and risk premiums, we now consider the relation between risk aversion and an individual's portfolio choice in a single-period context. While the portfolio choice problem that we analyze is very simple, many of its insights extend to the more complex environments that will be covered in later chapters of this book. We shall demonstrate that absolute and relative risk aversion play important roles in determining how portfolio choices vary with an individual's level of wealth. Moreover, we show that when given a choice between a risk-free asset and a risky asset, a risk-averse individual always chooses at least some positive investment in the risky asset if it pays a positive risk premium.

The model's assumptions are as follows. Assume there is a riskless security that pays a rate of return equal to r_f. In addition, for simplicity, suppose there is just one risky security that pays a stochastic rate of return equal to $\tilde{r}$. Also, let W_0 be the individual's initial wealth, and let A be the dollar amount that the individual invests in the risky asset at the beginning of the period. Thus, $W_0 - A$ is the initial investment in the riskless security. Denoting the individual's end-of-period wealth as $\widetilde{W}$, it satisfies

$$\widetilde{W} = (W_0 - A)(1 + r_f) + A(1 + \tilde{r}) \tag{1.41}$$
$$= W_0(1 + r_f) + A(\tilde{r} - r_f)$$

Note that in the second line of equation (1.41), the first term is the individual's return on wealth when the entire portfolio is invested in the risk-free asset, while the second term is the difference in return gained by investing A dollars in the risky asset.

We assume that the individual cares only about consumption at the end of this single period. Therefore, maximizing end-of-period consumption is equivalent to maximizing end-of-period wealth. Assuming that the individual is a von Neumann–Morgenstern expected utility maximizer, she chooses her portfolio by maximizing the expected utility of end-of-period wealth:

$$\max_A E[U(\widetilde{W})] = \max_A E\left[U\left(W_0(1 + r_f) + A(\tilde{r} - r_f)\right)\right] \tag{1.42}$$

The solution to the individual's problem in (1.42) must satisfy the following first-order condition with respect to A:

$$E\left[U'\left(\widetilde{W}\right)\left(\tilde{r} - r_f\right)\right] = 0 \tag{1.43}$$

This condition determines the amount, A, that the individual invests in the risky asset.[16] Consider the special case in which the expected rate of return on the risky asset equals the risk-free rate. In that case, $A = 0$ satisfies the first-order condition. To see this, note that when $A = 0$, then $\widetilde{W} = W_0(1 + r_f)$ and, therefore, $U'(\widetilde{W}) = U'(W_0(1 + r_f))$ are nonstochastic. Hence, $E[U'(\widetilde{W})(\tilde{r} - r_f)] = U'(W_0(1 + r_f))E[\tilde{r} - r_f] = 0$. This result is reminiscent of our earlier finding that a risk-averse individual would not choose to accept a fair lottery. Here, the fair lottery is interpreted as a risky asset that has an expected rate of return just equal to the risk-free rate.

Next, consider the case in which $E[\tilde{r}] - r_f > 0$. Clearly, $A = 0$ would not satisfy the first-order condition, because $E[U'(\widetilde{W})(\tilde{r} - r_f)] = U'(W_0(1 + r_f))E[\tilde{r} - r_f] > 0$ when $A = 0$. Rather, when $E[\tilde{r}] - r_f > 0$, condition (1.43) is satisfied only when $A > 0$. To see this, let r^h denote a realization of $\tilde{r}$ such that it exceeds r_f, and let W^h be the corresponding level of $\widetilde{W}$. Also, let r^l denote a realization of $\tilde{r}$ such that it is lower than r_f, and let W^l be the corresponding level of $\widetilde{W}$. Obviously, $U'(W^h)(r^h - r_f) > 0$ and $U'(W^l)(r^l - r_f) < 0$. For $U'(\widetilde{W})(\tilde{r} - r_f)$ to average to zero for all realizations of $\tilde{r}$, it must be the case that $W^h > W^l$ so that $U'(W^h) < U'(W^l)$ due to the concavity of the utility function. This is because $E[\tilde{r}] - r_f > 0$, so the average realization of r^h is farther above r_f than the average realization of r^l is below r_f. Therefore, to make $U'(\widetilde{W})(\tilde{r} - r_f)$ average to zero, the positive $(r^h - r_f)$ terms need to be given weights, $U'(W^h)$, that are smaller than the weights, $U'(W^l)$, that multiply the negative $(r^l - r_f)$ realizations. This can occur only if $A > 0$ so that $W^h > W^l$. The implication is that an individual will always hold at least some positive amount of the risky asset if its expected rate of return exceeds the risk-free rate.[17]

Now, we can go further and explore the relationship between A and the individual's initial wealth, W_0. Using the envelope theorem, we can differentiate the first-order condition to obtain[18]

---

16. The second-order condition for a maximum, $E[U''(\widetilde{W})(\tilde{r} - r_f)^2] \leq 0$, is satisfied because $U''(\widetilde{W}) \leq 0$ due to the assumed concavity of the utility function.

17. Related to this is the notion that a risk-averse expected utility maximizer should accept a small lottery with a positive expected return. In other words, such an individual should be close to risk-neutral for small-scale bets. However, Matthew Rabin and Richard Thaler (Rabin and Thaler 2001) claim that individuals frequently reject lotteries (gambles) that are modest in size yet have positive expected returns. From this they argue that concave expected utility is not a plausible model for predicting an individual's choice of small-scale risks.

18. The envelope theorem is used to analyze how the maximized value of the objective function and the control variable change when one of the model's parameters changes. In our context, define $f(A, W_0) \equiv E[U(\widetilde{W})]$ so that $v(W_0) = \max_A f(A, W_0)$ is the maximized value of the

$$E\left[U''(\widetilde{W})(\tilde{r}-r_f)(1+r_f)\right]dW_0 + E\left[U''(\widetilde{W})(\tilde{r}-r_f)^2\right]dA = 0 \tag{1.44}$$

or

$$\frac{dA}{dW_0} = \frac{(1+r_f)E\left[U''(\widetilde{W})(\tilde{r}-r_f)\right]}{-E\left[U''(\widetilde{W})(\tilde{r}-r_f)^2\right]} \tag{1.45}$$

The denominator of (1.45) is positive because concavity of the utility function ensures that $U''(\widetilde{W})$ is negative. Therefore, the sign of the expression depends on the numerator, which can be of either sign because realizations of $(\tilde{r}-r_f)$ can turn out to be both positive and negative.

To characterize situations in which the sign of (1.45) can be determined, let us first consider the case where the individual has absolute risk aversion that is decreasing in wealth. As before, let r^h denote a realization of $\tilde{r}$ such that it exceeds r_f, and let W^h be the corresponding level of $\widetilde{W}$. Then for $A \geq 0$, we have $W^h \geq W_0(1+r_f)$. If absolute risk aversion is decreasing in wealth, this implies

$$R\left(W^h\right) \leq R\left(W_0(1+r_f)\right) \tag{1.46}$$

where, as before, $R(W) = -U''(W)/U'(W)$. Multiplying both terms of (1.46) by $-U'(W^h)(r^h-r_f)$, which is a negative quantity, the inequality sign changes:

$$U''(W^h)(r^h-r_f) \geq -U'(W^h)(r^h-r_f)R\left(W_0(1+r_f)\right) \tag{1.47}$$

Next, we again let r^l denote a realization of $\tilde{r}$ that is lower than r_f and define W^l to be the corresponding level of $\widetilde{W}$. Then for $A \geq 0$, we have $W^l \leq W_0(1+r_f)$. If absolute risk aversion is decreasing in wealth, this implies

$$R(W^l) \geq R\left(W_0(1+r_f)\right) \tag{1.48}$$

---

objective function when the control variable, A, is optimally chosen. Also define $A(W_0)$ as the value of A that maximizes f for a given value of W_0. Then applying the chain rule, we have $\frac{dv(W_0)}{dW_0} = \frac{\partial f(A,W_0)}{\partial A}\frac{dA(W_0)}{dW_0} + \frac{\partial f(A(W_0),W_0)}{\partial W_0}$. But since $\frac{\partial f(A,W_0)}{\partial A} = 0$, from the first-order condition, this simplifies to just $\frac{dv(W_0)}{dW_0} = \frac{\partial f(A(W_0),W_0)}{\partial W_0}$. Again applying the chain rule to the first-order condition, one obtains $\frac{\partial(\partial f(A(W_0),W_0)/\partial A)}{\partial W_0} = 0 = \frac{\partial^2 f(A(W_0),W_0)}{\partial A^2}\frac{dA(W_0)}{dW_0} + \frac{\partial^2 f(A(W_0),W_0)}{\partial A\partial W_0}$. Rearranging gives us $\frac{dA(W_0)}{dW_0} = -\frac{\partial^2 f(A(W_0),W_0)}{\partial A\partial W_0} \big/ \frac{\partial^2 f(A(W_0),W_0)}{\partial A^2}$, which is equation (1.45).

Multiplying (1.48) by $-U'(W^l)(r^l - r_f)$, which is positive, so that the sign of (1.48) remains the same, we obtain

$$U''(W^l)(r^l - r_f) \geq -U'(W^l)(r^l - r_f)R\left(W_0(1 + r_f)\right) \tag{1.49}$$

Notice that inequalities (1.47) and (1.49) are of the same form. The inequality holds whether the realization is $\tilde{r} = r^h$ or $\tilde{r} = r^l$. Therefore, if we take expectations over all realizations, where $\tilde{r}$ can be either higher than or lower than r_f, we obtain

$$E\left[U''(\widetilde{W})(\tilde{r} - r_f)\right] \geq -E\left[U'(\widetilde{W})(\tilde{r} - r_f)\right]R\left(W_0(1 + r_f)\right) \tag{1.50}$$

Since the first term on the right-hand side is just the first-order condition, inequality (1.50) reduces to

$$E\left[U''(\widetilde{W})(\tilde{r} - r_f)\right] \geq 0 \tag{1.51}$$

Thus, the first conclusion that can be drawn is that declining absolute risk aversion implies $dA/dW_0 > 0$; that is, the individual invests an increasing amount of wealth in the risky asset for larger amounts of initial wealth. For two individuals with the same utility function but different initial wealths, the wealthier one invests a greater dollar amount in the risky asset if utility is characterized by decreasing absolute risk aversion. While not shown here, the opposite is true, namely, that the wealthier individual invests a smaller dollar amount in the risky asset if utility is characterized by increasing absolute risk aversion.

Thus far, we have not said anything about the *proportion* of initial wealth invested in the risky asset. To analyze this issue, we need the concept of relative risk aversion. Define

$$\eta \equiv \frac{dA}{dW_0}\frac{W_0}{A} \tag{1.52}$$

which is the elasticity measuring the proportional increase in the risky asset for an increase in initial wealth. Adding $1 - \frac{A}{A}$ to the right-hand side of (1.52) gives

$$\eta = 1 + \frac{(dA/dW_0)W_0 - A}{A} \tag{1.53}$$

Substituting the expression dA/dW_0 from equation (1.45), we have

$$\eta = 1 + \frac{W_0(1 + r_f)E\left[U''(\widetilde{W})(\tilde{r} - r_f)\right] + AE\left[U''(\widetilde{W})(\tilde{r} - r_f)^2\right]}{-AE\left[U''(\widetilde{W})(\tilde{r} - r_f)^2\right]} \tag{1.54}$$

Collecting terms in $U''(\widetilde{W})(\tilde{r} - r_f)$, this can be rewritten as

$$\eta = 1 + \frac{E\left[U''(\widetilde{W})(\tilde{r} - r_f)\{W_0(1+r_f) + A(\tilde{r} - r_f)\}\right]}{-AE\left[U''(\widetilde{W})(\tilde{r} - r_f)^2\right]} \tag{1.55}$$

$$= 1 + \frac{E\left[U''(\widetilde{W})(\tilde{r} - r_f)\widetilde{W}\right]}{-AE\left[U''(\widetilde{W})(\tilde{r} - r_f)^2\right]}$$

The denominator is always positive. Therefore, we see that the elasticity, η, is greater than one, so that the individual invests proportionally more in the risky asset with an increase in wealth, if $E\left[U''(\widetilde{W})(\tilde{r} - r_f)\widetilde{W}\right] \geq 0$. Can we relate this to the individual's risk aversion? The answer is yes and the derivation is almost exactly the same as that just given.

Consider the case where the individual has *relative* risk aversion that is decreasing in wealth. Let r^h denote a realization of $\tilde{r}$ such that it exceeds r_f, and let W^h be the corresponding level of $\widetilde{W}$. Then for $A \geq 0$, we have $W^h \geq W_0(1 + r_f)$. If relative risk aversion, $R_r(W) \equiv WR(W)$, is decreasing in wealth, this implies

$$W^h R(W^h) \leq W_0(1 + r_f)R\left(W_0(1 + r_f)\right) \tag{1.56}$$

Multiplying both terms of (1.56) by $-U'(W^h)(r^h - r_f)$, which is a negative quantity, the inequality sign changes:

$$W^h U''(W^h)(r^h - r_f) \geq -U'(W^h)(r^h - r_f)W_0(1 + r_f)R\left(W_0(1 + r_f)\right) \tag{1.57}$$

Next, let r^l denote a realization of $\tilde{r}$ such that it is lower than r_f, and let W^l be the corresponding level of $\widetilde{W}$. Then for $A \geq 0$, we have $W^l \leq W_0(1 + r_f)$. If relative risk aversion is decreasing in wealth, this implies

$$W^l R(W^l) \geq W_0(1 + r_f)R\left(W_0(1 + r_f)\right) \tag{1.58}$$

Multiplying (1.58) by $-U'(W^l)(r^l - r_f)$, which is positive, so that the sign of (1.58) remains the same, we obtain

$$W^l U''(W^l)(r^l - r_f) \geq -U'(W^l)(r^l - r_f)W_0(1 + r_f)R\left(W_0(1 + r_f)\right) \tag{1.59}$$

Notice that inequalities (1.57) and (1.59) are of the same form. The inequality holds whether the realization is $\tilde{r} = r^h$ or $\tilde{r} = r^l$. Therefore, if we take expectations over all realizations, where $\tilde{r}$ can be either higher than or lower than r_f, we obtain

$$E\left[\widetilde{W}U''(\widetilde{W})(\tilde{r} - r_f)\right] \geq -E\left[U'(\widetilde{W})(\tilde{r} - r_f)\right]W_0(1 + r_f)R(W_0(1 + r_f)) \tag{1.60}$$

Since the first term on the right-hand side is just the first-order condition, inequality (1.60) reduces to

$$E\left[\widetilde{W}U''(\widetilde{W})(\tilde{r}-r_f)\right] \geq 0 \tag{1.61}$$

Thus, we see that an individual with decreasing relative risk aversion has $\eta > 1$ and invests proportionally more in the risky asset as wealth increases. The opposite is true for increasing relative risk aversion: $\eta < 1$ so that this individual invests proportionally less in the risky asset as wealth increases. The following table provides another way of writing this section's main results.

Risk Aversion	Investment Behavior
Decreasing Absolute	$\frac{\partial A}{\partial W_0} > 0$
Constant Absolute	$\frac{\partial A}{\partial W_0} = 0$
Increasing Absolute	$\frac{\partial A}{\partial W_0} < 0$
Decreasing Relative	$\frac{\partial A}{\partial W_0} > \frac{A}{W_0}$
Constant Relative	$\frac{\partial A}{\partial W_0} = \frac{A}{W_0}$
Increasing Relative	$\frac{\partial A}{\partial W_0} < \frac{A}{W_0}$

A point worth emphasizing is that absolute risk aversion indicates how the investor's dollar amount in the risky asset changes with changes in initial wealth, whereas relative risk aversion indicates how the investor's portfolio proportion (or portfolio weight) in the risky asset, A/W_0, changes with changes in initial wealth.

1.4 Summary

This chapter is a first step toward understanding how an individual's preferences toward risk affect his portfolio behavior. It was shown that if an individual's risk preferences satisfied specific plausible conditions, then her behavior could be represented by a von Neumann–Morgenstern expected utility function. In turn, the shape of the individual's utility function determines a measure of risk aversion that is linked to two concepts of a risk premium. The first one is the monetary payment that the individual is willing to pay to avoid a risk, an example being a premium paid to insure against a property/casualty loss. The second is the rate of return in excess of a riskless rate that the individual requires to hold a risky asset, which is the common definition of a security risk premium used in the finance literature. Finally, it was shown how an individual's absolute and relative risk aversion affect his choice between a risky and risk-free asset. In particular, individuals with decreasing (*increasing*) relative risk aversion invest proportionally more (*less*) in the risky asset as their wealth increases. Though based on a simple single-period, two-asset portfolio choice model, this insight generalizes to the more complex portfolio choice problems that will be studied in later chapters.

1.5 Exercises

1. Suppose there are two lotteries $P = \{p_1, \ldots, p_n\}$ and $P^* = \{p_1^*, \ldots, p_n^*\}$. Let $V(p_1, \ldots, p_n) = \sum_{i=1}^{n} p_i U_i$ be an individual's expected utility function defined over these lotteries. Let $W(p_1, \ldots, p_n) = \sum_{i=1}^{n} p_i Q_i$ where $Q_i = a + b U_i$ and a and b are constants. If $P^* \succ P$, so that $V(p_1^*, \ldots, p_n^*) > V(p_1, \ldots, p_n)$, must it be the case that $W(p_1^*, \ldots, p_n^*) > W(p_1, \ldots, p_n)$? In other words, is W also a valid expected utility function for the individual? Are there any restrictions needed on a and b for this to be the case?

2. (Allais paradox) Asset A pays \$1,500 with certainty, while asset B pays \$2,000 with probability 0.8 or \$100 with probability 0.2. If offered the choice between asset A or B, a particular individual would choose asset A. Suppose, instead, that the individual is offered the choice between asset C and asset D. Asset C pays \$1,500 with probability 0.25 or \$100 with probability 0.75, while asset D pays \$2,000 with probability 0.2 or \$100 with probability 0.8. If asset D is chosen, show that the individual's preferences violate the independence axiom.

3. Verify that the HARA utility function in equation (1.33) becomes the constant absolute-risk-aversion utility function when $\beta = 1$ and $\gamma = -\infty$. Hint: recall that $e^a = \lim_{x \to \infty} \left(1 + \frac{a}{x}\right)^x$.

4. Consider the individual's portfolio choice problem given in equation (1.42). Assume $U(W) = \ln(W)$ and the rate of return on the risky asset equals

$$\widetilde{r} = \begin{cases} 4r_f & \text{with probability } \frac{1}{2} \\ -r_f & \text{with probability } \frac{1}{2}. \end{cases}$$

Solve for the individual's proportion of initial wealth invested in the risky asset, A/W_0.

5. An expected-utility-maximizing individual has constant relative-risk-aversion utility, $U(W) = W^\gamma / \gamma$, with relative-risk-aversion coefficient of $\gamma = -1$. The individual currently owns a product that has a probability p of failing, an event that would result in a loss of wealth that has a present value equal to L. With probability $1 - p$, the product will not fail and no loss will result. The individual is considering whether to purchase an extended warranty on this product. The warranty costs C and would insure the individual against

loss if the product fails. Assuming that the cost of the warranty exceeds the expected loss from the product's failure, determine the individual's level of wealth at which she would be just indifferent between purchasing or not purchasing the warranty.

6. In the context of the portfolio choice problem in equation (1.42), show that an individual with increasing relative risk aversion invests proportionally less in the risky asset as her initial wealth increases.

7. Consider the following four assets whose payoffs are as follows:

$$\text{Asset A} = \begin{cases} X & \text{with probability } p_x \\ 0 & \text{with probability } 1 - p_x \end{cases}$$

$$\text{Asset B} = \begin{cases} Y & \text{with probability } p_y \\ 0 & \text{with probability } 1 - p_y \end{cases}$$

$$\text{Asset C} = \begin{cases} X & \text{with probability } \alpha p_x \\ 0 & \text{with probability } 1 - \alpha p_x \end{cases}$$

$$\text{Asset D} = \begin{cases} Y & \text{with probability } \alpha p_y \\ 0 & \text{with probability } 1 - \alpha p_y \end{cases}$$

where $0 < X < Y$, $p_y < p_x$, $p_x X < p_y Y$, and $\alpha \in (0, 1)$.

a. When given the choice of asset C versus asset D, an individual chooses asset C. Could this individual's preferences be consistent with von Neumann–Morgenstern expected utility theory? Explain why or why not.

b. When given the choice of asset A versus asset B, an individual chooses asset A. This same individual, when given the choice between asset C and asset D, chooses asset D. Could this individual's preferences be consistent with von Neumann–Morgenstern expected utility theory? Explain why or why not.

8. An individual has expected utility of the form

$$E\left[U\left(\widetilde{W}\right)\right] = E\left[-e^{-b\widetilde{W}}\right]$$

where $b > 0$. The individual's wealth is normally distributed as $N(\overline{W}, \sigma_{\widetilde{W}}^2)$. What is this individual's *certainty equivalent* level of wealth?

CHAPTER 2

Mean-Variance Analysis

The preceding chapter studied an investor's choice between a risk-free asset and a single risky asset. This chapter adds realism by giving the investor the opportunity to choose among multiple risky assets. As a University of Chicago graduate student, Harry Markowitz wrote a path-breaking article on this topic (Markowitz 1952).[1] Markowitz's insight was to recognize that, in allocating wealth among various risky assets, a risk-averse investor should focus on the expectation and the risk of her combined portfolio's return, a return that is affected by the individual assets' diversification possibilities. Because of diversification, the attractiveness of a particular asset when held in a portfolio can differ from its appeal when it is the sole asset held by an investor.

Markowitz proxied the risk of a portfolio's return by the variance of its return. Of course, the variance of an investor's total portfolio return depends on the return variances of the individual assets included in the portfolio. But portfolio return variance also depends on the covariances of the individual assets' returns. Hence, in selecting an optimal portfolio, the investor needs to consider how the comovement of individual assets' returns affects diversification possibilities.

A rational investor would want to choose a portfolio of assets that efficiently trades off higher expected return for lower variance of return. Interestingly, not all portfolios that an investor can create are efficient in this sense. Given the expected

---

1. His work on portfolio theory, of which this article was the beginning, won him a share of the Nobel prize in economics in 1990. Initially, the importance of his work was not widely recognized. Milton Friedman, a member of Markowitz's doctoral dissertation committee and later also a Nobel laureate, questioned whether the work met the requirements for an economics Ph.D. See (Bernstein 1992).

returns and covariances of returns on individual assets, Markowitz solved the investor's problem of constructing an efficient portfolio. His work has had an enormous impact on the theory and practice of portfolio management and asset pricing.

Intuitively, it makes sense that investors would want their wealth to earn a high average return with as little variance as possible. However, in general, an individual who maximizes expected utility may care about moments of the distribution of wealth in addition to its mean and variance.[2] Though Markowitz's mean-variance analysis fails to consider the effects of these other moments, in later chapters of this book we will see that his model's insights can be generalized to more complicated settings.

The next section outlines the assumptions on investor preferences and the distribution of asset returns that would allow us to simplify the investor's portfolio choice problem to one that considers only the mean and variance of portfolio returns. We then analyze a risk-averse investor's preferences by showing that he has indifference curves that imply a trade-off of expected return for variance. Subsequently, we show how a portfolio can be allocated among a given set of risky assets in a mean-variance efficient manner. We solve for the *efficient frontier*, defined as the set of portfolios that maximizes expected returns for a given variance of returns, and show that any two frontier portfolios can be combined to create a third. In addition, we show that a fundamental simplification to the investor's portfolio choice problem results when one of the assets included in the investor's choice set is a risk-free asset. The final section of this chapter applies mean-variance analysis to a problem of selecting securities to hedge the risk of commodity prices. This application is an example of how modern portfolio analysis has influenced the practice of risk management.

2.1   Assumptions on Preferences and Asset Returns

Suppose an expected-utility-maximizing individual invests her beginning-of-period wealth, W_0, in a particular portfolio of assets. Let $\tilde{R}_p$ be the random return

---

2. For example, expected utility can depend on the skewness (the third moment) of the return on wealth. The observation that some people purchase lottery tickets even though these investments have a negative expected rate of return suggests that their utility is enhanced by positive skewness. Alan Kraus and Robert Litzenberger (Kraus and Litzenberger 1976) developed a single-period portfolio selection and asset pricing model that extends Markowitz's analysis to consider investors who have a preference for skewness. Their results generalize Markowitz's model, but his fundamental insights are unchanged. For simplicity, this chapter focuses on the orginal Markowitz framework. Recent empirical work by Campbell Harvey and Akhtar Siddique (Harvey and Siddique 2000) examines the effect of skewness on asset pricing.

on this portfolio, so that the individual's end-of-period wealth is $\widetilde{W} = W_0\widetilde{R}_p$.[3] Denote this individual's end-of-period utility by $U(\widetilde{W})$. Given W_0, for notational simplicity we write $U(\widetilde{W}) = U(W_0\widetilde{R}_p)$ as just $U(\widetilde{R}_p)$, because $\widetilde{W}$ is completely determined by $\widetilde{R}_p$.

Let us express $U(\widetilde{R}_p)$ by expanding it in a Taylor series around the mean of $\widetilde{R}_p$, denoted as $E[\widetilde{R}_p]$. Let $U'(\cdot)$, $U''(\cdot)$, and $U^{(n)}(\cdot)$ denote the first, second, and nth derivatives of the utility function:

$$U(\widetilde{R}_p) = U\left(E[\widetilde{R}_p]\right) + \left(\widetilde{R}_p - E[\widetilde{R}_p]\right) U'\left(E[\widetilde{R}_p]\right)$$

$$+ \tfrac{1}{2}\left(\widetilde{R}_p - E[\widetilde{R}_p]\right)^2 U''\left(E[\widetilde{R}_p]\right) + \cdots$$

$$+ \tfrac{1}{n!}\left(\widetilde{R}_p - E[\widetilde{R}_p]\right)^n U^{(n)}\left(E[\widetilde{R}_p]\right) + \cdots \tag{2.1}$$

Now let us investigate the conditions that would make this individual's expected utility depend only on the mean and variance of the portfolio return. We first analyze the restrictions on the form of utility, and then the restrictions on the distribution of asset returns, that would produce this result.

Note that if the utility function is quadratic, so that all derivatives of order 3 and higher are equal to zero ($U^{(n)} = 0$, $\forall\, n \geq 3$), then the individual's expected utility is

$$E\left[U(\widetilde{R}_p)\right] = U\left(E[\widetilde{R}_p]\right) + \tfrac{1}{2}E\left[\left(\widetilde{R}_p - E[\widetilde{R}_p]\right)^2\right] U''\left(E[\widetilde{R}_p]\right)$$

$$= U\left(E[\widetilde{R}_p]\right) + \tfrac{1}{2}V[\widetilde{R}_p]U''\left(E[\widetilde{R}_p]\right) \tag{2.2}$$

where $V[\widetilde{R}_p]$ is the variance of the return on the portfolio.[4] Therefore, for any probability distribution of the portfolio return, $\widetilde{R}_p$, quadratic utility leads to expected utility that depends only on the mean and variance of $\widetilde{R}_p$.

Next, suppose that utility is not quadratic but any general increasing, concave form. Are there particular probability distributions for portfolio returns that make expected utility, again, depend only on the portfolio return's mean and variance? Such distributions would need to be fully determined by their means and variances; that is, they must be two-parameter distributions whereby higher-order moments could be expressed in terms of the first two moments (mean and variance). Many distributions, such as the gamma, normal, and lognormal, satisfy this criterion. But in the context of an investor's portfolio selection problem, such

---

3. Thus, $\widetilde{R}_p$ is defined as one plus the rate of return on the portfolio.

4. The expected value of the second term in the Taylor series, $E\left[\left(\widetilde{R}_p - E[\widetilde{R}_p]\right) U'\left(E[\widetilde{R}_p]\right)\right]$, equals zero.

distributions need to satisfy another condition. Since an individual is able to choose which assets to combine into a portfolio, all portfolios created from a combination of individual assets or other portfolios must have distributions that continue to be determined by their means and variances. In other words, we need a distribution such that if the individual assets' return distributions depend on just mean and variance, then the return on a combination (portfolio) of these assets has a distribution that depends on just mean and variance. The only distributions that satisfy this "additivity" restriction is the stable family of distributions, and among this family the only distribution that has finite variance is the normal (Gaussian) distribution. A portfolio (sum) of assets whose returns are multivariate normally distributed also has a return that is normally distributed.

To verify that expected utility depends only on the portfolio return's mean and variance when this return is normally distributed, note that the third, fourth, and all higher central moments of the normal distribution are either zero or a function of the variance: $E\big[(\widetilde{R}_p - E[\widetilde{R}_p])^n\big] = 0$ for n odd, and $E\big[(\widetilde{R}_p - E[\widetilde{R}_p])^n\big] = \frac{n!}{(n/2)!}\big(\frac{1}{2}V[\widetilde{R}_p]\big)^{n/2}$ for n even. Therefore, in this case the individual's expected utility equals

$$E\left[U(\widetilde{R}_p)\right] = U\left(E[\widetilde{R}_p]\right) + \tfrac{1}{2}V[\widetilde{R}_p]U''\left(E[\widetilde{R}_p]\right) + 0 + \frac{1}{8}\left(V[\widetilde{R}_p]\right)^2 U''''\left(E[\widetilde{R}_p]\right)$$

$$+ 0 + \cdots + \frac{1}{(n/2)!}\left(\frac{1}{2}V[\widetilde{R}_p]\right)^{n/2} U^{(n)}\left(E[\widetilde{R}_p]\right) + \cdots \qquad (2.3)$$

which depends only on the mean and variance of the portfolio return.

In summary, restricting utility to be quadratic or restricting the distribution of asset returns to be normal allows us to write $E[U(\widetilde{R}_p)]$ as a function of only the mean, $E[\widetilde{R}_p]$, and the variance, $V[\widetilde{R}_p]$, of the portfolio return. Are either of these assumptions realistic? If not, it may be unjustified to suppose that only the first two moments of the portfolio return distribution matter to the individual investor.

The assumption of quadratic utility clearly is problematic. As mentioned earlier, quadratic utility displays negative marginal utility for levels of wealth greater than the "bliss point," and it has the unattractive characteristic of increasing absolute risk aversion. There are also difficulties with the assumption of normally distributed asset returns. When asset returns measured over any finite time period are normally distributed, there exists the possibility that their end-of-period values could be negative since realizations from the normal distribution have no lower (or upper) bound. This is an unrealistic description of returns for many assets such as stocks and bonds because, being limited-liability assets, their minimum value is nonnegative.[5]

As will be demonstrated in Chapter 12, the assumption of normal returns can be modified if we generalize the model to have multiple periods and assume that asset rates of return follow continuous-time, stochastic processes. In that context, one can assume that assets' rates of return are *instantaneously* normally distributed, which implies that if their means and variances are constant over infinitesimal intervals, then over any finite interval asset values are lognormally distributed. This turns out to be a better way of modeling limited-liability assets because the lognormal distribution bounds these assets' values to be no less than zero. When we later study continuous-time, multiperiod models, we shall see that the results derived here assuming a single-period, discrete-time model continue to hold, under particular conditions, in the more realistic multiperiod context. Moreover, in more complex multiperiod models that permit assets to have time-varying return distributions, we will show that optimal portfolio choices are straightforward generalizations of the mean-variance results derived in this chapter.

2.2   Investor Indifference Relations

Therefore, let us proceed by assuming that the individual's utility function, U, is a general concave utility function and that individual asset returns are normally distributed. Hence, a portfolio of these assets has a return $\widetilde{R}_p$ that is normally distributed with probability density function $f(R; \overline{R}_p, \sigma_p^2)$, where we use the shorthand notation $\overline{R}_p \equiv E[\widetilde{R}_p]$ and $\sigma_p^2 \equiv V[\widetilde{R}_p]$. In this section we analyze an investor's "tastes," that is, the investor's risk–expected return preferences when utility depends on the mean (expected return) and variance (risk) of the return on wealth. The following section analyzes investment "technologies" represented by the combinations of portfolio risk and expected return that can be created from different portfolios of individual assets. Historically, mean-variance analysis has been illustrated graphically, and we will follow that convention while also providing analytic results.

Note that an investor's expected utility can then be written as

$$E\left[U\left(\widetilde{R}_p\right)\right] = \int_{-\infty}^{\infty} U(R)f(R; \overline{R}_p, \sigma_p^2)dR \tag{2.4}$$

---

5. A related problem is that many standard utility functions, such as constant relative risk aversion, are not defined for negative values of portfolio wealth.

To gain insight regarding this investor's preferences over portfolio risk and expected return, we wish to determine the characteristics of this individual's indifference curves in portfolio mean-variance space. An indifference curve represents the combinations of portfolio mean and variance that would give the individual the same level of expected utility.[6] To understand this relation, let us begin by defining $\tilde{x} \equiv \frac{\tilde{R}_p - \overline{R}_p}{\sigma_p}$. Then

$$E\left[U\left(\tilde{R}_p\right)\right] = \int_{-\infty}^{\infty} U(\overline{R}_p + x\sigma_p)n(x)dx \tag{2.5}$$

where $n(x) \equiv f(x; 0, 1)$ is the standardized normal probability density function, that is, the normal density having a zero mean and unit variance. Now consider how expected utility varies with changes in the mean and variance of the return on wealth. Taking the partial derivative with respect to $\overline{R}_p$:

$$\frac{\partial E\left[U\left(\tilde{R}_p\right)\right]}{\partial \overline{R}_p} = \int_{-\infty}^{\infty} U'n(x)dx > 0 \tag{2.6}$$

since U' is always greater than zero. Next, take the partial derivative of equation (2.5) with respect to σ_p^2:

$$\frac{\partial E\left[U\left(\tilde{R}_p\right)\right]}{\partial \sigma_p^2} = \frac{1}{2\sigma_p}\frac{\partial E\left[U\left(\tilde{R}_p\right)\right]}{\partial \sigma_p} = \frac{1}{2\sigma_p}\int_{-\infty}^{\infty} U'xn(x)dx \tag{2.7}$$

While U' is always positive, x ranges between $-\infty$ and $+\infty$. Because x has a standard normal distribution, which is symmetric, for each positive realization there is a corresponding negative realization with the same probability density. For example, take the positive and negative pair $+x_i$ and $-x_i$. Then

---

6. Indifference curves are used in microeconomics to analyze an individual's choice of consuming different quantities of multiple goods. For example, if utility, $u(x, y)$, derives from consuming two goods, with x being the quantity of good X consumed and y being the quantity of good Y consumed, then an indifference curve is the locus of points in X, Y space that gives a constant level of utility, that is, combinations of goods X and Y for which the individual would be indifferent between consuming. Mathematically, these combinations are represented as the points (x, y) such that $u(x, y) = \overline{U}$, a constant. In this section, we employ a similar concept but where expected utility depends on the mean and variance of the return on wealth.

$n(+x_i) = n(-x_i)$. Comparing the integrand of equation (2.7) for equal absolute realizations of x, we can show

$$U'(\overline{R}_p + x_i\sigma_p)x_in(x_i) + U'(\overline{R}_p - x_i\sigma_p)(-x_i)n(-x_i) \qquad (2.8)$$

$$= U'(\overline{R}_p + x_i\sigma_p)x_in(x_i) - U'(\overline{R}_p - x_i\sigma_p)x_in(x_i)$$

$$= x_in(x_i)\left[U'(\overline{R}_p + x_i\sigma_p) - U'(\overline{R}_p - x_i\sigma_p)\right] < 0$$

because

$$U'(\overline{R} + x_i\sigma_p) < U'(\overline{R} - x_i\sigma_p) \qquad (2.9)$$

due to the assumed concavity of U; that is, the individual is risk averse so that $U'' < 0$. Thus, comparing $U'x_in(x_i)$ for each positive and negative pair, we conclude that

$$\frac{\partial E\left[U\left(\tilde{R}_p\right)\right]}{\partial \sigma_p^2} = \frac{1}{2\sigma_p}\int_{-\infty}^{\infty} U'xn(x)dx < 0 \qquad (2.10)$$

which is the intuitive result that higher portfolio variance, without higher portfolio expected return, reduces a risk-averse individual's expected utility.

Finally, an indifference curve is the combinations of portfolio mean and variance that leaves expected utility unchanged. In other words, it is combinations of $(\overline{R}_p, \sigma_p^2)$ that satisfy the equation $E[U(\tilde{R}_p)] = \overline{U}$, a constant. Higher levels of $\overline{U}$ denote different indifference curves providing a greater level of utility. If we totally differentiate this equation, we obtain

$$dE\left[U\left(\tilde{R}_p\right)\right] = \frac{\partial E\left[U\left(\tilde{R}_p\right)\right]}{\partial \sigma_p^2}d\sigma_p^2 + \frac{\partial E\left[U\left(\tilde{R}_p\right)\right]}{\partial \overline{R}_p}d\overline{R}_p = 0 \qquad (2.11)$$

which, based on our previous results, tells us that each indifference curve is positively sloped in $\left(\overline{R}_p, \sigma_p^2\right)$ space:

$$\frac{d\overline{R}_p}{d\sigma_p^2} = -\frac{\partial E\left[U\left(\tilde{R}_p\right)\right]}{\partial \sigma_p^2}\bigg/\frac{\partial E\left[U\left(\tilde{R}_p\right)\right]}{\partial \overline{R}_p} > 0 \qquad (2.12)$$

Thus, the indifference curve's slope in equation (2.12) quantifies the extent to which the individual requires a higher portfolio mean for accepting a higher portfolio variance.

Indifference curves are typically drawn in mean–standard deviation space, rather than mean-variance space, because standard deviations of returns are in

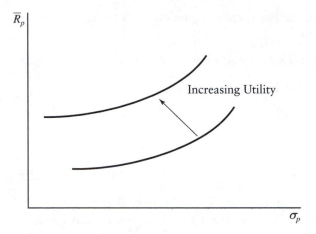

Figure 2.1 ——— Indifference Curves

the same unit of measurement as returns or interest rates (rather than squared returns). Figure 2.1 illustrates such a graph, where the arrow indicates an increase in the utility level, $\overline{U}$.[7] It is left as an end-of-chapter exercise to show that the curves are convex due to the assumed concavity of the utility function.

Having analyzed an investor's preferences over different combinations of portfolio means and standard deviations (or variances), let us consider next what portfolio means and standard deviations are possible given the available distributions of returns for individual assets.

2.3   The Efficient Frontier

The individual's optimal choice of portfolio mean and variance is determined by the point where one of these indifference curves is tangent to the set of means and standard deviations for all feasible portfolios, what we might describe as the "risk versus expected return investment opportunity set." This set represents all possible ways of combining various *individual* assets to generate alternative combinations of *portfolio* mean and variance (or standard deviation). This set includes inefficient portfolios (those in the interior of the opportunity set) as well as efficient portfolios (those on the "frontier" of the set). Efficient portfolios are those that make best use of the benefits of diversification. As we shall later prove, efficient portfolios have the attractive characteristic that any two efficient portfolios can be used to create any other efficient portfolio.

---

7. Clearly, these indifference curves cannot "cross" (intersect), because we showed that utility is always increasing in expected portfolio return for a given level of portfolio standard deviation.

2.3.1 A Simple Example

To illustrate the effects of diversification, consider the following simple example. Suppose there are two assets, assets A and B, that have expected returns $\overline{R}_A$ and $\overline{R}_B$ and variances of σ_A^2 and σ_B^2, respectively. Further, the correlation between their returns is given by ρ. Let us assume that $\overline{R}_A < \overline{R}_B$ but $\sigma_A^2 < \sigma_B^2$. Now form a portfolio with a proportion ω invested in asset A and a proportion $1 - \omega$ invested in asset B.[8] The expected return on this portfolio is

$$\overline{R}_p = \omega \overline{R}_A + (1 - \omega)\overline{R}_B \tag{2.13}$$

The expected return of a portfolio is a simple weighted average of the expected returns of the individual financial assets. Expected returns are not fundamentally transformed by combining individual assets into a portfolio. The standard deviation of the return on the portfolio is

$$\sigma_p = \left[\omega^2 \sigma_A^2 + 2\omega(1 - \omega)\sigma_A \sigma_B \rho + (1 - \omega)^2 \sigma_B^2\right]^{\frac{1}{2}} \tag{2.14}$$

In general, portfolio risk, as measured by the portfolio's return standard deviation, is a nonlinear function of the individual assets' variances and covariances. Thus, risk is altered in a relatively complex way when individual assets are combined in a portfolio.

Let us consider some special cases regarding the correlation between the two assets. Suppose $\rho = 1$, so that the two assets are perfectly positively correlated. Then the portfolio standard deviation equals

$$\sigma_p = \left[\omega^2 \sigma_A^2 + 2\omega(1 - \omega)\sigma_A \sigma_B + (1 - \omega)^2 \sigma_B^2\right]^{\frac{1}{2}} \tag{2.15}$$

$$= |\omega \sigma_A + (1 - \omega)\sigma_B|$$

which is a simple weighted average of the individual assets' standard deviations. Solving (2.15) for asset A's portfolio proportion gives $\omega = (\sigma_B \pm \sigma_p)/(\sigma_B - \sigma_A)$. Then, by substituting for ω in (2.13), we obtain

$$\overline{R}_p = \overline{R}_B + \left[\frac{\pm\sigma_p - \sigma_B}{\sigma_B - \sigma_A}\right](\overline{R}_B - \overline{R}_A) \tag{2.16}$$

$$= \frac{\sigma_B \overline{R}_A - \sigma_A \overline{R}_B}{\sigma_B - \sigma_A} \pm \frac{\overline{R}_B - \overline{R}_A}{\sigma_B - \sigma_A}\sigma_p$$

Thus, the relationship between portfolio risk and expected return are two straight lines in σ_p, $\overline{R}_p$ space. They have the same intercept of $(\sigma_B \overline{R}_A - \sigma_A \overline{R}_B)/(\sigma_B - \sigma_A)$

---

8. It is assumed that ω can be any real number. A $\omega < 0$ indicates a short position in asset A, while $\omega > 1$ indicates a short position in asset B.

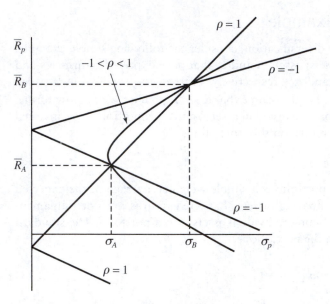

Figure 2.2 —— Efficient Frontier with Two Risky Assets

and have slopes of the same magnitude but opposite signs. The positively sloped line goes through the points $(\sigma_A, \overline{R}_A)$ and $(\sigma_B, \overline{R}_B)$ when $\omega = 1$ and $\omega = 0$, respectively. When $\omega = \sigma_B / (\sigma_B - \sigma_A) > 1$, indicating a short position in asset B, we see from (2.15) that all portfolio risk is eliminated ($\sigma_p = 0$). Figure 2.2 provides a graphical illustration of these relationships.

Next, suppose $\rho = -1$, so that the assets are perfectly negatively correlated. Then

$$\sigma_p = \left[(\omega \sigma_A - (1-\omega)\sigma_B)^2 \right]^{\frac{1}{2}} \tag{2.17}$$

$$= \left| \omega \sigma_A - (1-\omega)\sigma_B \right|$$

In a manner similar to the previous case, we can show that

$$\overline{R}_p = \frac{\sigma_A \overline{R}_B + \sigma_B \overline{R}_A}{\sigma_A + \sigma_B} \pm \frac{\overline{R}_B - \overline{R}_A}{\sigma_A + \sigma_B} \sigma_p \tag{2.18}$$

which, again, represents two straight lines in σ_p, $\overline{R}_p$ space. The intercept at $\sigma_p = 0$ is given by $\omega = \sigma_B / (\sigma_A + \sigma_B)$, so that all portfolio risk is eliminated with positive amounts invested in each asset. Furthermore, the negatively sloped line goes through the point $(\sigma_A, \overline{R}_A)$ when $\omega = 1$, while the positively sloped line goes through the point $(\sigma_B, \overline{R}_B)$ when $\omega = 0$. Figure 2.2 summarizes these risk–expected return constraints.

For either the $\rho = 1$ or $\rho = -1$ case, an investor would always choose a portfolio represented by the positively sloped lines because they give the highest average portfolio return for any given level of portfolio risk. These lines represent the so-called *efficient portfolio frontier*. The exact portfolio chosen by the individual would be where her indifference curve is tangent to the frontier.

When correlation between the assets is imperfect ($-1 < \rho < 1$), the relationship between portfolio expected return and standard deviation is not linear but, as illustrated in Figure 2.2, is hyperbolic. In this case, it is no longer possible to create a riskless portfolio, so that the portfolio having minimum standard deviation is one where $\sigma_p > 0$. We now set out to prove these assertions for the general case of n assets.

2.3.2 Mathematics of the Efficient Frontier

Robert C. Merton (Merton 1972) provided an analytical solution to the following portfolio choice problem: Given the expected returns and the matrix of covariances of returns for n individual assets, find the set of portfolio weights that minimizes the variance of the portfolio for each feasible portfolio expected return. The locus of these points in portfolio expected return–variance space is the portfolio frontier. This section presents the derivation of Merton's solution. We begin by specifying the problem's notation and assumptions.

Let $\overline{R} = (\overline{R}_1, \overline{R}_2, \ldots, \overline{R}_n)'$ be an $n \times 1$ vector of the expected returns of the n assets. Also let V be the $n \times n$ covariance matrix of the returns on the n assets. V is assumed to be of full rank.[9] Since it is a covariance matrix, it is also symmetric and positive definite. Next, let $\omega = (\omega_1, \omega_2, \ldots, \omega_n)'$ be an $n \times 1$ vector of portfolio proportions, such that ω_i is the proportion of total portfolio wealth invested in the ith asset. It follows that the expected return on the portfolio is given by

$$\overline{R}_p = \omega'\overline{R} \tag{2.19}$$

and the variance of the portfolio return is given by

$$\sigma_p^2 = \omega'V\omega \tag{2.20}$$

The constraint that the portfolio proportions must sum to 1 can be written as $\omega'e = 1$ where e is defined to be an $n \times 1$ vector of ones.

The problem of finding the portfolio frontier now can be stated as a quadratic optimization exercise: minimize the portfolio's variance subject to the constraints

---

9. This implies that there are no redundant assets among the n assets. An asset would be redundant if its return was an exact linear combination of the returns on other assets. If such an asset exists, it can be ignored, since its availability does not affect the efficient portfolio frontier.

that the portfolio's expected return equals $\overline{R}_p$ and the portfolio's weights sum to one.[10]

$$\min_{\omega} \tfrac{1}{2}\omega'V\omega + \lambda\left[\overline{R}_p - \omega'\overline{R}\right] + \gamma[1 - \omega'e] \tag{2.21}$$

The first-order conditions with respect to ω and the two Lagrange multipliers, λ and γ, are

$$V\omega - \lambda\overline{R} - \gamma e = 0 \tag{2.22}$$

$$\overline{R}_p - \omega'\overline{R} = 0 \tag{2.23}$$

$$1 - \omega'e = 0 \tag{2.24}$$

Solving (2.22), the optimal portfolio weights satisfy

$$\omega^* = \lambda V^{-1}\overline{R} + \gamma V^{-1}e \tag{2.25}$$

Pre-multiplying equation (2.25) by $\overline{R}'$, we have

$$\overline{R}_p = \overline{R}'\omega^* = \lambda\overline{R}'V^{-1}\overline{R} + \gamma\overline{R}'V^{-1}e \tag{2.26}$$

Pre-multiplying equation (2.25) by e', we have

$$1 = e'\omega^* = \lambda e'V^{-1}\overline{R} + \gamma e'V^{-1}e \tag{2.27}$$

Equations (2.26) and (2.27) are two linear equations in two unknowns, λ and γ. The solution is

$$\lambda = \frac{\delta\overline{R}_p - \alpha}{\varsigma\delta - \alpha^2} \tag{2.28}$$

$$\gamma = \frac{\varsigma - \alpha\overline{R}_p}{\varsigma\delta - \alpha^2} \tag{2.29}$$

where $\alpha \equiv \overline{R}'V^{-1}e = e'V^{-1}\overline{R}$, $\varsigma \equiv \overline{R}'V^{-1}\overline{R}$, and $\delta \equiv e'V^{-1}e$ are scalars. Note that the denominators of λ and γ, given by $\varsigma\delta - \alpha^2$, are guaranteed to be positive when V is of full rank.[11] Substituting for λ and γ in equation (2.25), we have

$$\omega^* = \frac{\delta\overline{R}_p - \alpha}{\varsigma\delta - \alpha^2}V^{-1}\overline{R} + \frac{\varsigma - \alpha\overline{R}_p}{\varsigma\delta - \alpha^2}V^{-1}e \tag{2.30}$$

---

10. In (2.21), the problem actually minimizes one-half the portfolio variance to avoid carrying an extra "2" in the first-order condition (2.22). The solution is the same as minimizing the total variance and only changes the scale of the Lagrange multipliers.

11. To see this, note that since V is positive definite, so is V^{-1}. Therefore, the quadratic form $(\alpha\overline{R} - \varsigma e)'V^{-1}(\alpha\overline{R} - \varsigma e) = \alpha^2\varsigma - 2\alpha^2\varsigma + \varsigma^2\delta = \varsigma(\varsigma\delta - \alpha^2)$ is positive. But since $\varsigma \equiv \overline{R}V^{-1}\overline{R}$ is a positive quadratic form, then $(\varsigma\delta - \alpha^2)$ must also be positive.

Collecting terms in $\overline{R}_p$ gives

$$\omega^* = a + b\overline{R}_p \tag{2.31}$$

where $a \equiv \frac{\varsigma V^{-1}e - \alpha V^{-1}\overline{R}}{\varsigma\delta - \alpha^2}$ and $b \equiv \frac{\delta V^{-1}\overline{R} - \alpha V^{-1}e}{\varsigma\delta - \alpha^2}$.

Equation (2.31) is both a necessary and sufficient condition for a frontier portfolio. Given $\overline{R}_p$, a portfolio must have weights satisfying (2.31) to minimize its return variance.

Having found the optimal portfolio weights for a given $\overline{R}_p$, the variance of the frontier portfolio is

$$\sigma_p^2 = \omega^{*\prime}V\omega^* = (a + b\overline{R}_p)'V(a + b\overline{R}_p) \tag{2.32}$$

$$= \frac{\delta\overline{R}_p^2 - 2\alpha\overline{R}_p + \varsigma}{\varsigma\delta - \alpha^2}$$

$$= \frac{1}{\delta} + \frac{\delta\left(\overline{R}_p - \frac{\alpha}{\delta}\right)^2}{\varsigma\delta - \alpha^2}$$

where the second line in equation (2.32) results from substituting in the definitions of a and b and simplifying the resulting expression. Equation (2.32) is a parabola in σ_p^2, $\overline{R}_p$ space and is graphed in Figure 2.3. From the third line in equation (2.32), it is obvious that the unique minimum is at the point $\overline{R}_p = R_{mv} \equiv \frac{\alpha}{\delta}$, which corresponds to a global minimum variance of $\sigma_{mv}^2 \equiv \frac{1}{\delta}$. Substituting $\overline{R}_p = \frac{\alpha}{\delta}$ into equation (2.30) shows that this minimum variance portfolio has weights $\omega_{mv} = \frac{1}{\delta}V^{-1}e$.

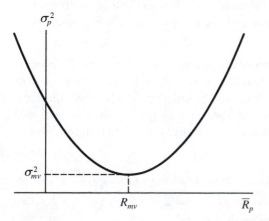

Figure 2.3 —— Frontier Portfolios

Each point on the parabola in Figure 2.3 represents an investor's lowest possible portfolio variance, given some target level of expected return, $\overline{R}_p$. However, an investor whose utility is increasing in expected portfolio return and is decreasing in portfolio variance would never choose a portfolio having $\overline{R}_p < R_{mv}$, that is, points on the parabola to the left of R_{mv}. This is because the frontier portfolio's variance actually increases as the target expected return falls when $\overline{R}_p < R_{mv}$, making this target expected return region irrelevant to an optimizing investor. Hence, the *efficient* portfolio frontier is represented only by the region $\overline{R}_p \geq R_{mv}$.

Traditionally, portfolios satisfying (2.32) are graphed in σ_p, $\overline{R}_p$ space. Taking the square root of both sides of equation (2.32), σ_p becomes a hyperbolic function of $\overline{R}_p$. When this is graphed as in Figure 2.4 with $\overline{R}_p$ on the vertical axis and σ_p on the horizontal one, only the upper arc of the hyperbola is relevant because, as just stated, investors would not choose target levels of $\overline{R}_p < R_{mv}$. Differentiating (2.32), we can also see that the hyperbola's slope equals

$$\frac{\partial \overline{R}_p}{\partial \sigma_p} = \frac{\varsigma\delta - \alpha^2}{\delta\left(\overline{R}_p - \frac{\alpha}{\delta}\right)} \sigma_p \tag{2.33}$$

The upper arc asymptotes to the straight line $\overline{R}_p = R_{mv} + \sqrt{\frac{\varsigma\delta-\alpha^2}{\delta}}\sigma_p$, while the lower arc, representing inefficient frontier portfolios, asymptotes to the straight line $\overline{R}_p = R_{mv} - \sqrt{\frac{\varsigma\delta-\alpha^2}{\delta}}\sigma_p$.[12]

2.3.3   Portfolio Separation

We now state and prove a fundamental result:

> Every portfolio on the mean-variance frontier can be replicated by a combination of any two frontier portfolios; and an individual will be indifferent between choosing among the n financial assets, or choosing a combination of just two frontier portfolios.

This remarkable finding has an immediate practical implication. If all investors have the same beliefs regarding the distribution of asset returns, namely, returns are distributed $N(\overline{R}, V)$ and, therefore, the frontier is (2.32), then they can form their individually preferred frontier portfolios by trading in as little as two frontier portfolios. For example, if a security market offered two mutual funds,

---

12. To see that the slope of the hyperbola asymptotes to a magnitude of $\sqrt{(\varsigma\delta - \alpha^2)/\delta}$, use (2.32) to substitute for $(\overline{R}_p - \frac{\alpha}{\delta})$ in (2.33) to obtain $\partial\overline{R}_p/\partial\sigma_p = \pm\sqrt{(\varsigma\delta - \alpha^2)}/\sqrt{\delta - 1/\sigma_p^2}$. Taking the limit of this expression as $\sigma_p \to \infty$ gives the desired result.

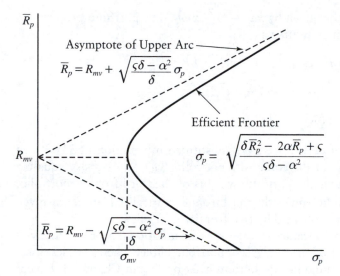

Figure 2.4 —— Efficient Frontier

each invested in a different frontier portfolio, any mean-variance investor could replicate his optimal portfolio by appropriately dividing his wealth between only these two mutual funds.[13]

The proof of this separation result is as follows. Let $\overline{R}_{1p}$ and $\overline{R}_{2p}$ be the expected returns on any two distinct frontier portfolios. Let $\overline{R}_{3p}$ be the expected return on a third frontier portfolio. Now consider investing a proportion of wealth, x, in the first frontier portfolio and the remainder, $(1-x)$, in the second frontier portfolio. Clearly, a value for x can be found that makes the expected return on this "composite" portfolio equal to that of the third frontier portfolio:[14]

$$\overline{R}_{3p} = x\overline{R}_{1p} + (1-x)\overline{R}_{2p} \tag{2.34}$$

In addition, because portfolios 1 and 2 are frontier portfolios, we can write their portfolio proportions as a linear function of their expected returns. Specifically, we have $\omega^1 = a + b\overline{R}_{1p}$ and $\omega^2 = a + b\overline{R}_{2p}$ where ω^i is the $n \times 1$ vector of optimal portfolio weights for frontier portfolio i. Now create a new portfolio with an $n \times 1$

---

13. To form his preferred frontier portfolio, an investor may require a short position in one of the frontier mutual funds. Since short positions are not possible with typical open-ended mutual funds, the better analogy would be that these funds are exchange-traded funds (ETFs), which do permit short positions.

14. x may be any positive or negative number.

vector of portfolio weights given by $x\omega^1 + (1-x)\omega^2$. The portfolio proportions of this new portfolio can be written as

$$x\omega^1 + (1-x)\omega^2 = x(a + b\overline{R}_{1p}) + (1-x)(a + b\overline{R}_{2p}) \tag{2.35}$$

$$= a + b(x\overline{R}_{1p} + (1-x)\overline{R}_{2p})$$

$$= a + b\overline{R}_{3p} = \omega^3$$

where, in the last line of (2.35), we have substituted in equation (2.34). Based on the portfolio weights of the composite portfolio, $x\omega^1 + (1-x)\omega^2$, equaling $a + b\overline{R}_{3p}$, which represents the portfolio weights of the third frontier portfolio, ω^3, this composite portfolio equals the third frontier portfolio. Hence, any given efficient portfolio can be replicated by two frontier portfolios.

Portfolios on the mean-variance frontier have an additional property that will prove useful to the next section's analysis of portfolio choice when a riskless asset exists and also to understanding equilibrium asset pricing in Chapter 3. Except for the global minimum variance portfolio, ω_{mv}, for each frontier portfolio one can find another frontier portfolio with which its returns have zero covariance. That is, one can find pairs of frontier portfolios whose returns are orthogonal. To show this, note that the covariance between two frontier portfolios, w^1 and w^2, is

$$\omega^{1\prime} V \omega^2 = (a + b\overline{R}_{1p})' V(a + b\overline{R}_{2p}) \tag{2.36}$$

$$= \frac{1}{\delta} + \frac{\delta}{\varsigma\delta - \alpha^2} \left(\overline{R}_{1p} - \frac{\alpha}{\delta}\right)\left(\overline{R}_{2p} - \frac{\alpha}{\delta}\right)$$

Setting this equal to zero and solving for $\overline{R}_{2p}$, the expected return on the portfolio that has zero covariance with portfolio ω^1 is

$$\overline{R}_{2p} = \frac{\alpha}{\delta} - \frac{\varsigma\delta - \alpha^2}{\delta^2\left(\overline{R}_{1p} - \frac{\alpha}{\delta}\right)} \tag{2.37}$$

$$= R_{mv} - \frac{\varsigma\delta - \alpha^2}{\delta^2\left(\overline{R}_{1p} - R_{mv}\right)}$$

Note that if $(\overline{R}_{1p} - R_{mv}) > 0$ so that frontier portfolio ω^1 is efficient, then equation (2.37) indicates that $\overline{R}_{2p} < R_{mv}$, implying that frontier portfolio ω^2 must be inefficient. We can determine the relative locations of these zero covariance portfolios by noting that in $\sigma_p, \overline{R}_p$ space, a line tangent to the frontier at the point $(\sigma_{1p}, \overline{R}_{1p})$ is of the form

$$\overline{R}_p = \overline{R}_0 + \left.\frac{\partial \overline{R}_p}{\partial \sigma_p}\right|_{\sigma_p = \sigma_{1p}} \sigma_p \tag{2.38}$$

where $\left.\dfrac{\partial \overline{R}_p}{\partial \sigma_p}\right|_{\sigma_p = \sigma_{1p}}$ denotes the slope of the hyperbola at point $(\sigma_{1p}, \overline{R}_{1p})$ and $\overline{R}_0$ denotes the tangent line's intercept at $\sigma_p = 0$. Using (2.33) and (2.32), we can solve for $\overline{R}_0$ by evaluating (2.38) at the point $(\sigma_{1p}, \overline{R}_{1p})$:

$$\overline{R}_0 = \overline{R}_{1p} - \left.\frac{\partial \overline{R}_p}{\partial \sigma_p}\right|_{\sigma_p = \sigma_{1p}} \sigma_{1p} = \overline{R}_{1p} - \frac{\varsigma\delta - \alpha^2}{\delta\left(\overline{R}_{1p} - \frac{\alpha}{\delta}\right)}\sigma_{1p}\sigma_{1p} \qquad (2.39)$$

$$= \overline{R}_{1p} - \frac{\varsigma\delta - \alpha^2}{\delta\left(\overline{R}_{1p} - \frac{\alpha}{\delta}\right)}\left[\frac{1}{\delta} + \frac{\delta\left(\overline{R}_{1p} - \frac{\alpha}{\delta}\right)^2}{\varsigma\delta - \alpha^2}\right]$$

$$= \frac{\alpha}{\delta} - \frac{\varsigma\delta - \alpha^2}{\delta^2\left(\overline{R}_{1p} - \frac{\alpha}{\delta}\right)}$$

$$= \overline{R}_{2p}$$

Hence, as shown in Figure 2.5, the intercept of the line tangent to frontier portfolio ω^1 equals the expected return of its zero-covariance counterpart, frontier portfolio ω^2.

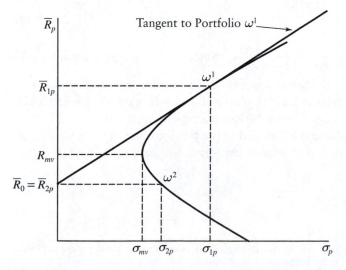

Figure 2.5 —— Frontier Portfolios with Zero Covariance

2.4   The Efficient Frontier with a Riskless Asset

Thus far, we have assumed that investors can hold only risky assets. An implication of our analysis was that while all investors would choose efficient portfolios of risky assets, these portfolios would differ based on the particular investor's level of risk aversion. However, as we shall now see, introducing a riskless asset can simplify the investor's portfolio choice problem. This augmented portfolio choice problem, whose solution was first derived by James Tobin (Tobin 1958), is one that we now consider.[15]

Assume that there is a riskless asset with return R_f. Let ω continue to be the $n \times 1$ vector of portfolio proportions invested in the risky assets. Now, however, the constraint $\omega'e = 1$ does not apply, because $1 - \omega'e$ is the portfolio proportion invested in the riskless asset. We can impose the restriction that the portfolio weights for all $n + 1$ assets sum to one by writing the expected return on the portfolio as

$$\overline{R}_p = R_f + \omega'(\overline{R} - R_f e) \tag{2.40}$$

The variance of the return on the portfolio continues to be given by $\omega'V\omega$. Thus, the individual's optimization problem is changed to

$$\min_{\omega} \tfrac{1}{2}\omega'V\omega + \lambda\left\{\overline{R}_p - \left[R_f + \omega'(\overline{R} - R_f e)\right]\right\} \tag{2.41}$$

In a manner similar to the previous derivation, the first-order conditions lead to the solution

$$\omega^* = \lambda V^{-1}(\overline{R} - R_f e) \tag{2.42}$$

where $\lambda \equiv \dfrac{\overline{R}_p - R_f}{(\overline{R} - R_f e)'V^{-1}(\overline{R} - R_f e)} = \dfrac{\overline{R}_p - R_f}{\varsigma - 2\alpha R_f + \delta R_f^2}$. Since V^{-1} is positive definite, λ is nonnegative when $\overline{R}_p \geq R_f$, the region of the efficient frontier where investors' expected portfolio return is at least as great as the risk-free return. Given (2.42), the amount optimally invested in the riskless asset is determined by $1 - e'\omega^*$. Note that since λ is linear in $\overline{R}_p$, so is ω^*, similar to the previous case of no riskless asset. The variance of the portfolio now takes the form

$$\sigma_p^2 = \omega^{*\prime}V\omega^* = \frac{(\overline{R}_p - R_f)^2}{\varsigma - 2\alpha R_f + \delta R_f^2} \tag{2.43}$$

---

15. Tobin's work on portfolio selection was one of his contributions cited by the selection committee that awarded him the Nobel prize in economics in 1981.

Taking the square root of each side of (2.43) and rearranging:

$$\overline{R}_p = R_f \pm \left(\varsigma - 2\alpha R_f + \delta R_f^2\right)^{\frac{1}{2}} \sigma_p \tag{2.44}$$

which indicates that the frontier is *linear* in σ_p, $\overline{R}_p$ space. Corresponding to the hyperbola for the no-riskless-asset case, the frontier when a riskless asset is included becomes two straight lines, each with an intercept of R_f but one having a positive slope of $\left(\varsigma - 2\alpha R_f + \delta R_f^2\right)^{\frac{1}{2}}$, the other having a negative slope of $-\left(\varsigma - 2\alpha R_f + \delta R_f^2\right)^{\frac{1}{2}}$. Of course, only the positively sloped line is the efficient portion of the frontier.

Since ω^* is linear in $\overline{R}_p$, the previous section's separation result continues to hold: any portfolio on the frontier can be replicated by two other frontier portfolios. However, when $R_f \neq R_{mv} \equiv \frac{\alpha}{\delta}$ holds, an even stronger separation principle obtains.[16] In this case, any portfolio on the linear efficient frontier can be replicated by two particular portfolios: one portfolio that is located on the "risky-asset-only" frontier and another portfolio that holds only the riskless asset.

Let us start by proving this result for the situation where $R_f < R_{mv}$. We assert that the efficient frontier given by the line $\overline{R}_p = R_f + \left(\varsigma - 2\alpha R_f + \delta R_f^2\right)^{\frac{1}{2}}\sigma_p$ can be replicated by a portfolio consisting of only the riskless asset and a portfolio on the risky-asset-only frontier that is determined by a straight line tangent to this frontier whose intercept is R_f. This situation is illustrated in Figure 2.6 where ω^A denotes the portfolio of risky assets determined by the tangent line having intercept R_f. If we can show that the slope of this tangent line equals $\left(\varsigma - 2\alpha R_f + \delta R_f^2\right)^{\frac{1}{2}}$, then our assertion is proved.[17] Let $\overline{R}_A$ and σ_A be the expected return and standard deviation of return, respectively, on this tangency

---

16. We continue to let R_{mv} denote the expected return on the minimum variance portfolio that holds only risky assets. Of course, with a riskless asset, the minimum variance portfolio would be one that holds only the riskless asset.

17. Note that if a proportion x is invested in any risky asset portfolio having expected return and standard deviation of $\overline{R}_A$ and σ_A, respectively, and a proportion $1-x$ is invested in the riskless asset having certain return R_f, then the combined portfolio has an expected return and standard deviation of $\overline{R}_p = R_f + x(\overline{R}_A - R_f)$ and $\sigma_p = x\sigma_A$, respectively. When graphed in $\overline{R}_p$, σ_p space, we can substitute for x to show that these combination portfolios are represented by the straight line $\overline{R}_p = R_f + \frac{R_A - R_f}{\sigma_A}\sigma_p$ whose intercept is R_f.

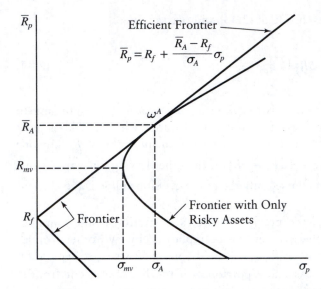

Figure 2.6 ——— Efficient Frontier with a Riskless Asset

portfolio. Then the results of (2.37) and (2.39) allow us to write the slope of the tangent as

$$\frac{\overline{R}_A - R_f}{\sigma_A} = \left[\frac{\alpha}{\delta} - \frac{\varsigma\delta - \alpha^2}{\delta^2 \left(R_f - \frac{\alpha}{\delta} \right)} - R_f \right] / \sigma_A \tag{2.45}$$

$$= \left[\frac{2\alpha R_f - \varsigma - \delta R_f^2}{\delta \left(R_f - \frac{\alpha}{\delta} \right)} \right] / \sigma_A$$

Furthermore, we can use (2.32) and (2.37) to write

$$\sigma_A^2 = \frac{1}{\delta} + \frac{\delta \left(\overline{R}_A - \frac{\alpha}{\delta} \right)^2}{\varsigma\delta - \alpha^2} \tag{2.46}$$

$$= \frac{1}{\delta} + \frac{\varsigma\delta - \alpha^2}{\delta^3 \left(R_f - \frac{\alpha}{\delta} \right)^2}$$

$$= \frac{\delta R_f^2 - 2\alpha R_f + \varsigma}{\delta^2 \left(R_f - \frac{\alpha}{\delta} \right)^2}$$

Substituting the square root of (2.46) into (2.45) gives[18]

$$\frac{\overline{R}_A - R_f}{\sigma_A} = \left[\frac{2\alpha R_f - \varsigma - \delta R_f^2}{\delta \left(R_f - \frac{\alpha}{\delta}\right)}\right] \frac{-\delta \left(R_f - \frac{\alpha}{\delta}\right)}{\left(\delta R_f^2 - 2\alpha R_f + \varsigma\right)^{\frac{1}{2}}} \tag{2.47}$$

$$= \left(\delta R_f^2 - 2\alpha R_f + \varsigma\right)^{\frac{1}{2}}$$

which is the desired result.

This result is an important simplification. If all investors agree on the distribution of asset returns (returns are distributed $N(\overline{R}, V)$), then they all consider the linear efficient frontier to be $\overline{R}_p = R_f + (\varsigma - 2\alpha R_f + \delta R_f^2)^{\frac{1}{2}}\sigma_p$ and all will choose to hold risky assets in the same relative proportions given by the tangency portfolio ω^A. Investors differ only in the amount of wealth they choose to allocate to this portfolio of risky assets versus the risk-free asset.

Along the efficient frontier depicted in Figure 2.7, the proportion of an investor's total wealth held in the tangency portfolio, $e'\omega^*$, increases as one moves to the right. At point $(\sigma_p, \overline{R}_p) = (0, R_f)$, $e'\omega^* = 0$ and all wealth is invested in the risk-free asset. In between points $(0, R_f)$ and $(\sigma_A, \overline{R}_A)$, which would be the case if, say, investor 1 had an indifference curve tangent to the efficient frontier at point $(\sigma_1, \overline{R}_{p1})$, then $0 < e'\omega^* < 1$ and positive proportions of wealth are invested in the risk-free asset and the tangency portfolio of risky assets. At point $(\sigma_A, \overline{R}_A)$, $e'\omega^* = 1$ and all wealth is invested in risky assets and none in the risk-free asset. Finally, to the right of this point, which would be the case if, say, investor 2 had an indifference curve tangent to the efficient frontier at point $(\sigma_2, \overline{R}_{p2})$, then $e'\omega^* > 1$. This implies a negative proportion of wealth in the risk-free asset. The interpretation is that investor 2 borrows at the risk-free rate to invest more than 100 percent of her wealth in the tangency portfolio of risky assets. In practical terms, such an investor could be viewed as buying risky assets "on margin," that is, leveraging her asset purchases with borrowed money.

It will later be argued that $R_f < R_{mv}$, the situation depicted in Figures 2.6 and 2.7, is required for asset market equilibrium. However, we briefly describe the implications of other parametric cases. When $R_f > R_{mv}$, the efficient frontier of $\overline{R}_p = R_f + (\varsigma - 2\alpha R_f + \delta R_f^2)^{\frac{1}{2}}\sigma_p$ is always above the risky-asset-only frontier. Along this efficient frontier, the investor short-sells the tangency portfolio of risky assets. This portfolio is located on the inefficient portion of the risky-asset-only frontier at the point where the line $\overline{R}_p = R_f - (\varsigma - 2\alpha R_f + \delta R_f^2)^{\frac{1}{2}}\sigma_p$ becomes

---

18. Because it is assumed that $R_f < \frac{\alpha}{\delta}$, the square root of (2.46) has an opposite sign in order for σ_A to be positive.

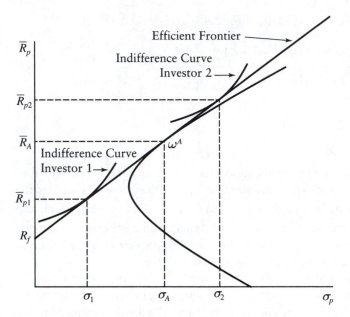

Figure 2.7 —— Investor Portfolio Choice

tangent. The proceeds from this short-selling are then wholly invested in the risk-free asset. Lastly, when $R_f = R_{mv}$, the portfolio frontier is given by the asymptotes illustrated in Figure 2.4. It is straightforward to show that $e'\omega^* = 0$ for this case, so that total wealth is invested in the risk-free asset. However, the investor also holds a risky, but zero net wealth, position in risky assets. In other words, the proceeds from short-selling particular risky assets are used to finance long positions in other risky assets.

2.4.1   An Example with Negative Exponential Utility

To illustrate our results, let us specify a form for an individual's utility function. This enables us to determine the individual's preferred efficient portfolio, that is, the point of tangency between the individual's highest indifference curve and the efficient frontier. Given a specific utility function and normally distributed asset returns, we show how the individual's optimal portfolio weights can be derived directly by maximizing expected utility.

As before, let $\widetilde{W}$ be the individual's end-of-period wealth and assume that she maximizes expected negative exponential utility:

$$U(\widetilde{W}) = -e^{-b\widetilde{W}} \tag{2.48}$$

where b is the individual's coefficient of absolute risk aversion. Now define $b_r \equiv b W_0$, which is the individual's coefficient of relative risk aversion at initial wealth W_0. Equation (2.48) can be rewritten:

$$U(\widetilde{W}) = -e^{-b_r \widetilde{W}/W_0} = -e^{-b_r \widetilde{R}_p} \tag{2.49}$$

where $\widetilde{R}_p$ is the total return (one plus the rate of return) on the portfolio.

In this problem, we assume that initial wealth can be invested in a riskless asset and n risky assets. As before, denote the return on the riskless asset as R_f and the returns on the n risky assets as the $n \times 1$ vector $\widetilde{R}$. Also as before, let $\omega = (\omega_1 \ldots \omega_n)'$ be the vector of portfolio weights for the n risky assets. The risky assets' returns are assumed to have a joint normal distribution where $\overline{R}$ is the $n \times 1$ vector of expected returns on the n risky assets and V is the $n \times n$ covariance matrix of returns. Thus, the expected return on the portfolio can be written $\overline{R}_p \equiv R_f + \omega'(\overline{R} - R_f e)$ and the variance of the return on the portfolio is $\sigma_p^2 \equiv \omega' V \omega$.

Now recall the properties of the lognormal distribution. If $\tilde{x}$ is a normally distributed random variable, for example, $\tilde{x} \sim N(\mu, \sigma^2)$, then $\tilde{z} = e^{\tilde{x}}$ is lognormally distributed. The expected value of $\tilde{z}$ is

$$E[\tilde{z}] = e^{\mu + \frac{1}{2}\sigma^2} \tag{2.50}$$

From (2.49), we see that if $\widetilde{R}_p = R_f + \omega'(\widetilde{R} - R_f e)$ is normally distributed, then $U(\widetilde{W})$ is lognormally distributed. Using equation (2.50), we have

$$E\left[U\left(\widetilde{W}\right)\right] = -e^{-b_r\left[R_f + \omega'(\overline{R} - R_f e)\right] + \frac{1}{2}b_r^2 \omega' V \omega} \tag{2.51}$$

The individual chooses portfolio weights by maximizing expected utility:

$$\max_{\omega} E\left[U\left(\widetilde{W}\right)\right] = \max_{\omega} -e^{-b_r\left[R_f + \omega'(\overline{R} - R_f e)\right] + \frac{1}{2}b_r^2 \omega' V \omega} \tag{2.52}$$

Because the expected utility function is monotonic in its exponent, the maximization problem in (2.52) is equivalent to

$$\max_{\omega} \; \omega'(\overline{R} - R_f e) - \frac{1}{2}b_r \omega' V \omega \tag{2.53}$$

The n first-order conditions are

$$\overline{R} - R_f e - b_r V \omega = 0 \tag{2.54}$$

Solving for ω, we obtain

$$\omega^* = \frac{1}{b_r} V^{-1}(\overline{R} - R_f e) \tag{2.55}$$

Thus, we see that the individual's optimal portfolio choice depends on b_r, her coefficient of relative risk aversion, and the expected returns and covariances of the assets. Comparing (2.55) to (2.42), note that

$$\frac{1}{b_r} = \lambda \equiv \frac{\overline{R}_p - R_f}{\left(\overline{R} - R_f e\right)' V^{-1}(\overline{R} - R_f e)} \tag{2.56}$$

so that the greater the investor's relative risk aversion, b_r, the smaller is her target mean portfolio return, $\overline{R}_p$, and the smaller is the proportion of wealth invested in the risky assets. In fact, multiplying both sides of (2.55) by W_0, we see that the absolute amount of wealth invested in the risky assets is

$$W_0 \omega^* = \frac{1}{b} V^{-1}(\overline{R} - R_f e) \tag{2.57}$$

Therefore, the individual with constant absolute risk aversion, b, invests a fixed dollar amount in the risky assets, independent of her initial wealth. As wealth increases, each additional dollar is invested in the risk-free asset. Recall that this same result was derived at the end of Chapter 1 for the special case of a single risky asset.

As in this example, constant absolute risk aversion's property of making risky asset choice independent of wealth often allows for simple solutions to portfolio choice problems when asset returns are assumed to be normally distributed. However, the unrealistic implication that both wealthy and poor investors invest the same dollar amount in risky assets limits the empirical applications of using this form of utility. As we shall see in later chapters of this book, models where utility displays constant relative risk aversion are more typical.

2.5 An Application to Cross-Hedging

The following application of mean-variance analysis is based on Anderson and Danthine (Anderson and Danthine 1981). Consider a one-period model of an individual or institution that is required to buy or sell a commodity in the future and would like to hedge the risk of such a transaction by taking positions in futures (or other financial securities) markets. Assume that this financial operator is committed at the beginning of the period, date 0, to buy y units of a risky commodity at the end of the period, date 1, at the then prevailing spot price p_1. For example, a commitment to buy could arise if the commodity is a necessary input in the operator's production process.[19] Conversely, $y < 0$ represents a commitment to sell $-y$ units of a commodity, which could be due to the operator producing a commodity that is nonstorable.[20] What is important is that, as of date 0, y is deterministic, while p_1 is stochastic.

There are n financial securities (for example, futures contracts) in the economy. Denote the date 0 price of the ith financial security as p_{i0}^s. Its date 1 price is p_{i1}^s, which is uncertain as of date 0. Let s_i denote the amount of the ith security purchased at date 0. Thus, $s_i < 0$ indicates a short position in the security.

Define the $n \times 1$ quantity and price vectors $s \equiv [s_1 \dots s_n]'$, $p_0^s \equiv [p_{10}^s \dots p_{n0}^s]'$, and $p_1^s \equiv [p_{11}^s \dots p_{n1}^s]'$. Also define $p^s \equiv p_1^s - p_0^s$ as the $n \times 1$ vector of security price changes. This is the profit at date 1 from having taken unit long positions in each of the securities (futures contracts) at date 0, so that the operator's profit from its security position is $p^{s'}s$. Also define the first and second moments of the date 1 prices of the spot commodity and the financial securities: $E[p_1] = \bar{p}_1$, $Var[p_1] = \sigma_{00}$, $E[p_1^s] = \bar{p}_1^s$, $E[p^s] = \bar{p}^s$, $Cov[p_{i1}^s, p_{j1}^s] = \sigma_{ij}$, $Cov[p_1, p_{i1}^s] = \sigma_{0i}$, and the $(n+1) \times (n+1)$ covariance matrix of the spot commodity and financial securities is

$$\Sigma = \begin{bmatrix} \sigma_{00} & \Sigma_{01} \\ \Sigma_{01}' & \Sigma_{11} \end{bmatrix} \tag{2.58}$$

where Σ_{11} is an $n \times n$ matrix whose i, jth element is σ_{ij}, and Σ_{01} is a $1 \times n$ vector whose ith element is σ_{0i}.

For simplicity, let us assume that y is fixed and, therefore, is not a decision variable at date 0. Then the end-of-period profit (wealth) of the financial operator, W, is given by

$$W = p^{s'}s - p_1 y \tag{2.59}$$

What the operator must decide is the date 0 positions in the financial securities. We assume that the operator chooses s in order to maximize the following objective function that depends linearly on the mean and variance of profit:

$$\max_s E[W] - \tfrac{1}{2}\alpha \, Var[W] \tag{2.60}$$

As was shown in the previous section's equation (2.53), this objective function results from maximizing expected utility of wealth when portfolio returns are

---

19. An example of this case would be a utility that generates electricity from oil.

20. For example, the operator could be a producer of an agricultural good, such as corn, wheat, or soybeans.

normally distributed and utility displays constant absolute risk aversion.[21] Substituting in for the operator's profit, we have

$$\max_{s} \ \bar{p}^{s\prime}s - \bar{p}_1 y - \tfrac{1}{2}\alpha \left[y^2 \sigma_{00} + s'\Sigma_{11}s - 2y\Sigma_{01}s \right] \tag{2.61}$$

The first-order conditions are

$$\bar{p}^s - \alpha \left[\Sigma_{11}s - y\Sigma'_{01} \right] = 0 \tag{2.62}$$

Thus, the optimal positions in financial securities are

$$s = \frac{1}{\alpha}\Sigma_{11}^{-1}\bar{p}^s + y\Sigma_{11}^{-1}\Sigma'_{01} \tag{2.63}$$

$$= \frac{1}{\alpha}\Sigma_{11}^{-1}\left(\bar{p}_1^s - p_0^s\right) + y\Sigma_{11}^{-1}\Sigma'_{01}$$

Let us first consider the case of $y = 0$. This can be viewed as the situation faced by a pure *speculator*, by which we mean a trader who has no requirement to hedge. If $n = 1$ and $\bar{p}_1^s > p_0^s$, the speculator takes a long position in (purchases) the security, while if $\bar{p}_1^s < p_0^s$, the speculator takes a short position in (sells) the security. The magnitude of the position is tempered by the volatility of the security ($\Sigma_{11}^{-1} = 1/\sigma_{11}$), and the speculator's level of risk aversion, α. However, for the general case of $n > 1$, an expected price decline or rise is not sufficient to determine whether a speculator takes a long or short position in a particular security. All of the elements in Σ_{11}^{-1} need to be considered, since a position in a given security may have particular diversification benefits.

For the general case of $y \neq 0$, the situation faced by a *hedger*, the demand for financial securities is similar to that of a pure speculator in that it also depends on price expectations. In addition, there are hedging components to the demand for financial assets, call them s^h :

$$s^h \equiv y\Sigma_{11}^{-1}\Sigma'_{01} \tag{2.64}$$

This is the solution to the problem $\min_s \ Var(W)$. Thus, even for a hedger, it is never optimal to minimize volatility (risk) unless risk aversion is infinitely large. Even a risk-averse, expected-utility-maximizing hedger should behave somewhat

---

21. Similar to the previous derivation, the objective function (2.60) can be derived from an expected utility function of the form $E\left[U\left(W\right)\right] = -\exp\left[-\alpha W\right]$ where α is the operator's coefficient of absolute risk aversion. Unlike the previous example, here the objective function is written in terms of total profit (wealth), not portfolio returns per unit wealth. Also, risky asset holdings, s, are in terms of absolute amounts purchased, not portfolio proportions. Hence, α is the coefficient of absolute risk aversion, not relative risk aversion.

like a speculator in that securities' expected returns matter. From definition (2.64), note that when $n = 1$, the pure hedging demand per unit of the commodity purchased, s^h/y, simplifies to[22]

$$\frac{s^h}{y} = \frac{Cov(p_1, p_1^s)}{Var(p_1^s)} \tag{2.65}$$

For the general case, $n > 1$, the elements of the vector $\Sigma_{11}^{-1}\Sigma_{01}'$ equal the coefficients $\beta_1, \ldots, \beta_n$ in the multiple regression model:

$$\Delta p_1 = \beta_0 + \beta_1 \Delta p_1^s + \beta_2 \Delta p_2^s + \cdots + \beta_n \Delta p_n^s + \varepsilon \tag{2.66}$$

where $\Delta p_1 \equiv p_1 - p_0$, $\Delta p_i^s \equiv p_{1i}^s - p_{0i}^s$, and ε is a mean-zero error term. An implication of (2.66) is that an operator might estimate the *hedge ratios*, s^h/y, by performing a statistical regression using a historical times series of the $n \times 1$ vector of security price changes. In fact, this is a standard way that practitioners calculate hedge ratios.

2.6 Summary

When the returns on individual assets are multivariate normally distributed, a risk-averse investor optimally chooses among a set of mean-variance efficient portfolios. Such portfolios make best use of the benefits of diversification by providing the highest mean portfolio return for a given portfolio variance. The particular efficient portfolio chosen by a given investor depends on her level of risk aversion. However, the ability to trade in only two efficient portfolios is sufficient to satisfy all investors, because any efficient portfolio can be created from any other two. When a riskless asset exists, the set of efficient portfolios has the characteristic that the portfolios' mean returns are linear in their portfolio variances. In such a case, a more risk-averse investor optimally holds a positive amount of the riskless asset and a positive amount of a particular risky-asset portfolio, while a less risk-averse investor optimally borrows at the riskless rate to purchase the same risky-asset portfolio in an amount exceeding his wealth.

This chapter provided insights on how individuals should optimally allocate their wealth among various assets. Taking the distribution of returns for all

---

22. Note that if the correlation between the commodity price and the financial security return were equal to 1, so that a perfect hedge exists, then (2.65) becomes $s^h/y = \sqrt{\sigma_{00}}/\sqrt{\sigma_{11}}$; that is, the hedge ratio equals the ratio of the commodity price's standard deviation to that of the security price.

available assets as given, we determined any individual's portfolio demands for these assets. Having now derived a theory of investor asset demands, the next chapter will consider the equilibrium asset pricing implications of this investor behavior.

2.7   Exercises

1. Prove that the indifference curves graphed in Figure 2.1 are convex if the utility function is concave. Hint: suppose there are two portfolios, portfolios 1 and 2, that lie on the same indifference curve, where this indifference curve has expected utility of $\overline{U}$. Let the mean returns on portfolios 1 and 2 be $\overline{R}_{1p}$ and $\overline{R}_{2p}$, respectively, and let the standard deviations of returns on portfolios 1 and 2 be σ_{1p} and σ_{2p}, respectively. Consider a third portfolio located in $(\overline{R}_p, \sigma_p)$ space that happens to be on a straight line between portfolios 1 and 2, that is, a portfolio having a mean and standard deviation satisfying $\overline{R}_{3p} = x\overline{R}_{1p} + (1-x)\overline{R}_{2p}$ and $\sigma_{3p} = x\sigma_{1p} + (1-x)\sigma_{2p}$ where $0 < x < 1$. Prove that the indifference curve is convex by showing that the expected utility of portfolio 3 exceeds $\overline{U}$. Do this by showing that the utility of portfolio 3 exceeds the convex combination of utilities for portfolios 1 and 2 for each standardized normal realization. Then integrate over all realizations to show this inequality holds for expected utilities.

2. Show that the covariance between the return on the minimum variance portfolio and the return on *any* other portfolio equals the variance of the return on the minimum variance portfolio. Hint: write down the variance of a portfolio that consists of a proportion x invested in the minimum variance portfolio and a proportion $(1-x)$ invested in any other portfolio. Then minimize the variance of this composite portfolio with respect to x.

3. Show how to derive the solution for the optimal portfolio weights for a frontier portfolio when there exists a riskless asset, that is, equation (2.42) given by $\omega^* = \lambda V^{-1}(\overline{R} - R_f e)$ where $\lambda \equiv \dfrac{\overline{R}_p - R_f}{\left(\overline{R} - R_f e\right)' V^{-1}(\overline{R} - R_f e)} = \dfrac{\overline{R}_p - R_f}{\varsigma - 2\alpha R_f + \delta R_f^2}$. The derivation is similar to the case with no riskless asset.

4. Show that when $R_f = R_{mv}$, the optimal portfolio involves $e'\omega^* = 0$.

5. Consider the mean-variance analysis covered in this chapter where there are n risky assets whose returns are jointly normally distributed. Assume that investors differ with regard to their (concave) utility functions and their initial wealths. Also assume that investors can lend at the risk-free rate, $R_f < R_{mv}$,

but investors are restricted from risk-free borrowing; that is, no risk-free borrowing is permitted.

a. Given this risk-free borrowing restriction, graphically show the efficient frontier for these investors in expected portfolio return–standard deviation space $(\overline{R}_p, \sigma_p)$.

b. Explain why only three portfolios are needed to construct this efficient frontier, and locate these three portfolios on your graph. (Note that these portfolios may not be unique.)

c. At least one of these portfolios will sometimes need to be sold short to generate the entire efficient frontier. Which portfolio(s) is it (label it on the graph) and in what range(s) of the efficient frontier will it be sold short? Explain.

6. Suppose there are n risky assets whose returns are multivariate normally distributed. Denote their $n \times 1$ vector of expected returns as $\overline{R}$ and their $n \times n$ covariance matrix as V. Let there also be a riskless asset with return R_f. Let portfolio a be on the mean-variance efficient frontier and have an expected return and standard deviation of $\overline{R}_a$ and σ_a, respectively. Let portfolio b be any other (not necessarily efficient) portfolio having expected return and standard deviation $\overline{R}_b$ and σ_b, respectively. Show that the correlation between portfolios a and b equals portfolio b's Sharpe ratio divided by portfolio a's Sharpe ratio, where portfolio i's Sharpe ratio equals $(\overline{R}_i - R_f)/\sigma_i$. (Hint: write the correlation as $Cov(R_a, R_b)/(\sigma_a \sigma_b)$, and derive this covariance using the properties of portfolio efficiency.)

7. A corn grower has utility of wealth given by $U(W) = -e^{-aW}$ where $a > 0$. This farmer's wealth depends on the total revenue from the sale of corn at harvest time. Total revenue is a random variable $\widetilde{s} = \widetilde{q}\widetilde{p}$, where $\widetilde{q}$ is the number of bushels of corn harvested and $\widetilde{p}$ is the spot price, net of harvesting costs, of a bushel of corn at harvest time. The farmer can enter into a corn futures contract having a current price of f_0 and a random price at harvest time of $\widetilde{f}$. If k is the number of short positions in this futures contract taken by the farmer, then the farmer's wealth at harvest time is given by $\widetilde{W} = \widetilde{s} - k(\widetilde{f} - f_0)$. If $\widetilde{s} \sim N(\overline{s}, \sigma_s^2)$, $\widetilde{f} \sim N(\overline{f}, \sigma_f^2)$, and $Cov(\widetilde{s}, \widetilde{f}) = \rho \sigma_s \sigma_f$, then solve for the optimal number of futures contract short positions, k, that the farmer should take.

8. Consider the standard Markowitz mean-variance portfolio choice problem where there are n risky assets and a risk-free asset. The risky assets' $n \times 1$ vector of returns, $\widetilde{R}$, has a multivariate normal distribution $N(\overline{R}, V)$, where $\overline{R}$ is the assets' $n \times 1$ vector of expected returns and V is a nonsingular $n \times n$ covariance matrix. The risk-free asset's return is given by $R_f > 0$.

As usual, assume no labor income so that the individual's end-of-period wealth depends only on her portfolio return; that is, $\widetilde{W} = W_0\widetilde{R}_p$, where the portfolio return is $\widetilde{R}_p = R_f + w'(\widetilde{R} - R_f e)$ where w is an $n \times 1$ vector of portfolio weights for the risky assets and e is an $n \times 1$ vector of 1s. Recall that we solved for the optimal portfolio weights, w^*, for the case of an individual with expected utility displaying constant absolute risk aversion, $E[U(\widetilde{W})] = E[-e^{-b\widetilde{W}}]$. Now, in this problem, consider the different case of an individual with expected utility displaying constant relative risk aversion, $E[U(\widetilde{W})] = E[\frac{1}{\gamma}\widetilde{W}^\gamma]$ where $\gamma < 1$. What is w^* for this constant relative-risk-aversion case? Hint: recall the efficient frontier and consider the range of the probability distribution of the tangency portfolio. Also consider what would be the individual's marginal utility should end-of-period wealth be nonpositive. This marginal utility will restrict the individual's optimal portfolio choice.

CHAPTER 3

CAPM, Arbitrage, and Linear Factor Models

In this chapter, we analyze the asset pricing implications of the previous chapter's mean-variance portfolio analysis. From one perspective, the Markowitz-Tobin portfolio selection rules form a normative theory instructing how an individual investor can best allocate wealth among various assets. However, these selection rules also could be interpreted as a positive or descriptive theory of how an investor actually behaves. If this latter view is taken, then a logical extension of portfolio selection theory is to consider the equilibrium asset pricing consequences of investors' individually rational actions. The portfolio choices of individual investors represent their particular demands for assets. By aggregating these investor demands and equating them to asset supplies, equilibrium asset prices can be determined. In this way, portfolio choice theory can provide a foundation for an asset pricing model. Indeed, such a model, the Capital Asset Pricing Model (CAPM), was derived at about the same time by four individuals: Jack Treynor, William Sharpe, John Lintner, and Jan Mossin.[1] CAPM has influenced financial practice in highly diverse ways. It has provided foundations for capital budgeting rules, for the regulation of utilities' rates of return, for performance evaluation of money managers, and for the creation of indexed mutual funds.

This chapter starts by deriving the CAPM and studying its consequences for assets' rates of return. The notion that investors might require higher rates of return for some types of risks but not others is an important insight of CAPM and extends to other asset pricing models. CAPM predicts that assets' risk premia

---

1. William Sharpe, a student of Harry Markowitz, shared the 1990 Nobel prize with Markowitz and Merton Miller. See (Treynor 1961), (Sharpe 1964), (Lintner 1965), and (Mossin 1966).

result from a single risk factor, the returns on the market portfolio of all risky assets which, in equilibrium, is a mean-variance efficient portfolio. However, it is not hard to imagine that a weakening of CAPM's restrictive assumptions could generate risk premia deriving from multiple factors. Hence, we then consider how assets' risk premia may be related when multiple risk factors generate assets' returns. We derive this relationship, not based on a model of investor preferences as was done in deriving CAPM, but based on the concept that competitive and efficient securities markets should not permit arbitrage.

As a prelude to considering a multifactor asset pricing model, we define and give examples of arbitrage. Arbitrage pricing is the primary technique for valuing one asset in terms of another. It is the basis of so-called relative pricing models, contingent claims models, or derivative pricing models. We look at some simple applications of arbitrage pricing and then study the multifactor Arbitrage Pricing Theory (APT) developed by Stephen Ross (Ross 1976). APT is the basis of the most popular empirical multifactor models of asset pricing.

3.1   The Capital Asset Pricing Model

In Chapter 2, we proved that if investors maximize expected utility that depends only on the expected return and variance of end-of-period wealth, then no matter what their particular levels of risk aversion, they would be interested only in portfolios on the efficient frontier. This mean-variance efficient frontier was the solution to the problem of computing portfolio weights that would maximize a portfolio's expected return for a given portfolio standard deviation or, alternatively, minimizing a portfolio's standard deviation for a given expected portfolio return. The point on this efficient frontier ultimately selected by a given investor was that combination of expected portfolio return and portfolio standard deviation that maximized the particular investor's expected utility. For the case of n risky assets and a risk-free asset, the optimal portfolio weights for the n risky assets were shown to be

$$\omega^* = \lambda V^{-1} \left(\overline{R} - R_f e \right) \tag{3.1}$$

where $\lambda \equiv \frac{\overline{R}_p - R_f}{\varsigma - 2\alpha R_f + \delta R_f^2}$, $\alpha \equiv \overline{R}' V^{-1} e = e' V^{-1} \overline{R}$, $\varsigma \equiv \overline{R}' V^{-1} \overline{R}$, and $\delta \equiv e' V^{-1} e$. The amount invested in the risk-free asset is then $1 - e' \omega^*$. Since λ is a scalar quantity that is linear in $\overline{R}_p$, which is the individual investor's equilibrium portfolio expected return, the weights in equation (3.1) are also linear in $\overline{R}_p$. $\overline{R}_p$ is determined by where the particular investor's indifference curve is tangent to the efficient frontier. Thus, because differences in $\overline{R}_p$ just affect the scalar, λ, we see that all investors, no matter what their degree of risk aversion, choose to hold the risky assets in the same *relative* proportions.

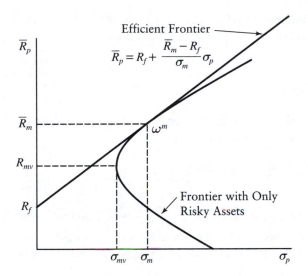

Figure 3.1 —— Capital Market Equilibrium

Mathematically, we showed that the efficient frontier is given by

$$\sigma_p = \frac{\overline{R}_p - R_f}{\left(\varsigma - 2\alpha R_f + \delta R_f^2\right)^{\frac{1}{2}}} \tag{3.2}$$

which, as illustrated in Figure 3.1, is linear when plotted in σ_p, $\overline{R}_p$ space.

3.1.1   Characteristics of the Tangency Portfolio

The efficient frontier, given by the line through R_f and ω^m, implies that investors optimally choose to hold combinations of the risk-free asset and the efficient frontier portfolio of risky assets having portfolio weights w^m. We can easily solve for this unique "tangency" portfolio of risky assets since it is the point where an investor would have a zero position in the risk-free asset; that is, $e'\omega^* = 1$, or $\overline{R}_p = \overline{R}'\omega^*$. Pre-multiplying (3.1) by e', setting the result to 1, and solving for λ, we obtain $\lambda = m \equiv [\alpha - \delta R_f]^{-1}$, so that

$$\omega^m = mV^{-1}(\overline{R} - R_f e) \tag{3.3}$$

Let us now investigate the relationship between this tangency portfolio and individual assets. Consider the covariance between the tangency portfolio and the individual risky assets. Define σ_M as the $n \times 1$ vector of covariances of the tangency portfolio with each of the n risky assets. Then using (3.3) we see that

$$\sigma_M = Vw^m = m(\overline{R} - R_f e) \tag{3.4}$$

Note that the variance of the tangency portfolio is simply $\sigma_m^2 = \omega^{m\prime} V \omega^m$. Accordingly, if we then pre-multiply equation (3.4) by $\omega^{m\prime}$, we obtain

$$\sigma_m^2 = \omega^{m\prime}\sigma_M = m\omega^{m\prime}(\overline{R} - R_f e) \qquad (3.5)$$

$$= m(\overline{R}_m - R_f)$$

where $\overline{R}_m \equiv \omega^{m\prime}\overline{R}$ is the expected return on the tangency portfolio.[2] Rearranging (3.4) and substituting in for m from (3.5), we have

$$(\overline{R} - R_f e) = \frac{1}{m}\sigma_M = \frac{\sigma_M}{\sigma_m^2}(\overline{R}_m - R_f) = \beta(\overline{R}_m - R_f) \qquad (3.6)$$

where $\beta \equiv \frac{\sigma_M}{\sigma_m^2}$ is the $n \times 1$ vector whose ith element is $\frac{Cov(\widetilde{R}_m, \widetilde{R}_i)}{Var(\widetilde{R}_m)}$. Equation (3.6) shows that a simple relationship links the excess expected return (expected return in excess of the risk-free rate) on the tangency portfolio, $(\overline{R}_m - R_f)$, to the excess expected returns on the individual risky assets, $(\overline{R} - R_f e)$.

3.1.2   Market Equilibrium

Now suppose that individual investors, each taking the set of individual assets' expected returns and covariances as fixed (exogenous), all choose mean-variance efficient portfolios. Thus, each investor decides to allocate his or her wealth between the risk-free asset and the unique tangency portfolio. Because individual investors demand the risky assets in the same relative proportions, we know that the *aggregate demands* for the risky assets will have the same relative proportions, namely, those of the tangency portfolio. Recall that our derivation of this result *does not* assume a "representative" investor in the sense of requiring all investors to have identical utility functions or beginning-of-period wealth. It *does* assume that investors have identical beliefs regarding the probability distribution of asset returns, that all risky assets can be traded, that there are no indivisibilities in asset holdings, and that there are no limits on borrowing or lending at the risk-free rate.

We can now define an equilibrium as a situation where asset returns are such that the investors' demands for the assets equal the assets' supplies. What determines the assets' supplies? One way to model asset supplies is to assume they are fixed. For example, the economy could be characterized by a fixed *quantity* of physical assets that produce random output at the end of the period. Such an economy is often referred to as an *endowment economy*, and we detail a model of this type in Chapter 6. In this case, equilibrium occurs by adjustment of the

---

2. Note that the elements of ω^m sum to 1 since the tangency portfolio has zero weight in the risk-free asset.

date 0 assets' prices so that investors' demands conform to the inelastic assets' supplies. The change in the assets' date 0 prices effectively adjusts the assets' return distributions to those which make the tangency portfolio and the net demand for the risk-free asset equal to the fixed supplies of these assets.

An alternative way to model asset supplies is to assume that the economy's asset return distributions are fixed but allow the quantities of these assets to be elastically supplied. This type of economy is known as a *production economy*, and a model of it is presented in Chapter 13. Such a model assumes that there are n risky, constant-returns-to-scale "technologies." These technologies require date 0 investments of physical capital and produce end-of-period physical investment returns having a distribution with mean $\overline{R}$ and a covariance matrix of V at the end of the period. Also, there could be a risk-free technology that generates a one-period return on physical capital of R_f. In this case of a fixed return distribution, supplies of the assets adjust to the demands for the tangency portfolio and the risk-free asset determined by the technological return distribution.

As it turns out, how one models asset supplies does not affect the results that we now derive regarding the equilibrium relationship between asset returns. We simply note that the tangency portfolio having weights ω^m must be the equilibrium portfolio of risky assets supplied in the market. Thus, equation (3.6) can be interpreted as an equilibrium relationship between the excess expected return on any asset and the excess expected return on the *market* portfolio. In other words, in equilibrium, the tangency portfolio chosen by all investors must be the market portfolio of all risky assets. Moreover, as mentioned earlier, the only case for which investors have a long position in the tangency portfolio is $R_f < R_{mv}$. Hence, for asset markets to clear, that is, for the outstanding stocks of assets to be owned by investors, the situation depicted in Figure 3.1 can be the only equilibrium efficient frontier.[3]

The Capital Asset Pricing Model's prediction that the market portfolio is mean-variance efficient is an important solution to the practical problem of identifying a mean-variance efficient portfolio. As a theory, CAPM justifies the practice of investing in a broad market portfolio of stocks and bonds. This insight has led to the growth of "indexed" mutual funds and exchange-traded funds (ETFs) that hold market-weighted portfolios of stocks and bonds.

Let's now look at some additional implications of CAPM when we consider realized, rather than expected, asset returns. Note that asset i's realized return,

---

3. This presumes that the tangency portfolio is composed of long positions in the individual risky assets; that is, $\omega_i^m > 0$ for $i = 1, \ldots, n$. While our derivation has not restricted the sign of these portfolio weights, since assets must have nonnegative supplies, equilibrium market clearing implies that assets' prices or individuals' choice of technologies must adjust (effectively changing $\overline{R}$ and/or V) to make the portfolio demands for individual assets nonnegative.

$\widetilde{R}_i$, can be defined as $\overline{R}_i + \tilde{v}_i$, where $\tilde{v}_i$ is the unexpected component of the asset's return. Similarly, the realized return on the market portfolio, $\widetilde{R}_m$, can be defined as $\overline{R}_m + \tilde{v}_m$, where $\tilde{v}_m$ is the unexpected part of the market portfolio's return. Substituting these into (3.6), we have

$$\widetilde{R}_i = R_f + \beta_i(\widetilde{R}_m - \tilde{v}_m - R_f) + \tilde{v}_i \tag{3.7}$$
$$= R_f + \beta_i(\widetilde{R}_m - R_f) + \tilde{v}_i - \beta_i\tilde{v}_m$$
$$= R_f + \beta_i(\widetilde{R}_m - R_f) + \widetilde{\varepsilon}_i$$

where $\widetilde{\varepsilon}_i \equiv \tilde{v}_i - \beta_i\tilde{v}_m$. Note that

$$Cov(\widetilde{R}_m, \widetilde{\varepsilon}_i) = Cov(\widetilde{R}_m, \tilde{v}_i) - \beta_i Cov(\widetilde{R}_m, \tilde{v}_m) \tag{3.8}$$
$$= Cov(\widetilde{R}_m, \widetilde{R}_i) - \beta_i Cov(\widetilde{R}_m, \widetilde{R}_m)$$
$$= \beta_i Var(\widetilde{R}_m) - \beta_i Var(\widetilde{R}_m) = 0$$

which, along with (3.7), implies that the total variance of risky asset i, σ_i^2, has two components:

$$\sigma_i^2 = \beta_i^2 \sigma_m^2 + \sigma_{\varepsilon_i}^2 \tag{3.9}$$

where $\beta_i^2 \sigma_m^2$ is proportional to the return variance of the market portfolios and $\sigma_{\varepsilon_i}^2$ is the variance of $\widetilde{\varepsilon}_i$, and it is orthogonal to the market portfolio's return. Since equation (3.8) shows that $\widetilde{\varepsilon}_i$ is the part of the return on risky asset i that is uncorrelated with the return on the market portfolio, this implies that equation (3.7) represents a regression equation. In other words, an unbiased estimate of β_i can be obtained by running an Ordinary Least Squares regression of asset i's excess return on the market portfolio's excess return. The orthogonal, mean-zero residual, $\widetilde{\varepsilon}_i$, is sometimes referred to as idiosyncratic, unsystematic, or diversifiable risk. This is the particular asset's risk that is eliminated or diversified away when the asset is held in the market portfolio. Since this portion of the asset's risk can be eliminated by the individual who invests optimally, there is no "price" or "risk premium" attached to it in the sense that the asset's equilibrium expected return is not altered by it.

To make clear what risk is priced, let us denote the covariance between the return on the ith asset and the return on the market portfolio as $\sigma_{Mi} = Cov(\widetilde{R}_m, \widetilde{R}_i)$, which is the ith element of σ_M. Also let ρ_{im} be the correlation between the return on the ith asset and the return on the market portfolio. Then equation (3.6) can be rewritten as

$$\overline{R}_i - R_f = \frac{\sigma_{Mi}}{\sigma_m} \frac{(\overline{R}_m - R_f)}{\sigma_m} \tag{3.10}$$

$$= \rho_{im}\sigma_i \frac{(\overline{R}_m - R_f)}{\sigma_m}$$

$$= \rho_{im}\sigma_i S_e$$

where $S_e \equiv \frac{(\overline{R}_m - R_f)}{\sigma_m}$ is the equilibrium excess return on the market portfolio per unit of market risk and is known as the market Sharpe ratio, named after William Sharpe, one of the developers of the CAPM. S_e can be interpreted as the market price of systematic or nondiversifiable risk. It is also referred to as the slope of the *capital market line*, where the capital market line is defined as the efficient frontier that connects the points R_f and ω^m in Figure 3.1. Now if we define ω_i^m as the weight of asset i in the market portfolio and V_i as the ith row of covariance matrix V, then

$$\frac{\partial \sigma_m}{\partial \omega_i^m} = \frac{1}{2\sigma_m} \frac{\partial \sigma_m^2}{\partial \omega_i^m} = \frac{1}{2\sigma_m} \frac{\partial \omega^{m\prime} V \omega^m}{\partial \omega_i^m} = \frac{1}{2\sigma_m} 2 V_i \omega^m = \frac{1}{\sigma_m} \sum_{j=1}^{N} \omega_j^m \sigma_{ij} \tag{3.11}$$

where σ_{ij} is the i, jth element of V. Since $\widetilde{R}_m = \sum_{j=1}^{n} \omega_j^m \widetilde{R}_j$, then $Cov(\widetilde{R}_i, \widetilde{R}_m) = Cov(\widetilde{R}_i, \sum_{j=1}^{n} \omega_j^m \widetilde{R}_j) = \sum_{j=1}^{n} \omega_j^m \sigma_{ij}$. Hence, (3.11) can be rewritten as

$$\frac{\partial \sigma_m}{\partial \omega_i^m} = \frac{1}{\sigma_m} Cov(\widetilde{R}_i, \widetilde{R}_m) = \rho_{im}\sigma_i \tag{3.12}$$

Thus, $\rho_{im}\sigma_i$ can be interpreted as the marginal increase in "market risk," σ_m, from a marginal increase of asset i in the market portfolio. In this sense, $\rho_{im}\sigma_i$ is the *quantity* of asset i's systematic or nondiversifiable risk. Equation (3.10) shows that this quantity of systematic risk, multiplied by the price of systematic risk, S_e, determines the asset's required excess expected return, or risk premium.

If a riskless asset does not exist so that all assets are risky, Fischer Black (Black 1972) showed that a similar asset pricing relationship exists. Here, we outline his *zero-beta CAPM*. Note that an implication of the portfolio separation result of section 2.3.3 is that since every frontier portfolio can be written as $\omega = a + b\overline{R}_p$, a linear combination of these frontier portfolios is also a frontier portfolio. Let W_i be the proportion of the economy's total wealth owned by investor i, and let ω^i be this investor's desired frontier portfolio so that $\omega^i = a + b\overline{R}_{ip}$. If there are a total of I investors, then the weights of the market portfolio are given by

$$\omega^m = \sum_{i=1}^{I} W_i \omega^i = \sum_{i=1}^{I} W_i \left(a + b\overline{R}_{ip} \right) \tag{3.13}$$

$$= a \sum_{i=1}^{I} W_i + b \sum_{i=1}^{I} W_i \overline{R}_{ip} = a + b\overline{R}_m$$

where $\overline{R}_m \equiv \sum_{i=1}^{I} W_i \overline{R}_{ip}$ and where the last equality of (3.13) uses the fact that the sum of the proportions of total wealth must equal 1. Equation (3.13) shows that the market portfolio, the aggregation of all individual investors' portfolios, is a frontier portfolio. Its expected return, $\overline{R}_m$, is a weighted average of the expected returns of the individual investors' portfolios. Because each individual investor optimally chooses a portfolio on the efficient portion of the frontier (the upper arc in Figure 2.4), then the market portfolio, being a weighted average, is also on the efficient frontier.

Now, let us compute the covariance between the market portfolio and any arbitrary portfolio of risky assets, not necessarily a frontier portfolio. Let this arbitrary risky-asset portfolio have weights ω^0, a random return of $\widetilde{R}_{0p}$, and an expected return of $\overline{R}_{0p}$. Then

$$Cov \left(\widetilde{R}_m, \widetilde{R}_{0p} \right) = \omega^{m\prime} V \omega^0 = \left(a + b\overline{R}_m \right)' V \omega^0 \tag{3.14}$$

$$= \left(\frac{\varsigma V^{-1}e - \alpha V^{-1}\overline{R}}{\varsigma\delta - \alpha^2} + \frac{\delta V^{-1}\overline{R} - \alpha V^{-1}e}{\varsigma\delta - \alpha^2} \overline{R}_m \right)' V \omega^0$$

$$= \frac{\varsigma e'V^{-1}V\omega^0 - \alpha \overline{R}'V^{-1}V\omega^0}{\varsigma\delta - \alpha^2}$$

$$+ \frac{\delta \overline{R}_m \overline{R}'V^{-1}V\omega^0 - \alpha \overline{R}_m e'V^{-1}V\omega^0}{\varsigma\delta - \alpha^2}$$

$$= \frac{\varsigma - \alpha\overline{R}_{0p} + \delta\overline{R}_m\overline{R}_{0p} - \alpha\overline{R}_m}{\varsigma\delta - \alpha^2}$$

Rearranging (3.14) gives

$$\overline{R}_{0p} = \frac{\alpha\overline{R}_m - \varsigma}{\delta\overline{R}_m - \alpha} + Cov \left(\widetilde{R}_m, \widetilde{R}_{0p} \right) \frac{\varsigma\delta - \alpha^2}{\delta\overline{R}_m - \alpha} \tag{3.15}$$

Rewriting the first term on the right-hand side of equation (3.15) and multiplying and dividing the second term by the definition of a frontier portfolio's variance given in Chapter 2's equation (2.32), equation (3.15) becomes

$$\overline{R}_{0p} = \frac{\alpha}{\delta} - \frac{\varsigma\delta - \alpha^2}{\delta^2\left(\overline{R}_m - \frac{\alpha}{\delta}\right)} + \frac{Cov\left(\widetilde{R}_m, \widetilde{R}_{0p}\right)}{\sigma_m^2} \left(\frac{1}{\delta} + \frac{\delta\left(\overline{R}_m - \frac{\alpha}{\delta}\right)^2}{\varsigma\delta - \alpha^2}\right) \frac{\varsigma\delta - \alpha^2}{\delta\overline{R}_m - \alpha}$$

$$= \frac{\alpha}{\delta} - \frac{\varsigma\delta - \alpha^2}{\delta^2\left(\overline{R}_m - \frac{\alpha}{\delta}\right)} + \frac{Cov\left(\widetilde{R}_m, \widetilde{R}_{0p}\right)}{\sigma_m^2} \left(\overline{R}_m - \frac{\alpha}{\delta} + \frac{\varsigma\delta - \alpha^2}{\delta^2\left(\overline{R}_m - \frac{\alpha}{\delta}\right)}\right)$$

$$(3.16)$$

From equation (2.39), we recognize that the first two terms on the right-hand side of (3.16) equal the expected return on the portfolio that has zero covariance with the market portfolio, call it $\overline{R}_{zm}$. Thus, equation (3.16) can be written as

$$\overline{R}_{0p} = \overline{R}_{zm} + \frac{Cov\left(\widetilde{R}_m, \widetilde{R}_{0p}\right)}{\sigma_m^2}\left(\overline{R}_m - \overline{R}_{zm}\right) \qquad (3.17)$$

$$= \overline{R}_{zm} + \beta_0\left(\overline{R}_m - \overline{R}_{zm}\right)$$

Since the portfolio having weights ω^0 can be any risky-asset portfolio, it includes a portfolio that invests solely in a single asset.[4] In this light, β_0 becomes the covariance of the individual asset's return with that of the market portfolio, and the relationship in equation (3.17) is identical to the previous CAPM result in equation (3.10) except that $\overline{R}_{zm}$ replaces R_f. Hence, when a riskless asset does not exist, we measure an asset's excess returns relative to $\overline{R}_{zm}$, the expected return on a portfolio that has a zero beta.

Because the CAPM relationship in equations (3.10) or (3.17) implies that assets' expected returns differ only due to differences in their betas, it is considered a single "factor" model, this risk factor being the return on the market portfolio. Stephen Ross (Ross 1976) derived a similar multifactor relationship, but starting from a different set of assumptions and using a derivation based on the arbitrage principle. Frequently in this book, we will see that asset pricing implications can often be derived based on investor risk preferences, as was done in the CAPM when we assumed investors cared only about the mean and variance of their portfolio's return. However, another powerful technique for asset pricing is to rule out the existence of arbitrage. We now turn to this topic, first by discussing the nature of arbitrage.

---

4. One of the elements of ω^0 would equal 1, while the rest would be zero.

3.2   Arbitrage

The notion of arbitrage is simple. It involves the possibility of getting something for nothing while having no possibility of loss. Specifically, consider constructing a portfolio involving both long and short positions in assets such that no initial wealth is required to form the portfolio.[5] If this zero-net-investment portfolio can sometimes produce a positive return but can never produce a negative return, then it represents an arbitrage: starting from zero wealth, a profit can sometimes be made but a loss can never occur. A special case of arbitrage is when this zero-net-investment portfolio produces a riskless return. If this certain return is positive (*negative*), an arbitrage is to buy (*sell*) the portfolio and reap a riskless profit, or "free lunch." Only if the return is zero would there be no arbitrage.

An arbitrage opportunity can also be defined in a slightly different context. If a portfolio that requires a nonzero initial net investment is created such that it earns a certain rate of return, then this rate of return must equal the current (competitive market) risk-free interest rate. Otherwise, there would also be an arbitrage opportunity. For example, if the portfolio required a positive initial investment but earned less than the risk-free rate, an arbitrage would be to (short-) sell the portfolio and invest the proceeds at the risk-free rate, thereby earning a riskless profit equal to the difference between the risk-free rate and the portfolio's certain (lower) rate of return.[6]

In efficient, competitive asset markets where arbitrage trades are feasible, it is reasonable to think that arbitrage opportunities are rare and fleeting. Should arbitrage temporarily exist, then trading by investors to earn this profit will tend to move asset prices in a direction that eliminates the arbitrage opportunity. For example, if a zero-net-investment portfolio produces a riskless positive return, as investors create (buy) this portfolio, the prices of the assets in the portfolio will be bid up. The cost of creating the portfolio will then exceed zero. The portfolio's cost will rise until it equals the present value of the portfolio's riskless return, thereby eliminating the arbitrage opportunity. Hence, for competitive asset markets where it is also feasible to execute arbitrage trades, it may be reasonable to assume that

---

5. Proceeds from short sales (or borrowing) are used to purchase (take long positions in) other assets.

6. Arbitrage defined in this context is really equivalent to the previous definition of arbitrage. For example, if a portfolio requiring a positive initial investment produces a certain rate of return in excess of the riskless rate, then an investor should be able to borrow the initial funds needed to create this portfolio and pay an interest rate on this loan that equals the risk-free interest rate. That the investor should be able to borrow at the riskless interest rate can be seen from the fact that the portfolio produces a return that is always sufficient to repay the loan in full, making the borrowing risk-free. Hence, combining this initial borrowing with the nonzero portfolio investment results in an arbitrage opportunity that requires zero initial wealth.

equilibrium asset prices reflect an absence of arbitrage opportunities. As will be shown, this assumption leads to a law of one price: if different assets produce exactly the same future payoffs, then the current prices of these assets must be the same. This simple result has powerful asset pricing implications.

However, as a word of caution, not all asset markets meet the conditions required to justify arbitrage pricing. For some markets, it may be impossible to execute pure arbitrage trades due to significant transactions costs and/or restrictions on short-selling or borrowing. In such cases of limited arbitrage, the law of one price can fail.[7] Alternative methods, such as those based on a model of investor preferences, are required to price assets.

3.2.1   Examples of Arbitrage Pricing

An early use of the arbitrage principle is the *covered interest parity* condition that links spot and forward foreign exchange markets to foreign and domestic money markets. To illustrate, let $F_{0\tau}$ be the current date 0 forward price for exchanging one unit of a foreign currency τ periods in the future. This forward price represents the dollar price to be paid τ periods in the future for delivery of one unit of foreign currency τ periods in the future. In contrast, let S_0 be the spot price of foreign exchange, that is, the current date 0 dollar price of one unit of foreign currency to be delivered immediately. Also let R_f be the per-period risk-free (money market) return for borrowing or lending in dollars over the period 0 to τ, and denote as R_f^* the per-period risk-free return for borrowing or lending in the foreign currency over the period 0 to τ.[8]

Now construct the following portfolio that requires zero net wealth. First, we sell forward (take a short forward position in) one unit of foreign exchange at price $F_{0\tau}$.[9] This contract means that we are committed to delivering one unit of foreign exchange at date τ in return for receiving $F_{0\tau}$ dollars at date τ. Second, let us also purchase the present value of one unit of foreign currency, $1/R_f^{*\tau}$, and invest it in a foreign bond yielding the per-period return, R_f^*. In terms of the domestic currency, this purchase costs $S_0/R_f^{*\tau}$, which we finance by borrowing dollars at the per-period return R_f.

What happens at date τ as a result of these trades? When date τ arrives, we know that our foreign currency investment yields $R_f^{*\tau}/R_f^{*\tau} = 1$ unit of the foreign

---

7. Andrei Shleifer and Robert Vishny (Shleifer and Vishny 1997) discuss why the conditions needed to apply arbitrage pricing are not present in many asset markets.

8. For example, if the foreign currency is the Japanese yen, R_f^* would be the per-period return for a yen-denominated risk-free investment or loan.

9. Taking a long or short position in a forward contract requires zero initial wealth, as payment and delivery all occur at the future date τ.

currency. This is exactly what we need to satisfy our short position in the forward foreign exchange contract. For delivering this foreign currency, we receive $F_{0\tau}$ dollars. But we also now owe a sum of $R_f^{\tau} S_0 / R_f^{*\tau}$ due to our dollar borrowing. Thus, our net proceeds at date τ are

$$F_{0\tau} - R_f^{\tau} S_0 / R_f^{*\tau} \tag{3.18}$$

Note that these proceeds are nonrandom; that is, the amount is known at date 0 since it depends only on prices and riskless rates quoted at date 0. If this amount is positive, then we should indeed create this portfolio as it represents an arbitrage. If, instead, this amount is negative, then an arbitrage would be for us to sell this portfolio; that is, we reverse each trade just discussed (i.e., take a long forward position, and invest in the domestic currency financed by borrowing in foreign currency markets). Thus, the only instance in which arbitrage would not occur is if the net proceeds are zero, which implies

$$F_{0\tau} = S_0 R_f^{\tau} / R_f^{*\tau} \tag{3.19}$$

Equation (3.19) is referred to as the *covered interest parity* condition.

The forward exchange rate, $F_{0\tau}$, represents the dollar price for buying or selling a foreign currency at date τ, a future date when the foreign currency's dollar value is unknown. Though $F_{0\tau}$ is the price of a risky cashflow, it has been determined without knowledge of the utility functions of investors or their expectations regarding the future value of the foreign currency. The reason for this simplification is due to the *law of one price*, which states that in the absence of arbitrage, equivalent assets (or contracts) must have the same price. A forward contract to purchase a unit of foreign currency can be replicated by buying, at the spot exchange rate S_0, a foreign currency investment paying the per-period risk-free return R_f^* and financing this by borrowing at the dollar risk-free return R_f. In the absence of arbitrage, these two methods for obtaining foreign currency in the future must be valued the same. Given the spot exchange rate, S_0, and the foreign and domestic money market returns, R_f^* and R_f, the forward rate is pinned down. Thus, when applicable, pricing assets or contracts by ruling out arbitrage is attractive in that assumptions regarding investor preferences or beliefs are not required.

To motivate how arbitrage pricing might apply to a very simple version of the CAPM, suppose that there is a risk-free asset that returns R_f and multiple risky assets. However, assume that only a single source of (market) risk determines all risky-asset returns and that these returns can be expressed by the linear relationship

$$\widetilde{R}_i = a_i + b_i \widetilde{f} \tag{3.20}$$

where $\tilde{R}_i$ is the return on the ith asset and $\tilde{f}$ is the single risk factor generating all asset returns, where it is assumed that $E[\tilde{f}] = 0$. a_i is asset i's expected return, that is, $E[\tilde{R}_i] = a_i$. b_i is the sensitivity of asset i to the risk factor and can be viewed as asset i's beta coefficient. Note that this is a highly simplified example in that all risky assets are perfectly correlated with each other. Assets have no idiosyncratic risk (residual component $\tilde{\varepsilon}_i$). A generalized model with idiosyncratic risk will be presented in the next section.

Now suppose that a portfolio of two assets is constructed, where a proportion of wealth of ω is invested in asset i and the remaining proportion of $(1 - \omega)$ is invested in asset j. This portfolio's return is given by

$$\tilde{R}_p = \omega a_i + (1 - \omega)a_j + \omega b_i \tilde{f} + (1 - \omega)b_j \tilde{f} \tag{3.21}$$

$$= \omega(a_i - a_j) + a_j + \left[\omega(b_i - b_j) + b_j\right]\tilde{f}$$

If the portfolio weights are chosen such that

$$\omega^* = \frac{b_j}{b_j - b_i} \tag{3.22}$$

then the uncertain (random) component of the portfolio's return is eliminated. The absence of arbitrage then requires that $R_p = R_f$, so that

$$R_p = \omega^*(a_i - a_j) + a_j = R_f \tag{3.23}$$

or

$$\frac{b_j(a_i - a_j)}{b_j - b_i} + a_j = R_f$$

which implies

$$\frac{a_i - R_f}{b_i} = \frac{a_j - R_f}{b_j} \equiv \lambda \tag{3.24}$$

This condition states that the expected return in excess of the risk-free rate, per unit of risk, must be equal for all assets, and we define this ratio as λ. λ is the risk premium per unit of the factor risk. The denominator, b_i, can be interpreted as asset i's quantity of risk from the single risk factor, while $a_i - R_f$ can be thought of as asset i's compensation or premium in terms of excess expected return given to investors for holding asset i. Thus, this no-arbitrage condition is really a law of one price in that the *price of risk*, λ, which is the risk premium divided by the quantity of risk, must be the same for all assets.

Equation (3.24) is a fundamental relationship, and similar law-of-one-price conditions hold for virtually all asset pricing models. For example, we can rewrite the CAPM equation (3.10) as

$$\frac{\overline{R}_i - R_f}{\rho_{im}\sigma_i} = \frac{(\overline{R}_m - R_f)}{\sigma_m} \equiv S_e \tag{3.25}$$

so that the ratio of an asset's expected return premium, $\overline{R}_i - R_f$, to its quantity of market risk, $\rho_{im}\sigma_i$, is the same for all assets and equals the slope of the capital market line, S_e. We next turn to a generalization of the CAPM that derives from arbitrage pricing.

3.3 Linear Factor Models

The CAPM assumption that all assets can be held by all individual investors is clearly an oversimplification. Transactions costs and other trading "frictions" that arise from distortions such as capital controls and taxes might prevent individuals from holding a global portfolio of marketable assets. Furthermore, many assets simply are nonmarketable and cannot be traded.[10] The preeminent example of a nonmarketable asset is the value of an individual's future labor income, what economists refer to as the individual's *human capital*. Therefore, in addition to the risk from returns on a global portfolio of marketable assets, individuals are likely to face multiple sources of nondiversifiable risks. It is then not hard to imagine that, in equilibrium, assets' risk premia derive from more than a single risk factor. Indeed, the CAPM's prediction that risk from a market portfolio is the only source of priced risk has not received strong empirical support.[11]

This is a motivation for the multifactor Arbitrage Pricing Theory (APT) model. APT assumes that an individual asset's return is driven by multiple risk factors and by an idiosyncratic component, though the theory is mute regarding the sources of these multiple risk factors. APT is a relative pricing model in the sense that it determines the risk premia on all assets relative to the risk premium for each of the

---

10. Richard Roll (Roll 1977) has argued that CAPM is not a reasonable theory, because a true "market" portfolio consisting of all risky assets cannot be observed or owned by investors. Moreover, empirical tests of CAPM are infeasible because proxies for the market portfolio (such as the S&P 500 stock index) may not be mean-variance efficient, even if the true market portfolio is. Conversely, a proxy for the market portfolio could be mean-variance efficient even though the true market portfolio is not.

11. Ravi Jagannathan and Ellen McGrattan (Jagannathan and McGrattan 1995) review the empirical evidence for CAPM.

factors and each asset's sensitivity to each factor.[12] It does not make assumptions regarding investor preferences but uses arbitrage pricing to restrict an asset's risk premium. The main assumptions of the model are that the returns on all assets are linearly related to a finite number of risk factors and that the number of assets in the economy is large relative to the number of factors. Let us now detail the model's assumptions.

Assume that there are k risk factors and n assets in the economy, where $n > k$. Let b_{iz} be the sensitivity of the ith asset to the zth risk factor, where $\tilde{f}_z$ is the random realization of risk factor z. Also let $\tilde{\varepsilon}_i$ be the idiosyncratic risk component specific to asset i, which by definition is independent of the k risk factors, $\tilde{f}_1, \ldots, \tilde{f}_k$, and the specific risk component of any other asset j, $\tilde{\varepsilon}_j$. $\tilde{\varepsilon}_i$ must be independent of the risk factors or else it would affect all assets, thus not being truly a specific source of risk to just asset i. If a_i is the expected return on asset i, then the return-generating process for asset i is given by the linear factor model

$$\tilde{R}_i = a_i + \sum_{z=1}^{k} b_{iz}\tilde{f}_z + \tilde{\varepsilon}_i \tag{3.26}$$

where $E[\tilde{\varepsilon}_i] = E[\tilde{f}_z] = E[\tilde{\varepsilon}_i\tilde{f}_z] = 0$, and $E[\tilde{\varepsilon}_i\tilde{\varepsilon}_j] = 0$ for $i \neq j$. For simplicity, we also assume that $E[\tilde{f}_z\tilde{f}_x] = 0$ for $z \neq x$; that is, the risk factors are mutually independent. In addition, let us further assume that the risk factors are normalized to have a variance equal to one, so that $E[\tilde{f}_z^2] = 1$. As it turns out, these last two assumptions are not important, as a linear transformation of correlated risk factors can allow them to be redefined as independent, unit-variance risk factors.[13]

A final assumption is that the idiosyncratic risk (variance) for each asset is finite; that is,

$$E\left[\tilde{\varepsilon}_i^2\right] \equiv s_i^2 < S^2 \tag{3.27}$$

---

12. This is not much different from the CAPM. CAPM determined each asset's risk premium based on the single-factor market risk premium, $\overline{R}_m - R_f$, and the asset's sensitivity to this single factor, β_i. The only difference is that CAPM provides somewhat more guidance as to the identity of the risk factor, namely, the return on a market portfolio of all assets.

13. For example, suppose $\tilde{g}$ is a $k \times 1$ vector of mean-zero, correlated risk factors with $k \times k$ covariance matrix $E[\tilde{g}\tilde{g}'] = \Omega$. Then create a transformed $k \times 1$ vector of risk factors given by $\tilde{f} = \sqrt{\Omega^{-1}}\tilde{g}$. The covariance matrix of these transformed risk factors is $E[\tilde{f}\tilde{f}'] = \sqrt{\Omega^{-1}}E[\tilde{g}\tilde{g}']\sqrt{\Omega^{-1}} = I_k$ where I_k is a $k \times k$ identity matrix.

where S^2 is some finite number. Under these assumptions, note that $Cov(\widetilde{R}_i, \widetilde{f}_z) = Cov(b_{iz}\widetilde{f}_z, \widetilde{f}_z) = b_{iz}Cov(\widetilde{f}_z, \widetilde{f}_z) = b_{iz}$. Thus, b_{iz} is the covariance between the return on asset i and factor z.

In the simple example of the previous section, assets had no idiosyncratic risk, and their expected returns could be determined by ruling out a simple arbitrage. This was because a hedge portfolio, consisting of appropriate combinations of different assets, could be created that had a riskless return. Now, however, when each asset's return contains an idiosyncratic risk component, it is not possible to create a hedge portfolio having a purely riskless return. Instead, we will argue that if the number of assets is large, a portfolio can be constructed that has "close" to a riskless return, because the idiosyncratic components of assets' returns are diversifiable. While ruling out pure arbitrage opportunities is not sufficient to constrain assets' expected returns, we can use the notion of *asymptotic arbitrage* to argue that assets' expected returns will be "close" to the relationship that would result if they had no idiosyncratic risk. So let us now state what we mean by an asymptotic arbitrage opportunity.[14]

DEFINITION   Let a portfolio containing n assets be described by the vector of investment amounts in each of the n assets, $W^n \equiv [W_1^n\ W_2^n \ldots W_n^n]'$. Thus, W_i^n is the amount invested in asset i when there are n total assets in the economy. Consider a sequence of these portfolios where n is increasing, $n = 2, 3, \ldots$. Let σ_{ij} be the covariance between the returns on assets i and j. Then an asymptotic arbitrage exists if the following conditions hold:

(A) The portfolio requires zero net investment:

$$\sum_{i=1}^{n} W_i^n = 0$$

(B) The portfolio return becomes certain as n gets large:

$$\lim_{n \to \infty} \sum_{i=1}^{n} \sum_{j=1}^{n} W_i^n W_j^n \sigma_{ij} = 0$$

(C) The portfolio's expected return is always bounded above zero:

$$\sum_{i=1}^{n} W_i^n a_i \geq \delta > 0$$

---

14. This proof of Arbitrage Pricing Theory based on the concept of asymptotic arbitrage is due to Gur Huberman (Huberman 1982).

We can now state the Arbitrage Pricing Theorem (APT):

THEOREM   If no asymptotic arbitrage opportunities exist, then the expected return of asset i, $i = 1, \ldots, n$, is described by the following linear relation:

$$a_i = \lambda_0 + \sum_{z=1}^{k} b_{iz}\lambda_z + v_i \qquad (*)$$

where λ_0 is a constant, λ_z is the risk premium for risk factor $\widetilde{f}_z$, $z = 1, \ldots, k$, and the expected return deviations, v_i, satisfy

$$\sum_{i=1}^{n} v_i = 0 \qquad (i)$$

$$\sum_{i=1}^{n} b_{iz}v_i = 0, \quad z = 1, \ldots, k \qquad (ii)$$

$$\lim_{n \to \infty} \frac{1}{n} \sum_{i=1}^{n} v_i^2 = 0 \qquad (iii)$$

Note that condition (*iii*) says that the average squared error (deviation) from the pricing rule (∗) goes to zero as n becomes large. Thus, as the number of assets increases relative to the risk factors, expected returns will, on average, become closely approximated by the relation $a_i = \lambda_0 + \sum_{z=1}^{k} b_{iz}\lambda_z$. Also note that if the economy contains a risk-free asset (implying $b_{iz} = 0$, $\forall\, z$), the risk-free return will be approximated by λ_0.

Proof: For a given number of assets, $n > k$, think of running a cross-sectional regression of the a_i's on the b_{iz}'s. More precisely, project the dependent variable vector $a = [a_1, a_2, \ldots, a_n]'$ on the k explanatory variable vectors $b_z = [b_{1z}, b_{2z}, \ldots, b_{nz}]$, $z = 1, \ldots, k$. Define v_i as the regression residual for observation i, $i = 1, \ldots, n$. Denote λ_0 as the regression intercept and λ_z, $z = 1, \ldots, k$, as the estimated coefficient on explanatory variable z. The regression estimates and residuals must then satisfy

$$a_i = \lambda_0 + \sum_{z=1}^{k} b_{iz}\lambda_z + v_i \qquad (3.28)$$

where by the properties of an orthogonal projection (Ordinary Least Squares regression), the residuals sum to zero, $\sum_{i=1}^{n} v_i = 0$, and are orthogonal to the regressors, $\sum_{i=1}^{n} b_{iz}v_i = 0$, $z = 1, \ldots, k$. Thus, we have shown that (∗), (*i*), and (*ii*) can be satisfied. The last but most important part of the proof is to show that (*iii*) must hold in the absence of asymptotic arbitrage.

Thus, let us construct a zero-net-investment arbitrage portfolio with the following investment amounts:

$$W_i = \frac{v_i}{\sqrt{\sum_{i=1}^n v_i^2 n}} \tag{3.29}$$

so that greater amounts are invested in assets having the greatest relative expected return deviation. The total arbitrage portfolio return is given by

$$\tilde{R}_p = \sum_{i=1}^n W_i \tilde{R}_i \tag{3.30}$$

$$= \frac{1}{\sqrt{\sum_{i=1}^n v_i^2 n}} \left[\sum_{i=1}^n v_i \tilde{R}_i \right] = \frac{1}{\sqrt{\sum_{i=1}^n v_i^2 n}} \left[\sum_{i=1}^n v_i \left(a_i + \sum_{z=1}^k b_{iz} \tilde{f}_z + \tilde{\varepsilon}_i \right) \right]$$

Since $\sum_{i=1}^n b_{iz} v_i = 0$, $z = 1, \ldots, k$, this equals

$$\tilde{R}_p = \frac{1}{\sqrt{\sum_{i=1}^n v_i^2 n}} \left[\sum_{i=1}^n v_i \left(a_i + \tilde{\varepsilon}_i \right) \right] \tag{3.31}$$

Let us calculate this portfolio's mean and variance. Taking expectations, we obtain

$$E\left[\tilde{R}_p\right] = \frac{1}{\sqrt{\sum_{i=1}^n v_i^2 n}} \left[\sum_{i=1}^n v_i a_i \right] \tag{3.32}$$

since $E[\tilde{\varepsilon}_i] = 0$. Substituting in for $a_i = \lambda_0 + \sum_{z=1}^k b_{iz}\lambda_z + v_i$, we have

$$E\left[\tilde{R}_p\right] = \frac{1}{\sqrt{\sum_{i=1}^n v_i^2 n}} \left[\lambda_0 \sum_{i=1}^n v_i + \sum_{z=1}^k \left(\lambda_z \sum_{i=1}^n v_i b_{iz} \right) + \sum_{i=1}^n v_i^2 \right] \tag{3.33}$$

and since $\sum_{i=1}^n v_i = 0$ and $\sum_{i=1}^n v_i b_{iz} = 0$, this simplifies to

$$E\left[\tilde{R}_p\right] = \frac{1}{\sqrt{\sum_{i=1}^n v_i^2 n}} \sum_{i=1}^n v_i^2 = \sqrt{\frac{1}{n}\sum_{i=1}^n v_i^2} \tag{3.34}$$

To calculate the portfolio's variance, start by subtracting (3.32) from (3.31):

$$\tilde{R}_p - E\left[\tilde{R}_p\right] = \frac{1}{\sqrt{\sum_{i=1}^n v_i^2 n}} \left[\sum_{i=1}^n v_i \tilde{\varepsilon}_i \right] \tag{3.35}$$

Then, because $E[\tilde{\varepsilon}_i\tilde{\varepsilon}_j] = 0$ for $i \neq j$ and $E[\tilde{\varepsilon}_i^2] = s_i^2$, the portfolio variance is

$$E\left[\left(\tilde{R}_p - E\left[\tilde{R}_p\right]\right)^2\right] = \frac{\sum_{i=1}^n v_i^2 s_i^2}{n \sum_{i=1}^n v_i^2} < \frac{\sum_{i=1}^n v_i^2 S^2}{n \sum_{i=1}^n v_i^2} = \frac{S^2}{n} \tag{3.36}$$

Thus, as n becomes large ($n \to \infty$), the variance of the portfolio goes to zero; that is, the expected return on the portfolio becomes *certain*. This implies that in the limit, the actual return equals the expected return in (3.34):

$$\lim_{n\to\infty} \tilde{R}_p = E\left[\tilde{R}_p\right] = \sqrt{\frac{1}{n}\sum_{i=1}^n v_i^2} \tag{3.37}$$

and so if there are no asymptotic arbitrage opportunities, this certain return on the portfolio must equal zero. This is equivalent to requiring

$$\lim_{n\to\infty} \frac{1}{n}\sum_{i=1}^n v_i^2 = 0 \tag{3.38}$$

which is condition (*iii*). ∎

We see that APT, given by the relation $a_i = \lambda_0 + \sum_{z=1}^k b_{iz}\lambda_z$, can be interpreted as a multibeta generalization of CAPM. However, whereas CAPM says that its single beta should be the sensitivity of an asset's return to that of the market portfolio, APT gives no guidance as to what are the economy's multiple underlying risk factors. An empirical application of APT by Nai-Fu Chen, Richard Roll, and Stephen Ross (Chen, Roll, and Ross 1986) assumed that the risk factors were macroeconomic in nature, as proxied by industrial production, expected and unexpected inflation, the spread between long- and short-maturity interest rates, and the spread between high- and low-credit-quality bonds.

Other researchers have tended to select risk factors based on those that provide the "best fit" to historical asset returns.[15] The well-known Eugene Fama and Kenneth French (Fama and French 1993) model is an example of this. Its risk factors are returns on three different portfolios: a market portfolio of stocks (like CAPM), a portfolio that is long the stocks of small firms and short the stocks of large firms, and a portfolio that is long the stocks having high book-to-market ratios (value stocks) and short the stocks having low book-to-market ratios (growth stocks). The latter two portfolios capture the empirical finding that the stocks of smaller firms and those of value firms tend to have higher expected returns than would be predicted solely by the one-factor CAPM model. The

---

15. Gregory Connor and Robert Korajczk (Connor and Korajczyk 1995) survey empirical tests of the APT.

Fama-French model predicts that a given stock's expected return is determined by its three betas for these three portfolios.[16] It has been criticized for lacking a theoretical foundation for its risk factors.[17]

However, there have been some attempts to provide a rationale for the Fama-French model's good fit of asset returns. Heaton and Lucas (Heaton and Lucas 2000) provide a rationale for the additional Fama-French risk factors. They note that many stockholders may dislike the risks of small-firm and value stocks, the latter often being stocks of firms in financial distress and thereby requiring higher average returns. They provide empirical evidence that many stockholders are, themselves, entrepreneurs and owners of small businesses, so that their human capital is already subject to the risks of small firms with relatively high probabilities of failure. Hence, these entrepreneurs wish to avoid further exposure to these types of risks.

We will later develop another multibeta asset pricing model, namely, Robert Merton's Intertemporal Capital Asset Pricing Model (ICAPM) (Merton 1973a), which is derived from an intertemporal consumer-investor optimization problem. It is a truly dynamic model that allows for changes in state variables that could influence investment opportunities. While the ICAPM is sometimes used to justify the APT, the static (single-period) APT framework may not be compatible with some of the predictions of the more dynamic (multiperiod) ICAPM. In general, the ICAPM allows for changing risk-free rates and predicts that assets' expected returns should be a function of such changing investment opportunities. The model also predicts that an asset's multiple betas are unlikely to remain constant through time, which can complicate deriving estimates of betas from historical data.[18]

3.4 Summary

In this chapter we took a first step in understanding the equilibrium determinants of individual assets' prices and returns. The Capital Asset Pricing Model (CAPM)

---

16. A popular extension of the Fama-French three-factor model is the four-factor model proposed by Mark Carhart (Carhart 1997). His model adds a proxy for stock momentum.

17. Moreover, some researchers argue that what the model interprets as risk factors may be evidence of market inefficiency. For example, the low returns on growth stocks relative to value stocks may represent market mispricing due to investor overreaction to high growth firms. Josef Lakonishok, Andrei Shleifer, and Robert Vishny (Lakonishok, Shleifer, and Vishny 1994) find that various measures of risk cannot explain the higher average returns of value stocks relative to growth stocks.

18. Ravi Jagannathan and Zhenyu Wang (Jagannathan and Wang 1996) find that the CAPM better explains stock returns when stocks' betas are permitted to change over time and a proxy for the return on human capital is included in the market portfolio.

was shown to be a natural extension of Markowitz's mean-variance portfolio analysis. However, in addition to deriving CAPM from investor mean-variance risk preferences, we showed that CAPM and its multifactor generalization Arbitrage Pricing Theory (APT) could result from assumptions of a linear model of asset returns and an absence of arbitrage opportunities.

Arbitrage pricing will arise frequently in subsequent chapters, especially in the context of valuing derivative securities. Furthermore, future chapters will build on our single-period CAPM and APT results to show how equilibrium asset pricing is modified when multiple periods and time-varying asset return distributions are considered.

3.5 Exercises

1. Assume that individual investor k chooses between n risky assets in order to maximize the following utility function:

$$\max_{\{\omega_i^k\}} \overline{R}_k - \frac{1}{\theta_k} V_k$$

where the mean and variance of investor k's portfolio are $\overline{R}_k = \sum_{i=1}^n \omega_i^k \overline{R}_i$ and $V_k = \sum_{i=1}^n \sum_{j=1}^n \omega_i^k \omega_j^k \sigma_{ij}$, respectively, and where $\overline{R}_i$ is the expected return on risky asset i, and σ_{ij} is the covariance between the returns on risky asset i and risky asset j. ω_i^k is investor k's portfolio weight invested in risky asset i, so that $\sum_{i=1}^n \omega_i^k = 1$. θ_k is a positive constant and equals investor k's *risk tolerance*.

a. Write down the Lagrangian for this problem and show the first-order conditions.

b. Rewrite the first-order condition to show that the expected return on asset i is a linear function of the covariance between risky asset i's return and the return on investor k's optimal portfolio.

c. Assume that investor k has initial wealth equal to W_k and that there are $k = 1, \ldots, M$ total investors, each with different initial wealth and risk tolerance. Show that the equilibrium expected return on asset i is of a similar form to the first-order condition found in part (b), but depends on the *wealth-weighted risk tolerances* of investors and the *covariance of the return on asset i with the market portfolio*. Hint: begin by multiplying the first-order condition in part (b) by investor k's wealth times risk tolerance, and then aggregate over all investors.

2. Let the U.S. dollar ($)/Swiss franc (SF) spot exchange rate be $0.68 per SF and the one-year forward exchange rate be $0.70 per SF. The one-year interest rate for borrowing or lending dollars is 6.00 percent.

   a. What must be the one-year interest rate for borrowing or lending Swiss francs in order for there to be no arbitrage opportunity?

   b. If the one-year interest rate for borrowing or lending Swiss francs was less than your answer in part (a), describe the arbitrage opportunity.

3. Suppose that the Arbitrage Pricing Theory holds with $k = 2$ risk factors, so that asset returns are given by

$$\widetilde{R}_i = a_i + b_{i1}\widetilde{f}_1 + b_{i2}\widetilde{f}_2 + \widetilde{\varepsilon}_i$$

where $a_i \cong \lambda_{f0} + b_{i1}\lambda_{f1} + b_{i2}\lambda_{f2}$. Maintain all of the assumptions made in the notes and, in addition, assume that both λ_{f1} and λ_{f2} are positive. Thus, the positive risk premia imply that both of the two orthogonal risk factors are "priced" sources of risk. Now define two new risk factors from the original risk factors:

$$\widetilde{g}_1 = c_1\widetilde{f}_1 + c_2\widetilde{f}_2$$

$$\widetilde{g}_2 = c_3\widetilde{f}_1 + c_4\widetilde{f}_2$$

Show that there exists a $c_1, c_2, c_3,$ and c_4 such that $\widetilde{g}_1$ is orthogonal to $\widetilde{g}_2$, they each have unit variance, and $\lambda_{g1} > 0$, but that $\lambda_{g2} = 0$, where λ_{g1} and λ_{g2} are the risk premia associated with $\widetilde{g}_1$ and $\widetilde{g}_2$, respectively. In other words, show that any economy with two priced sources of risk can also be described by an economy with one priced source of risk.

CHAPTER 4

Consumption-Savings Decisions and State Pricing

P revious chapters studied the portfolio choice problem of an individual who maximizes the expected utility of his end-of-period wealth. This specification of an individual's decision-making problem may be less than satisfactory since, traditionally, economists have presumed that individuals derive utility from consuming goods and services, not by possessing wealth per se. Taking this view, our prior analysis can be interpreted as implicitly assuming that the individual consumes only at the end of the single investment period, and all end-of-period wealth is consumed. Utility from the individual consuming some of her initial beginning-of-period wealth was not modeled, so that all initial wealth was assumed to be saved and invested in a portfolio of assets.

In this chapter we consider the more general problem where an individual obtains utility from consuming at both the initial and terminal dates of her decision period and where nontraded labor income also may be received. This allows us to model the individual's initial consumption-savings decision as well as her portfolio choice decision. In doing so, we can derive relationships between asset prices and the individual's optimal levels of consumption that extend many of our previous results. We introduce the concept of a *stochastic discount factor* that can be used to value the returns on any asset. This stochastic discount factor equals each individual's marginal rate of substitution between initial and end-of-period consumption for each state of nature, that is, each random outcome.

After deriving this stochastic discount factor, we demonstrate that its volatility restricts the feasible excess expected returns and volatilities of all assets. Importantly, we discuss empirical evidence that appears inconsistent with this restriction for standard, time-separable utility functions, casting doubt on the usefulness of a utility-of-consumption-based stochastic discount factor. Fortunately, however, a stochastic discount factor for pricing assets need not rely on this consumption-based foundation. We provide an alternative derivation of a stochastic discount factor based on the assumptions of an absence of arbitrage and *market completeness*. Markets are said to be complete when there are a sufficient number of nonredundant assets whose returns span all states of nature.

The chapter concludes by showing how the stochastic discount factor approach can be modified to derive an asset valuation relationship based on *risk-neutral* probabilities. These probabilities transform the true probabilities of each state of nature to incorporate adjustments for risk premia. Valuation based on risk-neutral probabilities is used extensively to price assets, and this technique will be employed frequently in future chapters.

4.1   Consumption and Portfolio Choices

In this section we introduce an initial consumption-savings decision into an investor's portfolio choice problem. This is done by permitting the individual to derive utility from consuming at the beginning, as well as at the end, of the investment period. The assumptions of our model are as follows.

Let W_0 and C_0 be the individual's initial date 0 wealth and consumption, respectively. At date 1, the end of the period, the individual is assumed to consume all of his wealth, which we denote as C_1. The individual's utility function is defined over beginning- and end-of-period consumption and takes the following form:

$$U\left(C_0\right) + \delta E\left[U\left(\tilde{C}_1\right)\right] \tag{4.1}$$

where δ is a subjective discount factor that reflects the individual's rate of time preference and $E\left[\cdot\right]$ is the expectations operator conditional on information at date 0.[1] The multidate specification of utility in expression (4.1) is an example of a *time-separable* utility function. Time separability means that utility at a particular date (say, 0 or 1) depends only on consumption at that same date. Later chapters will analyze the implications of time separability and consider generalized multiperiod utility functions that permit utility to depend on past or expected future consumption.

Suppose that the individual can choose to invest in n different assets. Let P_i be the date 0 price per share of asset i, $i = 1, \ldots, n$, and let X_i be the date 1

---

1. δ is sometimes written as $\frac{1}{1+\rho}$ where ρ is the rate of time preference. A value of $\delta < 1$ ($\rho > 0$) reflects impatience on the part of the individual, that is, a preference for consuming early. A more general two-date utility function could be expressed as $U_0\left(C_o\right) + E\left[U_1\left(C_1\right)\right]$ where U_0 and U_1 are any different increasing, concave functions of consumption. Our presentation assumes $U_1\left(C\right) = \delta U_0\left(C\right)$, but the qualitative results we derive also hold for the more general specification.

random payoff of asset i. For example, a dividend-paying stock might have a date 1 random payoff of $\tilde{X}_i = \tilde{P}_{1i} + \tilde{D}_{1i}$, where $\tilde{P}_{1i}$ is the date 1 stock price and $\tilde{D}_{1i}$ is the stock's dividend paid at date 1. Alternatively, for a coupon-paying bond, $\tilde{P}_{1i}$ would be the date 1 bond price and $\tilde{D}_{1i}$ would be the bond's coupon paid at date 1.[2] Given this definition, we can also define $R_i \equiv X_i/P_i$ to be the random return on asset i. The individual may also receive labor income of y_0 at date 0 and random labor income of y_1 at date 1.[3] If ω_i is the proportion of date 0 savings that the individual chooses to invest in asset i, then his intertemporal budget constraint is

$$C_1 = y_1 + (W_0 + y_0 - C_0) \sum_{i=1}^{n} \omega_i R_i \tag{4.2}$$

where $(W_0 + y_0 - C_0)$ is the individual's date 0 savings. The individual's maximization problem can then be stated as

$$\max_{C_0, \{\omega_i\}} U(C_0) + \delta E[U(C_1)] \tag{4.3}$$

subject to equation (4.2) and the constraint $\sum_{i=1}^{n} \omega_i = 1$. The first-order conditions with respect to C_0 and the ω_i, $i = 1, \ldots, n$ are

$$U'(C_0) - \delta E\left[U'(C_1) \sum_{i=1}^{n} \omega_i R_i\right] = 0 \tag{4.4}$$

$$\delta E[U'(C_1) R_i] - \lambda = 0, \quad i = 1, \ldots, n \tag{4.5}$$

where $\lambda \equiv \lambda' / (W_0 + y_0 - C_0)$ and λ' is the Lagrange multiplier for the constraint $\sum_{i=1}^{n} \omega_i = 1$. The first-order conditions in (4.5) describe how the investor chooses between different assets. Substitute out for λ and one obtains

$$E[U'(C_1) R_i] = E[U'(C_1) R_j] \tag{4.6}$$

for any two assets, i and j. Equation (4.6) tells us that the investor trades off investing in asset i for asset j until their expected marginal utility–weighted returns are equal. If this were not the case, the individual could raise his total expected utility by investing more in assets whose marginal utility–weighted returns were

---

2. The coupon payment would be uncertain if default on the payment is possible and/or the coupon is not fixed but floating (tied to a market interest rate).

3. There is an essential difference between tangible wealth, W, and wage income, y. The present value of wage income, which is referred to as "human capital," is assumed to be a nontradeable asset. The individual can rebalance his tangible wealth to change his holdings of marketable assets, but his endowment of human capital (and its cashflows in the form of wage income) is assumed to be fixed.

relatively high and investing less in assets whose marginal utility–weighted returns were low.

How does the investor act to make the optimal equality of expected marginal utility–weighted returns in (4.6) come about? Note from (4.2) that C_1 becomes more positively correlated with R_i the greater is ω_i. Thus, the greater asset i's portfolio weight, the lower will be $U'(C_1)$ when R_i is high due to the concavity of utility. Hence, as ω_i becomes large, smaller marginal utility weights multiply the high realizations of asset i's return, and $E[U'(C_1)R_i]$ falls. Intuitively, this occurs because the investor becomes more undiversified by holding a larger proportion of asset i. By adjusting the portfolio weights for asset i and each of the other $n-1$ assets, the investor changes the random distribution of C_1 in a way that equalizes $E[U'(C_1)R_k]$ for all assets $k = 1, \ldots, n$, thereby attaining the desired level of diversification.

Another result of the first-order conditions involves the intertemporal allocation of resources. Substituting (4.5) into (4.4) gives

$$U'(C_0) = \delta E\left[U'(C_1)\sum_{i=1}^{n}\omega_i R_i\right] = \sum_{i=1}^{n}\omega_i \delta E[U'(C_1)R_i] \tag{4.7}$$

$$= \sum_{i=1}^{n}\omega_i \lambda = \lambda$$

Therefore, substituting $\lambda = U'(C_0)$, the first-order conditions in (4.5) can be written as

$$\delta E[U'(C_1)R_i] = U'(C_0), \quad i = 1, \ldots, n \tag{4.8}$$

or, since $R_i = X_i/P_i$,

$$P_i U'(C_0) = \delta E[U'(C_1)X_i], \quad i = 1, \ldots, n \tag{4.9}$$

Equation (4.9) has an intuitive meaning and, as will be shown in subsequent chapters, generalizes to multiperiod consumption and portfolio choice problems. It says that when the investor is acting optimally, he invests in asset i until the loss in marginal utility of giving up P_i dollars at date 0 just equals the expected marginal utility of receiving the random payoff of X_i at date 1. To see this more clearly, suppose that one of the assets pays a risk-free return over the period. Call it asset f so that R_f is the risk-free return (1 plus the risk-free interest rate). For the risk-free asset, equation (4.9) can be rewritten as

$$U'(C_0) = R_f \delta E[U'(C_1)] \tag{4.10}$$

which states that the investor trades off date 0 for date 1 consumption until the marginal utility of giving up \$1 of date 0 consumption just equals the expected marginal utility of receiving \$$R_f$ of date 1 consumption. For example, suppose that utility is of a constant relative-risk-aversion form: $U(C) = C^\gamma / \gamma$, for $\gamma < 1$. Then equation (4.10) can be rewritten as

$$\frac{1}{R_f} = \delta E\left[\left(\frac{C_0}{C_1}\right)^{1-\gamma}\right] \tag{4.11}$$

Hence, when the interest rate is high, so will be the expected growth in consumption. For the special case of there being only one risk-free asset and nonrandom labor income, so that C_1 is nonstochastic, equation (4.11) becomes

$$R_f = \frac{1}{\delta}\left(\frac{C_1}{C_0}\right)^{1-\gamma} \tag{4.12}$$

Taking logs of both sides of the equation, we obtain

$$\ln\left(R_f\right) = -\ln\delta + (1-\gamma)\ln\left(\frac{C_1}{C_0}\right) \tag{4.13}$$

Since $\ln(R_f)$ is the continuously compounded, risk-free interest rate and $\ln(C_1/C_0)$ is the growth rate of consumption, then we can define the elasticity of intertemporal substitution, ϵ, as

$$\epsilon \equiv \frac{\partial \ln\left(C_1/C_0\right)}{\partial \ln\left(R_f\right)} = \frac{1}{1-\gamma} \tag{4.14}$$

Hence, with power (constant relative-risk-aversion) utility, ϵ is the reciprocal of the coefficient of relative risk aversion. That is, the single parameter γ determines both risk aversion and the rate of intertemporal substitution.[4] When $0 < \gamma < 1$, ϵ exceeds unity and a higher interest rate raises second-period consumption more than one-for-one. This implies that if utility displays less risk aversion than logarithmic utility, this individual increases his savings as the interest rate rises. Conversely, when $\gamma < 0$, then $\epsilon < 1$ and a rise in the interest rate raises second-period consumption less than one-for-one, implying that such an individual decreases her initial savings when the return to savings is higher. For the logarithmic utility individual ($\gamma = 0$ and therefore, $\epsilon = 1$), a change in the interest rate has no effect on savings. These results can be interpreted as an individual's response to two effects from an increase in interest rates. The first is a *substitution*

---

4. An end-of-chapter exercise shows that this result extends to an environment with risky assets. In Chapter 14, we will examine a recursive utility generalization of multiperiod power utility for which the elasticity of intertemporal substitution is permitted to differ from the inverse of the coefficient of relative risk aversion. There these two characteristics of multiperiod utility are modeled by separate parameters.

effect that raises the return from transforming current consumption into future consumption. This higher benefit from initial savings provides an incentive to do more of it. The second effect is an *income effect* due to the greater return that is earned on a given amount of savings. This makes the individual better off and, ceteris paribus, would raise consumption in both periods. Hence, initial savings could fall and still lead to greater consumption in the second period. For $\epsilon > 1$, the substitution effect outweighs the income effect, while the reverse occurs when $\epsilon < 1$. When $\epsilon = 1$, the income and substitution effects exactly offset each other.

A main insight of this section is that an individual's optimal portfolio of assets is one where the assets' expected marginal utility–weighted returns are equalized. If this were not the case, the individual's expected utility could be raised by investing more (*less*) in assets whose average marginal utility–weighted returns are relatively high (*low*). It was also demonstrated that an individual's optimal consumption-savings decision involves trading off higher current marginal utility of consuming for higher expected future marginal utility obtainable from invested saving.

4.2   An Asset Pricing Interpretation

Until now, we have analyzed the consumption–portfolio choice problem of an individual investor. For such an exercise, it makes sense to think of the individual taking the current prices of all assets and the distribution of their payoffs as given when deciding on his optimal consumption–portfolio choice plan. Importantly, however, the first-order conditions we have derived might be reinterpreted as asset pricing relationships. They can provide insights regarding the connection between individuals' consumption behavior and the distribution of asset returns.

To see this, let us begin by rewriting equation (4.9) as

$$P_i = E\left[\frac{\delta U'(C_1)}{U'(C_0)}X_i\right] \tag{4.15}$$

$$= E[m_{01}X_i]$$

where $m_{01} \equiv \delta U'(C_1)/U'(C_0)$ is the marginal rate of substitution between initial and end-of-period consumption. For any individual who can trade freely in asset i, equation (4.15) provides a condition that equilibrium asset prices must satisfy. Condition (4.15) appears in the form of an asset pricing formula. The current asset price, P_i, is an expected discounted value of its payoffs, where the discount factor, m_{01}, is a random quantity because it depends on the random level of future consumption. Hence, m_{01} is also referred to as the *stochastic discount factor* for valuing asset returns. In states of nature where future consumption turns out to be high (due to high asset portfolio returns or high labor income), marginal utility, $U'(C_1)$, is low and the asset's payoffs in these states are not highly valued.

Conversely, in states where future consumption is low, marginal utility is high so that the asset's payoffs in these states are much desired. This insight explains why m_{01} is also known as the *state price deflator*. It provides a different discount factor (deflator) for different states of nature.

It should be emphasized that the stochastic discount factor, m_{01}, is the same for all assets that a particular investor can hold. It prices these assets' payoffs only by differentiating in which state of nature the payoff is made. Since m_{01} provides the core, or kernel, for pricing all risky assets, it is also referred to as the *pricing kernel*. Note that the random realization of m_{01} may differ across investors because of differences in random labor income that can cause the random distribution of C_1 to vary across investors. Nonetheless, the expected product of the pricing kernel and asset i's payoff, $E[m_{01}X_i]$, will be the same for all investors who can trade in asset i.

4.2.1 Real versus Nominal Returns

In writing down the individual's consumption–portfolio choice problem, we implicitly assumed that returns are expressed in real, or *purchasing power*, terms; that is, returns should be measured after adjustment for inflation. The reason is that an individual's utility should depend on the real, not nominal (currency denominated), value of consumption. Therefore, in the budget constraint (4.2), if C_1 denotes real consumption, then asset returns and prices (as well as labor income) need to be real values. Thus, if P_i^N and X_i^N are the initial price and end-of-period payoff measured in currency units (nominal terms), we need to deflate them by a price index to convert them to real quantities. Letting CPI_t denote the consumer price index at date t, the pricing relationship in (4.15) becomes

$$\frac{P_i^N}{CPI_0} = E\left[\frac{\delta U'(C_1)}{U'(C_0)}\frac{X_i^N}{CPI_1}\right] \tag{4.16}$$

or if we define $I_{ts} = CPI_s/CPI_t$ as 1 plus the inflation rate between dates t and s, equation (4.16) can be rewritten as

$$P_i^N = E\left[\frac{1}{I_{01}}\frac{\delta U'(C_1)}{U'(C_0)}X_i^N\right] \tag{4.17}$$

$$= E\left[M_{01}X_i^N\right]$$

where $M_{01} \equiv (\delta/I_{01}) U'(C_1)/U'(C_0)$ is the stochastic discount factor (pricing kernel) for discounting nominal returns. Hence, this nominal pricing kernel is simply the real pricing kernel, m_{01}, discounted at the (random) rate of inflation between dates 0 and 1.

4.2.2   Risk Premia and the Marginal Utility of Consumption

The relation in equation (4.15) can be rewritten to shed light on an asset's risk premium. Dividing each side of (4.15) by P_i results in

$$1 = E\left[m_{01}R_i\right] \tag{4.18}$$

$$= E\left[m_{01}\right]E\left[R_i\right] + Cov\left[m_{01}, R_i\right]$$

$$= E\left[m_{01}\right]\left(E\left[R_i\right] + \frac{Cov\left[m_{01}, R_i\right]}{E\left[m_{01}\right]}\right)$$

Recall from (4.10) that for the case of a risk-free asset, $E\left[\delta U'\left(C_1\right)/U'\left(C_0\right)\right] = E\left[m_{01}\right] = 1/R_f$. Then (4.18) can be rewritten as

$$R_f = E\left[R_i\right] + \frac{Cov\left[m_{01}, R_i\right]}{E\left[m_{01}\right]} \tag{4.19}$$

or

$$E\left[R_i\right] = R_f - \frac{Cov\left[m_{01}, R_i\right]}{E\left[m_{01}\right]} \tag{4.20}$$

$$= R_f - \frac{Cov\left[U'\left(C_1\right), R_i\right]}{E\left[U'\left(C_1\right)\right]}$$

Equation (4.20) states that the risk premium for asset i equals the negative of the covariance between the marginal utility of end-of-period consumption and the asset return divided by the expected end-of-period marginal utility of consumption. If an asset pays a higher return when consumption is high, its return has a negative covariance with the marginal utility of consumption, and therefore the investor demands a positive risk premium over the risk-free rate.

Conversely, if an asset pays a higher return when consumption is low, so that its return positively covaries with the marginal utility of consumption, then it has an expected return less than the risk-free rate. Investors will be satisfied with this lower return because the asset is providing a hedge against low consumption states of the world; that is, it is helping to smooth consumption across states.

4.2.3   The Relationship to CAPM

Now suppose there exists a portfolio with a random return of $\widetilde{R}_m$ that is perfectly negatively correlated with the marginal utility of date 1 consumption, $U'(\widetilde{C}_1)$, implying that it is also perfectly negatively correlated with the pricing kernel, m_{01}:

$$U'(\widetilde{C}_1) = -\kappa\, \widetilde{R}_m, \quad \kappa > 0 \tag{4.21}$$

Then this implies

$$Cov[U'(C_1),\, R_m] = -\kappa\, Cov[R_m,\, R_m] = -\kappa\, Var[R_m] \tag{4.22}$$

and

$$Cov[U'(C_1),\, R_i] = -\kappa\, Cov[R_m,\, R_i] \tag{4.23}$$

For the portfolio having return $\widetilde{R}_m$, the risk premium relation (4.20) is

$$E[R_m] = R_f - \frac{Cov[U'(C_1),\, R_m]}{E[U'(C_1)]} = R_f + \frac{\kappa\, Var[R_m]}{E[U'(C_1)]} \tag{4.24}$$

Using (4.20) and (4.24) to substitute for $E[U'(C_1)]$, and using (4.23), we obtain

$$\frac{E[R_m] - R_f}{E[R_i] - R_f} = \frac{\kappa\, Var[R_m]}{\kappa\, Cov[R_m,\, R_i]} \tag{4.25}$$

and rearranging:

$$E[R_i] - R_f = \frac{Cov[R_m,\, R_i]}{Var[R_m]}\left(E[R_m] - R_f\right) \tag{4.26}$$

or

$$E[R_i] = R_f + \beta_i\left(E[R_m] - R_f\right) \tag{4.27}$$

So we obtain the CAPM if the return on the market portfolio is perfectly negatively correlated with the marginal utility of end-of-period consumption, that is, perfectly negatively correlated with the pricing kernel. Note that for an arbitrary distribution of asset returns and nonrandom labor income, this will always be the case if utility is quadratic, because marginal utility is linear in consumption and consumption also depends linearly on the market's return. In addition, for the case of general utility, normally distributed asset returns, and nonrandom labor income, marginal utility of end-of-period consumption is also perfectly negatively correlated with the return on the market portfolio, because each investor's optimal portfolio is simply a combination of the market portfolio and the (nonrandom) risk-free asset. Thus, consistent with Chapters 2 and 3, under the assumptions needed for mean-variance analysis to be equivalent with expected utility maximization, asset returns satisfy the CAPM.

4.2.4   Bounds on Risk Premia

Another implication of the stochastic discount factor is that it places bounds on the means and standard deviations of individual securities and, therefore, determines an efficient frontier. To show this, rewrite the first line in equation (4.20) as

$$E\left[R_i\right] = R_f - \rho_{m_{01}, R_i} \frac{\sigma_{m_{01}} \sigma_{R_i}}{E\left[m_{01}\right]} \tag{4.28}$$

where $\sigma_{m_{01}}$, σ_{R_i}, and ρ_{m_{01}, R_i} are the standard deviation of the discount factor, the standard deviation of the return on asset i, and the correlation between the discount factor and the return on asset i, respectively. Rearranging (4.28) leads to

$$\frac{E\left[R_i\right] - R_f}{\sigma_{R_i}} = -\rho_{m_{01}, R_i} \frac{\sigma_{m_{01}}}{E\left[m_{01}\right]} \tag{4.29}$$

The left-hand side of (4.29) is the Sharpe ratio for asset i. Since $-1 \le \rho_{m_{01}, R_i} \le 1$, we know that

$$\left| \frac{E\left[R_i\right] - R_f}{\sigma_{R_i}} \right| \le \frac{\sigma_{m_{01}}}{E\left[m_{01}\right]} = \sigma_{m_{01}} R_f \tag{4.30}$$

This equation was derived by Robert Shiller (Shiller 1982), was generalized by Lars Hansen and Ravi Jagannathan (Hansen and Jagannathan 1991), and is known as a Hansen-Jagannathan bound. Given an asset's Sharpe ratio and the risk-free rate, equation (4.30) sets a lower bound on the volatility of the economy's stochastic discount factor. Conversely, given the volatility of the discount factor, equation (4.30) sets an upper bound on the maximum Sharpe ratio that any asset, or portfolio of assets, can attain.

If there exists an asset (or portfolio of assets) whose return is perfectly negatively correlated with the discount factor, m_{01}, then the bound in (4.30) holds with equality. As we just showed in equations (4.21) to (4.27), such a situation implies the CAPM, so that the slope of the capital market line, $S_e \equiv \frac{E[R_m] - R_f}{\sigma_{R_m}}$, equals $\sigma_{m_{01}} R_f$. Thus, the slope of the capital market line, which represents (efficient) portfolios that have a maximum Sharpe ratio, can be related to the standard deviation of the discount factor.

The inequality in (4.30) has empirical implications. $\sigma_{m_{01}}$ can be estimated if we could observe an individual's consumption stream and if we knew his or her utility function. Then, according to (4.30), the Sharpe ratio of any portfolio of traded assets should be less than or equal to $\sigma_{m_{01}} / E\left[m_{01}\right]$. For power utility, $U\left(C\right) = C^\gamma / \gamma$, $\gamma < 1$, so that $m_{01} \equiv \delta \left(C_1 / C_0\right)^{\gamma - 1} = \delta e^{(\gamma - 1) \ln(C_1 / C_0)}$. If C_1 / C_0 is assumed to be lognormally distributed, with parameters μ_c and σ_c, then

$$
\begin{aligned}
\frac{\sigma_{m01}}{E\left[m_{01}\right]} &= \frac{\sqrt{Var\left[e^{(\gamma-1)\ln(C_1/C_0)}\right]}}{E\left[e^{(\gamma-1)\ln(C_1/C_0)}\right]} \\[4pt]
&= \frac{\sqrt{E\left[e^{2(\gamma-1)\ln(C_1/C_0)}\right] - E\left[e^{(\gamma-1)\ln(C_1/C_0)}\right]^2}}{E\left[e^{(\gamma-1)\ln(C_1/C_0)}\right]} \\[4pt]
&= \sqrt{E\left[e^{2(\gamma-1)\ln(C_1/C_0)}\right]\Big/E\left[e^{(\gamma-1)\ln(C_1/C_0)}\right]^2 - 1} \\[4pt]
&= \sqrt{e^{2(\gamma-1)\mu_c + 2(\gamma-1)^2\sigma_c^2}\Big/e^{2(\gamma-1)\mu_c + (\gamma-1)^2\sigma_c^2} - 1} = \sqrt{e^{(\gamma-1)^2\sigma_c^2} - 1} \\[4pt]
&\approx (1-\gamma)\,\sigma_c
\end{aligned}
\tag{4.31}
$$

where in the fourth line of (4.31), the expectations are evaluated assuming C_1 is lognormally distributed.[5] Hence, with power utility and lognormally distributed consumption, we have

$$
\left|\frac{E\left[R_i\right] - R_f}{\sigma_{R_i}}\right| \leq (1-\gamma)\,\sigma_c
\tag{4.32}
$$

Suppose, for example, that R_i is the return on a broadly diversified portfolio of U.S. stocks, such as the S&P 500. Over the last 75 years, this portfolio's annual real return in excess of the risk-free (U.S. Treasury bill) interest rate has averaged 8.3 percent, suggesting $E\left[R_i\right] - R_f = 0.083$. The portfolio's annual standard deviation has been approximately $\sigma_{R_i} = 0.17$, implying a Sharpe ratio of $\frac{E[R_i] - R_f}{\sigma_{R_i}} = 0.49$. Assuming a "representative agent" and using per capita U.S. consumption data to estimate the standard deviation of consumption growth, researchers have come up with annualized estimates of σ_c between 0.01 and 0.0386.[6] Thus, even if a diversified portfolio of U.S. stocks was an efficient portfolio of risky assets, so that equation (4.32) held with equality, it would imply

---

5. The fifth line of (4.31) is based on taking a two-term approximation of the series $e^x = 1 + x + \frac{x^2}{2!} + \frac{x^3}{3!} + \cdots$, which is reasonable when x is a small positive number.
6. See John Y. Campbell (Campbell 1999) and Stephen G. Cecchetti, Pok-Sam Lam, and Nelson C. Mark (Cecchetti, Lam, and Mark 1994).

a value of $\gamma = 1 - \left(\frac{E[R_i] - R_f}{\sigma_{R_i}} \right) / \sigma_c$ between -11.7 and -48.[7] Since reasonable levels of risk aversion estimated from other sources imply values of γ much smaller in magnitude, say, in the range of -1 to -5, the inequality (4.32) appears not to hold for U.S. stock market data and standard specifications of utility.[8] In other words, consumption appears to be too smooth (σ_c is too low) relative to the premium that investors demand for holding stocks. This inconsistency between theory and empirical evidence was identified by Rajnish Mehra and Edward Prescott (Mehra and Prescott 1985) and is referred to as the *equity premium puzzle*. Attempts to explain this puzzle have involved using different specifications of utility and questioning whether the ex-post sample mean of U.S. stock returns is a good estimate of the a priori expected return on U.S. stocks.[9]

Even if one were to accept a high degree of risk aversion in order to fit the historical equity premium, additional problems may arise because this high risk aversion could imply an unreasonable value for the risk-free return, R_f. Under our maintained assumptions and using (4.10), the risk-free return satisfies

$$\frac{1}{R_f} = E\left[m_{01} \right] \tag{4.33}$$

$$= \delta E \left[e^{(\gamma - 1) \ln(C_1/C_0)} \right]$$

$$= \delta e^{(\gamma - 1)\mu_c + \frac{1}{2}(\gamma - 1)^2 \sigma_c^2}$$

and therefore

$$\ln\left(R_f \right) = -\ln(\delta) + (1 - \gamma)\, \mu_c - \frac{1}{2}\, (1 - \gamma)^2\, \sigma_c^2 \tag{4.34}$$

---

7. If the stock portfolio were less than efficient, so that a strict inequality held in (4.32), the magnitude of the risk-aversion coefficient would need to be even higher.

8. Rajnish Mehra and Edward Prescott (Mehra and Prescott 1985) survey empirical work, finding values of γ of -1 or more (equivalent to coefficients of relative risk aversion, $1 - \gamma$, of 2 or less).

9. Jeremy J. Siegel and Richard H. Thaler (Siegel and Thaler 1997) review this literature. It should be noted that recent survey evidence from academic financial economists (Welch 2000) finds that a consensus believes that the current equity risk premium is significantly lower than the historical average. Moreover, at the begining of 2006, the Federal Reserve Bank of Philadelphia's *Survey of Professional Forecasters* found that the median predicted annual returns over the next decade on the S&P 500 stock portfolio, the 10-year U.S. Treasury bond, and the 3-month U.S. Treasury bill are 7.00%, 5.00%, and 4.25%, respectively. This implies a much lower equity risk premium (7.00% − 4.25% = 2.75%) compared to the historical average difference between stocks and bills of 8.3%.

If we set $\delta = 0.99$, reflecting a 1 percent rate of time preference, and $\mu_c = 0.018$, which is the historical average real growth of U.S. per capita consumption, then a value of $\gamma = -11$ and $\sigma_c = 0.036$ implies

$$\ln\left(R_f\right) = -\ln(\delta) + (1-\gamma)\,\mu_c - \frac{1}{2}\,(1-\gamma)^2\,\sigma_c^2$$

$$= 0.01 + 0.216 - 0.093 = 0.133 \tag{4.35}$$

which is a real risk-free interest rate of 13.3 percent. Since short-term real interest rates have averaged about 1 percent in the United States, we end up with a *risk-free rate puzzle*.

The notion that assets can be priced using a stochastic discount factor, m_{01}, is attractive because the discount factor is independent of the asset being priced: it can be used to price any asset no matter what its risk. We derived this discount factor from a consumption–portfolio choice problem and, in this context, showed that it equaled the marginal rate of substitution between current and end-of-period consumption. However, the usefulness of this approach is in doubt since empirical evidence using aggregate consumption data and standard specifications of utility appears inconsistent with the discount factor equaling the marginal rate of substitution.[10] Fortunately, a general pricing relationship of the form $P_i = E_0\left[m_{01}X_i\right]$ can be shown to hold without assuming that m_{01} represents a marginal rate of substitution. Rather, it can be derived using alternative assumptions. This is the subject of the next section.

4.3 Market Completeness, Arbitrage, and State Pricing

We need not assume a consumption–portfolio choice structure to derive a stochastic discount factor pricing formula. Instead, our derivation can be based on the assumptions of a complete market and the absence of arbitrage, an approach pioneered by Kenneth Arrow and Gerard Debreu.[11] With these alternative assumptions, one can show that a law of one price holds and that a unique stochastic discount factor exists. This new approach makes transparent the derivation of relative pricing relationships and is an important technique for valuing contingent claims (derivatives).

---

10. As will be shown in Chapter 14, some specifications of time-inseparable utility can improve the consumption-based stochastic discount factor's ability to explain asset prices.

11. See Kenneth Arrow (Arrow 1953) reprinted in (Arrow 1964) and Gerard Debreu (Debreu 1959).

4.3.1   Complete Markets Assumptions

To illustrate, suppose once again that an individual can freely trade in n different assets. Also, let us assume that there are a finite number of end-of-period states of nature, with state s having probability π_s.[12] Let X_{si} be the cashflow generated by one share (unit) of asset i in state s. Also assume that there are k states of nature and n assets. The following vector describes the payoffs to financial asset i:

$$X_i = \begin{bmatrix} X_{1i} \\ \vdots \\ X_{ki} \end{bmatrix} \tag{4.36}$$

Thus, the per-share cashflows of the universe of all assets can be represented by the $k \times n$ matrix

$$X = \begin{bmatrix} X_{11} & \cdots & X_{1n} \\ \vdots & \ddots & \vdots \\ X_{k1} & \cdots & X_{kn} \end{bmatrix} \tag{4.37}$$

We will assume that $n = k$ and that X is of full rank. This implies that the n assets *span* the k states of nature, an assumption that indicates a complete market. We would still have a complete market (and, as we will show, unique state-contingent prices) if $n > k$, as long as the payoff matrix X has rank k. If the number of assets exceeds the number of states, some assets are redundant; that is, their cashflows in the k states are linear combinations of others. In such a situation, we could reduce the number of assets to k by combining them into k linearly independent (portfolios of) assets.

An implication of the assumption that the assets' returns span the k states of nature is that an individual can purchase amounts of the k assets so that she can obtain target levels of end-of-period wealth in each of the states. To show this complete markets result, let W denote an arbitrary $k \times 1$ vector of end-of-period levels of wealth:

$$W = \begin{bmatrix} W_1 \\ \vdots \\ W_k \end{bmatrix} \tag{4.38}$$

where W_s is the level of wealth in state s. To obtain W, the individual needs to purchase shares in the k assets at the initial date. Let the vector $N = [N_1 \ldots N_k]'$ be the number of shares purchased of each of the k assets. Hence, N must satisfy

$$XN = W \tag{4.39}$$

---

12. As is discussed later, this analysis can be extended to the case of an infinite number of states.

Because X is a nonsingular matrix of rank k, its inverse exists so that

$$N = X^{-1}W \tag{4.40}$$

Hence, because the assets' payoffs span the k states, arbitrary levels of wealth in the k states can be attained if initial wealth is sufficient to purchase the required shares, N. Denoting $P = [P_1 \ldots P_k]'$ as the $k \times 1$ vector of beginning-of-period, per-share prices of the k assets, then the amount of initial wealth required to produce the target level of wealth given in (4.38) is simply $P'N$.

4.3.2   Arbitrage and State Prices

Given our assumption of complete markets, the absence of arbitrage opportunities implies that the price of a new, redundant security or contingent claim can be valued based on the prices of the original k securities. For example, suppose a new asset pays a vector of end-of-period cashflows of W. In the absence of arbitrage, its price must be $P'N$. If its price exceeded $P'N$, an arbitrage would be to sell this new asset and purchase the original k securities in amounts N. Since the end-of-period liability from selling the security is exactly offset by the returns received from the k original securities, the arbitrage profit equals the difference between the new asset's price and $P'N$. Conversely, if the new asset's price were less than $P'N$, an arbitrage would be to purchase the new asset and sell the portfolio N of the k original securities.

Let's apply this concept of complete markets, no-arbitrage pricing to the special case of a security that has a payoff of 1 in state s and 0 in all other states. Such a security is referred to as a *primitive*, *elementary*, or *Arrow-Debreu* security. Specifically, elementary security "s" has the vector of cashflows

$$e_s = \begin{bmatrix} W_1 \\ \vdots \\ W_s \\ \vdots \\ W_k \end{bmatrix} = \begin{bmatrix} 0 \\ \vdots \\ 1 \\ \vdots \\ 0 \end{bmatrix} \tag{4.41}$$

Let p_s be the beginning-of-period price of elementary security s, that is, the price of receiving 1 in state s. Then as we just showed, its price in terms of the payoffs and prices of the original k assets must equal

$$p_s = P'X^{-1}e_s, \quad s = 1, \ldots, k \tag{4.42}$$

so that a unique set of state prices exists in a complete market.[13] Furthermore, we would expect that these elementary state prices should each be positive, since a unit amount of wealth received in any state will have a value greater than zero whenever individuals are assumed to be nonsatiated.[14] Hence the equations in (4.42) along with the conditions $p_s > 0 \; \forall s$ restrict the payoffs, X, and the prices, P, of the original k securities.

We can now derive a stochastic discount factor formula by considering the value of any other security or contingent claim in terms of these elementary state security prices. Note that the portfolio composed of the sum of all elementary securities gives a cashflow of 1 unit with certainty. The price of this portfolio defines the risk-free return, R_f, by the relation

$$\sum_{s=1}^{k} p_s = \frac{1}{R_f} \tag{4.43}$$

In general, let there be some multicashflow asset, a, whose cashflow paid in state s is X_{sa}. In the absence of arbitrage, its price, P_a, must equal

$$P_a = \sum_{s=1}^{k} p_s X_{sa} \tag{4.44}$$

Note that the relative pricing relationships that we have derived did not require using information on the state probabilities. However, let us now introduce these probabilities to see their relationship to state prices and the stochastic discount factor. Define $m_s \equiv p_s / \pi_s$ to be the price of elementary security s divided by the probability that state s occurs. Note that if, as was argued earlier, a sensible equilibrium requires $p_s > 0 \; \forall s$, then $m_s > 0 \; \forall s$ when there is a positive probability of each state occurring. Using this new definition, equation (4.44) can be written as

$$P_a = \sum_{s=1}^{k} \pi_s \frac{p_s}{\pi_s} X_{sa} \tag{4.45}$$

$$= \sum_{s=1}^{k} \pi_s m_s X_{sa}$$

$$= E\left[m X_a\right]$$

---

13. If markets were incomplete, for example, if n were the rank of X and $k > n$, then state prices would not be uniquely determined by the absence of arbitrage. The no-arbitrage conditions would place only n linear restrictions on the set of k prices, implying that there could be an infinity of possible state prices.

14. This would be the case whenever individuals' marginal utilities are positive for all levels of end-of-period consumption.

where m denotes a stochastic discount factor whose expected value is $\sum_{s=1}^{k} \pi_s m_s$, and X_a is the random cashflow of the multicashflow asset a. Equation (4.45) shows that the stochastic discount factor equals the prices of the elementary securities normalized by their state probabilities. Hence, we have shown that in a complete market that lacks arbitrage opportunities, a unique, positive-valued stochastic discount factor exists. When markets are incomplete, the absence of arbitrage, alone, cannot determine the stochastic discount factor. One would need to impose additional conditions, such as the previous section's assumptions on the form of individuals' utility, in order to determine the stochastic discount factor. For example, if different states of nature led to different realizations of an individual's nontraded labor income, and there did not exist assets that could span or insure against this wage income, then a unique stochastic discount factor may not exist. In this case of market incompleteness, a utility-based derivation of the stochastic discount factor may be required for asset pricing.

While the stochastic discount factor relationship of equation (4.45) is based on state prices derived from assumptions of market completeness and the absence of arbitrage, it is interesting to interpret these state prices in terms of the previously derived consumption-based discount factor. Note that since $p_s = \pi_s m_s$, the price of the elementary security paying 1 in state s is higher the greater the likelihood of the state s occurring and the greater the stochastic discount factor for state s. In terms of the consumption-based model, $m_s = \delta U'(C_{1s}) / U'(C_0)$ where C_{1s} is the level of consumption at date 1 in state s. Hence, the state s price, p_s, is greater when C_{1s} is low; that is, state s is a low-consumption state, such as an economic recession.

4.3.3 Risk-Neutral Probabilities

The state pricing relationship of equation (4.44) can be used to develop an important alternative formula for pricing assets. Define $\widehat{\pi}_s \equiv p_s R_f$ as the price of elementary security s times the risk-free return. Then

$$P_a = \sum_{s=1}^{k} p_s X_{sa} \tag{4.46}$$

$$= \frac{1}{R_f} \sum_{s=1}^{k} p_s R_f X_{sa}$$

$$= \frac{1}{R_f} \sum_{s=1}^{k} \widehat{\pi}_s X_{sa}$$

Now these $\widehat{\pi}_s$, $s = 1, \ldots, k$, have the characteristics of probabilities because they are positive, $\widehat{\pi}_s = p_s / \sum_{s=1}^{k} p_s > 0$, and they sum to 1, $\sum_{s=1}^{k} \widehat{\pi}_s = R_f \sum_{s=1}^{k} p_s = R_f / R_f = 1$. Using this insight, we can rewrite equation (4.46) as

$$P_a = \frac{1}{R_f} \sum_{s=1}^{k} \widehat{\pi}_s X_{sa}$$

$$= \frac{1}{R_f} \widehat{E}[X_a] \tag{4.47}$$

where $\widehat{E}[\cdot]$ denotes the expectation operator evaluated using the "pseudo" probabilities $\widehat{\pi}_s$ rather than the true probabilities π_s. Since the expectation in (4.47) is discounted by the risk-free return, we can recognize $\widehat{E}[X_a]$ as the certainty equivalent expectation of the cashflow X_a. In comparison to the stochastic discount factor approach, the formula works by modifying the probabilities of the cashflows in each of the different states, rather than discounting the cashflows by a different discount factor. To see this, note that since $m_s \equiv p_s / \pi_s$ and $R_f = 1/E[m]$, $\widehat{\pi}_s$ can be written as

$$\widehat{\pi}_s = R_f m_s \pi_s$$

$$= \frac{m_s}{E[m]} \pi_s \tag{4.48}$$

so that the pseudo probability transforms the true probability by multiplying by the ratio of the stochastic discount factor to its average value. In states of the world where the stochastic discount factor is greater than its average value, the pseudo probability exceeds the true probability. For example, if $m_s = \delta U'(C_{1s}) / U'(C_0)$, $\widehat{\pi}_s$ exceeds π_s in states of the world with relatively low consumption where marginal utility is high.

As a special case, suppose that in each state of nature, the stochastic discount factor equaled the risk-free discount factor; that is, $m_s = \frac{1}{R_f} = E[m]$. This circumstance implies that the pseudo probability equals the true probability and $P_a = E[mX_a] = E[X_a]/R_f$. Because the price equals the expected payoff discounted at the risk-free rate, the asset is priced as if investors are risk-neutral. Hence, this explains why $\widehat{\pi}_s$ is referred to as the *risk-neutral* probability and $\widehat{E}[\cdot]$ is referred to as the risk-neutral expectations operator. In comparison, the true probabilities, π_s, are frequently called the *physical*, or *statistical*, probabilities.

If the stochastic discount factor is interpreted as the marginal rate of substitution, then we see that $\widehat{\pi}_s$ is higher than π_s in states where the marginal utility of consumption is high (or the level of consumption is low). Thus, relative to the physical probabilities, the risk-neutral probabilities place extra probability weight on "bad" states and less probability weight on "good" states.

4.3.4   State Pricing Extensions

The complete markets pricing framework that we have just outlined is also known as *State Preference Theory* and can be generalized to an infinite number of states and elementary securities. Basically, this is done by defining probability densities of states and replacing the summations in expressions like (4.43) and (4.44) with integrals. For example, let states be indexed by all possible points on the real line between 0 and 1; that is, the state $s \in (0, 1)$. Also let $p(s)$ be the price (density) of a primitive security that pays 1 unit in state s, 0 otherwise. Further, define $X_a(s)$ as the cashflow paid by security a in state s. Then, analogous to (4.43), we can write

$$\int_0^1 p(s)\, ds = \frac{1}{R_f} \tag{4.49}$$

and instead of (4.44), we can write the price of security a as

$$P_a = \int_0^1 p(s)\, X_a(s)\, ds \tag{4.50}$$

In some cases, namely, where markets are intertemporally complete, State Preference Theory can be extended to allow assets' cashflows to occur at different dates in the future. This generalization is sometimes referred to as Time State Preference Theory.[15] To illustrate, suppose that assets can pay cashflows at both date 1 and date 2 in the future. Let s_1 be a state at date 1 and let s_2 be a state at date 2. States at date 2 can depend on which states were reached at date 1.

For example, suppose there are two events at each date, economic recession (r) or economic expansion (boom) (b). Then we could define $s_1 \in \{r_1, b_1\}$ and $s_2 \in \{r_1 r_2, r_1 b_2, b_1 r_2, b_1 b_2\}$. By assigning suitable probabilities and primitive security state prices for assets that pay cashflows of 1 unit in each of these six states, we can sum (or integrate) over both time and states at a given date to obtain prices of complex securities. Thus, when primitive security prices exist at all states for all future dates, essentially we are back to a single-period complete markets framework, and the analysis is the same as that derived previously.

4.4   Summary

This chapter began by extending an individual's portfolio choice problem to include an initial consumption-savings decision. With this modification, we showed that an optimal portfolio is one where assets' expected marginal utility–weighted returns are equalized. Also, the individual's optimal level of savings involves an

---

15. See Steward C. Myers (Myers 1968).

intertemporal trade-off where the marginal utility of current consumption is equated to the expected marginal utility of future consumption.

The individual's optimal decision rules can be reinterpreted as an asset pricing formula. This formula values assets' returns using a stochastic discount factor equal to the marginal rate of substitution between present and future consumption. Importantly, the stochastic discount factor is independent of the asset being priced and determines the asset's risk premium based on the covariance of the asset's return with the marginal utility of consumption. Moreover, this consumption-based stochastic discount factor approach places restrictions on assets' risk premia relative to the volatility of consumption. However, these restrictions appear to be violated when empirical evidence is interpreted using standard utility specifications.

This contrary empirical evidence does not automatically invalidate the stochastic discount factor approach to pricing assets. Rather than deriving discount factors as the marginal rate of substituting present for future consumption, we showed that they can be derived based on the alternative assumptions of market completeness and an absence of arbitrage. When assets' returns spanned the economy's states of nature, state prices for valuing any derivative asset could be derived. Finally, we showed how an alternative risk-neutral pricing formula could be derived by transforming the states' physical probabilities to reflect an adjustment for risk. Risk-neutral pricing is an important valuation tool in many areas of asset pricing, and it will be applied frequently in future chapters.

4.5   Exercises

1. Consider the one-period model of consumption and portfolio choice. Suppose that individuals can invest in a one-period bond that pays a riskless real return of R_{rf} and in a one-period bond that pays a riskless nominal return of R_{nf}. Derive an expression for R_{rf} in terms of R_{nf}, $E[I_{01}]$, and $Cov(M_{01}, I_{01})$.

2. Assume there is an economy with k states of nature and where the following asset pricing formula holds:

$$P_a = \sum_{s=1}^{k} \pi_s m_s X_{sa}$$
$$= E[mX_a]$$

Let an individual in this economy have the utility function $\ln(C_0) + E[\delta \ln(C_1)]$, and let C_0^* be her equilibrium consumption at date 0 and C_s^* be her equilibrium consumption at date 1 in state s, $s = 1, \ldots, k$. Denote the date 0 price of elementary security s as p_s, and derive an expression for it in terms of the individual's equilibrium consumption.

3. Consider the one-period consumption–portfolio choice problem. The individual's first-order conditions lead to the general relationship

   $$1 = E\left[m_{01}R_s\right]$$

   where m_{01} is the stochastic discount factor between dates 0 and 1, and R_s is the one-period stochastic return on any security in which the individual can invest. Let there be a finite number of date 1 states where π_s is the probability of state s. Also assume markets are complete and consider the above relationship for primitive security s; that is, let R_s be the rate of return on primitive (or elementary) security s. The individual's elasticity of intertemporal substitution is defined as

   $$\varepsilon^I \equiv \frac{R_s}{C_s/C_0}\frac{d\left(C_s/C_0\right)}{dR_s}$$

   where C_0 is the individual's consumption at date 0 and C_s is the individual's consumption at date 1 in state s. If the individual's expected utility is given by

   $$U\left(C_0\right) + \delta E\left[U\left(\tilde{C}_1\right)\right]$$

   where utility displays constant relative risk aversion, $U\left(C\right) = C^\gamma/\gamma$, solve for the elasticity of intertemporal substitution, ε^I.

4. Consider an economy with $k = 2$ states of nature, a "good" state and a "bad" state.[16] There are two assets, a risk-free asset with $R_f = 1.05$ and a second risky asset that pays cashflows

   $$X_2 = \begin{bmatrix} 10 \\ 5 \end{bmatrix}$$

   The current price of the risky asset is 6.

   a. Solve for the prices of the elementary securities p_1 and p_2 and the risk-neutral probabilities of the two states.

   b. Suppose that the physical probabilities of the two states are $\pi_1 = \pi_2 = 0.5$. What is the stochastic discount factor for the two states?

5. Consider a one-period economy with two end-of-period states. An option contract pays 3 in state 1 and 0 in state 2 and has a current price of 1. A forward contract pays 3 in state 1 and -2 in state 2. What are the one-period risk-free return and the risk-neutral probabilities of the two states?

6. This question asks you to relate the stochastic discount factor pricing relationship to the CAPM. The CAPM can be expressed as

   $$E\left[R_i\right] = R_f + \beta_i\gamma$$

---

16. I thank Michael Cliff of Virginia Tech for suggesting this example.

where $E[\cdot]$ is the expectation operator, R_i is the realized return on asset i, R_f is the risk-free return, β_i is asset i's beta, and γ is a positive market risk premium. Now, consider a stochastic discount factor of the form

$$m = a + bR_m$$

where a and b are constants and R_m is the realized return on the market portfolio. Also, denote the variance of the return on the market portfolio as σ_m^2.

a. Derive an expression for γ as a function of a, b, $E[R_m]$, and σ_m^2. Hint: you may want to start from the equilibrium expression $0 = E[m(R_i - R_f)]$.

b. Note that the equation $1 = E[mR_i]$ holds for all assets. Consider the case of the risk-free asset and the case of the market portfolio, and solve for a and b as a function of R_f, $E[R_m]$, and σ_m^2.

c. Using the formula for a and b in part (b), show that $\gamma = E[R_m] - R_f$.

7. Consider a two-factor economy with multiple risky assets and a risk-free asset whose return is denoted R_f. The economy's first factor is the return on the market portfolio, R_m, and the second factor is the return on a zero-net-investment portfolio, R_z. In other words, one can interpret the second factor as the return on a portfolio that is long one asset and short another asset, where the long and short positions are equal in magnitude (e.g., $R_z = R_a - R_b$) and where R_a and R_b are the returns on the assets that are long and short, respectively. It is assumed that $Cov(R_m, R_z) = 0$. The expected returns on all assets in the economy satisfy the APT relationship

$$E[R_i] = \lambda_0 + \beta_{im}\lambda_m + \beta_{iz}\lambda_z \qquad (*)$$

where R_i is the return on an arbitrary asset i, $\beta_{im} = Cov(R_i, R_m)/\sigma_m^2$, $\beta_{iz} = Cov(R_i, R_z)/\sigma_z^2$, and λ_m and λ_z are the risk premiums for factors 1 and 2, respectively.

Now suppose you are given the stochastic discount factor for this economy, m, measured over the same time period as the above asset returns. It is given by

$$m = a + bR_m + cR_z \qquad (**)$$

where a, b, and c are known constants. Given knowledge of this stochastic discount factor in equation (**), show how you can solve for λ_0, λ_m, and λ_z in (*) in terms of a, b, c, σ_m, and σ_z. Just write down the conditions that would allow you to solve for the λ_0, λ_m, and λ_z. You need not derive explicit solutions for the λ's since the conditions are nonlinear and may be tedious to manipulate.

PART II

MULTIPERIOD CONSUMPTION, PORTFOLIO CHOICE, AND ASSET PRICING

CHAPTER 5

A Multiperiod Discrete-Time Model of Consumption and Portfolio Choice

This chapter considers an expected-utility-maximizing individual's consumption and portfolio choices over many periods. In contrast to our previous single-period or static models, here the intertemporal or dynamic nature of the problem is explicitly analyzed. Solving an individual's multiperiod consumption and portfolio choice problem is of interest in that it provides a theory for an individual's optimal lifetime savings and investment strategies. Hence, it has normative value as a guide for individual financial planning. In addition, just as our single-period mean-variance portfolio selection model provided the theory of asset demands for the Capital Asset Pricing Model, a multiperiod portfolio choice model provides a theory of asset demands for a general equilibrium theory of intertemporal capital asset pricing. Combining this model of individuals' preferences over consumption and securities with a model of firm production technologies can lead to an equilibrium model of the economy that determines asset price processes.[1]

In the 1920s, Frank Ramsey (Ramsey 1928) derived optimal multiperiod consumption-savings decisions but assumed that the individual could invest in only a single asset paying a certain return. It was not until the late 1960s that Paul A. Samuelson (Samuelson 1969) and Robert C. Merton (Merton 1969) were able to solve for an individual's multiperiod consumption and portfolio choice decisions under uncertainty, that is, where both a consumption-savings choice and a portfolio allocation decision involving risky assets were assumed to occur

---

1. Important examples of such models were developed by John Cox, Jonathan Ingersoll, and Stephen Ross (Cox, Ingersoll, and Ross 1985a) and Robert Lucas (Lucas 1978).

each period.[2] Their solution technique involves stochastic dynamic programming. While this dynamic programming technique is not the only approach to solving problems of this type, it can sometimes be the most convenient and intuitive way of deriving solutions.[3]

The model we present allows an individual to make multiple consumption and portfolio decisions over a single planning horizon. This planning horizon, which can be interpreted as the individual's remaining lifetime, is composed of many decision periods, with consumption and portfolio decisions occurring once each period. The richness of this problem cannot be captured in the single-period models that we presented earlier. This is because with only one period, an investor's decision period and planning horizon coincide. Still, the results from our single-period analysis will be useful because often we can transform multiperiod models into a series of single-period ones, as will be illustrated next.

The consumption–portfolio choice model presented in this chapter assumes that the individual's decision interval is a discrete time period. Later in this book, we change the assumption to make the interval instantaneous; that is, the individual may make consumption and portfolio choices continuously. This latter assumption often simplifies problems and can lead to sharper results. When we move from discrete time to continuous time, continuous-time stochastic processes are used to model security prices.

The next section outlines the assumptions of the individual's multiperiod consumption-portfolio problem. Perhaps the strongest assumption that we make is that utility of consumption is time separable.[4] The following section shows how this problem can be solved. It introduces an important technique for solving multiperiod decision problems under uncertainty, namely, stochastic dynamic programming. The beauty of this technique is that decisions over a multiperiod horizon can be broken up into a series of decisions over a single-period horizon. This allows us to derive the individual's optimal consumption and portfolio choices by starting at the end of the individual's planning horizon and working backwards toward the present. In the last section, we complete our analysis by

---

2. Jan Mossin (Mossin 1968) solved for an individual's optimal multiperiod portfolio decisions but assumed the individual had no interim consumption decisions, only a utility of terminal consumption.

3. An alternative martingale approach to solving consumption and portfolio choice problems is given by John C. Cox and Chi-Fu Huang (Cox and Huang 1989). This approach will be presented in Chapter 12 in the context of a continuous-time consumption and portfolio choice problem.

4. Time-inseparable utility, where current utility can depend on past or expected future consumption, is discussed in Chapter 14.

deriving explicit solutions for the individual's consumption and portfolio holdings when utility is assumed to be logarithmic.

5.1   Assumptions and Notation of the Model

Consider an environment in which an individual chooses his level of consumption and the proportions of his wealth invested in n risky assets plus a risk-free asset. As was the case in our single-period models, it is assumed that the individual takes the stochastic processes followed by the prices of the different assets as given. The implicit assumption is that security markets are perfectly competitive in the sense that the (small) individual is a price-taker in security markets. An individual's trades do not impact the price (or the return) of the security. For most investors trading in liquid security markets, this is a reasonably realistic assumption. In addition, it is assumed that there are no transactions costs or taxes when buying or selling assets, so that security markets can be described as "frictionless."

An individual is assumed to make consumption and portfolio choice decisions at the start of each period during a T-period planning horizon. Each period is of unit length, with the initial date being 0 and the terminal date being T.[5]

5.1.1   Preferences

The individual is assumed to maximize an expected utility function defined over consumption levels and a terminal bequest. Denote consumption at date t as C_t, $t = 0, \ldots, T - 1$, and the terminal bequest as W_T, where W_t indicates the individual's level of wealth at date t. A general form for a multiperiod expected utility function would be $E_0 \left[\Upsilon \left(C_0, C_1, \ldots, C_{T-1}, W_T \right) \right]$, where we could simply assume that Υ is increasing and concave in its arguments. However, as a starting point, we will assume that Υ has the following *time-separable*, or *additively separable*, form:

$$E_0 \left[\Upsilon \left(C_0, C_1, \ldots, C_{T-1}, W_T \right) \right] = E_0 \left[\sum_{t=0}^{T-1} U \left(C_t, t \right) + B \left(W_T, T \right) \right] \tag{5.1}$$

where U and B are assumed to be increasing, concave functions of consumption and wealth, respectively. Equation (5.1) restricts utility at date t, $U \left(C_t, t \right)$, to

---

5. The following presentation borrows liberally from Samuelson (Samuelson 1969) and Robert C. Merton's unpublished MIT course 15.433 class notes "Portfolio Theory and Capital Markets."

depend only on consumption at that date and not previous levels of consumption or expected future levels of consumption. While this is the traditional assumption in multiperiod models, in later chapters we loosen this restriction and investigate utility formulations that are not time separable.[6]

5.1.2   The Dynamics of Wealth

At date t, the value of the individual's tangible wealth held in the form of assets equals W_t. In addition, the individual is assumed to receive wage income of y_t.[7] This beginning-of-period wealth and wage income are divided between consumption and savings, and then savings is allocated between n risky assets as well as a risk-free asset. Let R_{it} be the random return on risky asset i over the period starting at date t and ending at date $t + 1$. Also let R_{ft} be the return on an asset that pays a risk-free return over the period starting at date t and ending at date $t + 1$. Then if the proportion of date t saving allocated to risky asset i is denoted ω_{it}, we can write the evolution of the individual's tangible wealth as

$$W_{t+1} = \left(W_t + y_t - C_t\right) \left(R_{ft} + \sum_{i=1}^{n} \omega_{it} \left(R_{it} - R_{ft}\right)\right) \tag{5.2}$$

$$= S_t R_t$$

where $S_t \equiv W_t + y_t - C_t$ is the individual's savings at date t, and $R_t \equiv R_{ft} + \sum_{i=1}^{n} \omega_{it}(R_{it} - R_{ft})$ is the total return on the individual's invested wealth over the period from date t to $t + 1$.

Note that we have not restricted the distribution of asset returns in any way. In particular, the return distribution of risky asset i could change over time, so that the distribution of R_{it} could differ from the distribution of $R_{i\tau}$ for $t \neq \tau$. Moreover, the one-period risk-free return could be changing, so that $R_{ft} \neq R_{f\tau}$. Asset distributions that vary from one period to the next mean that the individual faces changing investment opportunities. Hence, in a multiperiod model, the individual's current consumption and portfolio decisions may be influenced not only by the asset return distribution for the current period, but also by the possibility that asset return distributions could change in the future.

The information and decision variables available to the individual at each date are illustrated in Figure 5.1. At date t, the individual knows her wealth at

---

6. Dynamic programming, the solution technique presented in this chapter, can also be applied to consumption and portfolio choice problems where an individual's utility is time inseparable.

7. Wage income can be random. The present value of wage income, referred to as human capital, is assumed to be a nontradeable asset. The individual can rebalance how his financial wealth is allocated among risky assets but cannot trade his human capital.

Information Variables

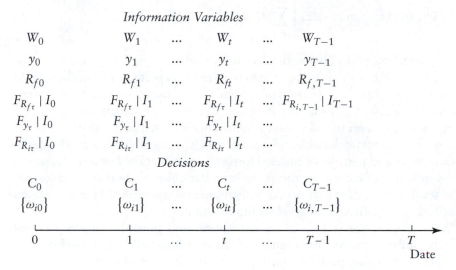

W_0	W_1	$\ldots$	W_t	$\ldots$	W_{T-1}
y_0	y_1	$\ldots$	y_t	$\ldots$	y_{T-1}
R_{f0}	R_{f1}	$\ldots$	R_{ft}	$\ldots$	$R_{f,T-1}$
$F_{R_{f\tau}} \mid I_0$	$F_{R_{f\tau}} \mid I_1$	$\ldots$	$F_{R_{f\tau}} \mid I_t$	$\ldots$	$F_{R_{i,T-1}} \mid I_{T-1}$
$F_{y_\tau} \mid I_0$	$F_{y_\tau} \mid I_1$	$\ldots$	$F_{y_\tau} \mid I_t$	$\ldots$	
$F_{R_{i\tau}} \mid I_0$	$F_{R_{i\tau}} \mid I_1$	$\ldots$	$F_{R_{i\tau}} \mid I_t$	$\ldots$	

Decisions

C_0	C_1	$\ldots$	C_t	$\ldots$	C_{T-1}
$\{\omega_{i0}\}$	$\{\omega_{i1}\}$	$\ldots$	$\{\omega_{it}\}$	$\ldots$	$\{\omega_{i,T-1}\}$

0	1	$\ldots$	t	$\ldots$	$T-1$	T

Date

Figure 5.1 —— Sequence of Individual's Consumption and Portfolio Choices

the start of the period, W_t; her wage income received at date t, y_t; and the risk-free interest rate for investing or borrowing over the period from date t to date $t+1$, R_{ft}. Conditional on information at date t, denoted by I_t, she also knows the distributions of future one-period risk-free rates and wage income, $F_{R_{f\tau}} | I_t$ and $F_{y_\tau} | I_t$, respectively, for dates $\tau = t+1, \ldots, T-1$. Lastly, the individual also knows the date t conditional distributions of the risky-asset returns for dates $\tau = t, \ldots, T-1$, given by $F_{R_{i\tau}} | I_t$. Date t information, I_t, includes all realizations of wage income and risk-free rates for all dates up until and including date t. I_t also includes all realizations of risky-asset returns for all dates up until and including date $t-1$. Moreover, I_t could include any other state variables known at date t that affect the distributions of future wages, risk-free rates, and risky-asset returns. Based on this information, the individual's date t decision variables are consumption, C_t, and the portfolio weights for the n risky assets, $\{\omega_{it}\}$, for $i = 1, \ldots, n$.

5.2 Solving the Multiperiod Model

We begin by defining an important concept that will help us simplify the solution to this multiperiod optimization problem. Let $J(W_t, t)$ denote the derived utility-of-wealth function. It is defined as follows:

$$J\left(W_t, I_t, t\right) \equiv \max_{C_s, \{\omega_{is}\}, \forall s, i} E_t \left[\sum_{s=t}^{T-1} U\left(C_s, s\right) + B\left(W_T, T\right) \right] \tag{5.3}$$

where "max" means to choose the decision variables C_s and $\{\omega_{is}\}$ for $s = t, t + 1, \ldots, T - 1$ and $i = 1, \ldots, n$ so as to maximize the expected value of the term in brackets. Note that J is a function of current wealth and all information up until and including date t. This information could reflect state variables describing a changing distribution of risky-asset returns and/or a changing risk-free interest rate, where these state variables are assumed to be exogenous to the individual's consumption and portfolio choices. However, by definition J is not a function of the individual's current or future decision variables, since they are assumed to be set to those values that maximize lifetime expected utility. Hence, J can be described as a "derived" utility-of-wealth function.

We will solve the individual's consumption and portfolio choice problem using backward dynamic programming. This entails considering the individual's multiperiod planning problem starting from her final set of decisions because, with one period remaining in the individual's planning horizon, the multiperiod problem has become a single-period one. We know from Chapter 4 how to solve for consumption and portfolio choices in a single-period context. Once we characterize the last period's solution for some given wealth and distribution of asset returns faced by the individual at date $T - 1$, we can solve for the individual's optimal decisions for the preceding period, those decisions made at date $T - 2$. This procedure is continued until we can solve for the individual's optimal decisions at the current date 0. As will be clarified next, by following this recursive solution technique, the individual's current decisions properly account for future optimal decisions that she will make in response to the evolution of uncertainty in asset returns and labor income.

5.2.1   The Final Period Solution

From the definition of J, note that[8]

$$J\left(W_T, T\right) = E_T \left[B\left(W_T, T\right) \right] = B\left(W_T, T\right) \tag{5.4}$$

Now working backwards, consider the individual's optimization problem when, at date $T - 1$, she has a single period left in her planning horizon.

---

8. To keep notation manageable, we suppress making information, I_t, an explicit argument of the indirect utility function. We use the shorthand notation $J\left(W_t, t\right)$ to refer to $J\left(W_t, I_t, t\right)$.

$$J\left(W_{T-1}, T-1\right) = \max_{C_{T-1}, \{\omega_{i, T-1}\}} E_{T-1}\left[U\left(C_{T-1}, T-1\right) + B\left(W_T, T\right)\right] \quad (5.5)$$

$$= \max_{C_{T-1}, \{\omega_{i, T-1}\}} U\left(C_{T-1}, T-1\right) + E_{T-1}\left[B\left(W_T, T\right)\right]$$

To clarify how W_T depends explicitly on C_{T-1} and $\{\omega_{i, T-1}\}$, substitute equation (5.2) for $t = T - 1$ into equation (5.5):

$$J\left(W_{T-1}, T-1\right)$$

$$= \max_{C_{T-1}, \{\omega_{i, T-1}\}} U\left(C_{T-1}, T-1\right) + E_{T-1}\left[B\left(S_{T-1}R_{T-1}, T\right)\right] \quad (5.6)$$

where it should be recalled that $S_{T-1} \equiv W_{T-1} + y_{T-1} - C_{T-1}$ and $R_{T-1} \equiv R_{f, T-1} + \sum_{i=1}^{n} \omega_{i, T-1}(R_{i, T-1} - R_{f, T-1})$. Equation (5.6) is a standard single-period consumption–portfolio choice problem. To solve it, we differentiate with respect to each decision variable, C_{T-1} and $\{\omega_{i, T-1}\}$, and set the resulting expressions equal to zero:

$$U_C\left(C_{T-1}, T-1\right) - E_{T-1}\left[B_W\left(W_T, T\right) R_{T-1}\right] = 0 \quad (5.7)$$

$$E_{T-1}\left[B_W\left(W_T, T\right)\left(R_{i, T-1} - R_{f, T-1}\right)\right] = 0, \quad i = 1, \ldots, n \quad (5.8)$$

where the subscripts on U and B denote partial differentiation.[9] Using the results in (5.8), we see that (5.7) can be rewritten as

$$U_C\left(C_{T-1}, T-1\right)$$

$$= E_{T-1}\left[B_W\left(W_T, T\right)\left(R_{f, T-1} + \sum_{i=1}^{n} \omega_{i, T-1}\left(R_{i, T-1} - R_{f, T-1}\right)\right)\right]$$

$$= R_{f, T-1} E_{T-1}\left[B_W\left(W_T, T\right)\right] \quad (5.9)$$

Conditions (5.8) and (5.9) represent $n + 1$ equations that determine the optimal choices of C_{T-1}^* and $\{\omega_{i, T-1}^*\}$. They are identical to the single-period model conditions (4.6) and (4.10) derived in the previous chapter but with the utility of bequest function, B, replacing the end-of-period utility function, U. If we substitute these optimal decision variables back into equation (5.6) and differentiate totally with respect to W_{T-1}, we have

---

9. Note that we apply the chain rule when differentiating $B\left(W_T, T\right)$ with respect to C_{T-1} since $W_T = S_{T-1}R_{T-1}$ depends on C_{T-1} through S_{T-1}.

$$J_W = U_C \frac{\partial C_{T-1}^*}{\partial W_{T-1}} + E_{T-1}\left[B_{W_T} \cdot \left(\frac{dW_T}{dW_{T-1}}\right)\right]$$

$$= U_C \frac{\partial C_{T-1}^*}{\partial W_{T-1}} + E_{T-1}\left[B_{W_T} \cdot \left(\frac{\partial W_T}{\partial W_{T-1}} + \sum_{i=1}^{n} \frac{\partial W_T}{\partial \omega_{i,T-1}^*} \frac{\partial \omega_{i,T-1}^*}{\partial W_{T-1}}\right.\right.$$

$$\left.\left. + \frac{\partial W_T}{\partial C_{T-1}^*} \frac{\partial C_{T-1}^*}{\partial W_{T-1}}\right)\right]$$

$$= U_C \frac{\partial C_{T-1}^*}{\partial W_{T-1}} + E_{T-1}\left[B_{W_T} \cdot \left(\sum_{i=1}^{n} \left[R_{i,T-1} - R_{f,T-1}\right] S_{T-1} \frac{\partial \omega_{i,T-1}^*}{\partial W_{T-1}}\right.\right.$$

$$\left.\left. + R_{T-1}\left(1 - \frac{\partial C_{T-1}^*}{\partial W_{T-1}}\right)\right)\right] \tag{5.10}$$

Using the first-order condition (5.8), $E_{T-1}\left[B_{W_T} \cdot \left(R_{i,T-1} - R_{f,T-1}\right)\right] = 0$, as well as (5.9), $U_C = R_{f,T-1}E_{T-1}\left[B_{W_T}\right]$, we see that (5.10) simplifies to $J_W = R_{f,T-1}E_{T-1}\left[B_{W_T}\right]$. Using (5.9) once again, this can be rewritten as

$$J_W\left(W_{T-1}, T-1\right) = U_C\left(C_{T-1}^*, T-1\right) \tag{5.11}$$

which is known as the "envelope condition." It says that the individual's optimal policy equates her marginal utility of current consumption, U_C, to her marginal utility of wealth (future consumption).

5.2.2   Deriving the Bellman Equation

Having solved the individual's problem with one period to go in her planning horizon, we next consider her optimal consumption and portfolio choices with two periods remaining, at date $T-2$. The individual's objective at this date is

$$J\left(W_{T-2}, T-2\right) = \max U\left(C_{T-2}, T-2\right) + E_{T-2}\left[U\left(C_{T-1}, T-1\right)\right.$$

$$\left. + B\left(W_T, T\right)\right] \tag{5.12}$$

The individual must maximize expression (5.12) by choosing C_{T-2} as well as $\{\omega_{i,T-2}\}$. However, note that she wishes to maximize an expression that is an expectation over utilities $U\left(C_{T-1}, T-1\right) + B\left(W_T, T\right)$ that depend on future decisions, namely, C_{T-1} and $\{\omega_{i,T-1}\}$. What should the individual assume these future values of C_{T-1} and $\{\omega_{i,T-1}\}$ to be? The answer comes from the *Principle of Optimality*. It states:

> An optimal set of decisions has the property that given an initial decision, the remaining decisions must be optimal with respect to the outcome that results from the initial decision.

The "max" in (5.12) is over all remaining decisions, but the Principle of Optimality says that whatever decision is made in period $T - 2$, given the outcome, the remaining decisions (for period $T - 1$) must be optimal (maximal). In other words,

$$\max_{\{(T-2),(T-1)\}} (Y) = \max_{\{T-2\}} \left[\max_{\{T-1,|\text{outcome from } (T-2)\}} (Y) \right] \tag{5.13}$$

This principle allows us to rewrite (5.12) as

$$J\left(W_{T-2}, T - 2\right) = \max_{C_{T-2},\{\omega_{i,T-2}\}} \left\{ U\left(C_{T-2}, T - 2\right) + \right. \tag{5.14}$$

$$\left. E_{T-2} \left[\max_{C_{T-1},\{\omega_{i,T-1}\}} E_{T-1} \left[U\left(C_{T-1}, T - 1\right) + B\left(W_T, T\right) \right] \right] \right\}$$

Then, using the definition of $J\left(W_{T-1}, T - 1\right)$ from (5.5), equation (5.14) can be rewritten as

$$J\left(W_{T-2}, T - 2\right) = \max_{C_{T-2},\{\omega_{i,T-2}\}} U\left(C_{T-2}, T - 2\right) + E_{T-2} \left[J\left(W_{T-1}, T - 1\right) \right]$$

$$\tag{5.15}$$

The recursive condition (5.15) is known as the (Richard) Bellman equation (Bellman 1957). It characterizes the individual's objective at date $T - 2$. What is important about this characterization is that if we compare it to equation (5.5), the individual's objective at date $T - 1$, the two problems are quite similar. The only difference is that in (5.15) we replace the known function of wealth next period, B, with another (known in principle) function of wealth next period, J. But the solution to (5.15) will be of the same form as that for (5.5).[10]

---

10. Using the envelope condition, it can be shown that the concavity of U and B ensures that $J(W, t)$ is a concave and continuously differentiable function of W. Hence, an interior solution to the second-to-last period problem exists.

5.2.3 The General Solution

Thus, the optimality conditions for (5.15) are

$$U_C\left(C_{T-2}^*, T-2\right) = E_{T-2}\left[J_W\left(W_{T-1}, T-1\right)R_{T-2}\right]$$

$$= R_{f,T-2}E_{T-2}\left[J_W\left(W_{T-1}, T-1\right)\right]$$

$$= J_W\left(W_{T-2}, T-2\right) \tag{5.16}$$

$$E_{T-2}\left[R_{i,T-2}J_W\left(W_{T-1}, T-1\right)\right] = R_{f,T-2}E_{T-2}\left[J_W\left(W_{T-1}, T-1\right)\right],$$

$$i = 1, \ldots, n \tag{5.17}$$

Based on the preceding pattern, inductive reasoning implies that for any $t = 0, 1, \ldots, T-1$, we have the Bellman equation:

$$J\left(W_t, t\right) = \max_{C_t, \{\omega_{i,t}\}} U\left(C_t, t\right) + E_t\left[J\left(W_{t+1}, t+1\right)\right] \tag{5.18}$$

and, therefore, the date t optimality conditions are

$$U_C\left(C_t^*, t\right) = E_t\left[J_W\left(W_{t+1}, t+1\right)R_t\right]$$

$$= R_{f,t}E_t\left[J_W\left(W_{t+1}, t+1\right)\right]$$

$$= J_W\left(W_t, t\right) \tag{5.19}$$

$$E_t\left[R_{i,t}J_W\left(W_{t+1}, t+1\right)\right] = R_{f,t}E_t\left[J_W\left(W_{t+1}, t+1\right)\right], \quad i = 1, \ldots, n \tag{5.20}$$

The insights of the multiperiod model conditions (5.19) and (5.20) are similar to those of a single-period model from Chapter 4. The individual chooses today's consumption such that the marginal utility of current consumption equals the derived marginal utility of wealth (the marginal utility of future consumption). Furthermore, the portfolio weights should be adjusted to equate all assets' expected marginal utility–weighted asset returns. However, solving for the individual's actual consumption and portfolio weights at each date, C_t^* and $\{\omega_{i,t}\}$, $t = 0, \ldots, T-1$, is more complex than for a single-period model. The conditions' dependence on the derived utility-of-wealth function implies that they depend on future contingent investment opportunities (the distributions of future asset returns $(R_{i,t+j}, R_{f,t+j}, j \geq 1)$, future income flows, y_{t+j}, and possibly, states of the world that might affect future utilities $(U\left(\cdot, t+j\right))$.

Solving this system involves starting from the end of the planning horizon and dynamically programing backwards toward the present. Thus, for the last period, T, we know that $J\left(W_T, T\right) = B\left(W_T, T\right)$. As we did previously, we substitute $B\left(W_T, T\right)$ for $J\left(W_T, T\right)$ in conditions (5.18) to (5.20) for date $T-1$ and solve for $J\left(W_{T-1}, T-1\right)$. This is then substituted into conditions (5.18) to (5.20) for date $T-2$ and one then solves for $J\left(W_{T-2}, T-2\right)$. If we proceed in this recursive manner, we eventually obtain $J(W_0, 0)$ and the solution is complete. These steps are summarized in the following table.

Step	Action
1	Construct $J(W_T, T)$.
2	Solve for C^*_{T-1} and $\{\omega_{i,T-1}\}$, $i = 1, \ldots, n$.
3	Substitute the decisions in step 2 to construct $J(W_{T-1}, T-1)$.
4	Solve for C^*_{T-2} and $\{\omega_{i,T-2}\}$, $i = 1, \ldots, n$.
5	Substitute the decisions in step 4 to construct $J(W_{T-2}, T-2)$.
6	Repeat steps 4 and 5 for date $T-3$.
7	Repeat step 6 for all prior dates until date 0 is reached.

By following this recursive procedure, we find that the optimal policy will be of the form[11]

$$C^*_t = g\left[W_t, y_t, I_t, t\right] \tag{5.21}$$

$$\omega^*_{it} = h\left[W_t, y_t, I_t, t\right] \tag{5.22}$$

Deriving analytical expressions for the functions g and h is not always possible, in which case numerical solutions satisfying the first-order conditions at each date can be computed. However, for particular assumptions regarding the form of utility, wage income, and the distribution of asset returns, such explicit solutions may be possible. The next section considers an example where this is the case.

5.3 Example Using Log Utility

To illustrate how solutions of the form (5.21) and (5.22) can be obtained, consider the following example where the individual has log utility and no wage income. Assume that $U(C_t, t) \equiv \delta^t \ln[C_t]$, $B(W_T, T) \equiv \delta^T \ln[W_T]$, and $y_t \equiv 0 \ \forall \ t$, where $\delta = \frac{1}{1+\rho}$ and ρ is the individual's subjective rate of time preference. Now at date $T - 1$, using condition (5.7), we have

---

11. When asset returns are serially correlated, that is, the date t distribution of asset returns depends on realized asset returns from periods prior to date t, the decision rules in (5.21) and (5.22) may depend on this prior, conditioning information. They will also depend on any other state variables known at time t and included in the date t information set I_t. This, however, does not affect the general solution technique. These prior asset returns are exogenous state variables that influence only the conditional expectations in the optimality conditions (5.19) and (5.20).

$$U_C(C_{T-1}, T-1) = E_{T-1}\left[B_W(W_T, T)R_{T-1}\right] \tag{5.23}$$

$$\delta^{T-1}\frac{1}{C_{T-1}} = E_{T-1}\left[\delta^T\frac{R_{T-1}}{W_T}\right] = E_{T-1}\left[\delta^T\frac{R_{T-1}}{S_{T-1}R_{T-1}}\right]$$

$$= \frac{\delta^T}{S_{T-1}} = \frac{\delta^T}{W_{T-1}-C_{T-1}}$$

or

$$C^*_{T-1} = \frac{1}{1+\delta}W_{T-1} \tag{5.24}$$

It is noteworthy that consumption for this log utility investor is a fixed proportion of wealth and is independent of investment opportunities, that is, independent of the distribution of asset returns. This is reminiscent of the result derived in Chapters 1 and 4: the income and substitution effects from a change in investment returns exactly offset each other for the log utility individual.

Turning to the first-order conditions with respect to the portfolio weights, conditions (5.8) imply

$$E_{T-1}\left[B_{W_T}R_{i,T-1}\right] = R_{f,T-1}E_{T-1}\left[B_{W_T}\right], \quad i = 1,\ldots,n$$

$$\delta^T E_{T-1}\left[\frac{R_{i,T-1}}{S_{T-1}R_{T-1}}\right] = \delta^T R_{f,T-1}E_{T-1}\left[\frac{1}{S_{T-1}R_{T-1}}\right]$$

$$E_{T-1}\left[\frac{R_{i,T-1}}{R_{T-1}}\right] = R_{f,T-1}E_{T-1}\left[\frac{1}{R_{T-1}}\right] \tag{5.25}$$

Furthermore, for the case of log utility we see that equation (5.25) equals unity, since from (5.9) we have

$$U_C(C_{T-1}, T-1) = R_{f,T-1}E_{T-1}\left[B_W(W_T, T)\right]$$

$$\frac{\delta^{T-1}}{C^*_{T-1}} = R_{f,T-1}E_{T-1}\left[\delta^T\frac{1}{S_{T-1}R_{T-1}}\right]$$

$$1 = \frac{\delta C^*_{T-1}R_{f,T-1}}{W_{T-1}-C^*_{T-1}}E_{T-1}\left[\frac{1}{R_{T-1}}\right]$$

$$1 = R_{f,T-1}E_{T-1}\left[\frac{1}{R_{T-1}}\right] \tag{5.26}$$

where we have substituted equation (5.24) in going from the third to the fourth line of (5.26). While we would need to make specific assumptions regarding the distribution of asset returns in order to derive the portfolio weights $\{\omega^*_{i,T-1}\}$

satisfying (5.25), note that the conditions in (5.25) are rather special in that they do not depend on W_{T-1}, C_{T-1}, or δ, but only on the particular distribution of asset returns that one assumes. The implication is that a log utility investor chooses assets in the same relative proportions, independent of his initial wealth. This, of course, is a consequence of log utility being a special case of constant relative-risk-aversion utility.[12]

The next step is to solve for $J\left(W_{T-1}, T-1\right)$ by substituting the date $T-1$ optimal consumption and portfolio rules into the individual's objective function. Denoting $R_t^* \equiv R_{f,t} + \sum_{i=1}^n \omega_{it}^*(R_{it} - R_{ft})$ as the individual's total portfolio return when assets are held in the optimal proportions, we have

$$
J\left(W_{T-1}, T-1\right) = \delta^{T-1} \ln\left[C_{T-1}^*\right] + \delta^T E_{T-1}\left[\ln\left[R_{T-1}^*\left(W_{T-1} - C_{T-1}^*\right)\right]\right]
$$

$$
= \delta^{T-1}\left(-\ln[1+\delta] + \ln[W_{T-1}]\right) +
$$

$$
\delta^T\left(E_{T-1}\left[\ln\left[R_{T-1}^*\right]\right] + \ln\left[\frac{\delta}{1+\delta}\right] + \ln\left[W_{T-1}\right]\right)
$$

$$
= \delta^{T-1}\left[(1+\delta)\ln\left[W_{T-1}\right] + H_{T-1}\right] \tag{5.27}
$$

where $H_{T-1} \equiv -\ln[1+\delta] + \delta\ln\left[\frac{\delta}{1+\delta}\right] + \delta E_{T-1}\left[\ln\left[R_{T-1}^*\right]\right]$. Notably, from equation (5.25) we saw that $\omega_{i,T-1}^*$ did not depend on W_{T-1}, and therefore R_{T-1}^* and H_{T-1} do not depend on W_{T-1}.

Next, let's move back one more period and consider the individual's optimal consumption and portfolio decisions at time $T-2$. From equation (5.15) we have

$$
J\left(W_{T-2}, T-2\right) = \max_{C_{T-2}, \{\omega_{i,T-2}\}} U\left(C_{T-2}, T-2\right) + E_{T-2}\left[J\left(W_{T-1}, T-1\right)\right]
$$

$$
= \max_{C_{T-2}, \{\omega_{i,T-2}\}} \delta^{T-2} \ln\left[C_{T-2}\right]
$$

$$
+ \delta^{T-1}E_{T-2}\left[(1+\delta)\ln\left[W_{T-1}\right] + H_{T-1}\right] \tag{5.28}
$$

Thus, using (5.16), the optimality condition for consumption is

$$
U_C\left(C_{T-2}^*, T-2\right) = E_{T-2}\left[J_W\left(W_{T-1}, T-1\right)R_{T-2}\right]
$$

$$
\frac{\delta^{T-2}}{C_{T-2}} = (1+\delta)\,\delta^{T-1}E_{T-2}\left[\frac{R_{T-2}}{S_{T-2}R_{T-2}}\right]
$$

$$
= \frac{(1+\delta)\,\delta^{T-1}}{W_{T-2} - C_{T-2}} \tag{5.29}
$$

---

12. Recall from section 1.3 that a one-period investor with constant relative risk aversion places constant proportions of wealth in a risk-free and a single risky asset.

or

$$C^*_{T-2} = \frac{1}{1 + \delta + \delta^2} W_{T-2} \tag{5.30}$$

Using (5.17), we then see that the optimality conditions for $\{\omega^*_{i,T-2}\}$ turn out to be of the same form as at $T - 1$:

$$E_{T-2}\left[\frac{R_{i,T-2}}{R^*_{T-2}}\right] = R_{f,T-2}E_{T-2}\left[\frac{1}{R^*_{T-2}}\right], \quad i = 1, \ldots, n \tag{5.31}$$

and, as in the case of $T - 1$, equation (5.31) equals unity, since

$$U_C\left(C_{T-2}, T - 2\right) = R_{f,T-2}E_{T-2}\left[J_W\left(W_{T-1}, T - 1\right)\right]$$

$$\frac{\delta^{T-2}}{C^*_{T-2}} = R_{f,T-2}\delta^{T-1}E_{T-2}\left[\frac{1 + \delta}{S_{T-2}R_{T-2}}\right]$$

$$1 = \frac{\delta\left(1 + \delta\right)C^*_{T-2}R_{f,T-2}}{W_{T-2} - C^*_{T-2}}E_{T-2}\left[\frac{1}{R_{T-2}}\right]$$

$$1 = R_{f,T-2}E_{T-2}\left[\frac{1}{R_{T-2}}\right] \tag{5.32}$$

Recognizing the above pattern, we see that the optimal consumption and portfolio rules for any prior date, t, are

$$C^*_t = \frac{1}{1 + \delta + \cdots + \delta^{T-t}} W_t = \frac{1 - \delta}{1 - \delta^{T-t+1}} W_t \tag{5.33}$$

$$E_t\left[\frac{R_{i,t}}{R^*_t}\right] = R_{ft}E_t\left[\frac{1}{R^*_t}\right] = 1, \quad i = 1, \ldots, n \tag{5.34}$$

Hence, we find that the consumption and portfolio rules are separable for a log utility individual. Equation (5.33) shows that the consumption-savings decision does not depend on the distribution of asset returns. Moreover, equation (5.34) indicates that the optimal portfolio proportions depend only on the distribution of one-period returns and not on the distribution of asset returns beyond the current period. This is described as *myopic behavior* because investment allocation decisions made by the multiperiod log investor are identical to those of a one-period log investor. Hence, the log utility individual's current period decisions are independent of the possibility of changing investment opportunities in future periods. It should be emphasized that these independence results are highly specific to the log utility assumption and do not occur with other utility functions. In general, it will be optimal for the individual to choose today's portfolio in a way that hedges against possible changes in tomorrow's investment opportunities. Such hedging demands for assets will become transparent when in Chapter 12 we consider the individual's consumption and portfolio choice problem in a continuous-time setting.

The consumption rule (5.33) shows that consumption is positive whenever wealth is. Since utility of consumption is undefined for logarithmic (or any other constant relative-risk-aversion) utility when consumption is nonpositive, what ensures that wealth is always positive? The individual's optimal portfolio choices will reflect this concern. While this example has not specified a specific distribution for asset returns, portfolio decisions in a discrete-time model can be quite sensitive to the requirement that wealth exceed zero. For example, suppose that the distribution of a risky asset's return had no lower bound, as would be the case if the distribution were normal. With logarithmic utility, the optimality conditions (5.34) imply that the individual avoids holding any normally distributed risky asset, since there is positive probability that a large negative return would make wealth negative as well.[13] In Chapter 12, we revisit the individual's intertemporal consumption and portfolio choices in a continuous-time environment. There we will see that the individual's ability to continuously reallocate her portfolio can lead to fundamental differences in asset demands. Individuals can maintain positive wealth even though they hold assets having returns that are instantaneously normally distributed. The intuition behind this difference in the discrete- versus continuous-time results is that the probability of wealth becoming negative decreases when the time interval between portfolio revisions decreases.

5.4   Summary

An individual's optimal strategy for making lifetime consumption-savings and portfolio allocation decisions is a topic having practical importance to financial planners. This chapter's analysis represents a first step in formulating and deriving a lifetime financial plan. We showed that an individual could approach this problem by a backward dynamic programming technique that first considered how decisions would be made when he reached the end of his planning horizon. For prior periods, consumption and portfolio decisions were derived using the recursive Bellman equation, which is based on the concept of a derived utility-of-wealth function. The multiperiod planning problem was transformed into a series of easier-to-solve one-period problems. While the consumption–portfolio choice problem in this chapter assumed that lifetime utility was time separable, in future

---

13. Note that this would not be the case for a risky asset having a return distribution that is bounded at zero, such as the lognormal distribution.

chapters we show that the Bellman equation solution technique often can apply to cases of time-inseparable lifetime utility.

Our general solution technique was illustrated for the special case of an individual having logarithmic utility and no wage income. It turned out that this individual's optimal consumption decision was to consume a proportion of wealth each period, where the proportion was a function of the remaining periods in the individual's planning horizon but not of the current or future distributions of asset returns. In other words, future investment opportunities did not affect the individual's current consumption-savings decision. Optimal portfolio allocations were also relatively simple because they depended only on the current period's distribution of asset returns.

Deriving an individual's intertemporal consumption and portfolio decisions has value beyond the application to financial planning. By summing all individuals' demands for consumption and assets, a measure of aggregate consumption and asset demands can be derived. When coupled with a theory of production technologies and asset supplies, these aggregate demands can provide the foundation for a general equilibrium theory of asset pricing. We turn to this topic in the next chapter.

5.5   Exercises

1. Consider the following consumption and portfolio choice problem. Assume that $U(C_t, t) = \delta^t [aC_t - bC_t^2]$, $B(W_T, T) = 0$, and $y_t \neq 0$, where $\delta = \frac{1}{1+\rho}$ and $\rho \geq 0$ is the individual's subjective rate of time preference. Further, assume that $n = 0$ so that there are no risky assets but there is a single-period riskless asset yielding a return of $R_{ft} = 1/\delta$ that is constant each period (equivalently, the risk-free interest rate $r_f = \rho$). Note that in this problem labor income is stochastic and there is only one (riskless) asset for the individual consumer-investor to hold. Hence, the individual has no portfolio choice decision but must decide only what to consume each period. In solving this problem, assume that the individual's optimal level of consumption remains below the "bliss point" of the quadratic utility function, that is, $C_t^* < \frac{1}{2}a/b, \forall t$.

   a. Write down the individual's wealth accumulation equation from period t to period $t + 1$.

   b. Solve for the individual's optimal level of consumption at date $T - 1$ and evaluate $J(W_{T-1}, T - 1)$. Hint: this is trivial.

   c. Continue to solve the individual's problem at date $T - 2$, $T - 3$, and so on and notice the pattern that emerges. From these results, solve for the individual's optimal level of consumption for any arbitrary date, $T - t$, in terms of the individual's expected future levels of income.

2. Consider the consumption and portfolio choice problem with power utility $U(C_t, t) \equiv \delta^t C_t^\gamma / \gamma$ and a power bequest function $B(W_T, T) \equiv \delta^T W_T^\gamma / \gamma$. Assume there is no wage income ($y_t \equiv 0 \ \forall t$) and a constant risk-free return equal to $R_{ft} = R_f$. Also, assume that $n = 1$ and the return of the single risky asset, R_{rt}, is independently and identically distributed over time. Denote the proportion of wealth invested in the risky asset at date t as ω_t.

   a. Derive the first-order conditions for the optimal consumption level and portfolio weight at date $T - 1$, C_{T-1}^* and ω_{T-1}^*, and give an explicit expression for C_{T-1}^*.

   b. Solve for the form of $J(W_{T-1}, T - 1)$.

   c. Derive the first-order conditions for the optimal consumption level and portfolio weight at date $T - 2$, C_{T-2}^* and ω_{T-2}^*, and give an explicit expression for C_{T-2}^*.

   d. Solve for the form of $J(W_{T-2}, T - 2)$. Based on the pattern for $T - 1$ and $T - 2$, provide expressions for the optimal consumption and portfolio weight at any date $T - t$, $t = 1, 2, 3, \ldots$.

3. Consider the multiperiod consumption and portfolio choice problem

$$\max_{C_s, \omega_s \forall s} E_t \left[\sum_{s=t}^{T-1} U(C_s, s) + B(W_T, T) \right]$$

Assume negative exponential utility $U(C_s, s) \equiv -\delta^s e^{-bC_s}$ and a bequest function $B(W_T, T) \equiv -\delta^T e^{-bW_T}$ where $\delta = e^{-\rho}$ and $\rho > 0$ is the (continuously compounded) rate of time preference. Assume there is no wage income ($y_s \equiv 0 \ \forall \ s$) and a constant risk-free return equal to $R_{fs} = R_f$. Also, assume that $n = 1$ and the return of the single risky asset, R_{rs}, has an identical and independent normal distribution of $N(\overline{R}, \sigma^2)$ each period. Denote the proportion of wealth invested in the risky asset at date s as ω_s.

   a. Derive the optimal portfolio weight at date $T - 1$, ω_{T-1}^*. Hint: it might be easiest to evaluate expectations in the objective function prior to taking the first-order condition.

   b. Solve for the optimal level of consumption at date $T - 1$, C_{T-1}^*. C_{T-1}^* will be a function of W_{T-1}, b, ρ, R_f, $\overline{R}$, and σ^2.

   c. Solve for the indirect utility function of wealth at date $T - 1$, $J(W_{T-1}, T - 1)$.

   d. Derive the optimal portfolio weight at date $T - 2$, ω_{T-2}^*.

   e. Solve for the optimal level of consumption at date $T - 2$, C_{T-2}^*.

4. An individual faces the following consumption and portfolio choice problem:

$$\max_{C_t, \omega_t \forall t} E_0 \left[\sum_{t=0}^{T-1} \delta^t \ln \left[C_t \right] + \delta^T \ln \left[W_T \right] \right]$$

where each period the individual can choose between a risk-free asset paying a time-varying return of R_{ft} over the period from t to $t+1$ and a single risky asset. The individual receives no wage income. The risky asset's return over the period from t to $t+1$ is given by

$$R_{rt} = \begin{cases} (1+u_t)\, R_{ft} & \text{with probability } \frac{1}{2} \\ (1+d_t)\, R_{ft} & \text{with probability } \frac{1}{2} \end{cases}$$

where $u_t > 0$ and $-1 < d_t < 0$. Let ω_t be the individual's proportion of wealth invested in the risky asset at date t. Solve for the individual's optimal portfolio weight ω_t^* for $t = 0, \ldots, T-1$.

CHAPTER 6

Multiperiod Market Equilibrium

The previous chapter showed how stochastic dynamic programming can be used to solve for an individual's optimal multiperiod consumption and portfolio decisions. In general, deriving an individual's decision rules for particular forms of utility and distributions of asset returns can be complex. However, even though simple solutions for individuals' decision rules may not exist, a number of insights regarding equilibrium asset pricing relationships often can be derived for an economy populated by such optimizing individuals. This is the topic of the first section of this chapter. Similar to what was shown in the context of Chapter 4's single-period consumption–portfolio choice model, here we find that an individual's first-order conditions from the multiperiod problem can be reinterpreted as equilibrium conditions for asset prices. This leads to empirically testable implications even when analytical expressions for the individuals' lifetime consumption and portfolio decisions cannot be derived. As we shall see, these equilibrium implications generalize those that we derived earlier for a single-period environment.

In the second section, we consider an important and popular equilibrium asset pricing model derived by Nobel laureate Robert E. Lucas (Lucas 1978). It is an endowment economy model of infinitely lived, representative individuals. The assumptions of the model, which determine individuals' consumption process, are particularly convenient for deriving the equilibrium price of the market portfolio of all assets. As will be shown, the model's infinite horizon gives rise to the possibility of speculative bubbles in asset prices. The last section of the chapter examines the nature of rational bubbles and considers what conditions could give rise to these nonfundamental price dynamics.

6.1   Asset Pricing in the Multiperiod Model

Recall that the previous chapter's Samuelson-Merton model of multiperiod consumption and portfolio choices assumed that an individual's objective was

$$\max_{C_s, \{\omega_{is}\}, \forall s, i} E_t \left[\sum_{s=t}^{T-1} U\left(C_s, s\right) + B\left(W_T, T\right) \right] \tag{6.1}$$

and that this problem of maximizing time-separable, multiperiod utility could be transformed into a series of one-period problems where the individual solved the Bellman equation:

$$J\left(W_t, t\right) = \max C_t, \{\omega_{i,t}\} U\left(C_t, t\right) + E_t \left[J\left(W_{t+1}, t+1\right) \right] \tag{6.2}$$

This led to the first-order conditions

$$U_C\left(C_t^*, t\right) = R_{f,t} E_t \left[J_W\left(W_{t+1}, t+1\right) \right]$$

$$= J_W\left(W_t, t\right) \tag{6.3}$$

$$E_t \left[R_{it} J_W\left(W_{t+1}, t+1\right) \right] = R_{f,t} E_t \left[J_W\left(W_{t+1}, t+1\right) \right], \ i = 1, \ldots, n \tag{6.4}$$

By making specific assumptions regarding the form of the utility function, the nature of wage income, and the distributions of asset returns at each date, explicit formulas for C_t^* and ω_{it}^* may be derived using backward dynamic programming. The previous chapter provided an example of such a derivation for the case of an individual with log utility and no wage income. However, under more general assumptions, the multiperiod model may have equilibrium implications even when analytical expressions for consumption and portfolio choices are not possible. This is the topic that we now consider.

6.1.1   The Multiperiod Pricing Kernel

Let us illustrate how equilibrium asset pricing implications can be derived from the individual's envelope condition (6.3), $U_C\left(C_t^*, t\right) = J_W\left(W_t, t\right)$. This condition conveys that under an optimal policy, the marginal value of financial wealth equals the marginal utility of consumption. Substituting the envelope condition evaluated at date $t+1$ into the right-hand side of the first line of (6.3), we have

$$U_C\left(C_t^*, t\right) = R_{f,t} E_t \left[J_W\left(W_{t+1}, t+1\right) \right]$$

$$= R_{f,t} E_t \left[U_C\left(C_{t+1}^*, t+1\right) \right] \tag{6.5}$$

Furthermore, substituting (6.4) into (6.3) and, again, using the envelope condition at date $t + 1$ allows us to write

$$U_C\left(C_t^*, t\right) = E_t\left[R_{it} J_W\left(W_{t+1}, t+1\right)\right]$$
$$= E_t\left[R_{it} U_C\left(C_{t+1}^*, t+1\right)\right] \tag{6.6}$$

or

$$1 = E_t\left[m_{t,t+1} R_{it}\right]$$
$$= R_{f,t} E_t\left[m_{t,t+1}\right] \tag{6.7}$$

where $m_{t,t+1} \equiv U_C\left(C_{t+1}^*, t+1\right)/U_C\left(C_t^*, t\right)$ is the stochastic discount factor, or pricing kernel, between dates t and $t + 1$. Equation (6.7) indicates that our previous asset pricing results derived from a single-period consumption–portfolio choice problem, such as equation (4.18), hold on a period-by-period basis even when we allow the consumption–portfolio choice problem to be a more complex multiperiod one. As before, we can interpret (6.6) and (6.7) as showing that the marginal rate of substitution between consumption at any two dates, such as t and $t + 1$, equals the marginal rate of transformation. Consumption at date t can be "transformed" into consumption at date $t + 1$ by investing in the riskless asset having return $R_{f,t}$ or by investing in a risky asset having the random return R_{it}.

A similar relationship can be derived for asset returns for any holding period, not just one of unit length. Note that if equation (6.6) for risky asset j is updated one period, $U_C(C_{t+1}^*, t+1) = E_{t+1}[R_{j,t+1} U_C(C_{t+2}^*, t+2)]$, and this is substituted into the right-hand side of the original (6.6), one obtains

$$U_C\left(C_t^*, t\right) = E_t\left[R_{it} E_{t+1}\left[R_{j,t+1} U_C\left(C_{t+2}^*, t+2\right)\right]\right]$$
$$= E_t\left[R_{it} R_{j,t+1} U_C\left(C_{t+2}^*, t+2\right)\right] \tag{6.8}$$

or

$$1 = E_t\left[R_{it} R_{j,t+1} m_{t,t+2}\right] \tag{6.9}$$

where $m_{t,t+2} \equiv U_C(C_{t+2}^*, t+2)/U_C(C_t^*, t)$ is the marginal rate of substitution, or the stochastic discount factor, between dates t and $t + 2$. In the preceding expressions, $R_{it} R_{j,t+1}$ is the return from a trading strategy that first invests in asset i over the period from t to $t + 1$, then invests in asset j over the period $t + 1$ to $t + 2$. Of course, i could equal j but need not, in general. By repeated substitution, (6.9) can be generalized to

$$1 = E_t\left[R_{t,t+k} m_{t,t+k}\right] \tag{6.10}$$

where $m_{t,t+k} \equiv U_C(C^*_{t+k}, t+k)/U_C(C^*_t, t)$ and $R_{t,t+k}$ is the return from any trading strategy involving multiple assets over the period from dates t to $t+k$.

Equation (6.10) says that optimizing consumers equate their expected marginal utilities across all time periods and all states. Its equilibrium implication is that the stochastic discount relationship holds for multiperiod returns generated from any particular trading strategy. This result implies that empirical tests of multiperiod, time-separable utility models using consumption data and asset returns can be constructed using a wide variety of investment returns and holding periods. Expressions such as (6.10) represent moment conditions that are often tested using generalized method-of-moments techniques.[1] As mentioned in Chapter 4, such consumption-based tests typically reject models that assume standard forms of time-separable utility. This has motivated a search for alternative utility specifications, a topic we will revisit in future chapters.

Lets us now consider a general equilibrium structure for this multiperiod consumption–portfolio choice model.

6.2   The Lucas Model of Asset Pricing

The Lucas model (Lucas 1978) derives the equilibrium prices of risky assets for an *endowment* economy. An endowment economy is one where the random process generating the economy's real output (e.g., Gross Domestic Product, or GDP) is taken to be exogenous. Moreover, it is assumed that output obtained at a particular date cannot be reinvested to produce more output in the future. Rather, all output on a given date can only be consumed immediately, implying that equilibrium aggregate consumption equals the exogenous level of output at each date. Assets in this economy represent ownership claims on output, so that output (and consumption) on a given date can also be interpreted as the cash dividends paid to asset holders. Because reinvestment of output is not permitted, so that the scale of the production process is fixed, assets can be viewed as being perfectly inelastically supplied.[2]

As we will make explicit shortly, these endowment economy assumptions essentially fix the process for aggregate consumption. Along with the assumption

---

1. See Lars Hansen and Kenneth Singleton (Hansen and Singleton 1983) and Lars Hansen and Ravi Jagannathan (Hansen and Jagannathan 1991).

2. An endowment economy is sometimes described as a "fruit tree" economy. The analogy refers to an economy whose production is represented by a fixed number of fruit trees. Each season (date), the trees produce a random amount of output in the form of perishable fruit. The only value to this fruit is to consume it immediately, as it cannot be reinvested to produce more fruit in the future. (Planting seeds from the fruit to increase the number of fruit trees is ruled out.) Assets represent ownership claims on the fixed number of fruit trees (orchards), so that the fruit produced on each date also equals the dividend paid to asset holders.

that all individuals are identical, that is, that there is a representative individual, the endowment economy assumptions fix the processes for individuals' consumptions. Thus, individuals' marginal rates of substitution between current and future consumptions are pinned down, and the economy's stochastic discount factor becomes exogenous. Furthermore, since the exogenous output-consumption process also represents the process for the market portfolio's aggregate dividends, that too is exogenous. This makes it easy to solve for the equilibrium price of the market portfolio.

In contrast, a *production* economy is, in a sense, the polar opposite of an endowment economy. A production economy allows for an aggregate consumption-savings (investment) decision. Not all of current output need be consumed, but some can be physically invested to produce more output using constant returns to scale (linear) production technologies. The random distribution of rates of return on these productive technologies is assumed to be exogenous. Assets can be interpreted as ownership claims on these technological processes and, therefore, their supplies are perfectly elastic, varying in accordance to the individual's reinvestment decision. Hence, the main difference between production and endowment economies is that production economies pin down assets' rates of return distribution and make consumption (and output) endogenous, whereas endowment economies pin down consumption and make assets' rates of return distribution endogenous. Probably the best-known asset pricing model based on a production economy was derived by John C. Cox, Jonathan E. Ingersoll, and Stephen A. Ross (Cox, Ingersoll, and Ross 1985a). We will study this continuous-time, general equilibrium model in Chapter 13.

6.2.1 Including Dividends in Asset Returns

The Lucas model builds on the multiperiod, time-separable utility model of consumption and portfolio choice. We continue with the stochastic discount factor pricing relationship of equation (6.7) but put more structure on the returns of each asset. Let the return on the ith risky asset, R_{it}, include a dividend payment made at date $t + 1$, $d_{i,t+1}$, along with a capital gain, $P_{i,t+1} - P_{it}$. Hence, P_{it} denotes the ex-dividend price of the risky asset at date t:

$$R_{it} = \frac{d_{i,t+1} + P_{i,t+1}}{P_{it}} \tag{6.11}$$

Substituting (6.11) into (6.7) and rearranging gives

$$P_{it} = E_t \left[\frac{U_C \left(C_{t+1}^*, t + 1 \right)}{U_C \left(C_t^*, t \right)} \left(d_{i,t+1} + P_{i,t+1} \right) \right] \tag{6.12}$$

Similar to what was done in equation (6.8), if we substitute for $P_{i,t+1}$ using equation (6.12) updated one period, and use the properties of conditional expectation, we have

$$P_{it} = E_t \left[\frac{U_C \left(C_{t+1}^*, t+1 \right)}{U_C \left(C_t^*, t \right)} \left(d_{i,t+1} + \frac{U_C \left(C_{t+2}^*, t+2 \right)}{U_C \left(C_{t+1}^*, t+1 \right)} \left(d_{i,t+2} + P_{i,t+2} \right) \right) \right]$$

$$= E_t \left[\frac{U_C \left(C_{t+1}^*, t+1 \right)}{U_C \left(C_t^*, t \right)} d_{i,t+1} + \frac{U_C \left(C_{t+2}^*, t+2 \right)}{U_C \left(C_t^*, t \right)} \left(d_{i,t+2} + P_{i,t+2} \right) \right]$$

$$(6.13)$$

Repeating this type of substitution, that is, solving forward the difference equation (6.13), gives us

$$P_{it} = E_t \left[\sum_{j=1}^{T} \frac{U_C \left(C_{t+j}^*, t+j \right)}{U_C \left(C_t^*, t \right)} d_{i,t+j} + \frac{U_C \left(C_{t+T}^*, t+T \right)}{U_C \left(C_t^*, t \right)} P_{i,t+T} \right] \qquad (6.14)$$

where the integer T reflects a large number of future periods. Now suppose utility reflects a rate of time preference, so that $U \left(C_t, t \right) = \delta^t u \left(C_t \right)$, where $\delta = \frac{1}{1+\rho} < 1$, so that the rate of time preference $\rho > 0$. Then (6.14) becomes

$$P_{it} = E_t \left[\sum_{j=1}^{T} \delta^j \frac{u_C \left(C_{t+j}^* \right)}{u_C \left(C_t^* \right)} d_{i,t+j} + \delta^T \frac{u_C \left(C_{t+T}^* \right)}{u_C \left(C_t^* \right)} P_{i,t+T} \right] \qquad (6.15)$$

If we have an infinitely lived individual or, equivalently, an individual whose utility includes a bequest that depends on the utility of his or her offspring, then we can consider the solution to (6.15) as the planning horizon, T, goes to infinity. If $\lim_{T\to\infty} E_t \left[\delta^T \frac{u_C(C_{t+T}^*)}{u_C(C_t^*)} P_{i,t+T} \right] = 0$, which (as discussed in the next section) is equivalent to assuming the absence of a speculative price "bubble," then

$$P_{it} = E_t \left[\sum_{j=1}^{\infty} \delta^j \frac{u_C \left(C_{t+j}^* \right)}{u_C \left(C_t^* \right)} d_{i,t+j} \right]$$

$$= E_t \left[\sum_{j=1}^{\infty} m_{t,t+j} d_{i,t+j} \right] \qquad (6.16)$$

Equation (6.16) is a present value formula, where the stochastic discount factors are the marginal rates of substitution between the present and the dates when the dividends are paid. This "discounted dividend" asset pricing formula holds for any individual following an optimal consumption–portfolio choice policy. Thus far, we have not made any strong assumptions about consumer homogeneity or the structure of the economy. For example, equation (6.16) would hold for a production economy with heterogeneous individuals.

6.2.2 Equating Dividends to Consumption

The Lucas model makes equation (6.16) into a general equilibrium model of asset pricing by assuming there is an infinitely lived *representative* individual, meaning that all individuals are identical with respect to utility and initial wealth. It also assumes that each asset is a claim on a real output process, where risky asset i pays a real dividend of d_{it} at date t. Moreover, the dividend from each asset is assumed to come in the form of a nonstorable consumption good that cannot be reinvested. In other words, this dividend output cannot be transformed into new investment in order to expand the scale of production. The only use for each asset's output is consumption. A share of risky asset i can be interpreted as an ownership claim on an exogenous dividend-output process that is fixed in supply. Assuming no wage income, it then follows that aggregate consumption at each date must equal the total dividends paid by all of the n assets at that date:

$$C_t^* = \sum_{i=1}^{n} d_{it} \tag{6.17}$$

Given the assumption of a representative individual, this individual's consumption can be equated to aggregate consumption.[3]

6.2.3 Asset Pricing Examples

With these endowment economy assumptions, the specific form of utility for the representative agent and the assumed distribution of the assets' dividend processes fully determine equilibrium asset prices. For example, if the representative individual is risk-neutral, so that u_C is a constant, then (6.16) becomes

$$P_{it} = E_t \left[\sum_{j=1}^{\infty} \delta^j d_{i,t+j} \right] \tag{6.18}$$

---

3. If one assumes that there are many representative individuals, each will have identical per capita consumption and receive identical per capita dividends. Hence, in (6.17), C_t^* and d_{it} can be interpreted as per capita quantities.

In words, the price of risky asset i is the expected value of dividends discounted by a constant factor, reflecting the constant rate of time preference.

Consider another example where utility is logarithmic, $u(C_t) = \ln C_t$. Also denote $d_t = \sum_{i=1}^{n} d_{it}$ to be the economy's aggregate dividends, which we know by (6.17) equals aggregate consumption. Then the price of risky asset i is given by

$$P_{it} = E_t \left[\sum_{j=1}^{\infty} \delta^j \frac{C_t^*}{C_{t+j}^*} d_{i,t+j} \right]$$

$$= E_t \left[\sum_{j=1}^{\infty} \delta^j \frac{d_t}{d_{t+j}} d_{i,t+j} \right] \tag{6.19}$$

Given assumptions regarding the distribution of the individual assets, the expectation in (6.19) can be computed. However, under this logarithmic utility assumption, we can obtain the price of the market portfolio of all assets even without any distributional assumptions. To see this, let P_t represent a claim on aggregate dividends. Then (6.19) becomes

$$P_t = E_t \left[\sum_{j=1}^{\infty} \delta^j \frac{d_t}{d_{t+j}} d_{t+j} \right]$$

$$= d_t \frac{\delta}{1 - \delta} \tag{6.20}$$

implying that the value of the market portfolio moves in step with the current level of dividends. It does not depend on the distribution of future dividends. Why? Higher expected future dividends, d_{t+j}, are exactly offset by a lower expected marginal utility of consumption, $m_{t,t+j} = \delta^j d_t/d_{t+j}$, leaving the value of a claim on this output process unchanged. This is consistent with our earlier results showing that a log utility individual's savings (and consumption) are independent of the distribution of asset returns. Since aggregate savings equals the aggregate demand for the market portfolio, no change in savings implies no change in asset demand. Note that this will not be the case for the more general specification of power (constant relative-risk-aversion) utility. If $u(C_t) = C_t^\gamma/\gamma$, then

$$P_t = E_t \left[\sum_{j=1}^{\infty} \delta^j \left(\frac{d_{t+j}}{d_t} \right)^{\gamma - 1} d_{t+j} \right]$$

$$= d_t^{1-\gamma} E_t \left[\sum_{j=1}^{\infty} \delta^j d_{t+j}^\gamma \right] \tag{6.21}$$

which does depend on the distribution of future aggregate dividends (output). Note from (6.21) that for the case of certainty $(E_t[d_{t+j}^\gamma] = d_{t+j}^\gamma)$, when $\gamma < 0$, higher future aggregate dividends reduce the value of the market portfolio; that is, $\partial P_t / \partial d_{t+j} = \gamma \delta^j (d_{t+j}/d_t)^{\gamma-1} < 0$. While this seems counterintuitive, recall that for $\gamma < 0$, individuals desire less savings (and more current consumption) when investment opportunities improve. Since current consumption is fixed at d_t in this endowment economy, the only way to bring higher desired consumption back down to d_t is for total wealth to decrease. In equilibrium, this occurs when the price of the market portfolio falls as individuals attempt to sell some of their portfolio in an (unsuccessful) attempt to raise consumption. Of course, the reverse story occurs when $0 < \gamma < 1$, as a desired rise in savings is offset by an increase in wealth via an appreciation of the market portfolio.

If we continue to assume power utility, we can also derive the value of a hypothetical riskless asset that pays a one-period dividend of \$1:

$$P_{ft} = \frac{1}{R_{ft}} = \delta E_t \left[\left(\frac{d_{t+1}}{d_t} \right)^{\gamma-1} \right] \tag{6.22}$$

Using aggregate U.S. consumption data, Rajnish Mehra and Edward C. Prescott (Mehra and Prescott 1985) used equations such as (6.21) and (6.22) with $d_t = C_t^*$ to see if a reasonable value of γ would produce a risk premium (excess average return over a risk-free return) for a market portfolio of U.S. common stocks that matched these stocks' historical average excess returns. They found that for reasonable values of γ, they could not come close to the historical risk premium, which at that time they estimated to be around 6 percent. They described this finding as the *equity premium puzzle*. As mentioned in Chapter 4, the problem is that for reasonable levels of risk aversion, aggregate consumption appears to vary too little to justify the high Sharpe ratio for the market portfolio of stocks. The moment conditions in (6.21) and (6.22) require a highly negative value of γ to fit the data.

6.2.4 A Lucas Model with Labor Income

The Lucas endowment economy model has been modified to study a wide array of issues. For example, Gurdip Bakshi and Zhiwu Chen (Bakshi and Chen 1996) studied a monetary endowment economy by assuming that a representative individual obtains utility from both real consumption and real money balances. In future chapters, we will present other examples of Lucas-type economies where utility is non-time-separable and where utility reflects psychological biases. In this section, we present a simplified version of a model by Stephen Cecchetti, Pok-sang

Lam, and Nelson Mark (Cecchetti, Lam, and Mark 1993) that modifies the Lucas model to consider nontraded labor income.[4]

As before, suppose that there is a representative agent whose financial wealth consists of a market portfolio of traded assets that pays an aggregate real dividend of d_t at date t. We continue to assume that these assets are in fixed supply and their dividend consists of a nonstorable consumption good. However, now we also permit each individual to be endowed with nontradeable human capital that is fixed in supply. The agent's return to human capital consists of a wage payment of y_t at date t that also takes the form of the nonstorable consumption good. Hence, equilibrium per capita consumption will equal

$$C_t^* = d_t + y_t \tag{6.23}$$

so that it is no longer the case that equilibrium consumption equals dividends. However, assuming constant relative-risk-aversion utility, the value of the market portfolio can still be written in terms of future consumption and dividends:

$$
\begin{aligned}
P_t &= E_t \left[\sum_{j=1}^{\infty} \delta^j \frac{u_C\left(C_{t+j}^*\right)}{u_C\left(C_t^*\right)} d_{t+j} \right] \\
&= E_t \left[\sum_{j=1}^{\infty} \delta^j \left(\frac{C_{t+j}^*}{C_t^*} \right)^{\gamma-1} d_{t+j} \right]
\end{aligned}
\tag{6.24}
$$

Because wage income creates a difference between aggregate dividends and equilibrium consumption, its presence allows us to assume separate random processes for dividends and consumption. For example, one might assume dividends and equilibrium consumption follow the lognormal processes:

$$\ln\left(C_{t+1}^*/C_t^*\right) = \mu_c + \sigma_c \eta_{t+1} \tag{6.25}$$

$$\ln\left(d_{t+1}/d_t\right) = \mu_d + \sigma_d \varepsilon_{t+1}$$

where the error terms are serially uncorrelated and distributed as

$$\begin{pmatrix} \eta_t \\ \varepsilon_t \end{pmatrix} \sim N\left(\begin{pmatrix} 0 \\ 0 \end{pmatrix}, \begin{pmatrix} 1 & \rho \\ \rho & 1 \end{pmatrix} \right) \tag{6.26}$$

---

4. They use a regime-switching version of this model to analyze the equity premium and risk-free rate puzzles. Based on Generalized Method of Moments (GMM) tests, they find that their model fits the first moments of the risk-free rate and the return to equity, but not the second moments.

It is left as an end-of-chapter exercise to show that with these assumptions regarding the distributions of C^*_{t+j} and d_{t+j}, when $\delta e^\alpha < 1$ one can compute the expectation in (6.24) to be

$$P_t = d_t \frac{\delta e^\alpha}{1 - \delta e^\alpha} \tag{6.27}$$

where

$$\alpha \equiv \mu_d - (1-\gamma)\,\mu_c + \frac{1}{2}\left[(1-\gamma)^2\,\sigma_c^2 + \sigma_d^2\right] - (1-\gamma)\,\rho\sigma_c\sigma_d \tag{6.28}$$

We can confirm that (6.27) equals (6.20) when $\gamma = 0$, $\mu_d = \mu_c$, $\sigma_c = \sigma_d$, and $\rho = 1$, which is the special case of log utility and no labor income. With no labor income ($\mu_d = \mu_c$, $\sigma_c = \sigma_d$, $\rho = 1$) but $\gamma \neq 0$, we have $\alpha = \gamma\mu_c + \frac{1}{2}\gamma^2\sigma_c^2$, which is increasing in the growth rate of dividends (and consumption) when $\gamma > 0$. As discussed in Chapter 4, this occurs because greater dividend growth leads individuals to desire increased savings since they have high intertemporal elasticity ($\varepsilon = 1/(1-\gamma) > 1$). An increase in desired savings reflects the substitution effect exceeding the income or wealth effect. Market clearing then requires the value of the market portfolio to rise, raising income or wealth to make desired consumption rise to equal the fixed supply. The reverse occurs when $\gamma < 0$, as the income or wealth effect will exceed the substitution effect.

For the general case of labor income where α is given by equation (6.28), note that a lower correlation between consumption and dividends (decline in ρ) increases α. Since $\partial P_t / \partial \alpha > 0$, this lower correlation raises the value of the market portfolio. Intuitively, this greater demand for the market portfolio results because it provides better diversification with uncertain labor income.

6.3 Rational Asset Price Bubbles

In this section we examine whether there are solutions other than (6.16) that can satisfy the asset price difference equation (6.15). Indeed, we will show that there are and that these alternative solutions can be interpreted as *bubble* solutions where the asset price deviates from its fundamental value. Potentially, these bubble solutions may be of interest because there appear to be numerous historical episodes during which movements in asset prices appear inconsistent with reasonable dynamics for dividends or outputs. In other words, assets do not appear to be valued according to their fundamentals. Examples include the Dutch tulip bulb bubble during the 1620s, the Japanese stock price bubble during the late 1980s, and the U.S. stock price bubble (particularly Internet-related stocks) during the late 1990s.[5] While some may conclude that these bubbles represent direct evidence of irrational behavior on the part of individual investors, might an argument be made that bubbles could be consistent with rational actions and beliefs? It is this possibility that we now consider.[6]

Let us start by defining $p_t \equiv P_{it} u_C (C_t)$ as the product of the asset price and the marginal utility of consumption, excluding the time preference discount factor, δ. Then equation (6.12) can be written as the difference equation:

$$E_t \left[p_{t+1} \right] = \delta^{-1} p_t - E_t \left[u_C \left(C_{t+1}^* \right) d_{i,t+1} \right] \tag{6.29}$$

where $\delta^{-1} = 1 + \rho > 1$ with ρ being the individual's subjective rate of time preference. The solution (6.16) to this equation is referred to as the *fundamental* solution. Let us denote it as f_t:

$$p_t = f_t \equiv E_t \left[\sum_{j=1}^{\infty} \delta^j u_C \left(C_{t+j}^* \right) d_{i,t+j} \right] \tag{6.30}$$

The sum in (6.30) converges as long as the marginal utility–weighted dividends are expected to grow more slowly than the time preference discount factor. For the Lucas endowment economy, assumptions regarding the form of utility and the distribution of the assets' dividends can ensure that this solution has a finite value.

While f_t satisfies (6.29), it is not the only solution. Solutions that satisfy (6.29) take the general form $p_t = f_t + b_t$, where the *bubble* component of the solution is any process that satisfies

$$E_t \left[b_{t+1} \right] = \delta^{-1} b_t \tag{6.31}$$

This is easily verified by substitution into (6.29):

$$E_t \left[f_{t+1} + b_{t+1} \right] = \delta^{-1} \left(f_t + b_t \right) - E_t \left[u_C \left(C_{t+1}^* \right) d_{i,t+1} \right]$$

$$E_t \left[f_{t+1} \right] + E_t \left[b_{t+1} \right] = \delta^{-1} f_t + \delta^{-1} b_t - E_t \left[u_C \left(C_{t+1}^* \right) d_{i,t+1} \right]$$

$$E_t \left[b_{t+1} \right] = \delta^{-1} b_t \tag{6.32}$$

---

5. Charles P. Kindleberger (Kindleberger 2001) gives an entertaining account of numerous asset price bubbles.

6. Of course, another possibility is that asset prices always equal their fundamental values, and sudden rises and falls in these prices reflect sudden changes in perceived fundamentals.

where in the last line of (6.32), we use the fact that f_t satisfies the difference equation. Note that since $\delta^{-1} > 1$, b_t explodes in expected value:

$$\lim_{i \to \infty} E_t \left[b_{t+i} \right] = \lim_{i \to \infty} \delta^{-i} b_t = \begin{cases} +\infty \text{ if } b_t > 0 \\ -\infty \text{ if } b_t < 0 \end{cases} \tag{6.33}$$

The exploding nature of b_t provides a rationale for interpreting the general solution $p_t = f_t + b_t$, $b_t \neq 0$, as a bubble solution. Only when $b_t = 0$ do we get the fundamental solution.

6.3.1 Examples of Bubble Solutions

Suppose that b_t follows a deterministic time trend; that is,

$$b_t = b_0 \delta^{-t} \tag{6.34}$$

Then the solution

$$p_t = f_t + b_0 \delta^{-t} \tag{6.35}$$

implies that the marginal utility–weighted asset price grows exponentially forever. In other words, we have an ever-expanding speculative bubble.

Next, consider a possibly more realistic modeling of a "bursting" bubble proposed by Olivier Blanchard (Blanchard 1979):

$$b_{t+1} = \begin{cases} (\delta q)^{-1} b_t + e_{t+1} & \text{with probability } q \\ z_{t+1} & \text{with probability } 1 - q \end{cases} \tag{6.36}$$

with $E_t \left[e_{t+1} \right] = E_t \left[z_{t+1} \right] = 0$. Note that this process satisfies the condition in (6.31), so that $p_t = f_t + b_t$ is again a valid bubble solution. In this case, the bubble continues with probability q each period but "bursts" with probability $1 - q$. If it bursts, it returns in expected value to zero, but then a new bubble would start. To compensate for the probability of a "crash," the expected return, conditional on not crashing, is higher than in the previous example of a never-ending bubble. The disturbance e_t allows bubbles to have additional noise and allows new bubbles to begin after the previous bubble has crashed. This bursting bubble model can be generalized to allow q to be stochastic.[7]

6.3.2 The Likelihood of Rational Bubbles

While these examples of bubble solutions indeed satisfy the asset pricing difference equation in (6.29), there may be additional economic considerations that rule

---

7. The reader is asked to show this in an exercise at the end of the chapter.

them out. One issue involves negative bubbles, that is, cases where $b_t < 0$. From (6.33) we see that individuals must expect that, at some future date $\tau > t$, the marginal utility–weighted price $p_\tau = f_\tau + b_\tau$ will become negative. Of course, since marginal utility is always positive, this implies that the asset price, $P_{it} = p_t/u_C\left(C_t\right)$, will also be negative. A negative price would be inconsistent with limited-liability securities, such as typical shareholders' equity (stocks). Moreover, if an individual can freely dispose of an asset, its price cannot be negative. Hence, negative bubbles can be ruled out.

Based on similar reasoning, Behzad Diba and Herschel Grossman (Diba and Grossman 1988) argue that many types of bubble processes, including bubbles that burst and start again, can also be ruled out. Their argument is as follows. Note that the general process for a bubble can be written as

$$b_t = \delta^{-t}b_0 + \sum_{s=1}^{t} \delta^{s-t}\varepsilon_s \tag{6.37}$$

where ε_s, $s = 1, \dots, t$ are mean-zero innovations. To avoid negative values of b_t (and negative expected future prices), realizations of ε_t must satisfy

$$\varepsilon_t \geq -\delta^{-1}b_{t-1}, \forall t \geq 0 \tag{6.38}$$

For example, suppose that $b_t = 0$, implying that, at the current date t, a bubble does not exist. Then from (6.38) and the requirement that ε_{t+1} have mean zero, it must be the case that $\varepsilon_{t+1} = 0$ with probability 1. This implies that if a bubble currently does not exist, it cannot get started next period or at any future period. The only possibility would be if a positive bubble existed on the first day of trading of the asset; that is, $b_0 > 0$.[8] Moreover, the bursting and then restarting bubble in (6.36) could only avoid a negative value of b_{t+1} if $z_{t+1} = 0$ with probability 1 and $e_{t+1} = 0$ whenever $b_t = 0$. Hence, this type of bubble would need to be positive on the first trading day, and once it bursts it could never restart.

Note, however, that arbitrage trading is unlikely to be a strong argument against a bursting bubble. While short-selling an asset with $b_t > 0$ would result in a profit when the bubble bursts, the short-seller could incur substantial losses beforehand. Over the near term, if the bubble continues, the market value of the short-seller's position could become sufficiently negative so as to wipe out his personal wealth.

Other arguments have been used to rule out positive bubbles. Similar to the assumptions underlying the Lucas model of the previous section, Jean Tirole

---

8. An implication is that an initial public offering (IPO) of stock should have a first-day market price that is above its fundamental value. Interestingly, Jay Ritter (Ritter 1991) documents that many IPOs initially appear to be overpriced since their subsequent returns tend to be lower than comparable stocks.

(Tirole 1982) considers a situation with a finite number of rational individuals and where the dividend processes for risky assets are exogenously given. In such an economy, individuals who trade assets at other than their fundamental prices are playing a zero-sum game, since the aggregate amounts of consumption and wealth are exogenous. Trading assets at prices having a bubble component only transfers claims on this fixed supply of wealth between individuals. Hence, a rational individual will not purchase an asset whose price already reflects a positive bubble component. This is because at a positive price, previous traders in the asset have already realized their gains and left a negative-sum game to the subsequent traders. The notion that an individual would believe that he can buy an asset at a positive bubble price and later sell it to another at a price reflecting an even greater bubble component might be considered a "greater fool" theory of speculative bubbles. However, this theory is not consistent with a finite number of fully rational individuals in most economic settings. Manual Santos and Michael Woodford (Santos and Woodford 1997) consider the possibility of speculative bubbles in a wide variety of economies, including those with overlapping generations of individuals. They conclude that the conditions necessary for rational speculative bubbles to exist are relatively fragile. Under fairly general assumptions, equilibria displaying rational price bubbles can be excluded.[9]

6.4   Summary

When individuals choose lifetime consumption and portfolio holdings in an optimal fashion, a multiperiod stochastic discount factor can be used to price assets. This is an important generalization of our earlier single-period pricing result. We also demonstrated that if an asset's dividends (cashflows) are modeled explicitly, the asset's price satisfies a discounted dividend formula. The Lucas endowment economy model took this discounted dividend formula a step further by equating aggregate dividends to aggregate consumption. This simplified valuing a claim on aggregate dividends, since now the value of this market portfolio could be expressed as an expectation of a function of only the future dividend (output) process.

   In an infinite horizon model, the possibility of rational asset price bubbles needs to be considered. In general, there are multiple solutions for the price of a risky asset. Bubble solutions represent nonstationary alternatives to the asset's

---

9. Of course, other considerations that are not fully consistent with rationality may give rise to bubbles. José Scheinkman and Wei Xiong (Scheinkman and Xiong 2003) present a model where individuals with heterogeneous beliefs think that particular information is more informative of asset fundamentals than it truly is. Bubbles arise due to a premium reflecting the option to sell assets to the more optimistic individuals.

fundamental value. However, when additional aspects of the economic environment are considered, the conditions that would give rise to rational bubbles appear to be rare.

6.5 Exercises

1. Two individuals agree at date 0 to a forward contract that matures at date 2. The contract is written on an underlying asset that pays a dividend at date 1 equal to D_1. Let f_2 be the date 2 random payoff (profit) to the individual who is the long party in the forward contract. Also let m_{0i} be the stochastic discount factor over the period from dates 0 to i where $i = 1, 2$, and let $E_0 [\cdot]$ be the expectations operator at date 0. What is the value of $E_0 [m_{02} f_2]$? Explain your answer.

2. Assume that there is an economy populated by infinitely lived representative individuals who maximize the lifetime utility function

$$E_0 \left[\sum_{t=0}^{\infty} -\delta^t e^{-ac_t} \right]$$

where c_t is consumption at date t and $a > 0$, $0 < \delta < 1$. The economy is a Lucas endowment economy (Lucas 1978) having multiple risky assets paying date t dividends that total d_t per capita. Write down an expression for the equilibrium per capita price of the market portfolio in terms of the assets' future dividends.

3. For the Lucas model with labor income, show that assumptions (6.25) and (6.26) lead to the pricing relationship of equations (6.27) and (6.28).

4. Consider a special case of the model of rational speculative bubbles discussed in this chapter. Assume that infinitely lived investors are risk-neutral and that there is an asset paying a constant, one-period risk-free return of $R_f = \delta^{-1} > 1$. There is also an infinitely lived risky asset with price p_t at date t. The risky asset is assumed to pay a dividend of d_t that is declared at date t and paid at the end of the period, date $t + 1$. Consider the price $p_t = f_t + b_t$ where

$$f_t = \sum_{i=0}^{\infty} \frac{E_t [d_{t+i}]}{R_f^{i+1}} \tag{6.39}$$

and

$$b_{t+1} = \begin{cases} \frac{R_f}{q_t} b_t + e_{t+1} & \text{with probability } q_t \\ z_{t+1} & \text{with probability } 1 - q_t \end{cases} \tag{6.40}$$

where $E_t \left[e_{t+1} \right] = E_t \left[z_{t+1} \right] = 0$ and where q_t is a random variable as of date $t-1$ but realized at date t and is uniformly distributed between 0 and 1.

a. Show whether or not $p_t = f_t + b_t$, subject to the specifications in (1) and (2), is a valid solution for the price of the risky asset.

b. Suppose that p_t is the price of a barrel of oil. If $p_t \geq p_{solar}$, then solar energy, which is in perfectly elastic supply, becomes an economically efficient perfect substitute for oil. Can a rational speculative bubble exist for the price of oil? Explain why or why not.

c. Suppose p_t is the price of a bond that matures at date $T < \infty$. In this context, the d_t for $t \leq T$ denotes the bond's coupon and principal payments. Can a rational speculative bubble exist for the price of this bond? Explain why or why not.

5. Consider an endowment economy with representative agents who maximize the following objective function:

$$\max_{C_s, \{\omega_{is}\}, \forall s, i} E_t \left[\sum_{s=t}^{T} \delta^s u \left(C_s \right) \right]$$

where $T < \infty$. Explain why a rational speculative asset price bubble could not exist in such an economy.

PART III

CONTINGENT CLAIMS PRICING

CHAPTER 7

Basics of Derivative Pricing

Chapter 4 showed how general pricing relationships for contingent claims could be derived in terms of an equilibrium stochastic discount factor or in terms of elementary securities. This chapter takes a more detailed look at this important area of asset pricing.[1] The field of contingent claims pricing experienced explosive growth following the seminal work on option pricing by Fischer Black and Myron Scholes (Black and Scholes 1973) and by Robert Merton (Merton 1973b). Research on contingent claims valuation and hedging continues to expand, with significant contributions coming from both academics and finance practitioners. This research is driving and is being driven by innovations in financial markets. Because research has given new insights into how potential contingent securities might be priced and hedged, financial service providers are more willing to introduce such securities to the market. In addition, existing contingent securities motivate further research by academics and practitioners whose goal is to improve the pricing and hedging of these securities.

We begin by considering two major categories of contingent claims, namely, forward contracts and option contracts. These securities are called *derivatives* because their cashflows derive from another "underlying" variable, such as an

---

1. The topics in this chapter are covered in greater detail in undergraduate and masters-level financial derivatives texts such as (McDonald 2002) and (Hull 2000). Readers with a background in derivatives at this level may wish to skip this chapter. For others without this knowledge, this chapter is meant to present some fundamentals of derivatives that provide a foundation for more advanced topics covered in later chapters.

asset price, interest rate, or exchange rate.[2] For the case of a derivative whose underlying is an asset price, we will show that the absence of arbitrage opportunities places restrictions on the derivative's value relative to that of its underlying asset.[3] In the case of forward contracts, arbitrage considerations alone may lead to an exact pricing formula. However, in the case of options, these no-arbitrage restrictions cannot determine an exact price for the derivative, but only bounds on the option's price. An exact option pricing formula requires additional assumptions regarding the probability distribution of the underlying asset's returns. The second section of this chapter illustrates how options can be priced using the well-known binomial option pricing technique. This is followed by a section covering different binomial model applications.

The next section begins with a reexamination of forward contracts and how they are priced. We then compare them to option contracts and analyze how the absence of arbitrage opportunities restricts option values.

7.1   Forward and Option Contracts

Chapter 3's discussion of arbitrage derived the link between spot and forward contracts for foreign exchange. Now we show how that result can be generalized to valuing forward contracts on any dividend-paying asset. Following this, we compare option contracts to forward contracts and see how arbitrage places limits on option prices.

7.1.1   Forward Contracts on Assets Paying Dividends

Similar to the notation introduced previously, let $F_{0\tau}$ be the current date 0 forward price for exchanging one share of an underlying asset τ periods in the future. Recall that this forward price represents the price agreed to at date 0 but to be paid at future date $\tau > 0$ for delivery at date τ of one share of the asset. The long (*short*) party in a forward contract agrees to purchase (*deliver*) the underlying asset in return for paying (*receiving*) the forward price. Hence, the date $\tau > 0$ payoff to the long party in this forward contract is $S_\tau - F_{0\tau}$, where S_τ is the spot price of one share of the underlying asset at the maturity date of the contract.[4] The short party's payoff is simply the negative of the long party's payoff. When the forward contract is initiated at date 0, the parties set the forward price, $F_{0\tau}$, to make the value of the contract equal zero. That is, by setting $F_{0\tau}$ at date 0,

---

2. Derivatives have been written on a wide assortment of other variables, including commodity prices, weather conditions, catastrophic insurance losses, and credit (default) losses.

3. Thus, our approach is in the spirit of considering the underlying asset as an elementary security and using no-arbitrage restrictions to derive implications for the derivative's price.

4. Obviously S_τ is, in general, random as of date 0 while $F_{0\tau}$ is known as of date 0.

the parties agree to the contract without one of them needing to make an initial payment to the other.

Let $R_f > 1$ be one plus the per-period risk-free rate for borrowing or lending over the time interval from date 0 to date τ. Also, let us allow for the possibility that the underlying asset might pay dividends during the life of the forward contract, and use the notation D to denote the date 0 present value of dividends paid by the underlying asset over the period from date 0 to date τ.[5] The asset's dividends over the life of the forward contract are assumed to be known at the initial date 0, so that D can be computed by discounting each dividend payment at the appropriate date 0 risk-free rate corresponding to the time until the dividend payment is made. In the analysis that follows, we also assume that risk-free interest rates are nonrandom, though most of our results in this section and the next continue to hold when interest rates are assumed to change randomly through time.[6]

Now we can derive the equilibrium forward price, $F_{0\tau}$, to which the long and short parties must agree in order for there to be no arbitrage opportunities. This is done by showing that the long forward contract's date τ payoffs can be exactly replicated by trading in the underlying asset and the risk-free asset. Then we argue that in the absence of arbitrage, the date 0 values of the forward contract and the replicating trades must be the same.

The following table outlines the cashflows of a long forward contract as well as the trades that would exactly replicate its date τ payoffs.

Date 0 Trade	Date 0 Cashflow	Date τ Cashflow
Long Forward Contract	0	$S_\tau - F_{0\tau}$
Replicating Trades		
1) Buy Asset and Sell Dividends	$-S_0 + D$	S_τ
2) Borrow	$R_f^{-\tau} F_{0\tau}$	$-F_{0\tau}$
Net Cashflow	$-S_0 + D + R_f^{-\tau} F_{0\tau}$	$S_\tau - F_{0\tau}$

Note that the payoff of the long forward party involves two cashflows: a positive cashflow of S_τ, which is random as of date 0, and a negative cashflow equal to $-F_{0\tau}$, which is certain as of date 0. The former cashflow can be replicated

---

5. In our context, "dividends" refer to any cashflows paid by the asset. For the case of a coupon-paying bond, the cashflows would be its coupon payments.

6. This is especially true for cases in which the underlying asset pays no dividends over the life of the contract, that is, $D = 0$. Also, some results can generalize to cases where the underlying asset pays dividends that are random, such as the case when dividend payments are proportional to the asset's value.

by purchasing one share of the underlying asset but selling ownership of the dividends paid by the asset between dates 0 and τ.[7] This would cost $S_0 - D$, where S_0 is the date 0 spot price of one share of the underlying asset. The latter cashflow can be replicated by borrowing the discounted value of $F_{0\tau}$. This would generate current revenue of $R_f^{-\tau} F_{0\tau}$. Therefore, the net cost of replicating the long party's cashflow is $S_0 - D - R_f^{-\tau} F_{0\tau}$. In the absence of arbitrage, this cost must be the same as the cost of initiating the long position in the forward contract, which is zero.[8] Hence, we obtain the no-arbitrage condition

$$S_0 - D - R_f^{-\tau} F_{0\tau} = 0 \tag{7.1}$$

or

$$F_{0\tau} = (S_0 - D)\, R_f^{\tau} \tag{7.2}$$

Equation (7.2) determines the equilibrium forward price of the contract. Note that if this contract had been initiated at a previous date, say, date -1, at the forward price $F_{-1\tau} = X$, then the date 0 value (replacement cost) of the long party's payoff, which we denote as f_0, would still be the cost of replicating the two cashflows:

$$f_0 = S_0 - D - R_f^{-\tau} X \tag{7.3}$$

---

7. In the absence of an explict market for selling the assets' dividends, the individual could borrow the present value of dividends, D, and repay this loan at the future dates when the dividends are received. This will generate a date 0 cashflow of D, and net future cashflows of zero since the dividend payments exactly cover the loan repayments.

8. If $S_0 - D - R_f^{-\tau} F_{0\tau} < 0$, the arbitrage would be to perform the following trades at date 0: 1) purchase one share of the stock and sell ownership of the dividends; 2) borrow $R_f^{-\tau} F_{0\tau}$; 3) take a short position in the forward contract. The date 0 net cashflow of these three transactions is $-(S_0 - D) + R_f^{-\tau} F_{0\tau} + 0 > 0$, by assumption. At date τ the individual would: 1) deliver the one share of the stock to satisfy the short forward position; 2) receive $F_{0\tau}$ as payment for delivering this one share of stock; 3) repay borrowing equal to $F_{0\tau}$. The date τ net cashflow of these three transactions is $0 + F_{0\tau} - F_{0\tau} = 0$. Hence, this arbitrage generates a positive cashflow at date 0 and a zero cashflow at date τ. Conversely, if $S_0 - D - R_f^{-\tau} F_{0\tau} > 0$, an arbitrage would be to perform the following trades at date 0: 1) short-sell one share of the stock and purchase rights to the dividends to be paid to the lender of the stock (in the absence of an explict market for buying the assets' dividends, the individual could lend out the present value of dividends, D, and receive payment on this loan at the future dates when the dividends are to be paid); 2) lend $R_f^{-\tau} F_{0\tau}$; 3) take a long position in the forward contract. The date 0 net cashflow of these three transactions is $(S_0 - D) - R_f^{-\tau} F_{0\tau} + 0 > 0$, by assumption. At date τ the individual would: 1) obtain one share of the stock from the long forward position and deliver it to satisfy the short sale obligation; 2) pay $F_{0\tau}$ to short party in forward contract; 3) receive $F_{0\tau}$ from lending agreement. The date τ net cashflow of these three transactions is $0 - F_{0\tau} + F_{0\tau} = 0$. Hence, this arbitrage generates a positive cashflow at date 0 and a zero cashflow at date τ.

However, as long as date 0 is following the initiation of the contract, the value of the payoff would not, in general, equal zero. Of course, the replacement cost of the short party's payoff would be simply $-f_0 = R_f^{-\tau} X + D - S_0$.

It should be pointed out that our derivation of the forward price in equation (7.2) did not require any assumption regarding the random distribution of the underlying asset price, S_τ. The reason for this is due to our ability to replicate the forward contract's payoff using a *static replication* strategy: all trades needed to replicate the forward contract's date τ payoff were done at the initial date 0. As we shall see, such a static replication strategy is not possible, in general, when pricing other contingent claims such as options. Replicating option payoffs will entail, in general, a *dynamic replication* strategy: trades to replicate an option's payoff at date τ will involve trades at multiple dates during the interval between dates 0 and τ. As will be shown, such a dynamic trading strategy requires some assumptions regarding the stochastic properties of the underlying asset's price. Typically, assumptions are made that result in the markets for the contingent claim and the underlying asset being dynamically complete.

As a prerequisite to these issues of option valuation, let us first discuss the basic features of option contracts and compare their payoffs to those of forward contracts.[9]

7.1.2 Basic Characteristics of Option Prices

The owner of a *call* option has the right, but not the obligation, to buy a given asset in the future at a pre-agreed price, known as the *exercise* price, or *strike* price. Similarly, the owner of a *put* option has the right, but not the obligation, to sell a given asset in the future at a pre-agreed price. For each owner (buyer) of an option, there is an option seller, also referred to as the option *writer*. If the owner of a call (*put*) option chooses to exercise, the seller must deliver (*receive*) the underlying asset or commodity in return for receiving (*paying*) the pre-agreed exercise price. Since an option always has a nonnegative payoff to the owner, this buyer of the option must make an initial payment, called the option's premium, to the seller of the option.[10]

Options can have different features regarding which future date(s) that exercise can occur. A *European* option can be exercised only at the maturity of the option contract, while an *American* option can be exercised at any time prior to the maturity of the contract.

---

9. Much of the next section's results are due to Robert C. Merton (Merton 1973b). For greater detail, see this article.

10. The owner of an option will choose to exercise it only if it is profitable to do so. The owner can always let the option expire unexercised, in which case its resulting payoff would be zero.

Let us define the following notation, similar to that used to describe a forward contract. Let S_0 denote the current date 0 price per share of the underlying asset, and let this asset's price at the maturity date of the option contract, τ, be denoted as S_τ. We let X be the exercise price of the option and denote the date t price of European call and put options as c_t and p_t, respectively. Then based on our description of the payoffs of call and put options, we can write the maturity values of European call and put options as

$$c_\tau = \max\left[S_\tau - X, 0\right] \qquad (7.4)$$

$$p_\tau = \max\left[X - S_\tau, 0\right] \qquad (7.5)$$

Now we recall that the payoffs to the long and short parties of a forward contract are $S_\tau - F_{0\tau}$ and $F_{0\tau} - S_\tau$, respectively. If we interpret the pre-agreed forward price, $F_{0\tau}$, as analogous to an option's pre-agreed exercise price, X, then we see that a call option's payoff equals that of the long forward payoff whenever the long forward payoff is positive, and it equals 0 when the long forward payoff is negative. Similarly, the payoff of the put option equals the short forward payoff when this payoff is positive, and it equals 0 when the short forward payoff is negative. Hence, assuming $X = F_{0\tau}$, we see that the payoff of a call option weakly dominates that of a long forward position, while the payoff of a put option weakly dominates that of a short forward position.[11] This is due to the consequence of option payoffs always being nonnegative, whereas forward contract payoffs can be of either sign.

Lower Bounds on European Option Values

Since a European call option's payoff is at least as great as that of a comparable long forward position, this implies that the current value of a European call must be at least as great as the current value of a long forward position. Hence, because equation (7.3) is the current value of a long forward position contract, the European call's value must satisfy

$$c_0 \geq S_0 - D - R_f^{-\tau} X \qquad (7.6)$$

Furthermore, because the call option's payoff is always nonnegative, its current value must also be nonnegative; that is, $c_0 \geq 0$. Combining this restriction with (7.6) implies

$$c_0 \geq \max\left[S_0 - D - R_f^{-\tau} X, 0\right] \qquad (7.7)$$

---

11. A payoff is said to dominate another when its value is strictly greater in all states of nature. A payoff weakly dominates another when its value is greater in some states of nature and the same in other states of nature.

By comparing a European put option's payoff to that of a short forward position, a similar argument can be made to prove that

$$p_0 \geq \max\left[R_f^{-\tau}X + D - S_0, 0\right] \tag{7.8}$$

An alternative proof is as follows. Consider constructing two portfolios at date 0:

Date 0:

- Portfolio A = a put option having value p_0 and a share of the underlying asset having value S_0

- Portfolio B = a bond having initial value of $R_f^{-\tau}X + D$

Then at date τ, these two portfolios are worth:

Date τ:

- Portfolio A = $\max\left[X - S_\tau, 0\right] + S_\tau + DR_f^\tau = \max\left[X, S_\tau\right] + DR_f^\tau$

- Portfolio B = $X + DR_f^\tau$

Since portfolio A's value at date τ is always at least as great as that of portfolio B, the absence of arbitrage implies that its value at date 0 must always be at least as great as that of portfolio B at date 0. Hence, $p_0 + S_0 \geq R_f^{-\tau}X + D$, proving result (7.8).

Put-Call Parity

Similar logic can be used to derive an important relationship that links the value of European call and put options that are written on the same underlying asset and that have the same maturity date and exercise price. This relationship is referred to as *put-call parity*:

$$c_0 + R_f^{-\tau}X + D = p_0 + S_0 \tag{7.9}$$

To show this, consider forming the following two portfolios at date 0:

Date 0:

- Portfolio A = a put option having value p_0 and a share of the underlying asset having value S_0

- Portfolio B = a call option having value c_0 and a bond with initial value of $R_f^{-\tau}X + D$

Then at date τ, these two portfolios are worth:

Date τ:

- Portfolio A = $\max\left[X - S_\tau, 0\right] + S_\tau + DR_f^\tau = \max\left[X, S_\tau\right] + DR_f^\tau$
- Portfolio B = $\max\left[0, S_\tau - X\right] + X + DR_f^\tau = \max\left[X, S_\tau\right] + DR_f^\tau$

Since portfolios A and B have exactly the same payoff, in the absence of arbitrage their initial values must be the same, proving the put-call parity relation (7.9). Note that if we rearrange (7.9) as $c_0 - p_0 = S_0 - R_f^{-\tau}X - D = f_0$, we see that the value of a long forward contract can be replicated by purchasing a European call option and writing (selling) a European put option.

American Options

Relative to European options, American options have the additional right that allows the holder (owner) to exercise the option prior to the maturity date. Hence, all other things being equal, an American option must be at least as valuable as a European option. Thus, if we let the uppercase letters C_0 and P_0 be the current values of American call and put options, respectively, then comparing them to European call and put options having equivalent underlying asset, maturity, and exercise price features, it must be the case that $C_0 \geq c_0$ and $P_0 \geq p_0$.

There are, however, cases where an American option's early exercise feature has no value, because it would not be optimal to exercise the option early. This situation occurs for the case of an American call option written on an asset that pays no dividends over the life of the option. To see this, note that inequality (7.7) says that prior to maturity, the value of a European call option must satisfy $c_0 \geq S_0 - R_f^{-\tau}X$. However, if an American call option is exercised prior to maturity, its value equals $C_0 = S_0 - X < S_0 - R_f^{-\tau}X < c_0$. This contradicts the condition $C_0 \geq c_0$. Hence, if a holder of an American call option wished to liquidate his position, it would always be better to sell the option, receiving C_0, rather than exercising it for the lower amount $S_0 - X$. By exercising early, the call option owner loses the time value of money due to paying X now rather than later. Note, however, that if the underlying asset pays dividends, early exercise of an American call option just prior to a dividend payment may be optimal. In this instance, early exercise would entitle the option holder to receive the asset's dividend payment, a payment that would be lost if exercise were delayed.

For an American put option that is sufficiently *in the money*, that is, S_0 is significantly less than X, it may be optimal to exercise the option early, selling the asset immediately and receiving $\$X$ now, rather than waiting and receiving $\$X$ at date τ (which would have a present value of $R_f^{-\tau}X$). Note that this does not necessarily violate inequality (7.8), since at exercise $P_0 = X - S_0$, which could be greater than $R_f^{-\tau} X + D - S_0$ if the remaining dividends were sufficiently small.

7.2 Binomial Option Pricing

The previous section demonstrated that the absence of arbitrage restricts the price of an option in terms of its underlying asset. However, the no-arbitrage assumption, alone, cannot determine an exact option price as a function of the underlying asset price. To do so, one needs to make an additional assumption regarding the distribution of returns earned by the underlying asset. As we shall see, particular distributional assumptions for the underlying asset can lead to a situation where the option's payoff can be replicated by trading in the underlying asset and a risk-free asset and, in general, this trading occurs at multiple dates. When such a dynamic replication strategy is feasible, the option market is said to be dynamically complete. Assuming the absence of arbitrage then allows us to equate the value of the option's payoff to the prices of more primitive securities, namely, the prices of the underlying asset and the risk-free asset. We now turn to a popular discrete-time, discrete-state model that produces this result.

The model presented in this section was developed by John Cox, Stephen Ross, and Mark Rubinstein (Cox, Ross, and Rubinstein 1979). It makes the assumption that the underlying asset, hereafter referred to as a stock, takes on one of only two possible values each period. While this may seem unrealistic, the assumption leads to a formula that often can accurately price options. This *binomial* option pricing technique is frequently applied by finance practitioners to numerically compute the prices of complex options. Here, we start by considering the pricing of a simple European option written on a non-dividend-paying stock.

In addition to assuming the absence of arbitrage opportunities, the binomial model assumes that the current underlying stock price, S, either moves up, by a proportion u, or down, by a proportion d, each period. The probability of an up move is π, so that the probability of a down move is $1 - \pi$. This two-state stock price process can be illustrated as

$$S \nearrow_{\searrow} \begin{array}{l} uS \quad \text{with probability } \pi \\ \\ dS \quad \text{with probability } 1 - \pi \end{array} \tag{7.10}$$

Denote R_f as one plus the risk-free interest rate for the period of unit length.

This risk-free return is assumed to be constant over time. To avoid arbitrage between the stock and the risk-free investment, we must have $d < R_f < u$.[12]

7.2.1   Valuing a One-Period Option

Our valuation of an option whose maturity can span multiple periods will use a backward dynamic programming approach. First, we will value the option when it has only one period left until maturity; then we will value it when it has two periods left until maturity; and so on until we establish an option formula for an arbitrary number of periods until maturity.

Let c equal the value of a European call option written on the stock and having a strike price of X. At maturity, $c = \max[0, S_\tau - X]$. Thus, *one period prior to maturity*:

$$c \nearrow \searrow \quad \begin{array}{l} c_u \equiv \max\left[0, uS - X\right] \quad \text{with probability} \pi \\[2em] c_d \equiv \max\left[0, dS - X\right] \quad \text{with probability } 1 - \pi \end{array} \tag{7.11}$$

What is c one period before maturity? Consider a portfolio containing Δ shares of stock and $\$B$ of bonds. It has current value equal to $\Delta S + B$. Then the value of this portfolio evolves over the period as

$$\Delta S + B \nearrow \searrow \quad \begin{array}{l} \Delta uS + R_f B \quad \text{with probability } \pi \\[2em] \Delta dS + R_f B \quad \text{with probability } 1 - \pi \end{array} \tag{7.12}$$

With two securities (the bond and stock) and two states of nature (up or down), Δ and B can be chosen to replicate the payoff of the call option:

$$\Delta uS + R_f B = c_u \tag{7.13}$$

$$\Delta dS + R_f B = c_d \tag{7.14}$$

---

12. If $R_f < d$, implying that the return on the stock is always higher than the risk-free return, an arbitrage would be to borrow at the risk-free rate and use the proceeds to purchase the stock. A profit is assured because the return on the stock would always exceed the loan repayment. Conversely, if $u < R_f$, implying that the return on the stock is always lower than the risk-free return, an arbitrage would be to short-sell the stock and use the proceeds to invest at the risk-free rate. A profit is assured because the risk-free return will always exceed the value of the stock to be repaid to the stock lender.

Solving for Δ and B that satisfy these two equations, we have

$$\Delta^* = \frac{c_u - c_d}{(u-d)\,S} \tag{7.15}$$

$$B^* = \frac{uc_d - dc_u}{(u-d)\,R_f} \tag{7.16}$$

Hence, a portfolio of Δ^* shares of stock and $\$B^*$ of bonds produces the same cashflow as the call option.[13] This is possible because the option market is complete. As was shown in Chapter 4, in this situation there are equal numbers of states and assets having independent returns so that trading in the stock and bond produces payoffs that span the two states. Now since the portfolio's return replicates that of the option, the absence of arbitrage implies

$$c = \Delta^*S + B^* \tag{7.17}$$

This analysis provides practical insights for option traders. Suppose an option writer wishes to hedge her position from selling an option, that is, insure that she will be able to cover her liability to the option buyer in all states of nature. Then her appropriate hedging strategy is to purchase Δ^* shares of stock and $\$B^*$ of bonds since, from equations (7.13) and (7.14), the proceeds from this hedge portfolio will cover her liability in both states of nature. Her cost for this hedge portfolio is $\Delta^*S + B^*$, and in a perfectly competitive options market, the premium received for selling the option, c, will equal this hedging cost.

Example: If $S = \$50$, $u = 2$, $d = .5$, $R_f = 1.25$, and $X = \$50$, then

$$uS = \$100, \quad dS = \$25, \quad c_u = \$50, \quad c_d = \$0$$

Therefore,

$$\Delta^* = \frac{50 - 0}{(2 - .5)\,50} = \frac{2}{3}$$

$$B^* = \frac{0 - 25}{(2 - .5)\,1.25} = -\frac{40}{3}$$

---

13. Δ^*, the number of shares of stock per option contract needed to replicate (or hedge) the option's payoff, is referred to as the option's *hedge ratio*. It can be verified from the formulas that for standard call options, this ratio is always between 0 and 1. For put options, it is always between -1 and 0. B^*, the investment in bonds, is negative for call options but positive for put options. In other words, the replicating trades for a call option involve buying shares in the underlying asset partially financed by borrowing at the risk-free rate. The replicating trades for a put option involve investing at the risk-free rate partially financed by short-selling the underlying asset.

so that

$$c = \Delta^* S + B^* = \frac{2}{3}(50) - \frac{40}{3} = \frac{60}{3} = \$20$$

If $c < \Delta^* S + B^*$, then an arbitrage is to short-sell Δ^* shares of stock, invest $\$ - B^*$ in bonds, and buy the call option. Conversely, if $c > \Delta^* S + B^*$, then an arbitrage is to write the call option, buy Δ^* shares of stock, and borrow $\$ - B^*$.

The resulting option pricing formula has an interesting implication. It can be rewritten as

$$c = \Delta^* S + B^* = \frac{c_u - c_d}{(u - d)} + \frac{u c_d - d c_u}{(u - d) R_f} \tag{7.18}$$

$$= \frac{\left[\frac{R_f - d}{u - d} \max[0, uS - X] + \frac{u - R_f}{u - d} \max[0, dS - X] \right]}{R_f}$$

which *does not* depend on the probability of an up or down move of the stock, π.

Thus, given S, investors will agree on the no-arbitrage value of the call option even if they do not agree on π. The call option formula does not *directly* depend on investors' attitudes toward risk. It is a *relative* (to the stock) pricing formula. This is reminiscent of Chapter 4's result (4.44) in which contingent claims could be priced based on state prices but without knowledge of the probability of different states occurring. Since π determines the stock's expected rate of return, $u\pi + d(1 - \pi) - 1$, this does not need to be known or estimated in order to solve for the no-arbitrage value of the option, c. However, we do need to know u and d, that is, the size of movements per period, which determine the stock's *volatility*.

Note also that we can rewrite c as

$$c = \frac{1}{R_f} \left[\widehat{\pi} c_u + (1 - \widehat{\pi}) c_d \right] \tag{7.19}$$

where $\widehat{\pi} \equiv \frac{R_f - d}{u - d}$.

Since $0 < \widehat{\pi} < 1$, $\widehat{\pi}$ has the properties of a probability. In fact, this is the *risk-neutral* probability, as defined in Chapter 4, of an up move in the stock's price. To see that $\widehat{\pi}$ equals the true probability π if individuals are risk-neutral, note that if the expected return on the stock equals the risk-free return, R_f, then

$$[u\pi + d(1 - \pi)] S = R_f S \tag{7.20}$$

which implies that

$$\pi = \frac{R_f - d}{u - d} = \widehat{\pi} \tag{7.21}$$

so that $\widehat{\pi}$ does equal π under risk neutrality. Thus, (7.19) can be expressed as

$$c_t = \frac{1}{R_f} \widehat{E} [c_{t+1}] \tag{7.22}$$

where, as in Chapter 4's equation (4.46), $\widehat{E} [\cdot]$ denotes the expectation operator evaluated using the risk-neutral probabilities $\widehat{\pi}$ rather than the true, or physical, probabilities π.

7.2.2 Valuing a Multiperiod Option

Next, consider the option's value with *two periods prior to maturity*. The stock price process is

$$
\begin{array}{ccc}
 & & u^2 S \\
 & uS \nearrow \\
 & \nearrow \quad \searrow \\
S & & duS \\
 & \searrow \quad \nearrow \\
 & dS \\
 & & \searrow \\
 & & d^2 S
\end{array}
\tag{7.23}
$$

so that the option price process is

$$
\begin{array}{ccc}
 & & c_{uu} \equiv \max [0, u^2 S - X] \\
 & c_u \nearrow \\
 & \nearrow \quad \searrow \\
c & & c_{du} \equiv \max [0, duS - X] \\
 & \searrow \quad \nearrow \\
 & c_d \\
 & & \searrow \\
 & & c_{dd} \equiv \max [0, d^2 S - X]
\end{array}
\tag{7.24}
$$

Using the results from our analysis when there was only one period to maturity, we know that

$$c_u = \frac{\widehat{\pi} c_{uu} + (1 - \widehat{\pi}) c_{du}}{R_f} \tag{7.25}$$

$$c_d = \frac{\widehat{\pi} c_{du} + (1 - \widehat{\pi}) c_{dd}}{R_f} \tag{7.26}$$

With two periods to maturity, the one-period-to-go cashflows of c_u and c_d can be replicated once again by the stock and bond portfolio composed of $\Delta^* = \frac{c_u - c_d}{(u-d)S}$ shares of stock and $B^* = \frac{uc_d - dc_u}{(u-d)R_f}$ of bonds. No arbitrage implies

$$c = \Delta^* S + B^* = \frac{1}{R_f} [\widehat{\pi} c_u + (1 - \widehat{\pi}) c_d] \tag{7.27}$$

which, as before, says that $c_t = \frac{1}{R_f}\widehat{E}[c_{t+1}]$. The market is not only complete over the last period but over the second-to-last period as well. Substituting in for c_u and c_d, we have

$$c = \frac{1}{R_f^2}\left[\widehat{\pi}^2 c_{uu} + 2\widehat{\pi}(1-\widehat{\pi})c_{ud} + (1-\widehat{\pi})^2 c_{dd}\right] \tag{7.28}$$

$$= \frac{1}{R_f^2}\left[\widehat{\pi}^2 \max\left[0, u^2S - X\right] + 2\widehat{\pi}(1-\widehat{\pi})\max\left[0, duS - X\right]\right]$$

$$+ \frac{1}{R_f^2}\left[(1-\widehat{\pi})^2 \max\left[0, d^2S - X\right]\right]$$

which can also be interpreted as $c_t = \frac{1}{R_f^2}\widehat{E}[c_{t+2}]$. This illustrates that when a market is complete each period, it becomes complete over the sequence of these individual periods. In other words, the option market is said to be *dynamically complete*. Even though the tree diagrams in (7.23) and (7.24) indicate that there are four states of nature two periods in the future (and three different payoffs for the option), these states can be spanned by a dynamic trading strategy involving just two assets. That is, we have shown that by appropriate trading in just two assets, payoffs in greater than two states can be replicated.

Note that c depends only on S, X, u, d, R_f, and the time until maturity, two periods. Repeating this analysis for three, four, five, ..., n periods prior to maturity, we always obtain

$$c = \Delta^* S + B^* = \frac{1}{R_f}\left[\widehat{\pi}c_u + (1-\widehat{\pi})c_d\right] \tag{7.29}$$

By repeated substitution for c_u, c_d, c_{uu}, c_{ud}, c_{dd}, c_{uuu}, and so on, we obtain the following formula, with *n periods prior to maturity*:

$$c = \frac{1}{R_f^n}\left[\sum_{j=0}^{n}\left(\frac{n!}{j!(n-j)!}\right)\widehat{\pi}^j(1-\widehat{\pi})^{n-j}\max\left[0, u^j d^{n-j}S - X\right]\right] \tag{7.30}$$

Similar to before, equation (7.30) can be interpreted as $c_t = \frac{1}{R_f^n}\widehat{E}[c_{t+n}]$, implying that the market is dynamically complete over any number of periods prior to the option's expiration. The formula in (7.30) can be further simplified by defining "*a*" as the minimum number of upward jumps of S for it to exceed X. Thus a is the smallest nonnegative integer such that $u^a d^{n-a}S > X$. Taking the natural logarithm of both sides, a is the minimum integer $> ln(X/Sd^n)/ln(u/d)$.

Therefore, for all $j < a$ (the option matures out-of-the-money),

$$\max \left[0, u^j d^{n-j} S - X \right] = 0 \tag{7.31}$$

while for all $j > a$ (the option matures in-the-money),

$$\max \left[0, u^j d^{n-j} S - X \right] = u^j d^{n-j} S - X \tag{7.32}$$

Thus, the formula for c can be rewritten:

$$c = \frac{1}{R_f^n} \left[\sum_{j=a}^{n} \left(\frac{n!}{j! \, (n-j)!} \right) \hat{\pi}^j \, (1-\hat{\pi})^{n-j} \left[u^j d^{n-j} S - X \right] \right] \tag{7.33}$$

Breaking up (7.33) into two terms, we have

$$c = S \left[\sum_{j=a}^{n} \left(\frac{n!}{j! \, (n-j)!} \right) \hat{\pi}^j \, (1-\hat{\pi})^{n-j} \left[\frac{u^j d^{n-j}}{R_f^n} \right] \right] \tag{7.34}$$

$$- XR_f^{-n} \left[\sum_{j=a}^{n} \left(\frac{n!}{j! \, (n-j)!} \right) \hat{\pi}^j \, (1-\hat{\pi})^{n-j} \right]$$

The terms in brackets in (7.34) are complementary binomial distribution functions, so that we can write (7.34) as

$$c = S\phi[a; n, \hat{\pi}'] - XR_f^{-n}\phi[a; n, \hat{\pi}] \tag{7.35}$$

where $\hat{\pi}' \equiv \left(\frac{u}{R_f} \right) \hat{\pi}$ and $\phi[a; n, \hat{\pi}]$ represents the probability that the sum of n random variables that equal 1 with probability $\hat{\pi}$ and 0 with probability $1 - \hat{\pi}$ will be $\geq a$. These formulas imply that c is the discounted expected value of the call's terminal payoff under the risk-neutral probability distribution.

If we define τ as the time until maturity of the call option and σ^2 as the variance per unit time of the stock's rate of return (which depends on u and d), then by taking the limit as the number of periods $n \to \infty$, but the length of each period $\frac{\tau}{n} \to 0$, the Cox-Ross-Rubinstein binomial option pricing formula converges to the well-known Black-Scholes-Merton option pricing formula:[14]

---

14. The intuition for why (7.36) is a limit of (7.35) is due to the Central Limit Theorem. As the number of periods becomes large, the sum of binomially distributed, random stock rates of return becomes normally distributed. Note that in the Black-Scholes-Merton formula, R_f is now the risk-free return per unit time rather than the risk-free return for each period. The relationship between σ and u and d will be discussed shortly. The Cox-Ross-Rubinstein binomial model (7.35) also can have a different continuous-time limit, namely, the jump-diffusion model that will be presented in Chapter 11.

$$c = SN(z) - XR_f^{-\tau}N\left(z - \sigma\sqrt{\tau}\right) \tag{7.36}$$

where $z \equiv \dfrac{\left[\ln\left(\frac{S}{XR_f^{-\tau}}\right) + \frac{1}{2}\sigma^2\tau\right]}{(\sigma\sqrt{\tau})}$ and $N(\cdot)$ is that cumulative standard normal distribution function.

7.3 Binomial Model Applications

Cox, Ross, and Rubinstein's binomial technique is useful for valuing relatively complicated options, such as those having American (early exercise) features. In this section we show how the model can be used to value an American put option and an option written on an asset that pays dividends.

Similar to our earlier presentation, assume that over each period of length Δt, stock prices follow the process

$$S \nearrow \quad\begin{array}{l} uS \quad \text{with probability } \pi \\ \\ dS \quad \text{with probability } 1 - \pi \end{array} \tag{7.37}$$

The results of our earlier analysis showed that the assumption of an absence of arbitrage allowed us to apply *risk-neutral* valuation techniques to derive the price of an option. Recall that, in general, this method of valuing a derivative security can be implemented by

1. setting the expected rate of return on all securities equal to the risk-free rate

2. discounting the expected value of future cashflows generated from (1) by this risk-free rate

For example, suppose we examine the value of the stock, S, in terms of the risk-neutral valuation method. Similar to the previous analysis, define R_f as the risk-free return per unit time, so that the risk-free return over a time interval Δt is $R_f^{\Delta t}$. Then we have

$$S = R_f^{-\Delta t}\hat{E}\left[S_{t+\Delta t}\right] \tag{7.38}$$

$$= R_f^{-\Delta t}\left[\hat{\pi}uS + (1 - \hat{\pi})dS\right]$$

where $\hat{E}[\cdot]$ represents the expectations operator under the condition that the expected rates of return on all assets equal the risk-free interest rate, which is not necessarily the assets' true expected rates of return. Rearranging (7.38), we obtain

$$R_f^{\Delta t} = \widehat{\pi} u + (1 - \widehat{\pi}) d \tag{7.39}$$

which implies

$$\widehat{\pi} = \frac{R_f^{\Delta t} - d}{u - d} \tag{7.40}$$

This is the same formula for $\widehat{\pi}$ as was derived earlier. Hence, risk-neutral valuation is consistent with this simple example.

7.3.1   Calibrating the Model

To use the binomial model to value actual options, the parameters u and d must be calibrated to fit the variance of the underlying stock. When estimating a stock's volatility, it is often assumed that stock prices are lognormally distributed. This implies that the continuously compounded rate of return on the stock over a period of length Δt, given by $\ln (S_{t+\Delta t}) - \ln (S_t)$, is normally distributed with a constant, per-period variance of $\Delta t \sigma^2$. As we shall see in Chapter 9, this constant variance assumption is also used in the Black-Scholes option pricing model. Thus, the sample standard deviation of a time series of historical log stock price changes provides us with an estimate of σ. Based on this value of σ, approximate values of u and d that result in the same variance for a binomial stock price distribution are[15]

$$u = e^{\sigma \sqrt{\Delta t}} \tag{7.41}$$

$$d = \frac{1}{u} = e^{-\sigma \sqrt{\Delta t}}$$

Hence, condition (7.41) provides a simple way of calibrating u and d to the stock's volatility, σ.

---

15. That the values of u and d in (7.41) result in a variance of stock returns given by $\sigma^2 \Delta t$ for sufficiently small Δt can be verified by noting that, in the binomial model, the variance of the end-of-period stock price is $E[S_{t+\Delta t}^2] - E[S_{t+\Delta t}]^2 = \pi u^2 S^2 + (1 - \pi) d^2 S^2 - [\pi S + (1 - \pi) dS]^2 = S^2 \{\pi u^2 + (1 - \pi) d^2 - [\pi u + (1 - \pi) d]^2\} = S^2 [e^{\alpha \Delta t} (e^{\sigma \sqrt{\Delta t}} + e^{-\sigma \sqrt{\Delta t}}) - 1 - e^{2\alpha \Delta t}]$, where $\pi = e^{\alpha \Delta t}$ and α is the (continuously compounded) expected rate of return on the stock per unit time. This implies that the variance of the return on the stock is $[e^{\alpha \Delta t} (e^{\sigma \sqrt{\Delta t}} + e^{-\sigma \sqrt{\Delta t}}) - 1 - e^{2\alpha \Delta t}]$. Expanding this expression in a series using $e^x = 1 + x + \frac{1}{2} x^2 + \frac{1}{6} x^3 + \cdots$ and then ignoring all terms of order $(\Delta t)^2$ and higher, it equals $\Delta t \sigma^2$.

Now consider the path of the stock price. Because we assumed $u = \frac{1}{d}$, the binomial process for the stock price has the simplified form:

$$
\begin{array}{c}
u^4 S \\
u^3 S \nearrow \searrow \\
u^2 S \nearrow \searrow \quad u^2 S \\
uS \nearrow \searrow \quad uS \nearrow \searrow \\
S \nearrow \searrow \quad S \nearrow \searrow \quad S \\
dS \nearrow \searrow \quad dS \nearrow \searrow \\
d^2 S \nearrow \searrow \quad d^2 S \\
d^3 S \nearrow \searrow \\
d^4 S
\end{array}
\tag{7.42}
$$

Given the stock price, S, and its volatility, σ, the above tree or "lattice" can be calculated for any number of periods using $u = e^{\sigma \sqrt{\Delta t}}$ and $d = e^{-\sigma \sqrt{\Delta t}}$.

7.3.2 Valuing an American Option

We can numerically value an option on this stock by starting at the last period and working back toward the first period. Recall that an American put option that is not exercised early will have a final period (date τ) value

$$
P_\tau = \max \left[0, X - S_\tau \right]
\tag{7.43}
$$

The value of the put at date $\tau - \Delta t$ is then the risk-neutral expected value discounted by $R_f^{-\Delta t}$:

$$
P_{\tau - \Delta t} = R_f^{-\Delta t} \hat{E} \left[P_\tau \right]
\tag{7.44}
$$

$$
= R_f^{-\Delta t} \left(\hat{\pi} P_{\tau, u} + (1 - \hat{\pi}) P_{\tau, d} \right)
$$

where $P_{\tau, u}$ is the date τ value of the option if the stock price changes by proportion u, while $P_{\tau, d}$ is the date τ value of the option if the stock price changes by proportion d. However, with an American put option, we need to check whether this value exceeds the value of the put if it were exercised early. Hence, the put option's value can be expressed as

$$
P_{\tau - \Delta t} = \max \left[X - S_{\tau - \Delta t}, \; R_f^{-\Delta t} \left(\hat{\pi} P_{\tau, u} + (1 - \hat{\pi}) P_{\tau, d} \right) \right]
\tag{7.45}
$$

Let us illustrate this binomial valuation technique with the following example: A stock has a current price of $S = \$80.50$ and a volatility $\sigma = 0.33$. If $\Delta t = \frac{1}{9}$ year, then $u = e^{\frac{.33}{\sqrt{9}}} = e^{.11} = 1.1163$ and $d = \frac{1}{u} = 0.8958$.

Thus the three-period tree for the stock price is

$$
\begin{array}{ccccc}
Date:0 & 1 & 2 & 3 \\
\end{array}
$$

Date : 0   1   2   3

```
                                        111.98
                            100.32 <
                 89.86 <                89.86
      S = 80.50 <          80.50 <
                 72.12 <                72.12
                            64.60 <
                                        57.86
```

Next, consider valuing an American put option on this stock that matures in $\tau = \frac{1}{3}$ years (4 months) and has an exercise price of $X = \$75$. Assume that the risk-free return is $R_f = e^{0.09}$; that is, the continuously compounded risk-free interest rate is 9 percent. This implies

$$
\widehat{\pi} = \frac{R_f^{\Delta t} - d}{u - d} = \frac{e^{\frac{0.09}{9}} - 0.8958}{1.1163 - 0.8958} = 0.5181
$$

We can now start at date 3 and begin filling in the tree for the put option:

Date : 0   1   2   3

```
                              P_uuu
                    P_uu <
          P_u <                P_uud
      P <           P_ud <
          P_d <                P_udd
                    P_dd <
                              P_ddd
```

Using $P_3 = \max\left[0, X - S_3\right]$, we have

$$
\begin{array}{ccccc}
Date:0 & 1 & 2 & 3 & \\
 & & & 0.00 & \\
 & & P_{uu} & & \\
 & P_u & & 0.00 & \\
P & & P_{ud} & & \\
 & P_d & & 2.88 & \\
 & & P_{dd} & & \\
 & & & 17.14 & \\
\end{array}
$$

Next, using $P_2 = \max\left[X - S_2,\ R_f^{-\Delta t}\left(\hat{\pi}P_{3,u} + (1-\hat{\pi})\,P_{3,d}\right)\right]$, we have

$$
\begin{array}{ccccc}
Date:0 & 1 & 2 & 3 & \\
 & & & 0.00 & \\
 & & 0.00 & & \\
 & P_u & & 0.00 & \\
P & & 1.37 & & \\
 & P_d & & 2.88 & \\
 & & 10.40^* & & \\
 & & & 17.14 & \\
\end{array}
$$

*Note that at P_{dd} the option is exercised early since

$$
\begin{aligned}
P_{dd} &= \max\left[X - S_2,\ R_f^{-\Delta t}\left(\hat{\pi}P_{3,u} + (1-\hat{\pi})\,P_{3,d}\right)\right] \\
&= \max\left[75 - 64.60,\ 9.65\right] = \$10.40
\end{aligned}
$$

Next, using $P_1 = \max \left[X - S_1, \; R_f^{-\Delta t} \left(\hat{\pi} P_{2,u} + (1 - \hat{\pi}) P_{2,d} \right) \right]$, we have

Date : 0 1   2   3

              0.00

        0.00

     0.65   0.00

  P 1.37

     5.66   2.88

        10.40*

              17.14

Note that the option is *not* exercised early at P_d since

$$P_d = \max \left[X - S_1, \; R_f^{-\Delta t} \left(\hat{\pi} P_{2,u} + (1 - \hat{\pi}) P_{2,d} \right) \right]$$
$$= \max [75 - 72.12, \, 5.66] = \$5.66$$

Finally, we calculate the value of the put at date 0 using

$$P_0 = \max \left[X - S_0, \; R_f^{-\Delta t} \left(\hat{\pi} P_{1,u} + (1 - \hat{\pi}) P_{1,d} \right) \right]$$
$$= \max [-5.5, \, 3.03] = \$3.03$$

and the final tree for the put is

Date : 0 1   2   3

              0.00

        0.00

     0.65   0.00

  3.03   1.37

     5.66   2.88

        10.40*

              17.14

7.3.3   Options on Dividend-Paying Assets

One can generalize the procedure shown in section 7.3.2 to allow for the stock (or portfolio of stocks such as a stock index) to *continuously* pay dividends that have a per unit time yield equal to δ; that is, for Δt sufficiently small, the owner of the stock receives a dividend of $\delta S \Delta t$. For this case of a dividend-yielding asset, we simply redefine

$$\widehat{\pi} = \frac{\left(R_f e^{-\delta}\right)^{\Delta t} - d}{u - d} \tag{7.46}$$

This is because when the asset pays a dividend yield of δ, its expected risk-neutral appreciation is $\left(R_f e^{-\delta}\right)^{\Delta t}$ rather than $R_f^{\Delta t}$.

For the case in which a stock is assumed to pay a known dividend yield, δ, at a *single point in time*, then if date $i\Delta t$ is *prior* to the stock going ex-dividend, the nodes of the stock price tree equal

$$u^j d^{i-j} S \qquad j = 0, 1, \ldots, i. \tag{7.47}$$

If the date $i\Delta t$ is *after* the stock goes ex-dividend, the nodes of the stock price tree equal

$$u^j d^{i-j} S \left(1 - \delta\right) \qquad j = 0, 1, \ldots, i. \tag{7.48}$$

The value of an option is calculated as before. We work backwards and again check for the optimality of early exercise.

7.4   Summary

In an environment where there is an absence of arbitrage opportunities, the price of a contingent claim is restricted by the price of its underlying asset. For some derivative securities, such as forward contracts, the contract's payoff can be replicated by the underlying asset and a riskless asset using a static trading strategy. In such a situation, the absence of arbitrage leads to a unique link between the derivative's price and that of its underlying asset without the need for additional assumptions regarding the asset's return distribution. For other types of derivatives, including options, static replication may not be possible. An additional assumption regarding the underlying asset's return distribution is necessary for valuing such derivative contracts. An example is the assumption that the underlying asset's returns are binomially distributed. In this case, an option's payoff can be dynamically replicated by repeated trading in a portfolio consisting of its underlying asset and a risk-free asset. Consistent with our earlier analysis, this situation of a dynamically complete market allows us to value derivatives using the risk-neutral approach. We also illustrated the flexibility of this binomial model by applying it to value options having an early exercise feature as well as options written on a dividend-paying asset.

As will be shown in Chapter 9, the binomial assumption is not the only way to obtain market completeness and a unique option pricing formula. If one assumes that investors can trade continuously in the underlying asset, and the underlying's returns follow a continuous-time diffusion process, then these alternative assumptions can also lead to market completeness. The next chapter prepares us for this important topic by introducing the mathematics of continuous-time stochastic processes.

7.5 Exercises

1. In light of this chapter's discussion of forward contracts on dividend-paying assets, reinterpret Chapter 3's example of a forward contract on a foreign currency. In particular, what are the "dividends" paid by a foreign currency?

2. What is the lower bound for the price of a three-month European put option on a dividend-paying stock when the stock price is $58, the strike price is $65, the annualized, risk-free return is $R_f = e^{0.05}$, and the stock is to pay a $3 dividend two months from now?

3. Suppose that c_1, c_2, and c_3 are the prices of European call options with strike prices X_1, X_2, and X_3, respectively, where $X_3 > X_2 > X_1$ and $X_3 - X_2 = X_2 - X_1$. All options are written on the same asset and have the same maturity. Show that

$$c_2 \le \frac{1}{2}(c_1 + c_3)$$

Hint: consider a portfolio that is long the option having a strike price of X_1, long the option having the strike price of X_3, and short two options having the strike price of X_2.

4. Consider the binomial (Cox-Ross-Rubinstein) option pricing model. The underlying stock pays no dividends and has the characteristic that $u = 2$ and $d = 1/2$. In other words, if the stock increases (*decreases*) over a period, its value doubles (*halves*). Also, assume that one plus the risk-free interest rate satisfies $R_f = 5/4$. Let there be two periods and three dates: 0, 1, and 2. At the initial date 0, the stock price is $S_0 = 4$. The following option is a type of *Asian* option referred to as an average price call. The option matures at date 2 and has a terminal value equal to

$$c_2 = \max\left[\frac{S_1 + S_2}{2} - 5, 0\right]$$

where S_1 and S_2 are the prices of the stock at dates 1 and 2, respectively. Solve for the no-arbitrage value of this call option at date 0, c_0.

5. Calculate the price of a three-month American put option on a non-dividend-paying stock when the stock price is $60, the strike price is $60, the annualized, risk-free return is $R_f = e^{0.10}$, and the annual standard deviation of the stock's rate of return is $\sigma = .45$, so that $u = 1/d = e^{\sigma\sqrt{\Delta\tau}} = e^{.45\sqrt{\Delta\tau}}$. Use a binomial tree with a time interval of one month.

6. Let the current date be t and let $T > t$ be a future date, where $\tau \equiv T - t$ is the number of periods in the interval. Let $A(t)$ and $B(t)$ be the date t prices of single shares of assets A and B, respectively. Asset A pays no dividends but asset B does pay dividends, and the present (date t) value of asset B's known dividends per share paid over the interval from t to T equals D. The per-period risk-free return is assumed to be constant and equal to R_f.

   a. Consider a type of forward contract that has the following features. At date t an agreement is made to exchange at date T one share of asset A for F shares of asset B. No payments between the parties are exchanged at date t. Note that F is negotiated at date t and can be considered a forward price. Give an expression for the equilibrium value of this forward price and explain your reasoning.

   b. Consider a type of European call option that gives the holder the right to buy one share of asset A in exchange for paying X shares of asset B at date T. Give the no-arbitrage lower bound for the date t value of this call option, $c(t)$.

   c. Derive a put-call parity relation for European options of the type described in part (b).

CHAPTER 8

Essentials of Diffusion Processes and Itô's Lemma

T his chapter covers the basic properties of continuous-time stochastic processes having continuous sample paths, commonly referred to as diffusion
processes. It describes the characteristics of these processes that are helpful for modeling many financial and economic time series. Modeling a variable
as a continuous-time, rather than a discrete-time, random process can allow for
different behavioral assumptions and sharper model results. A variable that follows a continuous-time stochastic process can display constant change yet be
observable at each moment in time. In contrast, a discrete-time stochastic process
implies that there is no change in the value of the variable over a fixed interval, or
that the change cannot be observed between the discrete dates. If an asset price
is modeled as a discrete-time process, it is natural to presume that no trading in
the asset occurs over the discrete interval. Often this makes problems that involve
hedging the asset's risk difficult, since portfolio allocations cannot be rebalanced
over the nontrading period. Thus, hedging risky-asset returns may be less than
perfect when a discrete-time process is assumed.[1]

Instead, if one assumes that asset prices follow continuous-time processes,
prices can be observed and trade can take place continuously. When asset prices

---

1. Imperfect hedging may, indeed, be a realistic phenomenon. However, in many situations
it may not be caused by the inability to trade during a period of time but due to discrete
movements (jumps) in asset prices. We examine how to model an asset price process that is
a mixture of a continuous process and a jump process in Chapter 11. Imperfect hedging can
also arise because transactions costs lead an individual to choose not to trade to hedge small price
movements. For models of portfolio choice in the presence of transactions costs, see work by
George Constantinides (Constantinides 1986) and Bernard Dumas and Elisa Luciano (Dumas
and Luciano 1991).

follow continuous sample paths, dynamic trading strategies that can fully hedge an asset's risk are possible. Making this continuous hedging assumption often simplifies optimal portfolio choice problems and problems of valuing contingent claims (derivative securities). It permits asset returns to have a continuous distribution (an infinite number of states), yet market completeness is possible because payoffs may be dynamically replicated through continuous trading. Such markets are characterized as dynamically complete.

The mathematics of continuous-time stochastic processes can be traced to Louis Bachelier's 1900 Sorbonne doctoral thesis, *Theory of Speculation*. He developed the mathematics of diffusion processes as a by-product of his modeling of option values. While his work predated Albert Einstein's work on Brownian motion by five years, it fell into obscurity until it was uncovered by Leonard J. Savage and Paul A. Samuelson in the 1950s. Samuelson (Samuelson 1965) used Bachelier's techniques to develop a precursor of the Black-Scholes option pricing model, but it was Robert C. Merton who pioneered the application of continuous-time mathematics to solve a wide variety of problems in financial economics.[2] The popularity of modeling financial time series by continuous-time processes continues to this day.

This chapter's analysis of continuous-time processes is done at an intuitive level rather than a mathematically rigorous one.[3] The first section examines Brownian motion, which is the fundamental building block of diffusion processes. We show how Brownian motion is a continuous-time limit of a discrete-time random walk. How diffusion processes can be developed by generalizing a pure Brownian motion process is the topic of the second section. The last section introduces Itô's lemma, which tells us how to derive the stochastic process for a function of a variable that follows a diffusion process. Itô's lemma is applied extensively in continuous-time financial modeling. It will be used frequently during the remainder of this book.

8.1   Pure Brownian Motion

Here we show how a Brownian motion process can be defined as the limit of a discrete-time process.[4] Consider the following stochastic process observed at date

---

2. See a collection of Merton's work in (Merton 1992).

3. The following books (in order of increasing rigor and difficulty) provide more in-depth coverage of the chapter's topics: (Neftci 1996), (Karlin and Taylor 1975), (Karlin and Taylor 1981), and (Karatzas and Shreve 1991).

4. Brownian motion is named after botanist Robert Brown, who in 1827 observed that pollen suspended in a liquid moved in a continuous, random fashion. In 1905, Albert Einstein explained this motion as the result of random collisions of water molecules with the pollen particle.

t, $z(t)$. Let Δt be a discrete change in time, that is, some time interval. The change in $z(t)$ over the time interval Δt is given by

$$z(t + \Delta t) - z(t) \equiv \Delta z = \sqrt{\Delta t} \, \tilde{\epsilon} \tag{8.1}$$

where $\tilde{\epsilon}$ is a random variable with $E[\tilde{\epsilon}] = 0$, $Var[\tilde{\epsilon}] = 1$, and $Cov[z(t + \Delta t) - z(t), \, z(s + \Delta t) - z(s)] = 0$ if $(t, \, t + \Delta t)$ and $(s, \, s + \Delta t)$ are nonoverlapping intervals. $z(t)$ is an example of a "random walk" process. Its standard deviation equals the square root of the time between observations.

Given the moments of $\tilde{\epsilon}$, we have $E[\Delta z] = 0$, $Var[\Delta z] = \Delta t$, and $z(t)$ has serially uncorrelated (independent) increments. Now consider the change in $z(t)$ over a fixed interval, from 0 to T. Assume T is made up of n intervals of length Δt. Then

$$z(T) - z(0) = \sum_{i=1}^{n} \Delta z_i \tag{8.2}$$

where $\Delta z_i \equiv z(i \cdot \Delta t) - z([i - 1] \cdot \Delta t) \equiv \sqrt{\Delta t} \, \tilde{\epsilon}_i$, and $\tilde{\epsilon}_i$ is the value of $\tilde{\epsilon}$ over the ith interval. Hence (8.2) can also be written as

$$z(T) - z(0) = \sum_{i=1}^{n} \sqrt{\Delta t} \, \tilde{\epsilon}_i = \sqrt{\Delta t} \sum_{i=1}^{n} \tilde{\epsilon}_i \tag{8.3}$$

Now note that the first two moments of $z(T) - z(0)$ are

$$E_0[z(T) - z(0)] = \sqrt{\Delta t} \sum_{i=1}^{n} E_0[\tilde{\epsilon}_i] = 0 \tag{8.4}$$

$$Var_0[z(T) - z(0)] = \left(\sqrt{\Delta t}\right)^2 \sum_{i=1}^{n} Var_0[\tilde{\epsilon}_i] = \Delta t \cdot n \cdot 1 = T \tag{8.5}$$

where $E_t[\cdot]$ and $Var_t[\cdot]$ are the mean and variance operators, respectively, conditional on information at date t. We see that holding T (the length of the time interval) fixed, the mean and variance of $z(T) - z(0)$ are independent of n.

8.1.1   The Continuous-Time Limit

Now let us perform the following experiment. Suppose we keep T fixed but let n, the number of intervening increments of length Δt, go to infinity. Can we say something else about the distribution of $z(T) - z(0)$ besides what its first two moments are? The answer is yes. Assuming that the $\tilde{\epsilon}_i$ are independent and identically distributed, we can state

$$p \lim_{n \to \infty} (z(T) - z(0)) = p \lim_{\Delta t \to 0} (z(T) - z(0)) \sim N(0, \, T) \tag{8.6}$$

In other words, $z(T) - z(0)$ has a *normal distribution* with mean zero and variance T. This follows from the *Central Limit Theorem*, which states that the sum of n independent, identically distributed random variables has a distribution that converges to the normal distribution as $n \to \infty$. Thus, the distribution of $z(t)$ over any finite interval, $[\,0,\ T\,]$, can be thought of as the sum of infinitely many small independent increments, $\Delta z_i = \sqrt{\Delta t}\,\tilde{\epsilon}_i$, which are realizations from an arbitrary distribution. However, when added together, these increments result in a normal distribution. Therefore, without loss of generality, we can assume that each of the $\tilde{\epsilon}_i$ have a standard (mean 0, variance 1) normal distribution.[5]

The limit of one of these minute independent increments can be defined as

$$dz(t) \equiv \lim_{\Delta t \to 0} \Delta z = \lim_{\Delta t \to 0} \sqrt{\Delta t}\,\tilde{\epsilon} \tag{8.7}$$

where $\tilde{\epsilon} \sim N(0,\ 1)$. Hence, $E[\,dz(t)\,] = 0$ and $Var[\,dz(t)\,] = dt$.[6] dz is referred to as a pure Brownian motion process, or a Wiener process, named after the mathematician Norbert Wiener, who in 1923 first proved its existence. We can now write the change in $z(t)$ over any finite interval $[\,0,\ T\,]$ as

$$z(T) - z(0) = \int_0^T dz(t) \sim N(0,\ T) \tag{8.8}$$

The integral in (8.8) is a *stochastic* or Itô integral, not the usual Riemann or Lebesgue integrals that measure the area under deterministic functions.[7] Note that $z(t)$ is a continuous process but constantly changing (by $\tilde{\epsilon}$ over each infinitesimal interval Δt), such that over any finite interval it has unbounded variation.[8] Hence, it is nowhere differentiable (very jagged); that is, its derivative $dz(t)/dt$ does not exist.

The step function in Figure 8.1 illustrates a sample path for $z\,(t)$ as a discrete-time random walk process with $T = 2$ and $n = 20$, so that $\Delta t = 0.1$. As $n \to \infty$, so that $\Delta t \to 0$, this random walk process becomes the continuous-time Brownian motion process also shown in the figure.

Brownian motion provides the basis for more general continuous-time stochastic processes. We next analyze such processes known as *diffusion* processes. Dif-

---

5. Note that sums of normally distributed random variables are also normally distributed. Thus, the Central Limit Theorem also applies to sums of normals.

6. That the $Var[dz\,(t)] = dt$ can be confirmed by noting that the sum of the variance over the interval from 0 to T is $\int_0^T dt = T$.

7. Kiyoshi Itô was a Japanese mathematician who developed the calculus of stochastic processes (Itô 1944, 1951).

8. This means that if you measured the length of the continuous process's path over a finite interval, it would be infinitely long.

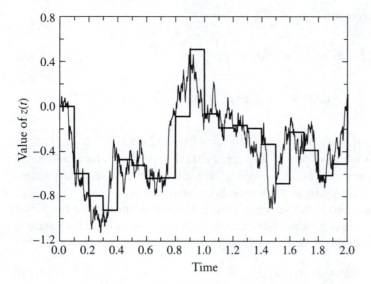

Figure 8.1 ——— Random Walk and Brownian Motion

fusion processes are widely used in financial economics and are characterized as continuous-time Markov processes having continuous sample paths.[9]

8.2 Diffusion Processes

To illustrate how we can build on the basic Wiener process, consider the process for dz multiplied by a constant, σ. Define a new process $x(t)$ by

$$dx(t) = \sigma \, dz(t) \tag{8.9}$$

Then over a discrete interval, $[0, T]$, $x(t)$ is distributed:

$$x(T) - x(0) = \int_0^T dx = \int_0^T \sigma \, dz(t) = \sigma \int_0^T dz(t) \sim N(0, \sigma^2 T) \tag{8.10}$$

Next, consider adding a deterministic (nonstochastic) change of $\mu(t)$ per unit of time to the $x(t)$ process:

$$dx = \mu(t)dt + \sigma \, dz \tag{8.11}$$

---

9. A stochastic process is said to be Markov if the date t probability distribution of its future date $T > t$ value depends only on the process's date t value, and not values at prior dates $s < t$. In other words, the process's future states are conditionally independent of past states, given information on its current state.

Now over any discrete interval, $[0, T]$, we have

$$x(T) - x(0) = \int_0^T dx = \int_0^T \mu(t)dt + \int_0^T \sigma \, dz(t) \tag{8.12}$$

$$= \int_0^T \mu(t)dt + \sigma \int_0^T dz(t) \sim N(\int_0^T \mu(t)dt, \, \sigma^2 T)$$

For example, if $\mu(t) = \mu$, a constant, then $x(T) - x(0) = \mu T + \sigma \int_0^T dz(t) \sim N(\mu T, \, \sigma^2 T)$. Thus, we have been able to generalize the standard trendless Wiener process to have a nonzero mean as well as any desired variance. The process $dx = \mu dt + \sigma dz$ is referred to as arithmetic Brownian motion.

In general, both μ and σ can be time varying. We permit them to be functions of calendar time, t, and/or functions of the contemporaneous value of the random variable, $x(t)$. In this case, the *stochastic differential equation* describing $x(t)$ is

$$dx(t) = \mu[x(t), \, t] \, dt + \sigma[x(t), \, t] \, dz \tag{8.13}$$

and is a continuous-time Markov process, by which we mean that the instantaneous change in the process at date t has a distribution that depends only on t and the current level of the state variable $x(t)$, and not on prior values of the $x(s)$, for $s < t$. The function $\mu[x(t), \, t]$, which denotes the process's instantaneous expected change per unit time, is referred to as the process's *drift*, while the instantaneous standard deviation per unit time, $\sigma[x(t), \, t]$, is described as the process's *volatility*.

The process in equation (8.13) can also be written in terms of its corresponding integral equation:

$$x(T) - x(0) = \int_0^T dx = \int_0^T \mu[x(t), \, t] \, dt + \int_0^T \sigma[x(t), \, t] \, dz \tag{8.14}$$

In this general case, $dx(t)$ could be described as being *instantaneously* normally distributed with mean $\mu[x(t), \, t] \, dt$ and variance $\sigma^2[x(t), \, t] \, dt$, but over any finite interval, $x(t)$ generally will not be normally distributed. One needs to know the functional form of $\mu[x(t), \, t]$ and $\sigma[x(t), \, t]$ to determine the discrete-time distribution of $x(t)$ implied by its continuous-time process. Shortly, we will show how this discrete-time probability can be derived.

8.2.1   Definition of an Itô Integral

An Itô integral is formally defined as a mean-square limit of a sum involving the discrete Δz_i processes. For example, when $\sigma[x(t), \, t]$ is a function of $x(t)$ and t, the

Itô integral in equation (8.14), $\int_0^T \sigma[x(t), t]\,dz$, is defined from the relationship

$$\lim_{n \to \infty} E_0\left[\left(\sum_{i=1}^{n} \sigma\left[x\left([i-1]\cdot\Delta t\right), [i-1]\cdot\Delta t\right]\Delta z_i - \int_0^T \sigma[x(t), t]\,dz\right)^2\right] = 0$$

(8.15)

where we see that within the parentheses of (8.15) is the difference between the Itô integral and its discrete-time approximation. An important Itô integral that will be used next is $\int_0^T [dz(t)]^2$. In this case, (8.15) gives its definition as

$$\lim_{n \to \infty} E_0\left[\left(\sum_{i=1}^{n} [\Delta z_i]^2 - \int_0^T [dz(t)]^2\right)^2\right] = 0$$

(8.16)

To better understand the properties of $\int_0^T [dz(t)]^2$, recall from (8.5) that

$$Var_0\left[z(T) - z(0)\right] = Var_0\left[\sum_{i=1}^{n} \Delta z_i\right] = E_0\left[\left(\sum_{i=1}^{n} \Delta z_i\right)^2\right]$$

$$= E_0\left[\sum_{i=1}^{n} [\Delta z_i]^2\right] = T$$

(8.17)

because increments of z are serially uncorrelated. Further, straightforward algebra shows that[10]

$$E_0\left[\left(\sum_{i=1}^{n} [\Delta z_i]^2 - T\right)^2\right] = 2T\Delta t$$

(8.18)

Hence, taking the limit as $\Delta t \to 0$, or $n \to \infty$, of the expression in (8.18), one obtains

$$\lim_{n \to \infty} E_0\left[\left(\sum_{i=1}^{n} [\Delta z_i]^2 - T\right)^2\right] = \lim_{\Delta t \to 0} 2T\Delta t = 0$$

(8.19)

---

10. This calculation uses the result that $E_0[(\Delta z_i)^2(\Delta z_j)^2] = (\Delta t)(\Delta t) = (\Delta t)^2$ for $i \neq j$ and $E_0[(\Delta z_i)^4] = 3(\Delta t)^2$ because the fourth moment of a normally distributed random variable equals 3 times its squared variance.

Comparing (8.16) with (8.19) implies that in the sense of mean-square convergence, we have the equality

$$\int_0^T \left[dz\,(t) \right]^2 = T \tag{8.20}$$

$$= \int_0^T dt$$

Since $\int_0^T \left[dz\,(t) \right]^2$ converges to $\int_0^T dt$ for any T, we can see that over an infinitesimally short time period, $\left[dz\,(t) \right]^2$ converges to dt.

To further generalize continuous-time processes, suppose that we have some variable, F, that is a function of the current value of a diffusion process, $x(t)$, and (possibly) also is a direct function of time. Can we then characterize the stochastic process followed by $F(x(t),\ t)$, which now depends on the diffusion process, $x(t)$? The answer is yes, and Itô's lemma shows us how to do it.

8.3   Functions of Continuous-Time Processes and Itô's Lemma

Itô's lemma also is known as the *fundamental theorem of stochastic calculus*. It gives the rule for finding the differential of a function of variables that follow stochastic differential equations containing Wiener processes. Here we state Itô's lemma for the case of a function of a single variable that follows a diffusion process.

ITÔ'S LEMMA (UNIVARIATE CASE):   Let the variable $x(t)$ follow the stochastic differential equation $dx(t) = \mu(x,t)\,dt + \sigma(x,t)\,dz$. Also let $F(x(t),\ t)$ be at least a twice-differentiable function. Then the differential of $F(x,\ t)$ is given by

$$dF = \frac{\partial F}{\partial x}\,dx + \frac{\partial F}{\partial t}\,dt + \frac{1}{2}\frac{\partial^2 F}{\partial x^2}\,(dx)^2 \tag{8.21}$$

where the product $(dx)^2 = \sigma(x,t)^2 dt$. Hence, substituting in for dx and $(dx)^2$, (8.21) can be rewritten:

$$dF = \left[\frac{\partial F}{\partial x}\,\mu(x,t) + \frac{\partial F}{\partial t} + \frac{1}{2}\frac{\partial^2 F}{\partial x^2}\,\sigma^2(x,t) \right] dt + \frac{\partial F}{\partial x}\,\sigma(x,t)\,dz \tag{8.22}$$

Proof: A formal proof is rather lengthy and only a brief, intuitive outline of a proof is given here.[11] Let us first expand $F(x(t + \Delta t), t + \Delta t)$ in a Taylor series around date t and the value of x at date t:

$$F(x(t + \Delta t), t + \Delta t) = F(x(t), t) + \frac{\partial F}{\partial x}\Delta x + \frac{\partial F}{\partial t}\Delta t + \frac{1}{2}\frac{\partial^2 F}{\partial x^2}(\Delta x)^2$$

$$+ \frac{\partial^2 F}{\partial x \partial t}\Delta x \Delta t + \frac{1}{2}\frac{\partial^2 F}{\partial t^2}(\Delta t)^2 + H \tag{8.23}$$

where $\Delta x \equiv x(t + \Delta t) - x(t)$ and H refers to terms that are multiplied by higher orders of Δx and Δt. Now a discrete-time approximation of Δx can be written as

$$\Delta x = \mu(x, t)\,\Delta t + \sigma(x, t)\,\sqrt{\Delta t}\tilde{\epsilon} \tag{8.24}$$

Defining $\Delta F \equiv F(x(t + \Delta t), t + \Delta t) - F(x(t), t)$ and substituting (8.24) in for Δx, equation (8.23) can be rewritten as

$$\Delta F = \frac{\partial F}{\partial x}\left(\mu(x, t)\,\Delta t + \sigma(x, t)\,\sqrt{\Delta t}\tilde{\epsilon}\right) + \frac{\partial F}{\partial t}\Delta t$$

$$+ \frac{1}{2}\frac{\partial^2 F}{\partial x^2}\left(\mu(x, t)\,\Delta t + \sigma(x, t)\,\sqrt{\Delta t}\tilde{\epsilon}\right)^2 \tag{8.25}$$

$$+ \frac{\partial^2 F}{\partial x \partial t}\left(\mu(x, t)\,\Delta t + \sigma(x, t)\,\sqrt{\Delta t}\tilde{\epsilon}\right)\Delta t + \frac{1}{2}\frac{\partial^2 F}{\partial t^2}(\Delta t)^2 + H$$

The final step is to consider the limit of equation (8.25) as Δt becomes infinitesimal; that is, $\Delta t \to dt$ and $\Delta F \to dF$. Recall from (8.7) that $\sqrt{\Delta t}\tilde{\epsilon}$ becomes dz and from (8.20) that $[\sqrt{\Delta t}\tilde{\epsilon}][\sqrt{\Delta t}\tilde{\epsilon}]$ becomes $[dz(t)]^2$ and converges to dt. Furthermore, it can be shown that all terms of the form $(\Delta t)^n$ where $n > 1$ go to zero as $\Delta t \to dt$. Hence, terms that are multiplied by $(\Delta t)^{\frac{3}{2}}$, $(\Delta t)^2$, $(\Delta t)^{\frac{5}{2}}$, ..., including all of the terms in H, vanish. The result is equation (8.22). Similar arguments show that[12]

$$(dx)^2 = \left(\mu(x, t)\,dt + \sigma(x, t)\,dz\right)^2 \tag{8.26}$$

$$= \sigma(x, t)^2\left(dz\right)^2 = \sigma(x, t)^2 dt \quad \blacksquare$$

---

11. For more details, see Chapter 3 of Merton (Merton 1992), Chapter 16 of Ingersoll (Ingersoll 1987), or Chapter 10 in Neftci (Neftci 1996). A rigorous proof is given in Karatzas and Shreve (Karatzas and Shreve 1991).

12. Thus, it may be helpful to remember that in the continuous-time limit, $(dz)^2 = dt$ but $dz\,dt = 0$ and $dt^n = 0$ for $n > 1$. This follows from thinking of the discrete approximation of dz as being proportional to $\sqrt{\Delta t}$, and any product that results in $(\Delta t)^n$ will go to zero as $\Delta t \to dt$ when n is strictly greater than 1.

Note from (8.22) that the dF process is similar to the dx process in that both depend on the same Brownian motion dz. Thus, while dF will have a mean (drift) and variance (volatility) that differs from dx, they both depend on the same source of uncertainty.

8.3.1   Geometric Brownian Motion

A process that is used in many applications is the geometric Brownian motion process. It is given by

$$dx = \mu x \, dt + \sigma x \, dz \tag{8.27}$$

where μ and σ are constants. It is an attractive process because if x starts at a positive value, it always remains positive. This is because its mean and variance are both proportional to its current value, x. Hence, a process like dx is often used to model the price of a limited-liability security, such as a common stock. Now consider the following function $F(x, t) = \ln(x)$. For example, if x is a security's price, then $dF = d(\ln x)$ represents this security's continuously compounded return. What type of process does $dF = d(\ln x)$ follow? Applying Itô's lemma, we have

$$dF = d(\ln x) = \left[\frac{\partial(\ln x)}{\partial x} \mu x + \frac{\partial(\ln x)}{\partial t} + \frac{1}{2} \frac{\partial^2(\ln x)}{\partial x^2} (\sigma x)^2 \right] dt$$

$$+ \frac{\partial(\ln x)}{\partial x} \sigma x \, dz$$

$$= \left[\mu + 0 - \frac{1}{2}\sigma^2 \right] dt + \sigma \, dz \tag{8.28}$$

Thus, we see that if x follows *geometric* Brownian motion, then $F = \ln x$ follows *arithmetic* Brownian motion. Since we know that

$$F(T) - F(0) \sim N\left((\mu - \frac{1}{2}\sigma^2) T, \ \sigma^2 T \right) \tag{8.29}$$

then $x(t) = e^{F(t)}$ has a lognormal distribution over any discrete interval (by the definition of a lognormal random variable). Hence, geometric Brownian motion is lognormally distributed over any time interval.

Figure 8.2 illustrates 300 simulated sample paths of geometric Brownian motion for $\mu = 0.10$ and $\sigma = 0.30$ over the period from $t = 0$ to 2, with $x(0) = 1$. These drift and volatility values are typical for a U.S. common stock. As the figure

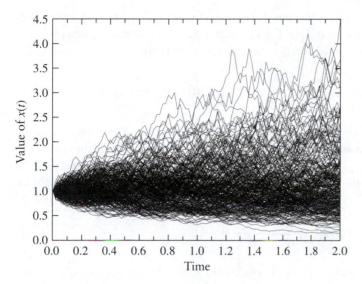

Figure 8.2 —— Geometric Brownian Motion Sample Paths

shows, the sample paths determine a frequency distribution at $T = 2$, which is skewed upward, as it should be since the discrete-time distribution is lognormal and bounded at zero.

8.3.2   Kolmogorov Equation

There are many instances where knowledge of a diffusion process's discrete-time probability distribution is very useful. As we shall see in future chapters, valuing a contingent claim often entails computing an expected value of its discounted terminal payoff at a specific future date. This discounted terminal payoff frequently depends on the value of a diffusion process, so that computing its expected value requires knowledge of the process's discrete-time probability distribution. Another situation where it is helpful to know a diffusion process's discrete-time distribution occurs when one wishes to estimate the process's drift and volatility parameters using time series data. Because time series data is typically sampled discretely rather than continuously, empirical techniques such as maximum likelihood estimation often require use of the process's discrete-time distribution.

A general method for finding the implied discrete-time probability distribution for a continuous-time process is to use the backward Kolmogorov equation. A heuristic derivation of this condition is as follows. Let $x(t)$ follow the general diffusion process given by equation (8.13). Also let $p(x, T; x_t, t)$ be the probability density function for x at date T given that it equals x_t at date t, where $T \geq t$. Applying Itô's lemma to this density function, one obtains[13]

$$dp = \left[\frac{\partial p}{\partial x_t} \mu(x_t, t) + \frac{\partial p}{\partial t} + \frac{1}{2} \frac{\partial^2 p}{\partial x_t^2} \sigma^2(x_t, t) \right] dt + \frac{\partial p}{\partial x_t} \sigma(x_t, t) \, dz \qquad (8.30)$$

Intuitively, one can see that only new information that was unexpected at date t should change the probability density of x at date T. In other words, for small $\Delta < T - t$, $E\left[p(x, T; x_{t+\Delta}, t + \Delta) \,|\, x(t) = x_t \right] = p(x, T; x_t, t)$.[14] This implies that the expected change in p should be zero; that is, the drift term in (8.30) should be zero:

$$\frac{1}{2}\sigma^2(x_t, t) \frac{\partial^2 p}{\partial x_t^2} + \mu[x_t, t]\frac{\partial p}{\partial x_t} + \frac{\partial p}{\partial t} = 0 \qquad (8.31)$$

Condition (8.31) is referred to as the backward Kolmogorov equation. This partial differential equation for $p(x, T; x_t, t)$ can be solved subject to the boundary condition that when t becomes equal to T, then x must equal x_t with probability 1. Formally, this boundary condition can be written as $p(x, t; x_t, t) = \delta(x - x_t)$, where $\delta(\cdot)$ is the Dirac delta function, which is defined as $\delta(0) = \infty$, $\delta(y) = 0$ for all $y \neq 0$, and $\int_{-\infty}^{\infty} \delta(y) \, dy = 1$.

For example, recall that if x_t follows geometric Brownian motion, then $\mu[x_t, t] = \mu x_t$ and $\sigma^2(x_t, t) = \sigma^2 x_t^2$ where μ and σ are constants. In this case the Kolmogorov equation becomes

$$\frac{1}{2}\sigma^2 x_t^2 \frac{\partial^2 p}{\partial x_t^2} + \mu x_t \frac{\partial p}{\partial x_t} + \frac{\partial p}{\partial t} = 0 \qquad (8.32)$$

By substitution into (8.32), it can be verified that the solution to this partial differential equation subject to the boundary condition that $p(x, t; x_t, t) = \delta(x - x_t)$ is[15]

---

13. In order to invoke Itô's lemma, we assume that the density function $p(x, T, x_t, t)$ is differentiable in t and twice differentiable in x_t. Under particular conditions, the differentiability of p can be proved, but this issue will not be dealt with here.

14. Essentially, this result derives from the *Law of Iterated Expectations*.

15. Methods for solving partial differential equations are beyond the scope of this book. However, if one makes the change in variable $y_t = \ln(x_t)$, then equation (8.32) can be transformed to a more simple partial differential equation with constant coefficients. Its solution is the probability density function of a normally distributed random variable. Reversing the change in variables to $x_t = e^{y_t}$ results in the lognormal density function.

$$p\left(x, T, x_t, t\right)$$

$$= \frac{1}{x\sqrt{2\pi\sigma^2\left(T-t\right)}} \exp\left[-\frac{\left(\ln x - \ln x_t - \left(\mu - \frac{1}{2}\sigma^2\right)\left(T-t\right)\right)^2}{2\sigma^2\left(T-t\right)}\right] \tag{8.33}$$

which is the lognormal probability density function for the random variable $x \in (0, \infty)$. Hence, the backward Kolmogorov equation verifies that a variable following geometric Brownian motion is lognormally distributed. For a diffusion process with general drift and volatility functions, $\mu(x, t)$ and $\sigma(x, t)$, it may not be easy or possible to find a closed-form expression solution for $p\left(x, T, x_t, t\right)$ such as in (8.33). Still, there are a number of instances where the Kolmogorov equation is valuable in deriving or verifying a diffusion's discrete-time distribution.[16]

8.3.3   Multivariate Diffusions and Itô's Lemma

In a number of portfolio choice and asset pricing applications that we will encounter in future chapters, one needs to derive the stochastic process for a function of several variables, each of which follows a diffusion process. So suppose we have m different diffusion processes of the form[17]

$$dx_i = \mu_i \, dt + \sigma_i \, dz_i \quad i = 1, \ldots, m, \tag{8.34}$$

and $dz_i dz_j = \rho_{ij}dt$, where ρ_{ij} has the interpretation of a correlation coefficient of the two Wiener processes. What is meant by this correlation? Recall that $dz_i dz_i = \left(dz_i\right)^2 = dt$. Now the Wiener process dz_j can be written as a linear combination of two other Wiener processes, one being dz_i, and another process that is uncorrelated with dz_i, call it dz_{iu}:

$$dz_j = \rho_{ij}dz_i + \sqrt{1 - \rho_{ij}^2}dz_{iu} \tag{8.35}$$

---

16. Andrew Lo (Lo 1988) provides additional examples where the backward Kolmogorov equation is used to derive discrete-time distributions. These examples include not only diffusion processes but the type of mixed jump-diffusion processes that we will examine in Chapter 11.

17. Note μ_i and σ_i may be functions of calendar time, t, and the current values of x_j, $j = 1, \ldots, m$.

Then from this interpretation of dz_j, we have

$$dz_j dz_j = \rho_{ij}^2 (dz_i)^2 + \left(1 - \rho_{ij}^2\right) (dz_{iu})^2 + 2\rho_{ij}\sqrt{1 - \rho_{ij}^2} dz_i dz_{iu} \qquad (8.36)$$

$$= \rho_{ij}^2 dt + \left(1 - \rho_{ij}^2\right) dt + 0$$

$$= dt$$

and

$$dz_i dz_j = dz_i \left(\rho_{ij} dz_i + \sqrt{1 - \rho_{ij}^2} dz_{iu}\right) \qquad (8.37)$$

$$= \rho_{ij} (dz_i)^2 + \sqrt{1 - \rho_{ij}^2} dz_i dz_{iu}$$

$$= \rho_{ij} dt + 0$$

Thus, ρ_{ij} can be interpreted as the proportion of dz_j that is perfectly correlated with dz_i.

We can now state, without proof, a multivariate version of Itô's lemma.

ITÔ'S LEMMA (MULTIVARIATE VERSION): Let $F(x_1, \ldots, x_m, t)$ be at least a twice-differentiable function. Then the differential of $F(x_1, \ldots, x_m, t)$ is given by

$$dF = \sum_{i=1}^{m} \frac{\partial F}{\partial x_i} dx_i + \frac{\partial F}{\partial t} dt + \frac{1}{2} \sum_{i=1}^{m} \sum_{j=1}^{m} \frac{\partial^2 F}{\partial x_i \partial x_j} dx_i dx_j \qquad (8.38)$$

where $dx_i dx_j = \sigma_i \sigma_j \rho_{ij} dt$. Hence, (8.38) can be rewritten as

$$dF = \left[\sum_{i=1}^{m} \left(\frac{\partial F}{\partial x_i} \mu_i + \frac{1}{2} \frac{\partial^2 F}{\partial x_i^2} \sigma_i^2 \right) + \frac{\partial F}{\partial t} + \sum_{i=1}^{m} \sum_{j>i}^{m} \frac{\partial^2 F}{\partial x_i \partial x_j} \sigma_i \sigma_j \rho_{ij} \right] dt$$

$$+ \sum_{i=1}^{m} \frac{\partial F}{\partial x_i} \sigma_i dz_i \qquad (8.39)$$

Equation (8.39) generalizes our earlier statement of Itô's lemma for a univariate diffusion, equation (8.22). Notably, we see that the process followed by a function of several diffusion processes inherits each of the processes' Brownian motions.

8.4 Summary

Diffusion processes and Itô's lemma are important tools for modeling financial time series, especially when individuals are assumed to be able to trade continuously. Brownian motion is the foundation of diffusion processes and is a continuous-time limit of a particular discrete-time random walk process. By modifying Brownian motion's instantaneous mean and variance, a wide variety of diffusion processes can be created. Itô's lemma tells us how to find the differential of a function of a diffusion process. As we shall see in the next chapter, Itô's lemma is essential for valuing a contingent claim when its payoff depends on the price of an underlying asset that follows a diffusion. This is because the contingent claim's value becomes a function of the underlying asset's value.

This chapter also showed that Itô's lemma could be used to derive the Kolmogorov equation, an important relation for finding the discrete-time distribution of a random variable that follows a diffusion process. Finally, we saw that multivariate diffusions are natural extensions of univariate ones and that the process followed by a function of several diffusions can be derived from a multivariate version of Itô's lemma.

8.5 Exercises

1. A variable, $x(t)$, follows the process

   $$dx = \mu dt + \sigma dz$$

   where μ and σ are constants. Find the process followed by $y(t) = e^{\alpha x(t) - \beta t}$.

2. Let P be a price index, such as the Consumer Price Index (CPI). Let M equal the nominal supply (stock) of money in the economy. For example, M might be designated as the amount of bank deposits and currency in circulation. Assume P and M each follow geometric Brownian motion processes

   $$\frac{dP}{P} = \mu_p dt + \sigma_p dz_p$$

   $$\frac{dM}{M} = \mu_m dt + \sigma_m dz_m$$

   with $dz_p dz_m = \rho dt$. Monetary economists define real money balances, m, to be $m = \frac{M}{P}$. Derive the stochastic process for m.

3. The value (price) of a portfolio of stocks, $S(t)$, follows a geometric Brownian motion process:

   $$dS/S = \alpha_s dt + \sigma_s dz_s$$

   while the dividend yield for this portfolio, $y(t)$, follows the process

   $$dy = \kappa (\gamma S - y) dt + \sigma_y y^{\frac{1}{2}} dz_y$$

   where $dz_s dz_y = \rho dt$ and κ, γ, and σ_y are positive constants. Solve for the process followed by the portfolio's dividends paid per unit time, $D(t) = yS$.

4. The Ornstein-Uhlenbeck process can be useful for modeling a time series whose value changes stochastically but which tends to revert to a long-run value (its unconditional or steady state mean). This continuous-time process is given by

$$dy(t) = \left[\alpha - \beta y(t)\right] dt + \sigma \, dz(t)$$

The process is sometimes referred to as an *elastic random walk*. $y(t)$ varies stochastically around its unconditional mean of α/β, and β is a measure of the strength of the variable's reversion to this mean.

   Find the distribution of $y(t)$ given $y(t_0)$, where $t > t_0$. In particular, find $E\left[y(t) \mid y(t_0)\right]$ and $Var\left[y(t) \mid y(t_0)\right]$. Hint: make the change in variables:

$$x(t) = \left(y(t) - \frac{\alpha}{\beta}\right) e^{\beta(t-t_0)}$$

and apply Itô's lemma to find the stochastic process for $x(t)$. The distribution and first two moments of $x(t)$ should be obvious. From this, derive the distribution and moments of $y(t)$.

CHAPTER 9

Dynamic Hedging and PDE Valuation

Having introduced diffusion processes and Itô's lemma in the previous chapter, we now apply these tools to derive the equilibrium prices of contingent claims. In this chapter asset prices are modeled as following diffusion processes. Because prices are permitted to vary continuously, it is feasible to also assume that individuals can choose to trade assets continuously. With the additional assumption that markets are "frictionless," this environment can allow the markets for a contingent claim, its underlying asset, and the risk-free asset to be dynamically complete.[1] Although the returns of the underlying asset and its contingent claim have a continuous distribution over any finite time interval, implying an infinite number of states for their future values, the future values of the contingent claim can be replicated by a dynamic trading strategy involving its underlying asset and the risk-free asset.

By way of three examples, we illustrate the Black-Scholes-Merton portfolio hedging argument that results in a partial differential equation (PDE) for a contingent claim's price. Solving this PDE subject to the appropriate boundary condition determines a unique price for the contingent security. Our first example is the well-known Fischer Black–Myron Scholes (Black and Scholes 1973) option pricing model. The second is the equilibrium term structure model of Oldrich Vasicek (Vasicek 1977). The final example combines aspects of the first two. It is Robert Merton's (Merton 1973b) option pricing model with stochastic interest rates.

---

1. Frictionless markets are characterized as having no direct trading costs or restrictions, that is, markets for which there are no transactions costs, taxes, short sales restrictions, or indivisibilities when trading assets.

As the next chapter will show, contingent claims prices also can be derived using alternative solution techniques: the martingale pricing approach, which involves computing expectations of a risk-neutral probability distribution; and the stochastic discount factor (pricing kernel) approach, where expectations are computed for the physical probability distribution. In some situations, it may be easier to derive contingent claims prices by solving the equilibrium PDE. In others, the martingale technique or stochastic discount factor approach may be simplest. All of these methods should be in a financial economist's toolbox.

9.1   Black-Scholes Option Pricing

The major insight of Black and Scholes (Black and Scholes 1973) is that when assets follow diffusion processes, an option's payoff can be replicated by continuous trading in its underlying asset and a risk-free asset. In the absence of arbitrage, the ability to replicate or "hedge" the option with the underlying stock and a risk-free asset restricts the option's value to bear a particular relationship to its underlying asset and the risk-free return. The Black-Scholes hedging argument is similar to that presented earlier in the context of the binomial option pricing model. The main difference is that the appropriate replicating portfolio changed only once per period in the binomial model, whereas in the Black-Scholes environment the replicating portfolio changes continuously. In the binomial model, market completion resulted from the assumption that at the end of each period there were only two states for the underlying asset's value. Under Black-Scholes assumptions, markets become dynamically complete due to the ability to trade continuously in the underlying asset whose price follows a continuous sample path.

9.1.1   Portfolio Dynamics in Continuous Time

A prerequisite for analyzing the Black-Scholes hedging of contingent claims is to consider the dynamics of a security portfolio in continuous time. The Black-Scholes hedge portfolio consists of a position in the contingent claim and its underlying asset, but we will begin by examining the general problem of an investor who can trade in any n different assets whose prices follow diffusion processes. Let us define $S_i(t)$ as the price per share of asset i at date t, where $i = 1, \ldots, n$. The instantaneous rate of return on the ith asset is assumed to satisfy the process

$$dS_i(t) / S_i(t) = \mu_i \, dt + \sigma_i \, dz_i \tag{9.1}$$

where its instantaneous expected return and variance, μ_i and σ_i^2, may be functions of time and possibly other asset prices or state variables that follow diffusion processes. For simplicity, assets are assumed to pay no cashflows (dividends or coupon payments), so that their total returns are given by their price changes.[2] An investor is assumed to form a portfolio of these assets and, in general, the portfolio may experience cash inflows and outflows. Thus, let $F(t)$ be the net cash outflow per unit time from the portfolio at date t. For example, $F(t)$ may be positive because the individual chooses to liquidate some of the portfolio to pay for consumption expenditures. Alternatively, $F(t)$ may be negative because the individual receives wage income that is invested in the securities.

To derive the proper continuous-time dynamics for this investor's portfolio, we will first consider the analogous discrete-time dynamics where each discrete period is of length h. We will then take the limit as $h \to 0$. Therefore, let $w_i(t)$ be the number of shares held by the investor in asset i from date t to $t + h$. The value of the portfolio at the beginning of date t is denoted as $H(t)$ and equals the prior period's holdings at date t prices:

$$H(t) = \sum_{i=1}^{n} w_i(t - h) S_i(t) \tag{9.2}$$

Given these date t prices, the individual may choose to liquidate some of the portfolio or augment it with new funds. The net cash outflow over the period is $F(t) h$, which must equal the net sales of assets. Note that $F(t)$ should be interpreted as the average liquidation rate over the interval from t to $t + h$:

$$-F(t) h = \sum_{i=1}^{n} [w_i(t) - w_i(t - h)] S_i(t) \tag{9.3}$$

To properly derive the limits of equations (9.2) and (9.3) as of date t and as $h \to 0$, we need to convert backward differences, such as $w_i(t) - w_i(t - h)$, to forward differences. We do this by updating one period, so that at the start of the next period, $t + h$, we have

$$-F(t + h) h = \sum_{i=1}^{n} [w_i(t + h) - w_i(t)] S_i(t + h)$$

$$= \sum_{i=1}^{n} [w_i(t + h) - w_i(t)] [S_i(t + h) - S_i(t)]$$

$$+ \sum_{i=1}^{n} [w_i(t + h) - w_i(t)] S_i(t) \tag{9.4}$$

---

2. This is not a critical assumption. What matters is the assets' expected rates of return and covariances, rather than their price changes per se. If an asset, such as a common stock or mutual fund, paid a dividend that was reinvested into new shares of the asset, then equation (9.1) would represent the percentage change in the value of the asset holding and thus the total rate of return.

and

$$H(t+h) = \sum_{i=1}^{n} w_i(t) S_i(t+h) \qquad (9.5)$$

Taking the limits of (9.4) and (9.5) as $h \to 0$ gives the results

$$-F(t) \ dt = \sum_{i=1}^{n} dw_i(t) \ dS_i(t) + \sum_{i=1}^{n} dw_i(t) \ S_i(t) \qquad (9.6)$$

and

$$H(t) = \sum_{i=1}^{n} w_i(t) \ S_i(t) \qquad (9.7)$$

Applying Itô's lemma to (9.7), we can derive the dynamics of the portfolio's value to be

$$dH(t) = \sum_{i=1}^{n} w_i(t) \ dS_i(t) + \sum_{i=1}^{n} dw_i(t) S_i(t) + \sum_{i=1}^{n} dw_i(t) \ dS_i(t) \qquad (9.8)$$

Substituting (9.6) into (9.8), we obtain

$$dH(t) = \sum_{i=1}^{n} w_i(t) \ dS_i(t) - F(t) \ dt \qquad (9.9)$$

Equation (9.9) says that the portfolio's value changes due to capital gains income less net cash outflows. Substituting (9.1) into (9.9), we arrive at

$$dH(t) = \sum_{i=1}^{n} w_i(t) \ dS_i(t) - F(t) \ dt$$

$$= \sum_{i=1}^{n} w_i(t) \left[\mu_i \ S_i dt + \sigma_i S_i \ dz_i \right] - F(t) \ dt \qquad (9.10)$$

Now, in some cases, rather than write a portfolio's dynamics in terms of the number of shares of each asset, $w_i(t)$, $i = 1, \ldots, n$, we may wish to write it in terms of each asset's proportion of the total portfolio value. If we define the proportion of $H(t)$ invested in asset i as $\omega_i(t) = w_i(t)S_i(t)/H(t)$, then (9.10) becomes

$$dH(t) = \sum_{i=1}^{n} \omega_i(t) H(t) \left[\mu_i dt + \sigma_i \ dz_i \right] - F(t) \ dt \qquad (9.11)$$

or

$$dH\left(t\right) = \left[\sum_{i=1}^{n} \omega_i\left(t\right) H\left(t\right) \mu_i - F\left(t\right)\right] dt + \sum_{i=1}^{n} \omega_i\left(t\right) H\left(t\right) \sigma_i \, dz_i \tag{9.12}$$

Note from (9.7) that $\sum_{i=1}^{n} \omega_i\left(t\right) = 1$; that is, the portfolio proportions invested in the n risky assets must sum to 1. However, consider the introduction of a new risk-free asset. If, in addition to n risky assets, there is an asset that pays an instantaneously risk-free rate of return, then this would correspond to an asset having an instantaneous standard deviation, σ_i, of zero and an expected rate of return, μ_i, equal to the instantaneous risk-free rate, which we denote as $r\left(t\right)$. In this case, the portfolio proportion invested in the risk-free asset equals $1 - \sum_{i=1}^{n} \omega_i\left(t\right)$. With this extension, equation (9.12) becomes

$dH\left(t\right)$

$$= \left[\sum_{i=1}^{n} \omega_i\left(t\right) \left(\mu_i - r\right) H\left(t\right) \mu_i + rH\left(t\right) - F\left(t\right)\right] dt + \sum_{i=1}^{n} \omega_i\left(t\right) H\left(t\right) \sigma_i \, dz_i$$

$$\tag{9.13}$$

Having derived the continuous-time dynamics of an investment portfolio, we now turn to the Black-Scholes approach to valuing contingent claims.

9.1.2 Black-Scholes Model Assumptions

The Black-Scholes model assumes that there is a contingent claim whose underlying asset pays no dividends. We will refer to this underlying asset as a stock, and its date t price per share, $S(t)$, is assumed to follow the diffusion process

$$dS = \mu S \, dt + \sigma S \, dz \tag{9.14}$$

where the instantaneous expected rate of return on the stock, μ, may be a function of S and t, that is, $\mu(S, t)$. However, the standard deviation of the stock's rate of return, σ, is assumed to be constant. It is also assumed that there is a risk-free asset that earns a constant rate of return equal to r per unit time. Hence, if an amount $B\left(t\right)$ is invested in the risk-free asset, this value follows the process

$$dB = rBdt \tag{9.15}$$

Now consider a European call option on this stock that matures at date T and has an exercise price of X. Denote the option's date t value as $c(S, t)$. We assume it is a function of both calendar time, t, and the current stock price, $S\left(t\right)$, since at the maturity date $t = T$, the option's payoff depends on $S\left(T\right)$:

$$c(S(T), T) = \max[\,0, \; S(T) - X] \tag{9.16}$$

Given that the option's value depends on the stock price and calendar time, what process does it follow prior to maturity?[3] Let us assume that $c(S, t)$ is a twice-differentiable function of S and is differentiable in t. Later, we will verify that the no-arbitrage value of $c(S, t)$ does indeed satisfy these conditions. Then we can apply Itô's lemma to state that the option's value must follow a process of the form

$$dc = \left[\frac{\partial c}{\partial S} \mu S + \frac{\partial c}{\partial t} + \frac{1}{2} \frac{\partial^2 c}{\partial S^2} \sigma^2 S^2 \right] dt + \frac{\partial c}{\partial S} \sigma S \, dz \tag{9.17}$$

Hence, the call option inherits the same source of risk as the underlying stock, reflected in the Wiener process dz.

9.1.3   The Hedge Portfolio

Now consider forming a portfolio that includes -1 unit of the option and a position in the underlying stock and the risk-free asset. Such a portfolio would reflect the wealth position of an option dealer who has just sold one call option to a customer and now attempts to hedge this liability by purchasing some of the underlying stock and investing or borrowing at the risk-free rate. We restrict this portfolio to require zero net investment; that is, after selling one unit of the call option and taking a hedge position in the underlying stock, the remaining surplus or deficit of funds is made up by borrowing or lending at the risk-free rate. Moreover, we require that the portfolio be self-financing, that is, $F(t) = 0$ $\forall t$, by which we mean that any surplus or deficit of funds from the option and stock positions are made up by investing or acquiring funds at the risk-free rate. Hence, if we let $w(t)$ be the number of shares invested in the stock, then this zero-net-investment, self-financing restriction implies that the amount invested in the risk-free asset for all dates t must be $B(t) = c(t) - w(t) S(t)$. Therefore, denoting the value of this hedge portfolio as $H(t)$ implies that its instantaneous return satisfies

$$dH(t) = -dc(t) + w(t) \, dS(t) + [c(t) - w(t) S(t)] r dt \tag{9.18}$$

Substituting (9.14) and (9.17) into (9.18), we obtain

$$dH(t) = - \left[\frac{\partial c}{\partial S} \mu S + \frac{\partial c}{\partial t} + \frac{1}{2} \frac{\partial^2 c}{\partial S^2} \sigma^2 S^2 \right] dt - \frac{\partial c}{\partial S} \sigma S \, dz$$

$$+ w(t) \left(\mu S \, dt + \sigma S \, dz \right) + [c(t) - w(t) S(t)] r dt \tag{9.19}$$

---

3. The option's value also depends on the risk-free rate, r, but since r is assumed to be constant, it need not be an explicit argument of the option's value.

Now consider selecting the number of shares invested in the stock in such a way as to offset the risk of the return on the option. Specifically, suppose that the option dealer chooses $w(t) = \partial c / \partial S$ units (shares) of the stock, which is the local sensitivity of the option's value to the value of the underlying stock, also known as the "hedge ratio."[4] Hence, the hedging portfolio involves maintaining a unit short position in the option and a position of $\partial c / \partial S$ shares of stock, with any surplus or deficit of funds required to maintain this hedge being invested or acquired at the risk-free rate. As will be verified, since $c(S, t)$ is a nonlinear function of S and t, $w(t) = \partial c / \partial S$ varies continuously over time as S and t change: the hedge portfolio's number of shares invested in the stock is not constant, but is continuously rebalanced.[5] However, as long as a position of $\partial c / \partial S$ shares of stock are held, we can substitute $w(t) = \partial c / \partial S$ into (9.19) to obtain

$$dH(t) = -\left[\frac{\partial c}{\partial S} \mu S + \frac{\partial c}{\partial t} + \frac{1}{2}\frac{\partial^2 c}{\partial S^2} \sigma^2 S^2\right] dt - \frac{\partial c}{\partial S} \sigma S\, dz$$

$$+ \frac{\partial c}{\partial S}\left(\mu S\, dt + \sigma S\, dz\right) + \left[c(t) - \frac{\partial c}{\partial S} S(t)\right] rdt$$

$$= \left[-\frac{\partial c}{\partial t} - \frac{1}{2}\sigma^2 S^2 \frac{\partial^2 c}{\partial S^2} + rc(t) - rS(t)\frac{\partial c}{\partial S}\right] dt \qquad (9.20)$$

Note that, by design, the return on this portfolio is instantaneously riskless. Not only do the dz terms in the first line of (9.20) drop out, but so do the terms that depend on the stock's drift, μ. By continually readjusting the number of shares held in the stock so that it always equals $\partial c / \partial S$, the risk of the option is perfectly hedged. Dynamic trading in the stock is able to replicate the risk of the option because both the option and stock depend on the same (continuous-time) Brownian motion process, dz. In this sense, when assets follow continuous-time stochastic processes, dynamic (continuous) trading can lead to a complete market and permit the pricing of contingent claims.

9.1.4   No-Arbitrage Implies a PDE

Since the rate of return on this "hedge" portfolio is riskless, to avoid arbitrage it must equal the competitive risk-free rate of return, r. But since we restricted the

---

4. $\partial c / \partial S$ is analogous to the hedge ratio Δ in the binomial option pricing model. Recall that the optimal choice of this hedge ratio was $\Delta^* = (c_u - c_d) / (uS - dS)$, which is essentially the same partial derivative.

5. Since $c(S, t)$ is yet to be determined, the question arises as to how $w(t) = \partial c / \partial S$ would be known to create the hedge portfolio. We will verify that if such a position in the stock is maintained, then a no-arbitrage value for the option, $c(S, t)$, is determined, which, in turn, makes known the hedge ratio $w(t) = \partial c / \partial S$.

hedge portfolio to require zero net investment at the initial date, say, $t = 0$, then $H(0) = 0$ and

$$dH(0) = rH(0) \, dt = r0dt = 0 \qquad (9.21)$$

This implies $H(t) = 0 \; \forall t$ so that $dH(t) = 0 \; \forall t$. This no-arbitrage condition along with (9.20) allows us to write

$$\frac{\partial c}{\partial t} + \frac{1}{2}\sigma^2 S^2 \frac{\partial^2 c}{\partial S^2} + rS\frac{\partial c}{\partial S} - rc = 0 \qquad (9.22)$$

which is the Black-Scholes partial differential equation. The call option's value must satisfy this partial differential equation subject to the boundary condition

$$c(S(T), \; T) = \max[\, 0, \; S(T) - X\,] \qquad (9.23)$$

The solution to (9.22) and (9.23) is[6]

$$c(S(t), \; t) = S(t)\, N(d_1) \; - \; X\, e^{-r\,(T-t)}\, N(d_2) \qquad (9.24)$$

where

$$d_1 = \frac{\ln(S(t)/X) + \left(r + \frac{1}{2}\sigma^2\right)(T - t)}{\sigma\sqrt{T - t}} \qquad (9.25)$$

$$d_2 = d_1 - \sigma\sqrt{T - t}$$

and $N(\cdot)$ is the standard normal distribution function. Similar to the binomial option pricing formula, the value of the call option does not depend on the stock's expected rate of return, μ, but on only its current price, $S(t)$, and volatility, σ. The value of a European put option follows immediately from put-call parity:[7]

$$p(S(t), \; t) = c(S(t), \; t) + X\, e^{-r\,(T-t)} - S(t) \qquad (9.26)$$

$$= S(t)\, N(d_1) \; - \; X\, e^{-r\,(T-t)}\, N(d_2) + X\, e^{-r\,(T-t)} - S(t)$$

$$= X\, e^{-r\,(T-t)}\, N(-d_2) - S(t) N(-d_1)$$

By taking the partial derivatives of (9.24) and (9.26) with respect to $S(t)$, the call and put options' hedge ratios are shown to be[8]

---

6. The solution can be derived using a separation of variables method (Churchill and Brown 1978) or a LaPlace transform method (Shimko 1992). Also, in Chapter 10, we will show how (9.24) can be derived using risk-neutral valuation.

7. The last line uses the symmetry property of the normal distribution $1 - N(x) = N(-x)$.

8. Deriving these partial derivatives is more tedious than it might first appear since d_1 and d_2 are both functions of $S(t)$. Note that $\partial c/\partial S = N(d_1) + Sn(d_1)\frac{\partial d_1}{\partial S} - Xe^{-r(T-t)}n(d_2)\frac{\partial d_2}{\partial S}$ where

$$\frac{\partial c}{\partial S} = N\left(d_1\right) \tag{9.27}$$

$$\frac{\partial p}{\partial S} = -N\left(-d_1\right) \tag{9.28}$$

which implies $0 < \partial c/\partial S < 1$ and $-1 < \partial p/\partial S < 0$. Hence, hedging a call option requires a long position in less than one share of the underlying stock, whereas hedging a put option requires a short position in less than one share of the underlying stock. Since d_1 is an increasing function of $S\left(t\right)$, the hedge portfolio for a call option increases the share amount in the stock as its price rises. A similar argument shows that the hedge portfolio for a put option increases the share amount sold short as the price of the stock falls. Thus, because $S\left(t\right)$ moves in a continuous fashion, so will the hedge portfolio's position in the stock. Finally, based on the solution in (9.24), we can verify that both $\partial^2 c/\partial S^2$ and $\partial c/\partial t$ exist, which justifies our use of Itô's lemma in deriving the process followed by the option's price.[9]

We now turn to another application of the Black-Scholes-Merton hedging argument for deriving security prices. However, rather than derive the price of a contingent security in terms of an underlying asset price, we next consider pricing securities that pay known (fixed) cashflows at different future dates. That is, we derive the relationship between the prices of different maturity bonds, also known as fixed-income securities. This provides an introduction into the literature on the term structure of interest rates (or bond yields).

9.2 An Equilibrium Term Structure Model

The previous section showed that in a continuous-time environment, the absence of arbitrage restricts a derivative's price in terms of its underlying asset's price. We now consider a second example of how the absence of arbitrage links security prices. When the prices of default-free bonds are assumed to be driven by

---

$n(d) = \frac{1}{\sqrt{2\pi}} \exp(\frac{1}{2}d^2)$ is the standard normal probability density function. This reduces to (9.27) because it can be shown that $Sn(d_1)\frac{\partial d_1}{\partial S} = Xe^{-r(T-t)}n(d_2)\frac{\partial d_2}{\partial S}$. Practitioners refer to the hedge ratios in (9.27) and (9.28) as the options' *deltas*.

9. Using (9.27) and (9.28), it is easy to see that $\partial^2 c/\partial S^2 = \partial^2 p/\partial S^2 = n\left(d_1\right)/[S\sigma\sqrt{T-t}] > 0$ where $n\left(x\right) = \partial N\left(x\right)/\partial x = e^{-x^2/2}/\sqrt{2\pi}$ is the standard normal probability density function. Hence, both call and put options are convex functions of the underlying asset price. Practitioners refer to this second derivative as the option's *gamma*. The larger an option's gamma, the larger is the required change in the hedge ratio for a given change in the underlying asset's price. The option's *theta* or *time decay* is given by $\partial c/\partial \left(T - t\right) = -Sn(d_1)\sigma/\left[2\left(T-t\right)\right] - rXe^{-r(T-t)}N(d_2)$.

continuous-time stochastic processes, continuous trading and the no-arbitrage condition can lead to equilibrium relationships between the prices of different maturity bonds. The simplest equilibrium bond pricing models assume that a single source of uncertainty affects bonds of all maturities. For these "one-factor" bond pricing models, it is often convenient to think of this uncertainty as being summarized by the yield on the shortest (instantaneous) maturity bond, $r(t)$.[10] This is the assumption we make in presenting the Oldrich Vasicek (Vasicek 1977) model of the term structure of interest rates.

Define $P(t, \tau)$ as the date t price of a bond that makes a single payment of $1 in τ periods, at date $T = t + \tau$. Hence, τ denotes this "zero-coupon" or "pure discount" bond's time until maturity. The instantaneous rate of return on the bond is given by $\frac{dP(t,\tau)}{P(t,\tau)}$. Also note that, by definition, $P(t, 0) = \$1$. The instantaneous yield, $r(t)$, is defined as

$$\lim_{\tau \to 0} \frac{dP(t, \tau)}{P(t, \tau)} \equiv r(t)\, dt \tag{9.29}$$

The Vasicek model assumes $r(t)$ follows an Ornstein-Uhlenbeck process:

$$dr(t) = \alpha\, [\bar{r} - r(t)]\, dt + \sigma_r dz_r \tag{9.30}$$

where α, $\bar{r}$, and σ_r are positive constants. The parameter σ_r measures the instantaneous volatility of $r(t)$, while α measures the strength of the process's mean reversion to $\bar{r}$, the unconditional mean value of the process. In discrete time, (9.30) is equivalent to a normally distributed, autoregressive (1) process.[11] Figure 9.1 illustrates a typical sample path for $r(t)$ that assumes the annualized parameter values of $r(0) = \bar{r} = 0.05$, $\alpha = 0.3$, and $\sigma_r = 0.02$.

Now assume that bond prices of all maturities depend on only a single source of uncertainty and that this single "factor" is summarized by the current level of $r(t)$.[12] Then we can write a τ-maturity bond's price as $P(r(t), \tau)$, and Itô's lemma implies that it follows the process

---

10. Other approaches to modeling the term structure of interest rates are considered in Chapter 17. For example, we will discuss research by David Heath, Robert Jarrow, and Andrew Morton (Heath, Jarrow, and Morton 1992) that assumes *forward* interest rates of all maturities are affected by one or more sources of risk.

11. The discrete-time expected value and variance implied by the continuous-time process in (9.30) are $E_t[r(t + \tau)] = \bar{r} + e^{-\alpha\tau}(r(t) - \bar{r})$ and $Var_t[r(t + \tau)] = \frac{\sigma_r^2}{2\alpha}(1 - e^{-2\alpha\tau})$, respectively. See exercise 4 at the end of Chapter 8.

12. For example, a central bank may implement monetary policy by changing the level of the short-term interest rate. Other macroeconomic effects on bond prices might be summarized in the level of the short rate.

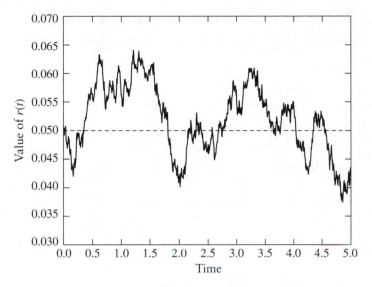

Figure 9.1 ——Ornstein-Uhlenbeck Interest Rate Process

$$dP\,(r,\tau)\ =\ \frac{\partial P}{\partial r}dr + \frac{\partial P}{\partial t}dt + \frac{1}{2}\frac{\partial^2 P}{\partial r^2}\,(dr)^2 \tag{9.31}$$

$$=\left[P_r\alpha\,(\bar r - r) + P_t + \tfrac{1}{2}P_{rr}\sigma_r^2\right]dt + P_r\sigma_r dz_r$$

$$=\mu_p\,(r,\tau)\,P\,(r,\tau)\,dt - \sigma_p\,(\tau)\,P\,(r,\tau)\,dz_r$$

where the subscripts on P denote partial derivatives and where $\mu_p\,(r,\tau) \equiv \dfrac{\left[P_r\alpha(\bar r - r) + P_t + \frac{1}{2}P_{rr}\sigma_r^2\right]}{P(r,\tau)}$ and $\sigma_p\,(\tau) \equiv -\dfrac{P_r\sigma_r}{P(r,\tau)}$ are the mean and standard deviation, respectively, of the bond's instantaneous rate of return.[13]

Consider forming a portfolio containing one bond of maturity τ_1 and $-\dfrac{\sigma_p(\tau_1)P(r,\tau_1)}{\sigma_p(\tau_2)P(r,\tau_2)}$ units of a bond with maturity τ_2. In other words, we have a unit long position in a bond of maturity τ_1 and a short position in a bond with maturity τ_2 in an amount that reflects the ratio of bond 1's return standard deviation to that of bond 2's. Since both bonds are driven by the same Wiener process, dz_r,

---

13. We define $\sigma_p\,(\tau) \equiv -P_r\sigma_r/P\,(r,\tau)$ rather than $\sigma_p\,(\tau) \equiv P_r\sigma_r/P\,(r,\tau)$ because it will turn out that $P_r < 0$. Hence, if we want both σ_r and σ_p to denote standard deviations, we need them to be positive. This choice of definition makes no material difference since the instantaneous variance of the change in the interest rate and the bond's rate of return will always be σ_r^2 and σ_p^2, respectively.

this portfolio is a hedged position. If we continually readjust the amount of the τ_2-maturity bonds to equal $-\frac{\sigma_p(\tau_1)P(r,\tau_1)}{\sigma_p(\tau_2)P(r,\tau_2)}$ as $r(t)$ changes, the value of this hedge portfolio, $H(t)$, is

$$H(t) = P(r, \tau_1) - \frac{\sigma_p(\tau_1) P(r, \tau_1)}{\sigma_p(\tau_2) P(r, \tau_2)} P(r, \tau_2) \tag{9.32}$$

$$= P(r, \tau_1) \left[1 - \frac{\sigma_p(\tau_1)}{\sigma_p(\tau_2)} \right]$$

Furthermore, the hedge portfolio's instantaneous return is

$$dH(t) = dP(r, \tau_1) - \frac{\sigma_p(\tau_1) P(r, \tau_1)}{\sigma_p(\tau_2) P(r, \tau_2)} dP(r, \tau_2) \tag{9.33}$$

$$= \mu_p(r, \tau_1) P(r, \tau_1) dt - \sigma_p(\tau_1) P(r, \tau_1) dz_r$$

$$\quad - \frac{\sigma_p(\tau_1)}{\sigma_p(\tau_2)} P(r, \tau_1) \mu_p(r, \tau_2) dt + \sigma_p(\tau_1) P(r, \tau_1) dz_r$$

$$= \mu_p(r, \tau_1) P(r, \tau_1) dt - \frac{\sigma_p(\tau_1)}{\sigma_p(\tau_2)} P(r, \tau_1) \mu_p(r, \tau_2) dt$$

where the second equality in (9.33) reflects substitution of (9.31). Since the portfolio return is riskless at each instant of time, the absence of arbitrage implies that its rate of return must equal the instantaneous riskless interest rate, $r(t)$:

$$dH(t) = \left[\mu_p(r, \tau_1) - \frac{\sigma_p(\tau_1)}{\sigma_p(\tau_2)} \mu_p(r, \tau_2) \right] P(r, \tau_1) dt \tag{9.34}$$

$$= r(t) H(t) dt = r(t) \left[1 - \frac{\sigma_p(\tau_1)}{\sigma_p(\tau_2)} \right] P(r, \tau_1) dt$$

Equating the terms that precede $P(r, \tau_1)$ on the first and second lines of (9.34), we see that an implication of this equation is

$$\frac{\mu_p(r, \tau_1) - r(t)}{\sigma_p(\tau_1)} = \frac{\mu_p(r, \tau_2) - r(t)}{\sigma_p(\tau_2)} \tag{9.35}$$

which relates the risk premiums or Sharpe ratios on the different maturity bonds.

9.2.1 A Bond Risk Premium

Equation (9.35) says that bonds' expected rates of return in excess of the instantaneous maturity rate, divided by their standard deviations, must be equal at all points in time. This equality of Sharpe ratios must hold for any set of bonds τ_1, τ_2, τ_3, and so on. Each of the different bonds' reward-to-risk ratios (Sharpe ratios) derives from the single source of risk represented by the dz_r process driving the short-term interest rate, $r(t)$. Hence, condition (9.35) can be interpreted as a law of one price that requires all bonds to have a uniform *market price of interest rate risk*.

To derive the equilibrium prices for bonds, we must specify the form of this market price of bond risk. Chapter 13 outlines a general equilibrium model by John Cox, Jonathan Ingersoll, and Stephen Ross, (Cox, Ingersoll, and Ross 1985a) and (Cox, Ingersoll, and Ross 1985b), that shows how this bond risk premium can be derived from individuals' preferences (utilities) and the economy's technologies. For now, however, we simply assume that the market price of bond risk is constant over time and equal to q. Thus, we have for any bond maturity, τ,

$$\frac{\mu_p(r, \tau) - r(t)}{\sigma_p(\tau)} = q \tag{9.36}$$

or

$$\mu_p(r, \tau) = r(t) + q\sigma_p(\tau) \tag{9.37}$$

which says that the expected rate of return on a bond with maturity τ equals the instantaneous risk-free rate plus a risk premium proportional to the bond's standard deviation. Substituting $\mu_p(r, \tau)$ and $\sigma_p(\tau)$ from Itô's lemma into (9.37) and simplifying, we obtain

$$P_r \alpha(\bar{r} - r) + P_t + \tfrac{1}{2}P_{rr}\sigma_r^2 = rP - q\sigma_r P_r \tag{9.38}$$

This can be rewritten as

$$\tfrac{\sigma_r^2}{2}P_{rr} + (\alpha\bar{r} + q\sigma_r - \alpha r) P_r - rP + P_t = 0 \tag{9.39}$$

Equation (9.39) is the equilibrium partial differential equation that all bonds must satisfy. Since $\tau \equiv T - t$, so that $P_t \equiv \frac{\partial P}{\partial t} = -\frac{\partial P}{\partial \tau} \equiv -P_\tau$, equation (9.39) can be rewritten as

$$\tfrac{\sigma_r^2}{2}P_{rr} + \left[\alpha(\bar{r} - \alpha r) + q\sigma_r\right] P_r - rP - P_\tau = 0 \tag{9.40}$$

and, solved subject to the boundary condition that at $\tau = 0$, the bond price equals $1; that is, $P(r, 0) = 1$. Doing so, gives the following solution:[14]

$$P(r(t), \tau) = A(\tau) e^{-B(\tau)r(t)} \tag{9.41}$$

where

$$B(\tau) \equiv \frac{1 - e^{-\alpha\tau}}{\alpha} \tag{9.42}$$

$$A(\tau) \equiv \exp\left[(B(\tau) - \tau)\left(\bar{r} + q\frac{\sigma_r}{\alpha} - \frac{1}{2}\frac{\sigma_r^2}{\alpha^2}\right) - \frac{\sigma_r^2 B(\tau)^2}{4\alpha}\right] \tag{9.43}$$

9.2.2   Characteristics of Bond Prices

Using equation (9.41), we see that

$$\sigma_p(\tau) = -\sigma_r \frac{P_r}{P} = \sigma_r B(\tau) = \frac{\sigma_r}{\alpha}\left(1 - e^{-\alpha\tau}\right) \tag{9.44}$$

which implies that a bond's rate of return standard deviation (volatility) is an increasing but concave function of its maturity, τ. Moreover, (9.44) confirms that as the bond approaches its maturity date, its price volatility shrinks to zero, $\sigma_p(\tau = 0) = 0$, since the instantaneous maturity bond's return is riskless. The tendency for price volatility to decrease over time is a fundamental property of finitely lived, fixed-income securities that distinguishes them from potentially infinitely lived securities such as common or preferred stocks. While it may be reasonable to assume as in (9.14) that the volatility of a stock's price need not be a function of calendar time, this cannot be the case for a zero-coupon bond.

Given that $\sigma_p(\tau)$ is an increasing function maturity, equation (9.37) says that a bond's expected rate of return increases (*decreases*) with its time until maturity if the market price of risk, q, is positive (*negative*). Since historical returns on longer-maturity bonds have exceeded those of shorter-maturity ones in most (though not all) countries, this suggests that q is likely to be positive.[15] Additional evidence on the value of q can be gleaned by observing the yields to maturity on different

---

14. The solution can be derived by "guessing" a solution of the form in (9.41) and substituting it into (9.40). Noting that the terms multiplied by $r(t)$ and those terms not multiplied by $r(t)$ must each be zero for all $r(t)$ leads to simple ordinary differential equations for $A(\tau)$ and $B(\tau)$. These equations are solved subject to the boundary condition $P(r, \tau = 0) = 1$, which implies $A(\tau = 0) = 1$ and $B(\tau = 0) = 0$. See Chapter 17 for details and a generalization to bond prices that are influenced by multiple factors.

15. See (Dimson, Marsh, and Staunton 2002) for an account of the historical evidence.

maturity bonds. A τ-maturity bond's continuously compounded yield to maturity, denoted $Y(r(t),\tau)$, can be derived from its price in (9.41):

$$Y(r(t),\tau) \equiv -\frac{1}{\tau}\ln[P(r(t),\tau)] \qquad (9.45)$$

$$= -\frac{1}{\tau}\ln[A(\tau)] + \frac{B(\tau)}{\tau}r(t)$$

$$= Y_\infty + [r(t) - Y_\infty]\frac{B(\tau)}{\tau} + \frac{\sigma_r^2 B(\tau)^2}{4\alpha\tau}$$

where $Y_\infty \equiv \bar{r} + q\frac{\sigma_r}{\alpha} - \frac{1}{2}\frac{\sigma_r^2}{\alpha^2}$. Note that $\lim_{\tau\to\infty} Y(r(t),\tau) = Y_\infty$, so that the yield to maturity on a very long maturity bond approaches Y_∞. Hence, the yield curve, which is the graph of $Y(r(t),\tau)$ as a function of τ, equals $r(t)$ at $\tau = 0$ and asymptotes to Y_∞ for τ large. When $r(t) \leq Y_\infty - \frac{\sigma_r^2}{4\alpha^2} = \bar{r} + q\frac{\sigma_r}{\alpha} - \frac{3\sigma_r^2}{4\alpha^2}$, the yield curve is monotonically increasing. When $Y_\infty - \frac{\sigma_r^2}{4\alpha^2} < r(t) < Y_\infty + \frac{\sigma_r^2}{2\alpha^2} = \bar{r} + q\frac{\sigma_r}{\alpha}$, the yield curve has a humped shape. A monotonically downward sloping, or "inverted," yield curve occurs when $\bar{r} + q\frac{\sigma_r}{\alpha} \leq r(t)$. Since the unconditional mean of the short rate is $\bar{r}$ and, empirically, the yield curve is normally upward sloping, this suggests that $\bar{r} < \bar{r} + q\frac{\sigma_r}{\alpha} - \frac{3\sigma_r^2}{4\alpha^2}$, or $q > \frac{3\sigma_r}{4\alpha}$. Therefore, a yield curve that typically is upward sloping is also evidence of a positive market price of bond risk.

9.3 Option Pricing with Random Interest Rates

This last example of the Black-Scholes hedging argument combines aspects of the first two in that we now consider option pricing in an environment where interest rates can be random. We follow Robert Merton (Merton 1973b) in valuing a European call option when the risk-free interest rate is stochastic and bond prices satisfy the Vasicek model. The main alteration to the Black-Scholes derivation is to realize that the call option's payoff, $\max[S(T) - X, 0]$, depends not only on the maturity date, T, and the stock price at that date, $S(T)$, but on the present value of the exercise price, X, which can be interpreted as the value of a default-free bond that pays X at its maturity date of T. Given the randomness of interest rates, even the value of this exercise price is stochastic prior to the option's maturity. This motivates us to consider the process of a bond maturing in $\tau \equiv T - t$ periods to be another underlying asset, in addition to the stock, affecting the option's value. Writing this bond price as $P(t,\tau)$, the option's value can now be expressed as $c\left(S\left(t\right), P\left(t, \tau\right), t\right)$. Consistent with the Vasicek model, we write this bond's process as

$$dP\left(t, \tau\right) = \mu_p\left(t, \tau\right) P\left(t, \tau\right) dt + \sigma_p\left(\tau\right) P\left(t, \tau\right) dz_p \tag{9.46}$$

where from equation (9.31) we define $dz_p \equiv -dz_r$. In general, the bond's return will be correlated with that of the stock, and we allow for this possibility by assuming $dz_p dz = \rho dt$. Given the option's dependence on both the stock and the bond, Itô's lemma says that the option price satisfies

$$dc = \left[\frac{\partial c}{\partial S} \mu S + \frac{\partial c}{\partial P} \mu_p P + \frac{\partial c}{\partial t} + \frac{1}{2} \frac{\partial^2 c}{\partial S^2} \sigma^2 S^2 + \frac{1}{2} \frac{\partial^2 c}{\partial P^2} \sigma_p^2 P^2 \right.$$

$$\left. + \frac{\partial^2 c}{\partial S \partial P} \rho \sigma \sigma_p SP \right] dt + \frac{\partial c}{\partial S} \sigma S \, dz + \frac{\partial c}{\partial P} \sigma_p P \, dz_p \tag{9.47}$$

$$\equiv \mu_c c \, dt + \frac{\partial c}{\partial S} \sigma S \, dz + \frac{\partial c}{\partial P} \sigma_p P \, dz_p$$

where $\mu_c c$ is defined as those bracketed terms in the first two lines of (9.47). Similar to our first example in which a dealer wishes to hedge the sale of an option, let us form a hedge portfolio consisting of a unit short position in the option, and a purchase of $w_s\left(t\right)$ units of the underlying stock, and a purchase of $w_p\left(t\right)$ units of the τ-maturity bond, where we also restrict the portfolio to require a zero net investment. The zero-net-investment restriction implies

$$c\left(t\right) - w_s\left(t\right) S\left(t\right) - w_p\left(t\right) P\left(t, \tau\right) = 0 \tag{9.48}$$

The hedge portfolio's return can then be written as

$$dH\left(t\right) = -dc(t) + w_s\left(t\right) dS\left(t\right) + w_p\left(t\right) dP\left(t, \tau\right) \tag{9.49}$$

$$= \left[-\mu_c c + w_s\left(t\right) \mu S + w_p\left(t\right) \mu_p P\right] dt$$

$$+ \left[-\frac{\partial c}{\partial S} \sigma S + w_s\left(t\right) \sigma S\right] dz$$

$$+ \left[-\frac{\partial c}{\partial P} \sigma_p P + w_p\left(t\right) \sigma_p P\right] dz_p$$

$$= \left[w_s\left(t\right) \left(\mu - \mu_c\right) S + w_p\left(t\right) \left(\mu_p - \mu_c\right) P\right] dt$$

$$+ \left[w_s\left(t\right) - \frac{\partial c}{\partial S}\right] \sigma S \, dz$$

$$+ \left[w_p\left(t\right) - \frac{\partial c}{\partial P}\right] \sigma_p P \, dz_p$$

where, in the last equality of (9.49), we have substituted in for c using the zero-net-investment condition (9.48). If $w_s(t)$ and $w_p(t)$ can be chosen to make the hedge portfolio's return riskless, then it must be the case that the terms in brackets in the last line of (9.49) can be made to equal zero. In other words, the following two conditions must hold:

$$w_s(t) = \frac{\partial c}{\partial S} \tag{9.50}$$

$$w_p(t) = \frac{\partial c}{\partial P} \tag{9.51}$$

but from the zero-net-investment condition (9.48), this can only be possible if it happens to be the case that

$$c = w_s(t) S + w_p(t) P$$

$$= S\frac{\partial c}{\partial S} + P\frac{\partial c}{\partial P} \tag{9.52}$$

By Euler's theorem, condition (9.52) holds if the option price is a homogeneous of degree 1 function of S and P.[16] What this means is that if the stock's price and the bond's price happened to increase by the same proportion, then the option's price would increase by that same proportion. That is, for $k > 0$, $c(kS(t), kP(t, \tau), t) = kc(S(t), P(t, \tau), t)$.[17] We assume this to be so and later verify that the solution indeed satisfies this homogeneity condition.

Given that condition (9.52) does hold, so that we can choose $w_s(t) = \partial c/\partial S$ and $w_p(t) = \partial c/\partial P$ to make the hedge portfolio's return riskless, then as in the first example the zero-net-investment portfolio's riskless return must equal zero in the absence of arbitrage:

$$w_s(t)(\mu - \mu_c)S + w_p(t)(\mu_p - \mu_c)P = 0 \tag{9.53}$$

or

$$\frac{\partial c}{\partial S}(\mu - \mu_c)S + \frac{\partial c}{\partial P}(\mu_p - \mu_c)P = 0 \tag{9.54}$$

---

16. A function $f(x_1, \ldots, x_n)$ is defined to be homogeneous of degree r (where r is an integer) if for every $k > 0$, then $f(kx_1, \ldots, kx_n) = k^r f(x_1, \ldots, x_n)$. Euler's theorem states that if $f(x_1, \ldots, x_n)$ is homogeneous of degree r and differentiable, then $\sum_{i=1}^{n} x_i \frac{\partial f}{\partial x_i} = rf$.

17. For example, suppose there was a general rise in inflation that increased the stock's and bond's prices but did not change their *relative* price, S/P. Then the homogeneity condition implies that the option's price would rise by the same increase in inflation.

which, using (9.52), can be rewritten as

$$\frac{\partial c}{\partial S}\mu S + \frac{\partial c}{\partial P}\mu_p P - \mu_c c = 0 \tag{9.55}$$

Substituting for $\mu_c c$ from (9.47), we obtain

$$-\frac{\partial c}{\partial t} - \frac{1}{2}\frac{\partial^2 c}{\partial S^2}\sigma^2 S^2 - \frac{1}{2}\frac{\partial^2 c}{\partial P^2}\sigma_p^2 P^2 - \frac{\partial^2 c}{\partial S \partial P}\rho\sigma\sigma_p SP = 0 \tag{9.56}$$

which, since $\tau \equiv T - t$, can also be written as

$$\frac{1}{2}\left[\frac{\partial^2 c}{\partial S^2}\sigma^2 S^2 + \frac{\partial^2 c}{\partial P^2}\sigma_p^2 P^2 + 2\frac{\partial^2 c}{\partial S \partial P}\rho\sigma\sigma_p SP\right] - \frac{\partial c}{\partial \tau} = 0 \tag{9.57}$$

Equation (9.57) is the equilibrium partial differential equation that the option's value must satisfy. Importantly, it does not depend on either the expected rate of return on the stock, μ, or the expected rate of return on the bond, μ_p. The appropriate boundary condition for a European call option is similar to before, with $c\left(S\left(T\right), P\left(T, 0\right), T\right) = c\left(S\left(T\right), 1, T\right) = \max\left[S\left(T\right) - X, 0\right]$, where we impose the condition $P\left(t = T, \tau = 0\right) = 1$. Robert Merton (Merton 1973b) shows that the solution to this equation is

$$c\left(S\left(t\right), P\left(t, \tau\right), \tau\right) = S(t)\, N(h_1) - P\left(t, \tau\right) X N(h_2) \tag{9.58}$$

where

$$h_1 = \frac{\ln\left(\frac{S(t)}{P(t,\tau)X}\right) + \frac{1}{2}v^2}{v} \tag{9.59}$$

$$h_2 = h_1 - v$$

where

$$v^2 = \int_0^\tau \left(\sigma^2 + \sigma_p\left(y\right)^2 - 2\rho\sigma\sigma_p\left(y\right)\right) dy \tag{9.60}$$

The solution is essentially the same as the Black-Scholes constant interest rate formula (9.24) but where the parameter v^2 replaces $\sigma^2\tau$. v^2 is the total variance of the ratio of the stock price to the discounted exercise price over the life of the option.[18] In other words, it is the variance of the ratio $\frac{S(t)}{P(t,\tau)X}$ from date t to date T, an interval of τ periods. Because the instantaneous variance of the bond, and hence the variance of the discounted exercise price, shrinks as the option

---

18. As one would expect, when interest rates are nonstochastic so that the volatility of bond prices is zero, that is, $\sigma_p\left(y\right) = 0$, then $v^2 = \sigma^2\tau$, and we obtain the standard Black-Scholes formula.

approaches maturity, this changing variance is accounted for by making $\sigma_p\left(y\right)$ a function of the time until maturity in (9.60). If we assume that the bond's volatility is that of the Vasicek model, $\sigma_p\left(y\right) = \frac{\sigma_r}{\alpha}\left(1 - e^{-\alpha y}\right)$, then (9.60) becomes

$$v^2 = \int_0^\tau \left(\sigma^2 + \frac{\sigma_r^2}{\alpha^2}\left(1 - 2e^{-\alpha y} + e^{-2\alpha y}\right) - 2\rho\sigma\frac{\sigma_r}{\alpha}\left(1 - e^{-\alpha y}\right)\right) dt \qquad (9.61)$$

$$= \sigma^2\tau + \frac{\sigma_r^2}{\alpha^3}\left(\alpha\tau + \frac{1 - e^{-2\alpha\tau}}{2} - 2\left(1 - e^{-\alpha\tau}\right)\right) - 2\rho\sigma\frac{\sigma_r}{\alpha^2}\left[\alpha\tau - \left(1 - e^{-\alpha\tau}\right)\right]$$

Finally, note that the solution is homogeneous of degree 1 in $S\left(t\right)$ and $P\left(t, \tau\right)$, which verifies condition (9.52).

9.4   Summary

Fischer Black, Myron Scholes, and Robert Merton made a fundamental discovery that profoundly changed the pricing of contingent securities. They showed that when an underlying asset follows a diffusion, and trade is allowed to occur continuously, a portfolio can be created that fully hedges the risk of the contingent claim. Therefore, in the absence of arbitrage, the hedge portfolio's return must be riskless, and this implies that the contingent claim's price must satisfy a particular partial differential equation subject to a boundary condition that its value must equal its terminal payoff. Solving this equation led to a surprising result: the contingent claim's value did not depend directly on the underlying security's expected rate of return, but only on its volatility. This was an attractive feature because estimating a risky asset's expected rate of return is much more difficult than estimating its volatility.[19]

As our second example illustrated, the Black-Scholes-Merton hedging argument can be used to derive models of the default-free term structure of interest rates. The pricing of different maturity bonds and of fixed-income derivatives is a large and ever-growing field of asset pricing. Chapter 17 is devoted solely to this subject. A related topic is the pricing of default-risky bonds. As the title of Black and Scholes's seminal paper suggests, it was readily recognized that a satisfactory model of option pricing could be applied to valuing the liabilities of corporations that were subject to default. This link between option pricing and credit risk also will be explored in Chapter 18.

---

19. The accuracy of estimates for a risky asset's expected rate of return is proportional to the time interval over which its average return is computed. In contrast, the accuracy of a risky asset's standard deviation of return is proportional to the number of times the return is sampled over any fixed time interval. See Merton (Merton 1980) and Chapter 9.3.2 of Campbell, Lo, and MacKinlay (Campbell, Lo, and MacKinlay 1997).

9.5 Exercises

1. Suppose that the price of a non-dividend-paying stock follows the process

$$dS = \alpha S dt + \beta S^{\gamma} dz$$

where α, β, and γ are constants. The risk-free interest rate equals a constant, r. Denote $p(S(t), t)$ as the current price of a European put option on this stock having an exercise price of X and a maturity date of T. Derive the equilibrium partial differential equation and boundary condition for the price of this put option using the Black-Scholes hedging argument.

2. Define $P(r(t), \tau)$ as the date t price of a pure discount bond that pays \$1 in τ periods. The bond price depends on the instantaneous maturity yield, $r(t)$, which follows the process

$$dr(t) = \alpha [\bar{r} - r(t)] dt + \sigma \sqrt{r} dz$$

where α, γ, and σ are positive constants. If the process followed by the price of a bond having τ periods until maturity is

$$dP(r, \tau) / P(r, \tau) = \mu(r, \tau) dt - \sigma_p(r, \tau) dz$$

and the market price of bond risk is

$$\frac{\mu(r, \tau) - r(t)}{\sigma_p(r, \tau)} = \lambda \sqrt{r}$$

then write down the equilibrium partial differential equation and boundary condition that this bond price satisfies.

3. The date t price of stock A, $A(t)$, follows the process

$$dA/A = \mu_A dt + \sigma_A dz$$

and the date t price of stock B, $B(t)$, follows the process

$$dB/B = \mu_B dt + \sigma_B dq$$

where σ_A and σ_B are constants and dz and dq are Brownian motion processes for which $dz dq = \rho dt$. Let $c(t)$ be the date t price of a European option written on the difference between these two stocks' prices. Specifically, at this option's maturity date, T, the value of the option equals

$$c(T) = \max [0, A(T) - B(T)]$$

a. Using Itô's lemma, derive the process followed by this option.

b. Suppose that you are an option dealer who has just sold (written) one of these options for a customer. You now wish to form a hedge portfolio composed of your unit short position in the option and positions in the two stocks. Let $H(t)$ denote the date t value of this hedge portfolio. Write down an equation for $H(t)$ that indicates the amount of shares of stocks A and B that should be held.

c. Write down the dynamics for $dH(t)$, showing that its return is riskless.

d. Assuming the absence of arbitrage, derive the equilibrium partial differential equation that this option must satisfy.

4. Let $S(t)$ be the date t price of an asset that continuously pays a dividend that is a fixed proportion of its price. Specifically, the asset pays a dividend of $\delta S(t)\,dt$ over the time interval dt. The process followed by this asset's price can be written as

$$dS = (\mu - \delta)\,S dt + \sigma S dz$$

where σ is the standard deviation of the asset's rate of return and μ is the asset's total expected rate of return, which includes its dividend payment and price appreciation. Note that the total rate of return earned by the owner of one share of this asset is $dS/S + \delta dt = \mu dt + \sigma dz$. Consider a European call option written on this asset that has an exercise price of X and a maturity date of $T > t$. Assuming a constant interest rate equal to r, use a Black-Scholes hedging argument to derive the equilibrium partial differential equation that this option's price, $c(t)$, must satisfy.

CHAPTER 10

Arbitrage, Martingales, and Pricing Kernels

In Chapters 4 and 7, we examined the asset pricing implications of market completeness in a discrete-time model. It was shown that when the number of nonredundant assets equaled the number of states of nature, markets were complete and the absence of arbitrage ensured that state prices and a state price deflator would exist. Pricing could be performed using risk-neutral valuation. The current chapter extends these results in a continuous-time environment. We formally show that when asset prices follow diffusion processes and trading is continuous, then the absence of arbitrage may allow us to value assets using a *martingale pricing* technique, a generalization of risk-neutral pricing. Under these conditions, a continuous-time stochastic discount factor, or pricing kernel, also exists.

These results were developed by John Cox and Stephen Ross (Cox and Ross 1976), John Harrison and David Kreps (Harrison and Kreps 1979), and John Harrison and Stanley Pliska (Harrison and Pliska 1981) and have proved to be very popular approaches to valuing a wide variety of contingent claims. Valuing contingent claims using risk-neutral pricing, or a pricing kernel method, can be an alternative to the previous chapter's partial differential equation approach.

The first section of this chapter reviews the derivation of the Black-Scholes partial differential equation and points out that this equation also implies that the market price of risk must be uniform for a contingent claim and its underlying asset. It also shows how the contingent claim's price process can be transformed into a driftless process by adjusting its Brownian motion process by the market price of risk and then deflating the contingent claim's price by that of a riskless asset. This driftless (zero expected change) process is known as a *martingale*. The contingent claim's value then can be computed as the expectation of its terminal value under this transformed process.

The second section derives the form of a continuous-time state price deflator that can also be used to price contingent claims. It also demonstrates how the continuous-time state price deflator transforms actual probabilities into risk-neutral probabilities. The third section shows how problems of valuing a contingent claim sometimes can be simplified by deflating the contingent claim's price by that of another risky asset. An example is given by valuing an option written on the difference between the prices of two risky assets. The final section of the chapter examines applications of the martingale approach. It is used to value an option written on an asset that pays a continuous dividend, examples of which include an option written on a foreign currency and an option written on a futures price. The martingale pricing technique is also applied to rederiving a model of the term structure of interest rates.

10.1   Arbitrage and Martingales

We begin by reviewing the Black-Scholes derivation of contingent claims prices. Let S be the value of a risky asset that follows a general scalar diffusion process

$$dS = \mu S dt + \sigma S dz \tag{10.1}$$

where both $\mu = \mu(S, t)$ and $\sigma = \sigma(S, t)$ may be functions of S and t and dz is a standard, pure Brownian motion (or Wiener) process. For ease of presentation, we assume that $S(t)$ is a scalar process. Later we discuss how multivariate processes can be handled by the theory, such that μ and σ can depend on other variables that follow diffusion processes (driven by additional Brownian motions) in addition to $S(t)$. In this way, asset values can depend on multiple sources of uncertainty.

Next let $c(S, t)$ denote the value of a contingent claim whose payoff depends solely on S and t. From Itô's lemma, we know that this value satisfies

$$dc = \mu_c c dt + \sigma_c c dz \tag{10.2}$$

where $\mu_c c = c_t + \mu S c_S + \frac{1}{2}\sigma^2 S^2 c_{SS}$ and $\sigma_c c = \sigma S c_S$, and the subscripts on c denote partial derivatives.

Similar to our earlier analysis, we employ a form of the Black-Scholes hedging argument by considering a portfolio of -1 units of the contingent claim and c_S units of the risky asset. The value of this portfolio, H, satisfies[1]

$$H = -c + c_S S \tag{10.3}$$

---

1. Unlike last chapter's derivation, we do not restrict this portfolio to be a zero-net-investment portfolio. As will be clear, the lack of this restriction does not change the nature of our results.

and the change in value of this portfolio over the next instant is

$$dH = -dc + c_S dS \tag{10.4}$$

$$= -\mu_c c\, dt - \sigma_c c\, dz + c_S \mu S\, dt + c_S \sigma S\, dz$$

$$= [c_S \mu S - \mu_c c]\, dt$$

Since the portfolio is riskless, the absence of arbitrage implies that it must earn the risk-free rate. Denoting the (possibly stochastic) instantaneous risk-free rate as $r(t)$, we have[2]

$$dH = [c_S \mu S - \mu_c c]\, dt = rH dt = r[-c + c_S S]dt \tag{10.5}$$

which implies

$$c_S \mu S - \mu_c c = r[-c + c_S S] \tag{10.6}$$

If we substitute $\mu_c c = c_t + \mu S c_S + \frac{1}{2}\sigma^2 S^2 c_{SS}$ into (10.6), we obtain the Black-Scholes equilibrium partial differential equation (PDE):

$$\frac{1}{2}\sigma^2 S^2 c_{SS} + rS c_S - rc + c_t = 0 \tag{10.7}$$

However, consider a different interpretation of equation (10.6). From Itô's lemma, we can substitute $c_S = \frac{\sigma_c c}{\sigma S}$ into (10.6) and rearrange to obtain

$$\frac{\mu - r}{\sigma} = \frac{\mu_c - r}{\sigma_c} \equiv \theta(t) \tag{10.8}$$

Condition (10.8) is the familiar no-arbitrage condition that requires a unique market price of risk, which we denote as $\theta(t)$. Then the stochastic process for the contingent claim can be written as

$$dc = \mu_c c\, dt + \sigma_c c\, dz = [rc + \theta\sigma_c c]\, dt + \sigma_c c\, dz \tag{10.9}$$

Note that the drift of this process depends on the market price of risk, $\theta(t)$, which may not be directly observable or easily estimated. We now consider an approach

---

2. For simplicity, we have assumed that the contingent claim's value depends only on a single risky asset price, $S(t)$. However, when the interest rate is stochastic, the contingent claim's value also might be a function of $r(t)$, that is, $c(S, r, t)$. If, for example, the interest rate followed the process $dr = \mu_r(r)\, dt + \sigma_r(r)\, dz_r$ where dz_r is an additional Wiener process affecting interest rate movements, then the contingent claim's process would be given by a bivariate version of Itô's lemma. Also, to create a portfolio that earns an instantaneous risk-free rate, the portfolio would need to include a bond whose price is driven by dz_r. Later, we discuss how our results generalize to multiple sources of uncertainty. However, the current univariate setting can be fully consistent with stochastic interest rates if the risky asset is, itself, a bond so that $S(r, t)$ and $dz = dz_r$. The contingent claim could then be interpreted as a fixed-income (bond) derivative security.

to valuing contingent claims that is an alternative to solving the PDE in (10.7) but that shares with it the benefit of not having to know $\theta\,(t)$. The next topic discusses how a contingent claim's risk premium can be eliminated by reinterpreting the probability distribution generating asset returns.

10.1.1   A Change in Probability: Girsanov's Theorem

Girsanov's theorem says that by shifting the Brownian motion process, one can change the drift of a diffusion process when this process is interpreted under a new probability distribution. Moreover, this shift in Brownian motion changes the future probability distribution for asset prices in a particular way. To see how this works, consider a new process $\widehat{z}_t = z_t + \int_0^t \theta\,(s)\,ds$, so that $d\widehat{z}_t = dz_t + \theta\,(t)\,dt$. Then substituting $dz_t = d\widehat{z}_t - \theta\,(t)\,dt$ in equation (10.9), it can be rewritten:

$$dc = \left[rc + \theta\sigma_c c\right]dt + \sigma_c c\left[d\widehat{z} - \theta dt\right]$$
$$= rcdt + \sigma_c cd\widehat{z} \tag{10.10}$$

Hence, converting from the Brownian motion process dz to $d\widehat{z}$, which removes the risk premium $\theta\sigma_c c$ from the drift term on the right-hand side of (10.9), results in the expected rate of return of c being equal to the risk-free rate *if* we were now to view $d\widehat{z}$, rather than dz, as a Brownian motion process. The probability distribution of future values of c that are generated by $d\widehat{z}$, a probability distribution that we define as the Q probability measure, is referred to as the risk-neutral probability measure.[3] This is in contrast to the actual probability distribution for c generated by the dz Brownian motion in (10.9), the original "physical," or "statistical," probability distribution that is denoted as the P measure.

Girsanov's theorem states that as long as $\theta\,(t)$ is well behaved in the sense that it follows a process that does not vary too much over time, then the probability density function for a random variable at some future date T, such as $c\,(T)$,

---

3. The idea of a probability measure (or distribution), P, is as follows. Define a set function, f, which assigns a real number to a set E, where E could be a set of real numbers, such as an interval on the real line. Formally, $f(E) \in R$. This function is *countably additive* if $f(\bigcup_{i=1}^{n} E_i) = \sum_{i=1}^{n} f(E_i)$ where $\langle E_i \rangle$ is a finite or countably infinite sequence of disjoint sets. A *measure* is defined as a nonnegative set function that is countably additive. Note that probabilities are measures since they assign a nonnegative probability to a particular set. For example, let the domain of a continuous probability distribution for a random variable, x, be the entire real line; that is, $\int_{-\infty}^{\infty} dP\,(x) = 1$ where P is the probability measure (probability distribution function). Now let a set $E_1 = [a, b]$ be an interval on this line. The probability of $x \in E_1$ is $f(E_1) = \int_a^b dP\,(x) \geq 0$. Similarly, if $E_2 = [c, d]$, which is assumed to be an interval that does not overlap with E_1, then $f(E_1 \bigcup E_2) = \int_a^b dP\,(x) + \int_c^d dP\,(x) = f(E_1) + f(E_2)$. Hence, probabilities are nonnegative and countably additive.

under the risk-neutral Q distribution bears a particular relationship to that of the physical P distribution.[4] Specifically, denote dP_T as the instantaneous change in the physical distribution function at date T generated by dz_t, which makes it the physical probability density function at date T.[5] Similarly, let dQ_T be the risk-neutral probability density function generated by $d\hat{z}_t$. Then Girsanov's theorem says that at some date t where $0 < t < T$, the relationship between the two probability densities at date T is

$$dQ_T = \exp\left[-\int_t^T \theta(u)\,dz - \frac{1}{2}\int_t^T \theta(u)^2\,du\right] dP_T$$

$$= (\xi_T/\xi_t)\,dP_T \tag{10.11}$$

where ξ_t is a positive random process that depends on $\theta(t)$ and z_t and is given by

$$\xi_\tau = \exp\left[-\int_0^\tau \theta(u)\,dz - \frac{1}{2}\int_0^\tau \theta(u)^2\,ds\right] \tag{10.12}$$

In other words, by multiplying the physical probability density at date T by the factor ξ_T/ξ_t, we can determine the risk-neutral probability density at date T. Since from (10.12) we see that $\xi_T/\xi_t > 0$, equation (10.11) implies that whenever dP_T has positive probability, so does dQ_T. Because they share this characteristic, the physical P measure and the risk-neutral Q measure are called *equivalent* probability measures in that any future value of c that has positive probability (density) under the physical measure also has positive probability (density) under the risk-neutral measure.[6] We can rearrange (10.11) to obtain

$$\frac{dQ_T}{dP_T} = \xi_T/\xi_t \tag{10.13}$$

which clarifies that ξ_T/ξ_t can be interpreted as the derivative of the risk-neutral measure Q_T with respect to the physical measure P_T. Indeed, ξ_T/ξ_t is known as the Radon-Nikodym derivative of Q with respect to P. Later in this chapter we

---

4. The restriction on $\theta(t)$ is that $E_t[\exp(\int_t^T \theta(u)^2\,du)] < \infty$, which is known as the Novikov condition. Ioannis Karatzas and Steven Shreve (Karatzas and Shreve 1991) give a formal statement and proof of Girsanov's theorem.

5. Recall that since a probability distribution function, P, is an integral over the probability density function, $\int dP$, the density function can be interpreted as the derivative of the probability distribution function.

6. An example illustrates this equivalency. Suppose in (10.1) that μ and σ are constant and the risk-free interest rate, r, is constant. Then the process $dS/S = \mu\,dt + \sigma\,dz$ has a discrete time lognormal distribution under the P measure. Under the Q measure the process is $dS/S = r\,dt + \sigma\,d\hat{z}$, which is also lognormally distributed but with r replacing μ. Since these lognormal distributions both have positive probability density over the domain from 0 to ∞, they are referred to as *equivalent*.

will return to an interpretation of this derivative ξ_T/ξ_t following a discussion of the continuous-time pricing kernel approach to valuing contingent securities.

In summary, we have seen that a transformation of a Brownian motion by the market price of risk transforms a security's expected rate of return to equal the risk-free rate. This transformation from the physical Brownian motion to a risk-neutral one also transforms the probability density functions for random variables at future dates.

10.1.2   Money Market Deflator

As a final step in deriving a new valuation formula for contingent claims, we now show that the contingent claim's appropriately deflated price process can be made driftless (a martingale) under the probability measure Q. Let $B(t)$ be the value of an investment in a "money market fund," that is, an investment in the instantaneous maturity risk-free asset.[7] Then

$$dB/B = r(t)dt \tag{10.14}$$

Note that $B(T) = B(t)\, e^{\int_t^T r(u)du}$ for any date $T \geq t$. Now define $C(t) \equiv c(t)/B(t)$ as the deflated price process for the contingent claim. Essentially, $C(t)$ is the value of the contingent claim measured in terms of the value of the riskless safe investment that grows at rate $r(t)$. A trivial application of Itô's lemma gives

$$
\begin{aligned}
dC &= \frac{1}{B}dc - \frac{c}{B^2}dB \\
&= \frac{rc}{B}dt + \frac{\sigma_c c}{B}d\widehat{z} - r\frac{c}{B}dt \\
&= \sigma_c C d\widehat{z}
\end{aligned}
\tag{10.15}
$$

Thus, the deflated price process under the equivalent probability measure generated by $d\widehat{z}$ is a driftless process: its expected change is zero. An implication of (10.15) is that the expectation under the risk-neutral, or Q, measure of any future value of C is the current value of C. This can be stated as

$$C(t) = \widehat{E}_t\left[C(T)\right] \; \forall T \geq t \tag{10.16}$$

---

7. An investment that earns the instantaneous maturity risk-free rate is sometimes referred to as a money market fund because money market mutual funds invest in short-maturity, high-credit quality (nearly risk-free) debt instruments.

where $\widehat{E}_t[\cdot]$ denotes the expectation operator under the probability measure generated by $d\widehat{z}$.[8] The mathematical name for a process such as (10.16) is a martingale, which is essentially a random walk in discrete time.[9]

To summarize, we showed that the absence of arbitrage implies the existence of an equivalent probability measure such that the deflated price process is a martingale. Note that (10.16) holds for any deflated contingent claim, including the deflated underlying risky asset, S/B, since we could define the contingent claim as $c = S$.

10.1.3 Feynman-Kac Solution

Now if we rewrite (10.16) in terms of the undeflated contingent claims price, we obtain

$$c(t) = B(t)\widehat{E}_t\left[c(T)\frac{1}{B(T)}\right] \tag{10.17}$$

$$= \widehat{E}_t\left[e^{-\int_t^T r(u)du}c(T)\right]$$

Equation (10.17) can be interpreted as a solution to the Black-Scholes partial differential equation (10.7) and, indeed, is referred to as the Feynman-Kac solution.[10] From a computational point of view, equation (10.17) says that we can price (value) a contingent security by taking the expected value of its discounted payoff, where we discount at the risk-free rate but also assume that when taking the expectation of $c(T)$ the rate of return on c (and all other asset prices, such as S) equals the risk-free rate, a rate that may be changing over time. As when the contingent security's value is found directly from the partial differential equation (10.7), no assumption regarding the market price of risk, $\theta(t)$, is required, because it was eliminated from all assets' return processes when converting to the Q measure. Equivalently, one can use equation (10.16) to value $c(t)/B(t)$ by taking expectations of the deflated price process, where this deflated process

---

8. Another common notation for this risk-neutral, or Q, measure expectation is $E_t^Q[\cdot]$.

9. More formally, define a family of information sets, I_t, that start at date $t = 0$ and continue for all future dates, $\{I_t, t \in [0, \infty]\}$. Also, assume that information at date t includes all information from previous dates, so that for $t_0 < t_1 < t_2$, $I_{t_0} \subseteq I_{t_1} \subseteq I_{t_2}$. Such a family of information sets is referred to as a *filtration*. A process is a martingale with respect to I_t if it satisfies $E[C(T)|I_t] = C(t)\ \forall t < T$ where I_t includes the value of $C(t)$, and $E[|C(T)|] < \infty$; that is, the unconditional expectation of the process is finite.

10. To solve (10.7), a boundary condition for the derivative is needed. For example, in the case of a European call option, it would be $c(T) = \max[0, S(T) - X]$. The solution given by (10.17) incorporates this boundary condition, $c(T)$.

has zero drift. Both of these procedures are continuous-time extensions of the discrete-time, risk-neutral valuation technique that we examined in Chapters 4 and 7.

10.2   Arbitrage and Pricing Kernels

This is not the first time that we have computed an expectation to value a security. Recall from the single- or multiperiod consumption–portfolio choice problem with time-separable utility that we obtained an Euler condition of the form[11]

$$c(t) = E_t \left[m_{t,T} c(T) \right] \tag{10.18}$$

$$= E_t \left[\frac{M_T}{M_t} c(T) \right]$$

where date $T \geq t$, $m_{t,T} \equiv M_T/M_t$ and $M_t = U_c(C_t, t)$ was the marginal utility of consumption at date t. In Chapter 4, we also showed in a discrete time–discrete state model that the absence of arbitrage implies that a stochastic discount factor, $m_{t,T}$, exists whenever markets are complete. We now show that this same result applies in a continuous-time environment whenever markets are dynamically complete. The absence of arbitrage opportunities, which earlier guaranteed the existence of an equivalent martingale measure, also determines a pricing kernel, or state price deflator, M_t. In fact, the concepts of an equivalent martingale measure and state pricing kernel are one and the same.

Note that we can rewrite (10.18) as

$$c(t) M_t = E_t \left[c(T) M_T \right] \tag{10.19}$$

which says that the deflated price process, $c(t) M_t$, is a martingale. But note the difference here versus our earlier analysis: the expectation in (10.19) is taken under the physical probability measure, P, while in (10.16) and (10.17) the expectation is taken under the risk-neutral measure, Q.

Since in the standard, time-separable utility portfolio choice model M_t is the marginal utility of consumption, this suggests that M_t should be a positive process even when we consider more general environments where a stochastic discount factor pricing relationship would hold. Hence, we assume that the state price deflator, M_t, follows a strictly positive diffusion process of the general form

$$dM = \mu_m dt + \sigma_m dz \tag{10.20}$$

---

11. In equation (10.18) we are assuming that the contingent claim pays no dividends between dates t and T.

Now consider the restrictions that the Black-Scholes no-arbitrage conditions place on μ_m and σ_m if (10.19) and (10.20) hold. For any arbitrary security or contingent claim, c, define $c^m = cM$ and apply Itô's lemma:

$$dc^m = cdM + Mdc + (dc)(dM) \tag{10.21}$$

$$= [c\mu_m + M\mu_c c + \sigma_c c\sigma_m] dt + [c\sigma_m + M\sigma_c c] dz$$

If $c^m = cM$ satisfies (10.19), that is, c^m is a martingale, then its drift in (10.21) must be zero, implying

$$\mu_c = -\frac{\mu_m}{M} - \frac{\sigma_c \sigma_m}{M} \tag{10.22}$$

Now consider the case in which c is the instantaneously riskless asset; that is, $c(t) = B(t)$ is the money market investment following the process in equation (10.14). This implies that $\sigma_c = 0$ and $\mu_c = r(t)$. Using (10.22) requires

$$r(t) = -\frac{\mu_m}{M} \tag{10.23}$$

In other words, the expected rate of change of the pricing kernel must equal minus the instantaneous risk-free interest rate.

Next, consider the general case where the asset c is risky, so that $\sigma_c \neq 0$. Using (10.22) and (10.23) together, we obtain

$$\mu_c = r(t) - \frac{\sigma_c \sigma_m}{M} \tag{10.24}$$

or

$$\frac{\mu_c - r}{\sigma_c} = -\frac{\sigma_m}{M} \tag{10.25}$$

Comparing (10.25) to (10.8), we see that

$$-\frac{\sigma_m}{M} = \theta(t) \tag{10.26}$$

Thus, the no-arbitrage condition implies that the form of the pricing kernel must be

$$dM/M = -r(t)\, dt - \theta(t)\, dz \tag{10.27}$$

Note that if we define $m_t \equiv \ln M_t$, then $dm = -\left[r + \frac{1}{2}\theta^2\right] dt - \theta dz$. Hence, in using the pricing kernel to value any contingent claim, we can rewrite (10.18) as

$$c(t) = E_t\left[c(T) M_T/M_t\right] = E_t\left[c(T) e^{m_T - m_t}\right] \tag{10.28}$$

$$= E_t\left[c(T) e^{-\int_t^T \left[r(u) + \frac{1}{2}\theta^2(u)\right] du - \int_t^T \theta(u) dz}\right]$$

Given processes for $r(t)$, $\theta(t)$, and the contingent claim's payoff, $c(T)$, in some instances it may be easier to compute (10.28) rather than, say, (10.16) or (10.17). Of course, in computing (10.28), we need to use the actual drift for c; that is, we compute expectations under the P measure, not the Q measure.

10.2.1   Linking the Valuation Methods

To better understand the connection between the pricing kernel (stochastic discount factor) approach and the martingale (risk-neutral) valuation approach, we now show how M_t is related to the change in probability distribution accomplished using Girsanov's theorem. Equating (10.17) to (10.28), we have

$$\widehat{E}_t \left[e^{-\int_t^T r(u)du} c(T) \right] = E_t \left[c(T) M_T/M_t \right] \tag{10.29}$$

$$= E_t \left[e^{-\int_t^T r(u)du} c(T) e^{-\int_t^T \frac{1}{2}\theta^2(u)du - \int_t^T \theta(u)dz} \right]$$

and then if we substitute using the definition of ξ_τ from (10.12), we have

$$\widehat{E}_t \left[e^{-\int_t^T r(u)du} c(T) \right] = E_t \left[e^{-\int_t^T r(u)du} c(T) \left(\xi_T/\xi_t \right) \right]$$

$$\widehat{E}_t \left[C(T) \right] = E_t \left[C(T) \left(\xi_T/\xi_t \right) \right] \tag{10.30}$$

$$\int C(T) \, dQ_T = \int C(T) \left(\xi_T/\xi_t \right) dP_T$$

where, you may recall, $C(t) = c(t)/B(t)$. From the first two lines of (10.30), we see that on both sides of the equation, the terms in brackets are exactly the same except that the expectation under P includes the Radon-Nikodym derivative ξ_T/ξ_t. As predicted by Girsanov's theorem, this factor transforms the physical probability density at date T to the risk-neutral probability density at date T. Furthermore, relating (10.29) to (10.30) implies

$$M_T/M_t = e^{-\int_t^T r(u)du} \left(\xi_T/\xi_t \right) \tag{10.31}$$

so that the continuous-time pricing kernel (stochastic discount factor) is the product of a risk-free rate discount factor and the Radon-Nikodym derivative. Hence, M_T/M_t can be interpreted as providing both discounting at the risk-free rate and transforming the probability distribution to the risk-neutral one. Indeed, if contingent security prices are deflated by the money market investment, thereby removing the risk-free discount factor, the second line of (10.30) shows that the pricing kernel, M_T/M_t, and the Radon-Nikodym derivative, ξ_T/ξ_t, are exactly the same.

Similar to the discrete-time case discussed in Chapter 4, the role of this derivative (ξ_T/ξ_t or M_T/M_t) is to adjust the risk-neutral probability, Q, to give it greater probability density for "bad" outcomes and less probability density for "good" outcomes relative to the physical probability, P. In continuous time, the extent to which an outcome, as reflected by a realization of dz, is bad or good depends on the sign and magnitude of its market price of risk, $\theta(t)$. This explains why in equation (10.27) the stochastic component of the pricing kernel is of the form $-\theta(t)\,dz$.

10.2.2 The Multivariate Case

The previous analysis has assumed that contingent claims prices depend on only a single source of uncertainty, dz. In a straightforward manner, the results can be generalized to permit multiple independent sources of risk. Suppose we had asset returns depending on an $n \times 1$ vector of independent Brownian motion processes, $\mathbf{dZ} = (dz_1 \ldots dz_n)'$ where $dz_i dz_j = 0$ for $i \neq j$.[12] A contingent claim whose payoff depended on these asset returns then would have a price that followed the process

$$dc/c = \mu_c dt + \Sigma_c \mathbf{dZ} \tag{10.32}$$

where Σ_c is a $1 \times n$ vector $\Sigma_c = (\sigma_{c1} \ldots \sigma_{cn})$.[13] Let the corresponding $n \times 1$ vector of market prices of risks associated with each of the Brownian motions be $\Theta = (\theta_1 \ldots \theta_n)'$. Then, it is straightforward to show that we would have the no-arbitrage condition

$$\mu_c - r = \Sigma_c \Theta \tag{10.33}$$

Equations (10.16) and (10.17) would still hold, and now the pricing kernel's process would be given by

$$dM/M = -r(t)\,dt - \Theta(t)'\,\mathbf{dZ} \tag{10.34}$$

10.3 Alternative Price Deflators

In previous sections, we found it convenient to deflate a contingent claim price by the money market fund's price, $B(t)$. Sometimes, however, it may be convenient to deflate or "normalize" a contingent claims price by the price of a different type of

---

12. The independence assumption is not important. If there are correlated sources of risk (Brownian motions), they can be redefined by a linear transformation to be represented by n orthogonal risk sources.

13. Both μ_c and the elements of Σ_c may be functions of state variables driven by the Brownian motion components of $\mathbf{dZ}$.

security. Such a situation can occur when a contingent claim's payoff depends on multiple risky assets. Let's now consider an example of this, in particular, where the contingent claim is an option written on the difference between two securities' (stocks') prices. The date t price of stock 1, $S_1(t)$, follows the process

$$dS_1/S_1 = \mu_1 dt + \sigma_1 dz_1 \tag{10.35}$$

and the date t price of stock 2, $S_2(t)$, follows the process

$$dS_2/S_2 = \mu_2 dt + \sigma_2 dz_2 \tag{10.36}$$

where σ_1 and σ_2 are assumed to be constants and dz_1 and dz_2 are Brownian motion processes for which $dz_1 dz_2 = \rho dt$. Let $C(t)$ be the date t price of a European option written on the difference between these two stocks' prices. Specifically, at this option's maturity date, T, the value of the option equals

$$C(T) = \max\left[0, S_1(T) - S_2(T)\right] \tag{10.37}$$

Now define $c(t) = C(t)/S_2(t)$, $s(t) \equiv S_1(t)/S_2(t)$, and $B(t) = S_2(t)/S_2(t) = 1$ as the deflated price processes, where the prices of the option, stock 1, and stock 2 are all normalized by the price of stock 2. With this normalized price system, the terminal payoff corresponding to (10.37) is now

$$c(T) = \max\left[0, s(T) - 1\right] \tag{10.38}$$

Applying Itô's lemma, the process for $s(t)$ is given by

$$ds/s = \mu_s dt + \sigma_s dz_3 \tag{10.39}$$

where $\mu_s \equiv \mu_1 - \mu_2 + \sigma_2^2 - \rho\sigma_1\sigma_2$, $\sigma_s dz_3 \equiv \sigma_1 dz_1 - \sigma_2 dz_2$, and $\sigma_s^2 = \sigma_1^2 + \sigma_2^2 - 2\rho\sigma_1\sigma_2$. Further, when prices are measured in terms of stock 2, the deflated price of stock 2 becomes the riskless asset, with the riskless rate of return given by $dB/B = 0dt$. That is, because the deflated price of stock 2 never changes, it returns a riskless rate of zero. Using Itô's lemma once again, the deflated option price, $c(s(t), t)$, follows the process

$$dc = \left[c_s\,\mu_s s + c_t + \frac{1}{2}c_{ss}\,\sigma_s^2 s^2\right] dt + c_s\sigma_s s\, dz_3 \tag{10.40}$$

With this normalized price system, the usual Black-Scholes hedge portfolio can be created from the option and stock 1. The hedge portfolio's value is given by

$$H = -c + c_s s \tag{10.41}$$

and the instantaneous change in value of the portfolio is

$$dH = -dc + c_s ds \tag{10.42}$$

$$= -\left[c_s \mu_s s + c_t + \frac{1}{2} c_{ss} \sigma_s^2 s^2 \right] dt - c_s \sigma_s s \, dz_3 + c_s \mu_s s \, dt + c_s \sigma_s s \, dz_3$$

$$= -\left[c_t + \frac{1}{2} c_{ss} \sigma_s^2 s^2 \right] dt$$

When measured in terms of stock 2's price, the return on this portfolio is instantaneously riskless. In the absence of arbitrage, it must earn the riskless return, which as noted previously equals zero under this deflated price system. Thus we can write

$$dH = -\left[c_t + \frac{1}{2} c_{ss} \sigma_s^2 s^2 \right] dt = 0 \tag{10.43}$$

which implies

$$c_t + \frac{1}{2} c_{ss} \sigma_s^2 s^2 = 0 \tag{10.44}$$

which is the Black-Scholes partial differential equation but with the risk-free rate, r, set to zero. Solving it subject to the boundary condition (10.38), which implies a unit exercise price, gives the usual Black-Scholes formula

$$c(s, t) = s \, N(d_1) - N(d_2) \tag{10.45}$$

where

$$d_1 = \frac{\ln(s(t)) + \frac{1}{2}\sigma_s^2 (T - t)}{\sigma_s \sqrt{T - t}} \tag{10.46}$$

$$d_2 = d_1 l - \sigma_s \sqrt{T - t}$$

To convert back to the undeflated price system, we simply multiply (10.45) by $S_2(t)$ and obtain

$$C(t) = S_1 \, N(d_1) - S_2 \, N(d_2) \tag{10.47}$$

Note that the option price does not depend on the nondeflated price system's risk-free rate, $r(t)$. Hence, the formula holds even for stochastic interest rates.

10.4 Applications

This section illustrates the usefulness of the martingale pricing technique. The first set of applications deals with options written on assets that continuously pay dividends. Examples include an option written on a foreign currency and an option written on a futures price. The second application is to value bonds of different maturities, which determines the term structure of interest rates.

10.4.1   Continuous Dividends

Many types of contingent claims depend on an underlying asset that can be interpreted as paying a continuous dividend that is proportional to the asset's price. Let us apply the risk-neutral pricing method to value an option on such an asset. Denote as $S(t)$ the date t price of an asset that continuously pays a dividend that is a fixed proportion of its price. Specifically, the asset pays a dividend of $\delta S(t)\, dt$ over the time interval dt. The process followed by this asset's price can be written as

$$dS = (\mu - \delta)\, S dt + \sigma S dz \tag{10.48}$$

where σ is the standard deviation of the asset's rate of return and μ is the asset's total expected rate of return, which includes its dividend payment and price appreciation. Similar to the assumptions of Black and Scholes, σ and δ are assumed to be constant, but μ may be a function of S and t. Now note that the total rate of return earned by the owner of one share of this asset is $dS/S + \delta dt = \mu dt + \sigma dz$. Consider a European call option written on this asset that has an exercise price of X and a maturity date of $T > t$, where we define $\tau \equiv T - t$. Assuming a constant interest rate equal to r, we use equation (10.17) to write the date t price of this option as

$$c(t) = \widehat{E}_t \left[e^{-r\tau} c(T) \right] \tag{10.49}$$

$$= e^{-r\tau} \widehat{E}_t \left[\max \left[S(T) - X, 0 \right] \right]$$

To calculate the expectation in (10.49), we need to consider the distribution of $S(T)$. Note that because μ could be a function of S and t, the distribution of $S(T)$ under the physical P measure cannot be determined until this functional relationship $\mu(S, t)$ is specified. However, (10.49) requires the distribution of $S(T)$ under the risk-neutral Q measure, and given the assumption of a constant risk-free rate, this distribution already is determined. As in (10.10), converting from the physical measure generated by dz to the risk-neutral measure generated by $d\widehat{z}$ removes the risk premium from the asset's expected rate of return. Hence, the risk-neutral process for the stock price becomes

$$dS = (r - \delta)\, S dt + \sigma S d\widehat{z} \tag{10.50}$$

Since $r - \delta$ and σ are constants, we know that S follows geometric Brownian motion, and hence is lognormally distributed, under Q. From our previous results, we also know that the risk-neutral distribution of $\ln[S(T)]$ is normal:

$$\ln [S(T)] \sim N \left(\ln [S(t)] + (r - \delta - \frac{1}{2}\sigma^2)\tau, \sigma^2\tau \right) \qquad (10.51)$$

Equation (10.49) can now be computed as

$$c(t) = e^{-r\tau}\widehat{E}_t [\max [S(T) - X, 0]] \qquad (10.52)$$

$$= e^{-r\tau} \int_X^\infty (S(T) - X)\, g(S(T))\, dS(T)$$

where $g(S_T)$ is the lognormal probability density function. This integral can be evaluated by making the change in variable

$$Y = \frac{\ln [S(T)/S(t)] - \left(r - \delta - \frac{1}{2}\sigma^2\right)\tau}{\sigma\sqrt{\tau}} \qquad (10.53)$$

which from (10.51) transforms the lognormally distributed $S(T)$ into the variable Y distributed $N(0, 1)$. The result is the modified Black-Scholes formula

$$c = Se^{-\delta\tau}N(d_1) - Xe^{-r\tau}N(d_2) \qquad (10.54)$$

where

$$d_1 = \frac{\ln (S/X) + \left(r - \delta + \frac{1}{2}\sigma^2\right)\tau}{\sigma\sqrt{\tau}}$$

$$d_2 = d_1 - \sigma\sqrt{\tau} \qquad (10.55)$$

Comparing this formula to Chapter 9's equations (9.24) and (9.25), the value of an option written on an asset that pays no dividends, the only difference is that the non-dividend-paying asset's price, $S(t)$, is replaced with the dividend-discounted price of the dividend-paying asset, $S(t)e^{-\delta\tau}$. The intuition behind this can be seen by realizing that if no dividends are paid, then $\widehat{E}_t[S(T)] = S(t)e^{r\tau}$. However, with dividends, the risk-neutral expected asset price appreciates at rate $r - \delta$, rather than r. This is because with dividends paid out at rate δ, expected price appreciation must be at rate $r - \delta$ to keep the total expected rate of return equal to $\delta + r - \delta = r$. Thus, the risk-neutral expectation of $S(T)$ is

$$\widehat{E}_t [S(T)] = S(t)e^{(r-\delta)\tau} \qquad (10.56)$$

$$= S(t)e^{-\delta\tau}e^{r\tau} = \overline{S}(t)e^{r\tau}$$

where we define $\overline{S}(t) \equiv S(t)e^{-\delta\tau}$. This shows that the value of an option on a dividend-paying asset with current price S equals the value of an option on a non-dividend-paying asset having current price $\overline{S} = Se^{-\delta\tau}$.

Formula (10.54) can be applied to an option on a foreign currency. If $S(t)$ is defined as the domestic currency value of a unit of foreign currency, that is, the spot exchange rate, then assuming this rate has a constant volatility gives it a process satisfying (10.48). Since purchase of a foreign currency allows the owner to invest it in an interest-earning asset yielding the foreign currency interest rate, r_f, the dividend yield will equal this foreign currency rate, $\delta = r_f$. Hence, $\widehat{E}_t [S(T)] = S(t) e^{(r - r_f)\tau}$, where the domestic and foreign currency interest rates are those for a risk-free investment having a maturity equal to that of the option. Note that this expression is the no-arbitrage value of the date t forward exchange rate having a time until maturity of τ, that is, $F_{t,\tau} = Se^{(r-r_f)\tau}$.[14] Therefore, equation (10.54) can be written as

$$c(t) = e^{-r\tau} \left[F_{t,\tau} N(d_1) - X N(d_2) \right] \tag{10.57}$$

where $d_1 = \frac{\ln[F_{t,\tau}/X] + \frac{\sigma^2}{2}\tau}{\sigma\sqrt{\tau}}$, and $d_2 = d_1 - \sigma\sqrt{\tau}$.

A final example is an option written on a futures price. Options are written on the futures prices of commodities, equities, bonds, and currencies. Futures prices are similar to forward prices.[15] Like a forward contract, futures contracts involve long and short parties, and if both parties maintain their positions until the maturity of the contract, their total profits equal the difference between the underlying asset's maturity value and the initial future price. The main difference between futures contracts and forward contracts is that a futures contract is "marked-to-market" daily; that is, the futures price for a particular maturity contract is recomputed daily and profits equal to the difference between today's and yesterday's future price are transferred (settled) from the short party to the long party on a daily basis. Thus, if F_{t,t^*} is the date t futures price for a contract maturing at date t^*, then the undiscounted profit (*loss*) earned by the long (*short*) party over the period from date t to date $T \leq t^*$ is simply $F_{T,t^*} - F_{t,t^*}$. Like forward contracts, there is no initial cost for the parties who enter into a futures contract. Hence, in a risk-neutral world, their expected profits must be zero. This implies that

$$\widehat{E}_t \left[F_{T,t^*} - F_{t,t^*} \right] = 0 \tag{10.58}$$

---

14. This is the same formula as (3.19) or (7.2) but with continuously compounded yields.

15. See (Cox, Ingersoll, and Ross 1981) and (Jarrow and Oldfield 1981) for a comparison of forward and futures contracts. If markets are frictionless, there are no arbitrage opportunities, and default-free interest rates are nonstochastic, then it can be shown that forward and futures prices are equivalent for contracts written on the same underlying asset and having the same maturity date. When interest rates are stochastic, then futures prices will be greater (*less*) than equivalent contract forward prices if the underlying asset is positively (*negatively*) correlated with short-term interest rates.

or that under the Q measure, the futures price is a martingale:

$$\widehat{E}_t \left[F_{T,t^*} \right] = F_{t,t^*} \qquad (10.59)$$

Thus, while under the Q measure a non-dividend-paying asset price would be expected to grow at rate r, a futures price would be expected to grow at rate 0. Hence, futures are like assets with a dividend yield $\delta = r$. From this, one can derive the value of a futures call option that matures in τ periods where $\tau \leq (t^* - t)$ as

$$c\left(t\right) = e^{-r\tau} \left[F_{t,t^*} N\left(d_1\right) - XN\left(d_2\right) \right] \qquad (10.60)$$

where $d_1 = \frac{\ln\left[F_{t,t^*}/X \right] + \frac{\sigma^2}{2}\tau}{\sigma\sqrt{\tau}}$, and $d_2 = d_1 - \sigma\sqrt{\tau}$. Note that this is similar in form to an option on a foreign currency written in terms of the forward exchange rate.

10.4.2   The Term Structure Revisited

The martingale pricing equation (10.17) can be applied to deriving the date t price of a default-free bond that matures in τ periods and pays \$1 at the maturity date $T = t + \tau$. This allows us to value default-free bonds in a manner that is an alternative to the partial differential equation approach of the previous chapter. Using the same notation as in Chapter 9, let $P\left(t, \tau\right)$ denote this bond's current price. Then, since $c\left(T\right) = P\left(T, 0\right) = 1$, equation (10.17) becomes

$$P\left(t, \tau\right) = \widehat{E}_t \left[e^{-\int_t^T r(u)du} 1 \right] \qquad (10.61)$$

We now rederive the Vasicek model using this equation. To apply equation (10.61), we need to find the risk-neutral (Q measure) process for the instantaneous maturity interest rate, $r\left(t\right)$. Recall that the physical (P measure) process for the interest rate was assumed to be the Ornstein-Uhlenbeck process

$$dr(t) = \alpha \left[\bar{r} - r\left(t\right) \right] dt + \sigma_r dz_r \qquad (10.62)$$

and that the market price of bond risk, q, was assumed to be a constant. This implied that the expected rate of return on all bonds satisfied

$$\mu_p \left(r, \tau\right) = r\left(t\right) + q\sigma_p \left(\tau\right) \qquad (10.63)$$

where $\sigma_p \left(\tau\right) = -P_r \sigma_r / P$. Thus, the physical process for a bond's price, given by equation (9.31), can be rewritten as

$$dP\left(r, \tau\right)/P\left(r, \tau\right) = \mu_p \left(r, \tau\right) dt - \sigma_p \left(\tau\right) dz_r \qquad (10.64)$$

$$= \left[r\left(t\right) + q\sigma_p \left(\tau\right) \right] dt - \sigma_p \left(\tau\right) dz_r$$

Now note that if we define the transformed Brownian motion process $d\widehat{z}_r = dz_r - qdt$, then equation (10.64) becomes

$$dP(t, \tau)/P(t, \tau) = \left[r(t) + q\sigma_p(\tau)\right]dt - \sigma_p(\tau)\left[d\widehat{z}_r + qdt\right] \qquad (10.65)$$

$$= r(t)dt - \sigma_p(\tau)d\widehat{z}_r$$

which is the risk-neutral, Q measure process for the bond price. This is so because under this transformation all bond prices now have an expected rate of return equal to the instantaneously risk-free rate, $r(t)$. Therefore, applying this same Brownian motion transformation to equation (10.62), we find that the instantaneous maturity interest rate process under the Q measure is

$$dr(t) = \alpha\left[\bar{r} - r(t)\right]dt + \sigma_r\left[d\widehat{z}_r + qdt\right]$$

$$= \alpha\left[\left(\bar{r} + \frac{q\sigma_r}{\alpha}\right) - r(t)\right]dt + \sigma_r d\widehat{z}_r \qquad (10.66)$$

Hence, we see that the risk-neutral process for $r(t)$ continues to be an Ornstein-Uhlenbeck process but with a different unconditional mean, $\bar{r} + q\sigma_r/\alpha$. Thus, we can use the valuation equation (10.61) to compute the discounted value of the bond's \$1 payoff, $P(t, \tau) = \widehat{E}_t\left[\exp\left(-\int_t^T r(u)\,du\right)\right]$, assuming $r(t)$ follows the process in (10.66). Doing so leads to the same solution given in the previous chapter, equation (9.41).[16]

The intuition for why (10.66) is the appropriate risk-neutral process for $r(t)$ is as follows. Note that if the market price of risk, q, is positive, then the risk-neutral mean, $\bar{r} + q\sigma_r/\alpha$, exceeds the physical process's mean, $\bar{r}$. In this case, when we use valuation equation $P(t, \tau) = \widehat{E}_t\left[\exp\left(-\int_t^T r(u)\,du\right)\right]$, the expected risk-neutral discount rate is greater than the physical expectation of $r(t)$. Therefore, ceteris paribus, the greater is q, the lower will be the bond's price, $P(t, \tau)$, and the greater will be its yield to maturity, $Y(t, \tau)$. Thus, the greater the market price of interest rate risk, the lower are bond prices and the greater are bond yields.

10.5   Summary

This chapter has covered much ground. Yet, many of its results are similar to discrete-time counterparts derived in Chapter 4. The martingale pricing method essentially is a generalization of risk-neutral pricing and is applicable in complete

---

16. Since the Ornstein-Uhlenbeck process in (10.66) is normally distributed, the integral $\int_t^T r(u)\,du$ is also normally distributed based on the idea that sums (an integral) of normals are normal. Hence, $\exp[-\int_t^T r(u)\,du]$ is lognormally distributed.

market economies when arbitrage opportunities are not present. A continuous-time state price deflator can also be derived when asset markets are dynamically complete. We demonstrated that this pricing kernel is expected to grow at minus the short-term interest rate and that the standard deviation of its growth is equal to the market price of risk. We also saw that contingent claims valuation often can be simplified by an appropriate normalization of asset prices. In some cases, this is done by deflating by the price of a riskless asset, and in others by deflating by a risky-asset price. A final set of results included showing how the martingale approach can be applied to valuing a contingent claim written on an asset that pays a continuous, proportional dividend. Important examples of this included options on foreign exchange and on futures prices. Also included was an illustration of how the martingale method can be applied to deriving the term structure of interest rates.

10.6 Exercises

1. In this problem, you are asked to derive the equivalent martingale measure and the pricing kernel for the case to two sources of risk. Let S_1 and S_2 be the values of two risky assets that follow the processes

$$dS_i/S_i = \mu_i dt + \sigma_i dz_i, i = 1, 2$$

where both μ_i and σ_i may be functions of S_1, S_2, and t, and dz_1 and dz_2 are two independent Brownian motion processes, implying $dz_1 dz_2 = 0$. Let $f(S_1, S_2, t)$ denote the value of a contingent claim whose payoff depends solely on S_1, S_2, and t. Also let $r(t)$ be the instantaneous, risk-free interest rate. From Itô's lemma, we know that the derivative's value satisfies

$$df = \mu_f f dt + \sigma_{f1} f dz_1 + \sigma_{f2} f dz_2$$

where $\mu_f f = f_3 + \mu_1 S_1 f_1 + \mu_2 S_2 f_2 + \frac{1}{2}\sigma_1^2 S_1^2 f_{11} + \frac{1}{2}\sigma_2^2 S_2^2 f_{22}, \sigma_{f1} f = \sigma_1 S_1 f_1, \sigma_{f2} f = \sigma_2 S_2 f_2$ and where the subscripts on f denote the partial derivatives with respect to its three arguments, S_1, S_2, and t.

   a. By forming a riskless portfolio composed of the contingent claim and the two risky assets, show that in the absence of arbitrage an expression for μ_f can be derived in terms of r, $\theta_1 \equiv \frac{\mu_1 - r}{\sigma_1}$, and $\theta_2 \equiv \frac{\mu_2 - r}{\sigma_2}$.

   b. Define the risk-neutral processes $d\widehat{z}_1$ and $d\widehat{z}_2$ in terms of the original Brownian motion processes, and then give the risk-neutral process for df in terms of $d\widehat{z}_1$ and $d\widehat{z}_2$.

   c. Let $B(t)$ be the value of a "money market fund" that invests in the instantaneous maturity, risk-free asset. Show that $F(t) \equiv f(t)/B(t)$ is a martingale under the risk-neutral probability measure.

   d. Let $M(t)$ be the state price deflator such that $f(t) M(t)$ is a martingale under the physical probability measure. If

$$dM = \mu_m dt + \sigma_{m1} dz_1 + \sigma_{m2} dz_2$$

   what must be the values of μ_m, σ_{m1}, and σ_{m2} that preclude arbitrage? Show how you solve for these values.

2. The Cox, Ingersoll, and Ross (Cox, Ingersoll, and Ross 1985b) model of the term structure of interest rates assumes that the process followed by the instantaneous maturity, risk-free interest rate is

$$dr = \alpha(\gamma - r) dt + \sigma\sqrt{r}dz$$

   where α, γ, and σ are constants. Let $P(t, \tau)$ be the date t price of a zero-coupon bond paying \$1 at date $t + \tau$. It is assumed that $r(t)$ is the only source of uncertainty affecting $P(t, \tau)$. Also, let $\mu_p(t, \tau)$ and $\sigma_p(t, \tau)$ be the instantaneous mean and standard deviation of the rate of return on this bond and assume

$$\frac{\mu_p(t, \tau) - r(t)}{\sigma_p(t, \tau)} = \beta\sqrt{r}$$

   where β is a constant.

   a. Write down the stochastic process followed by the pricing kernel (state price deflator), $M(t)$, for this problem, that is, the process dM/M. Also, apply Itô's lemma to derive the process for $m(t) \equiv \ln(M)$, that is, the process dm.

   b. Let the current date be 0 and write down the formula for the bond price, $P(0, \tau)$, in terms of an expectation of $m_\tau - m_0$. Show how this can be written in terms of an expectation of functions of integrals of $r(t)$ and β.

3. If the price of a non-dividend-paying stock follows the process $dS/S = \mu dt + \sigma dz$ where σ is constant, and there is a constant risk-free interest rate equal to r, then the Black-Scholes derivation showed that the no-arbitrage value of a standard call option having τ periods to maturity and an exercise price of X is given by $c = SN(d_1) - Xe^{-r\tau}N(d_2)$ where $d_1 = [\ln(S/X) + (r + \frac{1}{2}\sigma^2)\tau]/(\sigma\sqrt{\tau})$ and $d_2 = d_1 - \sigma\sqrt{\tau}$.

   A *forward start* call option is similar to this standard option but with the difference that the option exercise price, X, is initially a random variable. The exercise price is set equal to the contemporaneous stock price at a future date prior to the maturity of the option. Specifically, let the current date be 0 and the option maturity date be τ. Then at date t where $0 < t < \tau$, the option's exercise price, X, is set equal to the date t value of the stock, denoted as $S(t)$. Hence, $X = S(t)$ is a random variable as of the current date 0.

For a given date t, derive the date 0 value of this forward start call option. Hint: note the value of a standard call option when $S = X$, and then use a simple application of risk-neutral pricing to derive the value of the forward start option.

4. If the price of a non-dividend-paying stock follows the process $dS/S = \mu dt + \sigma dz$ where σ is constant, and there is a constant risk-free interest rate equal to r, then the Black-Scholes derivation showed that the no-arbitrage value of a standard call option having τ periods to maturity and an exercise price of X is given by $c = SN(d_1) - Xe^{-r\tau}N(d_2)$ where $d_1 = [\ln(S/X) + (r + \frac{1}{2}\sigma^2)\tau]/(\sigma\sqrt{\tau})$ and $d_2 = d_1 - \sigma\sqrt{\tau}$. Based on this result and a simple application of risk-neutral pricing, derive the value of the following *binary* options. Continue to assume that the underlying stock price follows the process $dS/S = \mu dt + \sigma dz$, the risk-free interest rate equals r, and the option's time until maturity equals τ.

   a. Consider the value of a *cash-or-nothing call*, cnc. If $S(T)$ is the stock's price at the option's maturity date of T, the payoff of this option is

$$cnc_T = \begin{cases} F & \text{if } S(T) > X \\ 0 & \text{if } S(T) \le X \end{cases}$$

   where F is a fixed amount. Derive the value of this option when its time until maturity is τ and the current stock price is S. Explain your reasoning.

   b. Consider the value of an *asset-or-nothing call*, anc. If $S(T)$ is the stock's price at the option's maturity date of T, the payoff of this option is

$$anc_T = \begin{cases} S(T) & \text{if } S(T) > X \\ 0 & \text{if } S(T) \le X \end{cases}$$

   Derive the value of this option when its time until maturity is τ and the current stock price is S. Explain your reasoning.

5. Outline a derivation of the form of the multivariate state price deflator given in equations (10.33) and (10.34).

6. Consider a continuous-time version of a Lucas endowment economy (Lucas 1978). It is assumed that there is a single risky asset (e.g., fruit tree) that produces a perishable consumption good that is paid out as a continuous dividend, g_t. This dividend satisfies the process

$$dg_t/g_t = \alpha dt + \sigma dz$$

where α and σ are constants. There is a representative agent who at date 0 maximizes lifetime consumption given by

$$E_0 \int_0^\infty U(C_t, t) \, dt$$

where $U(C_t, t) = e^{-\phi t} C_t^{\gamma} / \gamma$, $\gamma < 1$. Under the Lucas endowment economy assumption, we know that in equilibrium $C_t = g_t$.

a. Let $P_t(\tau)$ denote the date t price of a riskless discount (zero-coupon) bond that pays one unit of the consumption good in τ periods. Derive an (Euler equation) expression for $P_t(\tau)$ in terms of an expectation of a function of future dividends.

b. Let $m_{t,t+\tau} \equiv M_{t+\tau}/M_t$ be the stochastic discount factor (pricing kernel) for this economy. Based on your answer in part (a), write down the stochastic process for M_t. Hint: find an expression for M_t and then use Itô's lemma.

c. Based on your previous answers, write down the instantaneous, risk-free real interest rate. Is it constant or time varying?

CHAPTER 11

Mixing Diffusion and Jump Processes

We have studied the nature and application of diffusion processes, which are continuous-time stochastic processes whose uncertainty derives from Brownian motions. While these processes have proved useful in modeling many different types of economic and financial time series, they may be unrealistic for modeling random variables whose values can change very significantly over a short period of time. This is because diffusion processes have continuous sample paths and cannot model discontinuities, or "jumps," in their values. In some situations, it may be more accurate to allow for large, sudden changes in value. For example, when the release of significant new information results in an immediate, substantial change in the market value of an asset, then we need to augment the diffusion process with another type of uncertainty to capture this discontinuity in the asset's price. This is where Poisson jump processes can be useful. In particular, we can model an economic or financial time series as the sum of diffusion (Brownian motion–based) processes and jump processes.

The first section of this chapter introduces the mathematics of a process that is a mixture of a jump process and a diffusion process. Section 11.2 shows how Itô's lemma can be extended to derive the process of a variable that is a function of a mixed jump-diffusion process. It comes as no surprise that this function inherits the risk of both the Brownian motion component as well as the jump component of the underlying process. Section 11.3 revisits the problem of valuing a contingent claim, but now assumes that the underlying asset's price follows a mixed jump-diffusion process. Our analysis follows that of Robert Merton (Merton 1976), who first analyzed this subject. In general, the inclusion of a jump process means that a contingent claim's risk cannot be perfectly hedged by trading in the underlying asset. In this situation of market incompleteness, additional assumptions regarding the price of jump risk need to be made in order to value derivative securities. We show how an option can be valued when the underlying asset's jump risk is perfectly diversifiable. The problem of option valuation when the underlying asset is the market portfolio of all assets is also discussed.

11.1 Modeling Jumps in Continuous Time

Consider the following continuous-time process:

$$dS/S = (\mu - \lambda k) \, dt + \sigma \, dz + \gamma \, (Y) \, dq \tag{11.1}$$

where dz is a standard Wiener (Brownian motion) process and $q\,(t)$ is a Poisson counting process that increases by 1 whenever a Poisson-distributed event occurs. Specifically, $dq\,(t)$ satisfies

$$dq = \begin{cases} 1 & \text{if a jump occurs} \\ 0 & \text{otherwise} \end{cases} \tag{11.2}$$

During each time interval, dt, the probability that $q\,(t)$ will augment by 1 is $\lambda\,(t)\,dt$, where $\lambda\,(t)$ is referred to as the Poisson intensity. When a Poisson event does occur, say, at date $\hat{t}$, then there is a discontinuous change in S equal to $dS = \gamma\,(Y)\,S$ where γ is a function of $Y\,(\hat{t})$, which may be a random variable realized at date $\hat{t}$.[1] In other words, if a Poisson event occurs at date $\hat{t}$, then $dS\,(\hat{t}) = S\,(\hat{t}^{+}) - S\,(\hat{t}^{-}) = \gamma\,(Y)\,S\,(\hat{t}^{-})$, or

$$S\,(\hat{t}^{+}) = [1 + \gamma\,(Y)]\,S\,(\hat{t}^{-}) \tag{11.3}$$

Thus, if $\gamma\,(Y) > 0$, there is an upward jump in S; whereas, if $\gamma\,(Y) < 0$, there is a downward jump in S. Now we can define $k \equiv E[\gamma\,(Y)]$ as the expected proportional jump given that a Poisson event occurs, so that the expected change in S from the jump component $\gamma\,(Y)\,dq$ over the time interval dt is $\lambda\,k\,dt$. Therefore, if we wish to let the parameter μ denote the instantaneous total expected rate of return (rate of change) on S, we need to subtract off $\lambda\,k\,dt$ from the drift term of S:

$$E[dS/S] = E[(\mu - \lambda k)\,dt] + E[\sigma\,dz] + E[\gamma\,(Y)\,dq] \tag{11.4}$$

$$= (\mu - \lambda k)\,dt + 0 + \lambda\,k\,dt = \mu\,dt$$

The sample path of $S(t)$ for a process described by equation (11.1) will be continuous most of the time, but can have finite jumps of differing signs and

---

1. The date, or "point," of a jump, $\hat{t}$, is associated with the attribute or "mark" $Y\,(\hat{t})$. Hence, $(\hat{t}, Y\,(\hat{t}))$ is referred to as a *marked point process*, or space-time point process.

amplitudes at discrete points in time, where the timing of the jumps depends on the Poisson random variable $q(t)$ and the jump sizes depend on the random variable $Y(t)$. If $S(t)$ is an asset price, these jump events can be thought of as times when important information affecting the value of the asset is released.

Jump-diffusion processes can be generalized to a multivariate setting where the process for $S(t)$ can depend on multiple Brownian motion and Poisson jump components. Moreover, the functions μ, σ, λ, and γ may be time varying and depend on other variables that follow diffusion or jump-diffusion processes. In particular, if $\lambda(t)$ depends on a random state variable $x(t)$, where for example, $dx(t)$ follows a diffusion process, then $\lambda(t, x(t))$ is called a doubly stochastic Poisson process or Cox process. Wolfgang Runggaldier (Runggaldier 2003) gives an excellent review of univariate and multivariate specifications for jump-diffusion models. For simplicity, in this chapter we restrict our attention to univariate models.[2] Let us next consider an extension of Itô's lemma that covers univariate jump-diffusion processes.

11.2   Itô's Lemma for Jump-Diffusion Processes

Let $c(S, t)$ be the value of a variable that is a twice-differentiable function of $S(t)$, where $S(t)$ follows the jump-diffusion process in equation (11.1). For example, $c(S, t)$ might be the value of a derivative security whose payoff depends on an underlying asset having the current price $S(t)$. Itô's lemma can be extended to the case of mixed jump-diffusion processes, and this generalization implies that the value $c(S, t)$ follows the process

$$dc = c_s \left[(\mu - \lambda k)S\, dt + \sigma S\, dz \right] + \frac{1}{2}c_{ss}\sigma^2 S^2\, dt + c_t\, dt$$
$$+ \left\{ c\left([1 + \gamma(Y)]S,\ t\right) - c(S,\ t) \right\} dq \tag{11.5}$$

where subscripts on c denote its partial derivatives. Note that the first line on the right-hand side of equation (11.5) is the standard form for Itô's lemma when $S(t)$ is restricted to following a diffusion process. The second line is what is new. It states that when S jumps, the contingent claim's value has a corresponding jump and moves from $c(S, t)$ to $c([1 + \gamma(Y)]S, t)$. Now define $\mu_c dt$ as the instantaneous expected rate of return on c per unit time, that is, $E[dc/c]$. Also, define σ_c as the standard deviation of the instantaneous rate of return on c,

---

2. In Chapter 18, we consider examples of default risk models where λ and γ are permitted to be functions of other state variables that follow diffusion processes.

conditional on a jump not occurring. Then we can rewrite equation (11.5) as

$$dc/c = \left[\mu_c - \lambda k_c\,(t)\right] dt + \sigma_c dz + \gamma_c\,(Y)\,dq \tag{11.6}$$

where

$$\mu_c \equiv \frac{1}{c}\left[c_s\,(\mu - \lambda k)\,S + \frac{1}{2}c_{ss}\sigma^2 S^2 + c_t\right] + \lambda k_c\,(t) \tag{11.7}$$

$$\sigma_c \equiv \frac{c_s}{c}\sigma S \tag{11.8}$$

$$\gamma_c = [c\,([1 + \gamma\,(Y)]S,\ t) - c\,(S,t)]/c\,(S,t) \tag{11.9}$$

$$k_c\,(t) \equiv E_t\,[c\,([1 + \gamma\,(Y)]S,\ t) - c\,(S,t)]/c\,(S,t) \tag{11.10}$$

Here, $k_c\,(t)$ is the expected proportional jump of the variable $c\,(S,t)$ given that a Poisson event occurs. In general, $k_c\,(t)$ is time varying. Let us now apply these results to valuing a contingent claim that depends on an asset whose price follows a jump-diffusion process.

11.3 Valuing Contingent Claims

This section follows work by Robert Merton (Merton 1976). For simplicity, the analysis that follows assumes that λ is constant over time and that $\gamma\,(Y) = (Y - 1)$. Thus, if a jump occurs, the discontinuous change in S is $dS = (Y - 1)S$. In other words, $S\,(\hat{t}^-)$ goes to $S\,(\hat{t}^+) = YS\,(\hat{t}^-)$, where $\hat{t}$ is the date of the jump. It is also assumed that successive random jump sizes, $(\tilde{Y} - 1)$, are independently and identically distributed.

Note that if μ and σ are constants, so that the continuous component of $S(t)$ is lognormally distributed, then conditional upon there being n jumps in the interval $(0,\ t)$,

$$\tilde{S}(t) = S(0)\,e^{(\mu - \frac{1}{2}\sigma^2 - \lambda k)\,t + \sigma\,(\tilde{z}_t - z_0)}\,\tilde{y}(n) \tag{11.11}$$

where $\tilde{z}_t - z_0 \sim N(0,\ t)$ is the change in the Brownian motion process from date 0 to date t. Jump uncertainty is reflected in the random variable $\tilde{y}\,(n)$, where $\tilde{y}(0) = 1$ and $\tilde{y}(n) = \prod_{i=1}^{n} \tilde{Y}_i$ for $n \geq 1$ where $\{\tilde{Y}_i\}_{i=1}^{n}$ is a set of independent identically distributed jumps. A verification of (11.11) is left as an exercise.

Similar to a Black-Scholes hedge portfolio, let us now consider an investment that includes a contingent claim (for example, a call option), its underlying asset, and the riskless asset.[3] Let the contingent claim's price be c and assume

---

3. Our analysis regarding the return on a portfolio containing the underlying asset, the contingent claim, and the risk-free asset differs somewhat from our orginal Black-Scholes presentation, because here we write the portfolio's return in terms of the assets' portfolio proportions instead

the underlying asset's price follows the jump-diffusion process given in equation (11.1) with $\gamma\,(Y) = (Y - 1)$. Furthermore, assume that the risk-free interest rate is a constant equal to r per unit time. Denote the proportions of the portfolio invested in the underlying asset, contingent claim, and risk-free asset as ω_1, ω_2, and $\omega_3 = 1 - \omega_1 - \omega_2$, respectively. The instantaneous rate of return on this portfolio, denoted dH/H, is given by

$$dH/H = \omega_1\, dS/S + \omega_2\, dc/c + (1 - \omega_1 - \omega_2)r\, dt \tag{11.12}$$

$$= \left[\, \omega_1(\mu - r) + \omega_2(\mu_c - r) + r - \lambda(\omega_1 k + \omega_2 k_c)\,\right] dt$$

$$+\; (\omega_1\sigma + \omega_2\sigma_c)\, dz + \left[\omega_1\gamma\,(Y) + \omega_2\gamma_c\,(Y)\right] dq$$

11.3.1 An Imperfect Hedge

Consider the possibility of choosing ω_1 and ω_2 in order to eliminate the risk from jumps. Note that while jumps occur simultaneously in the asset and the contingent claim, that is, jump risk is perfectly dependent for these two securities, these risks are not necessarily linearly dependent. This is because the contingent claim price, $c(S,\,t)$, is generally a nonlinear function of the asset price. Unlike Brownian motion–generated movements, jumps result in nonlocal changes in S and $c(S,\,t)$. When the underlying asset's jump size $(\widetilde{Y} - 1)$ is random, the ratio between the size of the jump in S and the size of the jump in c, which is $\gamma\big(\widetilde{Y}\big)/\gamma_c\big(\widetilde{Y}\big)$, is unpredictable. Hence, a predetermined hedge ratio, ω_1/ω_2, that would eliminate all portfolio risk does not exist.[4] The implication is that one cannot perfectly replicate the contingent claim's payoff by a portfolio composed of the underlying asset and the risk-free asset. In this sense, the market for the contingent claim is incomplete.

Instead, suppose we pick ω_1 and ω_2 to eliminate only the risk from the continuous Brownian motion movements. This Black-Scholes hedge implies setting $\omega_1^*/\omega_2^* = -\sigma_c/\sigma = -c_s S/c$ from our definition of σ_c. This leads to the process for the value of the portfolio:

$$dH/H = [\omega_1^*\,(\mu - r) + \omega_2^*\,(\mu_c - r) + r - \lambda\,(\omega_1^* k + \omega_2^* k_c)]\, dt$$

$$+ \left[\omega_1^*\gamma\,(Y) + \omega_2^*\gamma_c\,(Y)\right] dq \tag{11.13}$$

---

of units of their shares. To do this, we do not impose the requirement that the portfolio require zero net investment ($H\,(t) = 0$), since then portfolio proportions would be undefined. However, as before, we do require that the portfolio be self-financing.

4. If the size of the jump is deterministic, a hedge that eliminates jump risk is possible. Alternatively, Phillip Jones (Jones 1984) shows that if the underlying asset's jump size has a discrete (finite state) distribution and a sufficient number of different contingent claims are written on this asset, a hedge portfolio that combines the underlying asset and these multiple contingent claims could also eliminate jump risk.

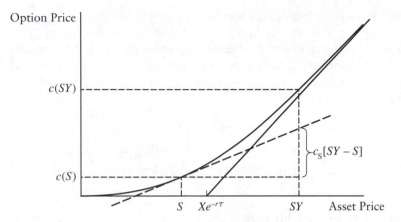

Figure 11.1 ——Hedge Portfolio Return with Jump

The return on this portfolio is a pure jump process. The return is deterministic, except when jumps occur. Using the definitions of γ, γ_c, and $\omega_1^* = -\omega_2^* c_s S/c$, we see that the portfolio jump term, $\left[\omega_1^* \gamma\,(Y) + \omega_2^* \gamma_c\,(Y)\right] dq$, equals

$$\begin{cases} \omega_2^* \left[\frac{c(S\widetilde{Y},t)-c(S,t)}{c(S,t)} - c_s(S,t)\frac{S\widetilde{Y}-S}{c(S,t)} \right] & \text{if a jump occurs} \\ 0 & \text{otherwise} \end{cases} \tag{11.14}$$

Now consider the case when the contingent claim is a European option on a stock with a time until expiration of τ and a strike price X. What would be the pattern of profits and losses on the (quasi-) hedge portfolio? We can answer this question by noting that if the rate of return on the underlying asset is independent of its price level, as is the case in equation (11.1), then the absence of arbitrage restricts the option price to a convex function of the asset price.[5] The option's convexity implies that $c(SY, t) - c(S, t) - c_s(S, t)[SY - S] \geq 0$ for all Y and t. This is illustrated in Figure 11.1 where the convex solid line gives the value of a call option as a function of its underlying asset's price.

From this fact and (11.14), we see that the unanticipated return on the hedge portfolio has the same sign as ω_2^*. This means that $\omega_1^* k + \omega_2^* k_c$, the expected portfolio value jump size, also has the same sign as ω_2^*. Therefore, an option writer who follows this Black-Scholes hedge by being short the option ($\omega_2^* < 0$) and long the underlying asset earns, most of the time, more than the portfolio's expected rate of return. However, on those rare occasions when the underlying asset price

---

5. For a proof, see Theorem 8.10 in Chapter 8 of (Merton 1992), which reproduces (Merton 1973b).

jumps, a relatively large loss is incurred. Thus in "quiet" times, option writers appear to make positive excess returns. However, during infrequent "active" times, option writers suffer large losses.

11.3.2   Diversifiable Jump Risk

Since the hedge portfolio is not riskless but is exposed to jump risk, we cannot use the previous no-arbitrage argument to equate the hedge portfolio's rate of return to the risk-free rate. The hedge portfolio is exposed to jump risk and, in general, there may be a "market price" to such risk. One assumption might be that this jump risk is the result of purely firm specific information and, hence, the jump risk is perfectly diversifiable. This would imply that the market price of jump risk is zero. In this case, all of the risk of the hedge portfolio is diversifiable, so that its expected rate of return must equal the risk-free rate, r. Making this assumption implies

$$\omega_1^*(\mu - r) + \omega_2^*(\mu_c - r) + r = r \tag{11.15}$$

or

$$\omega_1^*/\omega_2^* = -\sigma_c/\sigma = -(\mu_c - r)/(\mu - r) \tag{11.16}$$

Now denote T as the maturity date of the contingent claim, and let us use the time until maturity $\tau \equiv T - t$ as the second argument for $c(S, \cdot)$ rather than calendar time, t. Hence, $c(S, \tau)$ is the price of the contingent claim when the current asset price is S and the time until maturity of the contingent claim is τ. With this redefinition, note that $c_\tau = -c_t$. Using (11.16) and substituting in for μ_c and σ_c from the definitions (11.7) and (11.8), we obtain the equilibrium partial differential equation

$$\frac{1}{2}\sigma^2 S^2 c_{ss} + (r - \lambda k)S c_s - c_\tau - rc + \lambda E_t \left[c(S\tilde{Y}, \tau) - c(S, \tau) \right] = 0 \tag{11.17}$$

For a call option, this is solved subject to the boundary conditions $c(0, \tau) = 0$ and $c(S(T), 0) = \max[S(T) - X, 0]$. Note that when $\lambda = 0$, equation (11.17) is the standard Black-Scholes equation, which we know has the solution

$$b(S, \tau, X, \sigma^2, r) \equiv S N(d_1) - Xe^{-r\tau} N(d_2) \tag{11.18}$$

where $d_1 = [\ln(S/X) + (r + \frac{1}{2}\sigma^2)\tau] / (\sigma\sqrt{\tau})$ and $d_2 = d_1 - \sigma\sqrt{\tau}$. Robert Merton (Merton 1976) shows that the general solution to (11.17) is

$$c(S, \tau) = \sum_{n=0}^{\infty} \frac{e^{-\lambda\tau}(\lambda\tau)^n}{n!} E_t \left[b(S\tilde{y}(n) e^{-\lambda k\tau}, \tau, X, \sigma^2, r) \right] \tag{11.19}$$

where, you may recall, $\tilde{y}(0) = 1$ and $\tilde{y}(n) = \prod_{i=1}^{n} \tilde{Y}_i$ for $n \geq 1$. The intuition behind the formula in (11.19) is that the option is a probability-weighted average of expected Black-Scholes option prices. Note that if the underlying asset price followed (11.1), then conditional on no jumps occurring over the life of the option, risk-neutral valuation would imply that the Black-Scholes option price would be $b(Se^{-\lambda k \tau}, \tau, X, \sigma^2, r)$.[6] Similarly, conditional on one jump occurring, risk-neutral valuation would imply that the option price would be $b(Sy(1)e^{-\lambda k \tau}, \tau, X, \sigma^2, r)$. Conditional on two jumps, it would be $b(Sy(2)e^{-\lambda k \tau}, \tau, X, \sigma^2, r)$, and thus for n jumps, it would be $b(Sy(n)e^{-\lambda k \tau}, \tau, X, \sigma^2, r)$.

Since $\frac{e^{-\lambda \tau}(\lambda \tau)^n}{n!}$ is the probability of n jumps occurring, we see that (11.19) is the jump-probability-weighted average of expected option values conditioned over all possible numbers of jumps.

11.3.3   Lognormal Jump Proportions

Under particular assumptions regarding the distribution of $\tilde{Y}$, solutions to (11.19) can be calculated numerically or, in some cases, in closed form. Here, we consider a case that leads to a closed-form solution, namely, the case in which $\tilde{Y}$ is lognormally distributed. Thus, if $E[\ln \tilde{Y}] \equiv \alpha - \frac{1}{2}\delta^2$ where $var[\ln \tilde{Y}] \equiv \delta^2$, then $E[\tilde{Y}] = e^{\alpha} = 1 + k$. Hence, $\alpha \equiv \ln(1 + k)$. Given this assumption, if μ is assumed to be constant, the probability density for $\ln[S(t + \tau)]$, conditional on the value of $S(t)$, is

$$\sum_{n=0}^{\infty} g(\ln[S(t + \tau)/S(t)] \mid n)h(n) \tag{11.20}$$

where $g(\cdot \mid n)$ is the conditional density function given that n jumps occur during the interval between t and $t + \tau$, and $h(n)$ is the probability that n jumps occur between t and $t + \tau$. The values of these expressions are

$$g\left(\ln\left[\frac{S(t+\tau)}{S(t)}\right] \mid n\right) \equiv \frac{\exp\left[-\frac{\left(\ln\left[\frac{S(t+\tau)}{S(t)}\right] - \left(\mu - \lambda k + \frac{n\alpha}{\tau} - \frac{v_n^2}{2}\right)\tau\right)^2}{2v_n^2\tau}\right]}{\sqrt{2\pi v_n^2 \tau}} \tag{11.21}$$

$$h(n) \equiv \frac{e^{-\lambda \tau}(\lambda \tau)^n}{n!} \tag{11.22}$$

---

6. Recall that since the drift is $\mu - \lambda k$, and risk-neutral valuation sets $\mu = r$, then λk is like a dividend yield. Hence, $b(Se^{-\lambda k \tau}, \tau, X, \sigma^2, r)$ is the Black-Scholes formula for an asset with a dividend yield of λk.

where $v_n^2 \equiv \sigma^2 + n\delta^2/\tau$ is the "average" variance per unit time. From (11.21), we see that conditional on n jumps occurring, $\ln[S(t+\tau)/S(t)]$ is normally distributed. Using the Cox-Ross risk-neutral (equivalent martingale) transformation, which allows us to set $\mu = r$, we can compute the date t risk-neutral expectation of $\max[S(T) - X, 0]$, discounted by the risk-free rate, and conditional on n jumps occurring. This is given by

$$E_t[\, b(S\tilde{y}(n)e^{-\lambda k \tau}, \tau, X, \sigma^2, r)\,] = e^{-\lambda k \tau}(1+k)^n \, b(S, \tau, X, v_n^2, r_n)$$

$$= e^{-\lambda k \tau}(1+k)^n \, b_n(S, \tau) \qquad (11.23)$$

where $b_n(S, \tau) \equiv b(S, \tau, X, v_n^2, r_n)$ and where $r_n \equiv r - \lambda k + n\gamma/\tau$. The actual value of the option is then the weighted average of these conditional values, where each weight equals the probability that a Poisson random variable with characteristic parameter $\lambda \tau$ will take on the value n. Defining $\lambda' \equiv \lambda(1+k)$, this equals

$$c(S, \tau) = \sum_{n=0}^{\infty} \frac{e^{-\lambda \tau}(\lambda \tau)^n}{n!} e^{-\lambda k \tau} (1+k)^n \, b_n(S, \tau)$$

$$= \sum_{n=0}^{\infty} \frac{e^{-\lambda' \tau}(\lambda' \tau)^n}{n!} \, b_n(S, \tau) \qquad (11.24)$$

11.3.4 Nondiversifiable Jump Risk

In some circumstances, it is unrealistic to assume that jump risk is nonpriced risk. For example, David Bates (Bates 1991) investigated the U.S. stock market crash of 1987, an event that certainly was not firm specific but affected the entire market for equities. Similar work by Vasanttilak Naik and Moon Lee (Naik and Lee 1990) considered nondiversifiable jump risk. The models in these articles assume that aggregate wealth in the economy follows a mixed jump-diffusion process. This could result from a representative agent, Cox, Ingersoll, and Ross–type production economy in which technologies follow a jump-diffusion process and individuals select investments in these technologies such that their optimally invested aggregate wealth follows a mixed jump-diffusion process (Bates 1991). Or it can simply be assumed that the economy is a Lucas-type endowment economy and there is an exogenous firm dividend process that follows a mixed jump-diffusion process, and these dividends cannot be invested but must be consumed (Naik and Lee 1990).

In both articles, jumps in aggregate wealth or consumption (endowment) are assumed to be of the lognormal type that we assumed earlier. Further, representative individuals are assumed to have constant relative-risk-aversion utility. These assumptions allow the authors to solve for the general equilibrium price of jump risk. Given this setup, contingent claims, which are assumed to be in zero net supply, can be priced. For example, the formula for a call option derived by Bates has a series solution that is similar in form to equation (11.24).

11.3.5   Black-Scholes versus Jump-Diffusion Model

Having derived a model for pricing options written on an underlying asset whose price follows a jump-diffusion process, the natural question to ask is whether this makes any difference vis-à-vis the Black-Scholes option pricing model, which does not permit the underlying's price to jump. The answer is yes, and the jump-diffusion model appears to better fit the actual prices of many options written on stocks, stock indices, and foreign exchange. In most types of options, the Black-Scholes model underprices out-of-the-money and in-the-money options relative to at-the-money-options. What this means is that the prices of actual options whose exercise price is substantially different from the current price of the underlying are priced higher than the theoretical Black-Scholes price, while the prices of actual options whose exercise price is close to the current price of the underlying are priced lower than the theoretical Black-Scholes price. This phenomenon has been described as a *volatility smile* or *volatility smirk*.[7]

This empirical deficiency can be traced to the Black-Scholes model's assumption that the underlying's terminal price has a risk-neutral distribution that is lognormal. Apparently, investors price actual options under the belief that the risk-neutral distribution has much fatter "tails" than those of the lognormal distribution. In other words, investors price securities as if they believe that extreme asset prices are more likely than what would be predicted by a lognormal distribution, because actual in- and out-of-the-money options are priced relatively high versus the Black-Scholes theoretical prices. A model that permits the underlying asset's price to jump, with jumps possibly being both positive and negative, can generate a distribution for the asset's price that has fatter tails than the lognormal. The possibility of jumps makes extreme price changes more likely and, indeed,

---

7. Note that if the Black-Scholes model correctly priced all options having the same maturity date and the same underlying asset but different exercise prices, there would be one volatility parameter, σ, consistent with all of these options. However, the implied volatilities, σ, needed to fit in- and, especially, out-of-the-money call options are greater than the volatility parameter needed to fit at-the-money options. Hence, when implied volatility is graphed against call options' exercise prices, it forms an inverted hump, or "smile," or in the case of equity index options, a downward sloping curve, or "smirk." These characteristics of option prices are equivalent to the Black-Scholes model giving relatively low prices for in- and out-of-the-money options because options prices are increasing functions of the underlying's volatility, σ. The Black-Scholes model needs relatively high estimated volatility for in- and out-of-the-money options versus at-the-money options. If a (theoretically correct) single volatility parameter were used for all options, in- and out-of-the-money options would be relatively underpriced by the model. See (Hull 2000) for a review of this issue.

the jump-diffusion option pricing model can better match the market prices of many types of options.

However, there are other aspects of actual option prices for which even the standard jump-diffusion model cannot account. The volatility parameters implied by actual option prices change over time and appear to follow a mean-reverting stochastic process. To account for this empirical time variation, *stochastic volatility* option pricing models have been developed. These models start by assuming that the underlying asset price follows a diffusion process such as $dS/S = \mu dt + \sigma dz$, but where the volatility, σ, is stochastic. The volatility follows a mean-reverting process of the form $d\sigma = \alpha(\sigma) dt + \beta(\sigma) dz_\sigma$, where dz_σ is another Brownian motion process possibly correlated with dz. Similar to the jump-diffusion model, one must assign a market price of risk associated with the volatility uncertainty reflected in the dz_σ term.[8]

While stochastic volatility option pricing models also produce fatter-tailed distributions relative to the lognormal, empirically these distributions do not tend to be fat enough to explain volatility smiles and smirks. To capture both time variation in volatilities and cross-sectional differences in volatility due to different degrees of "moneyness" (volatility smiles or smirks), it appears that an option pricing model that allows for both stochastic volatility and jumps is required.[9] For recent reviews of the empirical option pricing literature, see (Bates 2002) and (Bakshi, Cao, and Chen 1997).

11.4 Summary

Allowing for the possibility of discontinuous movements can add realism to the modeling of asset prices. For example, a firm's stock price might experience a sudden, large change upon the public announcement that it is involved in a corporate merger. While the mixed jump-diffusion process captures such asset price dynamics, it complicates the valuation of contingent claims written on such an asset. In general, we showed that the contingent claim's payoff cannot be perfectly replicated by a dynamic trading strategy involving the underlying asset and risk-free asset. In this situation of market incompleteness, additional theory that assigns a market risk premium to jump risk is required to determine the contingent claim's value.

The additional complications in deriving jump-diffusion models of option pricing appear worthwhile. Because jumps increase the likelihood of extreme price movements, they generate a risk-neutral distribution of asset prices whose

---

8. Steven Heston (Heston 1993) developed a popular stochastic volatility model.
9. David Bates (Bates 1996) derived an option pricing model that combines both jumps and stochastic volatility and estimated its parameters using options on foreign exchange.

tails are fatter than the Black-Scholes model's lognormal distribution. Since the actual prices of many types of options appear to reflect significant probabilities of extreme movements in the underlying's price, the jump-diffusion model has better empirical performance.

Having seen that pricing contingent claims sometimes requires specifying market prices of risk, the following chapters turn to the subject of deriving equilibrium risk premia for assets in continuous-time economies. As a preliminary, we revisit the individual's consumption and portfolio choice problem when asset prices, and the individual's consumption and portfolio choices, can change continuously. Based on this structure of consumption and asset demands, we then derive assets' risk premia in a general equilibrium, continuous-time economy.

11.5 Exercises

1. Verify that (11.11) holds by using Itô's lemma to find the process followed by $\ln(S(t))$.

2. Let $S(t)$ be the U.S. dollar price of a stock. It is assumed to follow the process

$$dS/S = \left[\mu_s - \lambda k\right] dt + \sigma_s dz_s + \gamma\left(\tilde{Y}\right) dq \tag{*}$$

where dz_s is a standard Wiener process, $q(t)$ is a Poisson counting process, and $\gamma\left(\tilde{Y}\right) = \left(\tilde{Y} - 1\right)$. The probability that q will jump during the time interval dt is λdt. $k \equiv E\left[\tilde{Y} - 1\right]$ is the expected jump size. Let F be the foreign exchange rate between U.S. dollars and Japanese yen, denominated as U.S. dollars per yen. F follows the process

$$dF/F = \mu_f dt + \sigma_f dz_f$$

where $dz_s dz_f = \rho dt$. Define $x(t)$ as the Japanese yen price of the stock whose U.S. dollar price follows the process in (*). Derive the stochastic process followed by $x(t)$.

3. Suppose that the instantaneous-maturity, default-free interest rate follows the jump-diffusion process

$$dr(t) = \kappa\left[\theta - r(t)\right] dt + \sigma dz + r\gamma(Y) dq$$

where dz is a standard Wiener process and $q(t)$ is a Poisson counting process having the arrival rate of λdt. The arrival of jumps is assumed to be independent of the Wiener process, dz. $\gamma(Y) = (Y - 1)$ where $Y > 1$ is a known positive constant.

a. Define $P(r, \tau)$ as the price of a default-free discount bond that pays \$1 in τ periods. Using Itô's lemma for the case of jump-diffusion processes, write down the process followed by $dP(r, \tau)$.

b. Assume that the market price of jump risk is zero, but that the market price of Brownian motion (dz) risk is given by ϕ, so that $\phi = [\alpha_p - r(t)]/\sigma_p$, where $\alpha_p(r, \tau)$ is the expected rate of return on the bond and $\sigma_p(\tau)$ is the standard deviation of the bond's rate of return from Brownian motion risk (not including the risk from jumps). Derive the equilibrium partial differential equation that the value $P(r, \tau)$ must satisfy.

4. Suppose that a security's price follows a jump-diffusion process and yields a continuous dividend at a constant rate of δdt. For example, its price, $S(t)$, follows the process

$$dS/S = [\mu(S, t) - \lambda k - \delta] dt + \sigma(S, t)\, dz + \gamma(\tilde{Y})dq$$

where $q(t)$ is a Poisson counting process and $\gamma(\tilde{Y}) = (\tilde{Y} - 1)$. Also let $k \equiv E[\tilde{Y} - 1]$; let the probability of a jump be λdt; and denote $\mu(S, t)$ as the asset's total expected rate of return. Consider a forward contract written on this security that is negotiated at date t and matures at date T where $\tau = T - t > 0$. Let $r(t, \tau)$ be the date t continuously compounded, risk-free interest rate for borrowing or lending between dates t and T. Assuming that one can trade continuously in the security, derive the equilibrium date t forward price using an argument that rules out arbitrage. Hint: some information in this problem is extraneous. The solution is relatively simple.

PART IV

ASSET PRICING IN CONTINUOUS TIME

CHAPTER 12

Continuous-Time Consumption and Portfolio Choice

Until now our applications of continuous-time stochastic processes have focused on the valuation of contingent claims. In this chapter we revisit the topic introduced in Chapter 5, namely, an individual's intertemporal consumption and portfolio choice problem. However, rather than assume a discrete-time setting, we now examine this problem where asset prices are subject to continuous, random changes and an individual can adjust consumption and portfolio allocations at any time. Specifically, this chapter assumes that an individual maximizes a time-separable expected utility function that depends on the rate of consumption at all future dates. The savings of this individual are allocated among assets whose returns follow diffusion processes of the type first introduced in Chapter 8. Hence, in this environment, the values of the individual's portfolio holdings and total wealth change constantly and, in general, it is optimal for the individual to make continuous rebalancing decisions.

The continuous-time consumption and portfolio choice problem just described was formulated and solved in two papers by Robert Merton (Merton 1969; Merton 1971). This work was the foundation of his model of intertemporal asset pricing (Merton 1973a), which we will study in the next chapter. As we discuss next, allowing individuals to rebalance their portfolios continuously can lead to qualitatively different portfolio choices compared to those where portfolios can only be adjusted at discrete dates. This, in turn, means that the asset pricing implications of individuals' decisions in continuous time can sometimes differ from those of a discrete-time model. Continuous trading may enable markets to be dynamically complete and lead to sharper asset pricing results. For this reason, continuous-time consumption and portfolio choice models are often used in financial research on asset pricing. Much of our analysis in later chapters will be based on such models.

By studying consumption and portfolio choices in continuous time, the effects of time variation in assets' return distributions, that is, changing investment opportunities, become transparent. As will be shown, individuals' portfolio choices include demands for assets that are the same as those derived from the single-period mean-variance analysis of Chapter 2. However, portfolio choices also include demands for assets that hedge against changes in investment opportunities. This is a key insight that differentiates single-period and multiperiod models and has implications for equilibrium asset pricing.

The next section outlines the assumptions of an individual's consumption and portfolio choice problem for a continuous-time environment. Then, similar to what was done in solving for an individual's decisions in discrete time, we introduce and apply a continuous-time version of stochastic dynamic programming to derive consumption and portfolio demands. This technique leads to a nonlinear partial differential equation that can be solved to obtain optimal decision rules. Portfolio behaviors for both constant investment opportunities and changing investment opportunities are analyzed. We next present an alternative martingale approach to finding an individual's optimal consumption and portfolio choices. This martingale technique is most applicable to situations when markets are dynamically complete and involves computing an expectation of future discounted consumption rates or solving a Black-Scholes–type linear partial differential equation for wealth. We illustrate this solution method by an example where an individual faces risky-asset returns that are negatively correlated with investment opportunities.

12.1 Model Assumptions

Let us assume that an individual allocates his wealth between n different risky assets plus a risk-free asset. Define $S_i(t)$ as the price of the ith risky asset at date t. This asset's instantaneous rate of return is assumed to satisfy the process[1]

$$dS_i(t) / S_i(t) = \mu_i(x, t) \ dt + \sigma_i(x, t) \ dz_i \tag{12.1}$$

where $i = 1, \ldots, n$ and $(\sigma_i \, dz_i)(\sigma_j \, dz_j) = \sigma_{ij} \, dt$. In addition, let the instantaneous risk-free return be denoted as $r(x, t)$. It is assumed that μ_i, σ_i, and r may be

---

1. Equation (12.1) expresses a risky asset's rate of return process in terms of its proportional price change, dS_i/S_i. However, if the asset pays cashflows (e.g., dividends or coupons), then $S_i(t)$ can be reinterpreted as the value of an investment in the risky asset where all cashflows are reinvested. What is essential is the asset's return process, not whether returns come in the form of cash payouts or capital gains.

functions of time and a $k \times 1$ vector of state variables, which we denote by $x(t) = (x_1 \ldots x_k)'$. When the μ_i, σ_i, and/or r are time varying, the investor is said to face changing investment opportunities. The state variables affecting the moments of the asset prices can, themselves, follow diffusion processes. Let the ith state variable follow the process

$$dx_i = a_i(x, t)\, dt + b_i(x, t)\, d\zeta_i \tag{12.2}$$

where $i = 1, \ldots, k$. The process $d\zeta_i$ is a Brownian motion with $(b_i\, d\zeta_i)(b_j\, d\zeta_j) = b_{ij}\, dt$ and $(\sigma_i\, dz_i)(b_j\, d\zeta_j) = \phi_{ij}\, dt$. Hence, equations (12.1) and (12.2) indicate that up to $n + k$ sources of uncertainty (Brownian motion processes) affect the distribution of asset returns.

We denote the value of the individual's wealth portfolio at date t as W_t and define C_t as the individual's date t rate of consumption per unit time. Also, let ω_i be the proportion of total wealth allocated to risky asset i, $i = 1, \ldots, n$. Similar to our analysis in Chapter 9 and treating consumption as a net cash outflow from the individual's wealth portfolio, we can write the dynamics of wealth as[2]

$$
\begin{aligned}
dW &= \left[\sum_{i=1}^{n} \omega_i dS_i/S_i + \left(1 - \sum_{i=1}^{n} \omega_i\right) rdt \right] W - Cdt \\
&= \sum_{i=1}^{n} \omega_i(\mu_i - r)W\, dt + (rW - C)\, dt + \sum_{i=1}^{n} \omega_i W \sigma_i\, dz_i
\end{aligned} \tag{12.3}
$$

We can now state the individual's intertemporal consumption and portfolio choice problem:

$$\max_{C_s,\{\omega_{i,s}\},\forall s,i} E_t \left[\int_t^T U(C_s, s)\, ds + B(W_T, T) \right] \tag{12.4}$$

subject to the constraint (12.3).

The date t utility function, $U(C_t, t)$, is assumed to be strictly increasing and concave in C_t and the bequest function, $B(W_T, T)$, is assumed to be strictly increasing and concave in terminal wealth, W_T. This problem, in which the individual has time-separable utility of consumption, is analogous to the discrete-time problem studied in Chapter 5. The variables W_s and $x(s)$ are the date s

---

2. Our presentation assumes that there are no other sources of wealth, such as wage income. If the model is extended to include a flow of nontraded wage income received at date t, say, y_t, it could be incorporated into the individual's intertemporal budget constraint in a manner similar to that of consumption but with an opposite sign. In other words, the term $(C_t - y_t)$ would replace C_t in our derivation of the individual's dynamic budget constraint. Duffie, Fleming, Soner, and Zariphopoulou (Duffie et al. 1997) solve for optimal consumption and portfolio choices when the individual receives stochastic wage income.

state variables while the individual chooses the control variables C_s and $\omega_i(s)$, $i = 1, \ldots, n$, for each date s over the interval from dates t to T.

Note that some possible constraints have not been imposed. For example, one might wish to impose the constraint $C_t \geq 0$ (nonnegative consumption) and/or $\omega_i \geq 0$ (no short sales). However, for some utility functions, negative consumption is never optimal, so that solutions satisfying $C_t \geq 0$ would result even without the constraint.[3]

Before we attempt to solve this problem, let's digress to consider how stochastic dynamic programming applies to a continuous-time setting.

12.2   Continuous-Time Dynamic Programming

To illustrate the principles of dynamic programming in continuous time, consider a simplified version of the problem specified in conditions (12.3) to (12.4) where there is only one choice variable:

$$\max_{\{c\}} E_t \left[\int_t^T U(c_s, x_s)\, ds \right] \tag{12.5}$$

subject to

$$dx = a(x, c)\, dt + b(x, c)\, dz \tag{12.6}$$

where c_t is a *control* variable (such as a consumption and/or vector of portfolio proportions) and x_t is a *state* variable (such as wealth and/or a variable that changes investment opportunities, that is, a variable that affects the μ_i's and/or σ_i's). As in Chapter 5, define the indirect utility function, $J(x_t, t)$, as

$$J(x_t, t) = \max_{\{c\}} E_t \left[\int_t^T U(c_s, x_s)\, ds \right] \tag{12.7}$$

$$= \max_{\{c\}} E_t \left[\int_t^{t+\Delta t} U(c_s, x_s)\, ds + \int_{t+\Delta t}^T U(c_s, x_s)\, ds \right]$$

Now let us apply Bellman's *Principle of Optimality*. Recall that this concept says that an optimal policy must be such that for a given future realization of the state variable, $x_{t+\Delta t}$ (whose value may be affected by the optimal control policy at date

---

3. For example, if $\lim_{C_t \to 0} \frac{\partial U(C_t, t)}{\partial C_t} = \infty$, as would be the case if the individual's utility displayed constant relative risk aversion (power utility), then the individual would always avoid nonpositive consumption. However, other utility functions, such as constant absolute-risk-aversion (negative exponential) utility, do not display this property.

t and earlier), any remaining decisions at date $t + \Delta t$ and later must be optimal with respect to $x_{t+\Delta t}$. In other words, an optimal policy must be time consistent. This allows us to write

$$J(x_t,\ t) = \max_{\{c\}} E_t \left[\int_t^{t+\Delta t} U(c_s, x_s)\, ds + \max_{\{c\}} E_{t+\Delta t} \left[\int_{t+\Delta t}^{T} U(c_s, x_s)\, ds \right] \right]$$

$$= \max_{\{c\}} E_t \left[\int_t^{t+\Delta t} U(c_s, x_s)\, ds + J(x_{t+\Delta t},\ t + \Delta t) \right] \tag{12.8}$$

Equation (12.8) has the recursive structure of the Bellman equation that we derived earlier in discrete time. However, let us now go a step further by thinking of Δt as a short interval of time and approximate the first integral as $U(c_t, x_t)\,\Delta t$. Also, expand $J(x_{t+\Delta t},\ t + \Delta t)$ around the points x_t and t in a Taylor series to get

$$J(x_t,\ t) = \max_{\{c\}} E_t \left[U(c_t, x_t)\,\Delta t + J(x_t,\ t) + J_x \Delta x + J_t \Delta t \right. \tag{12.9}$$

$$\left. + \frac{1}{2} J_{xx}(\Delta x)^2 + J_{xt}(\Delta x)(\Delta t) + \frac{1}{2} J_{tt}(\Delta t)^2 + o(\Delta t) \right]$$

where $o\,(\Delta t)$ represents higher-order terms, say, $y\,(\Delta t)$, where $\lim_{\Delta t \to 0} \frac{y(\Delta t)}{\Delta t} = 0$. Based on our results from Chapter 8, the state variable's diffusion process (12.6) can be approximated as

$$\Delta x \approx a(x,\ c)\Delta t + b(x,\ c)\Delta z + o(\Delta t) \tag{12.10}$$

where $\Delta z = \sqrt{\Delta t}\,\tilde{\varepsilon}$ and $\tilde{\varepsilon} \sim N\,(0, 1)$. Substituting (12.10) into (12.9), and subtracting $J(x_t,\ t)$ from both sides, one obtains

$$0 = \max_{\{c\}} E_t \left[U(c_t, x_t)\Delta t + \Delta J + o(\Delta t) \right] \tag{12.11}$$

where

$$\Delta J = \left[J_t + J_x a + \frac{1}{2} J_{xx} b^2 \right] \Delta t + J_x b \Delta z \tag{12.12}$$

Equation (12.12) is just a discrete-time version of Itô's lemma. Next, note that in equation (12.11) the term $E_t \left[J_x b \Delta z \right] = 0$ and then divide both sides of (12.11) by Δt. Finally, take the limit as $\Delta t \to 0$ to obtain

$$0 = \max_{\{c\}} \left[U(c_t,\ x_t) + J_t + J_x a + \frac{1}{2} J_{xx} b^2 \right] \tag{12.13}$$

which is the stochastic, continuous-time Bellman equation analogous to the discrete-time Bellman equation (5.15). Equation (12.13) is sometimes rewritten as

$$0 = \max_{\{c\}} \left[U(c_t,\ x_t) + L[J] \right] \tag{12.14}$$

where $L[\cdot]$ is the *Dynkin operator*. This operator is the "drift" term (expected change per unit time) in $dJ(x, t)$ that one obtains by applying Itô's lemma to $J(x, t)$. In summary, equation (12.14) gives us a condition that the optimal stochastic control policy, c_t, must satisfy. Let us now return to the complete consumption and portfolio choice problem and apply this solution technique.

12.3   Solving the Continuous-Time Problem

Define the indirect utility-of-wealth function, $J(W, x, t)$, as

$$J(W, x, t) = \max_{C_s, \{\omega_{i,s}\}, \forall s, i} E_t \left[\int_t^T U(C_s, s)\, ds + B(W_T, T) \right] \tag{12.15}$$

and define L as the Dynkin operator with respect to the state variables W and x_i, $i = 1, \ldots, k$. In other words,

$$L[J] = \frac{\partial J}{\partial t} + \left[\sum_{i=1}^{n} \omega_i (\mu_i - r) W + (rW - C) \right] \frac{\partial J}{\partial W} + \sum_{i=1}^{k} a_i \frac{\partial J}{\partial x_i}$$

$$+ \frac{1}{2} \sum_{i=1}^{n} \sum_{j=1}^{n} \sigma_{ij} \omega_i \omega_j W^2 \frac{\partial^2 J}{\partial W^2} + \frac{1}{2} \sum_{i=1}^{k} \sum_{j=1}^{k} b_{ij} \frac{\partial^2 J}{\partial x_i \, \partial x_j}$$

$$+ \sum_{j=1}^{k} \sum_{i=1}^{n} W \omega_i \phi_{ij} \frac{\partial^2 J}{\partial W \partial x_j} \tag{12.16}$$

Thus, using equation (12.14), we have

$$0 = \max_{C_t, \{\omega_{i,t}\}} \left[U(C_t, t) + L[J] \right] \tag{12.17}$$

Given the concavity of U and B, equation (12.17) implies that the optimal choices of C_t and $\omega_{i,t}$ satisfy the conditions we obtain from differentiating $U(C_t, t) + L[J]$ and setting the result equal to zero. Hence, the first-order conditions are

$$0 = \frac{\partial U(C^*, t)}{\partial C} - \frac{\partial J(W, x, t)}{\partial W} \tag{12.18}$$

$$0 = W \frac{\partial J}{\partial W} (\mu_i - r) + W^2 \frac{\partial^2 J}{\partial W^2} \sum_{j=1}^{n} \sigma_{ij} \omega_j^* + W \sum_{j=1}^{k} \phi_{ij} \frac{\partial^2 J}{\partial x_j \, \partial W}, \quad i = 1, \ldots, n \tag{12.19}$$

Equation (12.18) is the envelope condition that we earlier derived in a discrete-time framework as equation (5.19), while equation (12.19) has the discrete-time analog (5.20). Defining the inverse marginal utility function as $G = [\partial U/\partial C]^{-1}$, condition (12.18) can be rewritten as

$$C^* = G\left(J_W, t\right) \tag{12.20}$$

where we write J_W as shorthand for $\partial J/\partial W$. Also, the n linear equations in (12.19) can be solved in terms of the optimal portfolio weights. Denote $\Omega \equiv [\sigma_{ij}]$ to be the $n \times n$ instantaneous covariance matrix whose i, jth element is σ_{ij}, and denote the i, jth element of the inverse of Ω to be v_{ij}; that is, $\Omega^{-1} \equiv [v_{ij}]$. Then the solution to (12.19) can be written as

$$\omega_i^* = -\frac{J_W}{J_{WW}W}\sum_{j=1}^{n} v_{ij}(\mu_j - r) - \sum_{m=1}^{k}\sum_{j=1}^{n}\frac{J_{Wx_m}}{J_{WW}W}\phi_{jm}v_{ij}, \quad i = 1, \ldots, n \tag{12.21}$$

Note that the optimal portfolio weights in (12.21) depend on $-J_W/\left(J_{WW}W\right)$, which is the inverse of relative risk aversion for lifetime utility of wealth.

Given particular functional forms for U and the μ_i's, σ_{ij}'s, and ϕ_{ij}'s, equations (12.20) and (12.21) are functions of the state variables W, x, and derivatives of J, that is, J_W, J_{WW}, and J_{Wx_i}. They can be substituted back into equation (12.17) to obtain a nonlinear partial differential equation (PDE) for J. For some specifications of utility and the processes for asset returns and the state variables, this PDE can be solved to obtain an analytic expression for J that, in turn, allows for explicit solutions for C^* and the ω_i^* based on (12.20) and (12.21). Examples of such analytical solutions are given in the next two sections. In general, however, one must resort to numerical solutions for J and, therefore, C^* and the ω_i^*.[4]

12.3.1   Constant Investment Opportunities

Let us consider the special case for which asset prices or returns are lognormally distributed, so that continuously compounded rates of return are normally distributed. This occurs when all of the μ_i's (including r) and σ_i's are constants.[5] This means that each asset's expected rate of return and variance of its rate of return do

---

4. Techniques for solving partial differential equations numerically are covered in Carrier and Pearson (Carrier and Pearson 1976), Judd (Judd 1998), and Rogers and Talay (Rogers and Talay 1997).

5. Recall that if μ_i and σ_i are constants, then dS_i/S_i follows geometric Brownian motion and $S_i(t) = S_i(0)\,e^{(\mu_i - \frac{1}{2}\sigma_i^2)t + \sigma_i(z_i(t) - z_i(0))}$ is lognormally distributed over any discrete period since $z_i(t) - z_i(0) \sim N(0, t)$. Therefore, the *return* on a unit initial investment over this period, $S_i(t)/S_i(0) = e^{(\mu_i - \frac{1}{2}\sigma_i^2)t + \sigma_i(z_i(t) - z_i(0))}$, is also lognormally distributed. The *continuously compounded rate of return*, equal to $\ln[S_i(t)/S_i(0)] = (\mu_i - \frac{1}{2}\sigma_i^2)t + \sigma_i(z_i(t) - z_i(0))$, is normally distributed.

not change; there is a *constant investment opportunity set*. Hence, investment and portfolio choice decisions are independent of the state variables, x, since they do not affect U, B, the μ_i's, or the σ_i's. The only state variable affecting consumption and portfolio choice decisions is wealth, W. This simplifies the above analysis, since now the indirect utility function J depends only on W and t, but not x.

For this constant investment opportunity set case, the optimal portfolio weights in (12.21) simplify to

$$\omega_i^* = -\frac{J_W}{J_{WW}W} \sum_{j=1}^{n} v_{ij}(\mu_j - r), \quad i = 1, \ldots, n \qquad (12.22)$$

Plugging (12.20) and (12.22) back into the optimality equation (12.17), and using the fact that $[v_{ij}] \equiv \Omega^{-1}$, we have

$$0 = U(G, t) + J_t + J_W(rW - G) - \frac{J_W^2}{2J_{WW}} \sum_{i=1}^{n} \sum_{j=1}^{n} v_{ij}(\mu_i - r)(\mu_j - r) \qquad (12.23)$$

The nonlinear partial differential equation (12.23) may not have an analytic solution for an arbitrary utility function, U. However, we can still draw some conclusions about the individual's investment behavior by looking at equation (12.22). This expression for the individual's optimal portfolio weights has an interesting implication, but one that might be intuitive given a constant investment opportunity set. Since v_{ij}, μ_j, and r are constants, the proportion of each risky asset that is optimally held will be proportional to $-J_W/(J_{WW}W)$, which depends only on the total wealth state variable, W. Thus, the proportion of wealth in risky asset i to risky asset k is a constant; that is,

$$\frac{\omega_i^*}{\omega_k^*} = \frac{\sum_{j=1}^{n} v_{ij}(\mu_j - r)}{\sum_{j=1}^{n} v_{kj}(\mu_j - r)} \qquad (12.24)$$

and the proportion of risky asset k to all risky assets is

$$\delta_k = \frac{\omega_k^*}{\sum_{i=1}^{n} \omega_i^*} = \frac{\sum_{j=1}^{n} v_{kj}(\mu_j - r)}{\sum_{i=1}^{n} \sum_{j=1}^{n} v_{ij}(\mu_j - r)} \qquad (12.25)$$

This means that each individual, no matter what her utility function, allocates her portfolio between the risk-free asset, paying return r, and a portfolio of the risky assets that holds the n risky assets in constant proportions, given by (12.25). Hence, two "mutual funds," one holding only the risk-free asset and the other holding a risky-asset portfolio with the weights in (12.25), would satisfy all investors. Only the investor's preferences; current level of wealth, W_t; and the investor's time horizon determine the amounts allocated to the risk-free fund and the risky one.

The implication is that with a constant investment opportunity set, one can think of the investment decision as being just a two-asset decision, where the choice is between the risk-free asset paying rate of return r and a risky asset having expected rate of return μ and variance σ^2 where

$$\mu \equiv \sum_{i=1}^{n} \delta_i \mu_i$$

$$\sigma^2 \equiv \sum_{i=1}^{n} \sum_{j=1}^{n} \delta_i \delta_j \sigma_{ij}$$

(12.26)

These results are reminiscent of those derived from the single-period mean-variance analysis of Chapter 2. In fact, the relative asset proportions given in (12.24) and (12.25) are exactly the same as those implied by the single-period mean-variance portfolio proportions given in equation (2.42).[6] The instantaneous means and covariances for the continuous-time asset price processes simply replace the previous means and covariances of the single-period, multivariate normal asset returns distribution. Again, we can interpret all investors as choosing along an efficient frontier, where the tangency portfolio is given by the weights in (12.25). But what is different in this continuous-time analysis is the assumption regarding the distribution in asset prices. In the discrete-time mean-variance analysis, we needed to assume that asset returns were normally distributed, whereas in the continuous-time context we specified that asset returns were lognormally distributed. This latter assumption is more attractive since most assets, like bonds and common stocks, have limited liability so that their values cannot become negative. The assumption of a lognormal return distribution embodies this restriction, whereas the assumption of normality does not.

The intuition for why we obtain the single-period Markowitz results in a continuous-time setting with lognormally distributed asset returns is as follows. By allowing continuous rebalancing, an individual's portfolio choice horizon is essentially a very short one; that is, the "period" is instantaneous. Since diffusion processes can be thought of as being instantaneously (locally) normally

---

6. Note that the ith element of (2.42) can be written as $w_i^* = \lambda \sum_{j=1}^{n} v_{ij}(\overline{R}_j - R_f)$, which equals (12.22) when $\lambda = -J_W / (J_{WW} W)$.

distributed, our continuous-time environment is as if the individual faces an infinite sequence of similar short portfolio selection periods with normally distributed asset returns.

Let's now look at a special case of the preceding general solution. Specifically, we assume that utility is of the hyperbolic absolute risk aversion (HARA) class.

HARA Utility

Recall from Chapter 1 that HARA utility functions are defined by

$$U(C, t) = e^{-\rho t} \frac{1 - \gamma}{\gamma} \left(\frac{\alpha C}{1 - \gamma} + \beta \right)^{\gamma} \tag{12.27}$$

and that this class of utility nests power (constant relative-risk-aversion), exponential (constant absolute-risk-aversion), and quadratic utility. Robert C. Merton (Merton 1971) derived explicit solutions for this class of utility functions. With HARA utility, optimal consumption given in equation (12.20) becomes

$$C^* = \frac{1 - \gamma}{\alpha} \left[\frac{e^{\rho t} J_W}{\alpha} \right]^{\frac{1}{\gamma - 1}} - \frac{(1 - \gamma)\beta}{\alpha} \tag{12.28}$$

and using (12.22) and (12.26), the proportion put in the risky-asset portfolio is

$$\omega^* = -\frac{J_W}{J_{WW} W} \frac{\mu - r}{\sigma^2} \tag{12.29}$$

This solution is incomplete since C^* and ω^* are in terms of J_W and J_{WW}. However, we solve for J in the following manner. Substitute (12.28) and (12.29) into the optimality equation (12.17) or, alternatively, directly simplify equation (12.23) to obtain

$$0 = \frac{(1 - \gamma)^2}{\gamma} e^{-\rho t} \left[\frac{e^{\rho t} J_W}{\alpha} \right]^{\frac{\gamma}{\gamma - 1}} + J_t$$

$$+ \left(\frac{(1 - \gamma)\beta}{\alpha} + rW \right) J_W - \frac{J_W^2}{J_{WW}} \frac{(\mu - r)^2}{2\sigma^2} \tag{12.30}$$

This is the partial differential equation for J that can be solved subject to a boundary condition for $J(W, T)$. Let us assume a zero bequest function, $B \equiv 0$, so that the appropriate boundary condition is $J(W, T) = 0$. The nonlinear partial differential equation in (12.30) can be simplified by a change in variable $Y = J^{\frac{\gamma}{\gamma - 1}}$. This puts it in the form of a Bernoulli-type equation and an analytic solution exists. The expression for the general solution is lengthy and can be found in (Merton 1971). Given this solution for J, one can then calculate J_W to solve for C^* and also calculate J_{WW} to solve for ω^*. It is interesting to note that for this class of HARA utility, C^* is of the form

$$C_t^* = aW_t + b \tag{12.31}$$

and

$$\omega_t^* = g + \frac{h}{W_t} \tag{12.32}$$

where a, b, g, and h are, at most, functions of time. For the special case of constant relative risk aversion where $U(C, t) = e^{-\rho t} C^\gamma / \gamma$, the solution is

$$J(W, t) = e^{-\rho t} \left[\frac{1 - e^{-a(T-t)}}{a} \right]^{1-\gamma} W^\gamma / \gamma \tag{12.33}$$

$$C_t^* = \frac{a}{1 - e^{-a(T-t)}} W_t \tag{12.34}$$

and

$$\omega^* = \frac{\mu - r}{(1 - \gamma)\sigma^2} \tag{12.35}$$

where $a \equiv \frac{\gamma}{1-\gamma} \left[\frac{\rho}{\gamma} - r - \frac{(\mu-r)^2}{2(1-\gamma)\sigma^2} \right]$. When the individual's planning horizon is infinite, that is, $T \to \infty$, a solution exists only if $a > 0$. In this case, we can see that by taking the limits of equations (12.33) and (12.34) as T becomes infinite, then $J(W, t) = e^{-\rho t} a^{\gamma-1} W^\gamma / \gamma$ and consumption is a constant proportion of wealth, $C_t^* = aW_t$.

As mentioned in the previous section, in a continuous-time environment when investment opportunities are constant, we obtain the single-period Markowitz result that an investor will optimally divide her portfolio between the risk-free asset and the tangency portfolio of risky assets given by (12.26). However, this does not imply that an investor with the same form of utility would choose the same portfolio weight in this tangency portfolio for both the continuous-time case and the discrete-time case. Indeed, the optimal portfolio choices can be qualitatively different. In particular, the constant relative-risk-averse individual's optimal portfolio weight (12.35) for the continuous-time case differs from what this individual would choose in the discrete-time Markowitz environment. As covered in an exercise at the end of Chapter 2, an individual with constant relative risk aversion and facing normally distributed risky-asset returns would choose to place his entire portfolio in the risk-free asset; that is, $\omega^* = 0$. The reason is that constant relative-risk-aversion utility is not a defined, real-valued function when end-of-period wealth is zero or negative: marginal utility becomes infinite as end-of-period wealth declines to zero. The implication is that such an investor would avoid assets that have a positive probability of making total end-of-period wealth nonpositive. Because risky assets with normally distributed returns have positive probability of having zero or negative values over a discrete period of time, a constant relative-risk-averse individual who cannot revise her portfolio continuously optimally chooses the corner solution where the entire portfolio consists of the risk-free asset.[7] In contrast, an interior portfolio choice occurs in the continuous-time context where constant investment opportunities imply lognormally distributed returns and a zero bound on the value of risky assets.

A couple of final observations regarding the optimal risky-asset portfolio holding (12.35) are, first, that it is decreasing in the individual's coefficient of relative risk aversion, $(1 - \gamma)$. This result is consistent with the received wisdom of financial planners that more risk-averse individuals should choose a smaller portfolio allocation in risky assets. However, the second observation is that this risky-asset allocation is independent of the time horizon, T, which runs counter to the conventional advice that individuals should reduce their allocations in risky assets (stocks) as they approach retirement. An extension of the portfolio choice model that endows individuals with riskless labor income whose present value declines as the individual approaches her retirement is one way of producing the result that the individual should allocate a decreasing proportion of her financial asset portfolio to risky assets.[8] In this case, riskless human capital (the present value of labor income) is large when the individual is young, and it substitutes for holding the risk-free in the individual's financial asset portfolio. As the individual ages, her riskless human capital declines and is replaced by more of the riskless asset in her financial portfolio.

12.3.2   Changing Investment Opportunities

Next, let us generalize the individual's consumption and portfolio choice problem by considering the effects of changing investment opportunities. To keep the analysis fairly simple, assume that there is a single state variable, x. That is, let $k = 1$ so that x is a scalar. We also simplify the notation by writing its process as

$$dx = a(x, t)\, dt + b(x, t)\, d\zeta \tag{12.36}$$

---

7. This portfolio corner solution result extends to the multiperiod discrete-time environment of Chapter 5. Note that this corner solution does not apply to constant absolute risk aversion where marginal utility continues to be positive and finite even when wealth is nonpositive. This is why portfolio choice models often assume that utility displays constant absolute risk aversion if asset returns are normally distributed.

8. Zvi Bodie, Robert Merton, and Paul Samuelson (Bodie, Merton, and Samuelson 1992) analyze the effects of labor income on lifetime portfolio choices. John Campbell and Luis Viceira (Campbell and Viceira 2002) provide a broader examination of lifetime portfolio allocation.

where $b\,d\zeta\,\sigma_i\,dz_i = \phi_i\,dt$. This allows us to write the optimal portfolio weights in (12.21) as

$$\omega_i^* = -\frac{J_W}{WJ_{WW}}\sum_{j=1}^{n} v_{ij}\left(\mu_j - r\right) - \frac{J_{Wx}}{WJ_{WW}}\sum_{j=1}^{n} v_{ij}\phi_j, \quad i = 1,\ldots,n \qquad (12.37)$$

or, written in matrix form,

$$\boldsymbol{\omega}^* = \frac{A}{W}\boldsymbol{\Omega}^{-1}\left(\boldsymbol{\mu} - re\right) + \frac{H}{W}\boldsymbol{\Omega}^{-1}\boldsymbol{\phi} \qquad (12.38)$$

where $\boldsymbol{\omega}^* = \left(\omega_1^* \ldots \omega_n^*\right)'$ is the $n \times 1$ vector of portfolio weights for the n risky assets; $\boldsymbol{\mu} = \left(\mu_1 \ldots \mu_n\right)'$ is the $n \times 1$ vector of these assets' expected rates of return; and e is an n-dimensional vector of ones, $\boldsymbol{\phi} = (\phi_1, \ldots, \phi_n)'$, $A = -\frac{J_W}{J_{WW}}$, and $H = -\frac{J_{Wx}}{J_{WW}}$. We will use **bold** type to denote vector or matrix variables, while regular type is used for scalar variables.

Note that A and H will, in general, differ from one individual to another, depending on the form of the particular individual's utility function and level of wealth. Thus, unlike in the constant investment opportunity set case (where $J_{Wx} = H = 0$), ω_i^*/ω_j^* is not the same for all investors; that is, a *two mutual fund theorem* does *not* hold. However, with one state variable, x, a *three fund theorem* does hold. Investors will be satisfied choosing between a fund holding only the risk-free asset, a second fund of risky assets that provides optimal instantaneous diversification, and a third fund composed of a portfolio of the risky assets that has the maximum absolute correlation with the state variable, x. The portfolio weights of the second fund are $\boldsymbol{\Omega}^{-1}\left(\boldsymbol{\mu} - re\right)$ and are the same ones representing the mean-variance efficient tangency portfolio that were derived for the case of constant investment opportunities. The portfolio weights for the third fund are $\boldsymbol{\Omega}^{-1}\boldsymbol{\phi}$. Note that these weights are of the same form as equation (2.64), which are the hedging demands derived in Chapter 2's cross-hedging example. They are the coefficients from a regression (or projection) of changes in the state variable on the returns of the risky assets. A/W and H/W, which depend on the individual's preferences, then determine the relative amounts that the individual invests in the second and third risky portfolios.

To gain more insight regarding the nature of the individual's portfolio holdings, recall the envelope condition $J_W = U_C$, which allows us to write $J_{WW} = U_{CC}\partial C/\partial W$. Therefore, A can be rewritten as

$$A = -\frac{U_C}{U_{CC}\left(\partial C/\partial W\right)} > 0 \qquad (12.39)$$

by the concavity of U. Also, since $J_{Wx} = U_{CC}\partial C/\partial x$, we have

$$H = -\frac{\partial C/\partial x}{\partial C/\partial W} \gtreqless 0 \tag{12.40}$$

Now the first vector of terms on the right-hand side of (12.38) represents the usual demand functions for risky assets chosen by a single-period, mean-variance utility maximizer. Since A is proportional to the reciprocal of the individual's absolute risk aversion, we see that the more risk averse the individual, the smaller A is and the smaller in magnitude is the individual's demand for any risky asset.

The second vector of terms on the right-hand side of (12.38) captures the individual's desire to hedge against "unfavorable" shifts in investment opportunities that would reduce optimal consumption. An unfavorable shift is defined as a change in x such that consumption falls for a given level of current wealth, that is, an increase in x if $\partial C/\partial x < 0$ and a decrease in x if $\partial C/\partial x > 0$. For example, suppose that Ω is a diagonal matrix, so that $v_{ij} = 0$ for $i \neq j$ and $v_{ii} = 1/\sigma_{ii} > 0$, and also assume that $\phi_i \neq 0.$[9] Then, in this special case, the hedging demand term for risky asset i in (12.38) simplifies to

$$H v_{ii} \phi_i = -\frac{\partial C/\partial x}{\partial C/\partial W} v_{ii} \phi_i > 0 \text{ iff } \frac{\partial C}{\partial x} \phi_i < 0 \tag{12.41}$$

Condition (12.41) says that if an increase in x leads to a decrease in optimal consumption ($\partial C/\partial x < 0$) and if x and asset i are positively correlated ($\phi_i > 0$), then there is a positive hedging demand for asset i; that is, $H v_{ii} \phi_i > 0$ and asset i is held in greater amounts than what would be predicted based on a simple single-period mean-variance analysis. The intuition for this result is that by holding more of asset i, one hedges against a decline in future consumption due to an unfavorable shift in x. If x increases, which would tend to decrease consumption ($\partial C/\partial x < 0$), then asset i would tend to have a high return ($\phi_i > 0$), which by augmenting wealth, W, helps neutralize the fall in consumption ($\partial C/\partial W > 0$). Hence, the individual's optimal portfolio holdings are designed to reduce fluctuations in consumption over his planning horizon.

To take a concrete example, suppose that x is a state variable that positively affects the expected rates of return on all assets, including the instantaneously risk-free asset. One simple specification of this is $r = x$ and $\mu = re + p = xe + p$, where p is a vector of risk premia for the risky assets. Thus, an increase in the risk-free rate r indicates an improvement in investment opportunities. Now recall from Chapter 4's equation (4.14) that in a simple certainty model with constant relative-risk-aversion utility, the elasticity of intertemporal substitution is given by $\epsilon = 1/(1 - \gamma)$. When $\epsilon < 1$, implying that $\gamma < 0$, it was shown that

---

9. Alternatively, assume Ω is nondiagonal but that $\phi_j = 0$ for $j \neq i$.

an increase in the risk-free rate leads to greater current consumption because the income effect is greater than the substitution effect. This result is consistent with equation (12.34) where, for the infinite horizon case of $T \rightarrow \infty$, we have $C_t = \frac{\gamma}{1-\gamma} \left[\frac{\rho}{\gamma} - r - \frac{(\mu-r)^2}{2(1-\gamma)\sigma^2} \right] W_t = \frac{\gamma}{1-\gamma} \left[\frac{\rho}{\gamma} - r - \frac{p^2}{2(1-\gamma)\sigma^2} \right] W_t$, so that $\partial C_t / \partial r = -\gamma W_t / (1 - \gamma)$.[10] Given empirical evidence that risk aversion is greater than log ($\gamma < 0$), the intuition from these simple models would be that $\partial C_t / \partial r > 0$ and is increasing in risk aversion.

From equation (12.41), we have

$$H v_{ii} \phi_i = -\frac{\partial C / \partial r}{\partial C / \partial W} v_{ii} \phi_i > 0 \text{ iff } \frac{\partial C}{\partial r} \phi_i < 0 \qquad (12.42)$$

Thus, there is a positive hedging demand for an asset that is negatively correlated with changes in the interest rate, r. An obvious candidate asset would be a bond with a finite time until maturity. For example, if the interest rate followed Vasicek's Ornstein-Uhlenbeck process (Vasicek 1977) given in equation (9.30) of Chapter 9, then any finite-maturity bond whose price process satisfied equations (9.31) and (9.44) would be perfectly negatively correlated with changes in r. Thus, bonds would be a hedge against adverse changes in investment opportunities since they would experience a positive return when r declines. Moreover, the greater an investor's risk aversion, the greater would be the hedging demand for bonds.

This insight may explain the Asset Allocation Puzzle described by Niko Canner, N. Gregory Mankiw, and David Weil (Canner, Mankiw, and Weil 1997). The puzzle relates to the choice of allocating one's portfolio among three asset classes: stocks, bonds, and cash (where cash refers to a short-maturity money market investment). The conventional wisdom of financial planners is to recommend that an investor hold a lower proportion of her portfolio in stocks and higher proportions in bonds and cash the more risk averse she is. If we consider cash to be the (instantaneous-maturity) risk-free investment paying the return of r, while bonds and stocks are each risky investments, Canner, Mankiw, and Weil point out that this advice is inconsistent with Markowitz's Two Fund Separation Theorem discussed in Chapter 2. While Markowitz's theory implies that more risk-averse individuals should hold more cash, it also implies that the optimal risky-asset portfolio (tangency portfolio) should be the same for all investors, so that investors' ratio of risky bonds to risky stocks should be identical irrespective of their risk aversions. Therefore, Canner, Mankiw, and Weil conclude that it

---

10. Technically, it is not valid to infer the derivative $\partial C / \partial r$ from the constant investment opportunities model where we derived optimal consumption assuming r was constant. However, as we shall see from an example later in this chapter, a similar result holds when we solve for optimal consumption using a model where investment opportunities are explicitly changing.

is puzzling that financial planners recommend a greater bonds-to-stocks mix for more risk-averse investors.

However, based on our previous analysis, specifically equation (12.42), we see that financial planners' advice is consistent with employing bonds as a hedge against changing investment opportunities and that the demand for this hedge increases with an investor's risk aversion. Hence, while the conventional wisdom is inconsistent with static, single-period portfolio rules, it is predicted by Merton's more sophisticated intertemporal portfolio rules.[11] One caveat with this explanation of the puzzle is that the Merton theory assumes that changing investment opportunities represent real, rather than nominal, variation in asset return distributions. If so, the optimal hedging instrument may be a real (inflation-indexed) bond. In contrast, the asset allocation advice of financial practitioners tends to be in terms of nominal (currency-denominated) bonds. Still, if nominal bond price movements result primarily from changes in real interest rates, rather than expected inflation, then in the absence of indexed bonds, nominal bonds may be the best available hedge against changes in real rates.[12]

The Special Case of Logarithmic Utility

Let us continue to assume that there is a single state variable affecting investment opportunities but now also specify that the individual has logarithmic utility and a logarithmic bequest function, so that in equation (12.15), $U(C_s, s) = e^{-\rho s} \ln (C_s)$ and $B(W_T, T) = e^{-\rho T} \ln (W_T)$. Logarithmic utility is one of the few cases in which analytical solutions for consumption and portfolio choices can be obtained when investment opportunities are changing. To derive the solution to (12.17) for log utility, let us consider a "trial" solution for the indirect utility function of the form $J(W, x, t) = d(t) U(W_t, t) + F(x, t) = d(t) e^{-\rho t} \ln (W_t) + F(x, t)$. Then optimal consumption in (12.20) would be

$$C_t^* = \frac{W_t}{d(t)} \tag{12.43}$$

and the first-order conditions for the portfolio weights in (12.37) simplify to

$$\omega_i^* = \sum_{j=1}^{n} v_{ij} \left(\mu_j - r \right) \tag{12.44}$$

---

11. Isabelle Bajeux-Besnainou, James Jordan, and Roland Portait (Bajeux-Besnainou, Jordan, and Portait 2001) were among the first to resolve this asset allocation puzzle based on Merton's intertemporal portfolio theory.

12. In 1997, the year the Canner, Mankiw, and Weil article was published, the United States Treasury began issuing inflation-indexed bonds called Treasury Inflation-Protected Securities (TIPS). Prior to this date, nominal bonds may have been feasible hedges against changing real returns. See research by Michael Brennan and Yihong Xia (Brennan and Xia 2002) and Chapter 3 of the book by John Campbell and Luis Viceira (Campbell and Viceira 2002).

since $J_{Wx} = 0$. Substituting these conditions into the Bellman equation (12.17), it becomes

$$0 = U\left(C_t^*, t\right) + J_t + J_W\left[rW_t - C_t^*\right] + a\left(x, t\right)J_x$$

$$+ \frac{1}{2}b\left(x, t\right)^2 J_{xx} + \frac{J_W^2}{2J_{WW}}\sum_{i=1}^{n}\sum_{j=1}^{n}v_{ij}\left(\mu_j - r\right)\left(\mu_i - r\right)$$

$$= e^{-\rho t}\ln\left[\frac{W_t}{d\left(t\right)}\right] + e^{-\rho t}\left[\frac{\partial d\left(t\right)}{\partial t} - \rho d\left(t\right)\right]\ln\left[W_t\right] + F_t + e^{-\rho t}d\left(t\right)r - e^{-\rho t}$$

$$+ a\left(x, t\right)F_x + \frac{1}{2}b\left(x, t\right)^2 F_{xx} - \frac{d\left(t\right)e^{-\rho t}}{2}\sum_{i=1}^{n}\sum_{j=1}^{n}v_{ij}\left(\mu_j - r\right)\left(\mu_i - r\right)$$

$$\tag{12.45}$$

or

$$0 = -\ln\left[d\left(t\right)\right] + \left[1 + \frac{\partial d\left(t\right)}{\partial t} - \rho d\left(t\right)\right]\ln\left[W_t\right] + e^{\rho t}F_t + d\left(t\right)r - 1$$

$$+ a\left(x, t\right)e^{\rho t}F_x + \frac{1}{2}b\left(x, t\right)^2 e^{\rho t}F_{xx} - \frac{d\left(t\right)}{2}\sum_{i=1}^{n}\sum_{j=1}^{n}v_{ij}\left(\mu_j - r\right)\left(\mu_i - r\right)$$

$$\tag{12.46}$$

Note that a solution to this equation must hold for all values of wealth. Hence, it must be the case that

$$\frac{\partial d\left(t\right)}{\partial t} - \rho d\left(t\right) + 1 = 0 \tag{12.47}$$

subject to the boundary condition $d\left(T\right) = 1$. The solution to this first-order ordinary differential equation is

$$d\left(t\right) = \frac{1}{\rho}\left[1 - \left(1 - \rho\right)e^{-\rho\left(T - t\right)}\right] \tag{12.48}$$

The complete solution to (12.46) is then to solve

$$0 = -\ln\left[d\left(t\right)\right] + e^{\rho t}F_t + d\left(t\right)r - 1 + a\left(x, t\right)e^{\rho t}F_x \tag{12.49}$$

$$+ \frac{1}{2}b\left(x, t\right)^2 e^{\rho t}F_{xx} - \frac{d\left(t\right)}{2}\sum_{i=1}^{n}\sum_{j=1}^{n}v_{ij}\left(\mu_j - r\right)\left(\mu_i - r\right)$$

subject to the boundary condition $F\left(x, T\right) = 0$ and where (12.48) is substituted in for $d\left(t\right)$. The solution to (12.49) depends on how r, the μ_i's, and Ω are assumed to depend on the state variable x. However, whatever assumptions are made regarding these variables' relationships to the state variable x, they will influence only the level of indirect utility via the value of $F\left(x, t\right)$ and will not change the form of the optimal consumption and portfolio rules. Thus, this verifies that our trial solution is, indeed, a valid form for the solution to the individual's problem. Substituting (12.48) into (12.43), consumption satisfies

$$C_t = \frac{\rho}{1 - (1 - \rho)\, e^{-\rho(T-t)}}\, W_t \tag{12.50}$$

which is the continuous-time counterpart to the log utility investor's optimal consumption that we derived for the discrete-time problem in Chapter 5, equation (5.33). Note also that the log utility investor's optimal portfolio weights given in (12.44) are of the same form as in the case of a constant investment opportunity set, equation (12.35) with $\gamma = 0$. Similar to the discrete-time case, the log utility investor may be described as behaving "myopically" in that she has no desire to hedge against changes in investment opportunities.[13] However, note that even with log utility, a difference from the constant investment opportunity set case is that since r, the μ_i's, and Ω depend, in general, on the constantly changing state variable x_t, the portfolio weights in equation (12.44) vary over time.

Recall that log utility is a very special case and, in general, other utility specifications lead to consumption and portfolio choices that reflect desires to hedge against investment opportunities. An example is given in the next section. After introducing an alternative solution technique, we solve for the consumption and portfolio choices of an individual with general power utility who faces changing investment opportunities.

12.4 The Martingale Approach to Consumption and Portfolio Choice

The preceding sections of this chapter showed how stochastic dynamic programming could be used to find an individual's optimal consumption and portfolio choices. An alternative to this dynamic programming method was developed by John Cox and Chi-Fu Huang (Cox and Huang 1989), Ioannis Karatzas, John Lehoczky, and Steven Shreve (Karatzas, Lehoczky, and Shreve 1987), and Stanley Pliska (Pliska 1986). Their solution technique uses a stochastic discount factor (state price deflator, or pricing kernel) for valuation, and so it is most applicable to an environment characterized by dynamically complete markets.[14] Recall that Chapter 10 demonstrated that when markets are complete, the absence of

---

13. The portfolio weights for the discrete-time case are given by (5.34). As discussed earlier, the log utility investor acts myopically because income and substitution effects from changing investment opportunities exactly cancel for this individual.

14. Hua He and Neil Pearson (He and Pearson 1991) have extended this martingale approach to an incomplete markets environment. Although in this case there exists an infinity of possible

arbitrage ensures the existence of a unique positive stochastic discount factor. Therefore, let us start by considering the necessary assumptions for market completeness.

12.4.1   Market Completeness Assumptions

As before, let there be n risky assets and a risk-free asset that has an instantaneous return $r(t)$. We modify the previous risky-asset return specification (12.1) to write the return on risky i as

$$dS_i/S_i = \mu_i dt + \mathbf{\Sigma}_i d\mathbf{Z}, \, i = 1, \ldots, n \tag{12.51}$$

where $\mathbf{\Sigma}_i = (\sigma_{i1} \ldots \sigma_{in})$ is a $1 \times n$ vector of volatility components and $d\mathbf{Z} = (dz_1 \ldots dz_n)'$ is an $n \times 1$ vector of independent Brownian motions.[15] The scalar μ_i, the elements of $\mathbf{\Sigma}_i$, and $r(t)$ may be functions of state variables driven by the Brownian motion elements of $d\mathbf{Z}$. Further, we assume that the n risky assets are nonredundant in the sense that their instantaneous covariance matrix is nonsingular. Specifically, if we let $\mathbf{\Sigma}$ be the $n \times n$ matrix whose ith row equals $\mathbf{\Sigma}_i$, then the instantaneous covariance matrix of the assets' returns, $\mathbf{\Omega} \equiv \mathbf{\Sigma}\mathbf{\Sigma}'$, has rank equal to n.

Importantly, we are assuming that any uncertain changes in the means and covariances of the asset return processes in (12.51) are driven only by the vector $d\mathbf{Z}$. This implies that changes in investment opportunities can be perfectly hedged by the n assets, and such an assumption makes this market dynamically complete. This differs from the assumptions of (12.1) and (12.2), because we exclude state variables driven by other, arbitrary Brownian motion processes, $d\zeta_i$, that cannot be perfectly hedged by the n assets' returns. Equivalently, if we assume there is a state variable affecting asset returns, say, x_i as represented in (12.2), then its Brownian motion process, $d\zeta_i$, must be a linear function of the Brownian motion

---

stochastic discount factors, their solution technique chooses what is referred to as a "minimax" martingale measure. This leads to a pricing kernel such that agents do not wish to hedge against the "unhedgeable" uncertainty.

15. Note that in (12.51), the independent Brownian motion components of $d\mathbf{Z}$, $dz_i, i = 1, \ldots, n$ are different from the possibly correlated Brownian motion processes dz_i defined in (12.1). Accordingly, the return on asset i in (12.51) depends on all n of the independent Brownian motion processes, while the return on asset i in (12.1) depends on only one of the correlated Brownian motion processes, namely, the ith one, dz_i. These different ways of writing the risky-asset returns are not important, because an orthogonal transformation of the n correlated Brownian motion processes in (12.1) can allow us to write asset returns as (12.51) where each asset return depends on all n independent processes. The reason for writing asset returns as (12.51) is that individual market prices of risk can be identified with each of the independent risk sources.

components of dZ. Hence, in this section there can be no more than n (not $n + k$) sources of uncertainty affecting the distribution of asset returns.

Given this structure, we showed in Chapter 10 that when arbitrage is not possible, a unique stochastic discount factor exists and follows the process

$$dM/M = -rdt - \Theta(t)' \, dZ \tag{12.52}$$

where $\Theta = (\theta_1 \ldots \theta_n)'$ is an $n \times 1$ vector of market prices of risks associated with each Brownian motion and where Θ satisfies

$$\mu_i - r = \Sigma_i \Theta, \, i = 1, \ldots, n \tag{12.53}$$

Notice that if we take the form of the assets' expected rates of return and volatilities as given, then equation (12.53) is a system of n linear equations that determine the n market prices of risk, Θ. Alternatively, if Θ and the assets' volatilities are taken as given, (12.53) determines the assets' expected rates of return.

12.4.2   The Optimal Consumption Plan

Now consider the individual's original consumption and portfolio choice problem in (12.4) and (12.3). A key to solving this problem is to view the individual's optimally invested wealth as an asset (literally, a portfolio of assets) that pays a continuous dividend equal to the individual's consumption. This implies that the return on wealth, equal to its change in value plus its dividend, can be priced using the stochastic discount factor. The current value of wealth equals the expected discounted value of the dividends (consumption) that it pays over the individual's planning horizon plus discounted terminal wealth.

$$W_t = E_t \left[\int_t^T \frac{M_s}{M_t} C_s ds + \frac{M_T}{M_t} W_T \right] \tag{12.54}$$

Equation (12.54) can be interpreted as an intertemporal budget constraint. This allows the individual's choice of consumption and terminal wealth to be transformed into a static, rather than dynamic, optimization problem. Specifically, the individual's problem can be written as the following Lagrange multiplier problem:[16]

---

16. By specifying the individual's optimal consumption problem as a static constrained optimization, it is straightforward to incorporate additional constraints into the Lagrange multiplier problem. For example, some forms of HARA utility may permit negative consumption. To prevent this, an additional constraint can be added to keep consumption nonnegative. For discussion of this issue, see Chapter 6 of Robert Merton's book (Merton 1992).

$$\max_{C_s \forall s \in [t,T], W_T} E_t \left[\int_t^T U\left(C_s, s\right) \, ds + B\left(W_T, T\right) \right]$$

$$+ \lambda \left(M_t W_t - E_t \left[\int_t^T M_s C_s ds + M_T W_T \right] \right) \tag{12.55}$$

Note that the problem in (12.55) does not explicitly address the portfolio choice decision. This will be determined later by deriving the individual's portfolio trading strategy required to finance his optimal consumption plan.

By treating the integrals in (12.55) as summations over infinite points in time, the first-order conditions for optimal consumption at each date and for terminal wealth are derived as

$$\frac{\partial U\left(C_s, s\right)}{\partial C_s} = \lambda M_s, \ \forall s \in [t, T] \tag{12.56}$$

$$\frac{\partial B\left(W_T, T\right)}{\partial W_T} = \lambda M_T \tag{12.57}$$

Similar to what we did earlier, define the inverse marginal utility function as $G = [\partial U / \partial C]^{-1}$ and the inverse marginal utility of bequest function as $G_B = [\partial B / \partial W]^{-1}$. This allows us to rewrite these first-order conditions as

$$C_s^* = G\left(\lambda M_s, s\right), \ \forall s \in [t, T] \tag{12.58}$$

$$W_T^* = G_B\left(\lambda M_T, T\right) \tag{12.59}$$

Except for the yet-to-be-determined Lagrange multiplier λ, equations (12.58) and (12.59) provide solutions to the optimal choices of consumption and terminal wealth. We can now solve for λ based on the condition that the discounted optimal consumption path and terminal wealth must equal the individual's initial endowment of wealth, W_t. Specifically, we substitute (12.58) and (12.59) into (12.54) to obtain

$$W_t = E_t \left[\int_t^T \frac{M_s}{M_t} G\left(\lambda M_s, s\right) \, ds + \frac{M_T}{M_t} G_B\left(\lambda M_T, T\right) \right] \tag{12.60}$$

Given the initial endowment of wealth, W_t, the distribution of the stochastic discount factor based upon its process in (12.52), and the forms of the utility and bequest functions (which determine G and G_B), the expectation in equation (12.60) can be calculated to determine λ as a function of W_t, M_t, and any date t state variables. Moreover, there is an alternative way to solve for W_t as a function of M_t, λ, and the date t state variables that may sometimes be easier to compute than equation (12.60). As demonstrated in Chapter 10, since wealth represents an asset or contingent claim that pays a dividend equal to consumption,

W_t must satisfy a particular Black-Scholes-Merton partial differential equation (PDE) similar to equation (10.7). The equivalence of the stochastic discount factor relationship in (12.60) and this PDE solution was shown to be a result of the assumptions of market completeness and an absence of arbitrage.

To derive the PDE corresponding to (12.60), let us assume for simplicity that there is a single state variable that affects the distribution of asset returns. That is, μ_i, the elements of Σ_i, and $r(t)$ may be functions of a single state variable, say, x_t. This state variable follows the process

$$dx = a(x, t)\, dt + \mathbf{B}(x, t)'\, \mathbf{dZ} \tag{12.61}$$

where $\mathbf{B}(x, t) = (B_1 \ldots B_n)'$ is an $n \times 1$ vector of volatilities multiplying the Brownian motion components of $\mathbf{dZ}$. Based on (12.60) and the fact that the processes for M_t in (12.52) and x_t in (12.61) are Markov processes, we know that the date t value of optimally invested wealth is a function of M_t and x_t and the individual's time horizon.[17] Hence, by Itô's lemma, the process followed by $W(M_t, x_t, t)$ satisfies

$$dW = W_M dM + W_x dx + \frac{\partial W}{\partial t} dt + \frac{1}{2} W_{MM} (dM)^2$$

$$+ W_{Mx} (dM)(dx) + \frac{1}{2} W_{xx} (dx)^2$$

$$= \mu_W dt + \Sigma_W' \mathbf{dZ} \tag{12.62}$$

where

$$\mu_W \equiv -rM W_M + a W_x + \frac{\partial W}{\partial t} + \frac{1}{2} \Theta' \Theta M^2 W_{MM} - \Theta' \mathbf{B} M W_{Mx} + \frac{1}{2} \mathbf{B}' \mathbf{B} W_{xx} \tag{12.63}$$

and

$$\Sigma_W \equiv -W_M M \Theta + W_x \mathbf{B} \tag{12.64}$$

Following the arguments of Black and Scholes in Chapter 10, the expected return on wealth must earn the instantaneous risk-free rate plus a risk premium, where this risk premium equals the market prices of risk times the sensitivities (volatilities) of wealth to these sources of risk. Specifically,

$$\mu_W + G(\lambda M_t, t) = rW_t + \Sigma_W' \Theta \tag{12.65}$$

---

17. This is because the expectation in (12.60) depends on the distribution of future values of the pricing kernel. From (12.52) and (12.53), the distribution clearly depends on its initial level, M_t, but also on r and Θ, which can vary with the state variable x.

Wealth's expected return, given by the left-hand side of (12.65), equals the expected change in wealth plus its consumption dividend. Substituting in for μ_W and Σ'_W leads to the PDE

$$0 = \frac{1}{2}\Theta'\Theta M^2 W_{MM} - \Theta'BM W_{Mx} + \frac{1}{2}B'B W_{xx} + (\Theta'\Theta - r)\,M W_M$$

$$+ (a - B'\Theta)\,W_x + \frac{\partial W}{\partial t} + G\left(\lambda M_t, t\right) - rW \qquad (12.66)$$

which is solved subject to the boundary condition that terminal wealth is optimal given the bequest motive; that is, $W\left(M_T, x_T, T\right) = G_B\left(\lambda M_T, T\right)$. Because this PDE is linear, as opposed to the nonlinear PDE for the indirect utility function, $J\left(W, x, t\right)$, that results from the dynamic programming approach, it may be relatively easy to solve, either analytically or numerically.

Thus, either equation (12.60) or (12.66) leads to the solution $W\left(M_t, x_t, t; \lambda\right) = W_t$ that allows us to determine λ as a function of W_t, M_t, and x_t, and this so-lution for λ can then be substituted into (12.58) and (12.59). The result is that consumption at any point in time and terminal wealth will depend only on the contemporaneous value of the pricing kernel, that is, $C_s^*\left(M_s\right)$ and $W_T^*\left(M_T\right)$. Note that when the individual follows this optimal policy, it is time consistent in the sense that should the individual resolve the optimal consumption problem at some future date, say, $s > t$, the computed value of λ will be the same as that derived at date t.

12.4.3   The Portfolio Allocation

Because we have assumed markets are dynamically complete, we know from the results of Chapters 9 and 10 that the individual's optimal process for wealth and its consumption dividend can be replicated by trading in the economy's underlying assets. Thus, our final step is to derive the portfolio allocation policy that finances the individual's consumption and terminal wealth rules. We can do this by comparing the process for wealth in (12.62) to the dynamics of wealth where the portfolio weights in the n risky assets are explicitly represented. Based on the assumed dynamics of asset returns in (12.51), equation (12.3) is

$$dW = \sum_{i=1}^{n} \omega_i(\mu_i - r)\,W\,dt + (rW - C_t)\,dt + W\sum_{i=1}^{n} \omega_i \Sigma_i dZ$$

$$= \omega'\left(\mu - re\right)W\,dt + (rW - C_t)\,dt + W\omega'\Sigma dZ \qquad (12.67)$$

where $\omega = \left(\omega_1 \ldots \omega_n\right)'$ is the $n \times 1$ vector of portfolio weights for the n risky assets and $\mu = \left(\mu_1 \ldots \mu_n\right)'$ is the $n \times 1$ vector of these assets' expected rates of return. Equating the coefficients of the Brownian motion components of the wealth processes in (12.67) and (12.62), we obtain $W\omega'\Sigma = \Sigma'_W$. Substituting in (12.64) for Σ_W and rearranging results gives

$$\omega = -\frac{MW_M}{W}\Sigma'^{-1}\Theta + \frac{W_x}{W}\Sigma'^{-1}B \tag{12.68}$$

Next, recall the no-arbitrage condition (12.53), and note that it can be written in the following matrix form:

$$\mu - re = \Sigma\Theta \tag{12.69}$$

Using (12.69) to substitute for Θ, equation (12.68) becomes

$$\omega = -\frac{MW_M}{W}\Sigma^{-1}\Sigma'^{-1}(\mu - re) + \frac{W_x}{W}\Sigma'^{-1}B$$

$$= -\frac{MW_M}{W}\Omega^{-1}(\mu - re) + \frac{W_x}{W}\Sigma'^{-1}B \tag{12.70}$$

These optimal portfolio weights are of the same form as what was derived earlier in (12.38) for the case where the state variable is perfectly correlated with asset returns.[18] A comparison shows that $MW_M = J_W/J_{WW}$ and $W_x = -J_{Wx}/J_{WW}$. Thus, given the solution for $W(M, x, t)$ in (12.60) or (12.66), equation (12.70) represents a derivation of the individual's optimal portfolio choices that is an alternative to the dynamic programming approach. Let us now use this martingale technique to solve a specific consumption–portfolio choice problem.

12.4.4   An Example

An end-of-chapter exercise asks you to use the martingale approach to derive the consumption and portfolio choices for the case of constant investment opportunities and constant relative-risk-aversion utility. As was shown earlier using the Bellman equation approach, this leads to the consumption and portfolio rules given by equations (12.34) and (12.35). In this section we consider another example analyzed by Jessica Wachter (Wachter 2002) that incorporates changing investment opportunities. A single state variable is assumed to affect the expected rate of return on a risky asset and, to ensure market completeness, this state variable is perfectly correlated with the risky asset's returns. Specifically, let there be a risk-free asset paying a constant rate of return of $r > 0$, and also assume there is a single risky asset so that equation (12.51) can be written simply as

$$dS/S = \mu(t)\,dt + \sigma\,dz \tag{12.71}$$

---

18. In this case, $\Omega^{-1}\phi = \Sigma'^{-1}B$.

The risky asset's volatility, σ, is assumed to be a positive constant but the asset's drift is permitted to vary over time. Specifically, let the single market price of risk be $\theta(t) = [\mu(t) - r]/\sigma$. It is assumed to follow the Ornstein-Uhlenbeck process

$$d\theta = a\left(\bar{\theta} - \theta\right)dt - b\,dz \tag{12.72}$$

where a, $\bar{\theta}$, and b are positive constants. Thus, the market price of risk is perfectly negatively correlated with the risky asset's return.[19] Wachter justifies the assumption of perfect negative correlation as being reasonable based on empirical studies of stock returns. Since $\mu(t) = r + \theta(t)\sigma$ and therefore $d\mu = \sigma\,d\theta$, this model implies that the expected rate of return on the risky asset is mean-reverting, becoming lower (*higher*) after its realized return has been high (*low*).[20]

The individual is assumed to have constant relative-risk-aversion utility and a zero bequest function, so that (12.55) becomes

$$\max_{C_s \forall s \in [t, T]} E_t\left[\int_t^T e^{-\rho s}\frac{C^\gamma}{\gamma}\,ds\right] + \lambda\left(M_t W_t - E_t\left[\int_t^T M_s C_s\,ds\right]\right) \tag{12.73}$$

where we have used the fact that it is optimal to set terminal wealth to zero in the absence of a bequest motive. The first-order condition corresponding to (12.58) is then

$$C_s^* = e^{-\frac{\rho s}{1-\gamma}}\left(\lambda M_s\right)^{-\frac{1}{1-\gamma}}, \ \forall s \in [t, T] \tag{12.74}$$

Therefore, the relationship between current wealth and this optimal consumption policy, equation (12.60), is

$$W_t = E_t\left[\int_t^T \frac{M_s}{M_t}e^{-\frac{\rho s}{1-\gamma}}\left(\lambda M_s\right)^{-\frac{1}{1-\gamma}}\,ds\right] \tag{12.75}$$

$$= \lambda^{-\frac{1}{1-\gamma}}M_t^{-1}\int_t^T e^{-\frac{\rho s}{1-\gamma}}E_t\left[M_s^{-\frac{\gamma}{1-\gamma}}\right]ds$$

Since $dM/M = -r\,dt - \theta\,dz$, the expectation in (12.75) depends only on M_t and the distribution of θ, which follows the Ornstein-Uhlenbeck process in (12.72). A solution for W_t can be obtained by computing the expectation in (12.75) directly.

---

19. Robert Merton (Merton 1971) considered a similar problem where the market price of risk was perfectly positively correlated with a risky asset's return.
20. Straightforward algebra shows that $\mu(t)$ follows the similar Ornstein-Uhlenbeck process $d\mu = a(\bar{\theta}\sigma + r - \mu)dt - \sigma b\,dz$.

Alternatively, one can solve for W_t using the PDE (12.66). For this example, the PDE is

$$0 = \frac{1}{2}\theta^2 M^2 W_{MM} + \theta b M W_{M\theta} + \frac{1}{2}b^2 W_{\theta\theta} + \left(\theta^2 - r\right) M W_M$$

$$+ \left[a\left(\bar{\theta} - \theta\right) + b\theta\right] W_\theta + \frac{\partial W}{\partial t} + e^{-\frac{\rho t}{1-\gamma}} \left(\lambda M_t\right)^{-\frac{1}{1-\gamma}} - rW \tag{12.76}$$

which is solved subject to the boundary condition $W\left(M_T, \theta_T, T\right) = 0$ since it is assumed there is no utility from leaving a bequest. Wachter discusses how the equations in (12.75) and (12.76) are similar to ones found in the literature on the term structure of interest rates. When $\gamma < 0$, so that the individual has risk aversion greater than that of a log utility maximizer, the solution is shown to be[21]

$$W_t = \left(\lambda M_t\right)^{-\frac{1}{1-\gamma}} e^{-\frac{\rho t}{1-\gamma}} \int_0^{T-t} H\left(\theta_t, \tau\right) d\tau \tag{12.77}$$

where $H\left(\theta_t, \tau\right)$ is the exponential of a quadratic function of θ_t given by

$$H\left(\theta_t, \tau\right) \equiv e^{\frac{1}{1-\gamma}\left[A_1(\tau)\frac{\theta_t^2}{2} + A_2(\tau)\theta_t + A_3(\tau)\right]} \tag{12.78}$$

and

$$A_1\left(\tau\right) \equiv \frac{2c_1\left(1 - e^{-c_3\tau}\right)}{2c_3 - \left(c_2 + c_3\right)\left(1 - e^{-c_3\tau}\right)}$$

$$A_2\left(\tau\right) \equiv \frac{4c_1 a\bar{\theta}\left(1 - e^{-c_3\tau/2}\right)^2}{c_3\left[2c_3 - \left(c_2 + c_3\right)\left(1 - e^{-c_3\tau}\right)\right]}$$

$$A_3\left(\tau\right) \equiv \int_0^\tau \left[\frac{b^2}{2\left(1 - \gamma\right)}A_2^2\left(s\right) + \frac{b^2}{2}A_1\left(s\right) + a\bar{\theta}A_2\left(s\right) + \gamma r - \rho\right] ds$$

with $c_1 \equiv \gamma/\left(1 - \gamma\right)$, $c_2 \equiv -2\left(a + c_1 b\right)$, and $c_3 \equiv \sqrt{c_2^2 - 4c_1 b^2/\left(1 - \gamma\right)}$. Equation (12.77) can be inverted to solve for the Lagrange multiplier, λ, but since we know from (12.74) that $\left(\lambda M_t\right)^{-\frac{1}{1-\gamma}} e^{-\frac{\rho t}{1-\gamma}} = C_t^*$, we can immediately rewrite (12.77) to derive the optimal consumption rule as

$$C_t^* = \frac{W_t}{\int_0^{T-t} H\left(\theta_t, \tau\right) d\tau} \tag{12.79}$$

---

21. This solution also requires $c_2^2 - 4c_1 b^2/\left(1 - \gamma\right) > 0$.

The positive function $H(\theta_t, \tau)$ can be given an economic interpretation. Recall that wealth equals the value of consumption from now until $T - t$ periods into the future. Therefore, since $\int_0^{T-t} H(\theta_t, \tau)\, d\tau = W_t / C_t^*$, the function $H(\theta_t, \tau)$ equals the value of consumption τ periods in the future scaled by current consumption.

Wachter shows that when $\gamma < 0$ and $\theta_t > 0$, so that the excess return on the risky asset, $\mu(t) - r$, is positive, then $\partial \left(C_t^* / W_t \right) / \partial \theta_t > 0$; that is, the individual consumes a greater proportion of wealth the larger the excess rate of return on the risky asset. This is what we would expect given our earlier analysis showing that the "income" effect dominates the "substitution" effect when risk aversion is greater than that of log utility. The higher expected rate of return on the risky asset allows the individual to afford more current consumption, which outweighs the desire to save more in order to take advantage of the higher expected return on wealth.

Let us next solve for this individual's optimal portfolio choice. The risky asset's portfolio weight that finances the optimal consumption plan is given by (12.70) for the case of a single risky asset:

$$\omega = -\frac{M W_M}{W} \frac{\mu(t) - r}{\sigma^2} - \frac{W_\theta}{W} \frac{b}{\sigma} \tag{12.80}$$

Using (12.77), we see that $-M W_M / W = 1 / (1 - \gamma)$. Moreover, it is straightforward to compute W_θ from (12.77), and by substituting these two derivatives into (12.80), we obtain

$$\omega = \frac{\mu(t) - r}{(1 - \gamma) \sigma^2} - \frac{b}{(1 - \gamma) \sigma} \frac{\int_0^{T-t} H(\theta_t, \tau) \left[A_1(\tau) \theta_t + A_2(\tau) \right] d\tau}{\int_0^{T-t} H(\theta_t, \tau)\, d\tau} \tag{12.81}$$

$$= \frac{\mu(t) - r}{(1 - \gamma) \sigma^2} - \frac{b}{(1 - \gamma) \sigma} \int_0^{T-t} \frac{H(\theta_t, \tau)}{\int_0^{T-t} H(\theta_t, \tau')\, d\tau'} \left[A_1(\tau) \theta_t + A_2(\tau) \right] d\tau$$

The first term is the familiar risky-asset demand whose form is the same as for the case of constant investment opportunities, equation (12.35). The second term on the right-hand side of (12.81) is the demand for hedging against changing investment opportunities. It can be interpreted as a consumption-weighted average of separate demands for hedging against changes in investment opportunities at all horizons from 0 to $T - t$ periods in the future, where the weight at horizon τ is $H(\theta_t, \tau) / \int_0^{T-t} H(\theta_t, \tau')\, d\tau'$.

It can be shown that $A_1(\tau)$ and $A_2(\tau)$ are negative when $\gamma < 0$, so that if $\theta_t > 0$, the term $\left[A_1(\tau) \theta_t + A_2(\tau) \right]$ is unambiguously negative and, therefore, the hedging demand is positive. Hence, individuals who are more risk averse than log utility place more of their wealth in the risky asset than would be the case if investment opportunities were constant. Because of the negative correlation between risky-asset returns and future investment opportunities, overweighting one's portfolio in the risky asset means that unexpectedly good returns today hedge against returns that are expected to be poorer tomorrow.

12.5 Summary

A continuous-time environment often makes the effects of asset return dynamics on consumption and portfolio decisions more transparent. Interestingly, when asset returns are assumed to be lognormally distributed so that investment opportunities are constant, the individual's optimal portfolio weights are similar in form to those of Chapter 2's single-period mean-variance model that assumed normally distributed asset returns. The fact that the mean-variance optimal portfolio weights could be derived in a multiperiod model with lognormal returns is an attractive result because lognormality is consistent with the limited-liability characteristics of most securities such as bonds and common stocks.

When assets' means and variances are time varying, so that investment opportunities are randomly changing, we found that portfolio allocation rules no longer satisfy the simple mean-variance demands. For cases other than log utility, portfolio choices include additional demand components that reflect a desire to hedge against unfavorable shifts in investment opportunities.

We presented two techniques for finding an individual's optimal consumption and portfolio decisions. The first is a continuous-time analog of the discrete-time dynamic programming approach studied in Chapter 5. This approach leads to a continuous-time Bellman equation, which in turn results in a partial differential equation for the derived utility of wealth. Solving for the derived utility of wealth allows one to then derive the individual's optimal consumption and portfolio choices at each point in time. The second is a martingale solution technique based on the insight that an individual's wealth represents an asset portfolio that pays dividends in the form of a stream of consumption. This permits valuation of the individual's optimal consumption stream using the economy's stochastic discount factor. After deriving the optimal consumption rule, one can then find the portfolio decisions that finance the individual's consumption plan.

This chapter's analysis of an individual's optimal consumption and portfolio decisions provides the foundation for considering the equilibrium returns of assets in a continuous-time economy. This is the topic that we address in the next chapter.

12.6 Exercises

1. Consider the following consumption and portfolio choice problem. An individual must choose between two different assets, a stock and a short (instantaneous) maturity, default-free bond. In addition, the individual faces a stochastic rate of inflation, that is, uncertain changes in the price level (e.g.,

the Consumer Price Index). The price level (currency price of the consumption good) follows the process

$$dP_t/P_t = \pi\, dt + \delta\, d\zeta$$

The nominal (currency value) of the stock is given by S_t. This nominal stock price satisfies

$$dS_t/S_t = \mu\, dt + \sigma\, dz$$

The nominal (currency value) of the bond is given by B_t. It pays an instantaneous nominal rate of return equal to i. Hence, its nominal price satisfies

$$dB_t/B_t = i\, dt$$

Note that $d\zeta$ and dz are standard Wiener processes with $d\zeta\, dz = \rho\, dt$. Also assume π, δ, μ, σ, and i are all constants.

a. What processes do the real (consumption good value) rates of return on the stock and the bond satisfy?

b. Let C_t be the individual's date t real rate of consumption and ω be the proportion of real wealth, W_t, that is invested in the stock. Give the process followed by real wealth, W_t.

c. Assume that the individual solves the following problem:

$$\max_{C,\omega} \; E_0 \int_0^\infty U\left(C_t, t\right) dt$$

subject to the real wealth dynamic budget constraint given in part (b). Assuming $U\left(C_t, t\right)$ is a concave utility function, solve for the individual's optimal choice of ω in terms of the indirect utility-of-wealth function.

d. How does ω vary with ρ? What is the economic intuition for this comparative static result?

2. Consider the individual's intertemporal consumption and portfolio choice problem for the case of a single risky asset and an instantaneously risk-free asset. The individual maximizes expected lifetime utility of the form

$$E_0 \left[\int_0^T e^{-\phi t} u\left(C_t\right) dt \right]$$

The price of the risky asset, S, is assumed to follow the geometric Brownian motion process

$$dS/S = \mu\, dt + \sigma\, dz$$

where μ and σ are constants. The instantaneously risk-free asset pays an instantaneous rate of return of r_t. Thus, an investment that takes the form of continually reinvesting at this risk-free rate has a value (price), B_t, that follows the process

$$dB/B = r_t dt$$

where r_t is assumed to change over time, following the Vasicek mean-reverting process (Vasicek 1977)

$$dr_t = a \left[b - r_t\right] dt + sd\zeta$$

where $dzd\zeta = \rho dt$.

a. Write down the intertemporal budget constraint for this problem.

b. What are the two state variables for this consumption–portfolio choice problem? Write down the stochastic, continuous-time Bellman equation for this problem.

c. Take the first-order conditions for the optimal choices of consumption and the demand for the risky asset.

d. Show how the demand for the risky asset can be written as two terms: one term that would be present even if r were constant and another term that exists due to changes in r (investment opportunities).

3. Consider the following resource allocation–portfolio choice problem faced by a university. The university obtains "utility" (e.g., an enhanced reputation for its students, faculty, and alumni) from carrying out research and teaching in two different areas: the "arts" and the "sciences." Let C_a be the number of units of arts activities "consumed" at the university and let C_s be the number of science activities consumed at the university. At date 0, the university is assumed to maximize an expected utility function of the form

$$E_0 \left[\int_0^\infty e^{-\phi t} u \left(C_a(t), C_s(t)\right) dt \right]$$

where $u \left(C_a, C_s\right)$ is assumed to be increasing and strictly concave with respect to the consumption levels. It is assumed that the cost (or price) of consuming a unit of arts activity is fixed at one. In other words, in what follows we express all values in terms of units of the arts activity, making units of the arts activity the numeraire. Thus, consuming C_a units of the arts activity always costs C_a. The cost (or price) of consuming one unit of science activity at date t is given by $S(t)$, implying that the university's expenditure on C_s

units of science activities costs SC_s. $S(t)$ is assumed to follow the process

$$dS/S = \alpha_s dt + \sigma_s d\zeta$$

where α_s and σ_s may be functions of S.

The university is assumed to fund its consumption of arts and sciences activities from its endowment. The value of its endowment is denoted W_t. It can be invested in either a risk-free asset or a risky asset. The risk-free asset pays a constant rate of return equal to r. The price of the risky asset is denoted P and is assumed to follow the process

$$dP/P = \mu dt + \sigma dz$$

where μ and σ are constants and $dz d\zeta = \rho dt$. Let ω denote the proportion of the university's endowment invested in the risky asset, and thus $(1 - \omega)$ is the proportion invested in the risk-free asset. The university's problem is then to maximize its expected utility by optimally selecting C_a, C_s, and ω.

a. Write down the university's intertemporal budget constraint, that is, the dynamics for its endowment, W_t.

b. What are the two state variables for this problem? Define a "derived utility of endowment" (wealth) function and write down the stochastic, continuous-time Bellman equation for this problem.

c. Write down the first-order conditions for the optimal choices of C_a, C_s, and ω.

d. Show how the demand for the risky asset can be written as two terms, a standard (single-period) portfolio demand term and a hedging term.

e. For the special case in which utility is given by $u(C_a, C_s) = C_a^\theta C_s^\beta$, solve for the university's optimal level of arts activity in terms of the level and price of the science activity.

4. Consider an individual's intertemporal consumption, labor, and portfolio choice problem for the case of a risk-free asset and a single risky asset. The individual maximizes expected lifetime utility of the form

$$E_0 \left\{ \int_0^T e^{-\phi t} u(C_t, L_t) \, dt + B(W_T) \right\}$$

where C_t is the individual's consumption at date t and L_t is the amount of labor effort that the individual exerts at date t. $u(C_t, L_t)$ is assumed to be an increasing concave function of C_t but a decreasing concave function of

L_t. The risk-free asset pays a constant rate of return equal to r per unit time and the price of the risky asset, S, satisfies the process

$$dS/S = \mu dt + \sigma dz$$

where μ and σ are constants. For each unit of labor effort exerted at date t, the individual earns an instantaneous flow of labor income of $L_t y_t dt$. The return to effort or wage rate, y_t, is stochastic and follows the process

$$dy = \mu_y(y) dt + \sigma_y(y) d\zeta$$

where $dz d\zeta = \rho dt$.

a. Letting ω be the proportion of wealth invested in the risky asset, write down the intertemporal budget constraint for this problem.

b. What are the state variables for this problem? Write down the stochastic, continuous-time Bellman equation for this problem.

c. Take the first-order conditions with respect to each of the individual's decision variables.

d. Show how the demand for the risky asset can be written as two terms: one term that would be present even if y were constant and another term that exists due to changes in y.

e. If $u(C_t, L_t) = \gamma \ln[C_t] + \beta \ln[L_t]$, solve for the optimal amount of labor effort in terms of the optimal level of consumption.

5. Consider an individual's intertemporal consumption and portfolio choice problem for the case of two risky assets (with no risk-free asset). The individual maximizes expected lifetime utility of the form

$$E_0 \left\{ \int_0^\infty e^{-\phi t} u(C_t) \, dt \right\}$$

where C_t is the individual's consumption at date t. The individual's portfolio can be invested in a stock whose price, S, follows the process

$$dS/S = \mu dt + \sigma dz$$

and a default-risky bond whose price, B, follows the process

$$dB = rBdt - Bdq$$

where dq is a Poisson counting process defined as

$$dq = \begin{cases} 1 & \text{if a default occurs} \\ 0 & \text{otherwise} \end{cases}$$

The probability of a default occurring over time interval dt is λdt. μ, σ, r, and λ are assumed to be constants. Note that the bond earns a rate of return equal to r when it does not default, but when default occurs, the total amount invested in the bond is lost; that is, the bond price goes to zero, $dB = -B$. We also assume that if default occurs, a new default-risky bond, following the same original bond price process given above, becomes available, so that the individual can always allocate her wealth between the stock and a default-risky bond.

a. Letting ω be the proportion of wealth invested in the stock, write down the intertemporal budget constraint for this problem.

b. Write down the stochastic, continuous-time Bellman equation for this problem. Hint: recall that the Dynkin operator, $L[J]$, reflects the drift terms from applying Itô's lemma to J. In this problem, these terms need to include the expected change in J from jumps in wealth due to bond default.

c. Take the first-order conditions with respect to each of the individual's decision variables.

d. Since this problem reflects constant investment opportunities, it can be shown that when $u(C_t) = c^\gamma / \gamma$, $\gamma < 1$, the derived utility-of-wealth function takes the form $J(W, t) = ae^{-\phi t}W^\gamma / \gamma$, where a is a positive constant. For this constant relative-risk-aversion case, derive the conditions for optimal C and ω in terms of current wealth and the parameters of the asset price processes. Hint: an explicit formula for ω in terms of all of the other parameters may not be possible because the condition is nonlinear in ω.

e. Maintaining the constant relative-risk-aversion assumption, what is the optimal ω if $\lambda = 0$? Assuming the parameters are such that $0 < \omega < 1$ for this case, how would a small increase in λ affect ω, the proportion of the portfolio held in the stock?

6. Show that a log utility investor's optimal consumption for the continuous-time problem, equation (12.50), is comparable to that of the discrete-time problem, equation (5.33).

7. Use the martingale approach to consumption and portfolio choice to solve the following problem. An individual can choose between a risk-free asset paying the interest rate r and a single risky asset whose price satisfies the geometric Brownian motion process

$$\frac{dS}{S} = \mu dt + \sigma dz$$

where r, μ, and σ are constants. This individual's lifetime utility function is time separable, has no bequest function, and displays constant relative risk aversion:

$$E_t \left[\int_t^T e^{-\rho s} \frac{C_s^\gamma}{\gamma} ds \right]$$

a. Assuming an absence of arbitrage, state the form of the market price of risk, θ, in terms of the asset return parameters and write down the process followed by the pricing kernel, dM/M. You need not give any derivations.

b. Write down the individual's consumption choice problem as a static maximization subject to a wealth constraint, where W_t is current wealth and λ is the Lagrange multiplier for the wealth constraint. Derive the first-order conditions for C_s $\forall s \in [t, T]$ and solve for the optimal C_s as a function of λ and M_s.

c. Write down the valuation equation for current wealth, W_t, in terms of λ, M_t, and an integral of expected functions of the future values of the pricing kernel. Given the previous assumptions that the asset price parameters are constants, derive the closed-form solution for this expectation.

d. From the answer in part (c), show that optimal consumption is of the form

$$C_t^* = \frac{a}{1 - e^{-a(T-t)}} W_t$$

where a is a function of r, ρ, γ, and θ.

e. Describe how you next would calculate the optimal portfolio proportion invested in the risky asset, ω, given the results of parts (a)–(d).

CHAPTER 13

Equilibrium Asset Returns

T his chapter considers the equilibrium pricing of assets for a continuous-time economy when individuals have time-separable utility. It derives the Intertemporal Capital Asset Pricing Model (ICAPM) that was developed by Robert Merton (Merton 1973a). One result of this model is to show that the standard single-period CAPM holds for the special case in which investment opportunities are assumed to be constant over time. This is an important modification of the CAPM, not only because the results are extended to a multiperiod environment but because the single-period model's assumption of a normal asset return distribution is replaced with a more attractive assumption of lognormally distributed returns. Since assets such as stocks and bonds have limited liability, the assumption of lognormal returns, which restricts asset values to be nonnegative, is more realistic.

When investment opportunities are changing, the standard "single-beta" CAPM no longer holds. Rather, a multibeta ICAPM is necessary for pricing assets. The additional betas reflect priced sources of risk from additional state variables that affect investment opportunities. However, as was shown by Douglas Breeden (Breeden 1979), the multibeta ICAPM can be collapsed into a single "consumption" beta model, the so-called Consumption Capital Asset Pricing Model (CCAPM). Thus, consistent with our consumption-based asset pricing results in Chapter 4, the continuous-time, multifactor ICAPM can be interpreted as a consumption-based asset pricing model.

The Merton ICAPM is not a fully general equilibrium analysis, because it takes the forms of the assets' return-generating processes as given. However, as this chapter demonstrates, this assumption regarding asset returns can be reconciled with the general equilibrium model of John Cox, Jonathan Ingersoll, and Stephen

Ross (CIR) (Cox, Ingersoll, and Ross 1985a). The CIR model is an example of a production economy that specifies the available productive technologies. These technologies are assumed to display constant returns to scale and provide us with a model of asset supplies that is an alternative to the Lucas endowment economy presented in Chapter 6. The CIR framework is useful for determining the equilibrium prices of contingent claims. The final section of this chapter gives an example of how the CIR model can be applied to determine the prices of various maturity bonds that are assumed to be in zero net supply.

13.1   An Intertemporal Capital Asset Pricing Model

Merton's ICAPM is based on the same assumptions made in the previous chapter regarding individuals' consumption and portfolio choices. Individuals can trade in a risk-free asset paying an instantaneous rate of return of $r(t)$ and in n risky assets, where the instantaneous rates of return for the risky assets satisfy

$$dS_i(t) / S_i(t) = \mu_i(x, t) \ dt + \sigma_i(x, t) \ dz_i \qquad (13.1)$$

where $i = 1, \ldots, n$, and $(\sigma_i \, dz_i)(\sigma_j \, dz_j) = \sigma_{ij} \, dt$. The risk-free return and the means and standard deviations of the risky assets can be functions of time and a $k \times 1$ vector of state variables that follow the processes

$$dx_i = a_i(x, t) \ dt + b_i(x, t) \ d\zeta_i \qquad (13.2)$$

where $i = 1, \ldots, k$, and $(b_i \, d\zeta_i)(b_j \, d\zeta_j) = b_{ij} \, dt$ and $(\sigma_i \, dz_i)(b_j \, d\zeta_j) = \phi_{ij} \, dt$. Now we wish to consider what must be the equilibrium relationships between the parameters of the asset return processes characterized by equations (13.1) and (13.2). Let us start by analyzing the simplest case first, namely, when investment opportunities are constant through time.

13.1.1   Constant Investment Opportunities

As shown in the previous chapter, when the risk-free rate and the parameters of assets' return processes are constants (r and the μ_i's, σ_i's, and σ_{ij}'s are all constants), the asset price processes in (13.1) are geometric Brownian motions and asset returns are lognormally distributed. In this case, the optimal portfolio choices of all individuals lead them to choose the same portfolio of risky assets. Individuals differ only in how they divide their total wealths between this common risky-asset portfolio and the risk-free asset. For this common risky-asset portfolio, it was shown in Chapter 12's equation (12.25) that the proportion of risky asset k to all risky assets is

$$\delta_k = \frac{\displaystyle\sum_{j=1}^{n} v_{kj}(\mu_j - r)}{\displaystyle\sum_{i=1}^{n}\sum_{j=1}^{n} v_{ij}(\mu_j - r)} \tag{13.3}$$

and in (12.26) that this portfolio's mean and variance are given by

$$\mu \equiv \sum_{i=1}^{n} \delta_i \mu_i$$

$$\sigma^2 \equiv \sum_{i=1}^{n}\sum_{j=1}^{n} \delta_i \delta_j \sigma_{ij} \tag{13.4}$$

Similar to our derivation of the single-period CAPM, in equilibrium this common risky-asset portfolio must be the market portfolio; that is, $\mu = \mu_m$ and $\sigma^2 = \sigma_m^2$. Moreover, the continuous-time market portfolio is exactly the same as that implied by the single-period CAPM, where the instantaneous means and covariances of the continuous-time asset return processes replace the means and covariances of CAPM's multivariate normal asset return distribution. This implies that the equilibrium asset returns in this continuous-time environment satisfy the same relationship as the single-period CAPM:

$$\mu_i - r = \beta_i \left(\mu_m - r\right), \qquad i = 1, \ldots, n \tag{13.5}$$

where $\beta_i \equiv \sigma_{im}/\sigma_m^2$ and σ_{im} is the covariance between the ith asset's rate of return and the market's rate of return. Thus, the constant investment opportunity set assumption replicates the standard, single-period CAPM. Yet, rather than asset returns being normally distributed as in the single-period CAPM, the ICAPM has asset returns being lognormally distributed.

While the standard CAPM results continue to hold for this more realistic intertemporal environment, the assumptions of a constant risk-free rate and unchanging asset return means and variances are untenable. Clearly, interest rates vary over time, as do the volatilities of assets such as common stocks.[1] Moreover, there is substantial evidence that mean returns on assets display predictable time

---

1. Not only do nominal interest rates vary over time, but there is also evidence that real interest rates do as well (Pennacchi 1991). Also, volatilities of stock returns have been found to follow mean-reverting processes. See, for example, (Bollerslev, Chou, and Kroner 1992) and (Andersen et al. 2001).

variation.[2] Let us next analyze equilibrium asset pricing for a model that permits such changing investment opportunities.

13.1.2   Stochastic Investment Opportunities

To keep the analysis simple, let us start by assuming that there is a single state variable, x. The system of n equations that a given individual's portfolio weights satisfy is given by the previous chapter's equation (12.19) with $k = 1$. It can be rewritten as

$$0 = -A(\mu_i - r) + \sum_{j=1}^{n} \sigma_{ij}\omega_j^* W - H\phi_i, \quad i = 1, \ldots, n \tag{13.6}$$

where you may recall that $A = -J_W/J_{WW} = -U_C/\left[U_{CC}\left(\partial C/\partial W\right)\right]$ and $H = -J_{Wx}/J_{WW} = -\left(\partial C/\partial x\right)/\left(\partial C/\partial W\right)$. Let's rewrite (13.6) in matrix form, using **bold** type to denote vectors and matrices while using regular type to indicate scalars. Also let the superscript p denote the pth individual's (person's) value of wealth, vector of optimal portfolio weights, and values of A and H. Then (13.6) becomes

$$A^p\left(\boldsymbol{\mu} - r\mathbf{e}\right) = \boldsymbol{\Omega}\boldsymbol{\omega}^p W^p - H^p\boldsymbol{\phi} \tag{13.7}$$

where $\boldsymbol{\mu} = (\mu_1, \ldots, \mu_n)'$, $\mathbf{e}$ is an n-dimensional vector of ones, $\boldsymbol{\omega}^p = (\omega_1^p, \ldots, \omega_n^p)'$, and $\boldsymbol{\phi} = (\phi_1, \ldots, \phi_n)'$. Now if we sum across all individuals and divide both sides by $\sum_p A^p$, we obtain

$$\boldsymbol{\mu} - r\mathbf{e} = a\boldsymbol{\Omega}\boldsymbol{\alpha} - h\boldsymbol{\phi} \tag{13.8}$$

where $a \equiv \sum_p W^p / \sum_p A^p$, $h \equiv \sum_p H^p / \sum_p A^p$, and $\boldsymbol{\alpha} \equiv \sum_p \boldsymbol{\omega}^p W^p / \sum_p W^p$ is the average investment in each asset across investors. These must be the market weights, in equilibrium. Hence, the ith row (ith risky-asset excess return) of equation (13.8) is

$$\mu_i - r = a\sigma_{im} - h\phi_i \tag{13.9}$$

To find the excess return on the market portfolio, we can pre-multiply (13.8) by $\boldsymbol{\alpha}'$ and obtain

$$\mu_m - r = a\sigma_m^2 - h\sigma_{mx} \tag{13.10}$$

---

2. For example, empirical evidence by Narasimhan Jegadeesh and Sheridan Titman (Jegadeesh and Titman 1993) find that abnormal stock returns appear to display positive serial correlation at short horizons up to about a year, a phenomenon described as "momentum." In contrast, there is some evidence (e.g., (Poterba and Summers 1988) and (Fama and French 1988)) that abnormal stock returns are negatively serially correlated over longer-term horizons.

where $\sigma_{mx} = \boldsymbol{\alpha}'\boldsymbol{\phi}$ is the covariance between the market portfolio and the state variable, x. Next, define $\eta \equiv \frac{\boldsymbol{\Omega}^{-1}\boldsymbol{\phi}}{e'\boldsymbol{\Omega}^{-1}\boldsymbol{\phi}}$. By construction, η is a vector of portfolio weights for the risky assets, where this portfolio has the maximum absolute correlation with the state variable, x. In this sense, it provides the best possible hedge against changes in the state variable.[3] To find the excess return on this optimal hedge portfolio, we can pre-multiply (13.8) by η' and obtain

$$\mu_\eta - r = a\sigma_{\eta m} - h\sigma_{\eta x} \tag{13.11}$$

where $\sigma_{\eta m}$ is the covariance between the optimal hedge portfolio and the market portfolio and $\sigma_{\eta x}$ is the covariance between the optimal hedge portfolio and the state variable, x. Equations (13.10) and (13.11) are two linear equations in the two unknowns, a and h. Solving for a and h and substituting them back into equation (13.9), we obtain

$$\mu_i - r = \frac{\sigma_{im}\sigma_{\eta x} - \phi_i\sigma_{mn}}{\sigma_m^2\sigma_{\eta x} - \sigma_{mx}\sigma_{mn}}\left(\mu_m - r\right) + \frac{\phi_i\sigma_m^2 - \sigma_{im}\sigma_{mx}}{\sigma_m^2\sigma_{\eta x} - \sigma_{mx}\sigma_{mn}}\left(\mu_\eta - r\right) \tag{13.12}$$

While the derivation is somewhat lengthy, it can be shown that (13.12) is equivalent to

$$\mu_i - r = \frac{\sigma_{im}\sigma_\eta^2 - \sigma_{in}\sigma_{mn}}{\sigma_m^2\sigma_\eta^2 - \sigma_{mn}^2}\left(\mu_m - r\right) + \frac{\sigma_{in}\sigma_m^2 - \sigma_{im}\sigma_{mn}}{\sigma_\eta^2\sigma_m^2 - \sigma_{mn}^2}\left(\mu_\eta - r\right)$$

$$\equiv \beta_i^m\left(\mu_m - r\right) + \beta_i^\eta\left(\mu_\eta - r\right) \tag{13.13}$$

where σ_{in} is the covariance between the return on asset i and that of the hedge portfolio. Note that $\sigma_{in} = 0$ if and only if $\phi_i = 0$. For the case in which the state variable, x, is uncorrelated with the market so that $\sigma_{mn} = 0$, equation (13.13) simplifies to

$$\mu_i - r = \frac{\sigma_{im}}{\sigma_m^2}\left(\mu_m - r\right) + \frac{\sigma_{in}}{\sigma_\eta^2}\left(\mu_\eta - r\right) \tag{13.14}$$

In this case, the first term on the right-hand side of (13.14) is that found in the standard CAPM. The assumption that x is uncorrelated with the market is not as restrictive as one might first believe, since one could redefine the state variable x as a factor that cannot be explained by current market returns, that is, a factor that is uncorrelated with the market.

An equation such as (13.13) can be derived when more than one state variable exists. In this case, there will be an additional "beta" for each state variable.

---

3. Note that the numerator of η, $\boldsymbol{\Omega}^{-1}\boldsymbol{\phi}$, is the $n \times 1$ vector of coefficients from a regression of dx on the n risky-asset returns, dS_i/S_i, $i - 1, \ldots, n$. Dividing these individual coefficients by their sum, $e'\boldsymbol{\Omega}^{-1}\boldsymbol{\phi}$, transforms them into portfolio weights.

The intertemporal capital asset pricing relations (ICAPM) given by (13.13) and (13.14) have a form similar to the Arbitrage Pricing Theory of Chapter 3. Indeed, the multifactor ICAPM has been used to justify empirical APT-type factor models. The ICAPM predicts that APT risk factors should be related to changes in investment opportunities. However, it should be noted that, in general, the ICAPM's betas may be time varying and not easy to estimate in a constant-coefficients, multifactor regression model.

13.1.3 An Extension to State-Dependent Utility

It is possible that individuals' utilities may be affected directly by the state of the economy. Here we briefly mention the consequences of allowing the state of nature, x, to influence utility by making it an argument of the utility function, $U\left(C_t, x_t, t\right)$. It is straightforward to verify that the form of the individual's continuous-time Bellman equation (12.17), the first-order conditions for consumption, C_t, and the portfolio weights, the ω_i's, remain unchanged from those specified in Chapter 12. Hence, our results on the equilibrium returns on assets, equation (13.13), continue to hold. The only change is in the interpretation of H, the individual's hedging demand coefficient. With state-dependent utility, by taking the total derivative of the envelope condition (12.18), one obtains

$$J_{Wx} = U_{CC}\frac{\partial C}{\partial x} + U_{Cx} \tag{13.15}$$

so that

$$H = -\frac{\partial C/\partial x}{\partial C/\partial W} - \frac{U_{Cx}}{U_{CC}\frac{\partial C}{\partial W}} \tag{13.16}$$

It can be shown that, in this case, individuals do not hold portfolios that minimize the variance of consumption. Rather, their portfolio holdings minimize the variance of marginal utility.

13.2 Breeden's Consumption CAPM

Douglas T. Breeden (Breeden 1979) provided a way of simplifying the asset return relationship given in Merton's ICAPM. Breeden's model shows that Chapter 4's single-period consumption–portfolio choice result that an asset's expected rate of return depends upon its covariance with the marginal utility of consumption can be generalized to a multiperiod, continuous-time context.

Breeden considers the same model as Merton and hence, in the case of multiple state variables, derives equation (12.38). Substituting in for A and H, equation (12.38) can be written in matrix form, and for the case of k (multiple) state variables the optimal portfolio weights for the pth investor are given by

$$\omega^p W^p = -\frac{U_C^p}{U_{CC}^p C_W^p}\boldsymbol{\Omega}^{-1}\left(\boldsymbol{\mu} - re\right) - \boldsymbol{\Omega}^{-1}\boldsymbol{\Phi}\mathbf{C}_x^p/C_W^p \tag{13.17}$$

where $C_W^p = \partial C^p / \partial W^p$, $\mathbf{C}_x^p = \left(\frac{\partial C^p}{\partial x_1} \cdots \frac{\partial C^p}{\partial x_k}\right)'$, and $\boldsymbol{\Phi}$ is the $n \times k$ matrix of covariances of asset returns with changes in the state variables; that is, its i,jth element is ϕ_{ij}. Pre-multiplying (13.17) by $C_W^p\boldsymbol{\Omega}$ and rearranging terms, we have

$$-\frac{U_C^p}{U_{CC}^p}\left(\boldsymbol{\mu} - re\right) = \boldsymbol{\Omega}_{W^p}C_W^p + \boldsymbol{\Phi}\mathbf{C}_x^p \tag{13.18}$$

where $\boldsymbol{\Omega}_{W^p}$ is the $n \times 1$ vector of covariances between asset returns with the change in wealth of individual p. Now individual p's optimal consumption, $C^p\left(W^p, \mathbf{x}, t\right)$, is a function of wealth, W^p; the vector of state variables, $\mathbf{x}$; and time, t. Thus, from Itô's lemma, we know that the stochastic terms for dC^p will be

$$C_W^p\left(\omega_1^p W^p \sigma_1 dz_1 + \cdots + \omega_n^p W^p \sigma_n dz_n\right) + \left(b_1 d\zeta_1\, b_2 d\zeta_2 \ldots b_k d\zeta_k\right)\mathbf{C}_x^p \tag{13.19}$$

Hence, the instantaneous covariances of asset returns with changes in individual p's consumption are given by calculating the instantaneous covariance between each asset (having stochastic term $\sigma_i dz_i$) with the terms given in (13.19). The result, in matrix form, is that the $n \times 1$ vector of covariances between asset returns and changes in the individual's consumption, denoted $\boldsymbol{\Omega}_{C^p}$, is

$$\boldsymbol{\Omega}_{C^p} = \boldsymbol{\Omega}_{W^p}C_W^p + \boldsymbol{\Phi}\mathbf{C}_x^p \tag{13.20}$$

Note that the right-hand side of (13.20) equals the right-hand side of (13.18), and therefore

$$\boldsymbol{\Omega}_{C^p} = -\frac{U_C^p}{U_{CC}^p}\left(\boldsymbol{\mu} - re\right) \tag{13.21}$$

Equation (13.21) holds for each individual, p. Next, define C as aggregate consumption per unit time and define $\mathcal{T}$ as an aggregate rate of risk tolerance, where

$$\mathcal{T} \equiv \sum_p -\frac{U_C^p}{U_{CC}^p} \tag{13.22}$$

Then (13.21) can be aggregated over all individuals to obtain

$$\boldsymbol{\mu} - re = \mathcal{T}^{-1}\boldsymbol{\Omega}_C \tag{13.23}$$

where $\boldsymbol{\Omega}_C$ is the $n \times 1$ vector of covariances between asset returns and changes in aggregate consumption. If we multiply and divide the right-hand side of (13.23) by current aggregate consumption, we obtain

$$\boldsymbol{\mu} - r\mathbf{e} = \left(\mathcal{F}/C\right)^{-1} \boldsymbol{\Omega}_{\ln C} \tag{13.24}$$

where $\boldsymbol{\Omega}_{\ln C}$ is the $n \times 1$ vector of covariances between asset returns and changes in the logarithm of consumption (percentage rates of change of consumption).

Consider a portfolio, m, with vector of weights $\boldsymbol{\omega}^m$. Pre-multiplying (13.24) by $\boldsymbol{\omega}^{m'}$, we have

$$\mu_m - r = \left(\mathcal{F}/C\right)^{-1} \sigma_{m, \ln C} \tag{13.25}$$

where μ_m is the expected return on portfolio m and $\sigma_{m, \ln C}$ is the (scalar) co-variance between returns on portfolio m and changes in the log of consumption. Using (13.25) to substitute for $\left(\mathcal{F}/C\right)^{-1}$ in (13.24), we have

$$\begin{aligned} \boldsymbol{\mu} - r\mathbf{e} &= \left(\boldsymbol{\Omega}_{\ln C}/\sigma_{m, \ln C}\right) \left(\mu_m - r\right) \\ &= \left(\boldsymbol{\beta}_C/\beta_{mC}\right) \left(\mu_m - r\right) \end{aligned} \tag{13.26}$$

where $\boldsymbol{\beta}_C$ and β_{mC} are the "consumption betas" of asset returns and of portfolio m's return. The consumption beta for any asset is defined as

$$\beta_{iC} = cov\left(dS_i/S_i, d \ln C\right)/var\left(d \ln C\right) \tag{13.27}$$

Portfolio m may be any portfolio of assets, not necessarily the market portfolio. Equation (13.26) says that the ratio of expected excess returns on any two assets or portfolios of assets is equal to the ratio of their betas measured relative to aggregate consumption. Hence, the risk of a security's return can be summarized by a single consumption beta. Aggregate optimal consumption, $C(W, \mathbf{x}, t)$, encompasses the effects of levels of wealth and the state variables and in this way is a sufficient statistic for the value of asset returns in different states of the world.

Breeden's consumption CAPM (CCAPM) is a considerable simplification relative to Merton's multibeta ICAPM. Furthermore, while the multiple state variables in Merton's model may not be directly identified or observed, and hence the multiple state variable "betas" may not be computed, Breeden's consumption beta can be computed given that we have data on aggregate consumption. However, as discussed earlier, the results of empirical tests using aggregate consumption data are unimpressive.[4] As in all of our earlier asset pricing models based on individuals' optimal consumption and portfolio choices, the CCAPM and ICAPM rely on the assumption of time-separable utility. When we depart from this restriction on

---

4. An exception is research by Martin Lettau and Sydney Ludvigson (Lettau and Ludvigson 2001), who find that the CCAPM is successful in explaining stock returns when the model's parameters are permitted to vary over time with the log consumption–wealth ratio.

utility, as we do in the next chapter, consumption-based models are able to better describe empirical distributions of asset prices.

The ICAPM and CCAPM are not general equilibrium models in a strict sense. While they model individuals' "tastes" by specifying the form of their utilities, they do not link the asset return processes in (13.1) and (13.2) to the economy's "technologies." A fully general equilibrium model would not start by specifying these assets' return processes but, rather, by specifying the economy's physical production possibilities. In other words, it would specify the economy's productive opportunities that determine the supplies of assets in the economy. By matching individuals' asset demands with the asset supplies, the returns on assets would then be determined endogenously. The Lucas endowment economy model in Chapter 6 was an example of this, and we now turn to another general equilibrium model, namely, Cox, Ingersoll, and Ross's production economy model.

13.3 A Cox, Ingersoll, and Ross Production Economy

In two companion articles (Cox, Ingersoll, and Ross 1985a; Cox, Ingersoll, and Ross 1985b), John Cox, Jonathan Ingersoll, and Stephen Ross (CIR) developed a continuous-time model of a production economy that is a general equilibrium framework for many of the asset pricing results of this chapter. Their model starts from basic assumptions regarding individuals' preferences and the economy's production possibilities. Individuals are assumed to have identical preferences and initial wealth as well as to maximize standard, time-separable utility similar to the lifetime utility previously specified in this and the previous chapter, namely, in (12.4).[5] The unique feature of the CIR model is the economy's technologies.

Recall that in the general equilibrium endowment economy model of Robert Lucas (Lucas 1978), technologies are assumed to produce perishable output (dividends) that could not be reinvested, only consumed. In this sense, these Lucas technologies are inelastically supplied. Individuals cannot save output and physically reinvest it to increase the productive capacity of the economy. Rather, in the Lucas economy, prices of the technologies adjust endogenously to make investors' changing demands equal to the technologies' fixed supplies. Given the technologies' distribution of future output (dividends), these prices determine the technologies' equilibrium rates of return.

In contrast, the CIR production economy makes the opposite assumption regarding the supply of technologies. Technologies are in perfectly elastic supply.

---

5. When individuals are assumed to have the same utility and initial wealth, we can think of there being a "representative" individual.

Individuals can save some of the economy's output and reinvest it, thereby changing the productive capacity of the economy. Assets' rates of return are pinned down by the economy's technologies' rates of return, and the amounts invested in these technologies become endogenous.

Specifically, CIR assumes that there is a single good that can be either consumed or invested. This "capital-consumption" good can be invested in any of n different risky technologies that produce an instantaneous change in the amount of the consumption good. If an amount η_i is physically invested in technology i, then the proportional change in the amount of this good that is produced is given by

$$\frac{d\eta_i(t)}{\eta_i(t)} = \mu_i(x, t) \ dt + \sigma_i(x, t) \ dz_i, \ i = 1, \ldots, n \tag{13.28}$$

where $(\sigma_i \ dz_i)(\sigma_j \ dz_j) = \sigma_{ij} \ dt$. μ_i is the instantaneous expected rate of change in the amount of the invested good and σ_i is the instantaneous standard deviation of this rate of change. Note that because μ_i and σ_i are independent of η_i, the change in the quantity of the good is linear in the amount invested. Hence, each technology is characterized by "constant returns to scale." μ_i and σ_i can vary with time and with a $k \times 1$ vector of state variables, $x(t)$. Thus, the economy's technologies for transforming consumption into more consumption can reflect changing (physical) investment opportunities. The ith state variable is assumed to follow the process

$$dx_i = a_i(x, t) \ dt + b_i(x, t) \ d\zeta_i \tag{13.29}$$

where $i = 1, \ldots, k$, and $(b_i \ d\zeta_i)(b_j \ d\zeta_j) = b_{ij} \ dt$ and $(\sigma_i \ dz_i)(b_j \ d\zeta_j) = \phi_{ij} \ dt$.

Note that equations (13.28) and (13.29) are nearly identical to our earlier modeling of financial asset returns, equations (13.1) and (13.2). Whereas $dS_i(t) / S_i(t)$ in (13.1) represented a security's proportional return, $d\eta_i(t) / \eta_i(t)$ in (13.28) represents a physical investment's proportional return. However, if each technology is interpreted as being owned by an individual firm, and each of these firms is financed entirely by shareholders' equity, then the rate of return on shareholders' equity of firm i, $dS_i(t) / S_i(t)$, equals the proportional change in the value of the firm's physical assets (capital), $d\eta_i(t) / \eta_i(t)$. Here, $dS_i(t) / S_i(t) = d\eta_i(t) / \eta_i(t)$ equals the instantaneous dividend yield where dividends come in the form of a physical capital-consumption good.

Like the Lucas endowment economy, we can think of the CIR production economy as arising from a set of production processes that pay physical dividends. The difference is that the Lucas economy's dividend is in the form of a consumption-only good, whereas the CIR economy's dividend is a capital-consumption good that can be physically reinvested to expand the capacities of the productive output processes. The CIR representative individuals must decide how much of their wealth (the capital-consumption good) to consume versus save and, of the amount saved, how to allocate it between the n different technologies (or firms).

Because equations (13.28) and (13.29) model an economy's production possibilities as constant returns-to-scale technologies, the distributions of assets' rates of return available to investors are exogenous. In one sense, this situation is not different from our earlier modeling of an investor's optimal consumption and portfolio choices. However, CIR's specification allows one to solve for the equilibrium prices of securities other than those represented by the n risky technologies. This is done by imagining there to be other securities that have zero net supplies. For example, there may be no technology that produces an instantaneously risk-free return; that is, $\sigma_i \neq 0 \; \forall \; i$. However, one can solve for the equilibrium riskless borrowing or lending rate, call it $r(t)$, for which the representative individuals would be just indifferent between borrowing or lending. In other words, r would be the riskless rate such that individuals choose to invest zero amounts of the consumption good at this rate. Since all individuals are identical, this amounts to the riskless investment having a zero supply in the economy, so that r is really a "shadow" riskless rate. Yet, this rate would be consistent, in equilibrium, with the specification of the economy's other technologies.

Let us solve for this equilibrium riskless rate in the CIR economy. The individual's consumption and portfolio choice problem is similar to that in Chapter 12, (12.4), except that the individual's savings are now allocated, either directly or indirectly through firms, to the n technologies. An equilibrium is defined as a set of interest rate, consumption, and portfolio weight processes $\{r, C^*, \omega_1^*, \ldots, \omega_n^*\}$ such that the representative individual's first-order conditions hold and markets clear: $\sum_{i=1}^{n} \omega_i = 1$ and $\omega_i \geq 0$. Note that because $\sum_{i=1}^{n} \omega_i = 1$, this definition of equilibrium implies that riskless borrowing and lending at the equilibrium rate r has zero net supply. Further, since the capital-consumption good is being physically invested in the technological processes, the constraint against short-selling, $\omega_i \geq 0$, applies.

To solve for the representative individual's optimal consumption and portfolio weights, note that since in equilibrium the individual does not borrow or lend, the individual's situation is exactly as if a riskless asset did not exist. Hence, the individual's consumption and portfolio choice problem is the same one as in the previous chapter but where the process for wealth excludes a risk-free asset. Specifically, the individual solves

$$\max_{C_s, \{\omega_{i,s}\}, \forall s, i} E_t \left[\int_t^T U(C_s, s) \, ds + B(W_T, T) \right] \tag{13.30}$$

subject to

$$dW = \sum_{i=1}^{n} \omega_i W \mu_i \, dt - C_t \, dt + \sum_{i=1}^{n} \omega_i W \sigma_i \, dz_i \tag{13.31}$$

and also subject to the condition $\sum_{i=1}^{n} \omega_i = 1$ and the constraint that $\omega_i \geq 0$. The individual's first-order condition for consumption is the usual one:

$$0 = \frac{\partial U\left(C^*, t\right)}{\partial C} - \frac{\partial J\left(W, x, t\right)}{\partial W} \tag{13.32}$$

but the first-order conditions with respect to the portfolio weights are modified slightly. If we let λ be the Lagrange multiplier associated with the equality $\sum_{i=1}^{n} \omega_i = 1$, then the appropriate first-order conditions for the portfolio weights are

$$\Psi_i \equiv \frac{\partial J}{\partial W} \mu_i W + \frac{\partial^2 J}{\partial W^2} \sum_{j=1}^{n} \sigma_{ij} \omega_j^* W^2 + \frac{\partial^2 J}{\partial x_i \, \partial W} \sum_{j=1}^{k} \phi_{ij} W - \lambda \leq 0$$

$$0 = \Psi_i \omega_i^* \quad i = 1, \ldots, n \tag{13.33}$$

The Kuhn-Tucker conditions in (13.33) imply that if $\Psi_i < 0$, then $\omega_i^* = 0$, so that in this case the ith technology would not be employed. Assuming that the parameters in (13.28) and (13.29) are such that all technologies are employed, that is, $\Psi_i = 0$ $\forall i$, then the solution to the system of equations in (13.33) is

$$\omega_i^* = -\frac{J_W}{J_{WW} W} \sum_{j=1}^{n} v_{ij} \mu_j - \sum_{m=1}^{k} \sum_{j=1}^{n} \frac{J_{Wx_m}}{J_{WW} W} v_{ij} \phi_{jm} + \frac{\lambda}{J_{WW} W^2} \sum_{j=1}^{n} v_{ij} \tag{13.34}$$

for $i = 1, \ldots, n$. Using our previously defined matrix notation, (13.34) can be rewritten as

$$\boldsymbol{\omega}^* = \frac{A}{W} \boldsymbol{\Omega}^{-1} \boldsymbol{\mu} - \frac{A\lambda}{J_W W^2} \boldsymbol{\Omega}^{-1} \mathbf{e} + \sum_{j=1}^{k} \frac{H_j}{W} \boldsymbol{\Omega}^{-1} \boldsymbol{\phi}_j \tag{13.35}$$

where $A = -J_W/J_{WW}$, $H_{nj} = -J_{Wx_i}/J_{WW}$, and $\boldsymbol{\phi}_j = (\phi_{1j}, \ldots, \phi_{nj})'$. These portfolio weights can be interpreted as a linear combination of $k + 2$ portfolios. The first two portfolios are mean-variance efficient portfolios in a single-period, Markowitz portfolio selection model: $\boldsymbol{\Omega}^{-1} \boldsymbol{\mu}$ is the portfolio on the efficient frontier that is tangent to a line drawn from the origin (a zero interest rate) while $\boldsymbol{\Omega}^{-1} \mathbf{e}$ is the global minimum variance portfolio.[6] The last k portfolios, $\boldsymbol{\Omega}^{-1} \boldsymbol{\phi}_j$, $j = 1, \ldots, k$, are held to hedge against changes in the technological risks (investment opportunities). The proportions of these $k + 2$ portfolios chosen depend on the individual's utility. An exact solution is found in the usual manner of substituting (13.35) and (12.18) into the Bellman equation. For specific functional forms, a value for the indirect utility function, $J\left(W, x, t\right)$, can be derived. This,

---

6. Recall that a linear combination of any two portfolios on the mean-variance frontier can create any other portfolio on the frontier.

along with the restriction $\sum_{i=1}^{n} \omega_i = 1$, allows the specific optimal consumption and portfolio weights to be determined.

Since in the CIR economy the riskless asset is in zero net supply, we know that the portfolio weights in (13.35) must be those chosen by the representative individual even if offered the opportunity to borrow or lend at rate r. Recall from the previous chapter's equation (12.21) that these conditions, rewritten in matrix notation, are

$$\boldsymbol{\omega}^* = \frac{A}{W} \boldsymbol{\Omega}^{-1} (\boldsymbol{\mu} - r\mathbf{e}) + \sum_{j=1}^{k} \frac{H_j}{W} \boldsymbol{\Omega}^{-1} \boldsymbol{\phi}_j, \quad i = 1, \ldots, n \tag{13.36}$$

Since the individual takes prices and rates as given, the portfolio choices given by the first-order conditions in (13.36)—namely, the case when a riskless asset exists—must therefore be the same as (13.35). By inspection, the weights in (13.35) and (13.36) are identical when $r = \lambda / (J_W W)$. Hence, substituting for λ in terms of the optimal portfolio weights, we can write the equilibrium interest as[7]

$$r = \frac{\lambda}{W J_W} \tag{13.37}$$

$$= \boldsymbol{\omega}^{*\prime} \boldsymbol{\mu} - \frac{W}{A} \boldsymbol{\omega}^{*\prime} \boldsymbol{\Omega} \boldsymbol{\omega}^* + \sum_{j=1}^{k} \frac{H_j}{A} \boldsymbol{\omega}^{*\prime} \boldsymbol{\phi}_j$$

Note that equation (13.37) is the same as the previously derived relationship (13.10) except that (13.37) is extended to k state variables. Hence, Merton's ICAPM, as well as Breeden's CCAPM, hold for the CIR economy.

The CIR model also can be used to find the equilibrium shadow prices of other securities that are assumed to have zero net supplies. Such "contingent claims" could include securities such as longer maturity bonds or options and futures. For example, suppose a zero-net-supply contingent claim has a payoff whose value could depend on wealth, time, and the state variables, $P(W, t, \{x_i\})$.[8] Itô's lemma implies that its price will follow a process of the form

$$dP = uP\,dt + P_W W \sum_{i=1}^{n} \omega_i^* \sigma_i dz_i + \sum_{i=1}^{k} P_{x_i} b_i d\zeta_i \tag{13.38}$$

---

7. To derive the second line in (13.37), it is easiest to write in matrix form the first-order condtions in (13.33) and assume these conditions all hold as equalities. Then solve for λ by pre-multiplying by $\boldsymbol{\omega}^{*\prime}$ and noting that $\boldsymbol{\omega}^{*\prime}\mathbf{e} = 1$.

8. A contingent claim whose payoff depends on the returns or prices of the technologies can be found by the Black-Scholes methodolgy described in Chapter 9.

where

$$uP = P_W \left(W\omega^{*\prime}\mu - C \right) + \sum_{i=1}^{k} P_{x_i} a_i + P_t + \frac{P_{WW} W^2}{2} \omega^{*\prime}\Omega\omega^*$$

$$+ \sum_{i=1}^{k} P_{Wx_i} W\omega^{*\prime}\phi_i + \frac{1}{2} \sum_{i=1}^{k} \sum_{j=1}^{k} P_{x_i x_j} b_{ij} \tag{13.39}$$

Using the Merton ICAPM result (13.9) extended to k state variables, the expected rate of return on the contingent claim must also satisfy[9]

$$u = r + \frac{W}{A} Cov\left(dP/P, dW/W \right) - \sum_{i=1}^{k} \frac{H_i}{A} Cov\left(dP/P, dx_i \right) \tag{13.40}$$

or

$$uP = rP + \frac{1}{A} Cov\left(dP, dW \right) - \sum_{i=1}^{k} \frac{H_i}{A} Cov\left(dP, dx_i \right)$$

$$= rP + \frac{1}{A} \left(P_W W^2 \omega^{*\prime}\Omega\omega^* + \sum_{i=1}^{k} P_{x_i} W\omega^{*\prime}\phi_i \right)$$

$$- \sum_{i=1}^{k} \frac{H_i}{A} \left(P_W W\omega^{*\prime}\phi_i + \sum_{j=1}^{k} P_{x_j} b_{ij} \right) \tag{13.41}$$

where in (13.40) we make use of the fact that the market portfolio equals the optimally invested wealth of the representative individual. Equating (13.39) and (13.41) and recalling the value of the equilibrium risk-free rate in (13.37), we obtain a partial differential equation for the contingent claim's value:[10]

$$0 = \frac{P_{WW} W^2}{2} \omega^{*\prime}\Omega\omega^* + \sum_{i=1}^{k} P_{Wx_i} W\omega^{*\prime}\phi_i + \frac{1}{2} \sum_{i=1}^{k} \sum_{j=1}^{k} P_{x_i x_j} b_{ij} + P_t +$$

$$P_W \left(rW - C \right) + \sum_{i=1}^{k} P_{x_i} \left[a_i - \frac{W}{A} \omega^{*\prime}\phi_i + \sum_{j=1}^{k} \frac{H_j b_{ij}}{A} \right] - rP \tag{13.42}$$

---

9. Condition (13.9) can be derived for the case of a contingent claim by using the fact that the contingent claim's weight in the market portfolio is zero.

10. It is straightforward to derive the valuation equation for a contingent claim that pays a continuous dividend at rate $\delta\left(W, x, t \right) dt$. In this case, the additional term $\delta\left(W, x, t \right)$ appears on the right-hand side of equation (13.42).

The next section illustrates how (13.37) and (13.42) can be used to find the risk-free rate and particular contingent claims for a specific case of a CIR economy.

13.3.1 An Example Using Log Utility

The example in this section is based on (Cox, Ingersoll, and Ross 1985b). It assumes that the representative individual's utility and bequest functions are logarithmic and of the form $U(C_s, s) = e^{-\rho s} \ln (C_s)$ and $B(W_T, T) = e^{-\rho T} \ln (W_T)$. For this specification, we showed in the previous chapter that the indirect utility function was separable and equaled $J(W, x, t) = d(t) e^{-\rho t} \ln (W_t) + F(x, t)$ where $d(t) = \frac{1}{\rho} \left[1 - (1 - \rho) e^{-\rho(T-t)} \right]$, so that optimal consumption satisfies equation (12.50) and the optimal portfolio proportions equal (12.44). Since $J_{Wx_i} = 0$, $H_i = 0$, and $A = W$, the portfolio proportions in (13.35) simplify to

$$\boldsymbol{\omega}^* = \boldsymbol{\Omega}^{-1} (\boldsymbol{\mu} - r\mathbf{e}) \tag{13.43}$$

where we have used the result that $r = \lambda / (J_W W)$. Using the market clearing condition $\mathbf{e}' \boldsymbol{\omega}^* = 1$, we can solve for the equilibrium risk-free rate:

$$r = \frac{\mathbf{e}' \boldsymbol{\Omega}^{-1} \boldsymbol{\mu} - 1}{\mathbf{e}' \boldsymbol{\Omega}^{-1} \mathbf{e}} \tag{13.44}$$

Substituting (13.44) into (13.43), we see that the optimal portfolio weights are

$$\boldsymbol{\omega}^* = \boldsymbol{\Omega}^{-1} \left[\boldsymbol{\mu} - \left(\frac{\mathbf{e}' \boldsymbol{\Omega}^{-1} \boldsymbol{\mu} - 1}{\mathbf{c}' \boldsymbol{\Omega}^{-1} \mathbf{e}} \right) \mathbf{e} \right] \tag{13.45}$$

Let us next assume that a single state variable, $x(t)$, affects all production processes in the following manner:

$$d\eta_i / \eta_i = \widehat{\mu}_i x \, dt + \widehat{\sigma}_i \sqrt{x} dz_i, \ i = 1, \ldots, n \tag{13.46}$$

where $\widehat{\mu}_i$ and $\widehat{\sigma}_i$ are assumed to be constants and the state variable follows the *square root process*[11]

$$dx = (a_0 + a_1 x) \, dt + b_0 \sqrt{x} d\zeta \tag{13.47}$$

where $dz_i d\zeta = \rho_i dt$. Note that this specification implies that the means and variances of the technologies' rates of return are proportional to the state variable. If $a_0 > 0$ and $a_1 < 0$, x is a nonnegative, mean-reverting random variable. A rise in x raises all technologies' expected rates of return but also increases their variances.

---

11. This process is a specific case of the more general *constant elasticity of variance process* given by $dx = (a_0 + a_1 x) \, dt + b_0 x^c dq$ where $c \in [0, 1]$.

We can write the technologies' $n \times 1$ vector of expected rates of return as $\mu = \widehat{\mu} x$ and their $n \times n$ matrix of rate of return covariances as $\Omega = \widehat{\Omega} x$. Using these distributional assumptions in (13.44), we find that the equilibrium interest rate is proportional to the state variable:

$$r = \frac{e' \widehat{\Omega}^{-1} \widehat{\mu} - 1}{e' \widehat{\Omega}^{-1} e} x = \alpha x \qquad (13.48)$$

where $\alpha \equiv \left(e' \widehat{\Omega}^{-1} \widehat{\mu} - 1 \right) / e' \widehat{\Omega}^{-1} e$ is a constant. This implies that the risk-free rate follows a square root process of the form

$$dr = \alpha\, dx = \kappa \left(\bar{r} - r \right) dt + \sigma \sqrt{r}\, d\zeta \qquad (13.49)$$

where $\kappa \equiv -a_1 > 0$, $\bar{r} \equiv -\alpha a_0 / a_1 > 0$, and $\sigma \equiv b_0 \sqrt{\alpha}$. CIR (Cox, Ingersoll, and Ross 1985b) state that when the parameters satisfy $2\kappa \bar{r} \geq \sigma^2$, then if $r(t)$ is currently positive, it will remain positive at all future dates $T \geq t$. This is an attractive feature if the model is used to characterize a nominal interest rate.[12]

Next, let us consider how to value contingent claims based on this example's assumptions. Specifically, let us consider the price of a default-free discount bond that pays one unit of the consumption good when it matures at date $T \geq t$. Since this bond's payoff is independent of wealth, and since logarithmic utility implies that the equilibrium interest rate and optimal portfolio proportions are independent of wealth, the price of this bond will also be independent of wealth. Hence, the derivatives P_W, P_{WW}, and P_{Wx} in the valuation equation (13.42) will all be zero. Moreover, since $r = \alpha x$, it will be insightful to think of r as the state variable rather than x, so that the date t bond price can be written as $P(r, t, T)$. With these changes, the valuation equation (13.42) becomes[13]

$$\frac{\sigma^2 r}{2} P_{rr} + \left[\kappa \left(\bar{r} - r \right) - \psi r \right] P_r - rP + P_t = 0 \qquad (13.50)$$

where ψ is a constant equal to $\widehat{\omega}' \widehat{\phi}$. $\widehat{\omega}$ equals the right-hand side of equation (13.45) but with μ replaced by $\widehat{\mu}$ and Ω replaced by $\widehat{\Omega}$, while $\widehat{\phi}$ is an $n \times 1$ vector of constants whose ith element is $\sigma \widehat{\sigma}_i \rho_i$. $\psi r = \omega^{*'} \phi$ is the covariance of interest rate changes with the proportional change in optimally invested wealth. In other words, it is the interest rate's "beta" (covariance with the market portfolio's return).

---

12. In contrast, recall from Chapter 9 that the Vasicek model (Vasicek 1977) assumes that the risk-free rate follows an Ornstein-Uhlenbeck process, which implies that r has a discrete-time normal distribution. Hence, the Vasicek model may be preferred for modeling a real interest rate since r can become negative. See (Pennacchi 1991) for such an application. It can be shown that the discrete-time distribution for the CIR interest rate process in (13.49) is a noncentral chi-square.

13. Recall that logarithmic utility implies $A = W$ and $H = 0$.

The partial differential equation (13.50), when solved subject to the boundary condition $P(r, T, T) = 1$, leads to the bond pricing formula

$$P(r, t, T) = A(\tau) e^{-B(\tau)r} \tag{13.51}$$

where $\tau = T - t$,

$$A(\tau) \equiv \left[\frac{2\theta e^{(\theta + \kappa + \psi)\frac{\tau}{2}}}{(\theta + \kappa + \psi)(e^{\theta\tau} - 1) + 2\theta} \right]^{2\kappa\bar{r}/\sigma^2} \tag{13.52}$$

$$B(\tau) \equiv \frac{2(e^{\theta\tau} - 1)}{(\theta + \kappa + \psi)(e^{\theta\tau} - 1) + 2\theta} \tag{13.53}$$

and $\theta \equiv \sqrt{(\kappa + \psi)^2 + 2\sigma^2}$. This CIR bond price can be contrasted with that of the Vasicek model derived in Chapter 9, equation (9.39). They are similar in having the same structure given in equation (13.51) but with different values for $A(\tau)$ and $B(\tau)$. Hence, the discount bond yield, $Y(r, \tau) \equiv -\ln[P(r, t, T)]/\tau = -\ln[A(\tau)]/\tau + B(\tau)r/\tau$, is linear in the state variable for both models.[14] But the two models differ in a number of ways. Recall that Vasicek directly assumed that the short rate, r, followed an Ornstein-Uhlenbeck process and derived the result that, in the absence of arbitrage, the market price of interest rate risk must be the same for bonds of all maturities. Using the notation of $\mu_p(r, \tau)$ and $\sigma_p(\tau)$ to be the mean and standard deviation of the return on a bond with τ periods to maturity, it was assumed that the market price of interest rate risk, $\left[\mu_p(r, \tau) - r\right]/\sigma_p(\tau)$, was a constant.

In contrast, the CIR model derived an equilibrium square root process for r based on assumptions of economic fundamentals (tastes and technologies). Moreover, the derivation of bond prices did not focus on the absence of arbitrage but rather the (zero-net-supply) market clearing conditions consistent with individuals' consumption and portfolio choices. Moreover, unlike the Vasicek model, the CIR derivation required no explicit assumption regarding the form of the market price of interest rate risk. Rather, this market price of risk was endogenous to the model's other assumptions regarding preferences and technologies. Let's solve for the market risk premium implicit in CIR bond prices.

Note that Itô's lemma says that the bond price follows the process

$$dP = P_r dr + \frac{1}{2} P_{rr} \sigma^2 r dt + P_t dt \tag{13.54}$$

$$= \left(\frac{1}{2} P_{rr} \sigma^2 r + P_r [\kappa(\bar{r} - r)] + P_t \right) dt + P_r \sigma \sqrt{r} d\zeta$$

---

14. Models having bond yields that are linear in the state variables are referred to as *affine* models of the term structure. Such models will be discussed further in Chapter 17.

In addition, rearranging (13.50) implies that $\frac{1}{2}P_{rr}\sigma^2 r + P_r\left[\kappa\left(\bar{r}-r\right)\right] + P_t = rP + \psi r P_r$. Substituting this into (13.54), it can be rewritten as

$$dP/P = r\left(1 + \psi\frac{P_r}{P}\right)dt + \frac{P_r}{P}\sigma\sqrt{r}d\zeta \tag{13.55}$$

$$= r\left(1 - \psi B\left(\tau\right)\right)dt - B\left(\tau\right)\sigma\sqrt{r}d\zeta$$

where we have used equation (13.51)'s result that $P_r/P = -B\left(\tau\right)$ in the second line of (13.55). Hence, we can write

$$\frac{\mu_p\left(r,\tau\right) - r}{\sigma_p\left(r,\tau\right)} = \frac{-\psi r B\left(\tau\right)}{\sigma\sqrt{r}B\left(\tau\right)} = -\frac{\psi\sqrt{r}}{\sigma} \tag{13.56}$$

so that the market price of interest rate risk is not constant, as in the Vasicek model, but is proportional to the square root of the interest rate. When $\psi < 0$, which occurs when the interest rate is negatively correlated with the return on the market portfolio (and bond prices are positively correlated with the market portfolio), bonds will carry a positive risk premium. CIR (Cox, Ingersoll, and Ross 1985b) argue that their equilibrium approach to deriving a market risk premium avoids problems that can occur when, following the no-arbitrage approach, an arbitrary form for a market risk premium is assumed. They show that some functional forms for market risk premia are inconsistent with the no-arbitrage assumption.

13.4   Summary

In a multiperiod, continuous-time environment, the Merton ICAPM shows that when investment opportunities are constant, the expected returns on assets satisfy the single-period CAPM relationship. For the more interesting case of changing investment opportunities, the CAPM relationship is generalized to include risk premia reflecting an asset's covariances with asset portfolios that best hedge against changes in investment opportunities. However, this multibeta relationship can be simplified to express an asset's expected return in terms of a single consumption beta.

The Cox, Ingersoll, and Ross model of a production economy helps to justify the ICAPM results by showing that they are consistent with a model that starts from more primitive assumptions regarding the nature of an economy's asset supplies. It also can be used to derive the economy's equilibrium risk-free interest rate and the shadow prices of contingent claims that are assumed to be in zero net supply. One important application of the model is a derivation of the equilibrium term structure of interest rates.

The next chapter builds on our results to this point by generalizing individuals' lifetime utility functions. No longer will we assume that utility is time separable.

Allowing for time-inseparable utility can lead to different equilibrium relation-ships between asset returns that can better describe empirical findings.

13.5 Exercises

1. Consider a CIR economy similar to the log utility example given in this chap-ter. However, instead of the productive technologies following the processes of equation (13.46), assume that they satisfy

$$dn_i/\eta_i = \widehat{\mu}_i x \, dt + \sigma_i dz_i, \, i = 1, \ldots, n$$

In addition, rather than assume that the state variable follows the process (13.47), suppose that it is given by

$$dx = (a_0 + a_1 x) \, dt + b_0 d\varsigma$$

where $dz_i d\varsigma = \rho_i dt$. It is assumed that $a_0 > 0$ and $a_1 < 0$.

a. Solve for the equilibrium risk-free interest rate, r, and the process it fol-lows, dr. What parametric assumptions are needed for the unconditional mean of r to be positive?

b. Derive the optimal (market) portfolio weights for this economy, ω^*. How does ω^* vary with r?

c. Derive the partial differential equation for $P(r, t, T)$, the date t price of a default-free discount bond that matures at date T. Does this equation look familiar?

2. Consider the intertemporal consumption–portfolio choice model and the Intertemporal Capital Asset Pricing Model of Merton and its general equi-librium specification by Cox, Ingersoll, and Ross.

a. What assumptions are needed for the single-period Sharpe-Treyner-Linter-Mossin CAPM results to hold in this multiperiod environment where consumption and portfolio choices are made continuously?

b. Briefly discuss the portfolio choice implications of a situation in which the instantaneous real interest rate, $r(t)$, is stochastic, following a mean-reverting process such as the square root process of Cox, Ingersoll, and Ross or the Ornstein-Uhlenbeck process of Vasicek. Specifically, suppose that individuals can hold the instantaneous-maturity risk-free asset, a long-maturity default-free bond, and equities (stocks) and that a rise in $r(t)$ raises all assets' expected rates of return. How would the results differ from the single-period Markowitz portfolio demands? In explaining your answer, discuss how the results are sensitive to utility displaying greater or lesser risk aversion compared to log utility.

3. Consider a continuous-time version of a Lucas endowment economy. Let C_t be the aggregate dividends paid at date t, which equals aggregate consumption at date t. It is assumed to follow the lognormal process

$$dC/C = \mu_c dt + \sigma_c dz_c \tag{1}$$

where μ_c and σ_c are constants. The economy is populated with representative individuals whose lifetime utility is of the form

$$E_t \left[\int_t^\infty e^{-\rho s} \frac{C_s^\gamma}{\gamma} ds \right] \tag{2}$$

a. Solve for the process followed by the continuous-time pricing kernel, M_t. In particular, relate the equilibrium instantaneous risk-free interest rate and the market price of risk to the parameters in equation (1) and utility function (2) above.

b. Suppose that a particular risky asset's price follows the process

$$dS/S = \mu_s dt + \sigma_s dz_s$$

where $dz_s dz_c = \rho_{sc} dt$. Derive a value for μ_s using the pricing kernel process.

c. From the previous results, show that Merton's Intertemporal Capital Asset Pricing Model (ICAPM) and Breeden's Consumption Capital Asset Pricing Model (CCAPM) hold between this particular risky asset and the market portfolio of all risky assets.

CHAPTER 14

Time-Inseparable Utility

In previous chapters, individuals' multiperiod utility functions were assumed to be time separable. In a continuous-time context, time-separable expected lifetime utility was specified as

$$E_t \left[\int_t^T U\left(C_s, s\right) \, ds \right] \qquad (14.1)$$

where $U\left(C_s, s\right)$ is commonly taken to be of the form

$$U\left(C_s, s\right) = e^{-\rho(s-t)} u\left(C_s\right) \qquad (14.2)$$

so that utility at date s depends only on consumption at date s and not consumption at previous or future dates. However, as was noted earlier, there is substantial evidence that standard time-separable utility appears inconsistent with the empirical time series properties of U.S. consumption data and the average returns on risky assets (common stocks) and risk-free investments. These empirical contradictions, referred to as the equity premium puzzle and the risk-free interest rate puzzle, have led researchers to explore lifetime utility functions that differ from function (14.1) by permitting more general time-inseparable forms.

In this chapter we consider two types of lifetime utility functions that are not time separable. The first type is a class of lifetime utility functions for which *past* consumption plays a role in determining current utility. These utility functions display *habit persistence*. We summarize two models of this type, one by George Constantinides (Constantinides 1990) and the other by John Campbell and John Cochrane (Campbell and Cochrane 1999). In addition to modeling habit persistence differently, these models provide interesting contrasts in terms of their assumptions regarding the economy's aggregate supplies of assets and the techniques we can use to solve them. Constantinides' *internal* habit persistence model is a simple example of a Cox, Ingersoll, and Ross production economy (Cox, Ingersoll, and Ross 1985a) where asset supplies are perfectly elastic. It is solved using a Bellman equation approach. Campbell and Cochrane present a model of *external* habit persistence or "Keeping Up with the Joneses" preferences. Their model assumes a Lucas endowment economy (Lucas 1978) where asset supplies are perfectly inelastic. Its solution is based on the economy's stochastic discount factor.

The second type of time-inseparable utility that we discuss is called *recursive utility*. From one perspective, recursive utility is the opposite of habit persistence because recursive utility functions make current utility depend on expected values of *future* utility, which in turn depends on *future* consumption. We illustrate this type of utility by considering the general equilibrium of an economy where representative consumer-investors have recursive utility. The specific model that we analyze is a continuous-time version of a discrete-time model by Maurice Obstfeld (Obstfeld 1994). A useful aspect of this model is that it enables us to easily distinguish between an individual's coefficient of relative risk aversion and his elasticity of intertemporal substitution.

By generalizing utility functions to permit habit persistence or to be recursive, we hope to provide better models of individuals' actual preferences and their resulting consumption and portfolio choice decisions. In this way, greater insights into the nature of equilibrium asset returns may be possible. Specifically, we can analyze these models in terms of their ability to resolve various asset pricing "puzzles," such as the equity premium puzzle and the risk-free rate puzzle that arise when utility is time separable. Let us first investigate how utility can be extended from the standard time-separable, constant relative-risk-aversion case to display habit persistence. We then follow this with an examination of recursive utility.

14.1   Constantinides' Internal Habit Model

The notion of habit persistence can be traced to the writings of Alfred Marshall (Marshall 1920), James Duesenberry (Duesenberry 1949), and more recently, Harl Ryder and Geoffrey Heal (Ryder and Heal 1973). It is based on the idea that an individual's choice of consumption affects not only utility today but directly affects utility in the near future because the individual becomes accustomed to today's consumption standard.

Let us illustrate this idea by presenting Constantinides' internal habit formation model, which derives a representative individual's consumption and portfolio choices in a simple production economy. It is based on the following assumptions.

14.1.1   Assumptions

Technology

A single capital-consumption good can be invested in up to two different technologies. The first is a risk-free technology whose output, B_t, follows the process

$$dB/B = r \, dt \tag{14.3}$$

The second is a risky technology whose output, η_t, follows the process

$$d\eta/\eta = \mu \, dt + \sigma \, dz \tag{14.4}$$

Note that the specification of technologies fixes the expected rates of return and variances of the safe and risky investments.[1] In this setting, individuals' asset demands determine equilibrium quantities of the assets supplied rather than asset prices. Since r, μ, and σ are assumed to be constants, there is a constant investment opportunity set.

Preferences

Representative agents maximize expected utility of consumption, C_t, of the form

$$E_0 \left[\int_0^\infty e^{-\rho t} u\left(\widehat{C}_t\right) \, dt \right] \tag{14.5}$$

where $u\left(\widehat{C}_t\right) = \widehat{C}_t^\gamma / \gamma$, $\gamma < 1$, $\widehat{C}_t = C_t - bx_t$, and

$$x_t \equiv e^{-at} x_0 + \int_0^t e^{-a(t-s)} C_s \, ds \tag{14.6}$$

Note that if $b = 0$, utility is of the standard time-separable form and displays constant relative risk aversion with a coefficient of relative risk aversion equal to $(1 - \gamma)$. The variable x_t is an exponentially weighted sum of past consumption, so that when $b > 0$, the quantity bx_t can be interpreted as a "subsistence," or "habit," level of consumption and $\widehat{C}_t = C_t - bx_t$ can be interpreted as "surplus" consumption. In this case, the specification in (14.5) assumes that the individual's utility depends on only the level of consumption in excess of the habit level. This models the notion that an individual becomes accustomed to a standard of living (habit), and current utility derives from only the part of consumption that is in excess of

---

1. In this model, the existence of a risk-free technology determines the risk-free interest rate. This differs from our earlier presentation of the Cox, Ingersoll, and Ross model (Cox, Ingersoll, and Ross 1985a) where risk-free borrowing and lending is assumed to be in zero net supply and the interest rate is an equilibrium rate determined by risky investment opportunities and individuals' preferences.

this standard. Alternatively, if $b < 0$ so that past consumption adds to rather than subtracts from current utility, then the model can be interpreted as one displaying *durability* in consumption rather than habit persistence.[2] Empirical evidence comparing habit formation versus durability in consumption is mixed.[3] Research that models utility as depending on the consumptions of multiple goods, where some goods display habit persistence and others display durability in consumption, may be a better approach to explaining asset returns.[4] However, for simplicity, here we assume the single-good, $b > 0$ case introduced by Constantinides.

The Constantinides model of habit persistence makes current utility depend on a linear combination of not only current consumption but past consumption through the variable x_t. Hence, it is not time separable. An increase in consumption at date t decreases current marginal utility, but it also increases the marginal utility of consumption at future dates because it raises the level of subsistence consumption. Of course, there are more general ways of modeling habit persistence, for example, $u(C_t, w_t)$ where w_t is any function of past consumption levels.[5] However, the linear habit persistence specification in (14.5) and (14.6) is attractive due to its analytical tractability.

Additional Parametric Assumptions

Let W_0 be the initial wealth of the representative individual. The following parametric assumptions are made to have a well-specified consumption and portfolio choice problem.

$$W_0 > \frac{bx_0}{r + a - b} > 0 \tag{14.7}$$

$$r + a > b > 0 \tag{14.8}$$

$$\rho - \gamma r - \frac{\gamma(\mu - r)^2}{2(1 - \gamma)\sigma^2} > 0 \tag{14.9}$$

$$0 \leq m \equiv \frac{\mu - r}{(1 - \gamma)\sigma^2} \leq 1 \tag{14.10}$$

---

2. Ayman Hindy and Chi-Fu Huang (Hindy and Huang 1993) consider such a model.

3. Empirical asset pricing tests by Wayne Ferson and George Constantinides (Ferson and Constantinides 1991) that used seasonally adjusted aggregate consumption data provided more support for habit persistence relative to consumption durability. In contrast, John Heaton (Heaton 1995) found more support for durability after adjusting for time-averaged data and seasonality.

4. Multiple-good models displaying durability and habit persistence and durability have been developed by Jerome Detemple, Christos Giannikos, and Zhihong Shi (Detemple and Giannikos 1996); (Giannikos and Shi 2006).

5. Jerome Detemple and Fernando Zapatero (Detemple and Zapatero 1991) consider a model that displays nonlinear habit persistence.

The reasons for making these parametric assumptions are the following. Note that C_t needs to be greater than bx_t for the individual to avoid infinite marginal utility.[6] Conditions (14.7) and (14.8) ensure that an admissible (feasible) consumption and portfolio choice strategy exists that enables $C_t > bx_t$.[7] To see this, note that the dynamics for the individual's wealth are given by

$$dW = \{[(\mu - r)\omega_t + r]W - C_t\} \, dt + \sigma \omega_t W \, dz \tag{14.11}$$

where ω_t, $0 \leq \omega_t \leq 1$ is the proportion of wealth that the individual invests in the risky technology. Now if $\omega_t = 0$ for all t, that is, one invests only in the riskless technology, and consumption equals a fixed proportion of wealth, $C_t = (r + a - b)W_t$, then

$$dW = \{rW - (r + a - b)W\} \, dt = (b - a) \, Wdt \tag{14.12}$$

which is a first-order differential equation in W having the initial condition that it equal W_0 at $t = 0$. Its solution is

$$W_t = W_0 e^{(b-a)t} > 0 \tag{14.13}$$

so that wealth always stays positive. This implies $C_t = (r + a - b) \, W_0 \, e^{(b-a)t} > 0$ and

$$C_t - bx_t$$

$$= (r + a - b) W_0 e^{(b-a)t} - b \left[e^{-at}x_0 + \int_0^t e^{-a(t-s)}(r + a - b) \, W_0 \, e^{(b-a)s} \, ds \right]$$

$$= (r + a - b) \, W_0 \, e^{(b-a)t} - \left[e^{-at}bx_0 + b(r + a - b)W_0 e^{-at} \int_0^t e^{bs} \, ds \right]$$

$$= (r + a - b) \, W_0 \, e^{(b-a)t} - \left[e^{-at}bx_0 + (r + a - b)W_0 e^{-at}(e^{bt} - 1) \right]$$

$$= e^{-at} \left[(r + a - b) W_0 - bx_0 \right] \tag{14.14}$$

which is greater than zero by assumption (14.7).

Condition (14.9) is a transversality condition. It ensures that if the individual follows an optimal policy (which will be derived next), the expected utility of

---

6. Note that $\lim_{C_t \to bx_t} (C_t - bx_t)^{-(1-\gamma)} = \infty$.

7. The ability to maintain $C_t > bx_t$ is possible when the underlying economy is assumed to be a production economy because individuals have the freedom of determining the aggregate level of consumption versus savings. This is not possible in an endowment economy where the path of C_t and, therefore, its exponentially weighted average, x_t, is assumed to be an exogenous stochastic process. For many random processes, there will be a positive probability that $C_t < bx_t$. Based on this observation, David Chapman (Chapman 1998) argues that many models that assume a linear habit persistence are incompatible with an endowment economy equilibrium.

consumption over an infinite horizon is finite. As will be seen, condition (14.10) ensures that the individual chooses to invest a nonnegative amount of wealth in the risky and risk-free technologies, since short-selling physical investments is infeasible. Recall from Chapter 12, equation (12.35), that m is the optimal choice of the risky-asset portfolio weight for the time-separable, constant relative-risk-aversion case.

14.1.2   Consumption and Portfolio Choices

The solution technique presented here uses a dynamic programming approach similar to that of (Sundaresan 1989) and our previous derivation of consumption and portfolio choices under time-separable utility.[8] The individual's maximization problem is

$$\max_{\{C_s,\, \omega_s\}} E_t \left[\int_t^\infty e^{-\rho s} \frac{[C_s - bx_s]^\gamma}{\gamma}\, ds \right] \equiv e^{-\rho t} J(W_t,\, x_t) \tag{14.15}$$

subject to the intertemporal budget constraint given by equation (14.11). Given the assumption of an infinite horizon, we can simplify the analysis by separating out the factor of the indirect utility function that depends on calendar time, t; that is, $\widehat{J}(W_t, x_t, t) = e^{-\rho t} J(W_t, x_t)$. The "discounted" indirect utility function depends on two state variables: wealth, W_t, and the state variable x_t, the current habit level of consumption. Since there are no changes in investment opportunities (μ, σ, and r are all constant), there are no other relevant state variables. Similar to wealth, x_t is not exogenous but depends on past consumption. We can work out its dynamics by taking the derivative of equation (14.6):

$$dx/dt = -ae^{-at}x_0 + C_t - a \int_0^t e^{-a(t-s)} C_s\, ds, \tag{14.16}$$

or

$$dx = \left(C_t - ax_t \right) dt \tag{14.17}$$

---

8. Interestingly, Mark Schroder and Costis Skiadas (Schroder and Skiadas 2002) show that consumption–portfolio choice models where an individual displays linear habit formation can be transformed into a consumption–portfolio model where the individual does not exhibit habit formation. This can often simplify solving such problems. Further, known solutions to time-separable or recursive utility consumption–portfolio choice problems can be transformed to obtain novel solutions that also display linear habit formation.

Thus, changes in x_t are instantaneously deterministic. The Bellman equation is then

$$0 = \max_{\{C_t, \omega_t\}} \{U(C_t, x_t, t) + L[e^{-\rho t}J]\}$$

$$= \max_{\{C_t, \omega_t\}} \{e^{-\rho t}\gamma^{-1}(C_t - bx_t)^{\gamma} + e^{-\rho t}J_W[((\mu - r)\omega_t + r)W - C_t]$$

$$+ \frac{1}{2}e^{-\rho t}J_{WW}\sigma^2\omega_t^2 W^2 + e^{-\rho t}J_x\left(C_t - ax_t\right) - \rho e^{-\rho t}J\} \tag{14.18}$$

The first-order conditions with respect to C_t and ω_t are

$$(C_t - bx_t)^{\gamma-1} = J_W - J_x, \quad \text{or}$$

$$C_t = bx_t + [J_W - J_x]^{\frac{1}{\gamma-1}} \tag{14.19}$$

and

$$(\mu - r)WJ_W + \omega_t\sigma^2 W^2 J_{WW} = 0, \quad \text{or}$$

$$\omega_t = -\frac{J_W}{J_{WW}W}\frac{\mu - r}{\sigma^2} \tag{14.20}$$

Note that the additional term $-J_x$ in (14.19) reflects the fact that an increase in current consumption has the negative effect of raising the level of subsistence consumption, which decreases future utility. The form of (14.20), which determines the portfolio weight of the risky asset, bears the same relationship to indirect utility as in the time-separable case.

Substituting (14.19) and (14.20) back into (14.18), we obtain the equilibrium partial differential equation:

$$\frac{1-\gamma}{\gamma}[J_W - J_x]^{\frac{\gamma}{1-\gamma}} - \frac{J_W^2}{J_{WW}}\frac{(\mu - r)^2}{2\sigma^2} + (rW - bx)J_W + (b - a)xJ_x - \rho J = 0 \tag{14.21}$$

From our previous discussion of the time-separable, constant relative-risk-aversion case ($a = b = x = 0$), when the horizon is infinite, we saw from (12.33) that a solution for J is of the form $J(W) = kW^{\gamma}$. For this previous case, $u = C^{\gamma}/\gamma$, $u_c = J_W$, and optimal consumption was a constant proportion of wealth:

$$C^* = (\gamma k)^{\frac{1}{(\gamma-1)}}W = W\left[\rho - r\gamma - \frac{1}{2}(\frac{\gamma}{1-\gamma})\frac{(\mu - r)^2}{\sigma^2}\right] / (1 - \gamma) \tag{14.22}$$

and

$$\omega^* = m \tag{14.23}$$

where m is defined in condition (14.10).

These results for the time-separable case suggest that the derived utility-of-wealth function for the time-inseparable case might have the form

$$J(W, x) = k_0[W + k_1 x]^\gamma \tag{14.24}$$

Making this guess, substituting it into (14.21), and setting the coefficients on x and W equal to zero, we find

$$k_0 = \frac{(r + a - b)h^{\gamma - 1}}{(r + a)\gamma} \tag{14.25}$$

where

$$h \equiv \frac{r + a - b}{(r + a)(1 - \gamma)}\left[\rho - \gamma r - \frac{\gamma(\mu - r)^2}{2(1 - \gamma)\sigma^2}\right] > 0 \tag{14.26}$$

and

$$k_1 = -\frac{b}{r + a - b} < 0 \tag{14.27}$$

Using equations (14.19) and (14.20), this implies

$$C_t^* = bx_t + h\left[W_t - \frac{bx_t}{r + a - b}\right] \tag{14.28}$$

and

$$\omega_t^* = m\left[1 - \frac{bx_t/W_t}{r + a - b}\right] \tag{14.29}$$

Interestingly, since $r + a > b$, by assumption, the individual always demands less of the risky asset compared to the case of no habit persistence. Thus we would expect lower volatility of wealth over time.

In order to study the dynamics of C_t^*, consider the change in the term $\left[W_t - \frac{bx_t}{r+a-b}\right]$. Recall that the dynamics of W_t and x_t are given in equations (14.11) and (14.17), respectively. Using these, one finds

$$d\left[W_t - \frac{bx_t}{r + a - b}\right] = \left\{[(\mu - r)\omega_t^* + r]W_t - C_t^* - b\frac{C_t^* - ax_t}{r + a - b}\right\} dt + \sigma\omega_t^* W_t\, dz \tag{14.30}$$

Substituting in for ω_t^* and C_t^* from (14.28) and (14.29), one obtains

$$d\left[W_t - \frac{bx_t}{r + a - b}\right] = \left[W_t - \frac{bx_t}{r + a - b}\right][n\, dt + m\sigma\, dz] \tag{14.31}$$

where

$$n \equiv \frac{r - \rho}{1 - \gamma} + \frac{(\mu - r)^2 (2 - \gamma)}{2(1 - \gamma)^2 \sigma^2} \tag{14.32}$$

Using this and (14.28), one can show[9]

$$\frac{dC_t}{C_t} = \left[n + b - \frac{(n + a)bx_t}{C_t} \right] dt + \left(\frac{C_t - bx_t}{C_t} \right) m\sigma \, dz \tag{14.33}$$

For particular parametric conditions, the ratio $\frac{bx_t}{C_t - bx_t}$ has a stationary distribution.[10] However, one sees from the stochastic term in (14.33), $\left(\frac{C_t - bx_t}{C_t} \right) m\sigma \, dz$, that consumption growth is smoother than in the case of no habit persistence. For a given equity (risky-asset) risk premium, this can imply relatively smooth consumption paths, even though risk aversion, γ, may not be of a very high magnitude. To see this, recall from Chapter 4's inequality (4.32) that the Hansen-Jagannathan (H-J) bound for the time-separable case can be written as

$$\left| \frac{\mu - r}{\sigma} \right| \leq (1 - \gamma) \, \sigma_c \tag{14.34}$$

In the current case of habit persistence, from (14.33) we see that the instantaneous standard deviation of consumption growth is

$$\sigma_{c,t} = \left(\frac{C_t - bx_t}{C_t} \right) m\sigma \tag{14.35}$$

$$= \left(\frac{\widehat{C}_t}{C_t} \right) \left[\frac{\mu - r}{(1 - \gamma) \, \sigma^2} \right] \sigma$$

where, recall, that $\widehat{C}_t \equiv C_t - bx_t$ is defined as surplus consumption. If we define $S_t \equiv \widehat{C}_t / C_t$ as the *surplus consumption ratio*, we can rearrange equation (14.35) to obtain

$$\frac{\mu - r}{\sigma} = \frac{(1 - \gamma) \, \sigma_{c,t}}{S_t} \tag{14.36}$$

Since $S_t \equiv \frac{C_t - bx_t}{C_t}$ is less than 1, we see by comparing (14.36) to (14.34) that habit persistence may help reconcile the empirical violation of the H-J bound. With habit persistence, the lower demand for the risky asset, relative to the time-separable case, can result in a higher equilibrium excess return on the risky

---

9. See Appendix A in (Constantinides 1990).
10. See Theorem 2 in (Constantinides 1990).

asset and, hence, may aid in explaining the "puzzle" of a large equity premium. However, empirical work by Wayne Ferson and George Constantinides (Ferson and Constantinides 1991) that tests linear models of habit persistence suggests that these models cannot produce an equity risk premium as large as that found in historical equity returns.

Let us next turn to another approach to modeling habit persistence where an individual's habit level depends on the behavior of other individuals and, hence, is referred to as an *external habit*.

14.2 Campbell and Cochrane's External Habit Model

The Campbell-Cochrane external habit persistence model is based on the following assumptions.

14.2.1 Assumptions

Technology

Campbell and Cochrane consider a discrete-time endowment economy. Date t aggregate consumption, which also equals aggregate output, is denoted C_t, and it is assumed to follow an independent and identically distributed lognormal process:

$$\ln(C_{t+1}) - \ln(C_t) = g + v_{t+1} \tag{14.37}$$

where $v_{t+1} \sim N(0, \sigma^2)$.

Preferences

It is assumed that there is a representative individual who maximizes expected utility of the form

$$E_0\left[\sum_{t=0}^{\infty} \delta^t \frac{(C_t - X_t)^\gamma - 1}{\gamma}\right] \tag{14.38}$$

where $\gamma < 1$ and X_t denotes the "habit level." X_t is related to past consumption in the following nonlinear manner. Define the surplus consumption ratio, S_t, as

$$S_t \equiv \frac{C_t - X_t}{C_t} \tag{14.39}$$

Then the log of surplus consumption is assumed to follow the autoregressive process[11]

$$\ln\left(S_{t+1}\right) = (1 - \phi) \ln\left(\overline{S}\right) + \phi \ln\left(S_t\right) + \lambda\left(S_t\right) v_{t+1} \tag{14.40}$$

where $\lambda\left(S_t\right)$, the *sensitivity function*, measures the proportional change in the surplus consumption ratio resulting from a shock to output growth. It is assumed to take the form

$$\lambda\left(S_t\right) = \frac{1}{\overline{S}}\sqrt{1 - 2\left[\ln\left(S_t\right) - \ln\left(\overline{S}\right)\right]} - 1 \tag{14.41}$$

and

$$\overline{S} = \sigma\sqrt{\frac{1 - \gamma}{1 - \phi}} \tag{14.42}$$

The lifetime utility function in (14.38) looks somewhat similar to (14.5) of the Constantinides model. However, whereas Constantinides assumes that an individual's habit level depends on his or her own level of past consumption, Campbell and Cochrane assume that an individual's habit level depends on everyone else's current and past consumption. Thus, in the Constantinides model, the individual's choice of consumption, C_t, affects his future habit level, bx_s, for all $s > t$, and he takes this into account in terms of how it affects his expected utility when he chooses C_t. This type of habit formation is referred to as *internal* habit. In contrast, in the Campbell and Cochrane model, the individual's choice of consumption, C_t, does not affect her future habit level, X_s, for all $s \geq t$, so that she views X_t as exogenous when choosing C_t. This type of habit formation is referred to as *external* habit or "Keeping Up with the Joneses." [12] The external habit assumption simplifies the representative agent's decision making because habit becomes an exogenous state variable that depends on aggregate, not the individual's, consumption.

14.2.2 Equilibrium Asset Prices

Because habit is exogenous to the individual, the individual's marginal utility of consumption is

$$u_c\left(C_t, X_t\right) = \left(C_t - X_t\right)^{\gamma - 1} = C_t^{\gamma - 1} S_t^{\gamma - 1} \tag{14.43}$$

---

11. This process is locally equivalent to $\ln\left(X_t\right) = \phi \ln\left(X_{t-1}\right) + \lambda \ln\left(C_t\right)$ or $\ln\left(X_t\right) = \lambda \sum_{i=0}^{\infty} \phi^i \ln\left(C_{t-i}\right)$. The reason for the more complicated form in (14.40) is that it ensures that consumption is always above habit since S_t is always positive. This precludes infinite marginal utility.

12. A similar modeling was developed by Andrew Abel (Abel 1990).

and the representative agent's stochastic discount factor is

$$m_{t,t+1} = \delta \frac{u_c \left(C_{t+1}, X_{t+1} \right)}{u_c \left(C_t, X_t \right)} = \delta \left(\frac{C_{t+1}}{C_t} \right)^{\gamma-1} \left(\frac{S_{t+1}}{S_t} \right)^{\gamma-1} \tag{14.44}$$

If we define r as the continuously compounded, risk-free real interest rate between dates t and $t + 1$, then it equals

$$r = -\ln \left(E_t \left[m_{t,t+1} \right] \right) = -\ln \left(\delta E_t \left[e^{-(1-\gamma)\ln(C_{t+1}/C_t)-(1-\gamma)\ln(S_{t+1}/S_t)} \right] \right) \tag{14.45}$$

$$= -\ln \left(\delta e^{-(1-\gamma)E_t[\ln(C_{t+1}/C_t)]-(1-\gamma)E_t[\ln(S_{t+1}/S_t)]+\frac{1}{2}(1-\gamma)^2 Var_t[\ln(C_{t+1}/C_t)+\ln(S_{t+1}/S_t)]} \right)$$

$$= -\ln(\delta) + (1-\gamma)g + (1-\gamma)(1-\phi)\left(\ln \bar{S} - \ln S_t \right) - \frac{(1-\gamma)^2 \sigma^2}{2} \left[1 + \lambda \left(S_t \right) \right]^2$$

Substituting in for $\lambda \left(S_t \right)$ from (14.41), equation (14.45) becomes

$$r = -\ln(\delta) + (1-\gamma)g - \frac{1}{2}(1-\gamma)(1-\phi) \tag{14.46}$$

which, by construction, turns out to be constant over time. One can also derive a relationship for the date t price of the market portfolio of all assets, denoted P_t. Recall that since we have an endowment economy, aggregate consumption equals the economy's aggregate output, which equals the aggregate dividends paid by the market portfolio. Therefore,

$$P_t = E_t \left[m_{t,t+1} \left(C_{t+1} + P_{t+1} \right) \right] \tag{14.47}$$

or, equivalently, one can solve for the price-dividend ratio for the market portfolio:

$$\frac{P_t}{C_t} = E_t \left[m_{t,t+1} \frac{C_{t+1}}{C_t} \left(1 + \frac{P_{t+1}}{C_{t+1}} \right) \right] \tag{14.48}$$

$$= \delta E_t \left[\left(\frac{S_{t+1}}{S_t} \right)^{\gamma-1} \left(\frac{C_{t+1}}{C_t} \right)^{\gamma} \left(1 + \frac{P_{t+1}}{C_{t+1}} \right) \right]$$

As in the Lucas model, this stochastic difference equation can be solved forward to obtain

$$\frac{P_t}{C_t} = \delta E_t \left[\left(\frac{S_{t+1}}{S_t} \right)^{\gamma-1} \left(\frac{C_{t+1}}{C_t} \right)^{\gamma} \left(1 + \delta \left(\frac{S_{t+2}}{S_{t+1}} \right)^{\gamma-1} \left(\frac{C_{t+2}}{C_{t+1}} \right)^{\gamma} \left(1 + \frac{P_{t+2}}{C_{t+2}} \right) \right) \right]$$

$$= E_t \left[\delta \left(\frac{S_{t+1}}{S_t} \right)^{\gamma-1} \left(\frac{C_{t+1}}{C_t} \right)^{\gamma} + \delta^2 \left(\frac{S_{t+2}}{S_t} \right)^{\gamma-1} \left(\frac{C_{t+2}}{C_t} \right)^{\gamma} + \cdots \right]$$

$$= E_t \left[\sum_{i=1}^{\infty} \delta^i \left(\frac{S_{t+i}}{S_t} \right)^{\gamma-1} \left(\frac{C_{t+i}}{C_t} \right)^{\gamma} \right] \qquad (14.49)$$

The solutions can then be computed numerically by simulating the lognormal processes for C_t and S_t. The distribution of C_{t+1}/C_t is lognormal and does not depend on the level of consumption, C_t, whereas the distribution of S_{t+1}/S_t does depend on the current level of S_t.[13] Hence, the value of the market portfolio relative to current output, P_t/C_t, varies only with the current surplus consumption ratio, S_t. By numerically calculating P_t/C_t as a function of S_t, Campbell and Cochrane can determine the market portfolio's expected returns and the standard deviation of returns as the level of S_t varies.

Note that in this model, the coefficient of relative risk aversion is given by

$$-\frac{C_t u_{cc}}{u_c} = \frac{1-\gamma}{S_t} \qquad (14.50)$$

and, as was shown in inequality (4.32), the relationship between the Sharpe ratio for any asset and the coefficient of relative risk aversion when consumption is lognormally distributed is approximately

$$\left| \frac{E[r_i] - r}{\sigma_{r_i}} \right| \leq -\frac{C_t u_{cc}}{u_c} \sigma_c = \frac{(1-\gamma)\sigma_c}{S_t} \qquad (14.51)$$

which has a similar form to that of the Constantinides internal habit model except, here, σ_c is a constant and, for the case of the market portfolio, $E[r_i]$ and σ_{r_i} will be time-varying functions of S_t. The coefficient of relative risk aversion will be relatively high when S_t is relatively low, that is, when consumption is low (a recession). Moreover, the model predicts that the equity risk premium increases during a recession (when $-\frac{C_t u_{cc}}{u_c}$ is high), a phenomenon that seems to be present in the postwar U.S. stock market. Campbell and Cochrane calibrate the model

---

13. Note that from (14.37) expected consumption growth, g, is a constant, but from (14.40) the expected growth in the surplus consumption ratio, $(1-\phi)[\ln(\overline{S}) - \ln(S_t)]$, is mean-reverting.

to U.S. consumption and stock market data.[14] Due to the different (nonlinear) specification for S_t vis-à-vis the model of Constantinides, they have relatively more success in fitting this model to data on asset prices.[15]

The next section introduces a class of time-inseparable utility that is much different from habit persistence in that current utility depends on expected future utility which, in turn, depends on future consumption. Hence, unlike habit persistence, in which utility depends on past consumption and is backward looking, recursive utility is forward looking.[16]

14.3   Recursive Utility

A class of time-inseparable utility known as recursive utility was developed by David Kreps and Evan Porteus (Kreps and Porteus 1978) and Larry Epstein and Stanley Zin (Epstein and Zin 1989). They analyze this type of utility in a discrete-time setting, while Darrell Duffie and Larry Epstein (Duffie and Epstein 1992a) study the continuous-time limit. In continuous time, recall that standard, time-separable utility can be written as

$$V_t = E_t \left[\int_t^T U\left(C_s, s\right) \, ds \right] \tag{14.52}$$

where $U\left(C_s, s\right)$ is often taken to be of the form $U\left(C_s, s\right) = e^{-\rho(s-t)} u\left(C_s\right)$. Recursive utility, however, is specified as

$$V_t = E_t \left[\int_t^T f\left(C_s, V_s\right) \, ds \right] \tag{14.53}$$

---

14. They generalize the model to allow dividends on the (stock) market portfolio to differ from consumption, so that dividend growth is not perfectly correlated with consumption growth. Technically, this violates the assumption of an endowment economy but, empirically, there is low correlation between growth rates of stock market dividends and consumption.

15. Empirical tests of the Campbell-Cochrane model by Thomas Tallarini and Harold Zhang (Tallarini and Zhang 2005) confirm that the model fits variation in the equity risk premium over the business cycle. However, while the model matches the mean returns on stocks, it fails to match higher moments such as the variance and skewness of stock returns. Another study by Martin Lettau and Harald Uhlig (Lettau and Uhlig 2000) embeds Campbell and Cochrane's external habit preferences in a production economy model having a labor-leisure decision. In this environment, they find that individuals' consumption and labor market decisions are counterfactual to their actual business cycle dynamics.

16. Utility can be both forward and backward looking in that it is possible to construct models that are recursive and also display habit persistence (Schroder and Skiadas 2002).

where f is known as an *aggregator function*. The specification is recursive in nature because current lifetime utility, V_t, depends on expected values of future lifetime utility, V_s, $s > t$. When f has appropriate properties, Darrell Duffie and Larry Epstein (Duffie and Epstein 1992b) show that a Bellman-type equation can be derived that characterizes the optimal consumption and portfolio choice policies for utility of this type. For particular functional forms, they have been able to work out a number of asset pricing models.

In the example to follow, we consider a form of recursive utility that is a generalization of standard power (constant relative-risk-aversion) utility in that it separates an individual's risk aversion from her elasticity of intertemporal substitution. This generalization is potentially important because, as was shown in Chapter 4, equation (4.14), multiperiod power utility restricts the elasticity of intertemporal substitution, ϵ, to equal $1/(1 - \gamma)$, the reciprocal of the coefficient of relative risk aversion. Conceptually, this may be a strong restriction. Risk aversion characterizes an individual's (portfolio) choices between assets of different risks and is a well-defined concept even in an atemporal (single-period) setting, as was illustrated in Chapter 1. In contrast, the elasticity of intertemporal substitution characterizes an individual's choice of consumption at different points in time and is inherently a temporal concept.

14.3.1 A Model by Obstfeld

Let us now consider the general equilibrium of an economy where representative consumer-investors have recursive utility. We analyze the simple production economy model of Maurice Obstfeld (Obstfeld 1994). This model makes the following assumptions.

Technology

A single capital-consumption good can be invested in up to two different technologies. The first is a risk-free technology whose output, B_t, follows the process

$$dB/B = rdt \tag{14.54}$$

The second is a risky technology whose output, η_t, follows the process

$$d\eta/\eta = \mu dt + \sigma dz \tag{14.55}$$

As in the Constantinides model's production economy, the specification of technologies fixes the expected rates of return and variances of the safe and risky investments. Individuals' asset demands will determine equilibrium quantities of the assets supplied rather than asset prices. Since r, μ, and σ are assumed to be constants, there is a constant investment opportunity set.

Preferences

Representative, infinitely lived households must choose between consuming (at rate C_s at date s) and investing the single capital-consumption good in the two technologies. The lifetime utility function at date t faced by each of these households, denoted V_t, is

$$V_t = E_t \int_t^\infty f(C_s, V_s) \, ds \qquad (14.56)$$

where f, the aggregator function, is given by

$$f(C_s, V_s) = \rho \frac{C_s^{1-\frac{1}{\epsilon}} - [\gamma V_s]^{\frac{\epsilon-1}{\epsilon\gamma}}}{\left(1 - \frac{1}{\epsilon}\right)[\gamma V_s]^{\frac{\epsilon-1}{\epsilon\gamma}-1}} \qquad (14.57)$$

Clearly, this specification is recursive in that current lifetime utility, V_t, depends on expected values of *future* lifetime utility, V_s, $s > t$. The form of equation (14.57) is ordinally equivalent to the continuous-time limit of the discrete-time utility function specified in (Obstfeld 1994). Recall that utility functions are ordinally equivalent; that is, they result in the same consumer choices, if the utility functions evaluated at equivalent sets of decisions produce values that are linear transformations of each other. It can be shown (see (Epstein and Zin 1989) and (Duffie and Epstein 1992a)) that $\rho > 0$ is the continuously compounded subjective rate of time preference; $\epsilon > 0$ is the household's elasticity of intertemporal substitution; and $1 - \gamma > 0$ is the household's coefficient of relative risk aversion. For the special case of $\epsilon = 1/(1-\gamma)$, the utility function given in (14.56) and (14.58) is (ordinally) equivalent to the time-separable, constant relative-risk-aversion case:

$$V_t = E_t \int_t^\infty e^{-\rho s} \frac{C_s^\gamma}{\gamma} \, ds \qquad (14.58)$$

Let ω_t be the proportion of each household's wealth invested in the risky asset (technology). Then the intertemporal budget constraint is given by

$$dW = [\omega(\mu - r)W + rW - C] \, dt + \omega \sigma W \, dz \qquad (14.59)$$

When the aggregator function, f, is put in a particular form by an ordinally equivalent change in variables, what Duffie and Epstein (Duffie and Epstein 1992b) refer to as a "normalization," then a Bellman equation can be used to solve the problem. The aggregator in (14.57) is in normalized form.

As before, let us define $J(W_t)$ as the maximized lifetime utility at date t:

$$J(W_t) = \max_{\{C_s,\omega_s\}} E_t \int_t^\infty f(C_s, V_s)\, ds \tag{14.60}$$

$$= \max_{\{C_s,\omega_s\}} E_t \int_t^\infty f(C_s, J(W_s))\, ds$$

Since this is an infinite horizon problem with constant investment opportunities, and the aggregator function, $f(C, V)$, is not an explicit function of calendar time, the only state variable is W.

The solution to the individual's consumption and portfolio choice problem is given by the continuous-time stochastic Bellman equation

$$0 = \max_{\{C_t,\omega_t\}} f[C_t, J(W_t)] + L[J(W_t)] \tag{14.61}$$

or

$$0 = \max_{\{C_t,\omega_t\}} f[C, J(W)] + J_W [\omega(\mu - r)W + rW - C] + \frac{1}{2} J_{WW}\omega^2\sigma^2 W^2$$

$$= \max_{\{C_t,\omega_t\}} \rho \frac{C^{1-\frac{1}{\epsilon}} - [\gamma J]^{\frac{\epsilon-1}{\epsilon\gamma}}}{\left(1 - \frac{1}{\epsilon}\right)[\gamma J]^{\frac{\epsilon-1}{\epsilon\gamma}-1}} + J_W [\omega(\mu - r)W + rW - C] + \frac{1}{2} J_{WW}\omega^2\sigma^2 W^2$$

$$\tag{14.62}$$

Taking the first-order condition with respect to C,

$$\rho \frac{C^{-\frac{1}{\epsilon}}}{[\gamma J]^{\frac{\epsilon-1}{\epsilon\gamma}-1}} - J_W = 0 \tag{14.63}$$

or

$$C = \left(\frac{J_W}{\rho}\right)^{-\epsilon} [\gamma J]^{\frac{1-\epsilon}{\gamma}+\epsilon} \tag{14.64}$$

Taking the first-order condition with respect to ω,

$$J_W (\mu - r)W + J_{WW}\omega\sigma^2 W^2 = 0 \tag{14.65}$$

or

$$\omega = -\frac{J_W}{J_{WW} W} \frac{\mu - r}{\sigma^2} \tag{14.66}$$

Substituting the optimal values for C and ω given by (14.64) and (14.66) into the Bellman equation (14.62), we obtain the partial differential equation:

$$\rho \frac{\left(\frac{J_W}{\rho}\right)^{1-\epsilon}[\gamma J]^{(\epsilon-1)\left[1-\frac{\epsilon-1}{\epsilon\gamma}\right]} - [\gamma J]^{\frac{1-\epsilon}{\epsilon\gamma}}}{\left(1-\frac{1}{\epsilon}\right)[\gamma J]^{\frac{\epsilon-1}{\epsilon\gamma}-1}} \tag{14.67}$$

$$+ J_W\left[-\frac{J_W}{J_{WW}}\frac{(\mu-r)^2}{\sigma^2} + rW - \left(\frac{J_W}{\rho}\right)^{-\epsilon}[\gamma J]^{\frac{1-\epsilon}{\gamma}+\epsilon}\right] + \frac{1}{2}\frac{J_W^2}{J_{WW}}\frac{(\mu-r)^2}{\sigma^2} = 0$$

or

$$\frac{\epsilon\rho}{\epsilon-1}\left[\left(\frac{J_W}{\rho}\right)^{-\epsilon}[\gamma J]^{\frac{1-\epsilon}{\gamma}+\epsilon} - \gamma J\right] \tag{14.68}$$

$$+ J_W\left[-\frac{J_W}{J_{WW}}\frac{(\mu-r)^2}{\sigma^2} + rW - \left(\frac{J_W}{\rho}\right)^{-\epsilon}[\gamma J]^{\frac{1-\epsilon}{\gamma}+\epsilon}\right] + \frac{1}{2}\frac{J_W^2}{J_{WW}}\frac{(\mu-r)^2}{\sigma^2} = 0$$

If one "guesses" that the solution is of the form $J(W) = (aW)^\gamma / \gamma$ and substitutes this into (14.68), one finds that $a = \alpha^{1/(1-\epsilon)}$ where

$$\alpha \equiv \rho^{-\epsilon}\left(\epsilon\rho + (1-\epsilon)\left[r + \frac{(\mu-r)^2}{2(1-\gamma)\sigma^2}\right]\right) \tag{14.69}$$

Thus, substituting this value for J into (14.64), we find that optimal consumption is a fixed proportion of wealth:

$$C = \alpha\rho^\epsilon W \tag{14.70}$$

$$= \left(\epsilon\rho + (1-\epsilon)\left[r + \frac{(\mu-r)^2}{2(1-\gamma)\sigma^2}\right]\right)W$$

and the optimal portfolio weight of the risky asset is

$$\omega = \frac{\mu-r}{(1-\gamma)\sigma^2} \tag{14.71}$$

which is the same as for an individual with standard constant relative risk aversion and time-separable utility. The result that the optimal portfolio choice depends only on risk aversion turns out to be an artifact of the model's assumption that investment opportunities are constant. Harjoat Bhamra and Raman Uppal (Bhamra and Uppal 2003) demonstrate that when investment opportunities are stochastic, the portfolio weight, ω, can depend on both γ and ϵ.

Note that if $\epsilon = 1/(1-\gamma)$, then equation (14.70) is the same as optimal consumption for the time-separable, constant relative-risk-aversion, infinite horizon case given in Chapter 12, equation (12.34), $C = \frac{\gamma}{1-\gamma} \left[\frac{\rho}{\gamma} - r - \frac{(\mu-r)^2}{2(1-\gamma)\sigma^2} \right] W$. Similar to the time-separable case, for an infinite horizon solution to exist, we need consumption to be positive in (14.70), which requires

$$\rho > \frac{1-\epsilon}{\epsilon} \left(r + [\mu - r]^2 / \left[2(1-\gamma)\sigma^2 \right] \right).$$

This will be the case when the elasticity of intertemporal substitution, ϵ, is sufficiently large. For example, assuming $\rho > 0$, this inequality is always satisfied when $\epsilon > 1$ but will not be satisfied when ϵ is sufficiently close to zero.

14.3.2 Discussion of the Model

Let us examine how optimal consumption depends on the model's parameters. Note that the term $r + [\mu - r]^2 / [2(1-\gamma)\sigma^2]$ in (14.70) can be rewritten using $\omega = (\mu - r) / [(1-\gamma)\sigma^2]$ from (14.71) as

$$r + \frac{(\mu - r)^2}{2(1-\gamma)\sigma^2} = r + \omega \frac{\mu - r}{2} \tag{14.72}$$

and can be interpreted as relating to the risk-adjusted investment returns available to individuals. From (14.70) we see that an increase in (14.72) increases consumption when $\epsilon < 1$ and reduces consumption when $\epsilon > 1$. This result provides intuition for the role of intertemporal substitution. When $\epsilon < 1$, the income effect from an improvement in investment opportunities dominates the substitution effect, so that consumption rises and savings fall. The reverse occurs when $\epsilon > 1$: the substitution effect dominates the income effect and savings rise.

We can also study how the growth rate of the economy depends on the model's parameters. Assuming $0 < \omega < 1$ and substituting (14.70) and (14.71) into (14.59), we have that wealth follows the geometric Brownian motion process:

$$dW/W$$
$$= \left[\omega^* (\mu - r) + r - \alpha\rho^\epsilon \right] dt + \omega^* \sigma \, dz \tag{14.73}$$
$$= \left[\frac{(\mu - r)^2}{(1-\gamma)\sigma^2} + r - \epsilon\rho - (1-\epsilon) \left(r + \frac{(\mu - r)^2}{2(1-\gamma)\sigma^2} \right) \right] dt + \frac{\mu - r}{(1-\gamma)\sigma} dz$$
$$= \left[\epsilon \left(r + \frac{(\mu - r)^2}{2(1-\gamma)\sigma^2} - \rho \right) + \frac{(\mu - r)^2}{2(1-\gamma)\sigma^2} \right] dt + \frac{\mu - r}{(1-\gamma)\sigma} dz$$

Since $C = \alpha\rho^\epsilon W$, the drift and volatility of wealth in (14.73) are also the drift and volatility of the consumption process, dC/C. Thus, consumption and wealth are both lognormally distributed and their continuously compounded growth, $d \ln C$, has a volatility, σ_c, and mean, g_c, equal to

$$\sigma_c = \frac{\mu - r}{(1 - \gamma) \sigma} \tag{14.74}$$

and

$$
\begin{aligned}
g_c &= \epsilon \left(r + \frac{(\mu - r)^2}{2 (1 - \gamma) \sigma^2} - \rho \right) + \frac{(\mu - r)^2}{2 (1 - \gamma) \sigma^2} - \frac{1}{2} \sigma_c^2 \\
&= \epsilon \left(r + \frac{(\mu - r)^2}{2 (1 - \gamma) \sigma^2} - \rho \right) - \frac{\gamma (\mu - r)^2}{2 (1 - \gamma)^2 \sigma^2}
\end{aligned} \tag{14.75}
$$

From (14.75) we see that if $r + [\mu - r]^2 / [2 (1 - \gamma) \sigma^2] > \rho$, then an economy's growth rate is higher the higher is intertemporal substitution, ϵ, since individuals save more. Also, consider how an economy's rate varies with the squared Sharpe ratio, $[\mu - r]^2 / \sigma^2$, a measure of the relative attractiveness of the risky asset. The sign of the derivative $\partial g_c / \partial \left([\mu - r]^2 / \sigma^2 \right)$ equals the sign of $\epsilon - \gamma / (1 - \gamma)$. For the time-separable, constant relative-risk-aversion case of $\epsilon = 1 / (1 - \gamma)$, this derivative is unambiguously positive, indicating that a higher μ or a lower σ would result in the economy growing faster. However, in the general case, the economy could grow slower if $\epsilon < \gamma / (1 - \gamma)$. Why? Although from (14.71) we see that individuals put a large proportion of their wealth into the faster-growing risky asset as the Sharpe ratio rises, a higher Sharpe ratio leads to greater consumption (and less savings) when $\epsilon < 1$. For $\epsilon < \gamma / (1 - \gamma)$, the effect of less savings dominates the portfolio effect and the economy is expected to grow more slowly.

Obstfeld points out that the integration of global financial markets that allows residents to hold risky foreign, as well as domestic, investments increases diversification and effectively reduces individuals' risky portfolio variance, σ^2. This reduction in σ would lead individuals to allocate a greater proportion of their wealth to the higher-yielding risky assets. If $\epsilon > \gamma / (1 - \gamma)$, financial market integration also would predict that countries would tend to grow faster.

It is natural to ask whether this recursive utility specification, which distinguishes between risk aversion and the intertemporal elasticity of substitution, can provide a better fit to historical asset returns compared to time-separable power utility. In terms of explaining the equity premium puzzle, from (14.74) we see that the risky-asset Sharpe ratio, $(\mu - r) / \sigma$, equals $(1 - \gamma) \sigma_c$, the same form as with time-separable utility. So, as discussed earlier, one would still need to assume that the coefficient of relative risk aversion $(1 - \gamma)$ were quite high in order to justify the equity risk premium. However, recursive utility has more hope of explaining the risk-free rate puzzle because of the additional degree of freedom added by the elasticity of substitution parameter, ϵ. If we substitute (14.74) into (14.75) and solve for the risk-free rate, we find

$$r = \rho + \frac{g_c}{\epsilon} - \left[1 - \gamma + \frac{\gamma}{\epsilon}\right]\frac{\sigma_c^2}{2} \tag{14.76}$$

Recall that for the time-separable case of $\epsilon = 1/(1 - \gamma)$, we have

$$r = \rho + (1 - \gamma)\,g_c - (1 - \gamma)^2\,\frac{\sigma_c^2}{2} \tag{14.77}$$

Because, empirically, $g_c \approx 0.018$ is large relative to $\sigma_c^2/2 \approx 0.03^2/2 = 0.00045$, the net effect of higher risk aversion, $1 - \gamma$, needed to fit the equity risk premium leads to too high a risk-free rate in (14.77). However, we see that the recursive utility specification in (14.76) potentially circumvents this problem because g_c is divided by ϵ rather than being multiplied by $1 - \gamma$.[17]

Empirical estimates of the elasticity of intertemporal substitution have been obtained by regressing consumption growth, $d \ln C$, on the real interest rate, r. From equations (14.73) and (14.75), we see that if the risky-asset Sharpe ratio, $(\mu - r)/\sigma$, is assumed to be independent of the level of the real interest rate, r, then the regression coefficient on the real interest should provide an estimate of ϵ. Tests using aggregate consumption data, such as (Hall 1988) and (Campbell and Mankiw 1989), generally find that ϵ is small, often indistinguishable from zero. However, other tests based on consumption data disaggregated at the state level (Beaudry and van Wincoop 1996) or at the household level (Attanasio and Weber 1993) find higher estimates for ϵ, often around 1. From (14.76) we see that a value of $\epsilon = 1$ would make r independent of risk aversion, γ, and, assuming ρ is small, could produce a reasonable value for the real interest rate.

14.4 Summary

The models presented in this chapter generalize the standard model of time-separable, power utility. For particular functional forms, an individual's consumption and portfolio choice problem can be solved using the same techniques that were previously applied to the time-separable case. For utility that displays habit persistence, we saw that the standard coefficient of relative risk aversion, $(1 - \gamma)$, is transformed to the expression $(1 - \gamma)/S_t$ where $S_t < 1$ is the surplus consumption ratio. Hence, habit persistence can make individuals behave in a

---

17. Philippe Weil (Weil 1989) appears to be the first to examine the equity premium and risk-free rate puzzles in the context of recursive utility.

very risk-averse fashion in order to avoid consuming below their habit or subsistence level. As a result, these models have the potential to produce aversion to holding risky assets sufficient to justify a high equity risk premium.

An attraction of recursive utility is that it distinguishes between an individual's level of risk aversion and his elasticity of intertemporal substitution, a distinction that is not possible with time-separable, power utility, which makes these characteristics reciprocals of one another. As a result, recursive utility can permit an individual to have high risk aversion while, at the same time, having a high elasticity of intertemporal substitution. Such a utility specification has the potential to produce both a high equity risk premium and a low risk-free interest rate that is present in historical data.

While recursive utility and utility displaying habit persistence might be considered nonstandard forms of utility, they are preference specifications that are considered to be those of rational individuals. In the next chapter we study utility that is influenced by psychological biases that might be described as irrational behavior. Such biases have been identified in experimental settings but have also been shown to be present in the actual investment behavior of some individuals. We examine how these biases might influence the equilibrium prices of assets.

14.5   Exercises

1. In the Constantinides habit persistence model, suppose that there are three, rather than two, technologies. Assume that there are the risk-free technology and two risky technologies:

$$dB/B = rdt$$
$$dS_1/S_1 = \mu_1 dt + \sigma_1 dz_1$$
$$dS_2/S_2 = \mu_2 dt + \sigma_2 dz_2$$

where $dz_1 dz_2 = \phi dt$. Also assume that the parameters are such that there is an interior solution for the portfolio weights (all portfolio weights are positive). What would be the optimal consumption and portfolio weights for this case?

2. Consider an endowment economy where a representative agent maximizes utility of the form

$$\max \sum_{t=0}^{\infty} \delta^t \frac{(C_t - X_t)^\gamma}{\gamma}$$

where X_t is a level of external habit and equals $X_t = \theta \overline{C}_{t-1}$, where $\overline{C}_{t-1}$ is aggregate consumption at date $t - 1$.

a. Write down an expression for the one-period, risk-free interest rate at date t, $R_{f,t}$.

b. If consumption growth, C_{t+1}/C_t, follows an independent and identical distribution, is the one-period riskless interest rate, $R_{f,t}$, constant over time?

3. The following problem is based on the work of Menzly, Santos, and Veronesi (Menzly, Santos, and Veronesi 2001). Consider a continuous-time endowment economy where agents maximize utility that displays external habit persistence. Utility is of the form

$$E_t \left[\int_0^\infty e^{-\rho t} \ln \left(C_t - X_t \right) dt \right]$$

and aggregate consumption (dividend output) follows the lognormal process

$$dC_t/C_t = \mu dt + \sigma dz$$

Define Y_t as the inverse surplus consumption ratio, that is, $Y_t \equiv \frac{C_t}{C_t - X_t} = \frac{1}{1-(X_t/C_t)} > 1$. It is assumed to satisfy the mean-reverting process

$$dY_t = k \left(\overline{Y} - Y_t \right) dt - \alpha \left(Y_t - \lambda \right) dz$$

where $\overline{Y} > \lambda \geq 1$ is the long-run mean of the inverse surplus, $k > 0$ reflects the speed of mean reversion, $\alpha > 0$. The parameter λ sets a lower bound for Y_t, and the positivity of $\alpha \left(Y_t - \lambda \right)$ implies that a shock to the aggregate output (dividend-consumption) process decreases the inverse surplus consumption ratio (and increases the surplus consumption ratio). Let P_t be the price of the market portfolio. Derive a closed-form expression for the price-dividend ratio of the market portfolio, P_t/C_t. How does P_t/C_t vary with an increase in the surplus consumption ratio?

4. Consider an individual's consumption and portfolio choice problem when her preferences display habit persistence. The individual's lifetime utility satisfies

$$E_t \left[\int_t^T e^{-\rho s} u \left(C_s, x_s \right) ds \right] \tag{1}$$

where C_s is date s consumption and x_s is the individual's date s level of habit. The individual can choose among a risk-free asset that pays a constant rate of return equal to r and n risky assets. The instantaneous rate of return on risky asset i satisfies

$$dP_i/P_i = \mu_i dt + \sigma_i dz_i, \ i = 1, \dots, n \tag{2}$$

where $dz_i dz_j = \sigma_{ij} dt$ and μ_i, σ_i, and σ_{ij} are constants. Thus, the individual's level of wealth, W, follows the process

$$dW = \sum_{i=1}^{n} \omega_i(\mu_i - r)W\, dt + (rW - C_t)\, dt + \sum_{i=1}^{n} \omega_i W \sigma_i\, dz_i \qquad (3)$$

where ω_i is the proportion of wealth invested in risky asset i. The habit level, x_s, is assumed to follow the process

$$dx = f\left(\overline{C}_t, x_t\right) dt \qquad (4)$$

where $\overline{C}_t$ is the date t consumption that determines the individual's habit.

a. Let $J\,(W, x, t)$ be the individual's derived utility-of-wealth function. Write down the continuous-time Bellman equation that $J\,(W, x, t)$ satisfies.

b. Derive the first-order conditions with respect to the portfolio weights, ω_i. Does the optimal portfolio proportion of risky asset i to risky asset j, ω_i/ω_j, depend on the individual's preferences? Why or why not?

c. Assume that the consumption, $\overline{C}_t$, in equation (4) is such that the individual's preferences display an internal habit, similar to the Constantinides model (Constantinides 1990). Derive the first-order condition with respect to the individual's date t optimal consumption, C_t.

d. Assume that the consumption, $\overline{C}_t$, in equation (4) is such that the individual's preferences display an external habit, similar to the Campbell-Cochrane model (Campbell and Cochrane 1999). Derive the first-order condition with respect to the individual's date t optimal consumption, C_t.

PART V

ADDITIONAL TOPICS IN ASSET PRICING

CHAPTER 15

Behavioral Finance and Asset Pricing

This chapter considers asset pricing when investors' asset demands incorporate some elements of irrationality. Irrationality can occur because investors' preferences are subject to psychological biases or because investors make systematic errors in judging the probability distribution of asset returns. Incorporating irrationality is a departure from von Neumann–Morgenstern expected utility maximization and the standard or classical economic approach. A model that incorporates some form of irrationality is unlikely to be useful for drawing normative conclusions regarding an individual's asset choice. Rather, such a model attempts to provide a positive or descriptive theory of how individuals actually behave. For this reason, the approach is referred to as "behavioral finance."

There is both experimental evidence as well as conventional empirical research documenting investor behavior that is inconsistent with von Neumann–Morgenstern expected utility theory. Numerous forms of cognitive biases and judgement errors appear to characterize the preferences of at least some individuals. Surveys by (Hirshleifer 2001), (Daniel, Hirshleifer, and Teoh 2001), and (Barberis and Thaler 2002) describe the evidence for these behavioral phenomena. However, to date there have been relatively few models that analyze how irrationality might affect equilibrium asset prices. This chapter examines two recent behavioral asset pricing models.

The first is an intertemporal consumption and portfolio choice model by Nicholas Barberis, Ming Huang, and Jesus Santos (Barberis, Huang, and Santos 2001) that incorporates two types of biases that are prominent in the behavioral finance literature. They are *loss aversion* and the *house money effect*. These biases fall within the general category of *prospect theory*. Prospect theory deviates from von Neumann–Morgenstern expected utility maximization because investor utility is a function of recent changes in, rather than simply the current level of, financial wealth. In particular, investor utility characterized by prospect theory may be more sensitive to recent losses than recent gains in financial wealth, this phenomenon being referred to as *loss aversion*. Moreover, losses following previous losses create more disutility than losses following previous gains. After a run-up in asset prices, the investor is less risk averse because subsequent losses would be "cushioned" by the previous gains. This is the so-called *house money* effect.[1]

An implication of this intertemporal variation in risk aversion is that after a substantial rise in asset prices, lower investor risk aversion can drive prices even higher. Hence, asset prices display volatility that is greater than that predicted by observed changes in fundamentals, such as changes in dividends. This also generates predictability in asset returns. A substantial recent fall (*rise*) in asset prices increases (*decreases*) risk aversion and expected asset returns. It can also imply a high equity risk premium because the "excess" volatility in stock prices leads loss-averse investors to demand a relatively high average rate of return on stocks.

Prospect theory assumes that investors are overly concerned with changes in financial wealth measured against some reference points, such as profits or losses measured from the times when assets were first purchased. They care about these holding period gains or losses more than would be justified by their effects on consumption, and this influences their risk-taking behavior. This psychological concept was advanced by Daniel Kahneman and Amos Tversky (Kahneman and Tversky 1979) and is based primarily on experimental evidence.[2] For example, Richard Thaler and Eric Johnson (Thaler and Johnson 1990) find that individuals faced with a sequence of gambles are more willing to take risk if they have made gains from previous gambles, evidence consistent with the house money effect. However, in a recent study of the behavior of traders of the Chicago Board of Trade's Treasury bond futures, Joshua Coval and Tyler Shumway (Coval and Shumway 2003) find evidence consistent with loss aversion but not the house money effect.

The second model presented in this chapter examines how equilibrium asset prices are affected when some investors are rational but others suffer from systematic optimism or pessimism. Leonid Kogan, Stephen Ross, Jiang Wang, and Mark Westerfied (Kogan et al. 2006) construct a simple endowment economy where rational and irrational investors are identical except that the irrational investors systematically misperceive the expected growth rate of the aggregate

---

1. This expression derives from the psychological misperception that a gambler's (unexpected) winnings are the casino house's money. The gambler views these winnings as different from his initial wealth upon entering the casino. Hence, the gambler is willing to bet more aggressively in the future because if the house's money is lost, the disutility of this loss will be small relative to the disutility of losing the same amount of his initial wealth.
2. Daniel Kahneman was awarded the Nobel prize in economics in 2002.

dividend process. Interestingly, it is shown that this economy can be transformed into one where the irrational traders can be viewed as acting rationally but their utilities are state dependent. This transformation of the problem allows it to be solved using standard techniques.

Kogan, Ross, Wang, and Westerfield's general equilibrium model shows that investors having irrational beliefs regarding the economy's fundamentals may not necessarily lose wealth to rational investors and be driven out of the asset market.[3] Moreover, in those instances where irrational individuals do lose wealth relative to the rational individuals, so that they do not survive in the long run, their trading behavior can significantly affect asset prices for substantial periods of time.

We now turn to the Barberis, Huang, and Santos model, which generalizes a standard consumption and portfolio choice problem to incorporate aspects of prospect theory.

15.1 The Effects of Psychological Biases on Asset Prices

The Barberis, Huang, and Santos model is based on the following assumptions.

15.1.1 Assumptions

In the discussion that follows, the model economy has the following characteristics.

Technology

A discrete-time endowment economy is assumed. The risky asset (or a portfolio of all risky assets) pays a stream of dividends in the form of perishable output. Denote the date t amount of this dividend as D_t. In the Economy I version of the Barberis, Huang, and Santos model, it is assumed that aggregate consumption equals dividends. This is the standard Lucas economy assumption (Lucas 1978). However, in the Economy II version of their model, which will be the focus of our analysis, the risky asset's dividends are distinct from aggregate consumption due to the assumed existence of nonfinancial, or labor, income.[4] Recall that we

---

3. This result was shown by Bradford De Long, Andrei Shleifer, Lawrence Summers, and Robert Waldmann (DeLong et al. 1991) in a partial equilibrium model.

4. Note that in a standard endowment economy, consumption and dividends are perfectly correlated since they equal each other in equilibrium. Empirically, it is obvious that aggregate consumption does not equal, nor is perfectly correlated with, aggregate stock dividends. Hence, to make the model more empirically relevant, the Economy II version of the model introduces nonfinancial income, which avoids the implication of perfect correlation.

studied this labor income extension of the standard Lucas economy in Chapter 6. Nonfinancial wealth can be interpreted as human capital and its dividend as labor income. Thus, in equilibrium, aggregate consumption, $\overline{C}_t$, equals dividends, D_t, plus nonfinancial income, Y_t, because both dividends and nonfinancial income are assumed to be perishable. Aggregate consumption and dividends are assumed to follow the joint lognormal process

$$\ln\left(\overline{C}_{t+1}/\overline{C}_t\right) = g_C + \sigma_C \eta_{t+1} \tag{15.1}$$

$$\ln\left(D_{t+1}/D_t\right) = g_D + \sigma_D \varepsilon_{t+1}$$

where the error terms are serially uncorrelated and distributed as

$$\begin{pmatrix} \eta_t \\ \varepsilon_t \end{pmatrix} \sim N\left(\begin{pmatrix} 0 \\ 0 \end{pmatrix}, \begin{pmatrix} 1 & \rho \\ \rho & 1 \end{pmatrix}\right) \tag{15.2}$$

The return on the risky asset from date t to date $t+1$ is denoted R_{t+1}. A one-period risk-free investment is assumed to be in zero net supply, and its return from date t to date $t+1$ is denoted $R_{f,t}$.[5] The equilibrium value for $R_{f,t}$ is derived next.

Preferences

Representative, infinitely lived individuals maximize lifetime utility of the form

$$E_0\left[\sum_{t=0}^{\infty}\left(\delta^t \frac{C_t^\gamma}{\gamma} + b_t \delta^{t+1} v\left(X_{t+1}, w_t, z_t\right)\right)\right] \tag{15.3}$$

where C_t is the individual's consumption at date t, $\gamma < 1$, and δ is a time discount factor. w_t denotes the value of the individual's risky-asset holdings at date t. X_{t+1} is defined as the total excess return or gain that the individual earned from holding the risky asset between date t and date $t+1$. Specifically, this risky-asset gain is assumed to be measured relative to the alternative of holding wealth in the risk-free asset and is given by

$$X_{t+1} \equiv w_t\left(R_{t+1} - R_{f,t}\right) \tag{15.4}$$

z_t is a measure of the individual's prior gains as a fraction of w_t. $z_t < (>)\ 1$ denotes a situation in which the investor has earned prior gains (*losses*) on the risky asset.

---

5. Since the risk-free asset is in zero net supply, the representative individual's equilibrium holding of this asset is zero. Similar to the case of the Cox, Ingersoll, and Ross model presented in Chapter 13, $R_{f,t}$ is interpreted as the shadow riskless return.

The prior gain factor, z_t, is assumed to follow the process

$$z_t = (1 - \eta) + \eta z_{t-1} \frac{\overline{R}}{R_t} \tag{15.5}$$

where $0 \leq \eta \leq 1$ and $\overline{R}$ is a parameter, approximately equal to the average risky-asset return, that makes the steady state value of z_t equal 1. If $\eta = 0$, $z_t = 1$ for all t. At the other extreme, when $\eta = 1$, z_t is smaller than z_{t-1} when risky-asset returns were relatively high last period, $R_t > \overline{R}$. Conversely, when $\eta = 1$ but $R_t < \overline{R}$, z_t is smaller than z_{t-1}. For intermediate cases of $0 < \eta < 1$, z_t adjusts partially to prior asset returns. In general, the greater η is, the longer the investor's memory in measuring prior gains from the risky asset.

The function $v(\cdot)$ characterizes the prospect theory effect of risky-asset gains on utility.[6] For the case of $z_t = 1$ (no prior gains or losses), this function displays pure loss aversion:

$$v(X_{t+1}, w_t, 1) = \begin{cases} X_{t+1} & \text{if } X_{t+1} \geq 0 \\ \lambda X_{t+1} & \text{if } X_{t+1} < 0 \end{cases} \tag{15.6}$$

where $\lambda > 1$. Hence, ceteris paribus, losses have a disproportionately bigger impact on utility. When $z_t \neq 1$, the function $v(\cdot)$ reflects the prospect theory's house money effect. In the case of prior gains ($z_t \leq 1$), the function takes the form

$$v(X_{t+1}, w_t, z_t) = \begin{cases} X_{t+1} & \text{if } R_{t+1} \geq z_t R_{f,t} \\ X_{t+1} + (\lambda - 1) w_t \left(R_{t+1} - z_t R_{f,t} \right) & \text{if } R_{t+1} < z_t R_{f,t} \end{cases} \tag{15.7}$$

The interpretation of this function is that when a return exceeds the cushion built by prior gains, that is, $R_{t+1} \geq z_t R_{f,t}$, it affects utility one-for-one. However, when the gain is less than the amount of prior gains, $R_{t+1} < z_t R_{f,t}$, it has a greater than one-for-one impact on disutility. In the case of prior losses ($z_t > 1$), the function becomes

$$v(X_{t+1}, w_t, z_t) = \begin{cases} X_{t+1} & \text{if } X_{t+1} \geq 0 \\ \lambda(z_t) X_{t+1} & \text{if } X_{t+1} < 0 \end{cases} \tag{15.8}$$

where $\lambda(z_t) = \lambda + k(z_t - 1)$, $k > 0$. Here we see that losses that follow previous losses are penalized at the rate of $\lambda(z_t)$, which exceeds λ and grows larger as prior losses become larger (z_t exceeds unity).

Finally, the prospect theory term in the utility function is scaled to make the risky-asset price-dividend ratio and the risky-asset risk premium stationary

---

6. Since $v(\cdot)$ depends only on the risky asset's returns, it is assumed that the individual is not subject to loss aversion on nonfinancial assets.

variables as aggregate wealth increases over time.[7] The form of this scaling factor is chosen to be

$$b_t = b_0 \overline{C}_t^{\gamma-1} \tag{15.9}$$

where $b_0 > 0$ and $\overline{C}_t$ is aggregate consumption at date t.[8]

15.1.2   Solving the Model

The state variables for the individual's consumption–portfolio choice problem are wealth, W_t, and z_t. Intuitively, since the aggregate consumption–dividend growth process in equation (15.1) is an independent, identical distribution, the dividend level is not a state variable. We start by assuming that the ratio of the risky-asset price to its dividend is a function of only the state variable z_t; that is, $f_t \equiv P_t/D_t = f_t(z_t)$, and then show that an equilibrium exists in which this is true.[9] Given this assumption, the return on the risky asset can be written as

$$R_{t+1} = \frac{P_{t+1} + D_{t+1}}{P_t} = \frac{1 + f(z_{t+1})}{f(z_t)} \frac{D_{t+1}}{D_t} \tag{15.10}$$

$$= \frac{1 + f(z_{t+1})}{f(z_t)} e^{g_D + \sigma_D \varepsilon_{t+1}}$$

It is also assumed that an equilibrium exists in which the risk-free return is constant; that is, $R_{f,t} = R_f$. This will be verified by the solution to the agent's first-order conditions. Making this assumption simplifies the form of the function v. From (15.7) and (15.8) it can be verified that v is proportional to w_t. Hence, $v(X_{t+1}, w_t, z_t)$ can be written as $v(X_{t+1}, w_t, z_t) = w_t \widehat{v}(R_{t+1}, z_t)$, where for $z_t < 1$

$$\widehat{v}(R_{t+1}, z_t) = \begin{cases} R_{t+1} - R_f & \text{if } R_{t+1} \geq z_t R_f \\ R_{t+1} - R_f + (\lambda - 1)\left(R_{t+1} - z_t R_f\right) & \text{if } R_{t+1} < z_t R_f \end{cases} \tag{15.11}$$

and for $z_t > 1$

$$\widehat{v}(R_{t+1}, z_t) = \begin{cases} R_{t+1} - R_f & \text{if } R_{t+1} \geq R_f \\ \lambda(z_t)\left(R_{t+1} - R_f\right) & \text{if } R_{t+1} < R_f \end{cases} \tag{15.12}$$

7. Without the scaling factor, as wealth (output) grows at rate g_D, the prospect theory term would dominate the conventional constant relative-risk-aversion term.

8. Because $\overline{C}_t$ is assumed to be aggregate consumption, the individual views b_t as an exogeneous variable.

9. This is plausible because the standard part of the utility function displays constant relative risk aversion. With this type of utility, optimal portfolio proportions would not be a function of wealth.

The individual's maximization problem is then

$$\max_{\{C_t, w_t\}} E_0 \left[\sum_{t=0}^{\infty} \left(\delta^t \frac{C_t^\gamma}{\gamma} + b_0 \delta^{t+1} \overline{C}_t^{\gamma-1} w_t \widehat{v} \left(R_{t+1}, z_t \right) \right) \right] \tag{15.13}$$

subject to the budget constraint

$$W_{t+1} = \left(W_t + Y_t - C_t \right) R_f + w_t \left(R_{t+1} - R_f \right) \tag{15.14}$$

and the dynamics for z_t given in (15.5). Define $\delta^t J \left(W_t, z_t \right)$ as the derived utility-of-wealth function. Then the Bellman equation for this problem is

$$J \left(W_t, z_t \right) = \max_{\{C_t, w_t\}} \frac{C_t^\gamma}{\gamma} + E_t \left[b_0 \delta \overline{C}_t^{\gamma-1} w_t \widehat{v} \left(R_{t+1}, z_t \right) + \delta J \left(W_{t+1}, z_{t+1} \right) \right] \tag{15.15}$$

Taking the first-order conditions with respect to C_t and w_t, one obtains

$$0 = C_t^{\gamma-1} - \delta R_f E_t \left[J_W \left(W_{t+1}, z_{t+1} \right) \right] \tag{15.16}$$

$$0 = E_t \left[b_0 \overline{C}_t^{\gamma-1} \widehat{v} \left(R_{t+1}, z_t \right) + J_W \left(W_{t+1}, z_{t+1} \right) \left(R_{t+1} - R_f \right) \right]$$

$$= b_0 \overline{C}_t^{\gamma-1} E_t \left[\widehat{v} \left(R_{t+1}, z_t \right) \right] + E_t \left[J_W \left(W_{t+1}, z_{t+1} \right) R_{t+1} \right]$$
$$- R_f E_t \left[J_W \left(W_{t+1}, z_{t+1} \right) \right] \tag{15.17}$$

It is straightforward (and left as an end-of-chapter exercise) to show that (15.16) and (15.17) imply the standard envelope condition

$$C_t^{\gamma-1} = J_W \left(W_t, z_t \right) \tag{15.18}$$

Substituting this into (15.16), one obtains the Euler equation

$$1 = \delta R_f E_t \left[\left(\frac{C_{t+1}}{C_t} \right)^{\gamma-1} \right] \tag{15.19}$$

Using (15.18) and (15.19) in (15.17) implies

$$0 = b_0 \overline{C}_t^{\gamma-1} E_t \left[\widehat{v} \left(R_{t+1}, z_t \right) \right] + E_t \left[C_{t+1}^{\gamma-1} R_{t+1} \right] - R_f E_t \left[C_{t+1}^{\gamma-1} \right]$$

$$= b_0 \overline{C}_t^{\gamma-1} E_t \left[\widehat{v} \left(R_{t+1}, z_t \right) \right] + E_t \left[C_{t+1}^{\gamma-1} R_{t+1} \right] - C_t^{\gamma-1} / \delta \tag{15.20}$$

or

$$1 = b_0 \left(\frac{\overline{C}_t}{C_t} \right)^{\gamma-1} \delta E_t \left[\widehat{v} \left(R_{t+1}, z_t \right) \right] + \delta E_t \left[R_{t+1} \left(\frac{C_{t+1}}{C_t} \right)^{\gamma-1} \right] \tag{15.21}$$

In equilibrium, conditions (15.19) and (15.21) hold with the representative agent's consumption, C_t, replaced with aggregate consumption, $\overline{C}_t$. Using the assumption in (15.1) that aggregate consumption is lognormally distributed, we can compute the expectation in (15.19) to solve for the risk-free interest rate:

$$R_f = e^{(1-\gamma)g_C - \frac{1}{2}(1-\gamma)^2 \sigma_C^2} / \delta \tag{15.22}$$

Using (15.1) and (15.10), condition (15.21) can also be simplified:

$$1 = b_0 \delta E_t \left[\hat{v} \left(R_{t+1}, z_t \right) \right] + \delta E_t \left[\frac{1 + f \left(z_{t+1} \right)}{f \left(z_t \right)} e^{g_D + \sigma_D \varepsilon_{t+1}} \left(e^{g_C + \sigma_C \eta_{t+1}} \right)^{\gamma - 1} \right] \tag{15.23}$$

or

$$1 = b_0 \delta E_t \left[\hat{v} \left(\frac{1 + f \left(z_{t+1} \right)}{f \left(z_t \right)} e^{g_D + \sigma_D \varepsilon_{t+1}}, z_t \right) \right] \tag{15.24}$$

$$+ \delta e^{g_D - (1-\gamma)g_C + \frac{1}{2}(1-\gamma)^2 \sigma_C^2 \left(1 - \rho^2 \right)} E_t \left[\frac{1 + f \left(z_{t+1} \right)}{f \left(z_t \right)} e^{(\sigma_D - (1-\gamma)\rho \sigma_C)\varepsilon_{t+1}} \right]$$

The price-dividend ratio, $P_t / D_t = f_t \left(z_t \right)$, can be computed numerically from (15.24). However, because $z_{t+1} = 1 + \eta \left(z_t \frac{\overline{R}}{R_{t+1}} - 1 \right)$ and $R_{t+1} = \frac{1 + f(z_{t+1})}{f(z_t)} e^{g_D + \sigma_D \varepsilon_{t+1}}$, z_{t+1} depends upon z_t, $f \left(z_t \right)$, $f \left(z_{t+1} \right)$, and ε_{t+1}; that is,

$$z_{t+1} = 1 + \eta \left(z_t \frac{\overline{R} f \left(z_t \right) e^{-g_D - \sigma_D \varepsilon_{t+1}}}{1 + f \left(z_{t+1} \right)} - 1 \right) \tag{15.25}$$

Therefore, (15.24) and (15.25) need to be solved jointly. Barberis, Huang, and Santos describe an iterative numerical technique for finding the function $f \left(\cdot \right)$. Given all other parameters, they guess an initial function, $f^{(0)}$, and then use it to solve for z_{t+1} in (15.25) for given z_t and ε_{t+1}. Then, they find a new candidate solution, $f^{(1)}$, using the following recursion that is based on (15.24):

$$f^{(i+1)} \left(z_t \right) = \delta e^{g_D - (1-\gamma)g_C + \frac{1}{2}(1-\gamma)^2 \sigma_C^2 \left(1 - \rho^2 \right)} \times$$

$$E_t \left[\left[1 + f^{(i)} \left(z_{t+1} \right) \right] e^{(\sigma_D - (1-\gamma)\rho \sigma_C)\varepsilon_{t+1}} \right] \tag{15.26}$$

$$+ f^{(i)} \left(z_t \right) b_0 \delta E_t \left[\hat{v} \left(\frac{1 + f^{(i)} \left(z_{t+1} \right)}{f^{(i)} \left(z_t \right)} e^{g_D + \sigma_D \varepsilon_{t+1}}, z_t \right) \right], \quad \forall z_t$$

where the expectations are computed using a Monte Carlo simulation of the ε_{t+1}. Given the new candidate function, $f^{(1)}$, z_{t+1} is again found from (15.25). The procedure is repeated until the function $f^{(i)}$ converges.

15.1.3 Model Results

For reasonable parameter values, Barberis, Huang, and Santos find that $P_t/D_t = f_t(z_t)$ is a decreasing function of z_t. The intuition was described earlier: if there were prior gains from holding the risky asset (z_t is low), then investors become less risk averse and bid up the price of the risky asset.

Using their estimate of $f(\cdot)$, the unconditional distribution of stock returns is simulated from a randomly generated sequence of ε_t's. Because dividends and consumption follow separate processes and stock prices have volatility exceeding that of dividend fundamentals, the volatility of stock prices can be made substantially higher than that of consumption. Moreover, because of loss aversion, the model can generate a significant equity risk premium for reasonable values of the consumption risk aversion parameter γ. Thus, the model provides an explanation for the "equity premium puzzle." Because the investor cares about stock volatility, per se, a large premium can exist even though stocks may not have a high correlation with consumption.[10]

The model also generates predictability in stock returns: returns tend to be higher following crashes (when z_t is high) and smaller following expansions (when z_t is low). An implication of this is that stock returns are negatively correlated at long horizons, a feature documented by empirical research such as (Fama and French 1988), (Poterba and Summers 1988), and (Richards 1997).

The Barberis, Huang, and Santos model is one with a single type of representative individual who suffers from psychological biases. The next model that we consider assumes that there are two types of representative individuals, those with rational beliefs and those with irrational beliefs regarding the economy's fundamentals. Important insights are obtained by analyzing the interactions of these two groups of investors.

15.2 The Impact of Irrational Traders on Asset Prices

The Kogan, Ross, Wang, and Westerfield model is based on the following assumptions.

15.2.1 Assumptions

The model is a simplified endowment economy with two different types of representative individuals, where one type suffers from either irrational optimism

---

10. Recall that in standard consumption asset pricing models, an asset's risk premium depends only on its return's covariance with consumption.

or pessimism regarding risky-asset returns. Both types of individuals maximize utility of consumption at a single, future date.[11]

Technology

There is a risky asset that represents a claim on a single, risky dividend payment made at the future date $T > 0$. The value of this dividend payment is denoted D_T, and it is the date T realization of the geometric Brownian motion process

$$dD_t/D_t = \mu dt + \sigma dz \qquad (15.27)$$

where μ and σ are constants, $\sigma > 0$, and $D_0 = 1$. Note that while the process in equation (15.27) is observed at each date $t \in [0, T]$, only its realization at date T determines the risky asset's single dividend payment, D_T. As with other endowment economies, it is assumed that the date T dividend payment is perishable output so that, in equilibrium, it equals aggregate consumption, $C_T = D_T$.

Also, it is assumed that there is a market for risk-free borrowing or lending where payment occurs with certainty at date T. In other words, individuals can buy or sell (issue) a zero-coupon bond that makes a default-free payment of 1 at date T. This bond is assumed to be in zero net supply; that is, the aggregate net amount of risk-free lending or borrowing is zero. However, because there are heterogeneous groups of individuals in the economy, some individuals may borrow while others will lend.

Preferences

All individuals in the economy have identical constant relative-risk-aversion utility defined over their consumption at date T. However, there are two different groups of representative individuals. The first group of individuals are rational traders who have a date 0 endowment equal to one-half of the risky asset and maximize the expected utility function

$$E_0 \left[\frac{C_{r,T}^{\gamma}}{\gamma} \right] \qquad (15.28)$$

where $C_{r,T}$ is the date T consumption of the rational traders and $\gamma < 1$. The second group of individuals are irrational traders. They also possess a date 0 endowment of one-half of the risky asset but incorrectly believe that the probability measure is different from the actual one. Rather than thinking that the aggregate

---

11. Alvaro Sandroni (Sandroni 2000) developed a discrete-time model with similar features that allows the different types of individuals to consume at multiple future dates.

dividend process is given by (15.27), the irrational traders incorrectly perceive the dividend process to be

$$dD_t/D_t = \left(\mu + \sigma^2\eta\right) dt + \sigma\, d\widehat{z} \tag{15.29}$$

where the irrational traders believe $d\widehat{z}$ is a Brownian motion, whereas in reality, $d\widehat{z} = dz - \sigma\eta\, dt$. The irrationality parameter, η, is assumed to be a constant. A positive value of η implies that the irrational individuals are too optimistic about the risky asset's future dividend payment, while a negative value of η indicates pessimism regarding the risky asset's payoff. Hence, rather than believe that the probability measure P is generated by the Brownian motion process dz, irrational traders believe that the probability measure is generated by $d\widehat{z}$, which we refer to as the probability measure $\widehat{P}$.[12] Therefore, an irrational individual's expected utility is

$$\widehat{E}_0 \left[\frac{C_{n,T}^{\gamma}}{\gamma} \right] \tag{15.30}$$

where $C_{n,T}$ is the date T consumption of the irrational trader.

15.2.2   Solution Technique

We start by showing that the irrational individual's utility can be reinterpreted as the state-dependent utility of a rational individual. Recall from Chapter 10 that as a result of Girsanov's theorem, a transformation of the type $d\widehat{z} = dz - \sigma\eta\, dt$ leads to $\widehat{P}$ and P being equivalent probability measures and that there exists a sequence of strictly positive random variables, ξ_t, that can transform one distribution to the other. Specifically, recall from equation (10.11) that Girsanov's theorem implies $d\widehat{P}_T = \left(\xi_T/\xi_0\right) dP_T$, where based on (10.12)

$$\xi_T = \exp\left[\int_0^T \sigma\eta\, dz - \frac{1}{2} \int_0^T (\sigma\eta)^2\, ds \right]$$

$$= e^{-\frac{1}{2}\sigma^2\eta^2 T + \sigma\eta(z_T - z_0)} \tag{15.31}$$

and where, without loss of generality, we have assumed that $\xi_0 = 1$. The second line in (15.31) follows because σ and η are assumed to be constants, implying that

---

12. It should be emphasized that the probability measure $\widehat{P}$ is not necessarily the risk-neutral probability measure. The dividend process is not an asset return process so that μ is not an asset's expected rate of return and η is not a risk premium.

ξ_t follows the lognormal process $d\xi/\xi = \sigma\eta dz$. Similar to (10.30), an implication of $d\widehat{P}_T = \xi_T dP_T$ is that an irrational trader's expected utility can be written as

$$\widehat{E}_0\left[\frac{C_{n,T}^\gamma}{\gamma}\right] = E_0\left[\xi_T\frac{C_{n,T}^\gamma}{\gamma}\right] \tag{15.32}$$

$$= E_0\left[e^{-\frac{1}{2}\sigma^2\eta^2 T + \sigma\eta(z_T - z_0)}\frac{C_{n,T}^\gamma}{\gamma}\right]$$

From (15.32) we see that the objective function of the irrational trader is observationally equivalent to that of a rational trader whose utility is state dependent. The state variable affecting utility, the Brownian motion z_T, is the same source of uncertainty determining the risky asset's dividend payment.

While the ability to transform the behavior of an irrational individual to that of a rational one may depend on the particular way that irrationality is modeled, this transformation allows us to use standard methods for determining the economy's equilibrium. Given the assumption of two different groups of representative individuals, we can solve for an equilibrium where the representative individuals act competitively, taking the price of the risky asset and the risk-free borrowing or lending rate as given. In addition, because there is only a single source of uncertainty, that being the risky asset's payoff, the economy is dynamically complete.

Given market completeness, let us apply the martingale pricing method introduced in Chapter 12. Each individual's lifetime utility function can be interpreted as of the form of (12.55) but with interim utility of consumption equaling zero and only a utility of terminal bequest being nonzero. Hence, based on equation (12.57), the result of each individual's static optimization is that his terminal marginal utility of consumption is proportional to the pricing kernel:

$$C_{r,T}^{\gamma-1} = \lambda_r M_T \tag{15.33}$$

$$\xi_T C_{n,T}^{\gamma-1} = \lambda_n M_T \tag{15.34}$$

where λ_r and λ_n are the Lagrange multipliers for the rational and irrational individuals, respectively. Substituting out for M_T, we can write

$$C_{r,T} = \left(\lambda\xi_T\right)^{-\frac{1}{1-\gamma}} C_{n,T} \tag{15.35}$$

where we define $\lambda \equiv \lambda_r/\lambda_n$. Also note that the individuals' terminal consumption must sum to the risky asset's dividend payment

$$C_{r,T} + C_{n,T} = D_T \tag{15.36}$$

Equations (15.35) and (15.36) allow us to write each individual's terminal consumption as

$$C_{r,T} = \frac{1}{1 + (\lambda \xi_T)^{\frac{1}{1-\gamma}}} D_T \tag{15.37}$$

Substituting (15.37) into (15.35), we also obtain

$$C_{n,T} = \frac{(\lambda \xi_T)^{\frac{1}{1-\gamma}}}{1 + (\lambda \xi_T)^{\frac{1}{1-\gamma}}} D_T \tag{15.38}$$

Similar to what was done in Chapter 13, the parameter $\lambda = \lambda_r/\lambda_n$ is determined by the individuals' initial endowments of wealth. Each individual's initial wealth is an asset that pays a dividend equal to the individual's terminal consumption. To value this wealth, we must determine the form of the stochastic discount factor used to discount consumption. As a prelude, note that the date t price of the zero-coupon bond that pays 1 at date $T > t$ is given by

$$P(t, T) = E_t [M_T/M_t] \tag{15.39}$$

In what follows, we deflate all asset prices, including the individuals' initial wealths, by this zero-coupon bond price. This is done for analytical convenience, though it should be noted that using the zero-coupon bond as the numeraire is somewhat different from using the value of a money market investment as the numeraire, as was done in Chapter 10. While the return on the zero-coupon bond over its remaining time to maturity is risk-free, its instantaneous return will not, in general, be risk-free.

Let us define $W_{r,0}$ and $W_{n,0}$ as the initial wealths, deflated by the zero-coupon bond price, of the rational and irrational individuals, respectively. They equal

$$W_{r,0} = \frac{E_0 [C_{r,T} M_T/M_0]}{E_0 [M_T/M_0]} = \frac{E_0 [C_{r,T} M_T]}{E_0 [M_T]} \tag{15.40}$$

$$= \frac{E_0 \left[C_{r,T} C_{r,T}^{\gamma-1}/\lambda_r \right]}{E_0 \left[C_{r,T}^{\gamma-1}/\lambda_r \right]} = \frac{E_0 \left[C_{r,T}^{\gamma} \right]}{E_0 \left[C_{r,T}^{\gamma-1} \right]}$$

$$= \frac{E_0 \left[\left[1 + (\lambda \xi_T)^{\frac{1}{1-\gamma}} \right]^{-\gamma} D_T^{\gamma} \right]}{E_0 \left[\left[1 + (\lambda \xi_T)^{\frac{1}{1-\gamma}} \right]^{1-\gamma} D_T^{\gamma-1} \right]}$$

where in the second line of (15.40) we used (15.33) to substitute for M_T, and then in the third line we used (15.37) to substitute for $C_{r,T}$. A similar derivation that uses (15.34) and (15.38) leads to

$$W_{n,0} = \frac{E_0\left[(\lambda\xi_T)^{\frac{1}{1-\gamma}}\left[1+(\lambda\xi_T)^{\frac{1}{1-\gamma}}\right]^{-\gamma}D_T^{\gamma}\right]}{E_0\left[\left[1+(\lambda\xi_T)^{\frac{1}{1-\gamma}}\right]^{1-\gamma}D_T^{\gamma-1}\right]} \tag{15.41}$$

Because it was assumed that the rational and irrational individuals are each initially endowed with equal one-half shares of the risky asset, then it must be the case that $W_{r,0} = W_{n,0}$. Equating the right-hand sides of equations (15.40) and (15.41) determines the value for λ. The expectations in these equations can be computed by noting that ξ_T satisfies (15.31) and is lognormally distributed and that

$$D_T/D_t = e^{\left[\mu-\frac{1}{2}\sigma^2\right](T-t)+\sigma(z_T-z_t)} \tag{15.42}$$

and is also lognormally distributed.[13] It is left as an end-of-chapter exercise to verify that the value of λ that solves the equality $W_{r,0} = W_{n,0}$ is given by

$$\lambda = e^{-\gamma\eta\sigma^2 T} \tag{15.43}$$

Given this value of λ, we have now determined the form of the pricing kernel and can solve for the equilibrium price of the risky asset. Define S_t as the date $t < T$ price of the risky asset deflated by the price of the zero-coupon bond. Then if we also define $\varepsilon_{T,t} \equiv \lambda\xi_T = \xi_t e^{-\gamma\eta\sigma^2 T-\frac{1}{2}\sigma^2\eta^2(T-t)+\sigma\eta(z_T-z_t)}$, the deflated risky-asset price can be written as

$$S_t = \frac{E_t\left[D_T M_T/M_t\right]}{E_t\left[M_T/M_t\right]} = \frac{E_t\left[\left(1+\varepsilon_{T,t}^{\frac{1}{1-\gamma}}\right)^{1-\gamma}D_T^{\gamma}\right]}{E_t\left[\left(1+\varepsilon_{T,t}^{\frac{1}{1-\gamma}}\right)^{1-\gamma}D_T^{\gamma-1}\right]} \tag{15.44}$$

While it is not possible to characterize in closed form the rational and irrational individuals' portfolio policies, we can still derive insights regarding equilibrium asset pricing.[14]

---

13. Recall that it was assumed that $D_0 = 1$. Note also that powers of ξ_T and D_T, such as D_T^{γ}, are also lognormally distributed.

14. Kogan, Ross, Wang, and Westerfield show that the individuals' demand for the risky asset, ω, satisfies the bound $|\omega| \leq 1 + |\eta| (2-\gamma)/(1-\gamma)$.

15.2.3   Analysis of the Results

For the limiting case of there being only rational individuals, that is, $\eta = 0$, then $\varepsilon_{T,t} = \xi_t = 1$ and from (15.44) the deflated stock price, $S_{r,t}$, is

$$S_{r,t} = \frac{E_t\left[D_T^\gamma\right]}{E_t\left[D_T^{\gamma-1}\right]} = D_t e^{\left[\mu-\sigma^2\right](T-t)+\sigma^2\gamma(T-t)} \tag{15.45}$$

$$= e^{\left[\mu-(1-\gamma)\sigma^2\right]T+\left[(1-\gamma)-\frac{1}{2}\right]\sigma^2 t+\sigma(z_t-z_0)}$$

A simple application of Itô's lemma shows that equation (15.45) implies that the risky asset's price follows geometric Brownian motion:

$$dS_{r,t}/S_{r,t} = (1-\gamma)\,\sigma^2 dt + \sigma\,dz \tag{15.46}$$

Similarly, when all individuals are irrational, the deflated stock price, $S_{n,t}$, is

$$S_{n,t} = e^{\left[\mu-(1-\gamma-\eta)\sigma^2\right]T+\left[(1-\gamma-\eta)-\frac{1}{2}\right]\sigma^2 t+\sigma(z_t-z_0)} = S_{r,t}e^{\eta\sigma^2(T-t)} \tag{15.47}$$

and its rate of return follows the process

$$dS_{n,t}/S_{n,t} = (1-\gamma-\eta)\,\sigma^2 dt + \sigma\,dz \tag{15.48}$$

Note that in (15.47) and (15.48) the effect of η is similar to γ. When all individuals are irrational, if η is positive, the higher expected dividend growth acts like lower risk aversion in that individuals find the risky asset, relative to the zero-coupon bond, more attractive. Equation (15.47) shows that this greater demand raises the deflated stock price relative to that in an economy with all rational individuals, while equation (15.48) indicates that it also lowers the stock's equilibrium expected rate of return.

It is also interesting to note that (15.46) and (15.48) indicate that when the economy is populated by only one type of individual, the volatility of the risky asset's deflated return equals σ. In contrast, when both types of individuals populate the economy, the risky asset's volatility, $\sigma_{S,t}$, always exceeds σ. Applying Itô's lemma to (15.44), Kogan, Ross, Wang, and Westerfield prove that the risky asset's volatility satisfies the following bounds:[15]

$$\sigma \le \sigma_{S,t} \le \sigma\,(1+|\eta|) \tag{15.49}$$

The conclusion is that a diversity of beliefs has the effect of raising the equilibrium volatility of the risky asset.

---

15. The proof is given in Appendix B of (Kogan et al. 2006). Below, we show that this bound is satisfied for the case of individuals with logarithmic utility.

For the special case in which rational and irrational individuals have logarithmic utility, that is, $\gamma = 0$, then (15.44) simplifies to

$$S_t = \frac{1 + E_t\left[\xi_T\right]}{E_t\left[(1 + \xi_T)\, D_T^{-1}\right]} \tag{15.50}$$

$$= D_t e^{\left[\mu - \sigma^2\right](T-t)} \frac{1 + \xi_t}{1 + \xi_t e^{-\eta\sigma^2(T-t)}}$$

$$= e^{\left[\mu - \frac{1}{2}\sigma^2\right]T - \frac{1}{2}\sigma^2(T-t) + \sigma(z_t - z_0)} \frac{1 + \xi_t}{1 + \xi_t e^{-\eta\sigma^2(T-t)}}$$

For this particular case, the risky asset's expected rate of return and variance, as a function of the distribution of wealth between the rational and irrational individuals, can be derived explicitly. Define

$$\alpha_t \equiv \frac{W_{r,t}}{W_{r,t} + W_{n,t}} = \frac{W_{r,t}}{S_t} \tag{15.51}$$

as the proportion of total wealth owned by the rational individuals. Using (15.40) and (15.44), we see that when $\gamma = 0$ this ratio equals

$$\alpha_t = \frac{E_t\left[\left(1 + \varepsilon_{T,t}^{\frac{1}{1-\gamma}}\right)^{-\gamma} D_T^\gamma\right]}{E_t\left[\left(1 + \varepsilon_{T,t}^{\frac{1}{1-\gamma}}\right)^{1-\gamma} D_T^\gamma\right]} = \frac{1}{1 + E_t\left[\xi_T\right]} = \frac{1}{1 + \xi_t} \tag{15.52}$$

Viewing S_t as a function of D_t and ξ_t as in the second line of (15.50), Itô's lemma can be applied to derive the mean and standard deviation of the risky asset's rate of return. The algebra is lengthy but results in the values

$$\sigma_{S,t} = \sigma + \eta\sigma \left[\frac{1}{1 + e^{-\eta\sigma^2(T-t)}\left(\alpha_t^{-1} - 1\right)} - \alpha_t \right] \tag{15.53}$$

and

$$\mu_{S,t} = \sigma_{S,t}^2 - \eta\sigma\left(1 - \alpha_t\right)\sigma_{S,t} \tag{15.54}$$

where we have used $\alpha_t = 1/\left(1 + \xi_t\right)$ to substitute out for ξ_t. Note that when $\alpha_t = 1$ or 0, equations (15.53) and (15.54) are consistent with (15.46) and (15.48) for the case of $\gamma = 0$.

Kogan, Ross, Wang, and Westerfield use their model to study how terminal wealth (consumption) is distributed between the rational and irrational individuals as the investment horizon, T, becomes large. The motivation for this comparative static exercise is the well-known conjecture made by Milton Friedman (Friedman 1953) that irrational traders cannot survive in a competitive market. The intuition is that when individuals trade based on the wrong beliefs, they will lose money to the rational traders, so that in the long run these irrational traders will deplete their wealth. Hence, in the long run, rational traders should control most of the economy's wealth and asset prices should reflect these rational individual's (correct) beliefs. The implication is that even when some individuals are irrational, markets should evolve toward long-run efficiency because irrational individuals will be driven to "extinction."

Kogan, Ross, Wang, and Westerfield introduce a definition of what would constitute the long-run dominance of rational individuals and, therefore, the relative extinction of irrational individuals. The *relative extinction* of an irrational individual would occur if

$$\lim_{T \to \infty} \frac{C_{n,T}}{C_{r,T}} = 0 \text{ a.s.} \tag{15.55}$$

which means that for arbitrarily small δ the probability of $\left| \lim_{T \to \infty} \frac{C_{n,T}}{C_{r,T}} \right| > \delta$ equals zero.[16] The relative extinction of a rational individual is defined symmetrically, and an individual is said to *survive relatively* in the long run if relative extinction does not occur.[17]

For the case of individuals having logarithmic utility, irrational individuals always suffer relative extinction. The proof of this is as follows. Rearranging (15.35), we have

$$\frac{C_{n,T}}{C_{r,T}} = \left(\lambda \xi_T \right)^{\frac{1}{1-\gamma}} \tag{15.56}$$

and for the case of $\gamma = 0$, (15.43) implies that $\lambda = 1$. Hence,

$$\frac{C_{n,T}}{C_{r,T}} = \xi_T \tag{15.57}$$

$$= e^{-\frac{1}{2}\sigma^2 \eta^2 T + \sigma \eta (z_T - z_0)}$$

---

16. In general, a sequence of random variables, say, X_t, is said to converge to X almost surely (a.s.) if for arbitrary δ, the probability $P\left(|\lim_{t \to \infty} X_t - X| > \delta \right) = 0$.

17. One could also define the *absolute extinction* of the irrational individual. This would occur if $\lim_{T \to \infty} C_{n,T} = 0$ almost surely, and an individual is said to *survive absolutely* in the long run if absolute extinction does not occur. Relative survival is sufficient for absolute survival, but the converse is not true. Similarly, absolute extinction implies relative extinction, but the converse is not true.

Based on the strong law of large numbers for Brownian motions, it can be shown that for any value of b

$$\lim_{T \to \infty} e^{aT + b(z_T - z_0)} = \begin{cases} 0 & a < 0 \\ \infty & a > 0 \end{cases} \tag{15.58}$$

where convergence occurs almost surely.[18] Since $-\frac{1}{2}\sigma^2\eta^2 < 0$ in (15.57), we see that equation (15.55) is proved.

The intuition for why irrational individuals become relatively extinct is due, in part, to the special properties of logarithmic utility. Note that the portfolio policy of the logarithmic rational individual is to maximize at each date t the utility

$$E_t\left[\ln C_{r,T}\right] = E_t\left[\ln W_{r,T}\right] \tag{15.59}$$

This is equivalent to maximizing the expected continuously compounded return per unit time:

$$E_t\left[\frac{1}{T-t} \ln\left(W_{r,T}/W_{r,t}\right)\right] = \frac{1}{T-t}\left[E_t\left[\ln\left(W_{r,T}\right)\right] - \ln\left(W_{r,t}\right)\right] \tag{15.60}$$

since $W_{r,t}$ is known at date t and $T - t > 0$. Thus, from (15.60) the rational log utility individual follows a portfolio policy that maximizes $E_t\left[d \ln W_{r,t}\right]$ at each point in time. This portfolio policy is referred to as the "growth-optimum port-folio" because it maximizes the (continuously compounded) return on wealth.[19] Now given that in the model economy there is a single source of uncertainty affecting portfolio returns, dz, the processes for the rational and irrational individuals' wealths can be written as

$$dW_{r,t}/W_{r,t} = \mu_{r,t}dt + \sigma_{r,t}dz \tag{15.61}$$

$$dW_{n,t}/W_{n,t} = \mu_{n,t}dt + \sigma_{n,t}dz \tag{15.62}$$

where, in general, the expected rates of returns and volatilities, $\mu_{r,t}$, $\mu_{n,t}$, $\sigma_{r,t}$, and $\sigma_{n,t}$, are time varying. Applying Itô's lemma, it is straightforward to show

---

18. See section 2.9.A of (Karatzas and Shreve 1991).

19. For the standard portfolio choice problem of selecting a portfolio from n risky assets and an instantaneously risk-free asset, we showed in equation (12.44) of Chapter 12 that the growth-optimum portfolio has the risky-asset portfolio weights $\omega_i^* = \sum_{j=1}^{n} v_{ij}(\mu_j - r)$. Note that this log utility investor's portfolio depends only on the current values of the investment opportunity set, and portfolio demands do not reflect a desire to hedge against changes in investment opportunities.

that the process followed by the log of the ratio of the individuals' wealth is

$$d \ln \left(\frac{W_{n,t}}{W_{r,t}} \right) = \left[\left(\mu_{n,t} - \frac{1}{2}\sigma_{n,t}^2 \right) - \left(\mu_{r,t} - \frac{1}{2}\sigma_{r,t}^2 \right) \right] dt + (\sigma_{n,t} - \sigma_{r,t}) \, dz$$

$$= E_t \left[d \ln W_{n,t} \right] - E_t \left[d \ln W_{r,t} \right] + (\sigma_{n,t} - \sigma_{r,t}) \, dz \qquad (15.63)$$

Since the irrational individual chooses a portfolio policy that deviates from the growth-optimum portfolio, we know that $E_t \left[d \ln W_{n,t} \right] - E_t \left[d \ln W_{r,t} \right] < 0$, and thus $E_t \left[d \ln \left(W_{n,t}/W_{r,t} \right) \right] < 0$, making $d \ln \left(W_{n,t}/W_{r,t} \right)$ a process that is expected to steadily decline as $t \longrightarrow \infty$, which verifies Friedman's conjecture that irrational individuals lose wealth to rational ones in the long run.

While irrational individuals lose influence in the long run, as indicated by equations (15.50), (15.53), and (15.54), their presence may impact the level and dynamics of asset prices for substantial periods of time prior to becoming "extinct." Moreover, if as empirical evidence suggests, individuals have constant relative-risk-aversion utility with $\gamma < 0$ so that they are more risk averse than logarithmic utility, it turns out that Friedman's conjecture may not always hold. To see this, let us compute (15.56) for the general case of $\lambda = e^{-\gamma \eta \sigma^2 T}$:

$$\frac{C_{n,T}}{C_{r,T}} = (\lambda \xi_T)^{\frac{1}{1-\gamma}} \qquad (15.64)$$

$$= e^{-\left[\gamma \eta + \frac{1}{2}\eta^2 \right] \frac{\sigma^2}{1-\gamma} T + \frac{\sigma \eta}{1-\gamma} (z_T - z_0)}$$

Thus, we see that the limiting behavior of $C_{n,T}/C_{r,T}$ is determined by the sign of the expression $\left[\gamma \eta + \frac{1}{2}\eta^2 \right]$ or $\eta \left(\gamma + \frac{1}{2}\eta \right)$. Given that $\gamma < 0$, the strong law of large numbers allows us to conclude

$$\lim_{T \longrightarrow \infty} \frac{C_{n,T}}{C_{r,T}} = \begin{cases} 0 & \eta < 0 & \text{rational trader survives} \\ \infty & 0 < \eta < -2\gamma & \text{irrational trader survives} \\ 0 & -2\gamma < \eta & \text{rational trader survives} \end{cases} \qquad (15.65)$$

When the irrational individual is pessimistic ($\eta < 0$) or strongly optimistic ($\eta > -2\gamma$), he becomes relatively extinct in the long run. However, when the irrational individual is moderately optimistic ($0 < \eta < -2\gamma$), the model has the opposite implication in that it is the rational individual who becomes relatively extinct in the long run. This parametric case is the reverse of Friedman's conjecture.

The intuition for these results comes from our previous discussion of a log utility investor's choice of the growth-optimal portfolio. When rational individuals are more risk averse than log utility ($\gamma < 0$), their demand for the risky asset is less than would be chosen by a log utility investor.[20] Ceteris paribus, the wealth of these $\gamma < 0$ investors would tend to grow more slowly than that of someone with log utility. When $\eta < 0$, irrationally pessimistic investors would demand even less of the risky asset than their rational counterparts, which would move them even farther away from the growth-optimal portfolio. Hence, in this case, a rational individual's wealth would tend to grow faster than the wealth of the irrational individual, so that the irrational individual would not survive in the long run.

When the irrational individual is optimistic ($\eta > 0$), her demand for the risky asset will exceed that of a rational investor. When her optimism is moderate, ($0 < \eta < -2\gamma$), her portfolio demand is closer to the growth-optimal portfolio than is the portfolio demanded by the rational individual. Therefore, in this case, the moderately optimistic individual's wealth grows faster than that of the rational individual, so that the rational individual suffers relative extinction in the long run. In contrast, when the irrational individual is strongly optimistic ($\eta > -2\gamma$), her demand for the risky asset is so great that her portfolio choice is farther from the growth-optimal portfolio than is the rational individual. For this case, the irrational individual's wealth tends to grow relatively slowly and, as in the pessimistic case, she does not survive in the long run.

The model outlined in this section is clearly a simplification of reality in that it assumes that individuals gain utility from only terminal, not interim, consumption. Interim consumption reduces the growth of wealth, and differences between rational and irrational individuals' consumption rates could affect their relative survivability. The model also assumes that rational and irrational individuals have the same preferences (levels of risk aversion). In general, an individual's portfolio choice, which affects his growth of wealth and survivability, is determined by risk aversion as well as beliefs. Hence, systematic differences between rational and irrational investors' risk aversions could influence the model's conclusions. In addition, one might expect that irrational individuals might learn over time of their mistakes since the historical distribution of the dividend process will tend to differ from their beliefs. The effect of such learning may be that irrationality could diminish with age.[21] Lastly, the model considers only one form of irrationality, namely, systematic optimism or pessimism. Other forms of irrationality have been identified that presumably would change the dynamics of wealth and of the

---

20. For example, recall from Chapter 12's analysis of the standard consumption–portfolio choice problem when investment opportunities are constant that equation (12.35), $\omega^* = \frac{\mu - r}{(1-\gamma)\sigma^2}$, implies that the demand for the risky asset decreases as risk aversion increases.

21. However, there is empirical psychological evidence (Lord, Ross, and Lepper 1979) showing that individuals tend to persist too strongly in their initial beliefs after being exposed to contrary information.

equilibrium prices of risky assets.[22] Yet, the main conclusions of the model, that irrational investors may have a significant impact on asset prices and that they may not necessarily become extinct, are likely to remain robust.

15.3 Summary

There is a growing body of experimental and empirical research documenting that individuals do not always form beliefs rationally and do not always make decisions consistent with expected utility theory. Analyzing the asset pricing implications of such behavior is at an early stage. This chapter attempted to present two of the few general equilibrium models that incorporate psychological biases or irrationality. Interestingly, these models can be solved using techniques similar to those previously employed to derive models of rational, expected-utility-maximizing individuals. Both models in this chapter embed rationality as a special case, which makes it easy to see how their behavioral assumptions specifically affect the models' results.

Currently, there is no consensus among financial economists regarding the importance of incorporating aspects of behavioral finance into asset pricing theories. Some criticize behavioral finance theories as ad hoc explanations of anomalies that are not always mutually consistent. It is especially unclear whether a behavioral paradigm will be universally successful in supplanting asset pricing theories built on von Neumann–Morgenstern expected utility. However, it is likely that research exploring the asset pricing implications of behavioral biases will grow in coming years.

15.4 Exercises

1. In the Barberis, Huang, and Santos model, verify that the first-order conditions (15.16) and (15.17) lead to the envelope condition (15.18).

2. In the Barberis, Huang, and Santos model, solve for the price-dividend ratio, P_t/D_t, for Economy II when utility is standard constant relative risk aversion, that is,

$$E_0 \left[\sum_{t=0}^{\infty} \delta^t \frac{C_t^{\gamma}}{\gamma} \right]$$

---

22. Recent models incorporating various forms of irrationality (Barberis, Shleifer, and Vishny 1998; Daniel, Hirshleifer, and Subrahmanyam 1998; and Hong and Stein 1999) have been constructed to explain the empirical phenomena that stock returns display short-run positive serial correlation (momentum) and long-run negative serial correlation (reversals or mean reversion). See pages 1551–1556 of John Campbell's survey of asset pricing (Campbell 2000) for a summary of these and other behavioral finance models.

3. In the Kogan, Ross, Wang, and Westerfield model, verify that $\lambda = e^{-\gamma \eta \sigma^2 T}$ satisfies the equality $W_{r,0} = W_{n,0}$.

4. In the Kogan, Ross, Wang, and Westerfield model, suppose that both representative individuals are rational but have different levels of risk aversion. The first type of representative individual maximizes utility of the form

$$E_0 \left[\frac{C_{r,T}^{\gamma_1}}{\gamma_1} \right]$$

and the second type of representative individual maximizes utility of the form

$$E_0 \left[\frac{C_{n,T}^{\gamma_2}}{\gamma_2} \right]$$

where $1 > \gamma_1 > \gamma_2$. Assuming $W_{r,0} = W_{n,0}$, solve for the equilibrium price of the risky asset deflated by the discount bond maturing at date T.

CHAPTER 16

Asset Pricing with Differential Information

The asset pricing models in prior chapters assumed that individuals have common information. Now we will consider arguably more realistic situations where individuals can have different private information about an asset's future payoff or value. Because the literature on asset pricing in the presence of private information is vast, this chapter is meant to provide only a taste of this research area.[1] However, the two models that we present in this chapter, those of Sanford Grossman (Grossman 1976) and Albert "Pete" Kyle (Kyle 1985), are probably the two most common modeling frameworks in this field of research. Familiarity with these two models provides a segue to much additional theoretical research.

A topic of particular interest is the influence of private information on a risky asset's equilibrium price. We start by analyzing the Grossman model that shows how individuals' information affects their demands for an asset and, via these demands, how private information is contained in the asset's equilibrium price. The model examines two equilibria: a "competitive," but not fully rational, equilibrium; and a fully revealing rational expectations equilibrium.

Following this, we examine an extension of the Grossman model that includes an additional source of uncertainty, namely, shifts in the supply of the risky asset. A model of this type was developed in a number of studies, including (Grossman and Stiglitz 1980), (Hellwig 1980), (Diamond and Verrecchia 1981), and (Grundy and McNichols 1989). Importantly, in a rational expectations equilibrium, this

---

1. More in-depth coverage of topics in this chapter includes books by Maureen O'Hara (O'Hara 1995) and Markus Brunnermeier (Brunnermeier 2001).

additional supply uncertainty makes the equilibrium asset price only partially reveal the private information of individuals.

We cover one additional model of a risky-asset market that also possesses an equilibrium where private information is partially revealed. It is Kyle's seminal market microstructure model. This model assumes a market for a particular security in which one agent, the so-called insider, has private information and trades with lesser-informed agents composed of a market maker and "noise" traders. The model solves for the strategic trading behavior of the insider and market maker and provides a theoretical framework for determining bid-ask spreads and the market impact of trades.

16.1   Equilibrium with Private Information

The model by Sanford Grossman (Grossman 1976) that we consider in this section examines how an investor's private information about a risky asset's future payoff affects her demand for that asset and, in turn, the asset's equilibrium price. In addition, it takes account of the idea that a rational individual can learn about others' private information from the risky asset's price, a concept known as "price discovery."

16.1.1   Grossman Model Assumptions

The Grossman model is based on the following assumptions.

Assets

This is a single-period portfolio choice problem. At the beginning of the period, traders can choose between a risk-free asset, which pays a known end-of-period return (1 plus the interest rate) of R_f, and a risky asset that has a beginning-of-period price of P_0 per share and an end-of-period random payoff (price) of $\widetilde{P}_1$ per share. The unconditional distribution of $\widetilde{P}_1$ is assumed to be normally distributed as $N(m, \sigma^2)$. The aggregate supply of shares of the risky asset is fixed at $\overline{X}$, but the risk-free asset is in perfectly elastic supply.

Trader Wealth and Preferences

There are n different traders. The ith trader has beginning-of-period wealth W_{0i} and is assumed to maximize expected utility over end-of-period wealth, $\widetilde{W}_{1i}$. Each trader is assumed to have constant absolute-risk-aversion (CARA) utility, but traders' levels of risk aversion are permitted to differ. Specifically, the form of the ith trader's utility function is assumed to be

$$U_i(\widetilde{W}_{1i}) = -e^{-a_i \widetilde{W}_{1i}}, \quad a_i > 0 \tag{16.1}$$

Trader Information

At the beginning of the period, the ith trader observes y_i, which is a realized value from the noisy signal of the risky-asset end-of-period value

$$\tilde{y}_i = \widetilde{P}_1 + \tilde{\epsilon}_i \qquad (16.2)$$

where $\tilde{\epsilon}_i \sim N(0, \sigma_i^2)$ and is independent of $\widetilde{P}_1$.

16.1.2 Individuals' Asset Demands

Let X_i be the number of shares of the risky asset chosen by the ith trader at the beginning of the period. Thus, the ith trader's wealth accumulation equation can be written as

$$\widetilde{W}_{1i} = R_f W_{0i} + \left[\widetilde{P}_1 - R_f P_0 \right] X_i \qquad (16.3)$$

Denote I_i as the information available to the ith trader at the beginning of the period. The trader's maximization problem is then

$$\max_{X_i} E\left[U_i(\widetilde{W}_{1i}) | I_i \right] = \max_{X_i} E\left[-e^{-a_i \left(R_f W_{0i} + \left[\widetilde{P}_1 - R_f P_0 \right] X_i \right)} | I_i \right] \qquad (16.4)$$

Since $\widetilde{W}_{1i}$ depends on $\widetilde{P}_1$, it is normally distributed, and due to the exponential form of the utility function, (16.4) is the moment-generating function of a normal random variable. Therefore, as we have seen earlier in the context of mean-variance analysis, the maximization problem is equivalent to

$$\max_{X_i} \left\{ E\left[\widetilde{W}_{1i} | I_i \right] - \frac{1}{2} a_i \operatorname{Var}\left[\widetilde{W}_{1i} | I_i \right] \right\} \qquad (16.5)$$

or

$$\max_{X_i} \left\{ X_i \left(E\left[\widetilde{P}_1 | I_i \right] - R_f P_0 \right) - \frac{1}{2} a_i X_i^2 \operatorname{Var}\left[\widetilde{P}_1 | I_i \right] \right\} \qquad (16.6)$$

The first-order condition with respect to X_i then gives us the optimal number of shares held in the risky asset:

$$X_i = \frac{E\left[\widetilde{P}_1 | I_i \right] - R_f P_0}{a_i \operatorname{Var}\left[\widetilde{P}_1 | I_i \right]} \qquad (16.7)$$

Equation (16.7) indicates that the demand for the risky asset is increasing in its expected excess return but declining in its price variance and the investor's risk aversion. Note that the CARA utility assumption results in the investor's demand for the risky asset being independent of wealth. This simplifies the derivation of the risky asset's equilibrium price.

16.1.3   A Competitive Equilibrium

Now consider an equilibrium in which each trader uses his knowledge of the unconditional distribution of $\widetilde{P}_1$ along with the conditioning information from his private signal, y_i, so that $I_i = \{y_i\}$. Then using Bayes rule and the fact that $\widetilde{P}_1$ and $\tilde{y}_i$ are jointly normally distributed with a squared correlation $\rho_i^2 \equiv \frac{\sigma^2}{\sigma^2 + \sigma_i^2}$, the ith trader's conditional expected value and variance of $\widetilde{P}_1$ are[2]

$$E\left[\widetilde{P}_1 \mid I_i\right] = m + \rho_i^2 \, (y_i - m)$$

$$\mathrm{Var}\left[\widetilde{P}_1 \mid I_i\right] = \sigma^2 \, (1 - \rho_i^2)$$

(16.8)

Substituting these into (16.7), we have

$$X_i = \frac{m + \rho_i^2 \, (y_i - m) - R_f \, P_0}{a_i \, \sigma^2 \, (1 - \rho_i^2)}$$

(16.9)

From the denominator of (16.9), one sees that the individual's demand for the risky asset is greater the lower his risk aversion, a_i, and the greater the precision of his signal (the closer is ρ_i to 1, that is, the lower is σ_i). Now by aggregating the individual traders' risky-asset demands for shares and setting the sum equal to the fixed supply of shares, we can solve for the equilibrium risky-asset price, P_0, that equates supply and demand:

$$\overline{X} = \sum_{i=1}^{n} \left[\frac{m + \rho_i^2 \, (y_i - m) - R_f \, P_0}{a_i \, \sigma^2 \, (1 - \rho_i^2)} \right]$$

$$= \sum_{i=1}^{n} \left[\frac{m + \rho_i^2 \, (y_i - m)}{a_i \, \sigma^2 \, (1 - \rho_i^2)} \right] - \sum_{i=1}^{n} \left[\frac{R_f \, P_0}{a_i \, \sigma^2 \, (1 - \rho_i^2)} \right]$$

(16.10)

or

$$P_0 = \frac{1}{R_f} \left[\sum_{i=1}^{n} \frac{m + \rho_i^2 \, (y_i - m)}{a_i \, \sigma^2 \, (1 - \rho_i^2)} - \overline{X} \right] \Big/ \left[\sum_{i=1}^{n} \frac{1}{a_i \, \sigma^2 \, (1 - \rho_i^2)} \right]$$

(16.11)

From (16.11) we see that the price reflects a weighted average of the traders' conditional expectations of the payoff of the risky asset. For example, the weight

---

2. A derivation of (16.8) is given as an end-of-chapter exercise. Note that ρ_i is the correlation coefficient since $\frac{\mathrm{cov}(\widetilde{P}_1, \tilde{y}_i)}{\sigma_{\widetilde{P}_1} \, \sigma_{\tilde{y}_i}} = \frac{\sigma^2}{\sigma \sqrt{\sigma^2 + \sigma_i^2}} = \rho_i$.

on the ith trader's conditional expectation, $m + \rho_i^2(y_i - m)$, is

$$\frac{1}{a_i\,\sigma^2\,(1-\rho_i^2)} \Bigg/ \left[\sum_{i=1}^{n} \frac{1}{a_i\,\sigma^2\,(1-\rho_i^2)} \right] \qquad (16.12)$$

The more precise (higher ρ_i) is trader i's signal or the lower is his risk aversion (lower a_i), the more aggressively he trades and, as a result, the more that the equilibrium price reflects his expectations.

16.1.4 A Rational Expectations Equilibrium

The solution for the price, P_0, in equation (16.11) can be interpreted as a competitive equilibrium: each trader uses information from his own signal and takes the price of the risky asset as given in formulating her demand for the risky asset. However, this equilibrium neglects the possibility that a trader might infer information about other traders' signals from the equilibrium price itself, what practitioners call "price discovery." In this sense, the previous equilibrium is not a rational expectations equilibrium. Why? Suppose traders initially formulate their demands according to equation (16.9), using only information about their own signals, and the price in (16.11) results. Then an individual trader could obtain information about the other traders' signals from the formula for P_0 in (16.11). Hence, this trader would have the incentive to change her demand from that initially formulated in (16.9). This implies that equation (16.11) would not be the rational expectations equilibrium price.

Therefore, to derive a fully rational expectations equilibrium, we need to allow traders' information sets to depend not only on their individual signals, but on the equilibrium price itself: $I_i = \{y_i, P_0^*(y)\}$ where $y \equiv (y_1\ y_2 \dots y_n)$ is a vector of the traders' individual signals and $P_0^*(y)$ is the rational expectations equilibrium price.[3]

In equilibrium, the aggregate demand for the shares of the risky asset must equal the aggregate supply, implying

$$\overline{X} = \sum_{i=1}^{n} \left[\frac{E\left[\widetilde{P}_1 \mid y_i,\ P_0^*(y) \right] - R_f\,P_0^*(y)}{a_i\,\mathrm{Var}\left[\widetilde{P}_1 \mid y_i,\ P_0^*(y) \right]} \right] \qquad (16.13)$$

---

3. The theory of a rational expectations equilibrium was introduced by John F. Muth (Muth 1961). Robert E. Lucas won the 1995 Nobel prize in economics for developing and applying rational expectations theory in several papers, including (Lucas 1972), (Lucas 1976), and (Lucas 1987).

Now one can show that a rational expectations equilibrium exists when investors' signals have independent forecast errors and have equal accuracies. Specifically, it is assumed that in (16.2) the ϵ_i's are independent and have the same variance, $\sigma_i^2 = \sigma_\epsilon^2$, for $i = 1, \ldots, n$.

THEOREM   There exists a rational expectations equilibrium with $P_0^*(y)$ given by

$$P_0^*(y) = \frac{1 - \rho^2}{R_f} m + \frac{\rho^2}{R_f} \bar{y} - \frac{\sigma^2 (1 - \rho^2)}{R_f \sum_{i=1}^n \frac{1}{a_i}} \overline{X} \tag{16.14}$$

where $\bar{y} \equiv \frac{1}{n} \sum_{i=1}^n y_i$ and $\rho^2 \equiv \frac{\sigma^2}{\sigma^2 + \frac{\sigma_\epsilon^2}{n}}$.

Proof: An intuitive outline of the proof is as follows.[4] Note that in (16.14) $P_0^*(y)$ is a linear function of $\bar{y}$ with a fixed coefficient of ρ^2/R_f. Therefore, if a trader observes $P_0^*(y)$ (and knows the structure of the model, that is, the other parameters), then he can invert this price formula to infer the value of $\bar{y}$. Now because all traders' signals were assumed to have equal precision (same σ_ϵ^2), the average signal, $\bar{y}$, is a sufficient statistic for the information contained in all of the other signals. Further, because of the assumed independence of the signals, the precision of this average of signals is proportional to the number of traders, n. Hence, the average signal would have the same precision as a single signal with variance $\frac{\sigma_\epsilon^2}{n}$. ∎

Now if individual traders' demands are given by equation (16.9) but where y_i is replaced with $\bar{y}$ and ρ_i is replaced with ρ, then by aggregating these demands and setting them equal to $\overline{X}$ as in equation (16.10), we end up with the solution in equation (16.14), which is consistent with our initial assumption that traders can invert $P_0^*(y)$ to find $\bar{y}$. Hence, $P_0^*(y)$ in equation (16.14) is the rational expectations equilibrium price of the risky asset.

Note that the information, $\bar{y}$, reflected in the equilibrium price is superior to any single trader's private signal, y_i. In fact, since $\bar{y}$ is a sufficient statistic for all traders' information, it makes knowledge of any single signal, y_i, redundant. The equilibrium would be the same if all traders received the same signal, $\bar{y} \sim N(m, \frac{\sigma_\epsilon^2}{n})$ or if they all decided to share information on their private signals among each other before trading commenced.

Therefore, the above equilibrium is a *fully revealing* rational expectations equilibrium. The equilibrium price fully reveals all private information, a condition

---

4. See the original Grossman article (Grossman 1976) for details.

defined as strong-form market efficiency.[5] This result has some interesting features in that it shows that prices can aggregate relevant information to help agents make more efficient investment decisions than would be the case if they relied solely on their private information and did not attempt to obtain information from the equilibrium price itself.

However, as shown by Sanford Grossman and Joseph Stiglitz (Grossman and Stiglitz 1980), this fully revealing equilibrium is not robust to some small changes in assumptions. Real-world markets are unlikely to be perfectly efficient. For example, suppose each trader needed to pay a tiny cost, c, to obtain his private signal, y_i. With any finite cost of obtaining information, the equilibrium would not exist, because each individual receives no additional benefit from knowing y_i given that they can observe $\bar{y}$ from the price. In other words, a given individual does not personally benefit from having private (inside) information in a fully revealing equilibrium. In order for individuals to benefit from obtaining (costly) information, we need an equilibrium where the price is only partially revealing. For this to happen, there needs to be one or more additional sources of uncertainty that add "noise" to individuals' signals, so that other agents cannot infer them perfectly. We now turn to an example of a noisy rational expectations equilibrium.

16.1.5   A Noisy Rational Expectations Equilibrium

Let us make the following changes to the Grossman model's assumptions along the lines of a model proposed by Bruce Grundy and Maureen McNichols (Grundy and McNichols 1989). Suppose that each trader begins the period with a random endowment of the risky asset. Specifically, trader i possesses ε_i shares of the risky asset so that her initial wealth is $W_{0i} = \varepsilon_i P_0$. The realization of ε_i is known only to trader i. Across all traders, the endowments, $\widetilde{\varepsilon}_i$, are independently and identically distributed with mean μ_X and variance $\sigma_X^2 n$. To simplify the problem, we assume that the number of traders is very large. If we define $\widetilde{X}$ as the *per capita* supply of the risky asset and let n go to infinity, then by the Central Limit Theorem, $\widetilde{X}$ is a random variable distributed $N\left(\mu_X, \sigma_X^2\right)$. Note that in the limit as $n \to \infty$, the correlation between $\widetilde{\varepsilon}_i$ and $\widetilde{X}$ becomes zero, so that trader i's observation of her own endowment, $\widetilde{\varepsilon}_i$, provides no information about the per capita supply, $\widetilde{X}$.

Next, let us modify the type of signal received by each trader to allow for a common error as well as a trader-specific error. Trader i is assumed to receive the signal

$$\tilde{y}_i = \widetilde{P}_1 + \widetilde{\omega} + \tilde{\epsilon}_i \tag{16.15}$$

---

5. This can be compared to semistrong form market efficiency where asset prices need only reflect all public information.

where $\tilde{\omega} \sim N(0, \sigma_{\omega}^2)$ is the common error independent of $\tilde{P}_1$ and, as before, the idiosyncratic error $\tilde{\epsilon}_i \sim N(0, \sigma_{\epsilon}^2)$ and is independent of $\tilde{P}_1$ and $\tilde{\omega}$. Because of the infinite number of traders, it is realistic to allow for a common error so that traders, collectively, would not know the true payoff of the risky asset.

Recall from the Grossman model that the rational expectations equilibrium price in (16.14) was a linear function of $\bar{y}$ and $\bar{X}$. In the current model, the aggregate supply of the risky asset is not fixed, but random. However, this suggests that the equilibrium price will be of the form

$$P_0 = \alpha_0 + \alpha_1 \bar{y} + \alpha_2 \tilde{X} \tag{16.16}$$

where now $\bar{y} \equiv \lim_{n \to \infty} \sum_i^n y_i / n = \tilde{P}_1 + \tilde{\omega}$.

Although some assumptions differ, trader i's demand for the risky asset continues to be of the form in (16.7). Now recall that in a rational expectations equilibrium, investor i's information set includes not only her private information but also the equilibrium price: $I_i = \{y_i, P_0\}$. Given the assumed structure in (16.16) and the assumed normal distribution for $\tilde{P}_1$, $\tilde{X}$, and y_i, then investor i optimally forecasts the end-of-period price as the projection

$$E\left[\tilde{P}_1 | I_i\right] = \beta_0 + \beta_1 P_0 + \beta_2 y_i \tag{16.17}$$

where

$$\begin{pmatrix} \beta_1 \\ \beta_2 \end{pmatrix} = \begin{pmatrix} \alpha_1^2 \left(\sigma^2 + \sigma_{\omega}^2\right) + \alpha_2^2 \sigma_X^2 & \alpha_1 \left(\sigma^2 + \sigma_{\omega}^2\right) \\ \alpha_1 \left(\sigma^2 + \sigma_{\omega}^2\right) & \sigma^2 + \sigma_{\omega}^2 + \sigma_{\epsilon}^2 \end{pmatrix}^{-1} \begin{pmatrix} \alpha_1^2 \sigma^2 \\ \sigma^2 \end{pmatrix}$$

$$\beta_0 = m - \beta_1 \left(\alpha_0 - \alpha_1 m - \alpha_2 \mu_X\right) - \beta_2 m \tag{16.18}$$

If we then average the X_i in (16.7) over all investors, one obtains

$$X = \frac{\beta_0 + \left(\beta_1 - R_f\right) P_0 + \beta_2 \bar{y}}{\bar{a} \mathrm{Var}\left[\tilde{P}_1 | I_i\right)} \tag{16.19}$$

$$= \frac{\beta_0}{\bar{a} \mathrm{Var}\left[\tilde{P}_1 | I_i\right]} + \frac{\beta_1 - R_f}{\bar{a} \mathrm{Var}\left[\tilde{P}_1 | I_i\right)} P_0 + \frac{\beta_2}{\bar{a} \mathrm{Var}\left[\tilde{P}_1 | I_i\right)} \bar{y}$$

where $\bar{a} \equiv 1 / \left(\lim_{n \to \infty} \frac{1}{n} \sum_i^n \frac{1}{a_i}\right)$ is the harmonic mean of the investors' risk aversions. Now note that we can rewrite equation (16.16) as

$$X = -\frac{\alpha_0}{\alpha_2} + \frac{1}{\alpha_2} P_0 - \frac{\alpha_1}{\alpha_2} \bar{y} \tag{16.20}$$

In a rational expectations equilibrium, the relationships between the variables X, P_0, and $\bar{y}$ must be consistent with the individual investors' expectations. This implies that the intercepts, and the coefficients on P_0 and on $\bar{y}$, must be identical in equations (16.19) and (16.20). By matching the intercepts and coefficients, we obtain three nonlinear equations in the three unknowns α_0, α_1, and α_2. Although explicit solutions for α_0, α_1, and α_2 cannot be obtained, we can still interpret some of the characteristics of the equilibrium. To see this, note that if the coefficients on $\bar{y}$ are equated, one obtains

$$-\frac{\alpha_1}{\alpha_2} = \frac{\beta_2}{\bar{a}\mathrm{Var}\left[\tilde{P}_1 \mid I_i\right)}} \qquad (16.21)$$

Using (16.18) to substitute for β_2 and the variance of the projection of $\tilde{P}_1$ on I_i to substitute for $\mathrm{Var}\left[\tilde{P}_1 \mid I_i\right)$, (16.21) can be rewritten as

$$-\frac{\alpha_1}{\alpha_2} = \frac{\sigma_X^2}{\bar{a}\left[\sigma_X^2\left(\sigma_\omega^2 + \sigma_\epsilon^2\right) + \left(\alpha_1/\alpha_2\right)^2 \sigma_\omega^2\sigma_\epsilon^2\right]} \qquad (16.22)$$

This is a cubic equation in α_1/α_2. The ratio α_1/α_2 is a measure of how aggressively an individual investor responds to his individual private signal, relative to the average signal, $\bar{y}$, reflected in P_0. To see this, note that if one uses (16.7), (16.19), (16.20), and $y_i - \bar{y} = \tilde{\epsilon}_i$, the individual's demand for the risky asset can be written as

$$X_i = \frac{\bar{a}}{a_i}\left(X - \frac{\alpha_1}{\alpha_2}\tilde{\epsilon}_i\right) \qquad (16.23)$$

From (16.23) one sees that if there were no information differences, each investor would demand a share of the average supply of the risky asset, X, in proportion to the ratio of the harmonic average of risk aversions to his own risk aversion. However, unlike the fully revealing equilibrium of the previous section, the individual investor cannot perfectly invert the equilibrium price to find the average signal in (16.16) due to the uncertain aggregate supply shift, X. Hence, individual demands do respond to private information as reflected by $\tilde{\epsilon}_i$. The ratio α_1/α_2 reflects the simultaneous equation problem faced by the investor in trying to sort out a shift in supply, X, from a shift in aggregate demand generated by $\bar{y}$. From (16.22) note that if $\sigma_\omega^2 \to \infty$ or $\sigma_\epsilon^2 \to \infty$, so that investors' private signals become uninformative, then $\alpha_1/\alpha_2 \to 0$ and private information has no impact on demands or the equilibrium price. If, instead, $\sigma_\omega^2 = 0$, so that there is no common error, then (16.22) simplifies to

$$-\frac{\alpha_1}{\alpha_2} = \frac{1}{\bar{a}\sigma_\epsilon^2} \qquad (16.24)$$

and (16.23) becomes

$$X_i = \frac{\bar{a}}{a_i}X - \frac{1}{a_i\sigma_\epsilon^2}\tilde{\epsilon}_i \qquad (16.25)$$

so that an individual's demand responds to her private signal in direct proportion to the signal's precision and indirect proportion to her risk aversion.

A general insight of this noisy rational expectations model is that an investor forms her asset demand based on her private signal but also attempts to extract the private signals of other investors from the asset's equilibrium price. We now study another signal extraction problem but where the signal is reflected in the quantity of an asset being traded. The problem is one of a market maker who is charged with setting a competitive market price of an asset when some trades reflect private information.

16.2   Asymmetric Information, Trading, and Markets

Let us now consider another model with private information that is pertinent to a security market organized by a market maker. This market maker, who might be thought of as a specialist on a stock exchange or a security dealer in an over-the-counter market, sets a risky asset's price with the recognition that he may be trading at that price with a possibly better-informed individual. Albert "Pete" Kyle (Kyle 1985) developed this model, and it has been widely applied to study market microstructure issues. The model is similar to the previous one in that the equilibrium security price partially reveals the better-informed individual's private information. Also like the previous model, there is an additional source of uncertainty that prevents a fully revealing equilibrium, namely, orders from uninformed "noise," or "liquidity" traders who provide camouflage for the better-informed individual's insider trades. The model's results provide insights regarding the factors affecting bid-ask spreads and the market impact of trades.

16.2.1   Kyle Model Assumptions

The Kyle model is based on the following assumptions.

Asset Return Distribution

The model is a single-period model.[6] At the beginning of the period, agents trade in an asset that has a random end-of-period liquidation value of $\tilde{v} \sim N\left(p_0, \sigma_v^2\right)$.

---

6. Kyle's paper (Kyle 1985) also contains a multiperiod continuous-time version of his single-period model. Jiang Wang (Wang 1993) has also constructed a continuous-time asset pricing model with asymmetrically informed investors who have constant absolute-risk-aversion utility.

Liquidity Traders

Noise traders have needs to trade that are exogenous to the model. It is assumed that they, as a group, submit a "market" order to buy $\tilde{u}$ shares of the asset, where $\tilde{u} \sim N\left(0, \sigma_u^2\right)$. $\tilde{u}$ and $\tilde{v}$ are assumed to be independently distributed.[7]

Better-Informed Traders

The single risk-neutral *insider* is assumed to have better information than the other agents. He knows with perfect certainty the realized end-of-period value of the risky security $\tilde{v}$ (but not $\tilde{u}$) and chooses to submit a market order of size x that maximizes his expected end-of-period profits.[8]

Competitive Market Maker

The single risk-neutral *market maker* (for example, a New York Stock Exchange specialist) receives the market orders submitted by the noise traders and the insider, which in total equal $\tilde{u} + \tilde{x}$. Importantly, the market maker cannot distinguish what part of this total order consists of orders made by noise traders and what part consists of the order of the insider. (The traders are anonymous.) The market maker sets the market price, p, and then takes the position $-\left(\tilde{u} + \tilde{x}\right)$ to clear the market. It is assumed that market making is a perfectly competitive profession, so that the market maker sets the price p such that, given the total order submitted, his profit at the end of the period is expected to be zero.

16.2.2 Trading and Pricing Strategies

Since the noise traders' order is exogenous, we need only consider the optimal actions of the market maker and the insider.

The market maker observes only the total order flow, $u + x$. Given this information, he must then set the equilibrium market price p that gives him zero expected profits. Since his end-of-period profits are $-\left(\tilde{v} - p\right)\left(u + x\right)$, this implies that the price set by the market maker satisfies

$$p = E\left[\tilde{v} \mid u + x\right] \tag{16.26}$$

---

7. Why rational noise traders submit these orders has been modeled by assuming they have exogenous shocks to their wealth and need to rebalance their portfolio (Spiegel and Subrahmanyam 1992) or by assuming that they have uncertainty regarding the timing of their consumption (Gorton and Pennacchi 1993).

8. This assumption can be weakened to the case of the insider having uncertainty over $\tilde{v}$ but having more information on $\tilde{v}$ than the other traders. One can also allow the insider to submit "limit" orders, that is, orders that are a function of the equilibrium market price (a demand schedule), as in another model by Kyle (Kyle 1989).

The information on the total order size is important to the market maker. The more positive the total order size, the more likely it is that x is large due to the insider knowing that v is greater than p_0. Thus, the market maker would tend to set p higher than otherwise. Similarly, the more negative is $u + x$, the more likely it is that x is low because the insider knows v is below p_0 and is submitting a sell order. In this case, the market maker would tend to set p lower than otherwise. Thus, the *pricing rule* of the market maker is a function of $x + u$, that is, $P(x + u)$.

Since the insider sets x, it is an endogenous variable that depends on $\tilde{v}$. The insider chooses x to maximize his expected end-of-period profits, $\tilde{\pi}$, given knowledge of v and the way that the market maker behaves in setting the equilibrium price:

$$\max_x E\left[\tilde{\pi} \mid v\right] = \max_x E\left[\left(v - P\left(x + \tilde{u}\right)\right) x \mid v\right] \tag{16.27}$$

An equilibrium in this model is a pricing rule chosen by the market maker and a trading strategy chosen by the insider such that 1) the insider maximizes expected profits, given the market maker's pricing rule; 2) the market maker sets the price to earn zero expected profits, given the trading strategy of the insider; and 3) the insider and market maker have rational expectations. That is, the equilibrium is a fixed point where each agent's actual behavior (e.g., pricing rule or trading strategy) is that which is expected by the other.

Insider's Trading Strategy

Suppose the market maker chooses a market price that is a linear function of the total order flow, $P(x + u) = \mu + \lambda(x + u)$. We will later argue that a linear pricing rule is optimal. If this is so, what is the insider's choice of x? From (16.27) we have

$$\max_x E\left[\left(v - P\left(x + \tilde{u}\right)\right) x \mid v\right] = \max_x E\left[\left(v - \mu - \lambda\left(x + \tilde{u}\right)\right) x \mid v\right] \tag{16.28}$$

$$= \max_x \left(v - \mu - \lambda x\right) x, \text{ since } E\left[\tilde{u}\right] = 0$$

Thus, the solution to the insider's problem in (16.28) is

$$x = \alpha + \beta v \tag{16.29}$$

where $\alpha = -\frac{\mu}{2\lambda}$ and $\beta = \frac{1}{2\lambda}$. Therefore, if the market maker uses a linear pricing rule, the optimal trading strategy for the insider is a linear trading rule.

Market Maker's Pricing Strategy

Next, let us return to the market maker's problem of choosing the market price that, conditional on knowing the total order flow, results in a competitive (zero) expected profit. Given the assumption that market making is a perfectly competitive profession, a market maker needs to choose the "best" possible estimate of $E\left[\tilde{v} \mid u + x\right]$ in setting the price $p = E\left[\tilde{v} \mid u + x\right]$. The maximum likelihood estimate of $E\left[\tilde{v} \mid u + x\right]$ is best in the sense that it attains maximum efficiency and is also the minimum-variance unbiased estimate.

Note that if the insider follows the optimal trading strategy, which according to equation (16.29) is $x = \alpha + \beta \tilde{v}$, then from the point of view of the market maker, $\tilde{v}$ and $y \equiv \tilde{u} + x = \tilde{u} + \alpha + \beta \tilde{v}$ are jointly normally distributed. Because v and y are jointly normal, the maximum likelihood estimate of the mean of v conditional on y is linear in y, that is, $E\left[\tilde{v} \mid y\right]$ is linear in y.[9] Hence, the previously assumed linear pricing rule is, in fact, optimal in equilibrium. Therefore, the market maker should use the maximum likelihood estimator, which in the case of v and y being normally distributed is equivalent to the "least squares" estimator. This estimator minimizes

$$E\left[\left(\tilde{v} - P\left(y\right)\right)^2\right] = E\left[\left(\tilde{v} - \mu - \lambda y\right)^2\right] \tag{16.30}$$

$$= E\left[\left(\tilde{v} - \mu - \lambda\left(\tilde{u} + \alpha + \beta \tilde{v}\right)\right)^2\right]$$

Thus, the optimal pricing rule equals $\mu + \lambda y$, where μ and λ minimize

$$\min_{\mu, \lambda} E\left[\left(\tilde{v}\left(1 - \lambda\beta\right) - \lambda\tilde{u} - \mu - \lambda\alpha\right)^2\right] \tag{16.31}$$

Recalling the assumptions $E\left[v\right] = p_0$, $E\left[\left(v - p_0\right)^2\right] = \sigma_v^2$, $E\left[u\right] = 0$, $E\left[u^2\right] = \sigma_u^2$, and $E\left[uv\right] = 0$, the objective function (16.31) can be written as

$$\min_{\mu, \lambda} \left(1 - \lambda\beta\right)^2 \left(\sigma_v^2 + p_0^2\right) + \left(\mu + \lambda\alpha\right)^2 + \lambda^2\sigma_u^2 - 2\left(\mu + \lambda\alpha\right)\left(1 - \lambda\beta\right)p_0 \tag{16.32}$$

The first-order conditions with respect to μ and λ are

$$\mu = -\lambda\alpha + p_0\left(1 - \lambda\beta\right) \tag{16.33}$$

$$0 = -2\beta\left(1 - \lambda\beta\right)\left(\sigma_v^2 + p_0^2\right) + 2\alpha\left(\mu + \lambda\alpha\right) + 2\lambda\sigma_u^2$$
$$- 2p_0\left[-\beta\left(\mu + \lambda\alpha\right) + \alpha\left(1 - \lambda\beta\right)\right] \tag{16.34}$$

Substituting $\mu + \lambda\alpha = p_0\left(1 - \lambda\beta\right)$ from (16.33) into (16.34), we see that (16.34) simplifies to

$$\lambda = \frac{\beta\sigma_v^2}{\beta^2\sigma_v^2 + \sigma_u^2} \tag{16.35}$$

---

9. Earlier in this chapter, we saw an example of this linear relationship in equation (16.8).

Substituting in for the definitions $\alpha = -\frac{\mu}{2\lambda}$ and $\beta = \frac{1}{2\lambda}$ in (16.33) and (16.34), we have

$$\mu = p_0 \tag{16.36}$$

$$\lambda = \frac{1}{2}\frac{\sigma_v}{\sigma_u} \tag{16.37}$$

In summary, the equilibrium price is

$$p = p_0 + \frac{1}{2}\frac{\sigma_v}{\sigma_u}(\tilde{u} + \tilde{x}) \tag{16.38}$$

where the equilibrium order submitted by the insider is

$$x = \frac{\sigma_u}{\sigma_v}(\tilde{v} - p_0) \tag{16.39}$$

16.2.3   Analysis of the Results

From (16.39), we see that the greater the volatility (amount) of noise trading, σ_u, the larger is the magnitude of the order submitted by the insider for a given deviation of v from its unconditional mean. Hence, the insider trades more actively on his private information the greater the "camouflage" provided by noise trading. Greater noise trading makes it more difficult for the market maker to extract the "signal" of insider trading from the noise. Note that if equation (16.39) is substituted into (16.38), one obtains

$$p = p_0 + \frac{1}{2}\frac{\sigma_v}{\sigma_u}\tilde{u} + \frac{1}{2}(\tilde{v} - p_0) \tag{16.40}$$

$$= \frac{1}{2}\left(\frac{\sigma_v}{\sigma_u}\tilde{u} + p_0 + \tilde{v}\right)$$

Thus, we see that only one-half of the insider's private information, $\frac{1}{2}\tilde{v}$, is reflected in the equilibrium price, so that the price is *not fully revealing*.[10] To obtain an equilibrium of incomplete revelation of private information, it is necessary to have a second source of uncertainty, namely, the amount of noise trading.

Using (16.39) and (16.40), we can calculate the insider's expected profits:

$$E[\tilde{\pi}] = E[x(v-p)] = E\left[\frac{\sigma_u}{\sigma_v}(\tilde{v} - p_0)\frac{1}{2}\left(v - p_0 - \frac{\sigma_v}{\sigma_u}\tilde{u}\right)\right] \tag{16.41}$$

---

10. A fully revealing price would be $p = \tilde{v}$.

Conditional on knowing v, that is, after learning the realization of v at the beginning of the period, the insider expects profits of

$$E\left[\tilde{\pi} \mid v\right] = \frac{1}{2}\frac{\sigma_u}{\sigma_v}\left(v - p_0\right)^2 \tag{16.42}$$

Hence, the larger v's deviation from p_0, the larger the expected profit. Unconditional on knowing $\tilde{v}$, that is, before the start of the period, the insider expects a profit of

$$E\left[\tilde{\pi}\right] = \frac{1}{2}\frac{\sigma_u}{\sigma_v}E\left[\left(\tilde{v} - p_0\right)^2\right] = \frac{1}{2}\sigma_u\sigma_v \tag{16.43}$$

which is proportional to the standard deviations of noise traders' orders and the end-of-period value of v.

Since, by assumption, the market maker sets the security price in a way that gives him zero expected profits, the expected profits of the insider equals the expected losses of the noise traders. In other words, it is the noise traders that lose, on average, from the presence of the insider. Due to the market maker's inability to distinguish between informed (insider) and uninformed (noise trader) orders, they are treated the same under his pricing rule. Thus, on average, noise traders' buy (*sell*) orders are executed at a higher (*lower*) price than p_0.

From equation (16.38), we see that $\lambda = \frac{1}{2}\frac{\sigma_v}{\sigma_u}$ is the amount that the market maker raises the price when the total order flow, $(u + x)$, goes up by 1 unit.[11] This can be thought of as relating to the security's bid-ask spread, that is, the difference in the price for sell orders versus buy orders, although here sell and buy prices are not fixed but are a function of the order size since the pricing rule is linear. Moreover, since the amount of order flow necessary to raise the price by \$1 equals $1/\lambda = 2\frac{\sigma_u}{\sigma_v}$, the model provides a measure of the "depth" of the market, or market "liquidity." The higher is the proportion of noise trading to the value of insider information, $\frac{\sigma_u}{\sigma_v}$, the deeper, or more liquid, is the market.

Intuitively, the more noise traders relative to the value of insider information, the less the market maker needs to adjust the price in response to a given order, since the likelihood of the order being that of a noise trader, rather than an insider, is greater. The more noise traders there are (that is, the greater is σ_u), the greater is the expected profit of the insider (see equation (16.43)) and the greater is the *total* expected loss of the noise traders. However, the expected loss per *individual* noise trader falls with the greater level of noise trading.[12]

---

11. It is now common in the market microstructure literature to refer to this measure of order flow and liquidity as "Kyle's lambda."

12. Gary Gorton and George Pennacchi (Gorton and Pennacchi 1993) derive this result by modeling individual liquidity traders.

16.3 Summary

The models considered in this chapter analyze the degree to which private information about an asset's future payoff or value is reflected in the asset's current price. An investor's private information affects an asset's price by determining the investor's desired demand (long or short position) for the asset, though the investor's demand also is tempered by risk aversion. More subtly, we saw that a rational investor can also learn about the private information of other investors through the asset's price itself, and this price discovery affects the investors' equilibrium demands. Indeed, under some circumstances, the asset's price may fully reveal all relevant private information such that any individual's private information becomes redundant.

Perhaps more realistically, there are non-information-based factors that affect the net supply or demand for an asset. These "noise" factors prevent investors from perfectly inferring the private information signals of others, resulting in an asset price that is less than fully revealing. Noise provides camouflage for investors with private information, allowing these traders to profit from possessing such information. Their profits come at the expense of liquidity traders since the greater the likelihood of private information regarding a security, the larger will be the security's bid-ask spread. Hence, this theory predicts that a security's liquidity is determined by the degree of noise (non-information-based) trading relative to insider (private-information-based) trading.

16.4 Exercises

1. Show that the maximization problem in objective function (16.6) is equivalent to the maximization problem in (16.4).

2. Show that the results in (16.8) can be derived from Bayes rule and the assumption that $\widetilde{P}_1$ and $\tilde{y}_i$ are normally distributed.

3. Consider a special case of the Grossman model. Traders can choose between holding a risk-free asset, which pays an end-of-period return of R_f, and a risky asset that has a beginning-of-period price of P_0 per share and an end-of-period payoff (price) of $\widetilde{P}_1$ per share. The unconditional distribution of $\widetilde{P}_1$ is assumed to be $N\left(m, \sigma^2\right)$. The risky asset is assumed to be a derivative security, such as a futures contract, so that its net supply equals zero.

   There are two different traders who maximize expected utility over end-of-period wealth, $\widetilde{W}_{1i}$, $i = 1, 2$. The form of the ith trader's utility function is

   $$U_i\left(\widetilde{W}_{1i}\right) = -e^{-a_i \widetilde{W}_{1i}}, a_i > 0$$

At the beginning of the period, the ith trader observes y_i, which is a noisy signal of the end-of-period value of the risky asset

$$y_i = \widetilde{P}_1 + \widetilde{\epsilon}_i$$

where $\epsilon_i \sim N\left(0, \sigma_\epsilon^2\right)$ and is independent of $\widetilde{P}_1$. Note that the variances of the traders' signals are the same. Also assume $E\left[\epsilon_1\epsilon_2\right] = 0$.

a. Suppose each trader does not attempt to infer the other trader's information from the equilibrium price, P_0. Solve for each of the traders' demands for the risky asset and the equilibrium price, P_0.

b. Now suppose each trader does attempt to infer the other's signal from the equilibrium price, P_0. What will be the rational expectations equilibrium price in this situation? What will be each of the traders' equilibrium demands for the risky asset?

4. In the Kyle model (Kyle 1985), replace the original assumption (see "Better-Informed Traders" on page 353) with the following new one:

The single risk-neutral *insider* is assumed to have better information than the other agents. He observes a signal of the asset's end-of-period value equal to

$$s = \widetilde{v} + \widetilde{\varepsilon}$$

where $\widetilde{\varepsilon} \sim N\left(0, \sigma_s^2\right)$, $0 < \sigma_s^2 < \sigma_v^2$, and $\widetilde{\varepsilon}$ is distributed independently of $\tilde{u}$ and $\tilde{v}$. The insider does not observe $\tilde{u}$ but chooses to submit a market order of size x that maximizes his expected end-of-period profits.

a. Suppose that the market maker's optimal price-setting rule is a linear function of the order flow

$$p = \mu + \lambda\left(u + x\right)$$

Write down the expression for the insider's expected profits given this pricing rule.

b. Take the first-order condition with respect to x and solve for the insider's optimal trading strategy as a function of the signal and the parameters of the market maker's pricing rule.

5. Consider a variation of the Kyle model (Kyle 1985). Replace the orginal assumption (see "Liquidity Traders" on page 353) with the following new one:

Noise traders have needs to trade that are exogenous to the model. It is assumed that they, as a group, submit a "market" order to buy $\tilde{u}$ shares of the asset, where $\tilde{u} \sim N\left(0, \sigma_u^2\right)$. $\tilde{u}$ and $\tilde{v}$ are assumed to be correlated with correlation coefficient ρ.

Note that the only change is that, instead of the original Kyle model's assumption that $\tilde{u}$ and $\tilde{v}$ are uncorrelated, they are now assumed to have nonzero correlation coefficient ρ.

a. Suppose that the market maker's optimal price-setting rule is a linear function of the order flow

$$p = \mu + \lambda\,(u + x)$$

Write down the expression for the insider's expected profits given this pricing rule. Hint: to find the conditional expectation of $\tilde{u}$, it might be helpful to write it as a weighted average of $\tilde{v}$ and another normal random variable uncorrelated with $\tilde{v}$.

b. Take the first-order condition with respect to x and solve for the insider's optimal trading strategy as a function of v and the parameters of the market maker's pricing rule.

c. For a given pricing rule (given μ and λ) and a realization of $v > p_0$, does the insider trade more or less when $\rho > 0$ compared to the case of $\rho = 0$? What is the intuition for this result? How might a positive value for ρ be interpreted as some of the liquidity traders being better-informed traders? What insights might this result have for a market with multiple insiders (informed traders)?

CHAPTER 17

Models of the Term Structure of Interest Rates

This chapter provides an introduction to the main approaches for modeling the term structure of interest rates and for valuing fixed-income derivatives. It is not meant to be a comprehensive review of this subject. The literature on term structure models is voluminous, and many surveys on this topic, including (Dai and Singleton 2004), (Dai and Singleton 2003), (Maes 2003), (Piazzesi 2005a), (Rebonato 2004), and (Yan 2001), have appeared in recent years. The more modest objective of this chapter is to outline the major theories for valuing default-free bonds and bond derivatives, such as Treasury bills, notes, bonds, and their derivatives. The next chapter analyzes the valuation of default-risky bonds.

This chapter is comprised of two main sections. The first discusses models used to derive the equilibrium bond prices of different maturities in terms of particular state variables. One way to think about these models is that the state variables are the models' "input," while the values of different maturity bonds are the models' "output." The second section covers models that value fixed-income derivatives, such as interest rate caps and swaptions, in terms of a given maturity structure of bond prices. In contrast, these models take the term structure of observed bond prices as the input and have derivative values as the models' output.

17.1 Equilibrium Term Structure Models

Equilibrium term structure models describe the prices (or, equivalently, the yields) of different maturity bonds as functions of one or more state variables or "factors." The Vasicek model (Vasicek 1977), introduced in Chapter 9 (see equation

9.41), and the Cox, Ingersoll, and Ross model (Cox, Ingersoll, and Ross 1985b), presented in Chapter 13 (see equation 13.51), were examples of single-factor models. The single factor in the Vasicek model was the instantaneous-maturity interest rate, denoted $r(t)$, which was assumed to follow the Ornstein-Uhlenbeck process (9.30). In Cox, Ingersoll, and Ross's one-factor model, the factor was a variable that determined the expected returns of the economy's production processes. In equilibrium, the instantaneous-maturity interest rate was proportional to this factor and inherited its dynamics. This interest rate followed the square root process in equation (13.49).

Empirical evidence finds that term structure movements are driven by multiple factors.[1] In many multifactor models, the factors are latent (unobserved) variables that are identified by data on the yields of different maturity bonds. Recently, however, economists have renewed their interest in models that link term structure factors with observed macroeconomic variables.[2] A motivation for these models is to better understand the relationship between the term structure of interest rates and the macroeconomy, with the potential of using term structure movements to forecast macroeconomic cycles.

Given the importance of multiple factors in term structure dynamics, let us generalize the pricing relationships for default-free, zero-coupon bonds that we developed in earlier chapters. We consider a situation where multiple factors determine bond prices and assume that there are n state variables, x_i, $i = 1, \ldots, n$, that follow the multivariate diffusion process

$$d\mathbf{x} = \mathbf{a}(t, \mathbf{x})\, dt + \mathbf{b}(t, \mathbf{x})\, \mathbf{dz} \tag{17.1}$$

where $\mathbf{x} = (x_1 \ldots x_n)'$; $\mathbf{a}(t, \mathbf{x})$ is an $n \times 1$ vector; $\mathbf{b}(t, \mathbf{x})$ is an $n \times n$ matrix; and $\mathbf{dz} = (dz_1 \ldots dz_n)'$ is an $n \times 1$ vector of independent Brownian motion processes so that $dz_i dz_j = 0$ for $i \neq j$.[3] This specification permits any general correlation structure for the state variables. Note that the instantaneous covariance matrix of the state variables is given by $\mathbf{b}(t, \mathbf{x})\, \mathbf{b}(t, \mathbf{x})'$.

---

1. For example, a principal components analysis by Robert Litterman and Jose Scheinkman (Litterman and Scheinkman 1988) finds that at least three factors are required to describe U.S. Treasury security movements. They relate these factors to the term structure's level, slope, and curvature.

2. Francis Diebold, Monika Piazzesi, and Glenn Rudebusch (Diebold, Piazzesi, and Rudebusch 2005) discuss empirical estimation of term structure models using macroeconomic factors. An example of this approach is given by Andrew Ang and Monika Piazzesi (Ang and Piazzesi 2003).

3. As discussed in Chapter 10, the independence assumption is not important. If there are correlated sources of risk (Brownian motions), they can be redefined by a linear transformation to be represented by n orthogonal risk sources.

Define $P(t, T, \mathbf{x})$ as the date t price of a default-free, zero-coupon bond that pays 1 at date T. Itô's lemma gives the process followed by this bond's price:

$$dP(t, T, \mathbf{x})/P(t, T, \mathbf{x}) = \mu_p(t, T, \mathbf{x})\, dt + \sigma_p(t, T, \mathbf{x})'\, d\mathbf{z} \qquad (17.2)$$

where the bond's expected rate of return equals

$$\mu_p(t, T, \mathbf{x}) = \left(\mathbf{a}(t, \mathbf{x})'\, \mathbf{P}_x + P_t + \tfrac{1}{2}\mathrm{Trace}\left[\mathbf{b}(t, \mathbf{x})\, \mathbf{b}(t, \mathbf{x})'\, \mathbf{P}_{xx}\right]\right) / P(t, T, \mathbf{x})$$

$$(17.3)$$

and $\sigma_p(t, T, \mathbf{x})$ is an $n \times 1$ vector of the bond's volatilities equal to

$$\sigma_p(t, T, \mathbf{x}) = \mathbf{b}(t, \mathbf{x})'\, \mathbf{P}_x/P(t, T, \mathbf{x}) \qquad (17.4)$$

and where $\mathbf{P}_x$ is an $n \times 1$ vector whose ith element equals the partial derivative P_{x_i}; $\mathbf{P}_{xx}$ is an $n \times n$ matrix whose i, jth element is the second-order partial derivative $P_{x_i x_j}$; and Trace[A] is the sum of the diagonal elements of a square matrix A.

Similar to the Black-Scholes hedging argument discussed in Chapter 9 and applied to derive the Vasicek model, we can form a hedge portfolio of $n + 1$ bonds having distinctly different maturities. By appropriately choosing the portfolio weights for these $n + 1$ bonds, the n sources of risk can be hedged so that the portfolio generates a riskless return. In the absence of arbitrage, this portfolio's return must equal the riskless rate, $r(t, \mathbf{x})$. Making this no-arbitrage restriction produces the implication that each bond's expected rate of return must satisfy

$$\mu_p(t, T, \mathbf{x}) = r(t, \mathbf{x}) + \Theta(t, \mathbf{x})'\sigma_p(t, T, \mathbf{x}) \qquad (17.5)$$

where $\Theta(t, \mathbf{x}) = (\theta_1 \ldots \theta_n)'$ is the $n \times 1$ vector of market prices of risks associated with each of the Brownian motions in $d\mathbf{z} = (dz_1 \ldots dz_n)'$. By equating (17.5) to the process for $\mu_p(t, T, \mathbf{x})$ given by Itô's lemma in (17.3), we obtain the equilibrium partial differential equation (PDE)

$$\tfrac{1}{2}\mathrm{Trace}\left[\mathbf{b}(t, \mathbf{x})\, \mathbf{b}(t, \mathbf{x})'\, \mathbf{P}_{xx}\right] + \left[\mathbf{a}(t, \mathbf{x}) - \mathbf{b}(t, \mathbf{x})\, \Theta\right]'\mathbf{P}_x - rP + P_t = 0 \quad (17.6)$$

Given functional forms for $\mathbf{a}(t, \mathbf{x})$, $\mathbf{b}(t, \mathbf{x})$, $\Theta(t, \mathbf{x})$, $r(t, \mathbf{x})$, this PDE can be solved subject to the boundary condition $P(T, T, \mathbf{x}) = 1$.

Note that equation (17.6) depends on the expected changes in the factors under the risk-neutral measure Q, $\mathbf{a}(t, \mathbf{x}) - \mathbf{b}(t, \mathbf{x})\, \Theta$, rather than the factors' expected changes under the physical measure P, $\mathbf{a}(t, \mathbf{x})$. Hence, to price bonds, one could simply specify only the factors' risk-neutral processes.[4] This insight is not surprising, because we saw in Chapter 10 that the Feynman-Kac solution to this PDE is the risk-neutral pricing equation (10.61):

$$P(t, T, \mathbf{x}) = \widehat{E}_t \left[e^{-\int_t^T r(s, \mathbf{x}) ds} \times 1 \right] \qquad (17.7)$$

In addition to the pricing relations (17.6) and (17.7), we saw that a third pricing approach can be based on the pricing kernel that follows the process

$$dM/M = -r(t, \mathbf{x}) dt - \mathbf{\Theta}(t, \mathbf{x})' d\mathbf{z} \qquad (17.8)$$

In this case, pricing can be accomplished under the physical measure based on the formula

$$P(t, T, \mathbf{x}) = E_t \left[\frac{M(T)}{M(t)} \times 1 \right] \qquad (17.9)$$

Thus far, we have placed few restrictions on the factors and their relationship to the short rate, $r(t, \mathbf{x})$, other than to assume that the factors follow the Markov diffusion processes (17.1). Let us next consider some popular parametric forms.

17.1.1   Affine Models

We start with models in which the yields of zero-coupon bonds are linear or "affine" functions of state variables. This class of models includes those of Oldrich Vasicek (Vasicek 1977) and John Cox, Jonathan Ingersoll, and Stephen Ross (Cox, Ingersoll, and Ross 1985b). Affine models are attractive because they lead to bond price formulas that are relatively easy to compute and because the parameters of the state variable processes can often be estimated using relatively straightforward econometric techniques.

Recall that a zero-coupon bond's continuously compounded yield, $Y(t, T, \mathbf{x})$, is defined from its price by the relation

$$P(t, T, \mathbf{x}) = e^{-Y(t, T, \mathbf{x})(T - t)} \qquad (17.10)$$

One popular class of models assumes that zero-coupon bonds' continuously compounded yields are affine functions of the factors. Defining the time until maturity as $\tau \equiv T - t$, this assumption can be written as

$$Y(t, T, \mathbf{x}) \tau = A(\tau) + \mathbf{B}(\tau)' \mathbf{x} \qquad (17.11)$$

where $A(\tau)$ is a scalar function and $\mathbf{B}(\tau)$ is an $n \times 1$ vector of functions that do not depend on the factors, $\mathbf{x}$. Because at maturity $P(T, T, \mathbf{x}) = 1$, equation (17.11)

---

4. However, if the factors are observable variables for which data are available, it may be necessary to specify their physical processes if empirical implementations of the model require estimates for $\mathbf{a}(\mathbf{x}, t)$ and $\mathbf{b}(\mathbf{x}, t)$.

implies that $A(0) = 0$ and $\mathbf{B}(0)$ is an $n \times 1$ vector of zeros. Another implication of (17.11) is that the short rate is also affine in the factors since

$$r(t, \mathbf{x}) = \lim_{T \to t} Y(t, T, \mathbf{x}) = \lim_{\tau \to 0} \frac{A(\tau) + \mathbf{B}(\tau)' \mathbf{x}}{\tau} \tag{17.12}$$

so that we can write $r(t, \mathbf{x}) = \alpha + \boldsymbol{\beta}' \mathbf{x}$, where $\alpha = \partial A(0) / \partial \tau$ is a scalar and $\boldsymbol{\beta} = \partial \mathbf{B}(0) / \partial \tau$ is an $n \times 1$ vector of constants.

Under what conditions regarding the factors' dynamics would the no-arbitrage, equilibrium bond yields be affine in the state variables? To answer this, let us substitute the affine yield assumption of (17.10) and (17.11) into the general no-arbitrage PDE of (17.6). Doing so, one obtains

$$\frac{1}{2}\mathbf{B}(\tau)' \mathbf{b}(t, \mathbf{x}) \mathbf{b}(t, \mathbf{x})' \mathbf{B}(\tau) - \left[\mathbf{a}(t, \mathbf{x}) - \mathbf{b}(t, \mathbf{x}) \boldsymbol{\Theta}\right]' \mathbf{B}(\tau) \\ + \frac{\partial A(\tau)}{\partial \tau} + \frac{\partial \mathbf{B}(\tau)'}{\partial \tau} \mathbf{x} = \alpha + \boldsymbol{\beta}' \mathbf{x} \tag{17.13}$$

Darrell Duffie and Rui Kan (Duffie and Kan 1996) characterize sufficient conditions for a solution to equation (17.13). Specifically, two of the conditions are that the factors' risk-neutral instantaneous expected changes and variances are affine in $\mathbf{x}$. In other words, if the state variables' risk-neutral drifts and variances are affine in the state variables, so are the equilibrium bond price yields. These conditions can be written as

$$\mathbf{a}(t, \mathbf{x}) - \mathbf{b}(t, \mathbf{x}) \boldsymbol{\Theta} = \kappa \left(\bar{\mathbf{x}} - \mathbf{x}\right) \tag{17.14}$$

$$\mathbf{b}(t, \mathbf{x}) = \boldsymbol{\Sigma} \sqrt{\mathbf{s}(\mathbf{x})} \tag{17.15}$$

where $\bar{\mathbf{x}}$ is an $n \times 1$ vector of constants, κ and $\boldsymbol{\Sigma}$ are $n \times n$ matrices of constants, and $\mathbf{s}(\mathbf{x})$ is an $n \times n$ diagonal matrix with the ith diagonal term

$$\mathbf{s}_i(\mathbf{x}) = s_{oi} + \mathbf{s}_{1i}' \mathbf{x} \tag{17.16}$$

where s_{oi} is a scalar constant and $\mathbf{s}_{1i}$ is an $n \times 1$ vector of constants. Now, because the state variables' covariance matrix equals $\mathbf{b}(t, \mathbf{x}) \mathbf{b}(t, \mathbf{x})' = \boldsymbol{\Sigma} \mathbf{s}(\mathbf{x}) \boldsymbol{\Sigma}'$, additional conditions are needed to ensure that this covariance matrix remains positive definite for all possible realizations of the state variable, $\mathbf{x}$. Qiang Dai and Kenneth Singleton (Dai and Singleton 2000) and Darrell Duffie, Damir Filipovic, and Walter Schachermayer (Duffie, Filipovic, and Schachermayer 2002) derive these conditions.[5]

---

5. These conditions can have important consequences regarding the correlation between the state variables. For example, if the state variables follow a multivariate Ornstein–Uhlenbeck process, so that the model is a multifactor extension of the Vasicek model given in (9.41), (9.42), and (9.43), then any general correlation structure between the state variables is permitted. Terence Langetieg (Langeteig 1980) has analyzed this model. However, if the state variables follow a multivariate square root process, so that the model is a multifactor extension of the Cox, Ingersoll, and Ross model given in (13.51), (13.52), and (13.53), then the correlation between the state variables must be nonnegative.

Given (17.14), (17.15), and (17.16), the partial differential equation in (17.13) can be rewritten as

$$\tfrac{1}{2} \mathbf{B}(\tau)' \, \mathbf{\Sigma s}(\mathbf{x}) \, \mathbf{\Sigma' B}(\tau) - \left[\boldsymbol{\kappa} \left(\overline{\mathbf{x}} - \mathbf{x} \right) \right]' \mathbf{B}(\tau) + \frac{\partial A(\tau)}{\partial \tau} + \frac{\partial \mathbf{B}(\tau)'}{\partial \tau} \mathbf{x} = \alpha + \boldsymbol{\beta}' \mathbf{x}$$

(17.17)

Note that this equation is linear in the state variables, $\mathbf{x}$. For the equation to hold for all values of $\mathbf{x}$, the constant terms in the equation must sum to zero and the terms multiplying each element of $\mathbf{x}$ must also sum to zero. These conditions imply

$$\frac{\partial A(\tau)}{\partial \tau} = \alpha + \left(\boldsymbol{\kappa} \overline{\mathbf{x}} \right)' \mathbf{B}(\tau) - \tfrac{1}{2} \sum_{i=1}^{n} \left[\mathbf{\Sigma' B}(\tau) \right]_i^2 s_{0i}$$

(17.18)

$$\frac{\partial \mathbf{B}(\tau)}{\partial \tau} = \boldsymbol{\beta} - \boldsymbol{\kappa}' \mathbf{B}(\tau) - \tfrac{1}{2} \sum_{i=1}^{n} \left[\mathbf{\Sigma' B}(\tau) \right]_i^2 s_{1i}$$

(17.19)

where $\left[\mathbf{\Sigma' B}(\tau) \right]_i$ is the ith element of the $n \times 1$ vector $\mathbf{\Sigma' B}(\tau)$. Equations (17.18) and (17.19) are a system of first-order ordinary differential equations that can be solved subject to the boundary conditions $A(0) = 0$ and $\mathbf{B}(0) = 0$. In some cases, such as a multiple state variable version of the Vasicek model (where $s_{1i} = 0 \; \forall i$), there exist closed-form solutions.[6] In other cases, fast and accurate numerical solutions to these ordinary differential equations can be computed using techniques such as a Runge-Kutta algorithm.

While affine term structure models require that the state variables' risk-neutral expected changes be affine in the state variables, there is more flexibility regarding the state variables' drifts under the physical measure. Note that the state variables' expected change under the physical measure is

$$\mathbf{a}(t, \mathbf{x}) = \boldsymbol{\kappa} \left(\overline{\mathbf{x}} - \mathbf{x} \right) + \mathbf{\Sigma} \sqrt{\mathbf{s}(\mathbf{x})} \, \mathbf{\Theta}$$

(17.20)

so that specification of the market prices of risk, $\mathbf{\Theta}$, is required to determine the physical drifts of the state variables. Qiang Dai and Kenneth Singleton (Dai and Singleton 2000) study the "completely affine" case where both the physical and risk-neutral drifts are affine, while Gregory Duffee (Duffee 2002) and Jefferson Duarte (Duarte 2004) consider extensions of the physical drifts that permit nonlinearities.[7] Because the means, volatilities, and risk premia of bond prices

---

6. Examples include (Langeteig 1980), (Pennacchi 1991), and (Jegadeesh and Pennacchi 1996).
7. Dai and Singleton analyze $\mathbf{\Theta} = \sqrt{\mathbf{s}(\mathbf{x})} \boldsymbol{\lambda}_1$ where $\boldsymbol{\lambda}_1$ is an $n \times 1$ vector of constants. Duffee considers the "essentially affine" modeling of the market price of risk of the form $\mathbf{\Theta} = \sqrt{\mathbf{s}(\mathbf{x})} \boldsymbol{\lambda}_1 +$

estimated from time series data depend on the physical moments of the state variables, the flexibility in choosing the parametric form for Θ can allow the model to better fit historical bond price data.

Example: Independent Factors

Consider the special case where κ and Σ are $n \times n$ diagonal matrices and the $n \times 1$ vector $\mathbf{s}_{1i}$ has all of its elements equal to zero except for its ith element. These assumptions imply that the risk-neutral drift term of each state variable depends only on its own level and that the state variables' covariance matrix, $\mathbf{b}(t, \mathbf{x})\mathbf{b}(t, \mathbf{x})' = \Sigma \mathbf{s}(\mathbf{x})\Sigma'$, is diagonal. Thus, this case is one where the processes for the state variables are independent of each other. Further, for simplicity, let $r(t, \mathbf{x}) = \alpha + \boldsymbol{\beta}'\mathbf{x} = \mathbf{e}'\mathbf{x}$, so that $\alpha = 0$ and $\boldsymbol{\beta} = \mathbf{e}$ is an $n \times 1$ vector of ones.[8] Given these parametric restrictions, the interest rate is the sum of independent state variables and the bond valuation equation (17.7) becomes

$$P(t, T, \mathbf{x}) = \widehat{E}_t \left[e^{-\int_t^T r(s, \mathbf{x})ds} \times 1 \right] \tag{17.21}$$

$$= \widehat{E}_t \left[e^{-\int_t^T \mathbf{e}'\mathbf{x}ds} \right]$$

$$= \prod_{i=1}^{n} \widehat{E}_t \left[e^{-\int_t^T x_i(s)ds} \right]$$

where the last line in (17.21) results from the independence assumption. The insight from (17.21) is that this multifactor term structure model can be interpreted as the product of n single-factor term structure models, where each state variable, x_i, is analogous to a different interest rate. For example, if $\mathbf{s}_i(\mathbf{x}) = s_{oi}$, so

---

$\sqrt{\mathbf{s}(\mathbf{x})}^{-}\lambda_2 \mathbf{x}$, where $\mathbf{s}(\mathbf{x})^{-}$ is an $n \times n$ diagonal matrix whose ith element equals $\left(s_{oi} + \mathbf{s}_{1i}'\mathbf{x}\right)^{-1}$ if $\inf\left(s_{oi} + \mathbf{s}_{1i}'\mathbf{x}\right) > 0$ and zero otherwise, and λ_2 is an $n \times n$ matrix of constants. This specification allows time variation in the market prices of risk for Gaussian state variables (such as state variables that follow Ornstein-Uhlenbeck processes), allowing their signs to switch over time. Duarte extends Duffee's modeling to add a square root term. This "semiaffine square root" model takes the form $\Theta = \Sigma^{-1}\lambda_0 + \sqrt{\mathbf{s}(\mathbf{x})}\lambda_1 + \sqrt{\mathbf{s}(\mathbf{x})}^{-}\lambda_2 \mathbf{x}$ where λ_0 is an $n \times 1$ vector of constants. See also work by Patrick Cheridito, Damir Filipovic, and Robert Kimmel (Cheridito, Filipovic, and Kimmel 2003) for extensions in modeling the market price of risk for affine models.

8. The assumptions regarding α and $\boldsymbol{\beta}$ are not restrictive to the results derived below. A nonzero α would add a multiplicative constant to bond prices and each state variable can be normalized by its $\boldsymbol{\beta}$ element to give a similar result.

that x_i follows an Ornstein-Uhlenbeck process, then $\widehat{E}_t \left[\exp \left(- \int_t^T x_i (s) \, ds \right) \right] = \exp \left[A_i (\tau) + B_i (\tau) x_i \right]$ where the functions $A_i (\tau)$ and $B_i (\tau)$ solve simplified versions of (17.18) and (17.19) and take similar forms to the Vasicek model formula in (9.41).[9] Another state variable, say, x_j, could have $s_j (x) = s_{1j} x_j$, so that it follows a square root constant elasticity of variance process. For this state variable, $\widehat{E}_t \left[\exp \left(- \int_t^T x_j (s) \, ds \right) \right] = \exp \left[A_j (\tau) + B_j (\tau) x_j \right]$ where the functions $A_j (\tau)$ and $B_j (\tau)$ satisfy simple versions of (17.18) and (17.19) and have solutions similar to the CIR model formula in (13.51).[10] Thus, using these prior single-factor model results, (17.21) can be written as

$$P (t, T, \mathbf{x}) = \prod_{i=1}^{n} \exp \left[A_i (\tau) + B_i (\tau) x_i \right] \tag{17.22}$$

Whether the assumption that state variables are independent is reasonable depends on the particular empirical context in which a term structure model is being used. Typically, there is a trade-off between more general correlation structures and model simplicity. Gaussian state variables (e.g., those following an Ornstein-Uhlenbeck process) allow for general correlation structures but do not restrict the state variables from becoming negative. State variables following square root processes can be restricted to maintain positive values but may be incapable of displaying negative correlation.

17.1.2   Quadratic Gaussian Models

Another class of models assumes that the yields of zero-coupon bonds are quadratic functions of normally distributed (Gaussian) state variables. Markus Leippold and Liuren Wu (Leippold and Wu 2002) provide a detailed discussion of these models. We can express the assumption that yields are a quadratic function of state variables by stating

$$Y (t, T, \mathbf{x}) \, \tau = A (\tau) + \mathbf{B} (\tau)' \mathbf{x} + \mathbf{x}' \mathbf{C} (\tau) \mathbf{x} \tag{17.23}$$

where $\mathbf{C} (\tau)$ is an $n \times n$ matrix and, with no loss of generality, can be assumed to be symmetric. Similar to our analysis of affine models, since $P (T, T, \mathbf{x}) = 1$, we must have $A (0) = 0$, $\mathbf{B} (0)$ equal to an $n \times 1$ vector of zeros, and $\mathbf{C} (0)$ equal to an $n \times n$ matrix of zeros. In addition, the yield on a bond of instantaneous

---

9. Due to slightly different notation, $A_i (\tau)$ equals $\ln[A (\tau)]$ in (9.43) and $B_i (\tau)$ equals $-B (\tau)$ in (9.42).

10. Because of slightly different notation, $A_j (\tau)$ equals $\ln[A (\tau)]$ in (13.52) and $B_j (\tau)$ equals $-B (\tau)$ in (13.53).

maturity must be of the form $r(t, \mathbf{x}) = \alpha + \boldsymbol{\beta}'\mathbf{x} + \mathbf{x}'\boldsymbol{\gamma}\mathbf{x}$, where $\alpha = \partial A(0)/\partial\tau$, $\boldsymbol{\beta} = \partial\mathbf{B}(0)/\partial\tau$, and $\boldsymbol{\gamma} = \partial\mathbf{C}(0)/\partial\tau$ is an $n \times n$ symmetric matrix of constants. Note that if $\boldsymbol{\gamma}$ is a positive semidefinite matrix and $\alpha - \frac{1}{4}\boldsymbol{\beta}'\boldsymbol{\gamma}^{-1}\boldsymbol{\beta} \geq 0$, then the interest rate can be restricted from becoming negative.[11] Substituting $P(t, T, \mathbf{x}) = \exp\left(-A(\tau) - \mathbf{B}(\tau)'\mathbf{x} - \mathbf{x}'\mathbf{C}(\tau)\mathbf{x}\right)$ into the general partial differential equation (17.6), we obtain

$$\frac{1}{2}\left[\left[\mathbf{B}(\tau) + 2\mathbf{C}(\tau)\mathbf{x}\right]'\mathbf{b}(t, \mathbf{x})\mathbf{b}(t, \mathbf{x})'\left[\mathbf{B}(\tau) + 2\mathbf{C}(\tau)\mathbf{x}\right]\right]$$
$$- \operatorname{Trace}\left[\mathbf{b}(t, \mathbf{x})'\mathbf{C}(\tau)\mathbf{b}(t, \mathbf{x})\right]$$
$$- \left[\mathbf{a}(t, \mathbf{x}) - \mathbf{b}(t, \mathbf{x})\boldsymbol{\Theta}\right]'\left[\mathbf{B}(\tau) + 2\mathbf{C}(\tau)\mathbf{x}\right]$$
$$+ \frac{\partial A(\tau)}{\partial\tau} + \frac{\partial\mathbf{B}(\tau)'}{\partial\tau}\mathbf{x} + \mathbf{x}'\frac{\partial\mathbf{C}(\tau)}{\partial\tau}\mathbf{x}$$
$$= \alpha + \boldsymbol{\beta}'\mathbf{x} + \mathbf{x}'\boldsymbol{\gamma}\mathbf{x} \tag{17.24}$$

In addition to yields being quadratic in the state variables, quadratic Gaussian models then assume that the vector of state variables, $\mathbf{x}$, has a multivariate normal (Gaussian) distribution. Specifically, it is assumed that $\mathbf{x}$ follows a multivariate Ornstein-Uhlenbeck process:

$$\mathbf{a}(t, \mathbf{x}) - \mathbf{b}(t, \mathbf{x})\boldsymbol{\Theta} = \kappa\left(\bar{\mathbf{x}} - \mathbf{x}\right) \tag{17.25}$$

$$\mathbf{b}(t, \mathbf{x}) = \boldsymbol{\Sigma} \tag{17.26}$$

Substituting these assumptions into the partial differential equation (17.24), one obtains

$$\frac{1}{2}\left[\left[\mathbf{B}(\tau) + 2\mathbf{C}(\tau)\mathbf{x}\right]'\boldsymbol{\Sigma}\boldsymbol{\Sigma}'\left[\mathbf{B}(\tau) + 2\mathbf{C}(\tau)\mathbf{x}\right]\right]$$
$$- \operatorname{Trace}\left[\boldsymbol{\Sigma}'\mathbf{C}(\tau)\boldsymbol{\Sigma}\right] - \left[\kappa\left(\bar{\mathbf{x}} - \mathbf{x}\right)\right]'\left[\mathbf{B}(\tau) + 2\mathbf{C}(\tau)\mathbf{x}\right]$$
$$+ \frac{\partial A(\tau)}{\partial\tau} + \frac{\partial\mathbf{B}(\tau)'}{\partial\tau}\mathbf{x} + \mathbf{x}'\frac{\partial\mathbf{C}(\tau)}{\partial\tau}\mathbf{x}$$
$$= \alpha + \boldsymbol{\beta}'\mathbf{x} + \mathbf{x}'\boldsymbol{\gamma}\mathbf{x} \tag{17.27}$$

For this equation to hold for all values of $\mathbf{x}$, it must be the case that the sums of the equation's constant terms, the terms proportional to the elements of $\mathbf{x}$, and

---

11. The lower bound for $r(t)$ is $\alpha - \frac{1}{4}\boldsymbol{\beta}'\boldsymbol{\gamma}^{-1}\boldsymbol{\beta}$, which occurs when $\mathbf{x} = -\frac{1}{2}\boldsymbol{\gamma}^{-1}\boldsymbol{\beta}$.

the terms that are products of the elements of **x** must each equal zero. This leads to the system of first-order ordinary differential equations

$$\frac{\partial A\,(\tau)}{\partial \tau} = \alpha + \left(\kappa \overline{\mathbf{x}}\right)' \mathbf{B}\,(\tau) - \tfrac{1}{2}\mathbf{B}\,(\tau)' \, \Sigma\Sigma'\mathbf{B}\,(\tau) + \text{Trace}\left[\Sigma'\mathbf{C}\,(\tau)\,\Sigma\right]$$

(17.28)

$$\frac{\partial \mathbf{B}\,(\tau)}{\partial \tau} = \beta - \kappa'\mathbf{B}\,(\tau) - 2\mathbf{C}\,(\tau)' \,\Sigma'\Sigma\mathbf{B}\,(\tau) + 2\mathbf{C}\,(\tau)' \, \kappa\overline{\mathbf{x}} \qquad (17.29)$$

$$\frac{\partial \mathbf{C}\,(\tau)}{\partial \tau} = \gamma - 2\kappa'\mathbf{C}\,(\tau) - 2\mathbf{C}\,(\tau)' \, \Sigma\Sigma'\mathbf{C}\,(\tau) \qquad (17.30)$$

which are solved subject to the aforementioned boundary conditions, $A\,(0) = 0$, $\mathbf{B}\,(0) = 0$, and $\mathbf{C}\,(0) = 0$.

Dong-Hyun Ahn, Robert Dittmar, and Ronald Gallant (Ahn, Dittmar, and Gallant 2002) show that the models of Francis Longstaff (Longstaff 1989), David Beaglehole and Mark Tenney (Beaglehole and Tenney 1992), and George Constantinides (Constantinides 1992) are special cases of quadratic Gaussian models. They also demonstrate that since quadratic Gaussian models allow a nonlinear relationship between yields and state variables, these models can outperform affine models in explaining historical bond yield data.

However, quadratic Gaussian models are more difficult to estimate from historical data because, unlike affine models, there is not a one-to-one mapping between bond yields and the elements of the vector of state variables. For example, suppose that at a given point in time, we observed bond yields of n different maturities, say, $Y\,(t, T_i, \mathbf{x})$, $i = 1, \ldots, n$. Denoting $\tau_i = T_i - t$, if yields are affine functions of the state variables, then $Y\,(t, T_i, \mathbf{x})\,\tau_i = A\,(\tau_i) + \mathbf{B}\,(\tau_i)'\,\mathbf{x}$, $i = 1, \ldots, n$, represents a set of n linear equations in the n elements of the state variable **x**. Solving these equations for the state variables $x_1, x_2, \ldots, x_n$ effectively allows one to observe the individual state variables from the observed yields. By observing a time series of these state variables, the parameters of their physical process could be estimated.

This approach cannot be used when yields are quadratic functions of the state variables since with $Y\,(t, T_i, \mathbf{x})\,\tau_i = A\,(\tau_i) + \mathbf{B}\,(\tau_i)'\,\mathbf{x} + \mathbf{x}'\mathbf{C}\,(\tau_i)\,\mathbf{x}$, there is not a one-to-one mapping between yields and state variables $x_1, x_2, \ldots, x_n$. There are multiple values of the state variable vector, **x**, consistent with the set of yields.[12] This difficulty requires a different approach to inferring the most likely state variable vector. Ahn, Dittmar, and Gallant use an efficient method of moments technique that simulates the state variable, **x**, to estimate the state variable vector that best fits the data.

---

12. For example, if $n = 1$, there are two state variable roots of the quadratic yield equation.

17.1.3   Other Equilibrium Models

Term structure models have been modified to allow state variable processes to differ from strict diffusions. Such models can no longer rely on the Black-Scholes hedging argument to identify market prices of risk and a risk-neutral pricing measure. Because fixed-income markets may not be dynamically complete, these models need to make additional assumptions regarding the market prices of risks that cannot be hedged.

A number of researchers, including Chang-Mo Ahn and Howard Thompson (Ahn and Thompson 1988), Sanjiv Das and Silverio Foresi (Das and Foresi 1996), Darrell Duffie, Jun Pan, and Kenneth Singleton (Duffie, Pan, and Singleton 2000), Sanjiv Das (Das 2002), and George Chacko and Sanjiv Das (Chacko and Das 2002), have extended equilibrium models to allow state variables to follow jump-diffusion processes. An interesting application of a model with jumps in a short-term interest rate is presented by Monika Piazzesi (Piazzesi 2005b) who studies the Federal Reserve's changes in the target federal funds rate.

Other affine equilibrium models have been set in discrete time, where the assumed existence of a discrete-time pricing kernel allows one to find solutions for equilibrium bond prices that have a recursive structure. Examples of models of this type include work by Tong-Sheng Sun (Sun 1992), David Backus and Stanley Zin (Backus and Zin 1994), V. Cvsa and Peter Ritchken (Cvsa and Ritchken 2001), and Qiang Dai, Anh Le, and Kenneth Singleton (Dai, Le, and Singleton 2006). Term structure models also have been generalized to include discrete regime shifts in the processes followed by state variables. See work by Vasant Naik and Moon Hoe Lee (Naik and Lee 1997) and Ravi Bansal and Hao Zhou (Bansal and Zhou 2002) for models of this type.

Let us now turn to fixed-income models whose primary purpose is not to determine the term structure of zero-coupon bond prices as a function of state variables. Rather, their objective is to determine the value of bond and interest rate–related derivatives as a function of a given term structure of bond prices.

17.2   Valuation Models for Interest Rate Derivatives

Models for valuing bonds and bond derivatives have different uses. The equilibrium models of the previous section can provide insights as to the nature of term structure movements. They allow us to predict how factor dynamics influence the prices of bonds of different maturities. Equilibrium models may also be of practical use to bond traders who wish to identify bonds of particular maturities that appear to be over- or underpriced based on their predicted model valuations. Such information could suggest profitable bond trading strategies.

However, bond prices are modeled for other objectives, such as the pricing of derivatives whose payoffs depend on the future prices of bonds or yields. Equilibrium models may be less than satisfactory for this purpose because it is bond derivatives, not the underlying bond prices themselves, that one wishes to value. In this context, one would like to use the observed market prices for bonds as an input into the valuation formulas for derivatives, not model the value of the underlying bonds themselves. For such a derivative-pricing exercise, one would like the model to "fit," or be consistent with, the observed market prices of the underlying bonds. The models that we will now consider are designed to have this feature.

17.2.1   Heath-Jarrow-Morton Models

The approach by David Heath, Robert Jarrow, and Andrew Morton (Heath, Jarrow, and Morton 1992) , hereafter referred to as HJM, differs from the previous equilibrium term structure models because it does not begin by specifying a set of state variables, $\mathbf{x}$, that determines the current term structure of bond prices. Rather, their approach takes the initial term structure of bond prices as given (observed) and then specifies how this term structure evolves in the future in order to value derivatives whose payoffs depend on future term structures. Because models of this type do not derive the term structure from more basic state variables, they cannot provide insights regarding how economic fundamentals determine the maturity structure of zero-coupon bond prices. Instead, HJM models are used to value fixed-income derivative securities: securities such as bond and interest rate options whose payoffs depend on future bond prices or yields.

An analogy to the HJM approach can be drawn from the risk-neutral valuation of equity options. Recall that in Chapter 10, equation (10.50), we assumed that the risk-neutral process for the price of a stock, $S(t)$, followed geometric Brownian motion, making this price lognormally distributed under the risk-neutral measure. From this assumption, and given the initial price of the stock, $S(t)$, the Black-Scholes formula for the value of a call option written on this stock was derived in equations (10.54) and (10.55). Note that we did not attempt to determine the initial value of the stock in terms of some fundamental state variables, say, $S(t, \mathbf{x})$. Rather, the initial stock price, $S(t)$, was taken as given and an assumption about this stock price's volatility, namely, that it was constant over time, was made.

The HJM approach to valuing fixed-income derivatives is similar but slightly more complex because it takes as given the entire initial term structure of bond prices, $P(t, T) \; \forall T \geq t$, not just a single asset (stock) price. It then assumes risk-neutral processes for how the initial observed bond prices change over time and does not attempt to derive these initial prices in terms of state variables, say,

$P(t, T, \mathbf{x})$. However, the way that HJM specify the processes followed by bond prices is somewhat indirect. They begin by specifying processes for bond *forward rates*. A fundamental result of the HJM analysis is to show that, in the absence of arbitrage, there must be a particular relationship between the drift and volatility parameters of forward rate processes and that only an assumption regarding the form of forward rate volatilities is needed for pricing derivatives.

Let us start by defining forward rates. Recall from Chapter 7 that a forward contract is an agreement between two parties where the long (*short*) party agrees to purchase (*deliver*) an underlying asset in return for paying (*receiving*) the forward price. Consider a forward contract agreed to at date t, where the contract matures at date $T \geq t$ and the underlying asset is a zero-coupon bond that matures at date $T + \tau$ where $\tau \geq 0$. Let $F(t, T, \tau)$ be the equilibrium forward price agreed to by the parties. Then this contract requires the long party to pay $F(t, T, \tau)$ at date T in return for receiving a cashflow of \$1 (the zero-coupon bond's maturity value) at date $T + \tau$. In the absence of arbitrage, the value of these two cashflows at date t must sum to zero, implying

$$-F(t, T, \tau) P(t, T) + P(t, T + \tau) = 0 \tag{17.31}$$

so that the equilibrium forward price equals the ratio of the bond prices maturing at dates $T + \tau$ and T, $F(t, T, \tau) = P(t, T + \tau) / P(t, T)$. From this forward price a continuously compounded forward rate, $f(t, T, \tau)$, is defined as

$$e^{-f(t, T, \tau)\tau} \equiv F(t, T, \tau) = \frac{P(t, T + \tau)}{P(t, T)} \tag{17.32}$$

$f(t, T, \tau) = -\left(\ln\left[P(t, T + \tau) / P(t, T)\right]\right) / \tau$ is the implicit per-period rate of return (interest rate) that the long party earns by investing \$$F(t, T, T + \tau)$ at date T and by receiving \$1 at date $T + \tau$. Now consider the case of such a forward contract where the underlying bond matures very shortly (e.g., the next day or instant) after the maturity of the forward contract. This permits us to define an instantaneous forward rate as

$$f(t, T) \equiv \lim_{\tau \to 0} f(t, T, \tau)$$

$$= \lim_{\tau \to 0} -\frac{\ln\left[P(t, T + \tau)\right] - \ln\left[P(t, T)\right]}{\tau} = -\frac{\partial \ln\left[P(t, T)\right]}{\partial T} \tag{17.33}$$

Equation (17.33) is a simple differential equation that can be solved to obtain

$$P(t, T) = e^{-\int_t^T f(t, s)ds} \tag{17.34}$$

Since this bond's continuously compounded yield to maturity is defined from the relation $P(t, T) = e^{-Y(t, T)(T - t)}$, we can write $Y(t, T) = \frac{1}{T - t} \int_t^T f(t, s)\,ds$. Thus, a bond's yield equals the average of the instantaneous forward rates for horizons out to the bond's maturity. In particular, the yield on an instantaneous-maturity bond is given by $r(t) = f(t, t)$.

Because the term structure of instantaneous forward rates, $f(t, T) \, \forall T \geq t$, can be determined from the term structure of bond prices, $P(t, T) \, \forall T \geq t$, or yields, $Y(t, T) \, \forall T \geq t$, specifying the evolution of forward rates over time is equivalent to specifying the dynamics of bond prices. HJM assume that forward rates for all horizons are driven by a finite-dimensional Brownian motion:

$$df(t, T) = \alpha(t, T) \, dt + \boldsymbol{\sigma}(t, T)' \, \mathbf{dz} \tag{17.35}$$

where $\boldsymbol{\sigma}(t, T)$ is an $n \times 1$ vector of volatility functions and $\mathbf{dz}$ is an $n \times 1$ vector of independent Brownian motions. Note that since there are an infinite number of instantaneous forward rates, one for each future horizon, equation (17.35) represents infinitely many processes that are driven by the same n Brownian motions.

Importantly, the absence of arbitrage places restrictions on $\alpha(t, T)$ and $\boldsymbol{\sigma}(t, T)$. To show this, let us start by deriving the process followed by bond prices, $P(t, T)$, implied by the forward rate processes. Note that since $\ln[P(t, T)] = -\int_t^T f(t, s) \, ds$, if we differentiate with respect to date t, we find that the process followed by the log bond price is

$$d\ln[P(t, T)] = f(t, t) \, dt - \int_t^T df(t, s) \, ds \tag{17.36}$$

$$= r(t) \, dt - \int_t^T \left[\alpha(t, s) \, dt + \boldsymbol{\sigma}(t, s)' \, \mathbf{dz}(t) \right] ds$$

Fubini's theorem allows us to switch the order of integration:

$$d\ln[P(t, T)] = r(t) \, dt - \int_t^T \alpha(t, s) \, ds dt - \int_t^T \boldsymbol{\sigma}(t, s)' \, ds \mathbf{dz}(t) \tag{17.37}$$

$$= r(t) \, dt - \alpha_I(t, T) \, dt - \boldsymbol{\sigma}_I(t, T)' \, \mathbf{dz}(t)$$

where we have used the shorthand notation $\alpha_I(t, T) \equiv \int_t^T \alpha(t, s) \, ds$ and $\boldsymbol{\sigma}_I(t, T) \equiv \int_t^T \boldsymbol{\sigma}(t, s) \, ds$ to designate these integrals that are known functions as of date t. Using Itô's lemma we can derive the bond's rate of return process from the log process in (17.37):

$$\frac{dP(t, T)}{P(t, T)} = \left[r(t) - \alpha_I(t, T) + \frac{1}{2}\boldsymbol{\sigma}_I(t, T)' \boldsymbol{\sigma}_I(t, T) \right] dt - \boldsymbol{\sigma}_I(t, T)' \, \mathbf{dz} \tag{17.38}$$

Now recall from (17.5) that the absence of arbitrage requires that the bond's expected rate of return equal the instantaneous risk-free return plus the product of the bond's volatilities and the market prices of risk. This is written as

$$r(t) - \alpha_I(t, T) + \frac{1}{2}\sigma_I(t, T)'\sigma_I(t, T) = r(t) - \Theta(t)'\sigma_I(t, T) \qquad (17.39)$$

or

$$\alpha_I(t, T) = \frac{1}{2}\sigma_I(t, T)'\sigma_I(t, T) + \Theta(t)'\sigma_I(t, T) \qquad (17.40)$$

Equations (17.38) and (17.40) show that the bond price process depends only on the instantaneous risk-free rate, the volatilities of the forward rates, and the market prices of risk. This no-arbitrage condition also has implications for the risk-neutral process followed by forward rates. If we substitute $dz = d\hat{z} - \Theta(t)\,dt$ in (17.35), we obtain

$$df(t, T) = [\alpha(t, T) - \sigma(t, T)'\Theta(t)]\,dt + \sigma(t, T)'\,d\hat{z}$$
$$= \hat{\alpha}(t, T)\,dt + \sigma(t, T)'\,d\hat{z} \qquad (17.41)$$

where $\hat{\alpha}(t, T) \equiv \alpha(t, T) - \sigma(t, T)'\Theta(t)$ is the risk-neutral drift observed at date t for the forward rate at date T. Define $\hat{\alpha}_I(t, T) \equiv \int_t^T \hat{\alpha}(t, s)\,ds$ as the integral over the drifts across all forward rates from date t to date T. Then using (17.40) we have

$$\hat{\alpha}_I(t, T) = \int_t^T \hat{\alpha}(t, s)\,ds = \int_t^T \alpha(t, s)\,ds - \int_t^T \sigma(t, s)'\,ds\Theta(t)$$
$$= \alpha_I(t, T) - \Theta(t)'\sigma_I(t, T)$$
$$= \frac{1}{2}\sigma_I(t, T)'\sigma_I(t, T) + \Theta(t)'\sigma_I(t, T) - \Theta(t)'\sigma_I(t, T)$$
$$= \frac{1}{2}\sigma_I(t, T)'\sigma_I(t, T) \qquad (17.42)$$

or $\int_t^T \hat{\alpha}(t, s)\,ds = \frac{1}{2}\left(\int_t^T \sigma(t, s)\,ds\right)'\left(\int_t^T \sigma(t, s)\,ds\right)$. This shows that in the absence of arbitrage, the risk-neutral drifts of forward rates are completely determined by their volatilities. Indeed, if we differentiate $\hat{\alpha}_I(t, T)$ with respect to T to recover $\hat{\alpha}(t, T)$, we obtain

$$df(t, T) = \sigma(t, T)'\sigma_I(t, T)\,dt + \sigma(t, T)'\,d\hat{z} \qquad (17.43)$$
$$= \left(\sigma(t, T)'\int_t^T \sigma(t, s)\,ds\right)dt + \sigma(t, T)'\,d\hat{z}$$

Equation (17.43) has an important implication, namely, that if we want to model the risk-neutral dynamics of forward rates in order to price fixed-income derivatives, we need only specify the form of the forward rates' volatility functions.[13] One can also use (17.43) to derive the risk-neutral dynamics of the instantaneous-maturity interest rate, $r(t) = f(t,t)$, which is required for discounting risk-neutral payoffs. Suppose dates are ordered such that $0 \leq t \leq T$. In integrated form, (17.43) becomes

$$f(t,T) = f(0,T) + \int_0^t \sigma(u,T)' \sigma_I(u,T)\, du + \int_0^t \sigma(u,T)'\, d\widehat{z}(u) \qquad (17.44)$$

and for $r(t) = f(t,t)$, this becomes

$$r(t) = f(0,t) + \int_0^t \sigma(u,t)' \sigma_I(u,t)\, du + \int_0^t \sigma(u,t)'\, d\widehat{z}(u) \qquad (17.45)$$

Differentiating with respect to t leads to[14]

$$
\begin{aligned}
dr(t) &= \frac{\partial f(0,t)}{\partial t} dt + \sigma(t,t)' \sigma_I(t,t)\, dt + \int_0^t \frac{\partial \sigma(u,t)' \sigma_I(u,t)}{\partial t}\, du\, dt \\
&\quad + \int_0^t \frac{\partial \sigma(u,t)'}{\partial t}\, d\widehat{z}(u)\, dt + \sigma(t,t)'\, d\widehat{z} \\
&= \frac{\partial f(0,t)}{\partial t} dt + \int_0^t \left[\sigma(u,t)' \sigma(u,t) + \frac{\partial \sigma(u,t)'}{\partial t} \sigma_I(u,t) \right] du\, dt \\
&\quad + \int_0^t \frac{\partial \sigma(u,t)'}{\partial t}\, d\widehat{z}(u)\, dt + \sigma(t,t)'\, d\widehat{z} \qquad (17.46)
\end{aligned}
$$

where we have used the fact that $\sigma_I(t,t) = 0$ and $\partial \sigma_I(u,t)/\partial t = \sigma(u,t)$.

With these results, one can now value fixed-income derivatives. As an example, define $C(t)$ as the current date t price of a European-type contingent claim that has a payoff at date T. This payoff is assumed to depend on the forward rate curve (equivalently, the term structure of bond prices or yields) at date T, which we write as $C(T, f(T, T+\delta))$ where $\delta \geq 0$. The contingent claim's risk-neutral valuation equation is

$$C(t, f(t, t+\delta)) = \widehat{E}_t \left[e^{-\int_t^T r(s)\, ds} C(T, f(T, T+\delta)) \mid f(t, t+\delta), \forall \delta \geq 0 \right]$$

$$(17.47)$$

---

13. In general, these volatility functions may be stochastic, as they could be specified to depend on current levels of the forward rates, that is, $\sigma(t, T, f(t, T))$.

14. Note that the dynamics of dr are more complicated than simply setting $T = t$ in equation (17.43), because both arguments of $f(t,t) = r(t)$ are varying simultaneously. Equation (17.46) is equivalent to $dr = df(t,t) + \frac{\partial f(t,u)}{\partial u}\big|_{u \to t} dt$.

where the expectation is conditioned on information of the current date t forward rate curve, $f(t, t + \delta)$ $\forall \delta \geq 0$. Equation (17.47) is the risk-neutral expectation of the claim's discounted payoff, conditional on information of all currently observed forward rates. In this manner, the contingent claim's formula can be assured of fitting the current term structure of interest rates, since the forward rate curve, $f(t, t + \delta)$, is an input. Only for special cases regarding the type of contingent claim and the assumed forward rate volatilities can the expectation in (17.47) be computed analytically. In general, it can be computed by a Monte Carlo simulation of a discrete-time analog to the continuous-time, risk-neutral forward rate and instantaneous interest rate processes in (17.43) and (17.46).[15]

Valuing American-type contingent claims using the HJM approach can be more complicated because, in general, one needs to discretize forward rates to produce a lattice (e.g., binomial tree) and check the nodes of the lattice to see if early exercise is optimal.[16] However, HJM forward rates will not necessarily follow Markov processes. From (17.43) and (17.46), one can see that if the forward rate volatility functions are specified to depend on the level of forward rates themselves, $\sigma(t, s, f(t, s))$, or the instantaneous risk-free rate, $\sigma(t, s, r(t))$, then the evolution of $f(t, T)$ and $r(t)$ depends on the entire history of forward rates between two dates such as 0 and t. It will be impossible to express forward rates as $f(0, T, x(0))$ and $f(t, T, x(t))$ where $x(t)$ is a set of finite state variables.[17] Non-Markov processes lead to lattice structures where the nodes do not recombine. This can make computation extremely time consuming because the number of nodes grows exponentially (rather than linearly in the case of recombining nodes) with the number of time steps. Hence, to value American contingent claims using the HJM framework, it is highly desirable to pick volatility structures that lead to forward rate processes that are Markov.[18] The next section gives two examples of HJM models that are Markov in a finite number of state variables.

---

15. An example is presented by Kaushik Amin and Andrew Morton (Amin and Morton 1994). They value Eurodollar futures and options assuming different one-factor ($n = 1$) specifications for forward rate volatilities. Their models are nested in the functional form $\sigma(t, T) = [\sigma_0 + \sigma_1(T - t)] e^{-\alpha(T-t)} f(t, T)^\gamma$.

16. Recall that this method was used in Chapter 7 to value an American option.

17. The reason why one may want to assume that forward rate volatilities depend on their own level is to preclude negative forward rates, a necessary condition if currency is not to dominate bonds in a nominal term structure model. For example, similar to the square root model of Cox, Ingersoll, and Ross, one could specify $\sigma(t, T) = \overline{\sigma}(t, T) f(t, T)^{\frac{1}{2}}$ or $\sigma(t, T) = \overline{\sigma}(t, T) r(t)^{\frac{1}{2}}$ where $\overline{\sigma}(t, T)$ is a deterministic function.

18. Note, also, that non-Markov short rate and forward rate processes imply that contingent claims cannot be valued by solving an equilibrium partial differential equation, such as was done in Chapter 9 in equation (9.40).

Examples: Markov HJM Models

General conditions on forward rate volatilities that lead to Markov structures are discussed in Koji Inui and Masaaki Kijima (Inui and Kijima 1998). In this section we give two different examples of Markov HJM models. The first is an example where forward rates, including the instantaneous-maturity interest rate, are Markov in one state variable. In the second example, rates are Markov in two state variables. In both examples, it is assumed that $n = 1$, so that there is a single Brownian motion process driving all forward rates.

Our first example assumes forward rate volatilities are deterministic. As shown by Andrew Carverhill (Carverhill 1994), this assumption results in HJM models that are Markov in one state variable. Here we consider a particular case of deterministic forward volatilities that decline exponentially with their time horizons:

$$\sigma(t, T) = \sigma_r e^{-\alpha(T-t)} \tag{17.48}$$

where σ_r and α are positive constants. From (17.38), this implies that the rate of return volatility of a zero-coupon bond equals

$$\sigma_I(t, T) \equiv \int_t^T \sigma(t, s)\, ds = \int_t^T \sigma_r e^{-\alpha(s-t)} ds = \frac{\sigma_r}{\alpha}\left(1 - e^{-\alpha(T-t)}\right) \tag{17.49}$$

Note that this volatility function is the same as the Vasicek model of the term structure given in (9.44). Hence, the bond price's risk-neutral process is $dP(t, T)/P(t, T) = r(t)\, dt - \frac{\sigma_r}{\alpha}\left(1 - e^{-\alpha(T-t)}\right) d\hat{z}$. To value contingent claims for this case, it remains to derive the instantaneous-maturity interest rate and its dynamics. From (17.45) and (17.46), we have

$$r(t) = f(0, t) + \int_0^t \frac{\sigma_r^2}{\alpha}\left(e^{-\alpha(t-u)} - e^{-2\alpha(t-u)}\right) du + \int_0^t \sigma_r e^{-\alpha(t-u)} d\hat{z}(u) \tag{17.50}$$

$$dr = \frac{\partial f(0, t)}{\partial t} dt + \int_0^t \left[\sigma_r^2 e^{-2\alpha(t-u)} - \sigma_r^2\left(e^{-\alpha(t-u)} - e^{-2\alpha(t-u)}\right)\right] du\, dt$$

$$- \int_0^t \alpha \sigma_r e^{-\alpha(t-u)} d\hat{z}(u)\, dt + \sigma_r d\hat{z} \tag{17.51}$$

Substituting (17.50) into (17.51) and simplifying leads to

$$dr = \frac{\partial f(0, t)}{\partial t} dt + \int_0^t \sigma_r^2 e^{-2\alpha(t-u)} du\, dt + \alpha\left[f(0, t) - r(t)\right] dt + \sigma_r d\hat{z}$$

$$= \alpha\left[\frac{1}{\alpha}\frac{\partial f(0, t)}{\partial t} + f(0, t) + \frac{\sigma_r^2}{2\alpha^2}\left(1 - e^{-2\alpha t}\right) - r(t)\right] dt + \sigma_r d\hat{z}$$

$$= \alpha\left[\bar{r}(t) - r(t)\right] dt + \sigma_r d\hat{z} \tag{17.52}$$

where $\bar{r}(t) \equiv \frac{1}{\alpha}\partial f(0,t)/\partial t + f(0,t) + \sigma_r^2(1 - e^{-2\alpha t})/(2\alpha^2)$ is the risk-neutral central tendency of the short-rate process that is a deterministic function of time. The process in (17.52) is Markov in that the only stochastic variable affecting its future distribution is the current level of $r(t)$. However, it differs from the standard Vasicek model, which assumes that the risk-neutral process for $r(t)$ has a long-run mean that is constant.[19] By making the central tendency, $\bar{r}(t)$, a particular deterministic function of the currently observed forward rate curve, $f(0,t) \forall t \geq 0$, the model's implied date 0 price of a zero-coupon bond, $P(0,T)$, coincides exactly with observed prices.[20] This model was proposed by John Hull and Alan White (Hull and White 1990; Hull and White 1993) and HJM (Heath, Jarrow, and Morton 1992) and is referred to as the "extended Vasicek" model.[21]

Let us illustrate this extended Vasicek model by valuing a European option maturing at date T, where the underlying asset is a zero-coupon bond maturing at date $T + \tau$. Since, as with the standard Vasicek model, the extended Vasicek model has bond return volatilities as a deterministic function of time, the expectation in (17.47) for the case of a European option has an analytic solution. Alternatively, the results of Merton (Merton 1973b) given in equations (9.58) to (9.60) on the pricing of options when interest rates are random can be applied to derive the solution. However, instead of Chapter 9's assumption of the underlying asset being an equity that follows geometric Brownian motion, the underlying asset is a bond that matures at date $T + \tau$. For a call option with exercise price X, the boundary condition is $c(T) = \max[P(T, T + \tau) - X, 0]$. This leads to the solution

$$c(t) = P(t, T + \tau) N(d_1) - P(t, T) X N(d_2) \tag{17.53}$$

$$= e^{-\int_t^{T+\tau} f(t,s)ds} N(d_1) - e^{-\int_t^{T} f(t,s)ds} X N(d_2)$$

where

$$d_1 = \left[\ln\left[P(t, T + \tau)/(P(t, T) X)\right] + \tfrac{1}{2}v(t, T)^2\right]/v(t, T), \quad d_2 = d_1 - v(t, T),$$

---

19. Recall from equation (10.66) that the unconditional mean of the risk-neutral interest rate is $\bar{r} + q\sigma_r/\alpha$, where $\bar{r}$ is the mean of the physical process and q is the market price of interest rate risk.

20. It is left as an exercise to verify that when $\bar{r}(t) \equiv \frac{1}{\alpha}\partial f(0,t)/\partial t + f(0,t) + \sigma_r^2(1 - e^{-2\alpha t})/(2\alpha^2)$, then $P(0,T) = \widehat{E}[\exp(-\int_0^T r(s)\,ds)] = \exp(-\int_0^T f(0,s)\,ds)$.

21. Hull and White show that, besides $\bar{r}(t)$, the parameters $\alpha(t)$ and $\sigma_r(t)$ also can be extended to be deterministic functions of time. With these extensions, $r(t)$ remains normally distributed and analytic solutions to options on discount bonds can be obtained. Making $\alpha(t)$ and $\sigma_r(t)$ time varying allows one to fit other aspects of the term structure, such as observed volatilities of forward rates.

and where[22]

$$v(t, T)^2 = \int_t^T \left[\sigma_I^2(t, u + \tau) + \sigma_I^2(t, u) - 2\rho\sigma_I(t, u + \tau)\sigma_I(t, u) \right] du$$

$$= \frac{\sigma_r^2}{2\alpha^3} \left(1 - e^{-2\alpha(T-t)} \right) \left(1 - e^{-\sigma\tau} \right)^2 \tag{17.54}$$

This solution illustrates a general principle of the HJM approach, namely, that formulas can be derived whose inputs match the initial term structure of bond prices ($P(t, T)$ and $P(t, T + \tau)$) or, equivalently, the initial forward rate curve ($f(t, s) \; \forall s \geq t$).

Our second example of a Markov HJM model is due to Peter Ritchken and L. Sankarasubramanian (Ritchken and Sankarasubramanian 1995), hereafter referred to as RS. They give general conditions on forward rate volatilities that result in term structure dynamics being Markov in two state variables. A particular example that satisfies these conditions is their example where forward rate volatilities take the form

$$\sigma(t, T) = \sigma_r r(t)^\gamma e^{-\alpha(T-t)} \tag{17.55}$$

where σ_r and α are positive constants. Thus, (17.55) specifies that the volatility of the short rate (when $T = t$) equals $\sigma_r r(t)^\gamma$. When $\gamma = 0$, we have our first example's extended Vasicek case of deterministic forward rates. However, empirical evidence indicates that interest rate volatility increases with the level of the short rate, so that it is desirable to obtain a Markov model with $\gamma > 0$. Similar to the derivation for $r(t)$ given for the extended Vasicek model, RS show that in this case the risk-neutral process for the instantaneous-maturity interest rate satisfies

$$dr(t) = \left(\alpha \left[f(0, t) - r(t) \right] + \phi(t) + \frac{\partial f(0, t)}{\partial t} \right) dt + \sigma_r r(t)^\gamma \, d\widehat{z} \tag{17.56}$$

where

$$\phi(t) = \int_0^t \sigma^2(s, t) \, ds$$

$$= \sigma_r^2 \int_0^t r(s)^{2\gamma} e^{-2\alpha(t-s)} ds \tag{17.57}$$

---

22. Note that when applying Merton's derivation to the case of the underlying asset being a bond, then ρ, the return correlation between bonds maturing at dates T and $T + \tau$, equals 1. This is because there is a single Brownian motion determining the stochastic component of returns.

Differentiating (17.57) with respect to t, one obtains the dynamics of $\phi(t)$ to be

$$d\phi(t) = \left(\sigma_r^2 r(t)^{2\gamma} - 2\alpha\phi(t) \right) dt \tag{17.58}$$

The variable $\phi(t)$ is an "integrated variance" factor that evolves stochastically when $\gamma \neq 0$.[23] It, along with the short rate, $r(t)$, are two state variables that determine the evolution of $r(t)$. In turn, this determines the bonds' risk-neutral processes. Recall that since a bond's rate of return volatility equals $\sigma_I(t, T) \equiv \int_t^T \sigma(t, s)\, ds = \int_t^T \sigma_r r(t)^\gamma e^{-\alpha(s-t)} ds = \frac{\sigma_r r(t)^\gamma}{\alpha} \left(1 - e^{-\alpha(T-t)}\right)$, its risk-neutral price process equals

$$dP(t, T)/P(t, T) = r(t)\, dt - \frac{\sigma_r r(t)^\gamma}{\alpha} \left(1 - e^{-\alpha(T-t)}\right) d\hat{z} \tag{17.59}$$

It is noteworthy that even when $\gamma = \frac{1}{2}$, the model differs from the CIR equilibrium model. Even though in both models the short rate's volatility, $\sigma_r \sqrt{r(t)}$, is the same, the RS model's requirement that it fit the observed term structure introduces a second stochastic state variable, $\phi(t)$, into the drift of the short rate process in (17.56).

In general, valuing fixed-income derivatives using the RS model does not lead to closed-form solutions. However, RS (Ritchken and Sankarasubramanian 1995) show that the risk-neutral processes for $r(t)$ and $\phi(t)$ can be discretized and Monte Carlo simulations performed to value contingent claims based on (17.47).

There are a number of other discrete-time models that can numerically value fixed-income derivatives based on calculations using binomial trees or lattices. These models can be viewed as discrete-time implementations of the continuous-time HJM approach in that they are designed to fit the initial term structure of bond prices and, possibly, bond volatilities. Thomas Ho and Sang Bin Lee (Ho and Lee 1986) first introduced the concept of pricing fixed-income derivatives by taking the initial term structure of bond prices as given and then making assumptions regarding the risk-neutral distribution of future interest rates. Their model is the discrete-time counterpart of the extended Vasicek model but with the mean reversion parameter, α, set to zero.[24] This binomial approach was modified for different risk-neutral interest rate dynamics by Fischer Black, Emanuel

---

23. Note that when $\gamma = 0$, one obtains $\phi(t) = \frac{\sigma_r^2}{2\alpha}(1 - e^{-2\alpha t})$, so that $\phi(t)$ is deterministic and the short rate process in (17.56) equals that of the extended Vasicek model in (17.52).

24. Thus, with zero mean reversion, an unattractive feature of this model is that the short rate is expected to explode over time. The Ho-Lee model is a mechanical way of calibrating a lattice that is consistent with an initial term structure of bond prices. The HJM approach can be viewed as a shortcut to accomplishing this because the extended Vasicek model provides an analytic solution that embeds the Ho-Lee assumptions.

Derman, and William Toy (Black, Derman, and Toy 1990) and Fischer Black and Piotr Karasinski (Black and Karasinski 1991). These discrete-time "no-arbitrage" models are fixed-income counterparts to the binomial model of Chapter 7 that was used to price equity derivatives.

17.2.2   Market Models

As shown in the previous section, HJM models begin with a particular specification for instantaneous-maturity, continuously compounded forward rates, and then derivative values are calculated based on these initial forward rates. However, instantaneous-maturity forward rates are not directly observable, and in many applications they must be approximated from data on bond yields or discrete-maturity forward or futures rates that are unavailable at every maturity. A class of models that is a variation on the HJM approach can sometimes avoid this approximation error and may lead to more simple, analytic solutions for particular types of derivatives. These models are known as "market models" and are designed to price derivatives whose payoffs are a function of a discrete maturity, rather than instantaneous-maturity, forward interest rate. Examples of such derivatives include interest rate caps and floors and swaptions. Let us illustrate the market model approach by way of these examples.

Example: An Interest Rate Cap

Consider valuing a European option written on a discrete forward rate, such as one based on the London Interbank Offer Rate (LIBOR). Define $L(t, T, \tau)$ as the date t annualized, τ-period compounded, forward interest rate for borrowing or lending over the period from future date T to $T + \tau$.[25] In terms of current date t discount bond prices ($P(t, t + \delta)$), forward price ($F(t, T, \tau)$), and continuously compounded forward rate ($f(t, T, \tau)$), this discrete forward rate is defined by the relation

$$\frac{P(t, T + \tau)}{P(t, T)} = F(t, T, \tau) = e^{-f(t,T,\tau)\tau} = \frac{1}{1 + \tau L(t, T, \tau)} \tag{17.60}$$

Note that when $T = t$, $P(t, t + \tau) = 1/[1 + \tau L(t, t, \tau)]$ defines $L(t, t, \tau)$ as the current "spot" τ-period LIBOR.[26] An example of an option written on LIBOR is a caplet that matures at date $T + \tau$ and is based on the realized spot rate $L(T, T, \tau)$.

---

25. The convention for LIBOR is to set the compounding interval equal to the underlying instrument's maturity. For example, if $\tau = \frac{1}{4}$ years, then three-month LIBOR is compounded quarterly. If $\tau = \frac{1}{2}$ years, then six-month LIBOR is compounded semiannually.

26. This modeling assumes that LIBOR is the yield on a default-free discount bond. However, LIBOR is not a fully default-free interest rate, such as a Treasury security rate. It represents

Assuming this caplet has an exercise cap rate X, its date $T + \tau$ payoff is

$$c\,(T + \tau) = \tau \max \left[L\,(T, T, \tau) - X, 0 \right] \tag{17.61}$$

that is, the option payoff at date $T + \tau$ depends on the τ-period spot LIBOR at date T.[27] Because uncertainty regarding the LIBOR rate is resolved at date T, which is τ period's prior to the caplet's settlement (payment) date, we can also write

$$
\begin{aligned}
c\,(T) &= P\,(T, T + \tau) \max \left[\tau L\,(T, T, \tau) - \tau X, 0 \right] \tag{17.62} \\
&= P\,(T, T + \tau) \max \left[\frac{1}{P\,(T, T + \tau)} - 1 - \tau X, 0 \right] \\
&= \max \left[1 - (1 + \tau X)\, P\,(T, T + \tau)\,, 0 \right] \\
&= \max \left[1 - \frac{1 + \tau X}{1 + \tau L\,(T, T, \tau)}, 0 \right]
\end{aligned}
$$

which illustrates that a caplet maturing at date $T + \tau$ is equivalent to a put option that matures at date T, has an exercise price of 1, and is written on a zero-coupon bond that has a payoff of $1 + \tau X$ at its maturity date of $T + \tau$. Similarly, a floorlet, whose date $T + \tau$ payoff equals $\tau \max \left[X - L\,(T, T, \tau)\,, 0 \right]$, can be shown to be equivalent to a call option on a zero-coupon bond.[28]

To value a caplet using a market model approach, let us first analyze the dynamics of $L\,(t, T, \tau)$. Rearranging (17.60) gives

$$\tau L\,(t, T, \tau) = \frac{P\,(t, T)}{P\,(t, T + \tau)} - 1 \tag{17.63}$$

We can derive the stochastic process followed by this forward rate in terms of the bond prices' risk-neutral processes. Note that from (17.38), along with $\mathbf{dz} = \mathbf{d\hat{z}} - \boldsymbol{\Theta}\,(t)\,dt$, we have $dP\,(t, T)\,/P\,(t, T) = r\,(t)\,dt - \boldsymbol{\sigma}_I\,(t, T)'\,\mathbf{d\hat{z}}$. Applying Itô's lemma to (17.63), we obtain

$$
\begin{aligned}
\frac{dL\,(t, T, \tau)}{L\,(t, T, \tau)} &= \left(\boldsymbol{\sigma}_I\,(t, T + \tau)' \left[\boldsymbol{\sigma}_I\,(t, T + \tau) - \boldsymbol{\sigma}_I\,(t, T) \right] \right) dt \tag{17.64} \\
&\quad + \left[\boldsymbol{\sigma}_I\,(t, T + \tau) - \boldsymbol{\sigma}_I\,(t, T) \right]'\,\mathbf{d\hat{z}}
\end{aligned}
$$

---

the borrowing rate of a large, generally high-credit-quality bank. Typically, the relatively small amount of default risk is ignored when applying market models to derivatives based on LIBOR.

27. Caplets are based on a notional principal amount, which here is assumed to be \$1. The value of a caplet having a notional principal of \$$N$ is simply N times the value of a caplet with a notional principal of \$1; that is, its payoff is $\tau N \max \left[L\,(T, T, \tau) - X, 0 \right]$.

28. Therefore, the HJM-extended Vasicek solution in (17.53) to (17.54) is one method for valuing a floorlet. A straightforward modification of this formula could also value a caplet.

In principle, now we could value a contingent claim written on $L(t, T, \tau)$ by calculating the claim's discounted expected terminal payoff assuming $L(t, T, \tau)$ follows the process in (17.64).[29] However, as will become clear, there is an alternative probability measure to the one generated by $d\hat{z}$ that can be used to calculate a contingent claim's expected payoff, and this alternative measure is analytically more convenient for this particular forward rate application.

To see this, consider the new transformation $d\tilde{z} = d\hat{z} + \sigma_I(t, T + \tau)\, dt = dz + [\Theta(t) + \sigma_I(t, T + \tau)]\, dt$. Substituting into (17.64) results in

$$\frac{dL(t, T, \tau)}{L(t, T, \tau)} = [\sigma_I(t, T + \tau) - \sigma_I(t, T)]'\, d\tilde{z} \tag{17.65}$$

so that under the probability measure generated by $d\tilde{z}$, the process followed by $L(t, T, \tau)$ is a martingale. This probability measure is referred to as the *forward rate measure* at date $T + \tau$. Note that since $L(t, T, \tau)$ is linear in the bond price $P(t, T)$ deflated by $P(t, T + \tau)$, the forward rate measure at date $T + \tau$ works by deflating all security prices by the price of the discount bond that matures at date $T + \tau$. This contrasts with the risk-neutral measure where security prices are deflated by the value of the money market account, which follows the process $dB(t) = r(t)B(t)\, dt$.

Not only does $L(t, T, \tau)$ follow a martingale under the forward measure, but so does the value of all other securities. To see this, let the date t price of a contingent claim be given by $c(t)$. In the absence of arbitrage, its price process is of the form

$$\frac{dc}{c} = [r(t) + \Theta(t)'\sigma_c(t)]\, dt + \sigma_c(t)'\, dz \tag{17.66}$$

Now define the deflated contingent claim's price as $C(t) = c(t)/P(t, T + \tau)$. Applying Itô's lemma gives

$$\frac{dC}{C} = [\Theta(t) + \sigma_I(t, T + \tau)]'[\sigma_c(t) + \sigma_I(t, T + \tau)]\, dt \tag{17.67}$$

$$+ [\sigma_c(t) + \sigma_I(t, T + \tau)]'\, dz$$

and making the forward measure transformation $d\tilde{z} = dz + [\Theta(t) + \sigma_I(t, T + \tau)]\, dt$, (17.67) becomes the martingale process

$$\frac{dC}{C} = [\sigma_c(t) + \sigma_I(t, T + \tau)]'\, d\tilde{z} \tag{17.68}$$

---

29. Specifically, if $c(t, L(t, T, \tau))$ is the contingent claim's value, it could be calculated as $\hat{E}_t\left[e^{-\int_t^T r(s)ds} c(T, L(T, T, \tau))\right]$ where $r(t)$ and $L(t, T, \tau)$ are assumed to follow risk-neutral processes.

so that $C(t) = \tilde{E}_t [C(t + \delta)] \; \forall \delta \geq 0$, where $\tilde{E}_t [\cdot]$ is the date t expectation under the forward measure. Now, to show why this transformation can be convenient, suppose that this contingent claim is the caplet described earlier. This deflated caplet's value is given by

$$C(t) = \tilde{E}_t [C(T + \tau)] \tag{17.69}$$

$$= \tilde{E}_t \left[\frac{\tau \max [L(T, T, \tau) - X, 0]}{P(T + \tau, T + \tau)} \right]$$

Noting that $C(t) = c(t) / P(t, T + \tau)$ and realizing that $P(T + \tau, T + \tau) = 1$, we can rewrite this as

$$c(t) = P(t, T + \tau) \, \tilde{E}_t [\tau \max [L(T, T, \tau) - X, 0]] \tag{17.70}$$

A common practice is to assume that $L(T, T, \tau)$ is lognormally distributed under the date $T + \tau$ forward measure.[30] This means that $\left[\sigma_I(t, T + \tau) - \sigma_I(t, T) \right]$ in (17.65) must be a vector of nonstochastic functions of time that can be calibrated to match observed bond or forward rate volatilities.[31] Noting that $L(t, T, \tau)$ also has a zero drift leads to a similar formula first proposed by Fischer Black (Black 1976) for valuing options on commodity futures:

$$c(t) = \tau P(t, T + \tau) \left[L(t, T, \tau) N(d_1) - X N(d_2) \right] \tag{17.71}$$

where $d_1 = \left[\ln (L(t, T, \tau) / X) + \frac{1}{2} v(t, T)^2 \right] / v(t, T), d_2 = d_1 - v(t, T)$, and

$$v(t, T)^2 = \int_t^T \left| \sigma_I(s, T + \tau) - \sigma_I(s, T) \right|^2 ds \tag{17.72}$$

Equation (17.71) is similar to equation (10.60) derived in Chapter 10 for the case of a call option on a forward or futures price where the underlying is lognormally distributed and interest rates are nonstochastic.

An interest rate cap is a portfolio of caplets written on the same τ-period LIBOR but maturing at different dates $T = T_1, T_2, \ldots, T_n$, where typically $T_{j+1} = T_j + \tau$. Standard practice is to value each individual caplet in the portfolio in the

---

30. Assuming a lognormal distribution for $L(t, T, \tau)$ is attractive because it prevents this discrete forward rate from becoming negative, thereby also restricting yields on discount bonds to be nonnegative. Note that if instantaneous-maturity forward rates are assumed to be lognormally distributed, HJM show that they will be expected to become infinite in finite time. This is inconsistent with arbitrage-free bond prices. Fortunately, such an explosion of rates does not occur when forward rates are discrete (Brace, Gatarek, and Musiela 1997).

31. Note that since $\sigma_I(t, t + \delta)$ is an integral of instantaneous forward rate volatilities, the lognormality of $\sigma_I(t, t + \tau) - \sigma_I(t, T)$ puts restrictions on instantaneous forward rates under an HJM modeling approach. However, we need not focus on this issue for pricing applications involving a discrete forward rate.

manner we have described, where the caplet maturing at date T_j is priced using the date $T_j + \tau$ forward measure. Often, caps are purchased by issuers of floating-rate bonds whose bond payments coincide with the caplet maturity dates. Doing so insures the bond issuer against having to make a floating coupon rate greater than X (plus a credit spread). Since a floating-rate bond's coupon rate payable at date $T + \tau$ is most commonly tied to the τ-period LIBOR at date T, caplet payoffs follow this same structure. Analogous to a cap, an interest rate floor is a portfolio of floorlets and can be valued using the same technique described in this section.

Example: A Swaption

Frequently, a market model approach is applied to value another common interest rate derivative, a swaption. A *swaption* is an option to become a party in an interest rate swap at a given future maturity date and at a prespecified swap rate. Let us, then, define the interest rate swap underlying this swaption. A standard ("plain vanilla") swap is an agreement between two parties to exchange fixed interest rate coupon payments for floating interest rate coupon payments at dates $T_1, T_2, \ldots, T_{n+1}$, where $T_{j+1} = T_j + \tau$ and τ is the maturity of the LIBOR of the floating-rate coupon payments. Thus, if K is the swap's fixed annualized coupon rate, then at date T_{j+1} the fixed-rate payer's net payment is $\tau[K - L(T_j, T_j, \tau)]$, whereas that of the floating-rate payer is exactly the opposite.[32]

Note that the swap's series of floating-rate payments plus an additional \$1 at date T_{n+1} can be replicated by starting with \$1 at time $T_0 = T_1 - \tau$ and repeatedly investing this \$1 in τ-maturity LIBOR deposits.[33] These are the same cashflows that one would obtain by investing \$1 in a floating-rate bond at date T_0. Similarly, the swap's series of fixed-rate payments plus an additional \$1 at date T_{n+1} can be replicated by buying a fixed-coupon bond that pays coupons of τK at each swap date and pays a principal of \$1 at its maturity date of T_{n+1}. Based on this insight, one can see that the value of a swap to the floating-rate payer is the difference between a fixed-coupon bond having coupon rate K, and a floating-coupon bond

---

32. Recall that $L(T_j, T_j, \tau)$ is the spot τ-period LIBOR at date T_j. Also, as discussed in the preceding footnote, this exchange is based on a notional principal of \$1. For a notional principal of \$$N$, all payments are multiplied by N.

33. Thus, \$1 invested at time T_0 produces a return of $1 + \tau L(T_0, T_0, \tau)$ at T_1. Keeping the cashflow of $\tau L(T_0, T_0, \tau)$ and reinvesting the \$1 will then produce a return of $1 + \tau L(T_1, T_1, \tau)$ at T_2. Keeping the cashflow of $\tau L(T_1, T_1, \tau)$ and reinvesting the \$1 will then produce a return of $1 + \tau L(T_2, T_2, \tau)$ at T_3. This process is repeated until at time T_{n+1} a final return of $1 + \tau L(T_n, T_n, \tau)$ is obtained.

having coupons tied to τ-period LIBOR. Thus, if $t \leq T_0 = T_1 - \tau$, then the date t value of the swap to the floating-rate payer is[34]

$$\tau K \sum_{j=1}^{n+1} P\left(t, T_j\right) + P\left(t, T_{n+1}\right) - P\left(t, T_0\right) \tag{17.73}$$

When a standard swap agreement is initiated at time T_0, the fixed rate K is set such that the value of the swap in (17.73) is zero. This concept of setting K to make the agreement fair (similar to forward contracts) can be extended to dates prior to T_0. One can define $s_{0,n}(t)$ as the forward swap rate that makes the date t value of the swap (starting at date T_0 and making n subsequent exchanges) equal to zero. Setting $K = s_{0,n}(t)$ and equating (17.73) to zero, one obtains

$$s_{0,n}(t) = \frac{P\left(t, T_0\right) - P\left(t, T_{n+1}\right)}{\tau \sum_{j=1}^{n+1} P\left(t, T_j\right)} \tag{17.74}$$

$$= \frac{P\left(t, T_0\right) - P\left(t, T_{n+1}\right)}{B_{1,n}(t)}$$

where $B_{1,n}(t) \equiv \tau \sum_{j=1}^{n+1} P(t, T_j)$ is a portfolio of zero-coupon bonds that each pay τ at the times of the swap's exchanges.

Now a standard swaption is an option to become either a fixed-rate payer or floating-rate payer at a fixed swap rate X at a specified future date. Thus, if the maturity of the swaption is date T_0, at which time the holder of the swaption has the right but not the obligation to become a fixed-rate payer (floating-rate receiver), this option's payoff equals[35]

$$c\left(T_0\right) = \max\left[B_{1,n}\left(T_0\right)\left[s_{0,n}\left(T_0\right) - X\right], 0\right] \tag{17.75}$$

$$= \max\left[1 - P\left(T_0, T_{n+1}\right) - B_{1,n}\left(T_0\right)X, 0\right]$$

Note from the first line of (17.75) that when the option is in the money, then $B_{1,n}\left(T_0\right)\left[s_{0,n}\left(T_0\right) - X\right]$ is the date T_0 value of the fixed-rate payer's savings from having the swaption relative to entering into a swap at the fair spot rate $s_{0,n}\left(T_0\right)$. In the second line of (17.75), we have substituted from (17.74)

---

34. Notice that $P\left(t, T_0\right)$ is the date t value of the floating-rate bond, while the remaining terms are the value of the fixed-rate bond.

35. The payoff of an option to be a floating-rate payer (fixed-rate receiver) is $\max[B_{1,n}(T_0)[X - s_{0,n}(T_0)], 0]$.

$s_{0,n}(T_0) B_{1,n}(T_0) = P(T_0, T_0) - P(T_0, T_{n+1}) = 1 - P(T_0, T_{n+1})$. This illustrates that a swaption is equivalent to an option on a coupon bond with coupon rate X and an exercise price of 1.

To value this swaption at date $t \leq T_0$, a convenient approach is to recognize from (17.75) that the swaption's payoff is proportional to $B_{1,n}(T_0) \equiv \tau \sum_{j=1}^{n+1} P(T_0, T_j)$. This suggests that $B_{1,n}(t)$ is a convenient deflator for valuing the swap. By normalizing all security prices by $B_{1,n}(t)$, we will value the swaption using the so-called forward swap measure.

Similar to valuation under the risk-neutral or forward measure of the previous section, let us define $C(t) = c(t)/B_{1,n}(t)$. Also define

$$d\bar{z} = dz + \left[\Theta(t) + \sigma_{B_{1,n}}(t)\right] dt$$

where $\sigma_{B_{1,n}}(t)$ is the date t vector of instantaneous volatilities of the zero-coupon bond portfolio's value, $B_{1,n}(t)$. Similar to the derivation in equations (17.66) to (17.68), we have

$$\frac{dC}{C} = \left[\sigma_c(t) + \sigma_{B_{1,n}}(t, T + \tau)\right]' d\bar{z} \tag{17.76}$$

so that all deflated asset prices under the forward swap measure follow martingale processes. Thus,

$$C(t) = \bar{E}_t\left[C(T_0)\right] \tag{17.77}$$

$$= \bar{E}_t\left[\frac{\max\left[B_{1,n}(T_0)\left[s_{0,n}(T_0) - X\right], 0\right]}{B_{1,n}(T_0)}\right]$$

$$= \bar{E}_t\left[\max\left[s_{0,n}(T_0) - X, 0\right]\right]$$

Rewritten in terms of the undeflated swaption's current value, $c(t) = C(t) B_{1,n}(t)$, (17.77) becomes

$$c(t) = B_{1,n}(t) \bar{E}_t\left[\max\left[s_{0,n}(T_0) - X, 0\right]\right] \tag{17.78}$$

so that the expected payoff under the forward swap measure is discounted by the current value of a portfolio of zero-coupon bonds that mature at the times of the swap's exchanges.

Importantly, note that $s_{0,n}(t) = \left[P(t, T_0) - P(t, T_{n+1})\right]/B_{1,n}(t)$ is the ratio of the difference between two security prices deflated by $B_{1,n}(t)$. In the absence of arbitrage, it must also follow a martingale process under the forward swap measure. A convenient and commonly made assumption is that this forward swap rate is lognormally distributed under the forward swap measure:

$$\frac{ds_{0,n}(t)}{s_{0,n}(t)} = \sigma_{s_{0,n}}(t)' d\bar{z} \tag{17.79}$$

so that $\sigma_{s_{0,n}}(t)$ is a vector of deterministic functions of time that can be calibrated to match observed forward swap volatilities or zero-coupon bond volatilities.[36] This assumption results in (17.78) taking a Black-Scholes-type form:

$$c(t) = B_{1,n}(t)\left[s_{0,n}(t) N(d_1) - X N(d_2)\right] \tag{17.80}$$

where $d_1 = \left[\ln\left(s_{0,n}(t)/X\right) + \frac{1}{2}v(t, T_0)^2\right]/v(t, T_0)$, $d_2 = d_1 - v(t, T_0)$, and

$$v^2(t, T_0) = \int_t^{T_0} \sigma_{s_{0,n}}(u)' \sigma_{s_{0,n}}(u)\, du \tag{17.81}$$

17.2.3 Random Field Models

The term structure models that we have studied thus far have specified a finite number of Brownian motion processes as the source of uncertainty determining the evolution of bond prices or forward rates. For example, the bond price processes in equilibrium models (see equation (17.2)) and HJM models (see equation (17.38)) were driven by an $n \times 1$ vector of Brownian motions, $\mathbf{dz}$. One implication of this is that a Black-Scholes hedge portfolio of n different maturity bonds can be used to perfectly replicate the risk of any other maturity bond. As shown in Chapter 10, in the absence of arbitrage, the fact that any bond's risk can be hedged with other bonds places restrictions on bonds' expected excess rates of return and results in a unique vector of market prices of risk, $\Theta(t)$, associated with $\mathbf{dz}$. This implies a bond price process of the form

$$dP(t, T)/P(t, T) = \left[r(t) + \Theta(t)'\sigma_p(t, T)\right] dt + \sigma_p(t, T)' \mathbf{dz} \tag{17.82}$$

Moreover, the Black-Scholes hedge, by making the market dynamically complete and by identifying a unique $\Theta(t)$ associated with $\mathbf{dz}$, allows us to perform risk-neutral valuation by the transformation $\mathbf{d\hat{z}} = \mathbf{dz} + \Theta(t)\, dt$ or valuation using the pricing kernel $dM/M = -r(t)\, dt - \Theta(t)' \mathbf{dz}$.

However, the elegance of these models comes with an empirical downside. The fact that all bond prices depend on the same $n \times 1$ vector $\mathbf{dz}$ places restrictions on

---

36. Applying Itô's lemma to (17.74) allows one to derive the volatility of $s_{0,n}(t)$ in terms of zero-coupon bond volatilities.

the covariance of bonds' rates of return. For example, when $n = 1$, the rates of return on all bonds are instantaneously perfectly correlated. While in these models the correlation can be made less perfect by increasing n, doing so introduces more parameters that require estimation.

A related empirical implication of (17.82) or (17.35) is that it restricts the possible future term structures of bond prices or forward rates. In other words, starting from the current date t set of bond prices $P(t, T) \ \forall T > t$, an arbitrary future term structure, $P(t + dt, T) \ \forall T > t + dt$, cannot always be achieved by any realization of $\mathbf{dz}$. This is because a given future term structure has an infinite number of bond prices (each of a different maturity), but the finiteness of $\mathbf{dz}$ allows matching this future term structure at only a finite number of maturity horizons.[37] Hence, models based on a finite $\mathbf{dz}$ are almost certainly inconsistent with future observed bond prices and forward rates. Because of this, empiricists must assume that data on bond prices (or yields) are observed with "noise" or that, in the case of HJM-type models, parameters (that the model assumes to be constant) must be recalibrated at each observation date to match the new term structure of forward rates.

Random field models are an attempt to avoid these empirical deficiencies. Research in this area includes that of David Kennedy (Kennedy 1994; Kennedy 1997), Robert Goldstein (Goldstein 2000), Pedro Santa-Clara and Didier Sornette (Santa-Clara and Sornette 2001), and Robert Kimmel (Kimmel 2004). These models specify that each zero-coupon bond price, $P(t, T)$, or each instantaneous forward rate, $f(t, T)$, is driven by a Brownian motion process that is unique to the bond's or rate's maturity, T. For example, a model of this type might assume that a bond's risk-neutral process satisfies

$$dP(t, T) / P(t, T) = r(t) \, dt + \sigma_p(t, T) \, d\widehat{z}_T \ \forall T > t \qquad (17.83)$$

where $d\widehat{z}_T(t)$ is a single Brownian motion process (under the risk-neutral measure) that is unique to the bond that matures at date T.[38] The set of Brownian motions for all zero-coupon bonds $\{ \widehat{z}_T(t) \}_{T > t}$ comprises a Brownian "field," or "sheet." This continuum of Brownian motions has two dimensions: calendar

---

37. For example, consider $n = 1$. In this case, all bond prices must either rise or fall with a given realization of dz. This model would not permit a situation where short-maturity bond prices fell but long-maturity bond prices rose. The model could produce a realization of dz that matched long-maturity bond prices or short-maturity bond prices, but not both.

38. An alternative way of specifying a random field model is to assume that the risk-neutral processes for instantaneous forward rates are of the form $df(t, T) = [\sigma(t, T) \int_t^T \sigma(t, s) c(t, T, s) \, ds] dt + \sigma(t, T) \, dz_T$, where $dz_{T_1} dz_{T_2} = c(t, T_1, T_2) \, dt$. This specification extends the HJM equation (17.43) to a random field driving forward rates.

time, t, and time to maturity, T. The elements affecting different bonds are linked by an assumed correlation structure:

$$d\widehat{z}_{T_1}(t)\, d\widehat{z}_{T_2}(t) = \rho\left(t, T_1, T_2\right) dt \tag{17.84}$$

where $\rho\left(t, T_1, T_2\right) > 0$ is specified to be a particular continuous, differentiable function with $\rho\left(t, T, T\right) = 1$ and $\frac{\partial \rho(t,T_1,T_2)}{\partial T_1}|_{T_1=T_2} = 0$. For example, one simple specification involving only a single parameter is $\rho\left(t, T_1, T_2\right) = e^{-\varrho|T_1 - T_2|}$, where ϱ is a positive constant.

One can also model the physical process for bond prices corresponding to (17.83). If $\theta_T(t)$ is the market price of risk associated with $d\widehat{z}_T(t)$, then making the transformation $dz_T = d\widehat{z}_T + \theta_T(t)\, dt$, one obtains

$$dP\left(t, T\right)/P\left(t, T\right) = \left[r\left(t\right) + \theta_T\left(t\right) \sigma_p\left(t, T\right)\right] dt + \sigma_p\left(t, T\right) dz_T \; \forall T > t \tag{17.85}$$

with $dz_T(t)$, $T > t$ satisfying the same correlation function as in (17.84). Analogous to the finite-factor pricing kernel process in (17.8), a pricing kernel for this random field model would be

$$dM/M = -r\left(t\right) dt - \int_t^\infty \left[\theta_T\left(t\right) dz_T\left(t\right)\right] dT \tag{17.86}$$

so that an integral of the products of market prices of risk and Brownian motions replaces the usual sum of these products that occur for the finite factor case.[39]

The benefit of a model like (17.83) and (17.84) is that a realization of the Brownian field can generate any future term structure of bond prices or forward rates and, hence, be consistent with empirical observation and not require model recalibration. Moreover, with only a few additional parameters, random field models can provide a flexible covariance structure among different maturity bonds. Specifically, unlike finite-dimensional equilibrium models or HJM models, the covariance matrix of different maturity bond returns or forward rates will always be nonsingular no matter how many bonds are included. This could be important when valuing particular fixed-income derivatives where the underlying is a portfolio of zero-coupon bonds, and the correlation between these bonds affects the overall portfolio volatility.

However, this rich covariance structure requires stronger theoretical assumptions for valuing derivatives compared to finite-dimensional diffusion models. A

---

39. Note, however, that a random field model is not the same as a standard finite factor model extended to an infinite number of factors. As shown in (17.85), a random field model has a single Brownian motion driving each bond price or forward rate. A factor model, such as (17.2) or (17.38), extended to infinite factors would have the same infinite set of Brownian motions driving each bond price.

given bond's return can no longer be perfectly replicated by a portfolio of other bonds, and thus a Black-Scholes hedging argument cannot be used to identify a unique market price of risk associated with each $dz_T(t)$.[40] The market for fixed-income securities is no longer dynamically complete. Hence, one must assume, perhaps due to an underlying preference-based general equilibrium model, that there exists particular $\theta_T(t)$ associated with each $dz_T(t)$ or, equivalently, that a risk-neutral pricing exists.

Random field models can be parameterized by assuming particular functions for bond price or forward rate volatilities. For example, Pierre Collin-Dufresne and Robert Goldstein (Collin-Dufresne and Goldstein 2003) propose a stochastic volatility model where, in equation (17.83), $\sigma_p(t, T) = \sigma(t, T)\sqrt{\Sigma(t)}$, where $\sigma(t, T)$ is a deterministic function and where $\Sigma(t)$ is a volatility factor, common to all bonds, that follows the square root process

$$d\Sigma(t) = \kappa\left(\overline{\Sigma} - \Sigma(t)\right)dt + \vartheta\sqrt{\Sigma(t)}d\widehat{z}_\Sigma \tag{17.87}$$

where $d\widehat{z}_\Sigma$ is a Brownian motion (under the risk-neutral measure) that is assumed to be independent of the Brownian field $\{d\widehat{z}_T\}$ $\forall T > t$. Based on this parameterization, which is similar to a one-factor affine model, they derive solutions for various interest rate derivatives.[41]

If, similar to David Kennedy (Kennedy 1994), one makes the more simple assumption that $\sigma_p(t, T)$ in (17.83) and $\rho(t, T_1, T_2)$ in (17.84) are deterministic functions, then options on bonds, such as caplets and floorlets, have a Black-Scholes-type valuation formula. For example, suppose as in the HJM-extended Vasicek case of (17.53) to (17.54) that we value a European call option that matures at date T, is written on a zero-coupon bond that matures at date $T + \tau$, and has an exercise price of X. Similar to (17.70), we can value this option using the date T forward rate measure:

$$c(t) = P(t, T)\widetilde{E}_t\left[\max\left[p(T, T + \tau) - X, 0\right]\right] \tag{17.88}$$

40. Robert Goldstein (Goldstein 2000) characterizes random field models of the term structure as being analogous to the APT model (Ross 1976). As discussed in Chapter 3, the APT assumes that a given asset's return depends on the risk from a finite number of factors along with the asset's own idiosyncratic risk. Thus, the asset is imperfectly correlated with any portfolio containing a finite number of other assets. Similarly, in a random field model, a given bond's return is imperfectly correlated with any portfolio containing a finite number of other bonds. Taking the analogy a step further, perhaps market prices of risk in a random field model can be characterized using the notion of asymptotic arbitrage, rather than exact arbitrage.

41. Robert Kimmel (Kimmel 2004) also derives models with stochastic volatility driven by multiple factors.

where $p(t, T + \tau) \equiv P(t, T + \tau)/P(t, T)$ is the deflated price of the bond that matures at date $T + \tau$. Applying Itô's lemma to the risk-neutral process for bond prices in (17.83), we obtain

$$\frac{dp(t, T + \tau)}{p(t, T + \tau)} = \sigma_p(t, T) \left[\sigma_p(t, T) - \rho(t, T, T + \tau) \sigma_p(t, T + \tau) \right] dt$$

$$+ \sigma_p(t, T + \tau) d\widehat{z}_{T+\tau} - \sigma_p(t, T) d\widehat{z}_T \tag{17.89}$$

We can rewrite $d\widehat{z}_{T+\tau} = \rho(t, T, T + \tau) d\widehat{z}_T + \sqrt{1 - \rho(t, T, T + \tau)^2} d\widehat{z}_{U,T}$, where $d\widehat{z}_{U,T}$ is a Brownian motion uncorrelated with $d\widehat{z}_T$, so that the stochastic component in (17.89) can be written as $\sigma_p(t, T + \tau) \sqrt{1 - \rho(t, T, T + \tau)^2} d\widehat{z}_{U,T}$ $+ [\sigma_p(t, T + \tau) \rho(t, T, T + \tau) - \sigma_p(t, T)] d\widehat{z}_T.$[42] Then making the transformation to the date T forward measure, $d\widetilde{z}_T = d\widehat{z}_T + \sigma_p(t, T)$, the process for $p(t, T + \tau)$ becomes

$$\frac{dp(t, T + \tau)}{p(t, T + \tau)} = \sigma_p(t, T + \tau) \sqrt{1 - \rho(t, T, T + \tau)^2} d\widehat{z}_{U,T}$$

$$+ \left[\sigma_p(t, T + \tau) \rho(t, T, T + \tau) - \sigma_p(t, T) \right] d\widetilde{z}_T$$

$$= \sigma(t, T, \tau) d\widetilde{z} \tag{17.90}$$

where

$$\sigma(t, T, \tau)^2 \equiv \sigma_p(t, T + \tau)^2 + \sigma_p(t, T)^2$$

$$- 2\rho(t, T, T + \tau) \sigma_p(t, T + \tau) \sigma_p(t, T) \tag{17.91}$$

Thus, $p(t, T + \tau)$ is lognormally distributed under the forward rate measure, so that (17.88) has the Black-Scholes-Merton-type solution

$$c(t) = P(t, T) \left[p(t, T + \tau) N(d_1) - X N(d_2) \right] \tag{17.92}$$

$$= P(t, T + \tau) N(d_1) - P(t, T) N(d_2)$$

where $d_1 = \left[\ln(p(t, T + \tau)/X) + \frac{1}{2} v(t, T)^2 \right]/v(t, T)$, $d_2 = d_1 - v(t, T)$, and

$$v(t, T)^2 = \int_t^T \sigma(u, T, \tau)^2 du \tag{17.93}$$

---

42. This rewriting puts the risk-neutral process for $p(t, T + \tau)$ in the form of our prior analysis in which the vector of Brownian motions, $d\widehat{z}$, was assumed to have independent elements. This allows us to make the transformation to the forward measure in the same manner as was done earlier.

and $\sigma\,(u, T, \tau)$ is defined in (17.91). While this formula is similar to the Vasicek-based ones in (9.58) and (17.53), the volatility function in (17.91) may permit a relatively more flexible form for matching observed data.

17.3 Summary

This chapter has outlined some of the important theoretical developments in modeling bond yield curves and valuing fixed-income securities. The chapter's presentation has been in the context of continuous-time models and, to keep its length manageable, many similar models set in discrete time have been omitted.[43] Moreover, questions regarding numerical implementation and parameter estimation for specific models could not be addressed in the short presentations given here.

There is a continuing search for improved ways of describing the term structure of bond prices and of valuing fixed-income derivatives. Researchers in this field have different objectives, and the models that we presented reflect this diversity. Much academic research focuses on analyzing equilibrium models in hopes of better understanding the underlying macroeconomic factors that shape the term structure of bond yields. In contrast, practitioner research concentrates on models that can value and hedge fixed-income derivatives. Their ideal model would match the initial term structure, provide a parsimonious structure for forward rate volatilities, and avoid negative, exploding forward rates. Unfortunately, a model with all of these characteristics is hard to find.

While in recent years research on term structure models has expanded, studies in the related field of default-risky fixed-income securities have grown even more rapidly. The next chapter takes up this topic of valuing defaultable bonds and credit derivatives.

17.4 Exercises

1. Consider the following example of a two-factor term structure model (Jegadeesh and Pennacchi 1996; Balduzzi, Das, and Foresi 1998). The instantaneous-maturity interest rate is assumed to follow the physical process

$$dr(t) = \alpha\,[\gamma\,(t) - r\,(t)]\,dt + \sigma_r dz_r$$

and the physical process for the interest rate's stochastic "central tendency," $\gamma\,(t)$, satisfies

$$d\gamma\,(t) = \delta\,[\overline{\gamma} - \gamma\,(t)]\,dt + \sigma_\gamma dz_\gamma$$

---

43. Treatments of models set in discrete time include books by Robert Jarrow (Jarrow 2002), Bruce Tuckman (Tuckman 2002), and Thomas Ho and Sang Bin Lee (Ho and Lee 2004).

where $dz_r dz_y = \rho dt$ and $\alpha > 0$, σ_r, $\delta > 0$, $\bar{\gamma} > 0$, σ_y, and ρ are constants. In addition, define the constant market prices of risk associated with dz_r and dz_y to be θ_r and θ_y. Rewrite this model using the affine model notation used in this chapter and solve for the equilibrium price of a zero-coupon bond, $P(t, T)$.

2. Consider the following one-factor quadratic Gaussian model. The single state variable, $x(t)$, follows the risk-neutral process

$$dx(t) = \kappa [\bar{x} - x(t)] dt + \sigma_x d\hat{z}$$

and the instantaneous-maturity interest rate is given by $r(t, x) = \alpha + \beta x(t) + \gamma x(t)^2$. Assume $\kappa, \bar{x}, \alpha$, and γ are positive constants and that $\alpha - \frac{1}{4}\beta^2/\gamma \geq 0$, where β also is a constant. Solve for the equilibrium price of a zero-coupon bond, $P(t, T)$.

3. Show that for the extended Vasicek model when $\bar{r}(t) \equiv \frac{1}{\alpha}\partial f(0, t)/\partial t + f(0, t) + \sigma_r^2(1 - e^{-2\alpha t})/(2\alpha^2)$, then $P(0, T) = \hat{E}\left[\exp\left(-\int_0^T r(s)\, ds\right)\right] = \exp\left(-\int_0^T f(0, s)\, ds\right)$.

4. Determine the value of an n-payment interest rate floor using the LIBOR market model.

CHAPTER 18

Models of Default Risk

T he bond pricing models in previous chapters assumed that bonds' promised cashflows are paid with certainty. Therefore, these models are most
applicable to valuing default-free bonds issued by a federal government,
which would include Treasury bills, notes, and bonds.[1] However, many debt
instruments, including corporate bonds, municipal bonds, and bank loans, have
default or "credit" risk. Valuing defaultable debt requires an extended modeling
approach. We now consider the two primary methods for modeling default
risk. The first, suggested in the seminal option pricing paper of Fischer Black
and Myron Scholes (Black and Scholes 1973) and developed by Robert Merton
(Merton 1974), Francis Longstaff and Eduardo Schwartz (Longstaff and Schwartz
1995), and others is called the "structural" approach. This method values a firm's
debt as an explicit function of the value of the firm's assets and its capital structure.

The second "reduced-form" approach more simply assumes that default is
a Poisson process with a possibly time-varying default intensity and default
recovery rate. This method views the exogenously specified default process as
the reduced form of a more complicated and complex model of a firm's assets
and capital structure. Examples of this approach include work by Robert Jarrow,
David Lando, and Stuart Turnbull (Jarrow, Lando, and Turnbull 1997), Dilip
Madan and Haluk Unal (Madan and Unal 1998), and Darrell Duffie and Kenneth

---

1. Default can be avoided on government bonds that promise a nominal (currency-valued)
payment if the government (or its central bank) has the power to print currency. However, if a
federal government relinquishes this power, as is the case for countries that adopted the Euro
supplied by the European Central Bank, default on government debt becomes a possibility.

Singleton (Duffie and Singleton 1999). This chapter provides an introduction to the main features of these two methods for incorporating default risk in bond values.

18.1 The Structural Approach

This section focuses on a model similar to that of Robert Merton (Merton 1974). It specifies the assets, debt, and shareholders' equity of a particular firm. Let $A(t)$ denote the date t value of a firm's assets. The firm is assumed to have a very simple capital structure. In addition to shareholders' equity, it has issued a single zero-coupon bond that promises to pay an amount B at date $T > t$. Also let $\tau \equiv T - t$ be the time until this debt matures. The firm is assumed to pay dividends to its shareholders at the continuous rate $\delta A(t)dt$, where δ is the firm's constant proportion of assets paid in dividends per unit time. The value of the firm's assets is assumed to follow the process

$$dA/A = (\mu - \delta)\, dt + \sigma\, dz \tag{18.1}$$

where μ denotes the instantaneous expected rate of return on the firm's assets and σ is the constant standard deviation of return on firm assets. Now let $D(t, T)$ be the date t market value of the firm's debt that is promised the payment of B at date T. It is assumed that when the debt matures, the firm pays the promised amount to the debtholders if there is sufficient asset value to do so. If not, the firm defaults (bankruptcy occurs) and the debtholders take ownership of all of the firm's assets. Hence, the payoff to debtholders at date T can be written as

$$\begin{aligned} D(T, T) &= \min\left[B, A(T)\right] \\ &= B - \max\left[0, B - A(T)\right] \end{aligned} \tag{18.2}$$

From the second line in equation (18.2), we see that the payoff to the debtholders equals the promised payment, B, less the payoff on a European put option written on the firm's assets and having exercise price equal to B. Hence, if we make the usual "frictionless" market assumptions, then the current market value of the debt can be derived to equal the present value of the promised payment less the value of a put option on the dividend-paying assets.[2] If we let $P(t, T)$ be the current date t price of a default-free, zero-coupon bond that pays \$1 at date T and assume that the default-free term structure satisfies the Vasicek model as specified earlier in (9.41) to (9.43), then using Chapter 9's results on the pricing of options when interest rates are random, we obtain

---

2. One needs to assume that the risk of the firm's assets, as determined by the dz process, is a tradeable risk, so that a Black-Scholes hedge involving the firm's debt can be constructed.

$$D(t, T) = P(t, T)B - P(t, T)BN(-h_2) + e^{-\delta\tau}AN(-h_1) \tag{18.3}$$

$$= P(t, T)BN(h_2) + e^{-\delta\tau}AN(-h_1)$$

where $h_1 = \left[\ln\left[e^{-\delta\tau}A/(P(t, T)B)\right] + \frac{1}{2}v^2\right]/v$, $h_2 = h_1 - v$, and $v(\tau)$ is given in (9.61). Note that if the default-free term structure is assumed to be deterministic, then we have the usual Black-Scholes value of $v = \sigma\sqrt{\tau}$. The promised yield to maturity on the firm's debt, denoted $R(t, T)$, can be calculated from (18.3) as $R(t, T) = \frac{1}{\tau}\ln[B/D(t, T)]$. Also, its credit spread, which is defined as the bond's yield less that of an equivalent maturity default-free bond, can be computed as $R(t, T) - \frac{1}{\tau}\ln[1/P(t, T)]$.

Based on this result, one can also solve for the market value of the firm's shareholders' equity, which we denote as $E(t)$. In the absence of taxes and other transactions costs, the value of investors' claims on the firm's assets, $D(t, T) + E(t)$, must equal the total value of the firm's assets, $A(t)$. This allows us to write

$$E(t) = A(t) - D(t, T) \tag{18.4}$$

$$= A - P(t, T)BN(h_2) - e^{-\delta\tau}AN(-h_1)$$

$$= A\left[1 - e^{-\delta\tau}N(-h_1)\right] - P(t, T)BN(h_2)$$

Shareholders' equity is similar to a call option on the firm's assets in the sense that at the debt's maturity date, equity holders receive the payment $\max[A(T) - B, 0]$. Shareholders' limited liability gives them the option of receiving the firm's residual value when it is positive. However, shareholders' equity differs from the standard European call option if the firm pays dividends prior to the debt's maturity. As is reflected in the first term in the last line of (18.4), the firm's shareholders, unlike the holders of standard options, receive these dividends.

Robert Merton (Merton 1974; Chapter 12 in Merton 1992) gives an in-depth analysis of the comparative statics properties of the debt and equity formulas similar to equations (18.3) and (18.4), as well as the firm's credit spread. Note that an equity formula such as (18.4) can be useful because for firms that have publicly traded shareholders' equity, observation of the firm's market value of equity and its volatility can be used to infer the market value and volatility of the firm's assets. The market value and volatility of the firm's assets can then be used as inputs into (18.3) so that the firm's default-risky debt can be valued. Such an exercise based on the Merton model has been done by the credit-rating firm Moody's KMV to forecast corporate defaults.[3]

---

3. For a description of the KMV application of the Merton model for forecasting defaults, see (Crosbie and Bohn 2002). Alan Marcus and Israel Shaked (Marcus and Shaked 1984) apply the Merton model to analyzing the default risk of commercial banks that have publicly traded shareholders' equity.

The Merton model's assumption that the firm has a single issue of zero-coupon debt is unrealistic, since it is commonly the case that firms have multiple coupon-paying debt issues with different maturities and different seniorities in the event of default. Modeling multiple debt issues and determining the point at which an asset deficiency triggers default is a complex task.[4] In response, some research has taken a different tack by assuming that when the firm's assets hit a lower boundary, default is triggered. This default boundary is presumed to bear a monotonic relation to the firm's total outstanding debt. With the initial value of the firm's assets exceeding this boundary, determining future default amounts to computing the first passage time of the assets through this boundary.

Francis Longstaff and Eduardo Schwartz (Longstaff and Schwartz 1995) developed such a model following the earlier work of Fischer Black and John Cox (Black and Cox 1976). They assume a default boundary that is constant over time and, when assets sink to the level of this boundary, bondholders are assumed to recover an exogenously given proportion of their bonds' face values. This contrasts with the Merton model, where in the case of default, bondholders recover $A(T)$, the stochastic value of firm assets at the bond's maturity date, which results in a loss of $B - A(T)$. In the Longstaff-Schwartz model, possible default occurs at a stochastic date, say, τ, defined by the first (passage) time that $A(\tau) = k$, where k is the predetermined default boundary. Bondholders are assumed to recover $\delta P(\tau, T) B$, where $\delta < 1$ is the recovery rate equaling a proportion of the market value of an otherwise equivalent default-free bond, $P(\tau, T) B$.[5] This exogenous recovery rate, δ, is permitted to differ for bonds with different maturity and seniority characteristics and might be estimated from the historical recovery rates of different types of bonds.

Pierre Collin-Dufresne and Robert Goldstein (Collin-Dufresne and Goldstein 2001) modify the Longstaff-Schwartz model to permit a firm's default boundary to be stochastic. Motivated by the tendency of firms to target their leverage ratios by partially adjusting their debt and equity over time, Collin-Dufresne and Goldstein permit the ratio of firm assets to firm debt (the default boundary) to follow a mean-reverting process with default triggered when this ratio declines to unity.[6] Chunsheng Zhou (Zhou 2001) and Jing-zhi Huang and Ming Huang (Huang

---

4. A study by Edward Jones, Scott Mason, and Eric Rosenfeld (Jones, Mason, and Rosenfeld 1984) is an example.

5. $P(\tau, T) B$ is the market value of a zero-coupon bond paying the face value of B at date T. However, Longstaff and Schwartz do not limit their analysis to defaultable zero-coupon bonds. Indeed, they value both fixed- and floating-coupon bonds assuming a Vasicek model of the term structure. Hence, in general, recovery equals a fixed proportion, δ, of the market value of an otherwise equivalent default-free (fixed- or floating-rate) bond.

6. More precisely, they assume that the risk-neutral process for the log of the ratio of firm debt to assets, say, $l(t) = \ln[k(t)/A(t)]$, follows an Ornstein-Uhlenbeck process. For an example

and Huang 2003) extend the Longstaff-Schwartz model in another direction by allowing the firm's assets to follow a mixed jump-diffusion process. In this case, assets can suddenly plunge below the default boundary, making default more abrupt than when assets have continuous sample paths. While these "first passage time" models seek to provide more realism than the more simple Merton model, they come at the cost of requiring numerical, rather than closed-form, solutions.[7]

For firms with complicated debt structures, these first passage time models simplify the determination of default by assuming it occurs when a firm's assets sink to a specified boundary. The interaction between default and the level and timing of particular promised bond payments are not directly modeled, except as they might affect the specification of the default boundary. In the next section, we consider the reduced-form approach, which goes a step further by not directly modeling either the firm's assets or its overall debt level.

18.2   The Reduced-Form Approach

With the reduced-form method, default need not be tied directly to the dynamics of a firm's assets and liabilities. As a result, this approach provides less insight regarding the link between a firm's balance sheet and its likelihood of default. However, because reduced-form models generate default based on an exogenous Poisson process, they may better capture the effects on default of additional unobserved factors and provide richer dynamics for the term structure of credit spreads.[8] Reduced-form modeling also can be convenient because, as will be

---

of a model displaying mean-reverting leverage in the context of commercial bank defaults, see (Pennacchi 2005).

7. An exception is the closed-form solutions obtained by Stijn Claessens and George Pennacchi (Claessens and Pennacchi 1996), who model default-risky sovereign debt such as Brady bonds.

8. In most structural models, (Zhou 2001) and (Huang and Huang 2003) are notable exceptions, a firm's assets are assumed to follow a diffusion process that has a continuous sample path. An implication of this is that default becomes highly unlikely for short horizons if the firm currently has a substantial difference between assets and liabilities. Hence, these models generate very small credit spreads for the short-maturity debt of credit worthy corporations, counter to empirical evidence that finds more significant spreads. Small spreads occur because default over a short horizon cannot come as a sudden surprise. This is not the case with reduced-form models, where sudden default is always possible due to its Poisson nature. Hence, these models can more easily match the significant credit spreads on short-term corporate debt. Darrell Duffie and David Lando (Duffie and Lando 2001) present a structural model where investors have less (accounting) information regarding the value of a firm's assets than do the firm's insiders. Hence, like the jump-diffusion models (Zhou 2001; Huang and Huang 2003), investors' valuation of the firm's assets can take discrete jumps when inside information is revealed. This model generates a Poisson default intensity equivalent to a particular reduced-form model.

shown, defaultable bonds are valued using techniques similar to those used to value default-free bonds.

To illustrate reduced-form modeling, we begin by analyzing a defaultable zero-coupon bond and, later, generalize the results to multiple-payment (coupon) bonds. As in the previous section, let $D(t, T)$ be the date t value of a default-risky, zero-coupon bond that promises to pay B at its maturity date of T. However, unlike the previous section's structural models where default was directly linked to the dynamics of the firm's capital structure, here we assume that a possible default event depends on a reduced-form process that only indirectly may be interpreted as depending on the firm's capital structure and possibly other macroeconomic factors that influence default. Specifically, default for a particular firm's bond is modeled as a Poisson process with a time-varying default intensity. Conditional on default having not occurred prior to date t, the instantaneous probability of default during the interval $(t, t + dt)$ is denoted $\lambda(t)\, dt$, where $\lambda(t)$ is the physical default intensity, or "hazard rate," and is assumed to be nonnegative.[9] The time-varying nature of $\lambda(t)$ may be linked to variation in state variables, as will be shown shortly.

Note from the definition of the instantaneous default intensity, $\lambda(t)$, one can compute the physical probability that the bond does *not* default over the discrete time interval from dates t to τ, where $t < \tau \leq T$. This probability is referred to as the bond's (physical) survival probability over the interval from dates t to τ and is given by

$$E_t\left[e^{-\int_t^{\tau} \lambda(u)du}\right] \tag{18.5}$$

18.2.1   A Zero-Recovery Bond

To determine $D(t, T)$, an assumption must be made regarding the payoff received by bondholders should the bond default. We begin by assuming that bondholders recover nothing if the bond defaults and, later, we generalize this assumption to permit a possible nonzero recovery value. With zero recovery, the bondholders' date T payoff is either $D(T, T) = B$ if there is no default or $D(T, T) = 0$ if default has occurred over the interval from t to T. Applying risk-neutral pricing, the date t value of the zero-recovery bond, denoted $D_Z(t, T)$, can be written as

$$D_Z(t, T) = \widehat{E}_t\left[e^{-\int_t^{T} r(u)du} D(T, T)\right] \tag{18.6}$$

---

9. Recall that in Chapter 11 we modeled jumps in asset prices as following a Poisson process with jump intensity λ. Here, a one-time default follows a Poisson process, and its intensity is explicitly time varying.

where $r(t)$ is the date t instantaneous default-free interest rate, and $\widehat{E}_t[\cdot]$ is the date t risk-neutral expectations operator. To compute this expression, we need to determine the expression for $D(T, T)$ in terms of the risk-neutral default intensity, rather than the physical default intensity. The risk-neutral default intensity will account for the market price of risk associated with the Poisson arrival of a default event.

To understand the role of default risk, suppose that both the default-free term structure and the firm's default intensity depend on a set of n state variables, x_i, $i = 1, \ldots, n$, that follow the multivariate Markov diffusion process[10]

$$d\mathbf{x} = \mathbf{a}(t, \mathbf{x})\, dt + \mathbf{b}(t, \mathbf{x})\, d\mathbf{z} \tag{18.7}$$

where $\mathbf{x} = (x_1 \ldots x_n)'$, $\mathbf{a}(t, \mathbf{x})$ is an $n \times 1$ vector, $\mathbf{b}(t, \mathbf{x})$ is an $n \times n$ matrix, and $d\mathbf{z} = (dz_1 \ldots dz_n)'$ is an $n \times 1$ vector of independent Brownian motion processes so that $dz_i dz_j = 0$ for $i \neq j$. As in the previous chapter, $\mathbf{x}(t)$ includes macroeconomic factors that affect the default-free term structure, but it now also includes firm-specific factors that affect the likelihood of default for the particular firm. Similar to (17.8), the stochastic discount factor for pricing the firm's default-risky bond will be of the form

$$dM/M = -r(t, \mathbf{x})\, dt - \boldsymbol{\Theta}(t, \mathbf{x})'\, d\mathbf{z} - \boldsymbol{\psi}(t, \mathbf{x}) \left[dq - \lambda(t, \mathbf{x})\, dt \right] \tag{18.8}$$

where $\boldsymbol{\Theta}(t, \mathbf{x})$ is an $n \times 1$ vector of the market prices of risk associated with the elements of $d\mathbf{z}$ and $\boldsymbol{\psi}(t, \mathbf{x})$ is the market price of risk associated with the actual default event. This default event is recorded by dq, which is a Poisson counting process similar to that described in equation (11.2) of Chapter 11. When default occurs, this Poisson counting process $q(t)$ jumps from 0 (the no-default state) to 1 (the absorbing default state) at which time $dq = 1$.[11] The risk-neutral default intensity, $\hat{\lambda}(t, \mathbf{x})$, is then given by $\hat{\lambda}(t, \mathbf{x}) = [1 - \boldsymbol{\psi}(t, \mathbf{x})]\lambda(t, \mathbf{x})$. Note that in this modeling context, default is a "doubly stochastic" process, also referred to as a Cox process.[12] Default depends on the Brownian motion vector $d\mathbf{z}$ that drives $\mathbf{x}$ and determines how the likelihood of default, $\hat{\lambda}(t, \mathbf{x})$, changes over time, but it also depends on the Poisson process dq that determines the arrival of default. Hence, default risk reflects two types of risk premia, $\boldsymbol{\Theta}(t, \mathbf{x})$ and $\boldsymbol{\psi}(t, \mathbf{x})$.

---

10. For concreteness our presentation assumes an equilibrium Markov state variable environment. However, much of our results on reduced-form pricing of defaultable bonds carries over to a non-Markov, no-arbitrage context, such as the Heath-Jarrow-Morton framework. See (Duffie and Singleton 1999), (Fan and Ritchken 2001), and (Ritchken and Sun 2003).

11. Recall from the discussion in Chapter 11 that jumps in an asset's value, as would occur when a bond defaults, cannot always be hedged. Thus, in general, it may not be possible to determine $\boldsymbol{\psi}(t, \mathbf{x})$ based on a no-arbitrage restriction. This market price of default risk may need to be determined from an equilibrium model of investor preferences.

12. Named after the statistician Sir David Cox (Cox 1955).

Based on the calculation of survival probability in (18.5), the value of the zero-recovery defaultable bond is

$$D_Z(t, T) = \widehat{E}_t \left[e^{- \int_t^T r(u)du} e^{- \int_t^T \hat{\lambda}(u)du} B \right] = \widehat{E}_t \left[e^{- \int_t^T [r(u)+\hat{\lambda}(u)]du} \right] B \quad (18.9)$$

Equation (18.9) shows that valuing this zero-recovery defaultable bond is similar to valuing a default-free bond except that we use the discount rate of $r(u) + \hat{\lambda}(u)$ rather than just $r(u)$. Given specific functional forms for $r(t, \mathbf{x})$, $\hat{\lambda}(t, \mathbf{x})$, and the risk-neutral state variable process (specifications of (18.7) and $\Theta(t, \mathbf{x})$), the expression in (18.9) can be computed.

18.2.2   Specifying Recovery Values

The value of a bond that has a possibly nonnegative recovery value in the event of default equals the value in (18.9) plus the present value of the amount recovered in default. Suppose that if the bond defaults at date τ where $t < \tau \leq T$, bondholders recover an amount $w(\tau, \mathbf{x})$ at date τ. Now note that the risk-neutral probability density of defaulting at time τ is

$$e^{- \int_t^\tau \hat{\lambda}(u)du} \hat{\lambda}(\tau) \quad (18.10)$$

In (18.10), $\hat{\lambda}(\tau)$ is discounted by $\exp\left[- \int_t^\tau \hat{\lambda}(u)\, du \right]$ because default at date τ is conditioned on not having defaulted previously. Therefore, the present value of recovery in the event of default, $D_R(t, T)$, is computed by integrating the expected discounted value of recovery over all possible default dates from t to T:

$$D_R(t, T) = \widehat{E}_t \left[\int_t^T e^{- \int_t^\tau r(u)du} w(\tau) e^{- \int_t^\tau \hat{\lambda}(u)du} \hat{\lambda}(\tau)\, d\tau \right]$$

$$= \widehat{E}_t \left[\int_t^T e^{- \int_t^\tau [r(u)+\hat{\lambda}(u)]du} \hat{\lambda}(\tau) w(\tau)\, d\tau \right] \quad (18.11)$$

Putting this together with (18.9) gives the bond's total value, $D(t, T) = D_Z(t, T) + D_R(t, T)$, as

$$D(t, T) = \widehat{E}_t \left[e^{- \int_t^T [r(s)+\hat{\lambda}(s)]ds} B + \int_t^T e^{- \int_t^\tau [r(s)+\hat{\lambda}(s)]ds} \hat{\lambda}(\tau) w(\tau)\, d\tau \right] \quad (18.12)$$

Recovery Proportional to Par Value

Let us consider some particular specifications for $w(\tau, \mathbf{x})$. One assumption used by several researchers is that bondholders recover at the default date τ a proportion of the bond's face, or par, value; that is, $w(\tau, \mathbf{x}) = \delta(\tau, \mathbf{x}) B$, where $\delta(\tau, \mathbf{x})$

is usually assumed to be a constant, say, $\bar{\delta}$.[13] In this case, (18.11) can be written as

$$D_R(t, T) = \bar{\delta} B \int_t^T k(t, \tau) \, d\tau \tag{18.13}$$

where

$$k(t, \tau) \equiv \widehat{E}_t \left[e^{-\int_t^\tau [r(u) + \hat{\lambda}(u)] du} \hat{\lambda}(\tau) \right] \tag{18.14}$$

has a closed-form solution when $r(u, \mathbf{x})$ and $\hat{\lambda}(u, \mathbf{x})$ are affine functions of $\mathbf{x}$ and the vector $\mathbf{x}$ in (18.7) has a risk-neutral process that is also affine.[14] In this case, the recovery value in (18.13) can be computed by numerical integration of $k(t, \tau)$ over the interval from t to T.

Recovery Proportional to Par Value, Payable at Maturity

An alternative recovery assumption is that if default occurs at date τ, the bond-holders recover a proportion $\delta(\tau, \mathbf{x})$ of the bond's face value, B, payable at the maturity date T.[15] This is equivalent to assuming that the bondholders recover a proportion $\delta(\tau, \mathbf{x})$ of the market value of a default-free discount bond paying B at date T; that is, $w(\tau, \mathbf{x}) = \delta(\tau, \mathbf{x}) P(\tau, T) B$. Under this assumption, (18.11) becomes

$$
\begin{aligned}
D_R(t, T) &= \widehat{E}_t \left[\int_t^T e^{-\int_t^\tau [r(u) + \hat{\lambda}(u)] du} \hat{\lambda}(\tau) \, \delta(\tau, \mathbf{x}) \, e^{-\int_\tau^T r(u) du} B \, d\tau \right] \\
&= \widehat{E}_t \left[\int_t^T e^{-\int_t^\tau \hat{\lambda}(u) du} \hat{\lambda}(\tau) \, \delta(\tau, \mathbf{x}) \, e^{-\int_t^T r(u) du} B \, d\tau \right] \\
&= \widehat{E}_t \left[e^{-\int_t^T r(u) du} \int_t^T e^{-\int_t^\tau \hat{\lambda}(u) du} \hat{\lambda}(\tau) \, \delta(\tau, \mathbf{x}) \, d\tau \right] B \tag{18.15}
\end{aligned}
$$

For the specific case of $\delta(\tau, x) = \bar{\delta}$, a constant, this expression can be simplified by noting that the term $\int_t^T \exp\left[-\int_t^\tau \hat{\lambda}(u) \, du\right] \hat{\lambda}(\tau) \, d\tau$ is the total risk-neutral probability of default for the period from date t to the maturity date T. Therefore,

---

13. Work by Darrell Duffie (Duffie 1998), David Lando (Lando 1998), and Dilip Madan and Haluk Unal (Madan and Unal 1998) makes this assumption. As reported by Gregory Duffee (Duffee 1999), the recovery rate, $\bar{\delta}$, estimated by Moody's for senior unsecured bondholders, is approxmately 44 percent.

14. This is shown in (Duffie, Pan, and Singleton 2000).

15. This specification has been studied by Robert Jarrow and Stuart Turnbull (Jarrow and Turnbull 1995) and David Lando (Lando 1998).

it must equal $1 - \exp\left[-\int_t^T \hat{\lambda}(u)\,du\right]$; that is, 1 minus the probability of surviving over the same period. Making this substitution and using (18.9), we have

$$D_R(t, T) = \widehat{E}_t\left[e^{-\int_t^T r(u)du}\left(1 - e^{-\int_t^T \hat{\lambda}(u)du}\right)\right]\delta B$$

$$= \widehat{E}_t\left[e^{-\int_t^T r(u)du} - e^{-\int_t^T [r(u)+\hat{\lambda}(u)]du}\right]\delta B$$

$$= \bar{\delta}BP(t, T) - \bar{\delta}D_Z(t, T) \qquad (18.16)$$

Therefore, the total value of the bond is

$$D(t, T) = D_Z(t, T) + D_R(t, T) = \left(1 - \bar{\delta}\right)D_Z(t, T) + \bar{\delta}BP(t, T) \qquad (18.17)$$

Hence, this recovery assumption amounts to requiring only a solution for the value of a zero-recovery bond.

Recovery Proportional to Market Value

Let us consider one additional recovery assumption analyzed by Darrell Duffie and Kenneth Singleton (Duffie and Singleton 1999). When default occurs, bondholders are assumed to recover a proportion of what was the bond's market value just prior to default. This is equivalent to assuming that the bond's market value jumps downward at the default date τ, suffering a proportional loss of $L(\tau, \mathbf{x})$. Specifically, at default $D(\tau^-, T)$ jumps to

$$D(\tau^+, T) = w(\tau, \mathbf{x}) = D(\tau^-, T)[1 - L(\tau, \mathbf{x})] \qquad (18.18)$$

By specifying a proportional loss in value at the time of default, the bond's dynamics become similar to the jump-diffusion model of asset prices presented in Chapter 11. Treating the defaultable bond as a contingent claim and applying Itô's lemma, its process prior to default is similar to equation (11.6):

$$dD(t, T)/D(t, T) = (\alpha_D - \lambda k_D)\,dt + \sigma_D'\mathbf{dz} - L(t, \mathbf{x})\,dq \qquad (18.19)$$

where α_D and the $n \times 1$ vector σ_D are given by the usual Itô's lemma expressions similar to (11.7) and (11.8). From (11.3) and (18.18), we have that when a jump occurs $[D(\tau^+, T) - D(\tau^-, T)]/D(\tau^-, T) = -L(\tau, \mathbf{x})$, which verifies the term $-L(t, \mathbf{x})\,dq$. Also, from (11.10), k_D, the expected jump size, is given by $k_D(\tau^-) \equiv E_{\tau^-}[D(\tau^+, T) - D(\tau^-, T)]/D(\tau^-, T) = -L(\tau, \mathbf{x})$, so that the drift term in (18.19) becomes $\alpha_D + \lambda(t, \mathbf{x})L(t, \mathbf{x})$.

Now under the risk-neutral measure, the defaultable bond's total expected rate of return, α_D, must equal the instantaneous-maturity, default-free rate, $r(t)$. Thus, we can write the bond's risk-neutral process prior to default as

$$dD\,(t,\,T)\,/D\,(t,\,T) = \left(r\,(t,\,\mathbf{x}) + \hat{\lambda}\,(t,\,\mathbf{x})\,\widehat{L}\,(t,\,\mathbf{x})\right)\,dt + \boldsymbol{\sigma}'_D\mathbf{d}\hat{\mathbf{z}} - \widehat{L}\,(t,\,\mathbf{x})\,dq$$

$$(18.20)$$

where $\widehat{L}\,(t,\,\mathbf{x})$ is the risk-neutral expected proportional loss given default.[16] The intuition of (18.20) is that because the bond has a risk-neutral expected loss given default of $\widehat{L}\,(t,\,\mathbf{x})$, and the risk-neutral instantaneous probability of default ($dq = 1$) is $\hat{\lambda}\,(t,\,\mathbf{x})$, when the bond does not default it must earn an excess expected return of $\hat{\lambda}\,(t,\,\mathbf{x})\,\widehat{L}\,(t,\,\mathbf{x})$ to make its unconditional risk-neutral expected return equal $r\,(t)$. Based on a derivation similar to that used to obtain (11.17) and (17.6), one can show that the defaultable bond's value satisfies the equilibrium partial differential equation

$$\tfrac{1}{2}\text{Trace}\left[\mathbf{b}\,(t,\,\mathbf{x})\,\mathbf{b}\,(t,\,\mathbf{x})'\,\mathbf{D}_{xx}\right] + \hat{\mathbf{a}}\,(t,\,\mathbf{x})'\,\mathbf{D}_x - R\,(t,\,\mathbf{x})\,D + D_t = 0 \qquad (18.21)$$

where $\mathbf{D}_x$ denotes the $n \times 1$ vector of first derivatives of $D\,(t,\,\mathbf{x})$ with respect to each of the factors and, similarly, $\mathbf{D}_{xx}$ is the $n \times n$ matrix of second-order mixed partial derivatives. In addition, $\hat{\mathbf{a}}\,(t,\,\mathbf{x}) = \mathbf{a}\,(t,\,\mathbf{x}) - \mathbf{b}\,(t,\,\mathbf{x})\,\boldsymbol{\Theta}$ is the risk-neutral drift of the factor process (18.7), and $R\,(t,\,\mathbf{x}) \equiv r\,(t,\,\mathbf{x}) + \hat{\lambda}\,(t,\,\mathbf{x})\,\widehat{L}\,(t,\,\mathbf{x})$ is the defaultable bond's risk-neutral drift in the process (18.20). Note that if the bond reaches the maturity date, T, without defaulting, then $D\,(T,\,T) = B$. This is the boundary condition for (18.21). The PDE (18.21) is in the form of a PDE for a standard contingent claim except that $R\,(t,\,\mathbf{x})$ has replaced $r\,(t,\,\mathbf{x})$ in the standard PDE. This insight allows us to write the PDE's Feynman-Kac solution as[17]

$$D\,(t,\,T) = \widehat{E}_t\left[e^{-\int_t^T R(u,\mathbf{x})du}\right]B \qquad (18.22)$$

where $R\,(t,\,\mathbf{x}) \equiv r\,(t,\,\mathbf{x}) + \hat{\lambda}\,(t,\,\mathbf{x})\,\widehat{L}\,(t,\,\mathbf{x})$ can be viewed as the "default-adjusted" discount rate. The product $s\,(t,\,\mathbf{x}) \equiv \hat{\lambda}\,(t,\,\mathbf{x})\,\widehat{L}\,(t,\,\mathbf{x})$ is interpreted as the "credit spread" on an instantaneous-maturity, defaultable bond. Since $\hat{\lambda}\,(t,\,\mathbf{x})$ and $\widehat{L}\,(t,\,\mathbf{x})$ are not individually identified in (18.22), when implementing this formula, one can simply specify a single functional form for $s\,(t,\,\mathbf{x})$.

---

16. As with the risk-neutral default intensity, $\hat{\lambda}\,(t,\,\mathbf{x})$, there may be a market price of recovery risk associated with $\widehat{L}\,(t,\,\mathbf{x})$ that distinguishes it from the physical expected loss at default, $L\,(t,\,\mathbf{x})$. This market price of recovery risk cannot, in general, be determined from a no-arbitrage restriction because recovery risk may be unhedgeable. Most commonly, modelers simply posit functional forms for risk-neutral variables in order to derive formulas for defaultable bond values. Differences between risk-neutral default intensities and losses at default and their physical counterparts might be inferred based on the market prices of defaultable bonds and historical (physical) default and recovery rates.

17. Recall from Chapter 10 that (10.17) was shown to be the Feynman-Kac solution to the Black-Scholes PDE (10.7). See Darrell Duffie and Kenneth Singleton (Duffie and Singleton 1999) for an alternative derivation of (18.22) that does not involve specification of factors or the bond's PDE.

18.2.3   Examples

Because default intensities and/or credit spreads must be nonnegative, a popular stochastic process for modeling these variables is the mean-reverting, square root process used in the term structure model of John Cox, Jonathan Ingersoll, and Stephen Ross (Cox, Ingersoll, and Ross 1985b). To take a very simple example, suppose that $\mathbf{x} = (x_1 \, x_2)'$ is a two-dimensional vector, $\widehat{\mathbf{a}}\,(t, \mathbf{x}) = (\kappa_1\,(\overline{x}_1 - x_1) \ \kappa_2\,(\overline{x}_2 - x_2))'$, and $\mathbf{b}\,(t, \mathbf{x})$ is a diagonal matrix with first and second diagonal elements of $\sigma_1\sqrt{x_1}$ and $\sigma_2\sqrt{x_2}$, respectively. If one assumes $r\,(t, \mathbf{x}) = x_1\,(t)$ and $\widehat{\lambda}\,(t, \mathbf{x}) = x_2\,(t)$, this has the implication that the default-free term structure and the risk-neutral default intensity are independent. Arguably, this is unrealistic since empirical work tends to find a negative correlation between default-free interest rates and the likelihood of corporate defaults.[18] Allowing for nonzero correlation between $r\,(t, \mathbf{x})$ and $\widehat{\lambda}\,(t, \mathbf{x})$ while restricting each to be positive is certainly feasible but comes at the cost of requiring numerical, rather than closed-form, solutions for defaultable bond values.[19] Hence, for simplicity of presentation, we maintain the independence assumption in the examples that follow.

With $r\,(t, \mathbf{x}) = x_1\,(t)$ and denoting $\overline{x}_1 = \overline{r}$, we obtain the Cox, Ingersoll, and Ross formula for the value of a default-free discount bond:[20]

$$P\,(t, T) = A_1\,(\tau)\,e^{-B_1(\tau)r(t)} \tag{18.23}$$

where

$$A_1\,(\tau) \equiv \left[\frac{2\theta_1 e^{(\theta_1+\kappa_1)\frac{\tau}{2}}}{(\theta_1 + \kappa_1)\,(e^{\theta_1\tau} - 1) + 2\theta_1}\right]^{2\kappa_1\overline{r}/\sigma_1^2} \tag{18.24}$$

$$B_1\,(\tau) \equiv \frac{2\,(e^{\theta_1\tau} - 1)}{(\theta_1 + \kappa_1)\,(e^{\theta_1\tau} - 1) + 2\theta_1} \tag{18.25}$$

---

18. This evidence is presented in work by Gregory Duffee (Duffee 1999) and Pierre Collin-Dufresne and Bruno Solnik (Collin-Dufresne and Solnik 2001).

19. For models with more flexible correlation structures that require numerical solutions, see examples given by Darrell Duffie and Kenneth Singleton (Duffie and Singleton 1999). Some research has dropped the restriction that $r\,(t)$ and $\widehat{\lambda}\,(t)$ (or $s\,(t) = \widehat{\lambda}\,(t)\,L\,(t)$) be positive by assuming these variables follow multivariate affine Gaussian processes. This permits general correlation between default-free interest rates and default intensities as well as closed-form solutions for defaultable bonds. The model in work by C.V.N. Krishnan, Peter Ritchken, and James Thomson (Krishnan, Ritchken, and Thomson 2004) is an example of this.

20. The formula in (18.23) to (18.25) is the same as (13.51) to (13.53) except that it is written in terms of the parameters of the risk-neutral, rather than physical, process for $r\,(t)$. Hence, relative to our earlier notation, $\kappa_1 = \kappa + \psi$, where the market price of interest-rate risk equals $\theta\,(t) = -\psi\sqrt{r}/\sigma_1$.

and $\theta_1 \equiv \sqrt{\kappa_1^2 + 2\sigma_1^2}$. Also with $\hat{\lambda}(t, \mathbf{x}) = x_2(t)$ and denoting $\bar{x}_2 = \bar{\lambda}$, then based on (18.9) and the assumed independence of $r(t)$ and $\hat{\lambda}(t)$, we can write the value of the zero-recovery bond as

$$D_Z(t, T) = \widehat{E}_t \left[e^{-\int_t^T [r(s) + \hat{\lambda}(s)] ds} \right] B$$

$$= \widehat{E}_t \left[e^{-\int_t^T r(s) ds} \right] \widehat{E}_t \left[e^{-\int_t^T \hat{\lambda}(s) ds} \right] B$$

$$= P(t, T) V(t, T) B \qquad (18.26)$$

where

$$V(t, T) = A_2(\tau) e^{-B_2(\tau)\hat{\lambda}(t)} \qquad (18.27)$$

and where $A_2(\tau)$ is the same as $A_1(\tau)$ in (18.24), and $B_2(\tau)$ is the same as $B_1(\tau)$ in (18.25) except that κ_2 replaces κ_1, σ_2 replaces σ_1, $\bar{\lambda}$ replaces $\bar{r}$, and $\theta_2 \equiv \sqrt{\kappa_2^2 + 2\sigma_2^2}$ replaces θ_1.

If we assume that recovery is a fixed proportion, $\bar{\delta}$, of par value, payable at maturity, then based on (18.17) the value of the defaultable bond equals

$$D(t, T) = \left(1 - \bar{\delta} \right) D_Z(t, T) + \bar{\delta} B P(t, T)$$

$$= \left[\bar{\delta} + \left(1 - \bar{\delta} \right) V(t, T) \right] P(t, T) B \qquad (18.28)$$

In (18.27), $V(t, T)$ is analogous to a bond price in the standard Cox, Ingersoll, and Ross term structure model, and as such it will be inversely related to $\hat{\lambda}(t)$ and strictly less than 1 whenever $\hat{\lambda}(t)$ is strictly positive, which can be ensured when $2\kappa_2\bar{\lambda} \geq \sigma_2^2$. Thus, (18.28) confirms that the defaultable bond's value declines as its risk-neutral default intensity rises.

A slightly different defaultable bond formula can be obtained when recovery is assumed to be proportional to market value and $s(t, \mathbf{x}) \equiv \hat{\lambda}(t, \mathbf{x}) \widehat{L}(t, \mathbf{x}) = x_2$ with the notation $\bar{x}_2 = \bar{s}$. In this case, (18.22) becomes

$$D(t, T) = \widehat{E}_t \left[e^{-\int_t^T [r(u) + s(u)] du} \right] B$$

$$= \widehat{E}_t \left[e^{-\int_t^T r(u) du} \right] \widehat{E}_t \left[e^{-\int_t^T s(u) du} \right] B$$

$$= P(t, T) S(t, T) B \qquad (18.29)$$

where

$$S(t, T) = A_2(\tau) e^{-B_2(\tau)s(t)} \qquad (18.30)$$

and where $A_2(\tau)$ is the same as $A_1(\tau)$ in (18.24), and $B_2(\tau)$ is the same as $B_1(\tau)$ in (18.25) except that κ_2 replaces κ_1, σ_2 replaces σ_1, $\bar{s}$ replaces $\bar{r}$, and $\theta_2 \equiv \sqrt{\kappa_2^2 + 2\sigma_2^2}$ replaces θ_1. This defaultable bond is priced similarly to a default-free bond except that the instantaneous-maturity interest rate, $R(t) = r(t) + s(t)$, is now the sum of two nonnegative square root processes. Hence, the defaultable bond is inversely related to $s(t)$ and can be strictly less than the default-free bond as $s(t)$ can always be positive when $2\kappa_2\bar{s} \geq \sigma_2^2$.

Coupon Bonds

Valuing the defaultable coupon bond of a particular issuer (e.g., corporation) is straightforward given the preceding analysis of defaultable zero-coupon bonds. Suppose that the issuer's coupon bond promises n cashflows, with the ith promised cashflow being equal to c_i and being paid at date $T_i > t$. Then the value of this coupon bond in terms of our zero-coupon bond formulas is

$$\sum_{i=1}^{n} D(t, T_i) \frac{c_i}{B} \tag{18.31}$$

Credit Default Swaps

Our results can also be applied to valuing credit derivatives. A credit default swap is a popular credit derivative that typically has the following structure. One party, the protection buyer, makes periodic payments until the contract's maturity date as long as a particular issuer, bond, or loan does not default. The other party, the protection seller, receives these payments in return for paying the difference between the bond or loan's par value and its recovery value if default occurs prior to the maturity of the swap contract. At the initial agreement date of this swap contract, the periodic payments are set such that the initial contract has a zero market value.

  We can use our previous analysis to value each side of this swap. Let the contract specify equal period payments of c at future dates $t + \Delta, t + 2\Delta, \ldots, t + n\Delta$.[21] Then recognizing that these payments are contingent on default not occurring and that they have zero value following a possible default event, their market value equals

$$\frac{c}{B} \sum_{i=1}^{n} D_Z(t, t + i\Delta) \tag{18.32}$$

---

21. A period of Δ = one-half year is common since these payments often coincide with an underlying coupon bond making semiannual payments.

where $D_Z(t, T)$ is the value of the zero-recovery bond given in (18.9). If we let $w(\tau, \mathbf{x})$ be the recovery value of the defaultable bond (or loan) underlying the swap contract, then assuming this bond's maturity date is $T \geq t + n\Delta$, the value of the swap protection can be computed similarly to (18.11) as

$$\widehat{E}_t\left[\int_t^{t+n\Delta} e^{-\int_t^\tau \left[r(u)+\hat{\lambda}(u)\right]du} \hat{\lambda}(\tau)\left[B - w(\tau)\right]d\tau\right] \tag{18.33}$$

The protection seller's payment in the event of default, $B - w(\tau)$, is often simplified by assuming recovery is a fixed proportion of par value, that is, $B - w(\tau) = B - \bar{\delta}B = B(1 - \bar{\delta})$. For this special case, (18.33) becomes

$$B\left(1 - \bar{\delta}\right)\int_t^{t+n\Delta} k(t, \tau)\,d\tau \tag{18.34}$$

where $k(t, \tau)$ is defined in (18.14). Given assumptions regarding the functional forms of $r(t, \mathbf{x})$, $\hat{\lambda}(t, \mathbf{x})$, and $w(t, \mathbf{x})$, and the state variables $\mathbf{x}$, the value of the swap payments, c, that equates (18.32) to (18.33) can be determined.

A general issue that arises when implementing the reduced-form approach to valuing risky debt is determining the proper current values $\hat{\lambda}(t)$, $s(t)$, or $w(t)$ that may not be directly observable. One or more of these default variables might be inferred by setting the actual market prices of one or more of an issuer's bonds to their theoretical formulas. Then, based on the "implied" values of $\hat{\lambda}(t)$, $s(t)$, or $w(t)$, one can determine whether a given bond of the same issuer is over- or underpriced relative to other bonds. Alternatively, these implied default variables could be used to set the price of a new bond of the same issuer or a credit derivative (such as a default swap) written on the issuer's bonds.

18.3 Summary

Research on credit risk has grown rapidly in recent years. In part, the expansion of this literature derives from a greater interest by financial institutions in credit risk management and credit derivatives.[22] New risk management practices and credit derivatives are being spawned as the techniques for quantifying and pricing credit

---

22. Interest in risk management has been stimulated by the adoption of risk-based capital standards formulated by the Basel Committee on Banking Supervision. This committee is composed of bank supervisors of the major developed countries. International bank capital standards were first devised in 1988 and are referred to as the Basel Capital Accord. A framework for revised capital standards that depend more intricately on credit and other risks, known as Basel II, was issued by the committee in June of 2004. The Basel II rules link a bank's minimum capital to its level of credit risk on bonds, loans, and credit derivatives. See (Basel Committee on Banking Supervision 2005).

risk evolve. This chapter introduced the two main branches of modeling default-able fixed-income securities. The structural approach models default based on the interaction between a firm's assets and its liabilities. Potentially, it can improve our understanding between capital structure and corporate bond and loan prices. In contrast, the reduced-form method abstracts from specific characteristics of a firm's financial structure. However, it can permit a more flexible modeling of default probabilities and may better describe actual the prices of an issuer's debt.

While this chapter has been limited to models of corporate defaults, the credit risk literature also encompasses additional topics such as consumer credit risk and the credit risk of (securitized) portfolios of loans and bonds. Interest by both academics and practitioners in the broad field of credit risk will undoubtedly continue.

18.4 Exercises

1. Consider the example given in the "structural approach" to modeling default risk. Maintain the assumptions made in the chapter but now suppose that a third party guarantees the firm's debtholders that if the firm defaults, the debtholders will receive their promised payment of B. In other words, this third-party guarantor will make a payment to the debtholders equal to the difference between the promised payment and the firm's assets if default occurs. (Banks often provide such a guarantee in the form of a letter of credit. Insurance companies often provide such a guarantee in the form of bond insurance.)

   What would be the fair value of this bond insurance at the initial date, t? In other words, what is the competitive bond insurance premium charged at date t?

2. Consider a Merton-type "structural" model of credit risk (Merton 1974). A firm is assumed to have shareholders' equity and two zero-coupon bonds that both mature at date T. The first bond is "senior" debt and promises to pay B_1 at maturity date T, while the second bond is "junior" (or subordinated) debt and promises to pay B_2 at maturity date T. Let $A(t)$, $D_1(t)$, and $D_2(t)$ be the date t values of the firm's assets, senior debt, and junior debt, respectively. Then the maturity values of the bonds are

$$D_1(T) = \begin{cases} B_1 & \text{if } A(T) \geq B_1 \\ A(T) & \text{otherwise} \end{cases}$$

$$D_2(T) = \begin{cases} B_2 & \text{if } A(T) \geq B_1 + B_2 \\ A(T) - B_1 & \text{if } B_1 + B_2 > A(T) \geq B_1 \\ 0 & \text{otherwise} \end{cases}$$

The firm is assumed to pay no dividends to its shareholders, and the value of shareholders' equity at date T, $E(T)$, is assumed to be

$$E(T) = \begin{cases} A(T) - (B_1 + B_2) & \text{if } A(T) \geq B_1 + B_2 \\ 0 & \text{otherwise} \end{cases}$$

Assume that the value of the firm's assets follows the process

$$dA/A = \mu dt + \sigma dz$$

where μ denotes the instantaneous expected rate of return on the firm's assets and σ is the constant standard deviation of return on firm assets. In addition, the continuously compounded, risk-free interest rate is assumed to be the constant r. Let the current date be t, and define the time until the debt matures as $\tau \equiv T - t$.

a. Give a formula for the current, date t, value of shareholders' equity, $E(t)$.

b. Give a formula for the current, date t, value of the senior debt, $D_1(t)$.

c. Using the results from parts (a) and (b), give a formula for the current, date t, value of the junior debt, $D_2(t)$.

3. Consider a portfolio of m different defaultable bonds (or loans), where the ith bond has a default intensity of $\lambda_i(t, \mathbf{x})$ where $\mathbf{x}$ is a vector of state variables that follows the multivariate diffusion process in (18.7). Assume that the only source of correlation between the bonds' defaults is through their default intensities. Suppose that the maturity dates for the bonds all exceed date $T > t$. Write down the expression for the probability that none of the bonds in the portfolio defaults over the period from date t to date T.

4. Consider the standard ("plain vanilla") swap contract described in Chapter 17. In equation (17.74) it was shown that under the assumption that each party's payments were default free, the equilibrium swap rate agreed to at the initiation of the contract, date T_0, equals

$$s_{0,n}(T_0) = \frac{1 - P(T_0, T_{n+1})}{\tau \sum_{j=1}^{n+1} P(T_0, T_j)}$$

where for this contract, fixed-interest-rate coupon payments are exchanged for floating-interest-rate coupon payments at the dates $T_1, T_2, \ldots, T_{n+1}$, where $T_{j+1} = T_j + \tau$ and τ is the maturity of the LIBOR of the floating-rate coupon payments. This swap rate formula is valid when neither of the parties have credit risk. Suppose, instead, that they both have the same credit risk and it is equivalent to the credit risk reflected in LIBOR interest rates. (Recall that LIBOR reflects the level of default risk for a large international bank.) Moreover, assume a reduced-form model of default with recovery proportional to market value, so that the value of a LIBOR discount bond promising \$1 at maturity date T_j is given by (18.22):

$$D\left(T_0, T_j\right) = \hat{E}_{T_0}\left[e^{-\int_{T_0}^{T_j} R(u, \mathbf{x}) du}\right]$$

where the default-adjusted instantaneous discount rate $R\left(t, \mathbf{x}\right) \equiv r\left(t, \mathbf{x}\right) + \hat{\lambda}\left(t, \mathbf{x}\right) \hat{L}\left(t, \mathbf{x}\right)$ is assumed to be the same for both parties. Assume that if default occurs at some date $\tau < T_{n+1}$, the counterparty whose position is in the money (whose position has positive value) suffers a proportional loss of $L\left(\tau, \mathbf{x}\right)$ in that position. Show that under these assumptions, the equilibrium swap rate is

$$s_{0,n}\left(T_0\right) = \frac{1 - D\left(T_0, T_{n+1}\right)}{\tau \sum_{j=1}^{n+1} D\left(T_0, T_j\right)}$$

References

Abel, A. B. (1990): "Asset Prices Under Habit Formation and Catching Up with the Joneses," *American Economic Review*, 80, 38–42.

Ahn, C.-M., and H. E. Thompson (1988): "Jump-Diffusion Processes and the Term Structure of Interest Rates," *Journal of Finance*, 43, 155–174.

Ahn, D.-H., R. F. Dittmar, and A. R. Gallant (2002): "Quadratic Term Structure Models: Theory and Evidence," *Review of Financial Studies*, 15, 243–288.

Amin, K. I., and A. J. Morton (1994): "Implied Volatility Functions in Arbitrage-Free Term Structure Models," *Journal of Financial Economics*, 35, 141–180.

Andersen, T. G., T. Bollerslev, F. X. Diebold, and H. Ebens (2001): "The Distribution of Realized Stock Return Volatility," *Journal of Financial Economics*, 61, 43–76.

Anderson, R. W., and J.-P. Danthine (1981): "Cross Hedging," *Journal of Political Economy*, 89(6), 1182–1196.

Ang, A., and M. Piazzesi (2003): "A No-Arbitrage Vector Autoregression of Term Structure Dynamics with Macroeconomic and Latent Variables," *Journal of Monetary Economics*, 50(4), 745–787.

Arrow, K. J. (1953): "The Role of Securities in the Optimal Allocation of Risk-Bearing," *Économétric*, 11, 41–48.

————(1964): "The Role of Securities in the Optimal Allocation of Risk-Bearing," *Review of Economics Studies*, 31(2), 91–96.

————(1971): *Essays in the Theory of Risk-Bearing*. North-Holland, Amsterdam.

Attanasio, O. P., and G. Weber (1993): "Consumption Growth, the Interest Rate, and Aggregation," *Review of Economic Studies*, 60(3), 631–649.

Backus, D., and S. Zin (1994): "Reverse Engineering the Yield Curve," National Bureau of Economic Review (NBER) Working Paper No. 4676, Cambridge, MA.

Bajeux-Besnainou, I., J. V. Jordan, and R. Portait (2001): "An Asset Allocation Puzzle: A Comment," *American Economic Review*, 91, 1170–1180.

Bakshi, G. S., and Z. Chen (1996): "Inflation, Asset Prices, and the Term Structure of Interest Rates in Monetary Economies," *Review of Financial Studies*, 9(1), 241–275.

Bakshi, G. S., C. Cao, and Z. Chen (1997): "Empirical Performance of Alternative Option Pricing Models," *Journal of Finance*, 52(5), 2003–2049.

Balduzzi, P., S. Das, and S. Foresi (1998): "The Central Tendency: A Second Factor in Bond Yields," *Review of Economics and Statistics*, 80(1), 62–72.

Bansal, R., and H. Zhou (2002): "The Term Structure of Interest Rates with Regime Shifts," *Journal of Finance*, 57, 1997–2043.

Barberis, N., and R. Thaler (2002): "A Survey of Behavioral Finance," National Bureau of Economic Review (NBER) Working Paper No. 9222, Cambridge, MA.

Barberis, N., M. Huang, and J. Santos (2001): "Prospect Theory and Asset Prices," *Quarterly Journal of Economics*, 116, 1–53.

Barberis, N., A. Shleifer, and R. Vishny (1998): "A Model of Investor Sentiment," *Journal of Financial Economics*, 49(3), 307–343.

Barsky, R. B., F. T. Juster, M. S. Kimball, and M. D. Shapiro (1997): "Preference Parameters and Behavioral Heterogeneity: An Experimental Approach in the Health and Retirement Study," *Quarterly Journal of Economics*, 112(2), 537–579.

Basel Committee on Banking Supervision (2005): "International Convergence of Capital Measurement and Capital Standards: A Revised Framework," Discussion Paper, Bank for International Settlements, Basel, Switzerland.

Bates, D. S. (1991): "The Crash of '87—Was It Expected? The Evidence from Options Markets," *Journal of Finance*, 46, 1009–1044.

———(1996): "Jumps and Stochastic Volatility: Exchange Rate Processes Implicit in Deutsche Mark Options," *Review of Financial Studies*, 9, 69–107.

———(2002): "Empirical Option Pricing: A Retrospection," *Journal of Econometrics*, 116, 387–404.

Beaglehole, D., and M. Tenney (1992): "A Nonlinear Equilibrium Model of the Term Structure of Interest Rates: Corrections and Additions," *Journal of Financial Economics*, 32, 345–454.

Beaudry, P., and E. van Wincoop (1996): "The Intertemporal Elasticity of Substitution: An Exploration Using a U.S. Panel of State Data," *Economica*, 63(251), 495–512.

Bellman, R. (1957): *Dynamic Programming*. Princeton University Press, Princeton, NJ.

Bernoulli, D. (1954): "Exposition of a New Theory on the Measurement of Risk," *Econometrica*, 22(1), 23–36.

Bernstein, P. L. (1992): *Capital Ideas: The Improbable Origins of Modern Wall Street*. Free Press, New York.

Bhamra, H. S., and R. Uppal (2003): "The Role of Risk Aversion and Intertemporal Substitution in Dynamic Consumption-Portfolio Choice with Recursive Utility," London Business School Working Paper.

Black, F. (1972): "Capital Market Equilibrium with Restricted Borrowing," *Journal of Business*, 45, 444–455.

———(1976): "The Pricing of Commodity Contracts," *Journal of Financial Economics*, 3, 167–179.

Black, F., and J. C. Cox (1976): "Valuing Corporate Securities: Some Effects of Bond Indenture Provisions," *Journal of Finance*, 31, 351–367.

Black, F., E. Derman, and W. Toy (1990): "A One-Factor Model of Interest Rates and Its Application to Treasury Bond Options," *Financial Analysts Journal*, 46(1), 33–39.

Black, F., and P. Karasinski (1991): "Bond and Option Pricing When Short Rates Are Lognormal," *Financial Analysts Journal*, 47(4), 52–59.

Black, F., and M. Scholes (1973): "The Pricing of Options and Corporate Liabilities," *Journal of Political Economy*, 81, 637–659.

Blanchard, O. J. (1979): "Speculative Bubbles, Crashes and Rational Expectations," *Economics Letters*, 3, 387–389.

Bodie, Z., R. C. Merton, and W. Samuelson (1992): "Labor Supply Flexibility and Portfolio Choice in a Life-Cycle Model," *Journal of Economic Dynamics and Control*, 16, 427–450.

Bollerslev, T., R. Y. Chou, and K. F. Kroner (1992): "ARCH Modeling in Finance: A Review of Theory and Empirical Evidence," *Journal of Econometrics*, 52, 5–59.

Brace, A., D. Gatarek, and M. Musiela (1997): "The Market Model of Interest Rate Dynamics," *Mathematical Finance*, 7(2), 127–147.

Breeden, D. T. (1979): "An Intertemporal Asset Pricing Model with Stochastic Consumption and Investment Opportunities," *Journal of Financial Economics*, 7, 265–296.

Brennan, M. J., and Y. Xia (2002): "Dynamic Asset Allocation Under Inflation," *Journal of Finance*, 57, 1201–1238.

Brunnermeier, M. K. (2001): *Asset Pricing Under Asymmetric Information: Bubbles, Crashes, Technical Analysis, and Herding*. Oxford University Press, Oxford.

Campbell, J. (1999): "Asset Prices, Consumption, and the Business Cycle," in *Handbook of Macroeconomics*, ed. by J. B. Taylor, and M. Woodford. North-Holland, Amsterdam.

Campbell, J. Y. (2000): "Asset Pricing at the Millennium," *Journal of Finance*, 55, 1515–1567.

Campbell, J. Y., and J. H. Cochrane (1999): "By Force of Habit: A Consumption Based Explanation of Aggregate Stock Market Behavior," *Journal of Political Economy*, 107(2), 205–251.

Campbell, J. Y., and N. G. Mankiw (1989): "Consumption, Income, and Interest Rates: Reinterpreting the Time Series Evidence," in *National Bureau of Economic Research Macroeconomics Annual*, ed. by O. J. Blanchard, and S. Fischer, vol. 4. MIT Press, Cambridge, MA.

Campbell, J. Y., and L. M. Viceira (2002): *Strategic Asset Allocation: Portfolio Choice for Long-Term Investors*. Oxford University Press, Oxford.

Campbell, J. Y., A. Lo, and C. MacKinlay (1997): *The Econometrics of Financial Markets*. Princeton University Press, Princeton, NJ.

Canner, N., N. G. Mankiw, and D. N. Weil (1997): "An Asset Allocation Puzzle," *American Economic Review*, 87, 181–191.

Carhart, M. M. (1997): "On Persistence in Mutual Fund Performance," *Journal of Finance*, 52, 57–82.

Carrier, G. F., and C. E. Pearson (1976): *Partial Differential Equations: Theory and Technique*. Academic Press, New York.

Carverhill, A. (1994): "When Is the Short Rate Markovian?" *Mathematical Finance*, 4, 305–312.

Cecchetti, S. G., P.-S. Lam, and N. C. Mark (1993): "The Equity Premium and the Risk-Free Rate: Matching the Moments," *Journal of Monetary Economics*, 31, 21–46.

———(1994): "Testing Volatility Restrictions on Intertemporal Marginal Rates of Substitution Implied by Euler Equations and Asset Returns," *Journal of Finance*, 49, 123–152.

Chacko, G., and S. Das (2002): "Pricing Interest Rate Derivatives: A General Approach," *Review of Financial Studies*, 15, 195–241.

Chapman, D. A. (1998): "Habit Formation and Aggregate Consumption," *Econometrica*, 66, 1223–1230.

Chen, N.-F., R. Roll, and S. A. Ross (1986): "Economic Forces and the Stock Market," *Journal of Business*, 59(3), 383–403.

Cheridito, P., D. Filipovic, and R. Kimmel (2003): "Market Price of Risk Specifications for Affine Models: Theory and Evidence," Princeton University Working Paper.

Churchill, R. V., and J. W. Brown (1978): *Fourier Series and Boundary Value Problems*. McGraw-Hill, New York.

Claessens, S., and G. G. Pennacchi (1996): "Estimating the Likelihood of Mexican Default from the Market Prices of Brady Bonds," *Journal of Financial and Quantitative Analysis*, 31(1), 109–126.

Collin-Dufresne, P., and R. S. Goldstein (2001): "Do Credit Spreads Reflect Stationary Leverage Ratios?" *Journal of Finance*, 56, 1929–1958.

———(2003): "Generalizing the Affine Framework to HJM and Random Field Models," Carnegie-Mellon University and Washington University Working Paper.

Collin-Dufresne, P., and B. Solnik (2001): "On the Term Structure of Default Premia in the Swap and LIBOR Markets," *Journal of Finance*, 56, 1095–1115.

Connor, G., and R. A. Korajczyk (1995): "The Arbitrage Pricing Theory and Multifactor Models of Asset Returns," in *Finance, Handbooks in Operations Research and Management Science*, ed. by R. A. Jarrow, V. Maksimovic, and W. T. Ziemba, vol. 4, chap. 23. North-Holland, Amsterdam.

Constantinides, G. M. (1986): "Capital Market Equilibrium with Transaction Costs," *Journal of Political Economy*, 94, 842–862.

———(1990): "Habit Formation: A Resolution of the Equity Premium Puzzle," *Journal of Political Economy*, 98(3), 519–543.

———(1992): "A Theory of the Nominal Term Structure of Interest Rates," *Review of Financial Studies*, 5, 531–552.

Coval, J. D., and T. Shumway (2003): "Do Behavioral Biases Affect Prices?" *Journal of Finance*, forthcoming.

Cox, D. R. (1955): "Some Statistical Methods Connected with Series of Events," *Journal of the Royal Statistical Society Series B*, 17(2), 129–164.

Cox, J., and S. A. Ross (1976): "The Valuation of Options for Alternative Stochastic Processes," *Journal of Financial Economics*, 3, 145–166.

Cox, J., S. A. Ross, and M. Rubinstein (1979): "Option Pricing: A Simplified Approach," *Journal of Financial Economics*, 7, 229–263.

Cox, J. C., and C.-F. Huang (1989): "Optimal Consumption and Portfolio Policies When Asset Prices Follow a Diffusion Process," *Journal of Economic Theory*, 49, 33–83.

Cox, J. C., J. E. Ingersoll, and S. A. Ross (1981): "The Relation Between Forward Prices and Futures Prices," *Journal of Financial Economics*, 9, 321–346.

——(1985a): "An Intertemporal General Equilibrium Model of Asset Prices," *Econometrica*, 53, 363–384.

——(1985b): "A Theory of the Term Structure of Interest Rates," *Econometrica*, 53, 385–408.

Crosbie, P. J., and J. R. Bohn (2002): *Modeling Default Risk*. KMV LLC, San Francisco.

Cvsa, V., and P. H. Ritchken (2001): "Pricing Claims Under Garch-Level Dependent Interest Rate Processes," *Management Science*, 47, 1693–1711.

Dai, Q., and K. Singleton (2000): "Specification Analysis of Affine Term Structure Models," *Journal of Finance*, 55, 1943–1978.

——(2003): "Term Structure Modeling in Theory and Reality," *Review of Financial Studies*, 16, 631–678.

——(2004): "Fixed-Income Pricing," in *Handbook of Economics and Finance*, ed. by G. Constantinides, M. Harris, and R. Stulz. North-Holland, Amsterdam.

Dai, Q., A. Le, and K. Singleton (2006): "Discrete-Time Dynamic Term Structure Models with Generalized Market Prices of Risk," UNC, NYU, and Stanford University Working Paper.

Daniel, K. D., D. Hirshleifer, and A. Subrahmanyam (1998): "Investor Psychology and Security Market Under- and Over-reactions," *Journal of Finance*, 53(6), 1839–1886.

Daniel, K. D., D. Hirshleifer, and S. H. Teoh (2001): "Investor Psychology in Capital Markets: Evidence and Policy Implications," Northwestern University Working Paper.

Das, S. R. (2002): "The Surprise Element: Jumps in Interest Rates," *Journal of Econometrics*, 106, 27–65.

Das, S. R., and S. Foresi (1996): "Exact Solutions for Bond and Option Prices with Systematic Jump Risk," *Review of Derivatives Research*, 1, 7–24.

Debreu, G. (1959): *Theory of Value*. Cowles Foundation Monograph 17, Yale University Press, New Haven, CT.

DeLong, J. B., A. Shleifer, L. Summers, and R. J. Waldmann (1991): "The Survival of Noise Traders in Financial Markets," *Journal of Business*, 64(1), 1–20.

Detemple, J., and C. Giannikos (1996): "Asset and Commodity Prices with Multi-attribute Durable Goods," *Journal of Economic Dynamics and Control*, 20, 1451–1504.

Detemple, J., and F. Zapatero (1991): "Asset Prices in an Exchange Economy with Habit Formation," *Econometrica*, 59, 1633–1658.

Diamond, D. W., and R. E. Verrecchia (1981): "Information Aggregation in a Noisy Rational Expectations Economy," *Journal of Financial Economics*, 9(3), 221–235.

Diba, B. T., and H. I. Grossman (1988): "The Theory of Rational Bubbles in Stock Prices," *Economic Journal*, 98, 746–754.

Diebold, F., M. Piazzesi, and G. Rudebusch (2005): "Modeling Bond Yields in Finance and Macroeconomics," *American Economic Review*, 95(2), 415–420.

Dimson, E., P. Marsh, and M. Staunton (2002): *Triumph of the Optimists: 101 Years of Global Investment Returns*. Princeton University Press, Princeton, NJ.

Duarte, J. (2004): "Evaluating an Alternative Risk Preference in Affine Term Structure Models," *Review of Financial Studies*, 17, 379–404.

Duesenberry, J. S. (1949): *Income, Saving, and the Theory of Consumer Behavior*. Harvard University Press, Cambridge, MA.

Duffee, G. (1999): "Estimating the Price of Default Risk," *Review of Financial Studies*, 12, 197–226.

———(2002): "Term Premia and Interest Rate Forecasts in Affine Models," *Journal of Finance*, 57, 405–443.

Duffie, D. (1998): "Defaultable Term Structure Models with Fractional Recovery of Par," Stanford University Working Paper.

Duffie, D., and L. Epstein (1992a): "Asset Pricing with Stochastic Differential Utility," *Review of Financial Studies*, 5, 411–436.

———(1992b): "Stochastic Differential Utility," *Econometrica*, 60, 353–394.

Duffie, D., and R. Kan (1996): "A Yield-Factor Model of Interest Rates," *Mathematical Finance*, 6, 379–406.

Duffie, D., and D. Lando (2001): "Term Structures of Credit Spreads with Incomplete Accounting Information," *Econometrica*, 69, 633–664.

Duffie, D., and K. Singleton (1999): "Modeling Term Structures of Defaultable Bonds," *Review of Financial Studies*, 12, 687–720.

Duffie, D., D. Filipovic, and W. Schachermayer (2002): "Affine Processes and Applications in Finance," *Annals of Applied Probability*, 13, 984–1053.

Duffie, D., J. Pan, and K. Singleton (2000): "Transform Analysis and Asset Pricing for Affine Jump-Diffusions," *Econometrica*, 68, 1343–1376.

Duffie, D., W. Fleming, M. Soner, and T. Zariphopoulou (1997): "Hedging in Incomplete Markets with HARA Utility," *Journal of Economic Dynamics and Control*, 21, 753–782.

Dumas, B., and E. Luciano (1991): "An Exact Solution to a Dynamic Portfolio Choice Problem Under Transactions Costs," *Journal of Finance*, 46, 577–596.

Epstein, L., and S. Zin (1989): "Substitution, Risk Aversion, and the Temporal Behavior of Consumption Growth and Asset Returns: A Theoretical Framework," *Econometrica*, 57, 937–969.

Fama, E. F., and K. R. French (1988): "Permanent and Temporary Components of Stock Prices," *Journal of Political Economy*, 96(2), 246–273.

———(1993): "Common Risk Factors in the Returns on Stocks and Bonds," *Journal of Financial Economics*, 33, 3–56.

Fan, R., and P. Ritchken (2001): "A Pricing Model for Credit Derivatives: Application to Default Swaps and Credit Spreads," Case Western Reserve University Working Paper.

Ferson, W. E., and G. M. Constantinides (1991): "Habit Persistence and Durability in Aggregate Consumption: Empirical Tests," *Journal of Financial Economics*, 29, 199–240.

Friedman, M. (1953): "The Case for Flexible Exchange Rates," in *Essays in Positive Economics*, ed. by M. Friedman. University of Chicago Press, Chicago, IL.

Giannikos, C., and Z. Shi (2006): "Does Durability Help Asset Pricing with Habit Formation Conform to U.S. Data?" Baruch College Working Paper.

Goldstein, R. (2000): "The Term Structure of Interest Rates as a Random Field," *Review of Financial Studies*, 13, 365–384.

Gorton, G. B., and G. G. Pennacchi (1993): "Security Baskets and Index-Linked Securities," *Journal of Business*, 66, 1–27.

Grossman, S. J. (1976): "On the Efficiency of Competitive Stock Markets Where Traders Have Diverse Information," *Journal of Finance*, 31, 573–585.

Grossman, S. J., and J. E. Stiglitz (1980): "On the Impossibility of Informationally Efficient Markets," *American Economic Review*, 70(3), 393–408.

Grundy, B. D., and M. McNichols (1989): "Trade and Revelation of Information Through Prices and Direct Disclosure," *Review of Financial Studies*, 2, 495–526.

Hall, R. E. (1988): "Intertemporal Substitution and Consumption," *Journal of Political Economy*, 96(2), 339–357.

Hansen, L. P., and R. Jagannathan (1991): "Implications of Security Market Data for Models of Dynamic Economies," *Journal of Political Economy*, 99(2), 225–262.

Hansen, L. P., and K. J. Singleton (1983): "Stochastic Consumption, Risk Aversion, and the Temporal Behavior of Asset Returns," *Journal of Political Economy*, 91, 249–265.

Harrison, J. M., and D. M. Kreps (1979): "Martingales and Arbitrage in Multiperiod Securities Markets," *Journal of Economic Theory*, 20, 381–408.

Harrison, J. M., and S. Pliska (1981): "Martingales and Stochastic Integrals and in Theory of Continuous Trading," *Stochastic Processes and Their Applications*, 11, 215–260.

Harvey, C. R., and A. Siddique (2000): "Conditional Skewness in Asset Pricing Tests," *Journal of Finance*, 55, 1263–1295.

He, H., and N. D. Pearson (1991): "Consumption and Portfolio Policies with Incomplete Markets and Short-Sale Constraints: The Infinite Dimensional Case," *Journal of Economic Theory*, 54, 259–304.

Heath, D., R. A. Jarrow, and A. Morton (1992): "Bond Pricing and the Term Structure of Interest Rates: A New Methodology for Contingent Claims Valuation," *Econometrica*, 60(1), 77–105.

Heaton, J. C. (1995): "An Empirical Investigation of Asset Pricing with Temporally Dependent Preference Specifications," *Econometrica*, 63, 681–717.

Heaton, J. C., and D. J. Lucas (2000): "Portfolio Choice and Asset Prices: The Importance of Entrepreneurial Risk," *Journal of Finance*, 55(3), 1163–1198.

Hellwig, M. F. (1980): "On the Aggregation of Information in Competitive Markets," *Journal of Economic Theory*, 22, 477–498.

Heston, S. (1993): "A Closed-Form Solution for Options with Stochastic Volatility with Applications to Bond and Currency Options," *Review of Financial Studies*, 6(2), 327–343.

Hindy, A., and C.-F. Huang (1993): "Optimal Consumption and Portfolio Rules with Durability and Local Substitution," *Econometrica*, 61, 85–121.

Hirshleifer, D. (2001): "Investor Psychology and Asset Pricing," *Journal of Finance*, 64(4), 1533–1597.

Ho, T., and S. B. Lee (1986): "Term Structure Movements and Pricing Interest Rate Contingent Claims," *Journal of Finance*, 41, 1011–1028.

———(2004): *The Oxford Guide to Financial Modeling: Applications for Capital Markets, Corporate Finance, Risk Management, and Financial Institutions.* Oxford University Press, New York.

Hong, H., and J. C. Stein (1999): "A Unified Theory of Underreaction, Momentum Trading and Overreaction in Asset Markets," *Journal of Finance*, 54(6), 2143–2184.

Huang, J.-Z., and M. Huang (2003): "How Much of the Corporate-Treasury Yield Spread Is Due to Credit Risk?" Penn State University, NYU, and Stanford Business School Working Paper.

Huberman, G. (1982): "A Simple Approach to Arbitrage Pricing Theory," *Journal of Economic Theory*, 28, 183–191.

Hull, J., and A. White (1990): "Pricing Interest Rate Derivative Securities," *Review of Financial Studies*, 3, 573–592.

———(1993): "One-Factor Interest-Rate Models and the Valuation of Interest-Rate Derivative Securities," *Journal of Financial and Quantitative Analysis*, 28, 235–254.

Hull, J. C. (2000): *Options, Futures, and Other Derivative Securities*, 4th ed. Prentice Hall, Upper Saddle River, NJ.

Ingersoll, J. E. (1987): *Theory of Financial Decision Making*. Rowman & Littlefield, Totowa, NJ.

Inui, K., and M. Kijima (1998): "A Markovian Framework in Heath-Jarrow-Morton Models," *Journal of Financial and Quantitative Analysis*, 33, 423–440.

Itô, K. (1944): "Stochastic Integral," *Proceedings of the Imperial Academy of Tokyo*, 20, 519–524.

———(1951): "On Stochastic Differential Equations," *Memoirs of the American Mathematical Society*, 4, 1–51.

Jagannathan, R., and E. McGrattan (1995): "The CAPM Debate," *Federal Reserve Bank of Minneapolis Quarterly Review*, 19(4), 2–17.

Jagannathan, R., and Z. Wang (1996): "The CAPM Is Alive and Well," *Journal of Finance*, 51(1), 3–53.

Jarrow, R. A. (2002): *Modelling Fixed Income Securities and Interest Rate Options*, 2nd ed. McGraw-Hill, New York.

Jarrow, R. A., and G. S. Oldfield (1981): "Forward Contracts and Futures Contracts," *Journal of Financial Economics*, 9, 373–382.

Jarrow, R. A., and S. M. Turnbull (1995): "Pricing Derivatives on Financial Securities Subject to Credit Risk," *Journal of Finance*, 50(1), 53–86.

Jarrow, R. A., D. Lando, and S. M. Turnbull (1997): "A Markov Model for the Term Structure of Credit Risk Spreads," *Review of Financial Studies*, 10(2), 481–523.

Jegadeesh, N., and G. Pennacchi (1996): "The Behavior of Interest Rates Implied by the Term Structure of Eurodollar Futures," *Journal of Money, Credit and Banking*, 28, 426–446.

Jegadeesh, N., and S. Titman (1993): "Returns to Buying Winners and Selling Losers: Implications for Stock Market Efficiency," *Journal of Finance*, 48(1), 65–91.

Jones, E., S. Mason, and E. Rosenfeld (1984): "Contingent Claims Analysis of Corporate Capital Structures: An Empirical Investigation," *Journal of Finance*, 39, 611–627.

Jones, E. P. (1984): "Option Arbitrage and Strategy with Large Price Changes," *Journal of Financial Economics*, 13, 91–113.

Judd, K. L. (1998): *Numerical Methods in Economics*. MIT Press, Cambridge, MA.

Kahneman, D., and A. Tversky (1979): "Prospect Theory: An Analysis of Decision Under Risk," *Econometrica*, 47, 263–291.

Karatzas, I., and S. E. Shreve (1991): *Brownian Motion and Stochastic Calculus*. Springer-Verlag, New York.

Karatzas, I., J. Lehoczky, and S. E. Shreve (1987): "Optimal Portfolio and Consumption Decisions for a 'Small Investor' on a Finite Horizon," *SIAM Journal of Control and Optimization*, 25, 1557–1586.

Karlin, S., and H. M. Taylor (1975): *A First Course in Stochastic Processes*. Academic Press, New York.

———(1981): *A Second Course in Stochastic Processes*. Academic Press, New York.

Kennedy, D. (1994): "The Term Structure of Interest Rates as a Gaussian Random Field," *Mathematical Finance*, 4, 247–258.

———(1997): "Characterizing Gaussian Models of the Term Structure of Interest Rates," *Mathematical Finance*, 7, 107–118.

Kimmel, R. L. (2004): "Modeling the Term Structure of Interest Rates: A New Approach," *Journal of Financial Economics*, 72, 143–183.

Kindleberger, C. P. (2001): *Manias, Panics, and Crashes: A History of Financial Crises*. Wiley, New York.

Kogan, L., S. Ross, J. Wang, and M. Westerfield (2006): "The Price Impact and Survival of Irrational Traders," *Journal of Finance*, 61, 195–229.

Kraus, A., and R. Litzenberger (1976): "Skewness Preference and the Valuation of Risk Assets," *Journal of Finance*, 31, 1085–1100.

Kreps, D., and E. Porteus (1978): "Temporal Resolution of Uncertainty and Dynamic Choice Theory," *Econometrica*, 46, 185–200.

Kreps, D. M. (1990): *A Course in Microeconomic Theory*. Princeton University Press, Princeton, NJ.

Krishnan, C., P. Ritchken, and J. Thomson (2004): "Monitoring and Controlling Bank Risk: Does Risky Debt Help?" *Journal of Finance*, 60, 343–377.

Kyle, A. S. (1985): "Continuous Auctions and Insider Trading," *Econometrica*, 53, 1315–1335.

———(1989): "Informed Speculation with Imperfect Competition," *Review of Economic Studies*, 56, 317–356.

Lakonishok, J., A. Shleifer, and R. W. Vishny (1994): "Contrarian Investment, Extrapolation and Risk," *Journal of Finance*, 49, 1541–1578.

Lando, D. (1998): "Cox Processes and Credit-Risky Securities," *Review of Derivatives Research*, 2, 99–120.

Langeteig, T. C. (1980): "A Multivariate Model of the Term Structure," *Journal of Finance*, 25, 71–97.

Leippold, M., and L. Wu (2002): "Asset Pricing Under the Quadratic Class," *Journal of Financial and Quantitative Analysis*, 37(2), 271–295.

Lettau, M., and S. Ludvigson (2001): "Resurrecting the (C)CAPM: A Cross-Sectional Test When Risk Premia Are Time-Varying," *Journal of Political Economy*, 109, 1238–1287.

Lettau, M., and H. Uhlig (2000): "Can Habit Formation Be Reconciled with Business Cycle Facts?" *Review of Economic Dynamics*, 3, 79–99.

Lintner, J. (1965): "The Valuation of Risky Assets and the Selection of Risky Investments in Stock Portfolios and Capital Budgets," *Review of Economics and Statistics*, 47, 13–37.

Litterman, R., and J. Scheinkman (1988): "Common Factors Affecting Bond Returns," *Journal of Fixed Income*, 1, 54–61.

Lo, A. W. (1988): "Maximum Likelihood Estimation of Generalized Ito Processes with Discretely Sampled Data," *Econometric Theory*, 4, 231–247.

Longstaff, F. (1989): "A Nonlinear General Equilibrium Model of the Term Structure of Interest Rates," *Journal of Financial Economics*, 23, 195–224.

Longstaff, F., and E. Schwartz (1995): "A Simple Approach to Valuing Risky Fixed and Floating Rate Debt," *Journal of Finance*, 50, 789–819.

Lord, C. G., L. Ross, and M. R. Lepper (1979): "Biased Assimilation and Attitude Polarization: The Effects of Prior Theories on Subsequently Considered Evidence," *Journal of Personality and Social Psychology*, 37(11), 2098–2109.

Lucas, R. E. (1972): "Expectations and the Neutrality of Money," *Journal of Economic Theory*, 4, 103–124.

Lucas, R. E., Jr. (1976): "Econometric Policy Evaluation: A Critique," in *The Phillips Curve and Labor Markets*. Vol. 1 of *Carnegie Rochester Conference Series on Public Policy*, pp. 19–46. North-Holland, Amsterdam.

———(1978): "Asset Prices in an Exchange Economy," *Econometrica*, 46, 1429–1445.

———(1987): *Models of Business Cycles*. Blackwell, New York.

Machina, M. J. (1987): "Choice Under Uncertainty: Problems Solved and Unsolved," *Journal of Economic Perspectives*, 1(1), 121–154.

Madan, D., and H. Unal (1998): "Pricing the Risks of Default," *Review of Derivatives Research*, 2, 121–160.

Maes, K. (2003): "Modeling the Term Structure of Interest Rates: Where Do We Stand?" Kleuven University and University of Amsterdam Working Paper.

Marcus, A. J., and I. Shaked (1984): "The Valuation of FDIC Deposit Insurance Using Option-Pricing Estimates," *Journal of Money, Credit and Banking*, 16, 446–460.

Markowitz, H. M. (1952): "Portfolio Selection," *Journal of Finance*, 7(1), 77–91.

Marshall, A. (1920): *Principles of Economics: An Introductory Volume*. Macmillan, London.

Mas-Colell, A., M. D. Whinston, and J. R. Green (1995): *Microeconomic Theory*. Oxford University Press, New York.

McDonald, R. L. (2002): *Derivatives Markets*. Addison-Wesley, Reading, MA.

Mehra, R., and E. Prescott (1985): "The Equity Premium: A Puzzle," *Journal of Monetary Economics*, 15, 145–161.

Menzly, L., T. Santos, and P. Veronesi (2001): "Habit Formation and the Cross Section of Stock Returns," Center for Research in Security Prices Working Paper No. 534, University of Chicago.

Merton, R. C. (1969): "Lifetime Portfolio Selection Under Uncertainty: The Continuous-Time Case," *Review of Economics and Statistics*, 51(3), 247–257.

———(1971): "Optimum Consumption and Portfolio Rules in a Continuous-Time Model," *Journal of Economic Theory*, 3(4), 373–413.

———(1972): "An Analytical Derivation of the Efficient Portfolio Frontier," *Journal of Financial and Quantitative Analysis*, 7, 1851–1872.

———(1973a): "An Intertemporal Capital Asset Pricing Model," *Econometrica*, 41(5), 867–887.

———(1973b): "Theory of Rational Option Pricing," *Bell Journal of Economics and Management Science*, 4, 141–183.

———(1974): "On the Pricing of Corporate Debt: The Risk Structure of Interest Rates," *Journal of Finance*, 29, 449–470.

————(1976): "Option Pricing When the Underlying Stock Returns are Discontinuous," *Journal of Financial Economics*, 3, 125–144.

————(1980): "On Estimating the Expected Return on the Market: An Exploratory Investigation," *Journal of Financial Economics*, 8, 323–361.

————(1992): *Continuous Time Finance*. Blackwell, Cambridge, MA.

Mossin, J. (1966): "Equilibrium in a Capital Asset Market," *Econometrica*, 34, 768–783.

————(1968): "Optimal Multiperiod Portfolio Policies," *Journal of Business*, 41(2), 215–229.

Muth, J. F. (1961): "Rational Expectations and the Theory of Price Movements," *Econometrica*, 29(3), 315–335.

Myers, S. C. (1968): "A Time-State Preference Model of Security Valuation," *Journal of Financial and Quantitative Analysis*, 3(1), 1–34.

Naik, V., and M. Lee (1990): "General Equilibrium Pricing of Options and the Market Portfolio with Discontinuous Returns," *Review of Financial Studies*, 3, 493–521.

Naik, V., and M. H. Lee (1997): "Yield Curve Dynamics with Discrete Shifts in Economic Regimes: Theory and Estimation," University of British Columbia Working Paper.

Neftci, S. N. (1996): *Introduction to the Mathematics of Financial Derivatives*. Academic Press, San Diego, CA.

Obstfeld, M. (1994): "Risk-Taking, Global Diversification, and Growth," *American Economic Review*, 84, 1310–1329.

O'Hara, M. (1995): *Market Microstructure Theory*. Blackwell, Oxford, UK.

Pennacchi, G. G. (1991): "Identifying the Dynamics of Real Interest Rates and Inflation: Evidence Using Survey Data," *Review of Financial Studies*, 4, 53–86.

————(2005): "Risk-Based Capital Standards, Deposit Insurance, and Procyclicality," *Journal of Financial Intermediation*, 14, 432–465.

Piazzesi, M. (2005a): "Affine Term Structure Models," in *Handbook of Financial Econometrics*, ed. by Y. Ait-Sahalia, and L. Hansen. Elsevier, Amsterdam.

————(2005b): "Bond Yields and the Federal Reserve," *Journal of Political Economy*, 113, 311–344.

Pliska, S. (1986): "A Stochastic Calculus Model of Continuous Trading: Optimal Portfolios," *Mathematics of Operations Research*, 11, 371–382.

Poterba, J. M., and L. H. Summers (1988): "Mean Reversion in Stock Returns: Evidence and Implications," *Journal of Financial Economics*, 22(1), 27–59.

Pratt, J. W. (1964): "Risk-Aversion in the Small and in the Large," *Econometrica*, 32(1), 122–136.

Rabin, M., and R. H. Thaler (2001): "Anomalies: Risk Aversion," *Journal of Economic Perspectives*, 15(1), 219–232.

Ramsey, F. P. (1928): "A Mathematical Theory of Saving," *Economic Journal*, 38(4), 543–559.

Rebonato, R. (2004): "Interest-Rate Term Structure Pricing Models: A Review," *Proceedings of the Royal Society of London*, 460, 667–728.

Richards, A. J. (1997): "Winner-Loser Reversals in National Stock Market Indices: Can They be Explained?" *Journal of Finance*, 52(5), 2129–2144.

Ritchken, P., and L. Sankarasubramanian (1995): "Volatility Structures of Forward Rates and the Dynamics of the Term Structure," *Mathematical Finance*, 5, 55–72.

Ritchken, P., and Z. Sun (2003): "On Correlation Effects and Systemic Risk in Credit Models," Case Western Reserve University Working Paper.

Ritter, J. R. (1991): "The Long-Run Performance of Initial Public Offerings," *Journal of Finance*, 46(1), 3–27.

Rogers, C. G., and D. Talay (1997): *Numerical Methods in Finance*. Cambridge University Press, Cambridge, UK.

Roll, R. W. (1977): "A Critique of the Asset Pricing Theory's Tests," *Journal of Financial Economics*, 4, 129–176.

Ross, S. A. (1976): "The Arbitrage Theory of Capital Asset Pricing," *Journal of Economic Theory*, 13, 341–360.

Runggaldier, W. (2003): "Jump-Diffusion Models," in *Finance, Handbook of Heavy Tailed Distributions in Finance*, ed. by S. T. Rachev, vol. 1, chap. 5, pp. 169–209. Elsevier, Amsterdam.

Ryder, H. E., and G. M. Heal (1973): "Optimum Growth with Intertemporally Dependent Preferences," *Review of Economic Studies*, 40, 1–43.

Samuelson, P. A. (1965): "Rational Theory of Warrant Pricing," *Industrial Management Review*, 6, 13–31.

———(1969): "Lifetime Portfolio Selection by Dynamic Stochastic Programming," *Review of Economics and Statistics*, 51(3), 239–246.

Sandroni, A. (2000): "Do Markets Favor Agents Able to Make Accurate Predictions?" *Econometrica*, 68, 1303–1342.

Santa-Clara, P., and D. Sornette (2001): "The Dynamics of the Forward Interest Rate Curve with Stochastic String Shocks," *Review of Financial Studies*, 14(1), 149–185.

Santos, M. S., and M. Woodford (1997): "Rational Asset Pricing Bubbles," *Econometrica*, 65(1), 19–57.

Scheinkman, J. A., and W. Xiong (2003): "Overconfidence and Speculative Bubbles," *Journal of Political Economy*, 111(6), 1183–1219.

Schroder, M., and C. Skiadas (2002): "An Isomorphism Between Asset Pricing Models With and Without Linear Habit Formation," *Review of Financial Studies*, 15(4), 1189–1221.

Sharpe, W. F. (1964): "Capital Asset Prices: A Theory of Market Equilibrium Under Conditions of Risk," *Journal of Finance*, 19, 425–442.

Shiller, R. J. (1982): "Consumption, Asset Markets, and Macroeconomic Fluctuations," *Carnegie Rochester Conference Series on Public Policy*, 17, 203–238.

Shimko, D. C. (1992): *Finance in Continuous Time: A Primer*. Kolb, Miami, FL.

Shleifer, A., and R. Vishny (1997): "The Limits to Arbitrage," *Journal of Finance*, 52(1), 35–55.

Siegel, J. J., and R. H. Thaler (1997): "Anomalies: The Equity Premium Puzzle," *Journal of Economic Perspectives*, 11, 191–200.

Spiegel, M., and A. Subrahmanyam (1992): "Informed Speculation and Hedging in a Noncompetitive Securities Market," *Review of Financial Studies*, 5, 307–329.

Sun, T.-S. (1992): "Real and Nominal Interest Rates: A Discrete-Time Model and Its Continuous-Time Limit," *Review of Financial Studies*, 5, 581–611.

Sundaresan, S. M. (1989): "Intertemporally Dependent Preferences and the Volatility of Consumption and Wealth," *Review of Financial Studies*, 2(1), 73–89.

Tallarini, T. D., and H. H. Zhang (2005): "External Habit and the Cyclicality of Expected Stock Returns," *Journal of Business*, 78, 1023–1048.

Thaler, R., and E. J. Johnson (1990): "Gambling with the House Money and Trying to Break Even: The Effects of Prior Outcomes on Risky Choice," *Management Science*, 36, 643–660.

Tirole, J. (1982): "On the Possibility of Speculation Under Rational Expectations," *Econometrica*, 50(5), 1163–1181.

Tobin, J. (1958): "Liquidity Preference as Behavior Towards Risk," *Review of Economic Studies*, 67, 65–86.

Treynor, J. L. (1961): "Toward a Theory of Market Value of Risky Assets," unpublished manuscript.

Tuckman, B. (2002): *Fixed Income Securities: Tools for Today's Markets*, 2nd ed. Wiley, New York.

Varian, H. R. (1992): *Microeconomic Analysis*, 3rd ed. W. W. Norton, New York.

Vasicek, O. A. (1977): "An Equilibrium Characterization of the Term Structure," *Journal of Financial Economics*, 5(2), 177–188.

von Neumann, J., and O. Morgenstern (1944): *Theory of Games and Economic Behavior*. Princeton University Press, Princeton, NJ.

Wachter, J. A. (2002): "Portfolio and Consumption Decisions Under Mean-Reverting Returns: An Exact Solution for Complete Markets," *Journal of Financial and Quantitative Analysis*, 37(1), 63–91.

Wang, J. (1993): "A Model of Intertemporal Asset Prices Under Asymmetric Information," *Review of Economic Studies*, 60, 249–282.

Weil, P. (1989): "The Equity Premium Puzzle and the Risk-Free Rate Puzzle," *Journal of Monetary Economics*, 24, 401–421.

Welch, I. (2000): "Views of Financial Economists on the Equity Premium and on Professional Controversies," *Journal of Business*, 73(4), 501–537.

Yan, H. (2001): "Dynamic Models of the Term Structure," *Financial Analysts Journal*, 57(4), 60–76.

Zhou, C. (2001): "The Term Structure of Credit Spreads with Jump Risk," *Journal of Banking and Finance*, 25, 2015–2040.

Index